Study and Practice of Meditation

Tibetan Interpretations of the Concentrations and Formless Absorptions

Leah Zahler

Snow Lion Publications
Ithaca, New York

Snow Lion Publications
P.O. Box 6483
Ithaca, NY 14851 USA
(607) 273-8519
www.snowlionpub.com

Printed in USA on acid-free recycled paper.

ISBN-10: 1-55939-325-4
ISBN-13: 978-1-55939-325-6

Library of Congress Cataloging-in-Publication Data

Zahler, Leah.
Study and practice of meditation : Tibetan interpretations of the concentrations and formless absorptions / Leah Zahler.
p. cm.
Includes translations from Tibetan.
Includes English translations of Tsoṅ-kha-pa Blo-bzaṅ-grags-pa's Bsam gzugs zin bris and Dkon-mchog 'Jigs-med-dbaṅ-po's Bsam gzugs chen mo las mdor bsdus te bkod pa bsam gzugs kyi rnam bźag legs bśad bum bzaṅ.
Includes bibliographical references.
ISBN-13: 978-1-55939-325-6 (alk. paper)
ISBN-10: 1-55939-325-4 (alk. paper)
1. Meditation--Dge-lugs-pa (Sect) I. Tsoṅ-kha-pa Blo-bzaṅ-grags-pa, 1357-1419. Bsam gzugs zin bris. English. II. Dkon-mchog 'Jigs-med-dbaṅ-po. Bsam gzugs chen mo las mdor bsdus te bkod pa bsam gzugs kyi rnam bźag legs bśad bum bzaṅ. English. III. Title.
BQ7805.Z35 2009
294.3'4435--dc22

2009003791

Study and Practice of Meditation

Contents

CHARTS

To the memory of my father, Carl Zahler,
and to my mother, Zella Zahler

ACKNOWLEDGMENTS

This book owes its existence to the help of many people. First, I would like to thank my dissertation advisor, Professor Jeffrey Hopkins, for his careful and rigorous guidance and for many hours of reading and discussion of the works translated here, as well as substantial portions of Jam-yang-shay-pa's *Great Exposition of the Concentrations and Formless Absorptions.* I would also like to thank the other members of my dissertation committee—Professor Karen Lang for her helpful suggestions and generous sharing of books and time, and Professors Paul Groner and Julian Hartt for their stimulating questions and suggestions. Others I would like to thank include Professor David Germano for discussing with me, from a Nying-ma perspective, issues relevant to Geluk/Nying-ma controversies; the late Richard B. Martin, South Asia Bibliographer and Curator of the Tibetan Collection at Alderman Library, as well as Paul G. Hackett, for helping me find Tibetan resources; Professor Joe B. Wilson, Jr., now of the University of North Carolina at Wilmington, who introduced me to Paṇ-chen Sö-nam-drak-pa's text in 1978; Dr. Harvey Aronson, formerly of the University of Virginia, for his efforts to give me a solid grounding in Vasubandhu's *Treasury of Manifest Knowledge;* Professor Georges Dreyfus, now of Williams College, for calling my attention to Jam-yang-shay-pa's text on hearing, thinking, and meditating and for many fruitful discussions, especially concerning the physical bases of the concentrations and formless absorptions, when he was at the University of Virginia; the many visiting Tibetan scholars at the University of Virginia, especially Lati Rinpoche, Denma Lochö Rinpoche, and the late Geshay Gedün Lodrö and Kensur Yeshey Tupden. I would also like to thank all my fellow Buddhist Studies graduate students for many free-flowing discussions of my work and theirs.

TECHNICAL NOTE

Tibetan and Sanskrit names and terms are phoneticized in the body of the text and transliterated, in parentheses, at their first occurrence. The system of transliteration followed for Tibetan is that of Turrell Wylie (see "A Standard System of Tibetan Transcription," *Harvard Journal of Asiatic Studies* 22 [1959], 261–67). For Sanskrit, the standard transliteration is used for names and terms cited in parentheses and in the glossaries. In the body of the text, *ch* is used for *c, sh* for *ś,* and *ṣh* for *ṣ* to facilitate pronunciation by English-speaking non-specialists.

In the translated texts, Indian or other Tibetan texts cited or referred to by the author are identified by author and a standard title, although the traditional Tibetan practice is often to use only a short title, without the author's name. The major exception is Vasubandhu's *Treasury of Manifest Knowledge,* also referred to simply as the *Treasury*, since modern Western academics as well as traditional Tibetan scholars often refer to it by a short title (the *Kośa*).

INTRODUCTION

The meditations known as the concentrations (*bsam gtan, dhyāna*) and formless absorptions (*gzugs med kyi snyoms 'jug, ārūpyasamāpatti*), best known in Europe, the Americas, and so forth from Theravāda scriptures and commentaries and from Vasubandhu's *Treasury of Manifest Knowledge (abhidharmakośa, chos mngon pa'i mdzod*) and its *Autocommentary* (*bhāṣya, bshad pa*), have become subjects of intensive study and debate in the Ge-luk (*dge lugs*) order of Tibetan Buddhism. Ge-luk-pa scholars have developed detailed textual presentations of the concentrations and formless absorptions, based on both (so called) Hīnayāna and Mahāyāna Indian sources and integrated them into the Mahāyānist educational system of the Ge-luk monastic universities in the context of the topic of the Perfections and their path-structure.

The present study gives an overview of several related Ge-luk scholastic presentations of the concentrations and formless absorptions, indicating both the commonly held points and a number of the debated ones. It is based on a text by Tsong-kha-pa (*tsong kha pa blo bzang grags pa*, 1357–1419), the founder of the Ge-luk order—*Notes on the Concentrations and Formless Absorptions* (*bsam gzugs zin bris*)—and two Ge-luk monastic textbooks (*yig cha*) for which it is the root text—"The Explanation of the Concentrations and Formless Absorptions" from Paṇ-chen Sö-nam-drak-pa's (*paṇ chen bsod nams grags pa*) *General Meaning of (Maitreya's) "Ornament for Clear Realization"* and Kön-chok-jik-may-wang-po's (*dkon mchog 'jigs med dbang po*) *Condensed Statement of (Jam-yang-shay-pa's) "Great Exposition of the Concentrations and Formless Absorptions."* Two of these texts—those by Tsong-kha-pa and Kön-chok-jik-may-wang-po—are translated in the second part of this study; the third has been previously published.[a] The discussion also draws on Jam-yang-shay-pa's *Great Exposition of the Concentrations and Formless Absorptions,* as well as oral commentaries by the contemporary Ge-luk-pa scholars Lati Rinpoche and Denma Lochö Rinpoche and the late Gedün Lodrö. It considers the two major Indian Manifest Knowledge (*chos mngon pa, abhidharma*) sources for the Ge-luk texts considered here—Vasubandhu's *Treasury of Manifest Knowledge* and its *Autocommentary,*[b] and Asaṅga's

---

[a] In Lati Rinpoche, Denma Lochö Rinpoche, Leah Zahler, Jeffrey Hopkins, *Meditative States in Tibetan Buddhism* (London: Wisdom Publications, 1983; revised edition, 1996).

[b] Available in Louis de La Vallée Poussin's French translation, which has, in turn, been translated into English by Leo M. Pruden: Louis de La Vallée Poussin, trans. and ed., *L'abhidharmakośa de Vasubandhu, Mélanges Chinois et Bouddhiques* 16 (reprinted 1971),

Summary of Manifest Knowledge (*abhidharmasamuccaya, mngon pa kun btus*), as well as another major source text by Asaṅga, his *Grounds of Hearers* (*śrāvakabhūmi, nyan sa*).[a] To clarify specific points, it also includes comparison with better-known Theravāda presentations, which have been translated into several languages, and consults a useful recent study of Theravāda presentations in Henepola Gunaratana's *The Path of Serenity and Insight: An Explanation of the Buddhist Jhānas*, which relies on untranslated Pāli subcommentaries to elucidate the presentations of the concentrations and formless absorptions in the Pāli canon and Buddhaghosa's *Path of Purification* (*visuddhimagga*).[b]

Structure of the Book and Chapter Summary

This work is in three parts: "Exposition," "Comparisons," and "Translations." The first part provides an overview and summary of Ge-luk presentations of the concentrations and formless absorptions. Chapter 1, "Ge-luk Presentations of the Concentrations and Formless Absorptions," initiates a discussion of religious scholarship. It also discusses the nature of the translated texts and their relationship to their sources, and examines their treatments of the various subtopics, which vary greatly; calm abiding and the mental contemplation of individual knowledge of the character, for example, are presented at great length, whereas the sections on the formless absorptions and the resultant-

---

cited hereafter as La Vallée Poussin; Leo M. Pruden, trans., *Abhidharmakośabhāṣyam by Louis de La Vallée Poussin*, 4 vols. (Berkeley: Asian Humanities Press, 1988–90), cited hereafter as Pruden.

[a] Walpola Rahula, trans., *Le Compendium de la super-doctrine (philosophie) (Abhidharmasamuccaya) d'Asaṅga* (Paris: École française d'extrême-orient, 1971); and for an English translation, *Abhidharmasamuccaya: The Compendium of the Higher Teaching (Philosophy) by Asaṅga*, trans. Sara Boin-Webb, (Fremont, Calif.: Asian Humanities Press, 2001). Two other major source texts by Asaṅga, his *Grounds of Hearers* and *Compendium of Ascertainments* (*viniścayasaṃgrahaṇī, gtan la dbab pa bsdu ba*), have not yet been translated into a Western language. Selected short passages of Asaṅga's *Grounds of Hearers* are translated in Alex Wayman, *Analysis of the Śrāvakabhūmi Manuscript*, University of California Publications in Classical Philology, vol. 17 (Berkeley and Los Angeles: University of California Press, 1961), although not in a way that indicated their place in the structure of the work as a whole or their significance in Asaṅga's presentation of calm abiding, special insight, and the concentrations and formless absorptions.

[b] Especially *The Collection of the Middle Length Sayings*, trans. I. B. Horner, Pali Text Society, first pub. 1954, 3 vols. (London: Luzac, 1967), and other Pali Text Society publications; Buddhaghosa, *Path of Purification* (*visuddhimagga*), trans. Ñyāṇamoli, 2 vols. (Berkeley and London: Shambhala, 1976). Henepola Gunaratana, *The Path of Serenity and Insight: An Explanation of the Buddhist Jhānas* (Motilal Banarsidass, 1985).

birth states are extremely short. Finally, the chapter compares the structure of the translated texts, which differ in the order in which they present the subtopics, and notes Jam-yang-shay-pa's contribution in introducing an obviously logical order, followed by Kön-chok-jik-may-wang-po in his condensation of Jam-yang-shay-pa's text. This is the order followed in the subsequent chapters of Part 1.

The second and third chapters present Jam-yang-shay-pa's—and, therefore, Kön-chok-jik-may-wang-po's—first two topics, which provide the background for the discussion of the meditations proper. The first topic, the physical bases of the concentrations and formless absorptions, is concerned with the types of beings who are capable or incapable of attaining those meditative absorptions; thus, it is also closely related to the topic of cosmology. The second, mental bases, is concerned not with the mental qualifications necessary for attainment of the concentrations and formless absorptions but, rather, with the ways in which certain consciousnesses, including the actual absorptions of the concentrations and formless absorptions, do or do not support—that is, act as bases of—certain other consciousnesses, especially path consciousnesses. The discussion of mental qualifications for attainment of the actual absorptions of the concentrations and formless absorptions, insofar as it relates to specific types of beings, is included in the topic of physical bases; insofar as it relates to the mental qualifications of beings capable by nature of attaining calm abiding and the concentrations and formless absorptions, it is included in the discussion of the prerequisites for cultivating and attaining calm abiding.

The next four chapters are concerned with calm abiding. Chapter 4 discusses the entity of calm abiding, the prerequisites for cultivating and attaining it, and the posture used in its cultivation. The last also includes a discussion of the process known as "the settling down of the winds"—that is, the use of meditation on the breath as a means of purifying the meditator's motivation—and, thereby, emphasizes the interdependence of mind and body in the cultivation of calm abiding.

Chapters 5 and 6 discuss objects of observation (*dmigs pa, ālambana*). Chapter 5 begins with a general discussion of Ge-luk presentations of objects of observation, starting with the general characteristics of objects of observation and the necessity of having one and continuing with practical points related to the choice of object of observation and whether—and if so, when—the meditator should change it. The chapter then proceeds to a discussion of the classic overview of the four types of object of observation set forth in Chapter 8 of the *Sūtra Unraveling the Thought* and explained, with slight differences in interpretation, in

Asaṅga's *Grounds of Hearers* and Kamalashīla's three texts called *Stages of Meditation.* Though confusing from a practical point of view, this classic layout is the point of departure of Ge-luk texts and oral presentations. The remainder of Chapter 5 and most of Chapter 6 discuss in detail the type called "objects of observation for purifying behavior" (*spyad pa rnam sbyong gi dmigs pa, caritaviśodanālambana*), used by beginners to pacify temporarily the five predominant afflictive emotions that prevent the attainment of calm abiding—namely, desire (*'dod chags, rāga*), hatred (*zhe dang, dveṣa*), obscuration (*gti mug, moha*), pride (*nga rgyal, māna*), and discursiveness (*rnam rtog, vikalpa*); they are pacified by meditating, respectively, on the unpleasant (*mi sdug pa, aśubha*), love (*byams pa, maitri*), dependent-arising (*rten cing 'brel bar 'byung ba, pratītyasamutpāda*), the divisions of the constituents (*khams, dhātu*), and the exhalation and inhalation of the breath (*dbugs 'byung rngub, ānāpana*).

Chapter 6 begins with a detailed discussion of breath meditation, based on Jam-yang-shay-pa's detailed explanations of the presentations in Vasubandhu's *Treasury of Manifest Knowledge* and Asaṅga's *Grounds of Hearers* and including, for purposes of comparison, examination of relevant Theravāda presentations of mindfulness of breathing in passages from the *Ānāpānasatisutta* and Buddhaghosa's *Path of Purification.* The chapter then completes the discussion of the four classic types of object of observation and introduces two other important sūtra-system objects of observation presented by Ge-luk-pa commentators—the body of a Buddha and one's own mind. The former, derived from Asaṅga's *Grounds of Hearers,* is the object of observation that Asaṅga, Tsong-kha-pa, and the Ge-luk textbook writers studied here consider best, especially for beginners. The latter, though derived from the *Sūtra Unraveling the Thought,* is somewhat disparaged, perhaps for sectarian reasons, by the Ge-luk-pa oral commentators cited here. The present Dalai Lama, however, recommends it and gives instructions, cited in Chapter 6, for its practice. The chapter also includes a brief discussion of the feasibility, or lack of it, of emptiness as an object of observation for beginners. Chapter 6 concludes with a discussion of what is known as finding the object of observation, for, once an object of observation has been correctly chosen, the meditator needs to achieve a basic level of proficiency in bringing it to mind at will, clearly and in its entirety, in order to proceed with the cultivation of calm abiding.

The first part of Chapter 7, "The Cultivation and Attainment of Calm Abiding," discusses the nine stages, known as the nine mental abidings (*sems gnas dgu, navākārā cittasthiti*), through which the meditator passes during the cultivation of calm abiding, as well as the five faults (*nyes dmigs, ādīnava*) encountered during the process and the eight means of overcoming them, known as antidotes, or applications (*'du byed pa, abhisaṃskāra*). In the ninth mental abiding, the meditator attains a stable, effortless meditation that is nevertheless not yet calm abiding. The second part of the chapter deals with the stages by which a meditator who has attained the ninth mental abiding goes on to achieve calm abiding, which, according to Ge-luk presentations, is characterized by a heightened mental capacity known as special pliancy (*shin tu sbyangs pa, praśrabdhi*). The chapter then discusses states, said to be attained simultaneously with calm abiding, that point toward attainments beyond it, since calm abiding, though attained gradually with great effort, is, among other things, the lowest mind of the Form Realm and the first of the seven preparations for the first concentration, known as the mental contemplation of a mere beginner (*las dang po pa tsam gyi yid byed*). Chapter 7 concludes with a brief discussion of controversial issues raised by Ge-luk presentations of calm abiding.

To progress beyond calm abiding, the meditator must develop the ability to analyze without disturbing the calm abiding already achieved. Thus, Chapter 8, "The Preparations," begins with a presentation of the four attributes of preparatory training (*sngon 'gro'i sbyor ba'i khyad par bzhi*) cultivated in order to strengthen this capacity. The chapter then considers problematic aspects of the brief expositions of special insight in Ge-luk presentations of the concentrations and formless absorptions—mainly, that the Ge-luk-pa writers considered here, especially Kön-chok-jik-may-wang-po and Jam-yang-shay-pa, cite the explanations of special insight in Asaṅga's *Grounds of Hearers* and the *Sūtra Unraveling the Thought,* which are important Indian sources for the topic of the concentrations and formless absorptions, whereas the main Ge-luk presentations of special insight are based on the work of Chandrakīrti, as interpreted by Tsong-kha-pa. The discussion here follows the example of modern Ge-luk-pa scholars and assimilates the explanation of special insight to that of the mental contemplation of individual knowledge of the character (*mtshan nyid so sor rig pa'i yid byed, lakṣaṇapratisaṃvedīmanaskāra*), the second preparation for the first contemplation and the first of Asaṅga's seven mental contemplations.

The chapter continues with a general explanation of preparations (*nyer bsdogs, sāmantaka*)—that is, the stages by which a meditator who has achieved calm abiding progresses to the next higher level. To do so, the meditator must separate from afflictive emotions pertaining to the lower level, the level he or she wishes to leave. This separation may be either a deep but temporary suppression of those afflictive emotions, in the mundane path, or, in the supramundane path, a radical eradication of them that leads to liberation from cyclic existence; in either case, the preparations are the means of effecting such a separation in order to attain an actual meditative absorption (*dngos gzhi'i snyoms 'jug, maulasamāpatti*) of the next higher level. Thus, the preparations are discussed in relation to the mundane and supramundane paths, which, in turn, are related to the three realms and nine levels of traditional Buddhist cosmology. The preparations for the first concentration are presented individually, in detail, as an example of the method for attaining the actual meditative absorptions of all the concentrations and formless absorptions.

The topic of the preparations extends to the presentation of the transitional periods between the attainment of calm abiding and the attainment of an actual meditative absorption of the first concentration, and between the attainment of any actual meditative absorption and the next higher one, the same detailed gradualist approach that marked the Ge-luk presentation of calm abiding. The Ge-luk synthesis of Vasubandhu's and Asaṅga's presentations of the transitional period between levels represents Ge-luk system-building at its strongest. Whereas Vasubandhu's *Treasury of Manifest Knowledge* posits eight preparations—meaning eight transitional periods between levels—without specifying their content or dividing them into stages, Asaṅga, in his *Grounds of Hearers*, divides this period into seven mental contemplations (*yid la byed pa, manaskāra*) that define the psychological stages of the meditator's progress. The strength of the Ge-luk synthesis lies in their careful comparison and differentiation of Vasubandhu's and Asaṅga's presentations, even while combining them into a single system. Moreover, on the basis of their own reasoning, as well as close readings of the source texts, they distinguish between preparations and Asaṅga's seven mental contemplations, the last of which is not a preparation but an actual meditative absorption, and they assign to calm abiding the status of a preparation—the mental contemplation of a mere beginner. Thus, in addition to their contributions to the psychology of meditation, Ge-luk expositions of the preparations for the concentrations and formless absorptions provide a developed example of Buddhist scholarly system-building based on reasoning.

Chapter 9, "The Meditative Absorptions of the Concentrations and Formless Absorptions," summarizes Ge-luk presentations of the meditative absorptions of the concentrations and formless absorptions, based primarily on Vasubandhu's *Treasury of Manifest Knowledge,* except for a few key passages from Asaṅga's *Compendium of Ascertainments* (*viniścaya-saṃgrahaṇī, gtan la dbab pa bsdu ba*). The Ge-luk presentations are similar in their main outline to the Theravāda presentation in Buddhaghosa's *Path of Purification;* although the differences are interesting, they are minor and are not discussed here. This chapter indicates how Ge-luk discussions of the meditative absorptions of the concentrations and formless absorptions provide an ideal model of sūtra-system Bodhisattva practice while accounting for the attainments of Hīnayāna and non-Buddhist meditators.

The second part, "Comparisons," consists of three chapters dealing with the reasons for the study of the concentrations and formless absorptions and the educational system in which they are studied. The first two chapters present two of the topics that provide reasons for the study of the concentrations and formless absorptions. Chapter 10, "The Concentrations and Formless Absorptions in the Life of Shākyamuni Buddha," briefly compares the significance of those meditative absorptions in two biographical accounts known to Tibetans—Bu-tön's (*bu ston*, 1290-1364) *History of Buddhism*, which relies on the *Extensive Sport Sūtra* (*rgya cher rol pa'i mdo, lalitavistarasūtra*), and Ashvaghoṣha's *Buddha's Deeds (buddhacarita, sangs rgyas kyi spyod pa*)—and in accounts in the Theravāda discourses. The chapter shows that although the concentrations and formless absorptions figured less prominently in Bu-tön's account of the Buddha's life than in the other two, Bu-tön retained significant elements, echoes of which appear in Ge-luk presentations of the concentrations and formless absorptions.

Chapter 11, "The Relationship of the Concentrations and Formless Absorptions to Traditional Buddhist Cosmology," shows how Buddhist cosmology is traditionally presented as a map of cyclic existence and the physical and mental states possible within it. This chapter discusses the relationship of the rebirth levels of the Form and Formless Realms to the cultivation and attainment, in a given lifetime, of the corresponding meditative absorption, and introduces the distinction between the mundane path (*'jig rten pa'i lam, laukikamārga*), which is held to lead only to high rebirths within cyclic existence, and the supramundane path (*'jig rten las 'das pa'i lam, lokottaramārga*), which is held to lead to liberation from cyclic existence. (The methods for cultivating the mundane and supramundane paths are discussed in greater detail in Chapter 8, "The Preparations.") This distinction, recognized by both Theravādins and Ge-luk-pas, allows Buddhist commentators to acknowledge the skill and high attainments of Indian non-Buddhist meditators while asserting the superiority of the motivation and goals of

Buddhist practice.

Since the concentrations and formless absorptions are studied in Ge-luk monastic universities as part of the extensive topic of the Perfections (*phar phyin, pāramitā*), Chapter 12, "The Concentrations and Formless Absorptions in Ge-luk Monastic Education," discusses the place of the concentrations and formless absorptions in that topic, which by providing a major Mahāyāna scriptural source—the Perfection of Wisdom sūtras—also provides a context for their study in a Mahāyāna educational system. This chapter gives an overview of the topic of the Perfection of Wisdom and its major Indian and Tibetan commentaries, introduces the major categories, and discusses in greater detail those aspects that emphasize the practitioner's Mahāyāna motivation and the place of the concentrations and formless absorptions in the practice of Bodhisattvas, as well as those that provide a theoretical basis for a Bodhisattva's engagement in Hīnayāna practices *as a Mahāyānist.* This chapter then turns to a comparison of Ge-luk-pa treatments of these topics with other academic approaches and finishes with a discussion of the dynamics of study and meditation as aspects of Ge-luk religious practice.

Part Three presents translations of the aforementioned texts by Tsong-kha-pa and Kön-chok-jik-may-wang-po.

PART ONE: *EXPOSITION*

1 GE-LUK PRESENTATIONS OF THE CONCENTRATIONS AND FORMLESS ABSORPTIONS

RELIGIOUS SCHOLARSHIP

The two Ge-luk texts translated here are works of religious scholarship. This statement makes two points. First, they *are* works of scholarship in that they are, as Robert Thurman remarked of similar Ge-luk works, essentially secondary material, and they perform functions we expect of scholarship, especially in their evaluations of Indian and earlier Tibetan sources.[a] Second, they are works of *religious* scholarship; thus, questions have been raised concerning their status in a Western academic context. As Donald S. Lopez has demonstrated, using the anthropologist Kenneth L. Pike's distinction between emic and etic views of cultures—that is, between views from within the system and from outside the system—the approach of Ge-luk scholars to Indian Buddhism is essentially emic, despite the factors of time and distance that separate them from their Indian sources. Lopez also shows with regard to his own area of interest, Svātantrika, that their system is synthetic, since Ge-luk scholars "were forced to construct a Svātantrika system from the sources before them."[b]

A similar case can be made with regard to Ge-luk presentations of calm abiding (*zhi gnas, śamatha*), special insight (*lhag mthong, vipaśyanā*), and the concentrations (*bsam gtan, dhyāna*) and formless absorptions (*gzugs med kyi snyoms 'jug, ārūpyasamāpatti*). These meditations, as far as we know, were probably not practiced in Tibet past the level of special insight, although presentations of them are studied as part of the program of education for the ge-shay (*dge bshes*) degree. Moreover, although the concentrations and formless absorptions are studied as a subtopic of the Perfections, the details of the system are synthesized largely from Manifest Knowledge sources—mainly from Asaṅga's *Summary of Manifest Knowledge,* as well as his more detailed presentation of

---

[a] Robert A. F. Thurman, remarks at the AAR annual meeting, 1983.

[b] Donald S. Lopez, *A Study of Svātantrika* (Ithaca, NY: Snow Lion Publications, 1987), pp. 27–30, citing Kenneth L. Pike, *Language in Relation to a Unified Theory of the Structure of Human Behavior,* 2nd rev. ed. (The Hague: Mouton and Co., 1967).

the concentrations and formless absorptions in *Grounds of Hearers,* but also from Vasubandhu's *Treasury of Manifest Knowledge* and his autocommentary on it, the *Explanation of the "Treasury of Manifest Knowledge"* (*abhidharmakośabhāṣya, chos mngon pa'i mdzod kyi tshig le'ur byas pa*). Kamalashīla's three texts called *Stages of Meditation* (*bhāvanākrama, sgom rim*) are also important sources. Tsong-kha-pa used these sources and others in his *Notes on the Concentrations and Formless Absorptions,* translated here, and in his earlier, more extensive treatment of the topic in his commentary on the topic of the Perfections, the *Golden Rosary of Eloquence* (*legs bshad gser gyi phreng ba;* see below, pp. 16-26ff., for a more detailed discussion of sources). Thus, Ge-luk-pas study presentations of the concentrations and formless absorptions out of what Lopez calls "the strong sense of tradition that characterizes [Tsong-kha-pa's] work and that of his followers,"[a] and these presentations, too, must be regarded as synthetic.

It could be argued that, like Talmudic scholarship—the best-known example of an emic, synthetic system of scholarship in a Western religious tradition—Ge-luk scholarship deserves to be made an object of academic study in its own right, for, like traditional Jews, Ge-luk-pas value study as an important part of a religious life. Thus, the academic study of the religious scholarship of both traditions is an important part of the study of their spirituality.

Ge-luk-pas consider study to be an aspect of hearing (*thos pa, śruta*) within the triad of hearing, thinking (*bsam pa, cintā*), and meditating (*sgom pa, bhāvanā*). This triad goes far back in Buddhist religious scholarship. The *locus classicus* for it is a verse in Vasubandhu's *Treasury of Manifest Knowledge* and the Vaibhāṣhika–Sautrāntika dispute on the second half of the verse, recorded in Vasubandhu's *Autocommentary.*[b] The first half of the verse gives the order and circumstances in which the members of the triad occur:

---

[a] Ibid., p. 29.

[b] La Vallée Poussin notes that this triad also occurs in Pāli sources. (La Vallée Poussin, 16:4, p. 143 n. 1). Robert Gimello, in a study of Indian/Chinese Buddhist perspectives, mentions two other classic sources that also influenced Ge-luk-pa writers: Kamalashīla's *Stages of Meditation* (*bhāvanākrama, sgom rim* [ed. Giuseppe Tucci, *Minor Buddhist Texts,* II [Rome: Istituto Italiano per il Medio ed Estremo Oriente, 1958], pp. 187 ff.) and, as an influence on Kamalashīla, Asaṅga's *Compendium of the Mahāyāna* (*mahāyānasaṃgraha, theg pa chen po bsdus pa* [P5549, vol. 112; trans. by Étienne Lamotte, *La Somme du Grand Véhicule d'Asaṅga,* first pub. 1939, vol. 2 [Louvain: Institut Orientaliste, 1973]) (Robert Gimello, "Mysticism in Its Contexts," *Mysticism and Religious Traditions,* ed. Steven T. Katz [New York: Oxford University Press, 1983], p. 88).

> Established in correct conduct, possessing hearing and thinking,
> One is fit for meditation [6.5a–b].[a]

The second half gives the Vaibhāṣhika (*bye brag smra ba, vaibhāṣika*) explanation of the awarenesses (*blo, dhī, buddhi*) or wisdoms (*shes rab, prajñā*), arisen from hearing, thinking, and meditating—that is, the consciousnesses (*rnam shes, vijñāna*) a person comes to have when he or she has developed hearing, thinking, and meditating, respectively, to their highest possible degree.

> Awarenesses arisen from hearing, and so forth,
> Have as objects name, both [name and meaning], or meaning [6.5c–d].[b]

The *Autocommentary* dispute involves the status of the wisdom arisen from thinking (*bsam byung gi shes rab, cintāmayīprajñā*) as set forth in the second half of the verse. According to the Vaibhāṣhika position, stated in the verse and the *Autocommentary* paraphrase, the first of the three wisdoms, that arisen from hearing (*thos byung gi shes rab, śrutamayīprajñā*), has name (*ming, nāman*) as its object—that is, the words setting forth whatever topic is being considered; the third, the wisdom arisen from meditation (*sgom byung gi shes rab, bhāvanāmayīprajñā*), has the meaning (*don, artha*) as its object, and the second, the wisdom arisen from thinking, has as its object both the name and the meaning. The *Autocommentary* uses as an example someone learning to swim, who at first holds on to a flotation device and eventually swims independently but, during the intermediate phase, sometimes holds on and sometimes lets go.[c]

The Sautrāntika objection, also given in Vasubandhu's *Autocommentary*, is that the Vaibhāṣhika position does not really account for the wisdom arisen from thinking; if the wisdom arisen from hearing has name as its object and that arisen from meditation has meaning as its object, that arisen from thinking, which is said to have both name and meaning as its object, is not established as anything specific; it may as well not exist. The Sautrāntika position, summarized in the

---

[a] Vasubandhu, *Treasury of Manifest Knowledge*, 6.5a–b (P5591, vol. 115, 243.5.6–7; Shastri, p. 891; La Vallée Poussin, 16:4, p. 142; Pruden, vol. 3, p. 911).

[b] Vasubandhu, *Treasury of Manifest Knowledge*, 6.5c–d (P5591, vol. 115, 244.1.1; Shastri, p. 891; La Vallée Poussin, 16:4, p. 143; Pruden, vol. 3, p. 912).

[c] Vasubandhu, *Autocommentary on the "Treasury of Manifest Knowledge,"* 6.5c–d (P5591, vol. 115, 244.1.1–4; Shastri, vol. 3, p. 891; La Vallée Poussin, 16:4, p. 143; Pruden, vol. 3, p. 912). See also Harvey B. Aronson, "The Buddhist Path: A Translation of the First Dalai Lama's *Path of Liberation*," Part II, *Tibet Journal* 5:4 (1980), 29.

commentary of Gen-dun-drup (*dge 'dun grub*, Dalai Lama I, 1391–1475), is that the wisdoms arisen from hearing, thinking, and meditating are, respectively, those "(1) arisen from valid authoritative scripture; (2) arisen from examination by reasoning; and (3) arisen from meditative stabilization (*ting nge 'dzin, samādhi*)."[a]

This position, too, is open to question. In his short text called *Analytical Delineation of the Presentation of the Three—Hearing, Thinking, and Meditating* (*thos bsam sgom gsum gyi rnam bzhag mtha' dpyod kyi sgo nas gtan la 'bebs pa lta ngan mun sel*), Jam-yang-shay-pa uses the Vaibhāṣhika–Sautrāntika dispute in Vasubandhu's *Autocommentary*, which he summarizes in Tibetan debate format, as the point of departure for his exposition of "the system of Tsong-kha-pa and his spiritual sons." He begins by refuting what amounts to the Sautrāntika presentation of the wisdom arisen from meditation, a position also held by earlier Tibetan scholars, in order to establish the importance of analytical meditation (*dpyad sgom*)—that is, of a reasoning process not only in thinking but also in meditation itself and in states arisen from meditation. In brief, he argues that the Sautrāntika position entails that "whatever is meditation is necessarily only stabilizing meditation (*'jog sgom*)"—an absurd position from the point of view of Tsong-kha-pa's system. This, in turn, entails the absurd consequence that "whatever is meditation is necessarily meditation that is only one-pointed meditative stabilization"; if the opponent accepts that, the counterexample is "analytical meditation that is a cultivation of special insight," since, "for the cultivation of special insight, one must meditate mainly analytically." To support this line of reasoning, he cites Tsong-kha-pa's [*Great*] *Exposition of the Stages of the Path* and Tsong-kha-pa's main Indian sources for this point, the *Sūtra Unraveling the Thought* (*samdhinirmocanasūtra, dgongs pa nges par 'grel pa'i mdo*) and Asaṅga's *Summary of Manifest Knowledge*.[b] These two texts set forth the basic Mahāyāna presentation of the path accepted by both Chittamātrins and Mādhyamikas; in citing Asaṅga's *Summary of Manifest Knowledge*, Jam-yang-shay-pa is using the main Mahāyāna Manifest Knowledge text as a corrective to the

---

[a] Aronson, "The Buddhist Path," p. 29; see Vasubandhu, *Treasury of Manifest Knowledge* (P5591, vol. 115, 244.1.5–7; Shastri, vol. 3, p. 892; La Vallée Poussin, 16:4, p. 143; Pruden, vol. 3, p. 912).

[b] Jam-yang-shay-pa, *Analytical Delineation of the Presentation of the Three—Hearing, Thinking, and Meditating: Clearing Away the Darkness of Bad Views* (*thos bsam sgom gsum gyi rnam bzhag mtha' dpyod kyi sgo nas gtan la 'bebs pa lta ngan mun sel*; Varanasi: Pleasure of Elegant Sayings Printing Press, 1964), pp. 2–5. (Also in Jam-yang-shay-pa, *Collected Works*, vol. 12, 436–72.) Thanks to Georges Dreyfus for calling my attention to this text.

main Hīnayāna one.

Once meditation and the wisdom arisen from meditation are held to include analytical as well as stabilizing meditation, as is the case according to Jam-yang-shay-pa's definitions of them—so that a "[state] arisen from meditation one-pointedly observes, from the point of view of either analytical or stabilizing meditation, the meaning of what has been ascertained by [a wisdom] arisen from thinking"[a]—the stages that precede meditation and the wisdom arisen from it are correspondingly raised one notch. Thus, according to Jam-yang-shay-pa, a wisdom arisen from thinking is an inferential cognition (*rjes dpag, anumāna*)—that is, not merely a reasoning process or a conclusion arrived at by a reasoning process but a consciousness fully convinced of that conclusion; the reasoning process leading to the inferential cognition that is a wisdom arisen from thinking—technically, the use of the four reasonings (*rigs pa, yukti*)—is included in the definition of "thinking." The object of this reasoning is "the meaning of what has been heard."[b]

The meaning and status of "hearing" are also extended. According to Jam-yang-shay-pa, "hearing" includes "newly apprehending a word or meaning in the Tripiṭaka, and so forth, that has not been heard."[c] Mention of "the Tripiṭaka, and so forth" establishes that hearing, in this context, is a religious activity. The definition also includes the two divisions "in terms of the mode of hearing"—"the hearing of words and the hearing of meanings."[d] The hearing of words is obvious; it is the mere apprehension of a word or its parts (its syllables). Essentially, this is the basic meaning of "hearing" stated in Vasubandhu's *Treasury of Manifest Knowledge*.[e] As an illustration of the hearing of meanings, however, Jam-yang-shay-pa gives the hearing of "proofs by means of many reasons that sound is impermanent,"[f] and he defines a wisdom arisen from hearing as

> an intelligence that distinguishes doctrines generated from the valid cognition of another, a spiritual guide or scripture, although it does not by its own power gain a state arisen from

---

[a] Ibid., p. 21.

[b] Ibid., pp. 18–19.

[c] Ibid., p. 17.

[d] Ibid., p. 22.

[e] Ibid., p. 22. Jam-yang-shay-pa cites Asaṅga's *Grounds of Hearers* with regard to the hearing of syllables.

[f] Ibid., p. 22.

thinking.[a]

Thus, the hearing of meanings can include the hearing of the steps of a reasoning process, and a wisdom arisen from hearing includes an ability to follow and understand a teacher's or a text's presentation of a reasoning process and the conclusion to be drawn from it. Indeed, according to a verse, appended to a Lo-sel-ling College textbook on the topic of Awareness and Knowledge (*blo rig*), which gives a generally-agreed-on Ge-luk position relating that topic to the presentation of hearing, thinking, and meditating, a wisdom arisen from hearing is a correctly assuming consciousness (*yid dpyod, *manaḥ parīkṣā*).[b] Thus, although Jam-yang-shay-pa does not do so, his definition of a wisdom arisen from hearing can be interpreted to include not only a general understanding derived from hearing but also any stage of the reasoning process short of an actual inferential cognition.

According to contemporary Ge-luk scholars, the term "hearing" also includes silent reading. Thus, the Ge-luk-pas have extended the meaning of "hearing" to include not only the mere hearing or reading of words but the activities associated with the study and assimilation of scripture and commentaries on scripture. Indeed, it would not be an exaggeration to say that the entire Ge-luk educational system, including the study of monastic textbooks and the Indian and Tibetan texts selectively cited in them, is included in the religious activity called hearing. Thus, the study of these textbooks in a Western academic context can increase understanding of a major component of Ge-luk-pa religious life.

THE MAJOR GE-LUK TEXTS DISCUSSED HERE

This study is based on two monastic textbooks—the section on the concentrations and formless absorptions from Paṇ-chen Sö-nam-drak-pa's *General Meaning of (Maitreya's) "Ornament for Clear Realization"* (*phar phyin spyi don*) and Kön-chok-jik-may-wang-po's *Condensed Statement of*

---

[a] Ibid., p. 18.

[b] Lati Rinpoche, *Mind in Tibetan Buddhism: Oral Commentary on Ge-shay Jam-bel-sam-pel's* Presentation of Awareness and Knowledge, ed. and trans. Elizabeth Napper (Ithaca, NY: Snow Lion Publications, 1980), Tibetan text, p. 25; this verse is not translated by Napper. Thanks to William A. Magee for calling my attention to it.

Since the writers of both this Awareness and Knowledge text and the appended verse are from Lo-sel-ling College of Dre-bung Monastic University, whereas Jam-yang-shay-pa is the main textbook writer of Go-mang College, differences can be expected in the details of the presentation, but the two colleges agree on the main outline.

(Jam-yang-shay-pa's) "Great Exposition of the Concentrations and Formless Absorptions" (bsam gzugs chen mo las mdor bsdus te bkod pa)—and a brief work by Tsong-kha-pa, the founder of the Ge-luk order of Tibetan Buddhism—his *Notes on the Concentrations and Formless Absorptions.*[a] This is the text on which both textbook writers base their discussions of the preparations for, and actual meditative absorptions of, the concentrations and formless absorptions. It is their "root text," as Jam-yang-shay-pa calls it in his single explicit reference to it, in the section on the seven mental contemplations in his *Great Exposition of the Concentrations and Formless Absorptions,*[b] and it is obvious that he, as well as the writers of the two textbooks discussed here, often had it clearly in mind and paraphrased it without acknowledgment. Nevertheless, they seldom refer to it explicitly. Rather, they quote extensively from Tsong-kha-pa's early work on the topic of the Perfections, his *Golden Rosary of Eloquence*—probably because of its many citations of Indian sources and of the opinions of earlier Tibetan scholars. However, it is the *Notes,* as Gedün Lodrö points out, that represents Tsong-kha-pa's own system; precisely because of the many references to other opinions in the *Golden Rosary,* it is difficult to tell from that work what Tsong-kha-pa's own system is; "thus, it is easy to become confused."[c] Therefore, it is useful to refer to Tsong-kha-pa's *Notes on the Concentrations and Formless Absorptions* when there is doubt concerning Tsong-kha-pa's position.

Tsong-kha-pa's *Notes* grounds the other two texts discussed here. It grounds them historically because it precedes them and because they are derived from it, and doctrinally because their authors are Tsong-kha-pa's followers and, despite their often divergent positions on subtle points, are trying to present his system accurately. Thus, it serves as a point of reference beyond and preceding the partisanship of intercollegial monastic debate. Ge-luk monastics are loyal to their colleges' textbooks, and the textbooks themselves contain debates and sometimes instruct students in debate—a style of debate that involves

---

[a] Kön-chok-jik-may-wang-po's *Condensed Statement* and Tsong-kha-pa's *Notes* are translated in Part 3 of this work. The translation of Paṇ-chen Sö-nam-drak-pa's section on the concentrations and formless absorptions has been previously published (in Lati Rinpoche, Denma Lochö Rinpoche, Leah Zahler, Jeffrey Hopkins, *Meditative States in Tibetan Buddhism* [London: Wisdom Publications, 1983; revised edition, 1996])(cited hereafter as *Meditative States*).

[b] Jam-yang-shay-pa, *Concentrations,* 210.5.

[c] Gedün Lodrö, *Walking Through Walls: A Presentation of Tibetan Meditation,* trans. and ed. by Jeffrey Hopkins (Ithaca, NY: Snow Lion Publications, 1992), p. 175; hereafter cited as Gedün Lodrö, p. 342.

fiercely partisan adherence to the textbooks of the debater's college. Nevertheless, all Ge-luk-pas owe their primary allegiance to Tsong-kha-pa. The Fourteenth Dalai Lama remarked in a lecture to a group of Ge-luk-pa monastics, "If you are Ge-luk-pas, you should read Tsong-kha-pa, not just your own colleges' textbooks."[a]

Although the *Notes* does not show the concern, evident in the two *Exposition(s) of the Stages of the Path,* with drawing instructions for practice from the "great texts"—that is, the Indian source texts—and thus making scholarship serve practice, it is a straightforward, though compressed, presentation of the topic, the result of care in sifting through the mass of previous Indian and Tibetan scholarship but without any display of scholarship for its own sake. Except for summaries of the two major Indian systems—those of Vasubandhu's *Treasury of Manifest Knowledge* and Asaṅga's *Summary of Manifest Knowledge* and other works of Asaṅga—and one citation of Yashomitra's *Commentary on (Asaṅga's) "Summary of Manifest Knowledge,"* the process of sifting does not show, but the extent of it is clear from Kön-chok-jik-may-wang-po's and, especially, Jam-yang-shay-pa's citations of Tsong-kha-pa's *Golden Rosary* and of Tsong-kha-pa's Indian sources.

In two respects, Tsong-kha-pa's *Notes* is not a complete presentation of his system: it omits his presentations of calm abiding and special insight. Later Ge-luk writers derive their presentations of calm abiding from Tsong-kha-pa's *Great* and *Middling Exposition(s) of the Stages of the Path* and their presentations of special insight in the context of the concentrations and formless absorptions, for the most part, from Asaṅga's *Grounds of Hearers* and the *Sūtra Unraveling the Thought.* The later texts also distinguish explicitly—as Tsong-kha-pa does not here—between the seven preparations, of which calm abiding is the first, and the seven mental contemplations, of which the mental contemplation of individual knowledge of the character is the first.

The two monastic textbooks are of different types. Paṇ-chen Sö-nam-drak-pa's section on the concentrations and formless absorptions is part of a general meaning (*spyi don*) commentary, whereas Kön-chok-jik-may-wang-po's *Condensed Statement of (Jam-yang-shay-pa's) "Great Exposition of the Concentrations and Formless Absorptions"* is a final analysis (*mtha' dpyod*) of the topic. These differ especially in their use of debate. Although Paṇ-chen Sö-nam-drak-pa's section on the concentrations and formless absorptions is loosely organized, he presents the various

[a] Reported by Jeffrey Hopkins in conversation. See Jeffrey Hopkins, *Emptiness Yoga* (Ithaca, NY: Snow Lion Publications, 1987), p. 353.

topics in a fairly straightforward manner, and it is always clear what his position is. The entire section has only five debates. They serve to indicate major areas of controversy and the author's position with regard to them, but they do not explore the fine points of those controversies. Kön-chok-jik-may-wang-po's text, on the other hand, is mainly a debate manual. As is customary in such texts, each major topic has three sections—a refutation of opinions the author considers mistaken, an exposition of his own system, and a final section in which the author dispels objections that might be made to his exposition. The first and third sections consist of a series of debates, and in the work by Jam-yang-shay-pa on which Kön-chok-jik-may-wang-po's text is based, even the middle, expository, sections sometimes include debates.

Ge-luk-pas consider Kön-chok-jik-may-wang-po to be the second incarnation of Jam-yang-shay-pa; if they are right, it would seem that Jam-yang-shay-pa saw a need to revise and clarify his earlier work on the concentrations and formless absorptions. In his condensation, Kön-chok-jik-may-wang-po has simplified Jam-yang-shay-pa's text and made it more accessible. Although Jam-yang-shay-pa's work is valuable for its detailed citations of Indian and Tibetan sources, revealing the process by which his system was synthesized, Kön-chok-jik-may-wang-po has eliminated most of these citations for the sake of clarity; he has also eliminated the extended discussions of minor points.

Above all, Kön-chok-jik-may-wang-po has simplified the debates and laid out his own and his opponents' positions in a straightforward manner instead of following the style of sustained sarcasm in which Jam-yang-shay-pa often makes his points—by stating sarcastically, for instance, that if the opponent's assertion on a given issue is correct, an Indian source text accepted by both parties must be wrong. Most writers of debate texts use this style on occasion, but Jam-yang-shay-pa is unusual in his evident pleasure in it and his ability to sustain it for pages on end. The bracketed additions in consequences and reasons in the translation—"it [absurdly] follows" and "because [according to you]"—are necessary for the Western reader's understanding of the various positions, but they weaken what is essentially an oral style. For Tibetans, as for many non-Tibetans, sarcasm is conveyed by voice and facial expression; a Tibetan debater does not have to be told in so many words that a consequence is absurd or that his own reason is being thrown back in his face. Jam-yang-shay-pa used his text to teach students how to present his positions in the debating courtyard; he often concludes a debate with instructions, beginning, "Fling such consequences as..., " that suggest how the student might extend the debate to related topics. It would seem, however, that even Jam-yang-shay-pa's followers in Go-mang College found his sustained sarcasm hard to bear. By tempering it and laying out the positions simply and clearly, Kön-chok-jik-may-wang-po has written a text to be read; his condensation serves as a guide to the complexities of Jam-yang-shay-pa's oral debate style.

Paṇ-chen Sö-nam-drak-pa's section on the concentrations and formless absorptions is part of a longer textbook on the topic of the Perfections. It appears there in the section on achieving engagement (*'jug sgrub, prasthānapratipatti;* see Chapter 12). Jam-yang-shay-pa also wrote a textbook on the topic of the Perfections, his *Final Analysis of the Perfections* (*phar phyin mtha' dpyod*), along with a short summation of Maitreya's principal topics, the *Eloquent Presentation of the Eight Categories and Seventy Topics* (*dngos po brgyad don bdun cu'i rnam bzhag legs par bshad pa*). There, he merely mentions the practice of the concentrations and formless absorptions as a division of achieving engagement,[a] whereas his *Great Exposition of the Concentrations and Formless Absorptions* discusses them at length as a topic in their own right, although still in the context of the Perfections.

THE RELATIONSHIP OF GE-LUK PRESENTATIONS OF THE CONCENTRATIONS AND FORMLESS ABSORPTIONS TO THEIR SOURCES

Since Ge-luk-pas study presentations of the concentrations and formless absorptions under the topic of the Perfections, the Indian sources for that topic (see Chapter 12) must be included among the sources for textbook presentations of the concentrations and formless absorptions. Tibetan commentaries on the Perfections—especially, for Ge-luk-pas, Tsong-kha-pa's *Golden Rosary of Eloquence*—must also be included. This early work by Tsong-kha-pa sets forth his method of applying Manifest Knowledge methods to the study of the Perfections (see pp. 59ff.), but its presentation of the concentrations and formless absorptions differs slightly from that in the later work translated here, his *Notes on the Concentrations and Formless Absorptions.*

However, the main Indian sources for the details of Ge-luk presentations of the concentrations and formless absorptions are not those for the topic of the Perfections but Manifest Knowledge texts and works based on or agreeing with them. The two main Manifest

---

[a] Jam-yang-shay-pa, *Seventy Topics,* 127.2.

Knowledge texts are Asaṅga's *Summary of Manifest Knowledge* and Vasubandhu's *Treasury of Manifest Knowledge*, together with its autocommentary, the *Explanation of the "Treasury of Manifest Knowledge."* Paṇ-chen Sö-nam-drak-pa, Jam-yang-shay-pa, and Kön-chok-jik-may-wang-po often refer to these as "the upper and lower Manifest Knowledges" (*mngon pa gong 'og*)—that is, respectively, the upper, or Mahāyāna, and the lower, or Hīnayāna, Manifest Knowledge.[a] Throughout his *Notes on the Concentrations and Formless Absorptions*, Tsong-kha-pa draws careful comparisons of the major points of the two Manifest Knowledge presentations.

A third category, overlapping the first two, is that of works dealing with the practical aspects of meditation. As will be discussed later (Chapter 12), the Perfection of Wisdom Sūtras describe the branches of the concentrations and formless absorptions in terms similar to those in the Pāli canon. Since the Perfection of Wisdom Sūtras raise the question of how a Bodhisattva should practice them, it is possible that they may have been practiced at that time, at least by a few yogic practitioners. In his *Grounds of Hearers*, Asaṅga gives detailed descriptions of the cultivation of calm abiding, special insight, and the preparations for the concentrations and formless absorptions, as well as the concentrations and formless absorptions themselves. The presentation in this work agrees with that of his *Summary of Manifest Knowledge* but is far more extensive. Tibetan textbook writers also quote his *Compendium of Ascertainments* to supplement the presentation in *Grounds of Hearers.*[b]

Other major Indian sources for Ge-luk presentations of calm abiding and special insight include Chapter 8 of the *Sūtra Unraveling the Thought;* Maitreya's *Ornament for the Mahāyāna Sūtras* (*mahāyānasūtrālaṃkāra, theg pa chen po'i mdo sde'i rgyan*) and *Differentiation of the Middle and the Extremes* (*madhyāntavibhaṅga, dbus dang mtha' rnam par 'byed pa*); Bhāvaviveka's *Heart of the Middle* (*madhyamakahṛdaya, dbu ma'i snying po*) and his autocommentary, the *Blaze of Reasoning* (*tarkajvālā, rtog ge 'bar ba*); and the three *Stages of Meditation* texts by Kamalashīla.[c]

Kamalashīla was an important figure in the first dissemination of Buddhism in Tibet. As Lopez points out, he

> was invited to Tibet to defend the Madhyamaka approach to the path against the arguments of a Northern Ch'an monk known as Ho-shang Mo-ho-yen. [He] presented his position in three texts, each entitled *Stages of Meditation*,...and was declared

---

[a] Gedün Lodrö, p. 17.

[b] Paṇ-chen Sö-nam-drak-pa, "Concentrations," 161b.1, 162b.1.

[c] Gedün Lodrö, pp. 21–22.

> the victor in the controversy that has come to be known as the Council of Lhasa (792–94).[a]

His victory established the dominance in Tibet not only of his philosophical views but also of his presentation of calm abiding and special insight. This presentation retained its authority, as both description and instruction for practice, even after the translation of Chandrakīrti's works into Tibetan and Atisha's avowal of Chandrakīrti's system during the second dissemination of Buddhism in Tibet in the eleventh century began to make Prāsaṅgika-Madhyamaka, rather than Kamalashīla's Yogāchāra-Svātantrika-Madhyamaka, the dominant philosophical system.[b] Ge-luk-pa scholars trace their presentations of calm abiding and special insight back to Atisha. According to Kensur Lekden,

> Atisha tends to follow the Yogāchāra-Svātantrika-Mādhyamikas with respect to the path, their description being renowned as the general Mahāyāna explanation.[c]

Atisha's *Lamp for the Path to Enlightenment* (*bodhipathapradīpa, byang chub lam gyi sgron ma*) and its autocommentary, written for his Tibetan disciples, became the model for later stages-of-the-path (*lam rim*) texts,[d] some of which included presentations of calm abiding and special insight. Although the concentrations and formless absorptions became and remained merely an academic topic, studied in the context of the Perfections, calm abiding and special insight were also taught in the stages-of-the-path tradition, which emphasized practice. Atisha's treatment of special insight, although brief, outlines four of the Prāsaṅgika reasonings for meditating on emptiness (*stong pa nyid, śūnyatā*)—those of the four extremes (*mtha', anta*), the vajra nodes (*rdo rje gzegs ma*), the lack of being one or many, and dependent-arising—and lays the groundwork for Ge-luk presentations, beginning with Tsong-kha-pa's.

His treatment of calm abiding is sketchy, however. He relies mainly on a work by his own guru, Bodhibhadra's *Chapter on the Collection of Meditative Stabilization* (*samādhisambhāraparivarta, ting nge 'dzin gyi tshogs kyi*

---

[a] Lopez, *Svātantrika*, pp. 15 and 435 n. 5. See also Donald S. Lopez, *The Heart Sūtra Explained: Indian and Tibetan Commentaries* (Albany, NY: State University of New York Press, 1988), pp. 11 and 189 n. 23.

[b] See Lopez, *Svātantrika*, p. 22.

[c] Hopkins, *Meditation on Emptiness*, p. 864 n. 527, citing the oral commentary of Kensur Lekden.

[d] Tenzin Gyatso, Dalai Lama XIV, Foreword to Richard Sherburne, S.J., trans., *A Lamp for the Path and Commentary of Atīśa* (London: Allen & Unwin 1983), p. vii.

le'u).[a] Although Bodhibhadra cites Maitreya's *Differentiation of the Middle and the Extremes* with regard to the five faults and the eight applications, or antidotes (*'du byed pa, abhisaṃskāra*),[b] he differs in some respects from later, specifically Ge-luk, presentations of calm abiding. The points of difference include the prerequisites (*tshogs bsten pa*) for calm abiding, objects of observation (*dmigs pa, ālambana*; Bodhibhadra lists objects of observation from both sūtra and mantra, without distinguishing between them), and, especially, the discussion of calm abiding with and without signs (*mtshan ma dang bcas pa'i zhi gnas* and *mtshan ma med pa'i zhi gnas*), the latter of which he equates with the wisdom of individual analysis (*so sor rtog pa'i shes rab*), which, in turn, is said to lead to special insight without signs (*mtshan ma med pa'i lhag mthong*).[c] Sherburne considers it "remarkable" that Atisha does not mention in this context the nine mental abidings "which have become so well known to Tibetan monks through Tsong-kha-pa's *Lam-rim chen-mo*" and suggests, "Perhaps Atīśa felt that teaching was too advanced for his audience."[d] According to Gedün Lodrö, however, the two systems—that of the five faults and eight antidotes, from Maitreya's *Differentiation of the Middle and the Extremes,* and that of the nine mental abidings, from Asaṅga's *Grounds of Hearers* and *Summary of Manifest Knowledge* and Maitreya's *Ornament for the Mahāyāna Sūtras*—were brought together only later, by Atisha's followers in the textual (*gzhung pa pa*) lineage of the Ka-dam-pa (*dka' gdams pa*) School.[e] The details of Atisha's system had to be filled in, from the "great texts" of Asaṅga and Maitreya and from Kamalashīla's three *Stages of Meditation,* before it could become the Ge-luk system as we know it.

Unfortunately, little is known about the development of the stages-of-the-path tradition between Atisha and Tsong-kha-pa; it is a virtually unresearched area. There seem to be no detailed Western studies of

---

[a] P5444; cited by Sherburne, p. 124 n. 9.

[b] Atisha, *Autocommentary on "A Lamp for the Path"* (*bodhimārgapradīpapañjika, byang chub lam gyi sgron ma'i dka' 'grel*), P5344, 37.5.1–4; Sherburne, p. 120. Sherburne notes that "Atīśa omits Bodhibhadra's acknowledgement of the source" (p. 125 n. 15).

[c] P5344, 38.1.7; Sherburne, pp. 122, 125 n. 25.

[d] Sherburne, p. 125 n. 13.

[e] Gedün Lodrö, pp. 193–94, 360. Gedün Lodrö explains the textual lineage as consisting of "those who engage in practice from the viewpoint of maintaining a continuum of explanation of the great texts," whereas the other main lineage of the Ka-dam-pa School, the preceptual (*gdams ngag pa*) lineage, "consists of those who mainly engage in practice by way of a transmission of quintessential instructions" (p. 193). The preceptual lineage was responsible for the texts giving quintessential instructions for training the mind (*blo sbyong*).

Tsong-kha-pa's citations of Ka-dam-pa scholars in his *Great Exposition of the Stages of the Path.* According to the *Blue Annals,*[a] Tsong-kha-pa's *Great Exposition of the Stages of the Path* was "mainly based" on the *Great Exposition of the Stages of the Teaching* (*bstan rim chen mo*) of Dro-lung-pa (*gro lung pa blo gros 'byung gnas*), who also wrote an *Exposition of the Stages of the Path* described by the *Blue Annals* as "extensive."[b] Dro-lung-pa is described as "the chief disciple" of the translator Ngok (*rngog lo tsa ba blo ldan shes rab,* 1059–1109), who composed a commentary on Atisha's *Lamp for the Path.*[c] The *Blue Annals* also mentions a tradition of teaching a *Great Exposition of the Stages of the Path* by Kor (*skor*) at Tag-jen (*stag can*) Monastery, although it is not clear from the context whether this text is by Kor the Great or by his successor as abbot at Tag-jen, Kor-jo-say (*skor jo sras*).[d] It would be especially valuable to know how and when the Indian source texts for the Ge-luk presentations of calm abiding and special insight—Tsong-kha-pa's "great texts"—were brought into the stages-of-the-path tradition, and by whom. In the texts translated here, Paṇ-chen Sö-nam-drak-pa cites the *Blue Small Text* (*be'u bum sngon po*) of Ge-shay Döl-pa-shay-rap-gya-tso (*dge bshes dol pa shes rab rgya mtsho,* 1059–1131) and an unidentified Ka-dam *Stages of the Path* to point out a subtle difference between their position and Tsong-kha-pa's with regard to the union of calm abiding and special insight.[e]

For Ge-luk-pas, Tsong-kha-pa's *Great Exposition of the Stages of the Path* is the stages-of-the-path text *par excellence.* It follows the order of his short text in verse, the *Concise Meaning of the Stages of the Path* (*lam rim bsdus don*), which, in turn, follows that of Atisha's *Lamp for the Path.* In both the *Great* and *Middling Exposition(s) of the Stages of the Path,* Tsong-kha-pa sets forth a system in which calm abiding and special insight realizing emptiness are attained by sūtra-system methods. Thus, both contain detailed presentations of calm abiding and special insight; both texts cite the main Indian sources but, unlike later monastic textbooks, are intended as instructions for practice.

In another short text in verse, the *Three Principal Aspects of the Path* (*lam gyi gtso bo rnam pa gsum*), Tsong-kha-pa teaches a system in which a meditator can gain experience with respect to all three aspects—the

---

[a] Gö-lo-tsa-wa (*'gos lo tsa ba gzhon nu dpal,* 1392–1481), *The Blue Annals* (*deb ther sngon po*), trans. George N. Roerich, first pub. 1949 (Delhi: Motilal Banarsidass, 1976), p. 314; see also p. 931.

[b] Ibid., p. 331; see also p. 326.

[c] Ibid, pp. 331, 326.

[d] Ibid., pp. 320, 318.

[e] Paṇ-chen Sö-nam-drak-pa, "Concentrations," 156b.4, and *Meditative States,* p. 76.

thought definitely to leave cyclic existence (*'khor ba, saṃsāra*), the altruistic mind of enlightenment (*byang chub kyi sems, bodhicitta*), and the correct view of emptiness—without first achieving calm abiding and special insight. According to this system, the meditator gains experience with respect to all three aspects and then enters the Vajra Vehicle. No mention is made of the cultivation of calm abiding and special insight. This system is the basis of such commentaries as the Fourth Paṇ-chen Lama's meditation manual, *Instructions on (Tsong-kha-pa's) "Three Principal Aspects of the Path,"* (*lam gyi gtso bo rnam pa gsum gyi khrid yig*) and is the system usually taught to beginners nowadays.[a]

In his works on the stages of the path, Tsong-kha-pa tries to resolve the tension between study and meditation that seems to persist among religious scholars even when study has been assigned a place in the religious life that is both important and subordinate to meditation. His commentaries on the Perfections are primarily works of religious scholarship, but in his stages-of-the-path texts he tries to teach meditators how to use the "great texts" themselves—that is, the Indian source texts—as instructions for practice. Commenting on Paṇ-chen Sö-nam-drak-pa's citation of Döl-pa-shay-rap-gya-tso's *Blue Small Text,* Denma Lochö Rinpoche remarked:

> Tsong-kha-pa said that we need to cause the great texts to appear as precepts [that is, instructions] for practice. This does not mean that we should have in our hands a small text [setting forth precepts]; rather, it means that all the great texts should appear as precepts to the mind.[b]

It is a point Tsong-kha-pa makes strongly and often, but he admits with regret that "those who know how to practice on the basis of the great texts appear as [rarely as] stars during the day."[c] Tsong-kha-pa himself seems to have been such a person, but the tension reappears among his followers. Although Ge-luk textbooks on calm abiding, special insight, and the concentrations and formless absorptions are not directed toward practice, in their presentations of calm abiding and special insight they cite not only the Indian source texts and Tibetan scholarly works

---

[a] Fourth Paṇ-chen Lama, *Instructions on the Three Principal Aspects of the Path,* in Geshe Lhundup Sopa and Jeffrey Hopkins, *Cutting through Appearances: The Practice and Theory of Tibetan Buddhism,* first published as *Practice and Theory of Tibetan Buddhism*, 1976 (Ithaca, NY: Snow Lion Publications, 1989), pp. 105–6.

[b] *Meditative States,* p. 176.

[c] Tsong-kha-pa, *Great Exposition of the Stages of the Path* (Dharamsala: shes rig par khang, no date), 665.5–6.

but also Tsong-kha-pa's *Great Exposition of the Stages of the Path* and other stages-of-the-path texts. Jam-yang-shay-pa cites, sometimes at length, the Fifth Dalai Lama's stages-of-the-path text, the *Sacred Word of Mañjushrī ('jam pa'i dbyangs kyi zhal lung)*,[a] which he refers to not only by its short title, in the usual manner of citations in monastic textbooks, but sometimes with laudatory epithets such as "the great good explanation without precedent" and "free of mistakes."[b] Although the balance between scholarship and practice advocated by Tsong-kha-pa remained rare among his followers, they continued to value it highly.

THE WEIGHT AND ORDER OF THE TOPICS

The monastic textbooks on the concentrations and formless absorptions reflect practice to some extent in the weight they give the various topics. The longest section in the textbooks considered here is that on calm abiding, a topic that is still also taught in the context of practice; the topic of calm abiding accounts for approximately thirty percent of Jam-yang-shay-pa's textbook, and of Kön-chok-jik-may-wang-po's condensation of it. Although actual special insight is treated fairly briefly in the context of the concentrations and formless absorptions, the analogous method for achieving so-called mundane special insight in the second of the preparations for the first concentration (*bsam gtan dang po, prathamadhyāna*), the mental contemplation of individual knowledge of the character, is treated at great length, as are the preparations generally. The actual meditative absorptions and branches (*yan lag, aṅga*) of the concentrations are also discussed in detail, although these sections are somewhat shorter. The discussions of the formless absorptions and the resultant-birth (*'bras bu skye ba*) states is extremely brief in all the texts.

Kön-chok-jik-may-wang-po's condensation of Jam-yang-shay-pa's text follows Jam-yang-shay-pa's order. According to Gedün Lodrö, this order is Jam-yang-shay-pa's own.[c] The major headings are as follows:

I. The basis of cultivation
   A. The physical basis (*lus rten*)
   B. The mental basis (*sems rten*)
II. The meditative stabilizations of the concentrations and formless

---

[a] Jam-yang-shay-pa, *Concentrations,* 135.6–136.1, 141.7, 156.7–157.1, 157.1–5; *Collected Works,* vol. 12, 123.2–3, 128.7–129.1, 142.5, 142.6–143.2.

[b] Ibid., 135.6, 141.7; *Collected Works,* vol. 12, 123.2, 128.7.

[c] Gedün Lodrö, p. 22.

absorptions that are to be cultivated

A. The preparations, which are the means of attainment
   1. Calm abiding and special insight, which include all meditative stabilizations
   2. The mode of entering into meditative absorption in the eight concentrations and formless absorptions by way of the seven mental contemplations (*yid byed, manaskāra*)

B. The actual meditative absorptions that are to be attained
   1. The explanation of the entities of the absorptions of the concentrations and formless absorptions
   2. The explanation of the features of the branches, objects of observation, and subjective aspects (*rnam pa, ākāra*)

III. The enumeration of the meditative stabilizations of Buddhas and Bodhisattvas in dependence upon that

The main topics are included in the first two sections, especially the second. In Kön-chok-jik-may-wang-po's condensation, the third, although listed as a main heading, is merely a brief concluding statement to the effect that there are limitless meditative stabilizations of Buddhas and Bodhisattvas that depend on each of the meditative absorptions;[a] although the threefold division into basis (*gzhi, vastu*), path (*lam, mārga*), and fruit (*'bras bu, phala*) is not used, it seems to be implicit in the three main headings. In simplified outline, then, omitting the third section, the main topics are:

The basis of cultivation
   The physical basis
   The mental basis
The preparations
   Calm abiding and special insight
   The seven mental contemplations
The actual meditative absorptions
   Their entities
   Their branches, objects of observation, and subjective aspects

When the third section is left out of consideration, the order is seen to be primarily a logical one, giving necessary background in the sections on the physical and mental bases and then proceeding mainly in the order of practice.

When one compares Jam-yang-shay-pa's order to Paṇ-chen

---

[a] Kön-chok-jik-may-wang-po, *Condensed Statement,* 604.3–5; Jam-yang-shay-pa, *Concentrations,* 416.3–418.2.

Sö-nam-drak-pa's, one can see how valuable Jam-yang-shay-pa's innovation is. Paṇ-chen Sö-nam-drak-pa's table of contents is as follows:

- I. The explanation of the concentrations
  - A. The explanation of the concentrations that are causal absorptions
    - 1. The explanation of the preparations for the first concentration
      - a. The explanation of the first concentration that is a causal absorption
    - 2. The explanation of the actual meditative absorptions that are concentrations
      - a. The explanation of the actual [first concentration]
      - b. The explanation of the second, third, and fourth concentrations that are causal absorptions
  - B. The explanation of the concentrations that are resultant births
- II. The explanation of the formless absorptions

Paṇ-chen Sö-nam-drak-pa's text presents two problems: the topics are not discussed in an obviously rational order, and the table of contents is not an accurate reflection of the topics discussed. Heading I.A.1.a is unnecessary; the discussion that follows belongs under the preceding head, the explanation of the preparations for the first concentration. Paṇ-chen Sö-nam-drak-pa begins with the second of the preparations, the mental contemplation of individual knowledge of the character. He then discusses the remaining preparations for the first concentration and goes on to discuss the last of the seven mental contemplations, the mental contemplation that is the fruit of final training (*sbyor ba mtha'i 'bras bu yid byed, prayoganiṣṭaphalamanaskāra*), which is not a preparation but an actual meditative absorption. Next, he discusses the relationship of the preparations to calm abiding and special insight, as well as other aspects of the preparations. Only then—without headings—does he begin the topics of calm abiding and special insight, even though the cultivation of calm abiding comes first in the order of practice. The sections on the resultant-birth concentrations and on the formless absorptions are brief, and the latter is followed by a long section that has no headings at all and includes discussions of topics related to the actual meditative absorptions, such as pure (*dag pa, śuddha*) and uncontaminated (*zag med, anāsrava*) absorptions, afflicted (*nyon mong can, kliṣṭa*) absorptions, the mode of leaving the lower level, and the branches of the concentrations. The topics of the physical and mental bases of the concentrations and formless absorptions are omitted.

In my presentation of the main points of the Ge-luk system, the order I will follow is mainly Jam-yang-shay-pa's, beginning with the physical basis of the concentrations and formless absorptions. Some topics not covered in the textbooks, such as posture and motivation in the cultivation of calm abiding, are filled in from oral presentations based on stages-of-the-path texts.

2 THE PHYSICAL BASES OF THE CONCENTRATIONS AND FORMLESS ABSORPTIONS

Kön-chok-jik-may-wang-po follows Jam-yang-shay-pa in dividing the topic of the basis of the concentrations and formless absorptions into two subtopics—the physical basis and mental bases. Paṇ-chen Sö-nam-drak-pa does not deal with either of these subtopics in his *General Meaning of (Maitreya's) "Ornament for Clear Realization"*; however, Lati Rinpoche, who usually follows Paṇ-chen Sö-nam-drak-pa, and Gedün Lodrö, who follows Jam-yang-shay-pa, both discuss the physical basis in their oral presentations.

The topic of the physical basis of the concentrations and formless absorptions deals with the question of who—that is, what types of person (*gang zag, pudgala*)—can achieve the concentrations and formless absorptions. As Gedün Lodrö points out, "achieve" here refers to both new achievement and the maintaining of states already achieved.[a] From the practitioner's point of view, the topic answers the question, "Am I included among those who can do it?"

THE MEANING OF "PHYSICAL BASIS"

The meaning of "basis" (*rten, āśraya*) in the term "physical basis" (*lus rten*) requires some explanation. Tibetan writers and scholars often refer to persons "having" a basis of the Desire Realm (*'dod khams, kāmadhātu*), the Form Realm (*gzugs khams, rūpadhātu*), or the Formless Realm (*gzugs med khams, ārūpyadhātu*). In this somewhat awkward phrase, "basis" is a technical term referring to the collection of aggregates (*phung po, skandha*) in dependence upon which the person is designated—that is, the basis of designation (*gdags gzhi*) of the person, since, according to Prāsaṅgika-Madhyamaka tenets (*grub mtha', siddhānta*), the person is not any of the aggregates and is not the collection of aggregates but, rather, is *designated* in dependence upon the collection of aggregates. Thus, beings of the Desire and Form Realms—technically, persons "having" Desire or Form Realm bases—have all five aggregates, so that the person is designated in dependence upon the collection of the form aggregate (*gzugs kyi phung po, rūpaskandha*) and the four mental aggregates, or the body and mind. This is the basis of

[a] Gedün Lodrö, p. 45.

the person.

In the topic of the physical basis, the term "physical basis" is used loosely, since it refers to beings of all three realms. Strictly speaking, only individuals of the Desire and Form Realms have a *physical* basis, since only they have a form aggregate—a body—as well as the four mental aggregates. Beings of the Formless Realm have only the mental aggregates and, therefore, have no physical bodies. Nevertheless, they are also discussed under this heading, since the term "mental basis" is used technically in a completely different context, which will be explained in the next chapter.

Classes of Beings Who Cannot Achieve the Concentrations and Formless Absorptions

Kön-chok-jik-may-wang-po begins the exposition of his own system by enumerating and eliminating those persons who cannot achieve the concentrations and formless absorptions. Lati Rinpoche and Gedün Lodrö both follow this method in their oral presentations.[a] From among the six realms of cyclic existence, the main groups of those who cannot cannot achieve the concentrations and formless absorptions are "beings in the three bad [trans]migrations—that is, hell beings (*dmyal ba, nāraka*) hungry ghosts (*yi dvags, preta*), and animals (*dud 'gro, tiryañc*)"; demigods (*lha ma yin, asura*); humans (*mi, manuṣya*) of the northern continent called Unpleasant Sound (*sgra mi nyan, kuru*); the higher types of gods (*lha, deva*) of the Desire Realm, and the gods of no discrimination (*'du shes med pa'i sems can, asaṃjñisattva*) in the Great Fruit Land (*'bras bu che, bṛhatphala*) of the Fourth Concentration (*bsam gtan bzhi pa, caturthadhyāna*).[b] All of these are said to have "strong fruitional obstructions (*rnam smin gyi sgrib pa, *vipākāvaraṇa*)," which Gedün Lodrö explains as meaning "that the actions, or karmas, that caused such persons to be reborn" as a being of any of these transmigrations "prevents such persons from engaging in virtuous activity"—at any rate, the type of virtuous activity required for generation of the concentrations and formless absorptions.[c]

Additional reasons are given for the inability of such beings to achieve the concentrations and formless absorptions. According to Lati Rinpoche, beings in the three bad transmigrations cannot because their

---

[a] *Meditative States*, pp. 48–50; Gedün Lodrö, pp. 45–55.

[b] *Meditative States*, pp. 48–49.

[c] Gedün Lodrö, p. 48; Kön-chok-jik-may-wang-po, *Condensed Statement*, 543.2.

suffering gives them no opportunity to do so.[a] Gedün Lodrö explains the sufferings of the bad transmigrations in greater detail in this context: "Hell beings not only have physical suffering but are particularly tormented by mental suffering"; hungry ghosts "are troubled by the sufferings of hunger and thirst" and, therefore, "are tremendously afflicted with jealousy of those who have food and drink," and animals, although they have less physical and mental suffering than hell beings and hungry ghosts, are too stupid to focus on an object of observation; Gedün Lodrö notes that "the faculties of hell beings and hungry ghosts are sharper than those of animals."[b] In addition to stupidity, animals also have the sufferings enumerated by Lati Rinpoche in his description of cyclic existence: they eat one another or constantly have to search for food or are used for human purposes.[c]

The fruitional obstruction of demigods is such that they "are strongly afflicted by jealousy."[d] As Gedün Lodrö explains, this occurs

> because their rebirths as demigods are impelled by an action (*las, karma*) conjoined with a mind of jealousy regarding the wealth and resources of the gods. While they accumulated the karma that caused their rebirth as demigods, they were overcome by jealousy and hatred of the gods and, as a fruition of this, are now continually troubled by the mental suffering of jealousy.[e]

According to Lati Rinpoche, humans of the northern continent, Unpleasant Sound, and the higher types of gods of the Desire Realm cannot achieve the concentrations and formless absorptions because they are unable to analyze. They cannot analyze because they

> experience a continuous wonderful fruition of past actions. Thus, they do not have untimely death; things go well for them, and they experience the fruition of good past actions so strongly that they do not have much to think about and, therefore, do not have strong power of thought.[f]

Gedün Lodrö cites commentaries on Vasubandhu's *Treasury of Manifest*

---

[a] *Meditative States,* p. 48.

[b] Gedün Lodrö, p. 46.

[c] *Meditative States,* pp. 35–36.

[d] *Meditative States,* p. 48; Gedün Lodrö, p. 47; Kön-chok-jik-may-wang-po, *Condensed Statement,* 543.4.

[e] Gedün Lodrö, p. 47.

[f] *Meditative States,* p. 49.

Knowledge as the sources for this point. He also suggests that the pleasant lives of such beings are mostly given over to ethically neutral (*lung du ma bstan pa, avyākṛta*) activity, since "they do not have any strong force of thought to engage in either virtue or non-virtue."[a]

Lati Rinpoche and Gedün Lodrö differ as to which of the higher Desire Realm gods cannot achieve the concentrations and formless absorptions and, to some extent, with regard to the reason. According to Lati Rinpoche, the three higher types cannot—mainly because, like humans of the northern continent, they cannot analyze. According to Gedün Lodrö, however, the four higher types of gods of the Desire Realm cannot do so. He divides the six types of Desire Realm gods into those who depend on the earth and those who are in the sky and holds that only the two lowest types, which depend on the earth, can generate the concentrations and formless absorptions; the four higher types, those who are in the sky, cannot because they cannot see the faults of the Desire Realm.[b] Kön-chok-jik-may-wang-po, however, gives a somewhat different presentation; according to him, all six types of gods of the Desire Realm can newly generate the concentrations and formless absorptions because all "have new generation of concentrative discipline" (*bsam gtan gyi sdom pa, dhyānasaṃvara;*[c] for a discussion of the topic of concentrative discipline, see pages 39–44).

Because of their fruitional obstruction, gods of no discrimination in the Great Fruit Land of the Fourth Concentration are also prevented from achieving the concentrations and formless absorptions by inability to analyze—in their case, according to Lati Rinpoche, because they are born into a meditative absorption without discrimination as a result of having cultivated such a meditative absorption in the previous lifetime.[d] Kön-chok-jik-may-wang-po also includes gods of no discrimination among those having a strong fruitional obstruction.[e] Gedün Lodrö, however, includes these gods in a "secondary group" of gods and humans unable to achieve the concentrations and formless absorptions—a group consisting of "humans or gods at a time of sleeping, fainting, the meditative absorption of cessation (*'gog pa'i snyoms 'jug, nirodhasamāpatti*), or the meditative equipoise of non-discrimination

---

a Gedün Lodrö, p. 47.

b Ibid., p. 54; *Meditative States*, p. 233, n. 1.

c Kön-chok-jik-may-wang-po, *Condensed Statement*, 543.5–6.

d *Meditative States*, pp. 43, 49.

e Kön-chok-jik-may-wang-po, *Condensed Statement*, 543.2.

(*'du shes me pa, asaṃjñā*)."[a] According to Gedün Lodrö, those who are born as gods of no discrimination have cultivated a meditative equipoise of non-discrimination because of intense concern with overcoming "coarse states of mind" and have also achieved an actual concentration; they

> mistake the factor which is pacification of coarse minds for liberation; thus, they view the meditative absorption of no discrimination as being a path to liberation and see birth in that level as liberation.[b]

Exceptions among Beings Otherwise Qualified to Generate the Concentrations and Formless Absorptions

The remaining types of sentient beings—that is, humans of the three continents other than Unpleasant Sound, the lower types of Desire Realm gods, and Form Realm gods other than those of non-discrimination—can achieve the concentrations and formless absorptions. Even among them, however, there are exceptions based on inability to analyze, disqualification due to genital abnormality, and the presence of strong karmic obstructions.

Inability to analyze. Gedün Lodrö lists as "the main human exceptions...those who are insane, those whose elements are physically disturbed, and beings emanated by another being."[c] He explains that beings of the last type cannot generate calm abiding or the concentrations and formless absorptions because they do not have minds of their own: they "are incapable of deciding to generate calm abiding because they depend on the mind of the emanator."[d] He also includes among

---

[a] Gedün Lodrö, p. 49.

[b] Ibid., p. 55. This meditative absorption, which is a Form Realm absorption, differs from the formless absorption of nothingness because "in the level of Nothingness there is no appearance of form, and one does not have the mistaken discrimination that the meditative absorption of no discrimination is a path to liberation and that birth at that level is liberation" (idem). Georges Dreyfus points out that the formless absorption of nothingness is achieved through contemplation of the faults of form, whereas a meditative absorption of no discrimination is not achieved in this way. Moreover, since gods of no discrimination are born in the Form Realm, they perceive form at the time of birth and death there, although probably not at other times (Georges Dreyfus in conversation).

[c] Gedün Lodrö, p. 47.

[d] Ibid., p. 47.

the main exceptions those humans who are "overpowered by poison"; such persons are suffering from a type of craziness, but not the natural insanity referred to above; rather, their minds are temporarily "affected by certain substances," including drugs such as marijuana and *datura*,[a] as well as manufactured drugs (in both the Tibetan and Western systems).[b] "These," he notes, "are the main cases of the mind's not abiding in a normal state."[c] Of humans in this main type, he adds that "not only can these people not generate calm abiding or an actual concentration; they also cannot generate a vow of individual emancipation, a Bodhisattva vow, or a tantric vow."[d]

Genital abnormality. Among the humans of the three continents other than Unpleasant Sound who cannot generate the concentrations and formless absorptions are those disqualified because of genital abnormality. It is important for modern Westerners to bear in mind that the abnormalities referred to here are anatomical abnormalities and the mental distortions thought to accompany them; there is no mention of sexual orientation

According to Kön-chok-jik-may-wang-po, persons so disqualified are neuter persons (*za ma, ṣaṇḍha*), eunuchs (*ma ning, paṇḍaka*), and androgynes (*mtshan gnyis pa, ubhayavyañjana*); Lati Rinpoche gives the second category as "the impotent" and appears to include what we generally think of as eunuchs among the neuter—those who "have neither male nor female organs." Such persons either "are born without such organs or...lose their organs through sickness, through the application of medicine, or through the organs' being cut off by a weapon." He explains impotent persons as those who have male or female organs but lack the sexual capacity of males and females. Androgynous humans, according to both Lati Rinpoche and Gedün Lodrö, are those who have both male and female organs.[e]

---

[a] This is identified by Gedün Lodrö as *da du ra,* apparently a Tibetan transliteration of the Hindi *dhatura,* from which the botanical name *Datura* is derived. In his note, Hopkins, citing Guy Newland, gives the Tibetan name of the plant as *thang phrom,* also spelled *thang khrom,* identified in Sarat Chandra Das's *Tibetan-English Dictionary* (p. 568) as *dhūstūra*, or thorn-apple (Gedün Lodrö, p. 52). The *Shorter Oxford English Dictionary* (p. 455) defines *Datura* as "A genus of poisonous plants (N.O. *Solanaceæ*), of which *D. Stramonium* is the Strammony or Thorn-apple; it is a powerful narcotic."

[b] Gedün Lodrö., pp. 47, 52.

[c] Ibid., p. 52.

[d] Ibid., p. 48.

[e] Kön-chok-jik-may-wang-po, *Condensed Statement,* 543.1; *Meditative States,* pp. 49, 38; Gedün Lodrö, p. 48.

In a detailed discussion of the term *paṇḍaka*, Leonard Zwilling suggests that *paṇḍakas*

According to Kön-chok-jik-may-wang-po, the reason people with genital abnormalities cannot newly generate the concentrations and formless absorptions is that they have strong afflictive obstructions (*nyon mongs kyi sgrib pa, kleśāvaraṇa*).[a] Lati Rinpoche explains that

> their minds are continuously held by such afflictive emotions as desire, anger, and jealousy. Because there is no time at which they are free of these afflictive emotions, they have no opportunity to cultivate paths

and, therefore, cannot newly attain the concentrations and formless absorptions.[b]

Gedün Lodrö distinguishes between the incapacity for such meditation of the neuter and the androgynous. According to him,

> Neuter beings, like those in the northern continent, are unable to carry anything through to a conclusion. They do not have sufficiently strong force of thought.[c]

The androgynous, however, are prevented from attaining calm abiding or the concentrations and formless absorptions because they have too many afflictive emotions:

> Androgynous humans, those who have both male and female signs, have the afflictive emotions of both male and female and thus have too many afflictive emotions to be able to generate calm abiding [or the concentrations and formless absorptions].[d]

With regard to the afflictive emotions of male and female, Gedün Lodrö explains:

> In general, we refer to the three poisons, the six root afflictive emotions (*rtsa ba'i nyon mongs, mūlakleśa*), and the twenty secondary afflictive emotions (*nye ba'i nyon mongs, upakleśa*). Both

---

were "a socially stigmatized class of passive, probably transvestite, homosexuals" and that the usual modern translation—"eunuch"—is utterly inadequate, since, although Yashomitra's list of types of *paṇḍaka* includes castrates, the word *eunuch* "implies intentional castration as opposed to accidental castration," whereas eunuchs were "virtually unknown in pre-Muslim India" (Leonard Zwilling, "Homosexuality as Seen in Indian Buddhist Texts," *Buddhism, Sexuality, and Gender*, ed. José Ignacio Cabezón [Albany, NY: State University of New York Press, 1992], pp. 209, 208, 204).

a Kön-chok-jik-may-wang-po, *Condensed Statement,* 543.1.

b *Meditative States,* p. 49.

c Gedün Lodrö, p. 48.

d Ibid., p. 48.

> males and females have all these. The male and female afflictive emotions that I was referring to are the desire each has for the other. Males have an attraction to females and females, to males. A person who had both types of desire would have a great deal.[a]

It is important to note that people with genital abnormalities cannot *newly* attain calm abiding and the concentrations and formless absorptions. Kön-chok-jik-may-wang-po does not say of them, as he does of those with strong karmic obstructions, that they "can neither newly generate meditative absorptions nor keep what has already been generated"; he says only that those with genital abnormalities "do not have new generation of these [meditative absorptions]."[b] According to Gedün Lodrö, those who had previously attained calm abiding or any of the concentrations and formless absorptions and later fell into one of the categories of genital abnormality through accident or illness would not necessarily lose their attainments; some people would be able to use their previous understanding to hold on to their attainments, but in the case of a strong accident, the attainment would deteriorate.[c] Thus, although humans capable of generating the concentrations and formless absorptions must be genitally normal males and females, Gedün Lodrö's qualification shows that the criterion of genital normality is not applied mechanically.

Strong karmic obstructions. Some humans are prevented from generating the concentrations and formless absorptions by strong karmic obstructions (*las sgrib, karmāvaraṇa*).[d] These karmic obstructions are the actions of abandoning the doctrine (*chos spong*) and the five heinous crimes (*mtshams med pa, ānantarya*). Abandoning the doctrine, in the narrowest technical sense, involves partisanship among Buddhists; it is a Buddhist's disparagement of another Buddhist position. The five heinous crimes, which bring immediate retribution at death, are those of killing one's father, killing one's mother, killing a Foe Destroyer (*dgra bcom pa, arhan*), maliciously causing the body of a Buddha to bleed, and causing division in the spiritual community (*dge 'dun, saṃgha*).

According to Jam-yang-shay-pa, the reason karmic obstructions prevent attainment of the concentrations and formless absorptions is

---

[a] Ibid., p. 53.

[b] Kön-chok-jik-may-wang-po, *Condensed Statement*, 543.1. Cf. ibid., 542.7.

[c] Gedün Lodrö, p. 54, and *Meditative States*, p. 233, n. 2.

[d] Kön-chok-jik-may-wang-po, *Condensed Statement*, 542.7–543.1; *Meditative States*, p. 49; Jam-yang-shay-pa, *Concentrations*, 21.2 ff.

that they "obstruct the Superior (*'phags pa, ārya*) paths and the special faith, and so forth, that are the virtuous roots for training in them."[a] Obviously, if even the virtuous roots (*dge ba'i rtsa ba, kuśalamūla*) necessary for training in the Superior paths are obstructed, it will be impossible to attain the Superior paths themselves. Jam-yang-shay-pa's reason is based on a passage concerning the Superior paths in Vasubandhu's *Autocommentary on the "Treasury of Manifest Knowledge,"*[b] in this context, Jam-yang-shay-pa is treating the concentrations and formless absorptions as analogous to the Superior paths. Thus, the virtuous roots necessary for training in the concentrations and formless absorptions are also obstructed. By his mention of virtuous roots, Jam-yang-shay-pa seems to imply that even to train in the Superior paths and the concentrations and formless absorptions one needs to accumulate a certain amount of merit; this position, based on the above-mentioned passage in Vasubandhu's *Autocommentary on the "Treasury of Manifest Knowledge,"* also accords with the assumptions of Tibetan practice generally.

Karmic obstructions are not held to be irreversible, however; Tibetan presentations of the concentrations and formless absorptions agree that persons who have committed the actions in question can become capable of generating the concentrations and formless absorptions if they engage in a means of purifying those actions. This position, too, accords with the assumptions of Tibetan practice. As Hopkins points out, "purification" here probably refers to the four powers explained in the context of confession of misdeeds.[c] The four are: (1) the object, or base; (2) contrition; (3) "an aspiration toward restraint"; (4) application of an antidote; this last, according to the Nying-ma scholar Khetsun Sangpo Rinpoche, "can be any virtuous practice."[d]

Concentrative Discipline

Jam-yang-shay-pa says of several types of beings that they cannot generate the concentrations and formless absorptions because they cannot

[a] Jam-yang-shay-pa, *Concentrations,* 21.5.

[b] Vasubandhu, *Autocommentary on the "Treasury of Manifest Knowledge,"* commentary to 4.96. P5591, vol. 115, 216.4.5. *Abhidharmakośa & Bhaṣya of Ācārya Vasubandhu,* ed. by Dwarikadas Shastri (Varanasi: Bauddha Bharati, 1971), Part 2, p. 723; cited hereafter as Shastri. La Vallée Poussin, 16:3, p. 203; Pruden, vol. 2, p. 679.

[c] Jeffrey Hopkins in conversation.

[d] Khetsun Sangpo Rinpoche, *Tantric Practice in Nying-ma* (Ithaca, NY: Gabriel/Snow Lion Publications, 1982), p. 142, where the four powers are explained in relation to the Vajrasattva meditation. He also explains them in relation to taking refuge, pp. 121–22.

generate concentrative discipline.[a] He uses this line of reasoning in relation to humans of the northern continent, Unpleasant Sound, who "do not have either the discipline of individual emancipation (*so mthar gyi sdom pa, pratimokṣasaṃvara*), concentrative discipline, or bad discipline (*sdom min, asaṃvara*)";[b] he also uses it in relation to humans with genital abnormalities and beings of the three bad transmigrations.[c] He mentions concentrative discipline in relation to the inability of demigods to generate the concentrations and formless absorptions, although he also mentions their "obstructions of jealousy."[d] Similarly, he gives ability to generate concentrative discipline as the reason that humans of the three continents other than Unpleasant Sound and "the six types of gods of the Desire Realm and transmigrators of the Form Realm" can generate the concentrations and formless absorptions.[e]

Kön-chok-jik-may-wang-po, in his condensation of Jam-yang-shay-pa's text, follows Jam-yang-shay-pa closely, although he does not mention concentrative discipline in relation to demigods; apparently, he considers their "very strong obstructions of jealousy and of [being that kind of] transmigrator" sufficient reason for their inability to generate the concentrations and formless absorptions.[f]

As the source for his discussion of concentrative discipline, Jam-yang-shay-pa cites Chapter 4 of Vasubandhu's *Treasury of Manifest Knowledge* and its *Autocommentary*.[g] According to the *Treasury*, concentrative discipline is one of three types of discipline (*sdom pa, saṃvara*); the other two are the discipline of individual emancipation (*so sor mthar pa, pratimokṣa*) and uncontaminated discipline.[h] Jam-yang-shay-pa's reason cited above (page 40) also mentions bad discipline (*sdom min, asaṃvara*)—literally, "non-discipline." All these, according to both the Vaibhāṣhika and Prāsaṅgika schools of tenets, are types of form—

---

[a] The usual term for concentrative discipline in Vasubandhu's *Treasury of Manifest Knowledge* (4.13d) and its *Autocommentary* is *dhyānaja* (*bsam gtan skyes*), "born of concentration," although *dhyānasaṃvara* also occurs (P5591, vol. 115, 197.2.7; Shastri, Part 2, p. 605; La Vallée Poussin, 16:3, p. 43; Pruden, vol. 2, p. 580).

[b] Jam-yang-shay-pa, *Concentrations*, 23.1.

[c] Ibid., 23.5–24.2.

[d] Ibid., 24.3–5: "the bases of concentrative restraint are definite as only [those of] gods and humans, and Vasubandhu's *Treasury of Manifest Knowledge* here does not explain demigods as gods."

[e] Ibid., 24.5–7, 25.1.

[f] Kön-chok-jik-may-wang-po, *Condensed Statement*, 543.4.

[g] Jam-yang-shay-pa, *Concentrations*, 24.3, 24.5 ff.

[h] Vasubandhu, *Treasury of Manifest Knowledge*, 4.13c–d (P5591, vol. 115, 197.2.7; Shastri, Part 2, p. 605; La Vallée Poussin, 16:3, p. 43; Pruden, vol. 2, p. 580).

specifically, non-revelatory form (*rnam par rig byed ma yin pa'i gzugs, avijñaptirūpa*).[a] According to Hopkins, non-revelatory forms are so called because they

> are continuations of virtue or sin and arise from revelatory actions of body or speech or arise from cultivating meditative stabilization. Since the motivations of these actions are not knowable by others, they are called 'non-revelatory forms.'[b]

Vasubandhu's *Treasury of Manifest Knowledge* lists three types of non-revelatory form: discipline, bad discipline, and something that is neither.[c]

Although the word "discipline" is used by Hopkins as a translation of *'dul ba* (*vinaya*), I am following La Vallée Poussin's translation of Vasubandhu's *Treasury*, and Pruden's translation of La Vallée Poussin, in using "discipline" to translate *sdom pa* (*saṃvara*) in this context, since it is probably the only English (and French) word that conveys both senses of *saṃvara*—"vow" and "restraint."[d] In the case of individual emancipation (*so sor thar pa, pratimokṣa*), the meaning is closer to that of "vow," whereas, for the other two types of *saṃvara*, the meaning is closer to that of "restraint."

The discipline of individual emancipation is a vow taken from someone else. Thus, Jam-yang-shay-pa states that humans of the northern continent do not have the discipline of individual emancipation because "they [can]not take something supreme [that is, a vow] from another [person, who is giving it]."[e] Bodhisattva and tantric vows are taken and given similarly.[f] The last, obviously, is not mentioned in Vasubandhu's *Treasury*, but it is worth noting that Gedün Lodrö remarks of humans whose minds are not in a normal state that they "cannot generate a vow of individual emancipation, a Bodhisattva vow, or a tantric vow."[g] A Go-mang scholar and, therefore, a follower of Jam-yang-shay-pa, he implicitly extends Jam-yang-shay-pa's line of reasoning, based on Vasubandhu's *Treasury*, to the other two types of *saṃvara*

---

[a] Jeffrey Hopkins in conversation.

[b] Jeffrey Hopkins, *Meditation on Emptiness* (London: Wisdom Publications, 1983), p. 234.

[c] Vasubandhu, *Treasury of Manifest Knowledge*, 4.13a–b (P5591, vol. 115, 197.2.6; Shastri, Part 2, p. 605; La Vallée Poussin, 16:3, p. 43; Pruden, vol. 2, p. 580.)

[d] *Meditation on Emptiness*, p. 532. Vasubandhu, *Treasury of Manifest Knowledge*, 4.13 (La Vallée Poussin, 16:3, p. 43; Pruden, vol. 2, p. 580).

[e] Jam-yang-shay-pa, *Concentrations*, 23.3.

[f] Jeffrey Hopkins in conversation, citing Ge-shay Pel-den Drak-pa.

[g] Gedün Lodrö, p. 48.

used in contemporary Tibetan practice.

Concentrative and uncontaminated disciplines are restraints rather than vows. They are induced by the mere attainment of certain minds—the former, by the mere attainment of a mind of the Form Realm (that is, by the initial attainment of calm abiding[a]) and the latter, by the mere attainment of an uncontaminated path. The mere attainment of such a mind leads the practitioner to refrain from certain actions. Thus, he or she acquires a restraint, or discipline.[b] Since concentrative discipline is form—non-revelatory form—beings of the Formless Realm, although able to generate the concentrations and formless absorptions, are not said to have concentrative discipline. Jam-yang-shay-pa cites Vasubandhu's *Treasury of Manifest Knowledge* (4.44a–b) and its *Autocommentary* to establish this point but does not discuss it.[c]

Bad discipline is an absence of restraint, a non-revelatory form produced by non-virtue—for example, the action of a butcher in killing animals.[d]

According to Jam-yang-shay-pa, then, many of the beings who cannot generate calm abiding and the concentrations and formless absorptions cannot do so because they cannot generate concentrative discipline; of some, he adds that they also cannot generate the other two types of discipline. The problem with this line of reasoning is its apparent circularity. Jam-yang-shay-pa is saying that such beings cannot generate calm abiding and the concentrations and formless absorptions because they cannot generate something—a form—that is induced by the mere attainment of calm abiding. He seems to be saying that such beings cannot achieve the cause because they cannot achieve the

---

[a] Jam-yang-shay-pa cites Vasubandhu's *Autocommentary on the "Treasury,"* 4.26a-b—"Those who possess concentration unquestionably possess concentrative discipline. Here the preparations are also indicated within the mention of concentrations"—to establish that those who have attained even a preparation for a concentration have concentrative discipline. (Jam-yang-shay-pa, *Concentrations,* 23.5; see La Vallée Poussin, 16:3, p. 59, Pruden, vol. 2, p. 591). For the reasoning establishing calm abiding as the first of the preparations, see page 199 below.

[b] Georges Dreyfus in conversation.

[c] Jam-yang-shay-pa, *Concentrations,* 25.2. Vasubandhu, *Treasury of Manifest Knowledge,* 4.44a–b (P5591, vol. 115, 204.7–205.1.1; Shastri, Part 2, p. 651; La Vallée Poussin, 16:3, p. 105; Pruden, vol. 2, p. 620). La Vallée Poussin notes that the Tibetan version he used skips part of this verse; it is also missing in Pruden, but the version cited by Jam-yang-shay-pa agrees with Shastri and La Vallée Poussin.

[d] *Meditation on Emptiness,* p. 234. Vasubandhu, *Autocommentary,* 4.36c–d. (P5591, vol. 115, 202.5.6–203.1.4; Shastri, Part 2, pp. 640–42; La Vallée Poussin, 16:3, p. 91; Pruden, vol. 2, p. 611.)

effect. As Hopkins remarks, this, "in general, is not very suitable reasoning." It is also somewhat misleading in this context, since it suggests that "concentrative discipline must be something beyond the discipline that takes place when one attains a [level of] concentration, and it is not."[a]

Georges Dreyfus holds that it is best not to emphasize the fact that concentrative discipline comes only with the attainment of a level of concentration. Rather, the argument should be based on the inability of such beings to generate any discipline at all. According to him, such beings lack ethical commitment. Therefore, they cannot have the discipline of individual emancipation and, for the same reason, cannot attain any type of meditative stabilization. Thus, they do not have concentrative discipline.[b]

Hopkins, perhaps more plausibly, takes the circularity of Jam-yang-shay-pa's reasoning into account and argues that it comes from the way the topic is presented in Jam-yang-shay-pa's sources. It is as though Jam-yang-shay-pa were saying, "Although there are no direct statements that such beings cannot attain the concentrations, we know that they cannot because there are explanations that they cannot have concentrative discipline."[c]

Jam-yang-shay-pa's source is Vasubandhu's *Treasury of Manifest Knowledge* and its *Autocommentary*. Vasubandhu's discussion of calm abiding and the concentrations and formless absorptions is divided among Chapter 6, which includes a presentation of calm abiding; Chapter 8, which presents the concentrations and formless absorptions as meditative states without stating what types of beings cannot and can attain them; and Chapter 4, which deals with the topic of karma. In the context of karma, Vasubandhu discusses concentrative discipline not in relation to the attainment of meditative states but in relation to the non-revelatory forms that carry continuations of virtuous and non-virtuous actions. It is from this discussion of non-revelatory forms that Jam-yang-shay-pa, whose concern *is* meditative states, must extrapolate his presentation of the types of beings that cannot and can attain those states.

---

[a] Jeffrey Hopkins in conversation.

[b] Georges Dreyfus in conversation.

[c] Jeffrey Hopkins in conversation.

Additional points discussed by Kön-chok-jik-may-wang-po and Gedün Lodrö

Kön-chok-jik-may-wang-po and Gedün Lodrö, who follow Jam-yang-shay-pa, discuss several other points concerning the physical basis. One of the most important concerns the capacity of beings in the bad transmigrations for acting virtuously and the difference between the type of virtuous action involved in generating the concentrations and formless absorptions, on the one hand, and the altruistic mind of enlightenment, on the other. Kön-chok-jik-may-wang-po establishes, in a debate, that beings in the three bad transmigrations can attain great love (*byams pa chen po, mahāmaitrī*), great compassion (*snying rje chen po, mahākaruṇā*), and the altruistic mind of enlightenment but cannot attain the four immeasurables (*tshad med bzhi, catvary apramāṇāni*).[a] They can attain the altruistic mind of enlightenment, as well as great love and great compassion, because they can newly generate the seven cause-and-effect quintessential instructions (*rgyu 'bras man ngag bdun*) for attaining the altruistic mind of enlightenment—great love and great compassion being the fourth and fifth of these.[b] However, they cannot generate the four immeasurables because the four immeasurables are actual meditative absorptions of concentrations, which cannot be attained in the bad transmigrations.

Gedün Lodrö, following Jam-yang-shay-pa's more detailed version of this debate in the *Great Exposition of the Concentrations and Formless Absorptions*,[c] discusses the problem presented by a sūtra statement that "there are cases of hell beings who newly saw the truth." The problem is that

> "newly seeing the truth" means that one is achieving the path of seeing (*mthong lam, darśanamārga*), and in order to achieve

[a] The four immeasurables are love (*byams pa, maitrī*), compassion (*snying rje, karuṇā*), joy (*dga' ba, muditā*), and equanimity (*btang snyoms, upekṣā*).

[b] The seven cause-and-effect quintessential instructions are (1) recognition of all sentient beings as having been one's mother, (2) mindfulness of their kindness, (3) the wish to repay their kindness, (4) great love, (5) great compassion, (6) the high resolve to free all beings from suffering, and (7) the decision to achieve Buddhahood for the sake of all sentient beings. Donald S. Lopez notes, "These seven were derived by Tsong-kha-pa in his *Lam rim chen mo* from a statement by Atīśa in the *Bodhimārgapradīpapañjikā*, in commentary on the tenth stanza of his *Bodhipathapradīpa*." (Donald S. Lopez, *The Heart Sūtra Explained: Indian and Tibetan Commentaries* [Albany, NY: State University of New York Press, 1988], p. 212 n. 5.)

[c] Jam-yang-shay-pa, *Concentrations*, 9.1–10.2.

> that path it is necessary to achieve the path of preparation (*sbyor lam, prayogamārga*), the sign of which is the attainment of the meditative stabilization which is a union of calm abiding and special insight. Thus, before that path, one must have achieved a full-fledged calm abiding.[a]

There are two answers. One is that, in this statement, "the word 'truth' does not refer to the path of seeing but to the generation of the altruistic mind of enlightenment"; Gedün Lodrö adds, "Indeed, many sūtras say that there are cases of hell beings, hungry ghosts, and nāgas (*klu*) who newly generate the altruistic mind of enlightenment during that lifetime and become Bodhisattvas."[b] The other is that "'seeing the truth' really does mean achieving the path of seeing, and the moment such a person attains the path of seeing, he or she ceases to be a hungry ghost or a hell being."[c]

The first answer, which Gedün Lodrö appears to favor, raises the question of how someone who cannot achieve calm abiding can nevertheless generate the altruistic mind of enlightenment. Gedün Lodrö's answer turns on the difference between wisdom analyzing an object and great faithful interest in and aspiration toward it. For calm abiding, a strong factor of wisdom is necessary:

> Although one does not engage in a great deal of analysis during [the cultivation of] calm abiding, being told about an object by someone else is not sufficient to cause that object to appear to your own mind; you yourself must investigate it carefully. For the generation of an altruistic mind of enlightenment, however, it is enough to be told that there is such a thing as Buddhahood, and if you come to believe that and can thereby generate great effort, the altruistic mind of enlightenment can be attained.[d]

According to Gedün Lodrö, it is better if one engages in analysis even in the generation of the altruistic mind of enlightenment, but analysis is not necessary; "non-artificial, spontaneous experience" of the altruistic mind of enlightenment—that is, the arising of the altruistic mind of enlightenment as strongly outside meditation as in a strong meditation

---

[a] Gedün Lodrö, p. 49.

[b] Ibid., p. 50.

[c] Ibid., p. 50.

[d] Ibid., p. 50.

session—is possible even without analysis.[a] Thus, beings such as hell beings and hungry ghosts, who are incapable of analysis because of their intense sufferings and therefore cannot generate the concentrations and formless absorptions, can nevertheless generate the altruistic mind of enlightenment.

Kön-chok-jik-may-wang-po also discusses whether meditative absorptions attained in a former rebirth can be retained—in particular, whether beings of the three bad transmigrations or humans of the northern continent, Unpleasant Sound, who cannot newly generate the concentrations and formless absorptions, can retain "possession of actual meditative absorptions already attained" in a previous lifetime in the Form or Formless Realm.[b] He establishes that they cannot, since the meditative absorption—or, one might say, the mind—of a being of the Form or Formless Realm who is about to die and who will definitely be reborn in the next lifetime in a bad transmigration or as a human of the northern continent degenerates before death. Such a being, just before death, has manifest afflictive emotions of the Desire Realm such as gross craving and, since it is impossible to manifest such afflictive emotions and an actual meditative absorption simultaneously, the meditative absorption is necessarily lost—not at the point of rebirth, as we might think, but just before death from the Form or Formless Realm.[c]

He makes several other points about beings in transition—beings of various types who are about to be reborn. Some of these points seem merely to involve verbal faults in debate. Others emphasize the changes such beings undergo—especially, that they become intermediate-state (*bar do, antarābhāva*) beings between their death at the end of one lifetime and their birth in the next. These points about such changes counteract the tendency to think of the status of the beings in question as fixed, even for the duration of a lifetime. For example, it is wrong to say that beings in the bad transmigrations necessarily have strong karmic obstructions in their mental continua. To someone who takes this position, he cites as a counterexample "someone in a bad transmigration who, having used up his [or her] strong karmic obstructions, is about to die and is definite to attain a [human] basis of leisure and fortune in the next life."[d] The point seems to be that one cannot make such generalizations about the entire lifetime of a being in a bad

---

[a] Ibid., p. 51.

[b] Kön-chok-jik-may-wang-po, *Condensed Statement,* 539.3.

[c] Ibid., 539.3–5.

[d] Ibid., 540.7–541.1.

transmigration; beings change during the course of a life in one of the bad transmigrations and have other predispositions in their continua; therefore, although they have strong karmic obstructions in their continua at the time of their birth in a bad transmigration, the karmic obstructions that caused them to be born there can be used up in that lifetime.

Kön-chok-jik-may-wang-po also discusses problems relating to the level of meditative absorption a being of a given rebirth level can cultivate; this is a problem with regard to beings of the Form and Formless Realms. Following Jam-yang-shay-pa, he maintains that, in general, beings of a given level can attain meditative absorptions of either their own or a higher level but would not usually cultivate actual meditative absorptions of levels lower than their own. The qualification "in general" is important, since there are exceptions. Hīnayāna Superiors born in the Peak of Cyclic Existence constitute the most noteworthy exception, since they cultivate a meditative absorption of the level of Nothingness as the mental basis of the uninterrupted path by which they become Foe Destroyers. Vasubandhu's *Treasury of Manifest Knowledge* (8.20a–b) is cited as the source for this point. The reason for the exception is the character of "the mind of the Peak of Cyclic Existence," which "has unclear discrimination" and, therefore, "is not suitable as a [mental] basis of a supramundane path that eliminates cyclic existence for the Hīnayāna." Therefore, Hīnayāna Superiors born in the Peak of Cyclic Existence can attain liberation from cyclic existence only after attaining a meditative absorption of the level immediately below their own—that of Nothingness. This is possible because the mind of the level of Nothingness is clearer than that of the Peak of Cyclic Existence and because the realms and objects of observation of the two levels are close.[a] The debate on this point leads to more detailed discussion of points relating to the meditative absorption of the peak of cyclic existence.[b]

Conclusion

The topic of the physical basis of the concentrations and formless absorptions is more than a mere list of types of person. Elementary though the topic seems, it presupposes essential Buddhist doctrines.

---

[a] Ibid., 541.1–542.2; Jam-yang-shay-pa, *Concentrations,* 28.7–29.7. Vasubandhu, *Treasury of Manifest Knowledge,* 8.20a–b (P5591, vol. 115, 202.5.6–203.1.4; Shastri, part 4, pp. 1145–46; La Vallée Poussin, 16:5, p. 175; Pruden, vol. 4, p. 1251.) See also Tsong-kha-pa, *Notes,* 18.2–4.

[b] Kön-chok-jik-may-wang-po, *Condensed Statement,* 542.4–7.

The doctrine of selflessness (*bdag med, nairātmya*), for instance, is implied by the very term "physical basis," with its reference to the basis of designation of the person—the collection of aggregates in dependence upon which the person is designated.

Of more obvious importance is the doctrine of actions and their effects. The classes of beings who cannot and can achieve the concentrations and formless absorptions are first delineated in terms of the six transmigrations of cyclic existence—the traditional Buddhist cosmology, which is produced by karma. (See Chapter 12.) Then, within the broad categories of beings who can achieve the concentrations and formless absorptions, exceptions are set forth—beings whose obstructions, like the six transmigrations themselves, are also produced by karma. What results from this method of delineation is a hierarchical ranking of present capacity, changeable in the long run by actions but often fixed for the duration of any given lifetime if the physical manifestation limits the mind based on it. Over many lifetimes, however, all beings are considered capable of attaining not only the concentrations and formless absorptions but also liberation from cyclic existence and Buddhahood. Given an audience of humans capable of cultivating calm abiding and the concentrations and formless absorptions in this lifetime, the hierarchical ranking presented in the topic of the physical basis of the concentrations and formless absorptions serves both to assure the members of the audience of their present capacity and to spur them to effort. Thus, this topic, together with the more technical discussion of mental bases, introduces the presentation of calm abiding and the remaining preparations for the concentrations and formless absorptions, as well as the actual meditative absorptions.

3 MENTAL BASES

From the discussion of the physical basis of the concentrations and formless absorptions, one would expect the topic of mental bases to deal with the mental qualifications necessary for their attainment—the type of mind beings who can attain them must have. It does not deal with that, however—at least, not in the usual sense. Indeed, mental qualifications and disqualifications are included in other topics; much is said in the topic of the physical basis about obvious types of mind that disqualify certain classes of beings from attaining the concentrations and formless absorptions—for example, jealousy in the case of the demigods, stupidity in the case of animals, and inability to analyze in the case of some humans and gods—and the topic of prerequisites (discussed in the next chapter) outlines the attitudes a practitioner must have in order to cultivate calm abiding and the concentrations and formless absorptions.

Although the topic of mental bases does not deal with the obvious types of mind already mentioned, Hopkins suggests that it may, nonetheless, have been introduced in answer to a qualm: someone may have thought, "If there is a physical basis, there must be a mental basis."[a] A mental basis, however, is not simply something that is both a mind and a basis, as one might think from the literal meaning of the term "mental basis" itself. The explicit refutation of this position, although it occurs only late in Jam-yang-shay-pa's discussion of mental bases—in the third debate of the third section, "Dispelling Objections"[b]—is essential to the discussion. To rule out this notion, Jam-yang-shay-pa gives a highly technical presentation of the relationships between consciousnesses, which will be addressed below (page 58). Specifically, the topic of mental bases deals with the ways in which certain consciousnesses do or do not support—that is, act as bases of—certain other consciousnesses. The discussion includes the mental bases of the concentrations and formless absorptions, as well as the way in which the concentrations and formless absorptions act as the mental bases of path consciousnesses, but it is not confined to the concentrations and formless absorptions; it also includes examples drawn from other topics.

Of the writers and oral commentators discussed here, neither

---

[a] Jeffrey Hopkins in conversation.

[b] Jam-yang-shay-pa, *Concentrations,* 42.3; Kön-chok-jik-may-wang-po, *Condensed Statement,* 547.1–2.

Paṇ-chen Sö-nam-drak-pa nor Lati Rinpoche, who follows the former's presentation, includes the topic of the mental basis, but the two Go-mang College writers, Jam-yang-shay-pa and Kön-chok-jik-may-wang-po, give brief but closely reasoned presentations of it, as does the Go-mang College scholar Gedün Lodrö. Since Kön-chok-jik-may-wang-po's condensation of Jam-yang-shay-pa's section on the topic is extremely compressed, it is necessary to go back to Jam-yang-shay-pa to understand how, and from what Tibetan and Indian sources, the various positions are developed. The main source of Jam-yang-shay-pa's method is Tsong-kha-pa's *Golden Rosary of Eloquence* (*legs bshad gser gyi phreng ba;* for a discussion of the two key citations, see pages 57–62).

THE GO-MANG PRESENTATION OF MENTAL BASES

In his oral commentary, Gedün Lodrö mainly follows Jam-yang-shay-pa; he has organized Jam-yang-shay-pa's main points into a detailed exposition of the topic and omitted some of Jam-yang-shay-pa's more complicated qualifications. His, and Jam-yang-shay-pa's, method of presenting mental bases is

> first to explain two other meanings of basis that would be inappropriate in the context of the mental basis of calm abiding and then to give the appropriate meaning.[a]

He also explains the mental bases of the concentrations and formless absorptions and of various path consciousnesses. The two types of basis he refutes as "inappropriate in the context of the mental basis of calm abiding" are: (1) a basis which is prior to that which it supports—(*snga phyi ba'i rten;* literally, "a basis involved in an earlier-and-later [sequence]")—and (2) a basis which is simultaneous with that which it supports (*dus mnyam pa'i rten*).[b] These are mentioned "for the sake of clarifying what the basis of calm abiding [and the concentrations and formless absorptions and path consciousnesses] is not."[c]

He draws his examples of the first type from the topic of Awareness and Knowledge, citing examples of a sense consciousness (*dbang shes, indriyajñāna*) and a mental consciousness (*yid kyi rnam shes, manovijñāna*). As an example of a sense consciousness, he mentions an eye consciousness (*mig gi rnam par shes pa, cakṣurvijñāna*) that apprehends a form, which "has three bases which are its causes." These are:

---

[a] Gedün Lodrö, p. 57.

[b] Ibid., p. 57.

[c] Ibid., p. 58.

> (1) the uncommon empowering condition (*thun mong ma yin pa'i bdag rkyen, asādhāranadhipatipratyaya*)—the eye sense power (*mig gi dbang po, cakṣurindriya*); (2) the immediately preceding condition (*de ma thag rkyen, samanantarapratyaya*)—the immediately preceding moment of consciousness that ceases just before the first moment of an eye consciousness; (3) the observed-object condition (*dmigs rkyen, ālambanapratyaya*)—the form which is the object of that eye consciousness.[a]

If one uses as an example of a mental consciousness "a mental consciousness that knows a pot,"

> the pot itself is the observed-object condition. The mind that induces the thought consciousness is its immediately preceding condition. Whether the basis of the thought that knows a pot is the term "pot" or a memory of a pot, that thought arises in dependence on a prior basis.[b]

A basis that precedes and is a cause of a sense or mental consciousness it supports must also be a different entity from that consciousness. However, the mental basis of calm abiding and of the concentrations and formless absorptions is not like any of the prior bases of either a sense or a mental consciousness: it does not precede, and is not a cause of, the consciousness of which it is the mental basis.[c] Indeed, according to Jam-yang-shay-pa, "Whatever is the mental basis of a consciousness must *not* be a cause of it."[d]

Jam-yang-shay-pa explains the fault that would be incurred if one asserted that the mental basis of a path consciousness is a prior basis that is the cause or substantial cause of that consciousness: there would be the unwanted consequence "that there are non-virtuous consciousnesses for which virtuous consciousnesses act as the mental basis."[e] Non-virtuous consciousnesses can precede virtuous consciousnesses and be their causes—specifically, their immediately preceding conditions, or substantial causes—but non-virtuous consciousnesses are not the mental bases of virtuous consciousnesses.

The second type of basis that is being refuted is one that is simultaneous with that which it supports but a different entity from it. Gedün

[a] Ibid., p. 58.

[b] Ibid., p. 58.

[c] Ibid., p. 58.

[d] Jam-yang-shay-pa, *Concentrations*, 36.5–6 (emphasis added).

[e] Ibid., 39.2–3; see also 38.1–2. Kön-chok-jik-may-wang-po, *Condensed Statement*, 546.4.

Lodrö gives as an example a table that supports, or is a basis of, a book resting on it.[a] This second type of basis is being refuted because it is a different entity from that which it supports. Jam-yang-shay-pa, continuing to draw examples from the bases of a virtuous consciousness, cites "a virtuous mind's depending upon virtuous predispositions (*bags chags, vāsanā*)."[b] These two are simultaneous but different entities, like a book resting on a table; the virtuous predispositions are not consciousnesses but non-associated compositional factors (*ldan min 'du byed, viprayuktasaṃskāra*) and, therefore, cannot act as the *mental* basis of a virtuous consciousness because "it does not occur that a non-associated compositional factor acts as the mental basis of a consciousness."[c]

The crucial point here is that the mental bases of calm abiding and of the concentrations and formless absorptions are of the same entity as the consciousnesses they support; they are not different entities from them. There is the complication, however, that they do not start out as the same entity; they *become* of the same entity when calm abiding or a given concentration or formless absorption has been attained. With regard to calm abiding, Gedün Lodrö explains that the mental basis of calm abiding

> ...is of the same entity as calm abiding itself. When one cultivates the nine mental abidings (*sems gnas dgu, navākārā cittasthiti*) that precede calm abiding, these nine are all minds included within the Desire Realm (*'dod khams, kāmadhātu*). When, however, after achieving these nine, one attains calm abiding, one has attained a mind that is included within an upper realm [in this case, the Form Realm (*gzugs khams, rūpadhātu*)].
>
> This mind is of the same entity as calm abiding. The mind included within an upper realm is itself calm abiding, and calm abiding is a mind included within an upper realm.[d]

Thus, it is the mind included within an upper realm that is the mental basis of calm abiding. Since the process by which the nine Desire Realm minds that precede calm abiding become the mind of the Form Realm that is its mental basis is a little difficult to understand, Gedün Lodrö gives an easier example—the way in which an actual meditative

---

[a] Gedün Lodrö, p. 58.

[b] Jam-yang-shay-pa, *Concentrations,* 39.3–4. This is a debatable illustration, since, as Hopkins suggests, it is by no means clear that the virtuous predispositions for a given virtuous consciousness still exist once that virtuous consciousness is produced.

[c] Ibid., 39.4–5.

[d] Gedün Lodrö, p. 59.

absorption of a concentration becomes the mental basis of the path of preparation; the person cultivating the path of preparation in this way would be someone on the path of accumulation (*tshogs lam, saṃbhāra-mārga*).

> ...at first the actual concentration and the path of preparation are different. However, when, within the mind of an actual concentration, one attains the path of preparation, then the concentration and the path of preparation are of one entity. The mind of the actual concentration becomes of the entity of the mind of the path of preparation. At this point, the two cannot be separated; the one is the other.[a]

This example is less complicated than that of calm abiding because, in this example, there is nothing corresponding to the nine mental abidings. In this example, the meditator is not cultivating an actual concentration but has already attained it and is using it to cultivate the path of preparation. At the beginning of the process, before the attainment of the path of preparation, the actual concentration and the path of preparation are said to be of different entities,[b] but once the path of preparation has been attained, they are of the same entity. Thus, they *become* of the same entity.

To illustrate further this example of how an actual concentration acts as the mental basis of the path of preparation, Gedün Lodrö also cites the example of iron in fire, which is used by Jam-yang-shay-pa and Kön-chok-jik-may-wang-po in the context of a general statement concerning the way in which "the absorption of the ninth mental abiding and those ranging from the first concentration to the peak of cyclic existence" act "as the mental bases of paths that depend on them."[c] What is exemplified here is not the mental bases of calm abiding and the concentrations and formless absorptions but, rather, the way in which the ninth mental abiding, calm abiding (implicitly), and the concentrations and formless absorptions act as mental bases of higher path consciousnesses. The example applies to the exemplified in that, "just as when iron is burned, the iron becomes of the entity of the fire, these [absorptions] act as the mental bases of paths by way of paths'

---

[a] Ibid., p. 59.

[b] Even though, as Hopkins suggests, this particular person's path of preparation does not yet exist.

[c] Gedün Lodrö, p. 59–60. Jam-yang-shay-pa, *Concentrations,* 39.8–40.1. Kön-chok-jik-may-wang-po uses Jam-yang-shay-pa's initial statement without further explanation (Kön-chok-jik-may-wang-po, *Condensed Statement,* 546.5–6).

becoming of their entities."[a] Hopkins points out that a distinction is made between *becoming of the entity of* fire (*me'i ngo bor song ba*) and *being* fire (*me yin pa*); a debater who asserted, "It follows that the subject, such iron, is fire" (*de lta bu'i lcags de chos can me yin par thal zer na*) would be challenged.[b] Thus, refuting the related position that "if something is the mental basis of a path it is necessarily that path because it exists in the mode of having become of its entity," Jam-yang-shay-pa points out that, although "there are cases in which a mental basis has become of the entity of something [else] and also is that,"[c] there are also instances of that not being the case; for example,

> whatever has become of the entity of hatred does not have to be hatred. This is because, although a mind that is associated with hatred is not hatred, it has become of the entity of [hatred].[d]

Gedün Lodrö's reference to the way in which an actual concentration becomes the mental basis of the path of preparation is a specific illustration of Jam-yang-shay-pa's general point, cited above (page 53), concerning the way in which absorptions act "as the mental bases of paths that depend on them." Applying the example of iron in fire to his illustration, Gedün Lodrö explains that

> [w]hen a piece of iron is placed in fire, the iron becomes red hot; at that point, it is impossible to distinguish or separate the iron from the fire. However, when the iron has just been placed in the fire and is just becoming red, the two can be separated. The texts do not spell out how this example applies [to the exemplified], but it is easy to understand. The fire is like the meditative equipoise which is an actual concentration, and the iron is like the path of preparation. If one takes an actual first concentration as one's basis and cultivates the path of preparation, when the path of preparation is attained the mental basis becomes [of the entity of] the path of preparation just as the iron takes on the nature of fire.[e]

---

[a] Jam-yang-shay-pa, *Concentrations,* 39.7–40.1; Kön-chok-jik-may-wang-po, *Condensed Statement,* 546.5–6.

[b] Jeffrey Hopkins in conversation.

[c] Jam-yang-shay-pa, *Concentrations,* 41.4–5.

[d] Ibid., 41.3. Cf. Kön-chok-jik-may-wang-po, *Condensed Statement,* 546.6–547.1.

[e] Gedün Lodrö, p. 59–60.

Thus, it is established with regard to calm abiding and the concentrations and formless absorptions, and also with regard to path consciousnesses that depend on them, that their mental bases are of one entity with them. But the question arises: Are they simultaneous within being of the same entity? Neither Jam-yang-shay-pa nor Gedün Lodrö ever explicitly states that they are. It could be argued with regard to this type of basis that support and supported become simultaneous only when they have become of one entity—that is, only after the state being cultivated has been attained. How, for instance—to use Gedün Lodrö's example—can an actual concentration serve as the mental basis of a path of preparation that has not yet been attained? However, neither Jam-yang-shay-pa nor Gedün Lodrö raises the question. One would have to say, from the order in which Jam-yang-shay-pa and Gedün Lodrö refute the other two types of basis (prior bases and bases that are simultaneous within being different entities from that which is supported) that they are implying that the mental bases of calm abiding, the concentrations and formless absorptions, and path consciousnesses dependent on them are another type of simultaneous basis—one that is the same entity as that which it supports.

Gedün Lodrö points out that there are other ways in which paths are generated. For example, when a Bodhisattva Superior—that is, a Bodhisattva on the path of seeing or the path of meditation (*sgom lam, bhāvanāmārga*)—directly realizes emptiness, the mind does not become of the entity of emptiness; rather, emptiness is the apprehended object. Although emptiness and the mind directly cognizing it are said to be like water poured into water, the cognizing mind—the subject—is not generated into the entity of the object. Indeed, a path of seeing or meditation *has* a mental basis, a meditative stabilization that has become of its entity,[a] but here Gedün Lodrö is not discussing that mental basis. What he is pointing out here is that emptiness is *not* that mental basis but, rather, the apprehended object.[b]

There are also ways in which paths are meditated on by persons who are not yet ready to attain them. One way is to generate the mind into a similitude of the state to be attained—that is, to cultivate a subjective aspect which is an aspect of that state. Gedün Lodrö gives as an example of this process the cultivation of a first-ground Bodhisattva's meditative stabilization by someone on the Mahāyāna path of accumulation. A Bodhisattva on the path of accumulation "neither takes this

---

[a] Jam-yang-shay-pa, *Concentrations,* 41.3–4.

[b] Gedün Lodrö, pp. 62–64.

path as the object nor generates his or her mind into the entity of that path"[a] because a first-ground Bodhisattva is someone on the path of seeing, whereas a Bodhisattva on the path of accumulation has not yet attained the path of preparation and, therefore, is not ready to attain a first-ground Bodhisattva's meditative stabilization.

Another method is to meditate "on that which has a similar type of realization." Gedün Lodrö's example here is meditation on the three exalted knowers (*mkhyen pa, jñāta*) by common beings (*so so'i skye bo, pṛthagjana*).

> For example, the exalted knower of bases (*gzhi shes, vastujñatā*) is of the same type of realization as direct realization of the selflessness of persons (*gang zag gi bdag med, pudgalanairātmya*). Thus, persons on the path of accumulation can take as their object a mind that exists in their own mental continuums—namely, their own [conceptual] realization of the selflessness of persons. Through meditating on this, they achieve the first moment of a continuum which later turns into the fruit of an actual exalted knower of bases.[b]

Another way of cultivating a path that has not yet been attained is that of aspirational prayer (*smon lam, praṇidhāna*), within an understanding of "the characteristics and types" of that which is to be attained. An example of this method is meditation on inconceivable hidden qualities in the continuum of a Buddha, which even a Bodhisattva Superior cannot perceive directly.[c]

Yet another method is analysis leading to a similitude of special insight. This is the way in which ordinary beings meditate on the eight categories of the Perfections.[d]

Gedün Lodrö mentions the last five types of meditation as types in which a mental basis does not become of the entity of a path. He emphasizes, however, that when texts speak of a mental basis, the method of understanding the mental basis is the same for all paths for which a mental basis is explained.[e] This method of understanding mental bases is set forth in Jam-yang-shay-pa's text on the concentrations and formless absorptions.

---

[a] Ibid., p. 61.
[b] Ibid., p. 62.
[c] Ibid., pp. 62–63.
[d] Ibid., p. 63.
[e] Ibid., p. 60.

JAM-YANG-SHAY-PA'S METHOD

In his section on mental bases, Jam-yang-shay-pa follows a method developed by Tsong-kha-pa. He relies mainly on two key citations from Tsong-kha-pa's *Golden Rosary,* one laying out Tsong-kha-pa's method and the principles governing mental bases and the other illustrating the method. The main citation is as follows:

> What are support and supported like? They are also not like a juniper supported in a tub [that supports it], or the supported in [the case of] a sprout that is generated from a seed. With regard to those which are explained as 'supported,' one uses the convention 'supported' for something that has been produced as an entity of whatsoever level. One should understand this mode for all mental bases of paths; it is a unique term of the Proponents of Manifest Knowledge.[a]

This passage occurs in the subsection on the clairvoyances (*mngon shes, abhijñā*) under the topic of preceptual instructions (*gdams ngag, avavāda*), the second topic of an exalted knower of all aspects (*rnam mkhyen, sarvākārajñatā*), which is the first of the eight categories of Maitreya's *Ornament for Clear Realization* (*abhisamayālaṃkāra, mngon rtogs rgyan*). It is a summary of an explanation of how the concentrations act as mental bases of the clairvoyances. Thus, it is an explanation not of the mental bases of the concentrations but of how the concentrations act as the mental bases of other consciousnesses and, beyond that, of

---

[a] *'o na/ rten dang brten par 'gyur tshul 'ji 'dra ba zhe na/ 'di ni mkhar gzhong la rgya shug brten pa dang/ sa bon las myu gu skye ba la de la (b)rten zhes pa lta bu yang min no// 'o na ci zhe na/ brten par bshad pa de rnams sa gang dang gang gi ngo bor skyes pa la brten pa'i tha snyed byas pa ste/ tshul 'di ni lam gyi sems rten thams cad la rig par bya ste/ chos mngon pa pa'i thun mong ma yin pa'i brda'o/* (Tsong-kha-pa, *Golden Rosary, Collected Works,* vol. 25 [New Delhi: Ngawang Gelek Demo, 1975], 276.3–5).

With regard to *(b)rten zhes pa,* Tsong-kha-pa, *Collected Works,* vol. 25 [New Delhi: Ngawang Gelek Demo, 1975], 276.4 reads *brten,* "supported," whereas both texts of Jam-yang-shay-pa's *Great Exposition of the Concentrations and Formless Absorptions* have *rten,* "support," "basis," in the actual citation, even though Jam-yang-shay-pa has *brten* in his paraphrase (Indian folio printing, 36.6, 36.7; Jam-yang-shay-pa, *Collected Works,* vol. 12, 34.6, 34.7). When the passage is seen as a whole, it is clear that *brten,* "supported," makes more sense, since Tsong-kha-pa continues, "With regard to those which are explained as 'supported,'..." Although a translation of Jam-yang-shay-pa's version would have to read, "They are also not like...the basis in [the case of] a sprout that is generated from a seed," the translation here has been changed from "basis" to "supported" to conform to the text of Tsong-kha-pa, *Collected Works,* vol. 25 [New Delhi: Ngawang Gelek Demo, 1975], 276.4.

how mental bases function in general.

That, indeed, is how Jam-yang-shay-pa uses the passage from Tsong-kha-pa's *Golden Rosary.* Following his usual method of citing source texts, he breaks this passage into several citations, each illustrating a different point. The first citation consists of the first two sentences of the passage:

> What are support and supported like? [They are not like] a juniper supported in a tub [that supports it], or the supported in [the case of] a sprout that is generated from a seed.[a]

Jam-yang-shay-pa uses these sentences to rule out the types of basis that the mental basis of a consciousness is not:

> ...the meaning of "dependence" in this [context] does not refer at all to a mode of dependence in which [things that are] earlier and later are different entities, like the supported [in the case of] a sprout that is generated from a seed, nor, even among the simultaneous, [to a mode of dependence in which support and supported] are different entities, like a juniper supported in a tub [that supports it].[b]

This means that a mental basis is not a prior basis, in which something supports and is the cause of something else that is a different entity from it, and that it is not a basis that is simultaneous with, but a different entity from, that which it supports. Gedün Lodrö's method of clarifying the mental basis of calm abiding by ruling out these two types of basis that the mental basis of calm abiding is not (cited above, page 50) is based on this passage, although he does not cite it.

The next group of citations establishes that what is being set forth is a general principle that applies to all mental bases of paths. The sentences in question are:

> With regard to those which are explained as 'supported,' one uses the convention 'supported' for something that has been produced as an entity of whatsoever level,[c]

and

> One should understand this mode for all mental bases of

---

[a] Jam-yang-shay-pa, *Concentrations,* 36.7.

[b] Ibid., 36.6.

[c] Ibid., 37.5 and 40.1.

paths;...[a]

Jam-yang-shay-pa's final citation from this passage is a statement of Tsong-kha-pa's method, which Jam-yang-shay-pa follows. Jam-yang-shay-pa repeats the beginning of the sentence just quoted and continues to the end of the passage:

> One should understand this mode for all mental bases of paths; it is a unique term of the Proponents of Manifest Knowledge.[b]

The method involves the application of the Manifest Knowledge mode of procedure to Mahāyāna topics not discussed in Manifest Knowledge texts—an extension of method especially important in works on the topic of the Perfections, such as Tsong-kha-pa's *Golden Rosary,* Jam-yang-shay-pa's own textbook on the Perfections, and his textbook on the topics of the concentrations and formless absorptions, which Ge-luk-pas traditionally study as a subtopic of the Perfections. In the passage cited, Tsong-kha-pa merely indicates the method, which Jam-yang-shay-pa explains in detail:

> This mode of a given path's becoming of the entity of a given mental basis is similar in all the paths for which a mental basis is explained—Mahāyāna [altruistic] mind generation (*theg chen sems bskyed, mahāyānacittotpāda*), and so forth—because, with respect to statements in the Manifest Knowledge—Vasubandhu's *Treasury of Manifest Knowledge,* and so forth—that the five paths, the four immeasurables, meditative stabilization on the unpleasant, counting the exhalation and inhalation of the breath,...and so forth, need certain mental bases, there is a purpose in [the authors'] analyzing whether or not it is suitable, when something is generated as the entity of something [else], for that path to be of the nature of that [basis].
>
> It is entailed [that if, with respect to statements in the Manifest Knowledge that certain paths need certain mental bases, there is a purpose in the authors' analyzing whether or not it is suitable, when something is generated as the entity of something else, for that path to be of the nature of that basis, this mode of a given path's becoming of the entity of a given mental basis is necessarily similar in all the paths for which a mental basis is explained—Mahāyāna altruistic mind generation, and

[a] Ibid., 37.7.

[b] Ibid., 40.4.

> so forth] because, with respect to the mere cause or substantial cause of something, the explanation of merely that is not sufficient as an explanation of the mental basis. This is because Tsong-kha-pa's *Golden Rosary of Eloquence* says,...[a]

and here Jam-yang-shay-pa cites Tsong-kha-pa's statement concerning the method of "the Proponents of Manifest Knowledge."[b] In the third debate of the third section, "Dispelling Objections," Jam-yang-shay-pa cites a Manifest Knowledge text, Vasubandhu's *Autocommentary on the "Treasury of Manifest Knowledge,"* to illustrate the Manifest Knowledge method; he justifies his distinction between a mental basis and a similar immediately preceding condition by showing that the distinction is to be found in Vasubandhu's *Autocommentary* and that neither Tsong-kha-pa nor "any of the great [Indian] texts of sūtra and tantra" speaks of a similar immediately preceding condition as a mental basis.[c]

Although, in general, the term "Manifest Knowledge" refers to both the Hīnayāna and Mahāyāna Manifest Knowledges—that is, respectively, to Vasubandhu's *Treasury of Manifest Knowledge* and Asaṅga's *Summary of Manifest Knowledge*—it is clear that in this context Jam-yang-shay-pa is referring mainly to Vasubandhu's *Treasury* and has relegated Asaṅga's work on Manifest Knowledge to "and so forth"—and indeed, Asaṅga's *Summary of Manifest Knowledge* does not consider the generation of an altruistic mind of enlightenment, although it includes other specifically Mahāyāna topics, such as the ten Bodhisattva grounds, and gives a Chittamātra analysis of traditional Manifest Knowledge topics. Thus, although there is a Mahāyāna Manifest Knowledge, the method of analyzing Mahāyāna topics according to the method of Vasubandhu's *Treasury* is not to be found in it.

Jam-yang-shay-pa's statement is convoluted. What he is saying, in brief, is that, because it is obvious from his presentation up to this point that a prior basis of a path is not its mental basis, another, better analysis of what a mental basis is has to be found. It is "this mode of a given path's becoming of the entity of a given mental basis." Jam-yang-shay-pa finds it in Vasubandhu's *Treasury*, for Vasubandhu has applied this analysis of the mental basis of a path to a number of topics common to Hīnayāna and Mahāyāna practice, several of which

[a] Ibid., 40.1–4.

[b] Ibid., 40.4.

[c] Ibid., 42.7, 43.6. Cf. Kön-chok-jik-may-wang-po, *Condensed Statement,* 547.1–3. Kön-chok-jik-may-wang-po merely states the distinction without citing any sources or discussing the method.

Jam-yang-shay-pa lists. Because Vasubandhu has applied this analysis to a wide range of topics, Jam-yang-shay-pa feels justified in applying it to "*all* the paths for which a mental basis is explained—Mahāyāna altruistic mind generation, and so forth" (emphasis mine), and cites Tsong-kha-pa as his authority for doing so.

Thus, the other citation from Tsong-kha-pa's *Golden Rosary* has to do with the mental basis of a Mahāyāna altruistic mind generation:

> The mental basis is the three: the faith that observes the Conqueror, compassion that observes sentient beings, and hearing the benefits of the [altruistic] mind of enlightenment.[a]

In Tsong-kha-pa's *Golden Rosary,* this passage occurs in the exposition of a Mahāyāna altruistic mind generation, the first topic of the first category, an exalted knower of all aspects. Jam-yang-shay-pa's quotes it in the first debate of the first section, "Refutation [of Mistaken Opinions]." In this debate, Jam-yang-shay-pa refutes the position that whatever is the mental basis of a consciousness necessarily acts as that consciousness's substantial cause. He discusses as a counterexample the faith that is a mental basis of a Mahāyāna altruistic mind generation but is not its substantial cause.[b] (There is another debate that deals with this topic in the third section, "Dispelling Objections."[c])

It is surprising, at first, to see this topic introduced in a text on the concentrations and formless absorptions. Its introduction is a reminder that, as was mentioned earlier, Ge-luk-pas traditionally study the concentrations and formless absorptions as a subtopic of the Perfections. With regard to mental bases in general, these debates bring out the point that an accompanying mental factor (*sems byung, caitta*)—in this case, faith—can act as the mental basis of a main mind (*rtso sems*), or even of other mental factors, since "there are cases of faith and aspiration individually acting as the mental bases of effort, concentration, and so forth."[d]

Aside from this point, a detailed discussion of the mental basis of an

---

[a] *sems rten ni/ rgyal ba la dmigs pa'i dad pa/ sems can la dmigs pa'i snying rje/ byang sems kyi phan yon thos pa dang gsum yin te/* (Tsong-kha-pa, *Collected Works,* vol. 25 [New Delhi: Ngawang Gelek Demo, 1975], 185.2–3; Jam-yang-shay-pa, *Concentrations,* 36.3–4.)

[b] Jam-yang-shay-pa, *Concentrations,* 35.5–36.5. In his condensation of this debate, Kön-chok-jik-may-wang-po uses "the faith that is a mental basis of a Mahāyāna altruistic mind generation" as the subject of one of the consequences he hurls at his opponent. (Kön-chok-jik-may-wang-po, *Condensed Statement,* 545.5).

[c] Ibid., 41.5–42.4; Kön-chok-jik-may-wang-po, *Condensed Statement,* 547.3–4.

[d] Ibid., 37.1–2; Kön-chok-jik-may-wang-po, *Condensed Statement,* 545.6.

altruistic mind generation is outside the scope of this book.

Jam-yang-shay-pa's introduction of the topic demonstrates that he is discussing mental bases in general and the principles that govern them, and that he is concerned with applying these principles as extensively as possible. Although he does not cite Tsong-kha-pa's statement concerning the mental basis of a Mahāyāna altruistic mind generation as an explicit illustration of the method developed through the main citation from Tsong-kha-pa's *Golden Rosary,* it functions as such an illustration, as is clear from the reference, in his exposition of his own system, to "*all* the paths for which a mental basis is explained—Mahāyāna [altruistic] mind generation, and so forth" (emphasis mine; see above, page 59). Nevertheless, although the discussion applies to a wide range of topics outside that of the concentrations and formless absorptions, Jam-yang-shay-pa includes it in his work on this topic because of the importance of calm abiding and the concentrations and formless absorptions as mental bases of other paths, such as the path of seeing.

4 CALM ABIDING: ENTITY, PREREQUISITES, POSTURE

The Ge-luk-pas present calm abiding as a stable, heightened meditative state in which the mind is focused tightly on an object of observation and both mind and object are clear and vibrant. A meditator who has calm abiding is able to focus the mind on the object of observation without distraction (*rnam par g.yeng ba, vikṣepa*), at will, for as long as he or she wishes, and has complete control over the process; this mental and physical serviceability is known as pliancy (*shin sbyangs, praśrabdhi*). Calm abiding is the goal of the type of meditation known as stabilizing meditation and is attained gradually as the result of steady practice. It is important as the foundation of higher Buddhist meditative states—especially special insight and later path consciousnesses such as those of the paths of seeing and meditation—and of the meditative states known as the concentrations and formless absorptions, which can be attained by both Buddhists and non-Buddhists.

TEXTBOOK DEFINITIONS

Kön-chok-jik-may-wang-po, abridging Jam-yang-shay-pa's definition slightly, defines calm abiding as "a meditative stabilization, arisen from meditation, which is conjoined with special pliancy." Jam-yang-shay-pa's definition glosses "special" (*khyad par can*) as "completely qualified" (*mtshan nyid rdzogs pa*).[a]

Jam-yang-shay-pa "unpacks" the definition to show why all four parts are necessary. His first point is that "the mention of meditative stabilization eliminates the possibility that another mind or mental factor is calm abiding." This means that calm abiding is a mental factor—namely, meditative stabilization; moreover, it is not any other mental factor and also is not a main mind (*gtso sems*).[b]

The remaining three points deal with the relationship between calm abiding and pliancy, a key term in the Ge-luk presentation of calm abiding. The mention of a state "arisen from meditation" eliminates the possibility of calm abiding's being any attainment subsequent [to meditative equipoise] (*rjes thob, pṛṣṭhalabdha*) that is conjoined with

---

[a] Kön-chok-jik-may-wang-po, *Condensed Statement*, 557.3; Jam-yang-shay-pa, *Concentrations*, 110.6.

[b] Jam-yang-shay-pa, *Concentrations*, 111.2–3.

pliancy. The mention of pliancy eliminates the possibility of calm abiding's being "a state arisen from meditation which is a Desire Realm mind (*'dod sems*)"; calm abiding is a mind of the Form Realm. Moreover, the mention of *special* pliancy eliminates the possibility of something's becoming a calm abiding "through being conjoined with coarse pliancy"—that is, as Gedün Lodrö points out, with the coarse pliancies initially generated after the attainment of the ninth mental abiding but before the attainment of calm abiding.[a]

TEXTBOOK ETYMOLOGIES

According to Kön-chok-jik-may-wang-po, who gives Jam-yang-shay-pa's etymology without alteration, calm abiding is so called because "the mind, having pacified (*zhi, śama*) distractions to external objects, abides (*gnas*) internally on an object of observation."[b] Jam-yang-shay-pa declines to discuss the formation of the word *śamatha* from the Sanskrit verbal roots.[c] Hopkins, referring to Pa-bong-ka's (*pha bong kha*, 1878–1941) *Lectures on the Stages of the Path*, gives the etymology similarly as

> the mind's abiding (*sthā, gnas*) on an internal object of observation upon the calming (*śama, zhi*) of distraction to the outside.[d]

In these etymologies, the *-tha* of *śamatha* is traditionally interpreted as being derived from the verbal root *sthā* ("stand"); it is therefore translated as *gnas* ("abide") in Tibetan. Whitney's *Sanskrit Grammar* explains *-tha* merely as a suffix indicating an action-noun, without relating it to the verbal root *sthā*.[e] According to Edgerton, however, *st* and *sth* were assimilated "to *tth*, initially *th*," so that *thā* became the equivalent root of *sthā* in Pāli and Prakrit.[f] It would be easy for someone who spoke a Middle Indic dialect in which this shift had occurred, and who also wrote Sanskrit, to derive the suffix *-tha* from the root *sthā* (or *thā*) and

---

[a] Jam-yang-shay-pa, *Concentrations*, 110.6–111.3; Gedün Lodrö, pp. 212–13.

[b] Kön-chok-jik-may-wang-po, *Condensed Statement*, 557.4. Jam-yang-shay-pa, *Concentrations*, 111.3–4.

[c] Jam-yang-shay-pa, *Concentrations*, 111.4.

[d] *Meditation on Emptiness*, p. 67.

[e] William Dwight Whitney, *Sanskrit Grammar*, rpt. 1975 (Cambridge, MA: Harvard University Press, 1889). *śamatha* seems to be of the type discussed in paragraph 1163.c: root (*sam*) + *a* + *-tha*; the *a* "is probably of thematic origin, though become a union-vowel."

[f] Franklin Edgerton, *Buddhist Hybrid Sanskrit Grammar and Dictionary*, first pub. 1953 (reprint: Delhi: Motilal Banarsidass, 1977), vol. 1, pp. 15 and 236–37. Thanks to Karen Lang for this point.

to transmit that etymology.

Near the end of his exposition of calm abiding, Jam-yang-shay-pa explains the related term "mental abiding" (*sems gnas, cittasthiti*)—the term applied to each of the nine mental abidings, or states of mind, that successively precede calm abiding—by citing a passage in Asaṅga's *Grounds of Hearers* that relates "calm abiding" to "mental abiding":

> What is calm abiding? It is the nine-aspected mental abiding (*sems gnas pa rnam pa dgu, navākārā cittasthiti*); since that mind is signless, without [coarse] conceptuality, and is pacified (*zhi ba*), thoroughly pacified (*rab tu zhi ba*), abides in [a state of being] pacified (*zhi ba la gnas*), and definitely has become unmixed [with coarse conceptuality], it is called calm abiding (*zhi gnas*).[a]

Jam-yang-shay-pa cites this passage to account for the literal translation of *sthiti* as *gnas* in the Tibetan translation of *cittasthiti* (*sems gnas*, "mental abiding"), and also, by implication, to account for *gnas* in the Tibetan translation of *śamatha* (*zhi gnas*, "calm abiding"). Although Western grammarians do not seem to explain the suffix *-tha*, as derived from the root *sthā* (or *thā*), *sthā* clearly *is* the root of *sthiti*. Jam-yang-shay-pa's citation from Asaṅga's *Grounds of Hearers* establishes (1) that Asaṅga saw the *-tha* of *śamatha* and the *sthiti* of *cittasthiti* as related and (2) that Tibetan translators also saw them as related and therefore used the same word to translate them in this context.

CALM ABIDING IN RELATION TO SPECIAL INSIGHT

Calm abiding is traditionally discussed in relation to special insight. Both Lati Rinpoche and Gedün Lodrö refer to a passage in the *Sūtra Unraveling the Thought* which "states that all good qualities of the three vehicles are fruits of calm abiding and special insight."[b] According to both scholars, this statement refers not only to calm abiding and special insight themselves but also to what Lati Rinpoche calls "similitudes of calm abiding or special insight"—that is, the meditations of similar

---

[a] Jam-yang-shay-pa, *Concentrations*, 160.6; *Collected Works*, vol. 12, 146.1. In the Asaṅga citation, *navākārā cittasthiti* is not translated as *sems gnas dgu*, the usual Tibetan short form, but literally, as *sems gnas pa rnam pa dgu*.

[b] Gedün Lodrö, p. 156; *Meditative States*, p. 50, both citing Chapter 8 of the *Sūtra Unraveling the Thought* (Étienne Lamotte, tr., *Saṃdhinirmocana Sūtra: L'explication des mystères* [Louvain: Université de Louvain, 1935], p. 277; see also the corresponding section in John Powers, *Wisdom of Buddha: Saṃdhinirmocana Sūtra* (Berkeley, Calif.: Dharma Publishing, 1995), and Thomas Cleary, *Buddhist Yoga: A Comprehensive Course* (Boston: Shambhala, 1995).

type by which calm abiding and special insight are cultivated. These are, respectively, stabilizing meditation and analytical meditation, and, according to Gedün Lodrö, "there is no practice of meditation that is not included within" these two.[a]

The Order of Cultivation

Ge-luk texts and oral presentations agree that calm abiding must be cultivated before special insight.[b] As the source for this position, Paṇ-chen Sö-nam-drak-pa cites Shāntideva's *Engaging in the Bodhisattva Deeds* (*bodhisattvacaryāvatāra, byang chub sems dpa'i spyod pa la 'jug pa*):

> Having understood that the afflictive emotions are overcome through special insight thoroughly endowed with calm abiding, one should first seek calm abiding.[c]

The textbooks and oral presentations also discuss certain apparent exceptions—that is, certain statements in the Indian source texts that appear to contradict the general position. The main one, cited by both Paṇ-chen Sö-nam-drak-pa and Kön-chok-jik-may-wang-po, as well as by the Go-mang scholar Gedün Lodrö, is from Asaṅga's *Summary of Manifest Knowledge:*

> Some have attained special insight but have not attained calm abiding; in dependence upon special insight they make effort at calm abiding.[d]

There are two ways of resolving this contradiction; both allow Ge-luk scholars to reconcile the statement in Asaṅga's *Summary of Manifest Knowledge*, which they are committed to accepting, with the general Ge-luk position. The first is to understand this statement as referring to the initial achievement of calm abiding and to interpret the terms "calm abiding" and "special insight" in this statement as *imputed* calm abiding and *imputed* special insight—that is, as stabilizing meditation and analytical meditation, respectively. According to this

---

[a] *Meditative States*, p. 50; Gedün Lodrö, p. 156.

[b] *Meditative States*, p. 51; Gedün Lodrö, p. 149.

[c] Shāntideva, *Engaging in the Bodhisattva Deeds*, 8.4, cited in Paṇ-chen Sö-nam-drak-pa, "Concentrations," 155a.1–2, *Meditative States*, p. 167.

[d] Asaṅga, *Summary of Manifest Knowledge*, cited in Paṇ-chen Sö-nam-drak-pa, "Concentrations," 155a.3. Also cited by Gedün Lodrö, p. 150. Walpola Rahula, trans., *Le Compendium de la super-doctrine (philosophie) (Abhidharmasamuccaya d'Asaṅga)* (Paris: École française d'extrême-orient, 1971), p. 126.

interpretation, people who make effort at calm abiding in dependence upon special insight have one of the five predominant afflictive emotions—desire, hatred, obscuration, pride, and discursiveness—and cannot succeed in attaining calm abiding unless they reduce that afflictive emotion by doing analytical meditation on the specific object of observation that is the antidote to that afflictive emotion—respectively, the unpleasant, love, dependent-arising, the divisions of the constituents, and the exhalation and inhalation of the breath.[a] Gedün Lodrö notes that

> "Imputed calm abiding" refers to the ninth mental abiding [preceding calm abiding], and "imputed special insight," to the experience of analytical meditation used to break down hatred [for instance]. Following this, the person will indeed achieve actual calm abiding...but the ninth mental abiding is achieved on the basis of an imputed special insight.[b]

According to the second method, an actual calm abiding can be achieved on the basis of an actual special insight, but such calm abiding will not be a *new* achievement of calm abiding. Gedün Lodrö gives the example of someone who achieves an actual absorption of the first concentration, which is a calm abiding. That person achieved an actual special insight at the time of the third of the preparations for the first concentration, the mental contemplation arisen from belief (*mos pa las byung ba'i yid byed, adhimokṣikamanaskāra*). However, the calm abiding of the first concentration is not this person's initial achievement of calm abiding; the initial achievement of calm abiding occurred earlier and was simultaneous with the attainment of the first of the preparations for the first concentration.[c]

Kön-chok-jik-may-wang-po further qualifies the basic position by discussing the status of the calm abiding and special insight experienced by Bodhisattvas on high Bodhisattva grounds (*sa, bhūmi*) and by briefly mentioning the other major exception, which occurs in Highest Yoga Tantra (*bla med kyi rgyud, anuttarayogatantra*) and is not

---

[a] *Meditative States*, p. 51; Gedün Lodrö, pp. 150–51. See the extended discussion of objects of observation for purifying behavior (*mkhas pa'i dmigs pa, mkhas par byed pa'i dmigs pa, kauśalyālambana*) in the next two chapters.

[b] Gedün Lodrö, p. 151.

[c] Ibid., pp. 151–52. This example is based on a passage from Asaṅga's *Actuality of the Grounds* (*bhūmivastu, sa'i dngos gzhi*, also known as *Grounds of Yogic Practice* [*yogācārya-bhūmi, rnal 'byor spyod pa'i sa*]), cited in Paṇ-chen Sö-nam-drak-pa, "Concentrations," 155a.5–6. Asaṅga's *Actuality of the Grounds.*

part of the presentations of the concentrations and formless absorptions. He also adds that it is possible to understand the view of emptiness through analytical meditation without first attaining calm abiding and mentions the realization of impermanence (*mi rtag pa, anitya*) and the generation of the altruistic mind of enlightenment as additional examples of realization attained through analytical meditation without previous attainment of calm abiding.[a]

The Benefits of Cultivating Each

In brief, the chief benefit of cultivating calm abiding is stability, and the chief benefit of cultivating special insight is wisdom. According to Lati Rinpoche, the stability attained with calm abiding allows the meditator to achieve other good qualities, such as clairvoyance, and ensures that his or her good qualities do not degenerate. Because the mind is set on an internal object of observation and thereby tamed, calm abiding also renders external sources of harm ineffective.[b] The wisdom attained through special insight is the wisdom necessary for uprooting afflictive emotions, the chief of which is ignorance (*ma rig pa, avidyā*).[c] Gedün Lodrö notes, more technically, that

> The first of the actual antidotes of any vehicle is an uninterrupted path (*bar chad med lam, ānantaryamārga*). The uncommon direct cause of an uninterrupted path is a meditative stabilization which is a union of calm abiding and special insight (*zhi lhag zung 'brel*). Therefore, it is definite that one must cultivate special insight.[d]

He also remarks that the achievement of special insight leads to clear perception not only of the meditator's object of observation but also of any other object to which the meditator's mind may be directed.[e]

Why It Is Necessary to Cultivate Both

Ge-luk-pas emphasize that it is necessary to cultivate both calm abiding and special insight. Lati Rinpoche compares a person who cultivates calm abiding but not special insight to "someone who has a strong body

---

a Kön-chok-jik-may-wang-po, *Condensed Statement*, 556.1–557.1.

b *Meditative States*, p. 50; Gedün Lodrö, p. 156.

c *Meditative States*, p. 51.

d Gedün Lodrö, p. 156.

e Ibid., p. 156.

but no eyes" and someone who tries to cultivate special insight but not calm abiding to "someone who has strong eyesight but a weak body; because he staggers, he cannot see forms steadily." The person who cultivates only calm abiding has stability but not wisdom, whereas the person who tries to cultivate only special insight "cannot see reality clearly."[a] Although Gedün Lodrö further emphasizes the importance of the intensity of clarity that comes with special insight and is necessary "for anything to serve as an antidote to ignorance,"[b] he agrees with this basic presentation. The general Ge-luk position is that the two types of meditation are necessary to each other; they must be balanced, and special insight itself is viewed as a union of calm abiding and special insight.[c]

Prerequisites

The topic of the physical basis of calm abiding and of the concentrations and formless absorptions answers the question, "What kinds of beings can achieve them?" For the would-be practitioner it answers the question, "Am *I* in the class of beings who can achieve them?" The topic of prerequisites, or "causal collection," is directed to those who know they are technically in the class of those able to achieve calm abiding and the higher meditative states and who want to know what further requirements there are, what physical situations and mental qualities the successful practitioner needs, what they themselves have to do to prepare themselves physically and mentally for such an achievement.

Paṇ-chen Sö-nam-drak-pa does not discuss the prerequisites of calm abiding. They are mentioned briefly by Kön-chok-jik-may-wang-po and discussed at greater length by Jam-yang-shay-pa, as well as in the oral commentaries of Lati Rinpoche and Gedün Lodrö. The liveliest discussion, and the most practical, is in the oral presentations. These draw not only on monastic textbooks but also on stages-of-the-path

[a] *Meditative States*, p. 51.

[b] Gedün Lodrö, p. 156.

[c] Paṇ-chen Sö-nam-drak-pa mentions exceptions to the general Ge-luk position that a union of calm abiding and special insight is attained simultaneously with special insight. These are "Ge-shay Dol-pa-shay-rap-gya-tso's (*dge bshes dol pa shes rab rgya mtsho*, 1059–1131)] *Blue Small Text* and a [Ka-dam (*bka' gdams*)] *Stages of the Path*, and so forth," which assert that a union of calm abiding and special insight is attained *after* the attainment of special insight. (Paṇ-chen Sö-nam-drak-pa, "Concentrations," 156b.3–4.) However, Denma Lochö Rinpoche notes that the difference between the general Ge-luk position and the position of those two texts "is very slight; it is a difference of only one moment" (*Meditative States*, p. 176).

texts, beginning with Tsong-kha-pa's, and from practical instructions based on these.

Kön-chok-jik-may-wang-po's condensation of Jam-yang-shay-pa's text mentions "the six [prerequisites] explained in Kamalashīla's *Stages of Meditation* and the thirty-four explained in Asaṅga's *Grounds of Hearers*."[a] Those usually explained, and still applied in practice, are the six from Kamalashīla's *Stages of Meditation:*

1. Staying in an agreeable place (*mthun pa'i yul na gnas pa*)
2. Having few desires (*'dod pa chung pa*)
3. Knowing satisfaction (*chog shes pa*)
4. Pure ethics (*tshul khrims dag pa*)
5. Thoroughly abandoning the commotion of many activities (*bya ba mang po'i 'du 'dzi yong su spang ba*)
6. Thoroughly abandoning thoughts of desire, and so forth (*'dod pa la sogs pa'i rnam rtog yongs su spang pa*)[b]

Lati Rinpoche notes that

> Of these six prerequisites, the first two...refer to the period before the beginning of cultivation, and the others, to the period during cultivation.[c]

The "agreeable place" mentioned in the first prerequisite has five qualities. Hopkins, following Pa-bong-ka's *Lectures on the Stages of the Path*, gives them as:

a. Good acquisitions
b. Salutary location
c. Salutary place
d. Salutary friends
e. Possession of the pleasant "articles" of yoga.[d]

"Good acquisitions" means that food and clothing are easily obtained and are attained by right livelihood, not by non-virtuous means.[e] "Salutary location" means that, if possible, the place should be one in

[a] Kön-chok-jik-may-wang-po, *Condensed Statement,* 557.4–5, abridged from Jam-yang-shay-pa, *Concentrations,* 111.4–113.1.

[b] Pa-bong-ka, *Lectures on the Stages of the Path,* adapted from a summary by Hopkins in *Meditation on Emptiness*, pp. 68–69; *Meditative States in Tibetan Buddhism* (London: Wisdom Publications, 1983), pp. 75–77; Gedün Lodrö, p. 25.

[c] *Meditative States*, p. 76.

[d] *Meditation on Emptiness*, p. 68.

[e] *Meditation on Emptiness*, p. 68; *Meditative States*, p. 75.

which a good meditator has previously practiced; if such a place cannot be found, the area should be peaceful and free of wild animals, harm from non-human spirits, and loud noises.[a] "Salutary place" means "an area in which the ground itself does not generate sickness but is conducive to good health."[b] Salutary friends, implies that, even when calm abiding is cultivated in a retreat, it should not be cultivated in a solitary retreat. Hopkins, following Pa-bong-ka, states:

> It is harmful for beginners to stay alone without friends, and thus one should have at least three companions whose views and behavior are concordant and whose presence promotes conscientiousness.[c]

According to Gedün Lodrö, these friends should, ideally, have achieved calm abiding, or at least be familiar with the process of cultivating it.[d] The fifth quality is "possession of the pleasant 'articles' of yoga." Hopkins, following Pa-bong-ka states:

> Through hearing and thinking one should eliminate false ideas with respect to the object of meditation and become skilled in the essentials of practice.[e]

Lati Rinpoche emphasizes the importance of also having books so that one can study the process of cultivating calm abiding.[f]

Although the second and third prerequisites—having few desires and knowing satisfaction—refer to different times, they may be considered as a pair. According to Pa-bong-ka, having few desires means that "one should not have desire for food, clothing, and so forth, either of good quality or in great quantity."[g] "Knowing satisfaction" means that "one should be satisfied with gaining only mediocre food and clothing"—that is, content with what one has. The purpose of these prerequisites is the avoidance of distraction.[h]

According to Pa-bong-ka, the fourth prerequisite, pure ethics,

---

[a] *Meditation on Emptiness*, p. 68; *Meditative States*, p. 75. Lati Rinpoche mentions freedom from loud noises under this heading, whereas Hopkins, following Pa-bong-ka, mentions it under the fourth, "salutary friends."

[b] *Meditative States*, p. 75; see also *Meditation on Emptiness*, p. 68.

[c] *Meditation on Emptiness*, p. 68.

[d] Gedün Lodrö, p. 29.

[e] *Meditation on Emptiness*, p. 68.

[f] *Meditative States*, p. 76.

[g] *Meditation on Emptiness*, p. 68.

[h] Ibid., p. 68.

involves the restraint and pacification of "ill behaviour of body and speech." The reason is that calm abiding requires "the pacification of subtle internal distraction." This, in turn, "depends on abandoning coarse external distractions;...for if one is dominated by coarse discursiveness, one's mind will not abide in a natural state."[a] Gedün Lodrö discusses this prerequisite in the more technical context of vows and the purification of past non-virtues (*mi dge ba, akuśala*). He notes that "pure ethics, as a prerequisite of calm abiding, does not necessarily involve having taken vows."[b] He also emphasizes the importance of confession (*bshags pa, deśanā*) and purification, both for those who have vows and for those who do not, especially "for someone who has committed murder....Otherwise, it would be impossible for that person to achieve calm abiding."[c]

According to Pa-bong-ka, the fifth prerequisite, thoroughly abandoning the commotion of many activities, will come "of its own accord if a meditator" has the second and third prerequisites. It is important because, if a meditator does not have it, "time will be passed in senseless activities and conversation." Activities a one-pointed meditator should avoid include not only senseless activities but even helpful ones such as the practice of medicine, as well as the performance of rites and the pursuit of "minor topic[s] of scholarship."[d]

There are several interpretations of the sixth prerequisite, "thoroughly abandoning thoughts of desire, and so forth." Jam-yang-shay-pa gives it as "the definite emergence which is a discarding of adherence to desire,"[e] thus implying that it is a type of definite emergence (*nges byung, niḥsaraṇa*), or renunciation. Lati Rinpoche emphasizes the importance of giving up "attachment to the attributes of the Desire Realm, the chief of which is the desire for copulation."[f] Gedün Lodrö also explains in detail what is included in "and so forth"—the abandonment of "coarse non-virtuous thoughts such as a wish to kill or steal, and also [of] thoughts whose motivation is neutral but might involve the generation of fright or fear."[g]

According to Lati Rinpoche, the six prerequisites are specifically for

---

[a] Ibid., pp. 68–69.

[b] Gedün Lodrö, p. 26; he specifically mentions "the vows of a monk or novice"; although he does not mention the vows of a layperson, they may be implied.

[c] Ibid., p. 30.

[d] *Meditation on Emptiness*, p. 69.

[e] *dod pa la zhen pa dor pa'i nges byung;* Jam-yang-shay-pa, *Concentrations,* 111.5.

[f] *Meditative States*, p. 76.

[g] Gedün Lodrö, p. 26.

people who are cultivating calm abiding in a retreat—classically, a six-month retreat, although, as Denma Lochö Rinpoche remarked, there is no guarantee that calm abiding can be attained in six months.[a] People who combine work with short meditation sessions

> should try to have as many of these prerequisites as possible, but it is not necessary to have them all....There are many levels of engagement in the practice.[b]

Gedün Lodrö, citing Atisha's *Lamp for the Path,* divides prerequisites into two types, "excellent and absolutely necessary." The latter "involve giving up non-virtuous conceptions and neutral ones causing fright." The others are excellent but "are not essential because there are some people who can engage in activities and also in the meantime achieve calm abiding."[c]

The thirty-four prerequisites explained in Asaṅga's *Grounds of Hearers* are barely mentioned and do not seem to be used in contemporary practice. Gedün Lodrö refers to them only briefly,[d] and in his exposition of his own system, Jam-yang-shay-pa, whose text Gedün Lodrö follows, merely cites the passages from Asaṅga's *Grounds of Hearers* in which they are listed, without giving any explanation. The thirty-four consist of fourteen prerequisites, explicitly so called; ten discriminations concordant in quality with the three trainings (*bslab pa, śikṣā*); and ten practices concordant with the three trainings.[e]

How to Set Up the Session

Oral presentations of calm abiding generally discuss the meditator's posture and motivation, topics not discussed in the monastic textbooks translated here. Posture and motivation are stages-of-the-path topics, practical in focus. They are discussed in the section on calm abiding in Tsong-kha-pa's *Great Exposition of the Stages of the Path,* which cites Asaṅga's *Grounds of Hearers* as its main Indian source, but Tsong-kha-pa's citations of Asaṅga have to be understood in the light of his Ga-dam-pa emphasis on taking the "great texts"—that is, the major Indian

---

a Lati Rinpoche in *Meditative States,* p. 76; Denma Lochö Rinpoche in meditation lectures.

b Lati Rinpoche in *Meditative States,* pp. 76–77.

c Gedün Lodrö, p. 30.

d Ibid., p. 29.

e Jam-yang-shay-pa, *Concentrations,* 111.5–6, 112.1–113.1.

source texts—as advice for practice.[a] Gedün Lodrö also cites Kamalashīla's *Stages of Meditation*.[b]

THE CUSHION

The discussion of posture is usually preceded by a description of the type of cushion the meditator should use. According to Ge-luk-pa teachers, the cushion should be square and "large enough for us to sit entirely on it." It should be higher in back than in the front, so that the buttocks are higher than the knees, mainly to cause the spine to straighten.[c] Lati Rinpoche holds that the materials placed under the cushion also have some influence on the meditator's progress. According to him, the Buddha's cushion was placed above crossed vajras. For ordinary people, however, he suggests a swastika drawn clockwise, to increase the meditator's mindfulness and ward off "obstructions, or obstructors, that might cause the mind to fluctuate." On top of the swastika, and immediately under the cushion, he suggests placing kusha grass (*Poa cynosuroides*) or quitch grass (*Agropyron repens*), the former "for the sake of the mind's remaining clear" and the latter, "for the sake of increasing the lifespan."[d]

POSTURE

The posture itself is traditionally said to have either seven or eight features. When seven features are listed, they are as follows:

1 *Legs and hands.* The legs should be in a cross-legged posture—if possible, in the vajra, or adamantine, cross-legged posture (*rdo rje skyil krung, vajrāsana*), with the left foot on the right thigh and the right foot on the left thigh; this is considered the best posture and is obligatory for people cultivating the stage of completion (*rdzogs rim, niṣpannakrama*) of Highest Yoga Tantra (*rnal 'byor bla med kyi rgyud, anuttarayogatantra*). However, for people cultivating calm abiding, the half-vajra posture, with the left foot on the right thigh and the right foot underneath, is also acceptable; it is often used by Tibetans. Another acceptable posture is that of Tārā, with the left

---

[a] Tsong-kha-pa, *Great Exposition of the Stages of the Path* (Dharamsala: shes rig par khang, no date), 663.2–5, 665.5–666.2.

[b] Gedün Lodrö, p. 32.

[c] Gedün Lodrö, p. 31; *Meditative States*, p. 77.

[d] *Meditative States*, p. 77.

foot against the inside of the right thigh and the bent right leg extended.[a] The Fourteenth Dalai Lama, giving contemporary practical instruction, says merely to place the legs in the most comfortable position.[b]

According to Gedün Lodrö, the hands should be "in the position of meditative equipoise (*mnyam bzhag, samāhita*), about four finger-widths below the navel with the left hand under the right and the two thumbs just touching"; the distance of the hands from the navel is determined by the fingers, not the thumbs.[c] According to the present Dalai Lama, "this placement of the hands has connection with the place inside the body where inner heat is generated."[d]

2 *Spine.* The spine should be "straight as an arrow," without leaning forward or backward.[e]

3 *Shoulders.* According to Gedün Lodrö, it is very important that the shoulders be level, with "no difference in height between the two shoulders."[f] Lati Rinpoche also notes that "we should not sit with raised shoulders, as though we had wings; it would become uncomfortable after a while."[g]

4 *Head and neck.* Descriptions of the posture agree that the neck should be bent a little.[h] From Lati Rinpoche's description, it is clear that bending the neck does not mean merely dropping the head forward; rather, "We should bend the head slightly, as if pressing the Adam's apple just a little, and the neck should be like the neck of a peacock."[i] Thus, the neck is seen as flexible; it is stretched first, like a peacock's, and then bent.

5 *Lips and teeth.* According to Gedün Lodrö, Asaṅga's *Grounds of Hearers* advises meditators to leave their lips and teeth as usual, according to their nature; the lips and teeth should not be forced either open or shut; although Tibetan commentaries differ concerning this point, according to Gedün Lodrö the reliable ones agree with

---

a *Meditative States*, pp. 78–79; Gedün Lodrö, p. 31.
b *Kindness, Clarity, and Insight*, p. 66.
c Gedün Lodrö, p. 31; see also *Meditative States*, p. 78.
d *Kindness, Clarity, and Insight*, p. 66.
e *Meditative States*, p. 78; *Kindness, Clarity, and Insight*, p. 66; Gedün Lodrö, p. 31.
f Gedün Lodrö, p. 32.
g *Meditative States*, p. 78.
h Gedün Lodrö, p. 31; also *Kindness, Clarity, and Insight*, p. 66.
i *Meditative States*, p. 78.

Asaṅga.[a]

6 *Tongue.* All presentations agree that "the tip of the tongue should be placed at the ridge just behind the upper teeth." This prevents excessive saliva from flowing while the meditator is in deep meditative equipoise and incapable of noticing it.[b]

7 *Eyes.* It is generally stated that the eyes should be aimed at the tip of the nose and neither opened wide nor tightly closed but, rather, partly closed.[c] The Fourteenth Dalai Lama gives a somewhat more flexible instruction:

> Let the eyes gaze downwards loosely—it is not necessary that they be directed to the end of the nose; they can be pointed toward the floor in front of you if this seems more natural.[d]

He adds that it is all right if the eyes sometimes close "of their own accord," and for a meditator to close them if he or she is bothered by visible objects. He cautions, however, that a meditator who sees a reddish appearance when the eyes are closed, or is bothered by sense objects when the eyes are open, is "too involved with the eye consciousness and thus should try to withdraw attention from the eye consciousness and put it with the mental consciousness."[e]

This posture is known as the seven features of Vairochana's (*rnam par snang mdzad, vairocana*) way of sitting because, as Lati Rinpoche explains:

> The Buddha Vairochana is the symbol of the purification of the form aggregate (*rūpaskandha, gzugs kyi phung po*), the body aggregate; since he is the Buddha who, symbolically, is mainly concerned with the body, it is his posture that is used for sitting.[f]

The main purpose of sitting in this way is to establish predispositions for attaining the Form Body (*gzugs sku, rūpakāya*) of a Buddha.[g]

---

[a] Gedün Lodrö, pp. 31–32; see also *Meditative States*, p. 78; *Kindness, Clarity, and Insight*, p. 66.

[b] *Meditative States*, p. 78; see also Gedün Lodrö, p. 32; *Kindness, Clarity, and Insight*, p. 66.

[c] Gedün Lodrö, p. 32; *Meditative States*, p. 78.

[d] *Kindness, Clarity, and Insight*, p. 66.

[e] Ibid., pp. 66–67.

[f] *Meditative States*, p. 78.

[g] *Meditative States*, p. 78; Gedün Lodrö, p. 38.

When eight features are listed, the eighth, in its simplest form, is simply the manner of breathing while cultivating calm abiding: "Breathing should be quiet and gentle."[a]

According to Gedün Lodrö, this posture has both common and uncommon purposes. Citing Asaṅga's *Grounds of Hearers*, he lists four purposes of the common type:

1. To facilitate the generation of pliancy, since pliancy is easily generated when the body is straightened well.
2. To facilitate progress, since, although the posture is difficult at first, once the practitioner has become used to the posture, it is easier to make progress in it than in postures in which the body is not straightened.
3. To make known that this mode of behavior is different from that of non-Buddhists.
4. To accord with the posture "recommended by Buddha and the Hearers" (*nyan thos, śrāvaka*).[b]

The uncommon purpose is to pacify afflictive emotions by causing winds to enter the central channel (*rtsa dbu ma*), since "this posture causes the winds (*rlung, prāṇa*) serving as the mounts (*bzhon pa*) of such coarse minds to be pacified."[c]

These explanations, as well as the traditional explanations of the individual features of the posture, emphasize the interdependence of the body, channels, winds, and mind. According to Gedün Lodrö:

> Because the body, channels, and mind do not exist self-sufficiently but are in a dependent relationship, when one is straightened all are straightened and when one goes bad all follow.[d]

MOTIVATION

For anyone wishing to achieve calm abiding, the basic motivation is simply the clear thought that one is meditating in order to achieve it.[e] Ge-luk-pas agree that *pure* motivation in this context is that of the Mahāyāna—the altruistic mind of enlightenment. A Hīnayāna

---

[a] *Meditative States*, p. 78.
[b] Gedün Lodrö, p. 33.
[c] Ibid., p. 33.
[d] Gedün Lodrö, p. 32; see also *Meditative States*, p. 77.
[e] Gedün Lodrö, p. 36.

motivation—the wish to get out of cyclic existence only for one's own sake—is not considered a pure motivation in this context, although it is not impure in general.[a] According to Gedün Lodrö, non-Buddhists can meditate on the breath and can achieve calm abiding, as well as the concentrations and formless absorptions, but lack the quintessential instructions (*man ngag, upadeśa*) for purifying motivation that are unique to Buddhists.[b]

Motivation is considered to be impure when an afflictive emotion, such as desire or anger (*khong khro, pratigha*), is present.[c] Gedün Lodrö identifies impure motivations as consisting mainly of the three poisons—desire, hatred, and obscuration. He explains:

> Even though the meditator will still retain them, he or she is seeking to suppress their manifest functioning at that time. The specific purpose for cleansing impure motivations before meditation is to dispel bad motivations connected with this lifetime, such as having hatred for enemies, attachment for friends, and so forth.[d]

Because of the interdependence of the body, channels, winds, and mind, the eighth feature of the posture—namely, the breath—becomes a means of purifying the meditator's motivation; Gedün Lodrö refers to the process as "the settling down of the winds."[e] The winds in question here are those of the afflictive emotions—that is, "the coarse winds that serve as the mounts of impure motivations and coarse thoughts"—which are expelled with the breath.[f]

The simplest method, explained by Lati Rinpoche, is to pacify any afflictive emotion that is present by counting "three, five, seven, nine, or twenty-one" breaths, beginning with the inhalations; the sharper the meditator's faculties, the fewer breaths will be required. Then, when the mind is "somewhat neutral" (*lung du ma bstan pa, avyākṛta*), the meditator establishes a pure motivation by cultivating the altruistic mind of enlightenment before turning to his or her usual object of observation.[g]

Gedün Lodrö presents three methods of meditating on the breath,

---

[a] Ibid., p. 37.

[b] Ibid., p. 40.

[c] *Meditative States*, p. 79.

[d] Gedün Lodrö, p. 37.

[e] Ibid., p. 34.

[f] Ibid., pp. 35, 39.

[g] *Meditative States*, p. 79.

in increasing order of difficulty; these can be used either by one person, who "progresses from one to the next as he or she increases in capacity," or by different persons, according to their initial capacity.[a] The first method involves attention to just exhalation and inhalation, not to *how* one is breathing—whether in long or short exhalations and inhalations—but simply to the fact of exhalation or inhalation; the meditator thinks, with each breath, either, "I am exhaling," or, "I am inhaling."[b]

The second method, called the "twenty-one cycles,"[c] is, essentially, the same method set forth by Lati Rinpoche, except that the number of breaths counted is always twenty-one.

The third method is known as "the nine-cycled dispelling of wind-corpses"—that is, of bad winds. Gedün Lodrö explains that "it is as if the coarse winds that serve as the mounts of impure motivations and coarse thoughts are expelled" with the breath. This method involves inhaling through the left nostril and exhaling through the right three times, inhaling through the right nostril and exhaling through the left three times, and then inhaling and exhaling through both nostrils three times; beginners can use the fingers to press closed the nostril not being used, but, according to Gedün Lodrö, this is unnecessary for advanced practitioners.[d] There are other systems that instruct the meditator to do each type of inhalation and exhalation once and then to repeat the series twice more.[e]

According to Gedün Lodrö, "This practice does not mainly rely on the exhalation and inhalation of the breath but on the imagination of it," since "in order to purify bad motivation, it is necessary to make it manifest."[f] Here "making it manifest" means visualizing it:

> Meditators should imagine or manifest their own impure motivation in the form of smoke, and with the exhalation of breath should expel all bad motivation. When inhaling they should imagine that all the blessings and good qualities of Buddhas and Bodhisattvas, in the form of bright light, are inhaled into

---

[a] Gedün Lodrö, p. 35.

[b] Gedün Lodrö, p. 35. Awareness of exhalations and inhalations as long or short constitutes the second and third aspects of the fifth feature, thorough purification through sixteen aspects (*rnam pa bcu drug yongs su sbyangs pa*), in the system of meditation on the breath in Asaṅga's *Grounds of Hearers* (Jam-yang-shay-pa, *Concentrations,* 116.1, 119.6; see page 118).

[c] Ibid., p. 35.

[d] Ibid., p. 35.

[e] Khetsun Sangpo Rinpoche, *Tantric Practice in Nying-ma,* pp. 197–98.

[f] Gedün Lodrö, pp. 35, 36.

> them. This practice is called purification by way of the descent of ambrosia (*bdud rtsi 'bebs sbyang*).[a]

According to Lati Rinpoche, who discusses this type of breath meditation in the context of the objects of observation for purifying behavior, this practice originated in Tibet and "is not mentioned in the Indian texts"; for that reason, although Lati Rinpoche considers it "helpful," he does not regard it as mandatory.[b]

To explain why observing the breath makes possible the establishment of a pure motivation, Gedün Lodrö, relying on Dharmakīrti's *Commentary on (Dignāga's) "Compilation of [Teachings on] Prime Cognition"* (*pramāṇavārttikakārikā, tshad ma rnam 'grel gyi gshig le'ur byas pa*), points out that "when strong desire manifests, hatred will not manifest and vice versa because desire and hatred are...different conceptions of a similar type"—similar in that both are mental factors—and therefore, in systems asserting six consciousnesses, cannot operate simultaneously in the continuum (*rgyud, saṃtāna*) of one person.[c] Similarly, it is impossible to have discursiveness or manifest afflictive emotions and, simultaneously, to focus on an object of observation. Gedün Lodrö emphasizes the importance of this initial period of observing the breath:

> As much as you are able to withdraw the mind during this period of meditative stabilization on the breath, so great will be your ability to do as you wish in meditative stabilization [on your main object of observation].[d]

Meditation on the breath pacifies all afflictive emotions somewhat; it especially pacifies discursiveness, or coarse conceptuality, thereby increasing the meditator's ability to focus not only on the breath but also on other objects of observation. Thus, although there are many possible objects of observation, this initial period of observing the breath for the sake of purifying motivation is important to a meditator's progress in observing any of them.

---

[a] Ibid., p. 37.

[b] *Meditative States*, pp. 86–87.

[c] Gedün Lodrö, pp. 39–40.

[d] Ibid., p. 41.

5 OBJECTS OF OBSERVATION: I

Ge-luk presentations of objects of observation are extremely complex. For the most part, they explain the categories of objects of observation set forth in Asaṅga's *Grounds of Hearers* and Kamalashīla's *Stages of Meditation,* which, in turn, systematize, in somewhat different ways, discussions of the topic in chapter 8 of the *Sūtra Unraveling the Thought.*[a] All these presentations include several overlapping categories, terminological divisions (*sgras brjod rigs kyi sgo nas dbye ba*) that are conceptually useful for a complete understanding of the nature and function of objects of observation but that sometimes seem to have little practical significance, especially for the beginning meditator. Moreover, although monastic textbooks discuss objects of observation in their sections on calm abiding, all the objects discussed are not objects of observation for the attainment of calm abiding. Mainly, they are presented as objects for calm abiding *and special insight* (*lhag mthong, vipaśyanā*), but a few are interpreted as objects of observation for higher levels.

It is also important to remember that the objects of observation discussed in the monastic textbooks and their Indian sources are mainly objects of observation for Buddhist meditators. Ge-luk textbooks and scholars admit that non-Buddhists can attain calm abiding and the concentrations and formless absorptions, that any virtuous (*dge ba, kuśala*) or ethically neutral object can serve as an object of observation, and that even some of the great Indian Buddhist meditators are said to have used neutral objects to achieve calm abiding; they cite and debate a well-known story about Nāgabodhi, an Indian Buddhist scholar-yogi who could not achieve calm abiding with the usual Buddhist objects of observation and was finally able to achieve it only by visualizing the horns of an ox growing from his head.[b] Nevertheless, they tend to disparage the use of neutral objects, usually typified by "a pebble or a stick."[c] Despite these difficulties, however, the Ge-luk presentations illuminate the range of possible objects of observation, the range of possibilities for directing and focusing the mind, and the range of

---

[a] Gedün Lodrö, p. 78. This statement is qualified by "for the most part" because Gedün Lodrö mentions briefly (pp. 140, 144–45) objects of observation used in tantra but not in the sūtra system.

[b] *Meditative States,* p. 91; *Meditation on Emptiness,* p. 69; Jam-yang-shay-pa, *Concentrations,* 93.2.

[c] Jam-yang-shay-pa, *Concentrations,* 89.4–92.3; Tsong-kha-pa, *Great Exposition of the Stages of the Path* (Dharamsala: shes rig par khang, no date), 673.2–3.

possible results.

The presupposition underlying Ge-luk discussions of the topic of objects of observation is that the meditator *has* an object of observation; mere withdrawal of the mind from sense objects is not the cultivation of calm abiding. A warning against cultivating a meditative equipoise of non-discrimination occurs during discussion of the physical basis of calm abiding and of the concentrations and formless absorptions. Moreover, with regard to meditation on emptiness (*stong pa nyid, śūnyatā*), Kön-chok-jik-may-wang-po and Jam-yang-shay-pa emphasize that "meditation on emptiness is not the same as withdrawing from conceptuality."[a]

General Characteristics of Objects of Observation

The object of observation of calm abiding is said to be internal—that is, mental. Ge-luk-pa scholars refute the position that a sense object—especially the object of an eye consciousness—can serve as object of observation for calm abiding. They hold that calm abiding is achieved with the mental consciousness, not with a sense consciousness: To achieve calm abiding, it is necessary to withdraw the mind inside, and, as Gedün Lodrö explains, "it is impossible to withdraw the mind inside unless the sense consciousnesses are stopped," since "the sense consciousnesses are by their very nature distracted to external objects."[b] Gedün Lodrö qualifies this position by noting, "The only person who can remain in a state of deep meditative equipoise while sense consciousnesses operate is a Buddha."[c]

According to Gedün Lodrö, the erroneous notion that calm abiding can be achieved with the eye consciousness "arises because, when the objects of observation of calm abiding are discussed, there is reference to something that we have seen, such as a picture of a Buddha."[d] The process of learning to visualize a given object of observation involves committing to memory a visual object previously seen (for example, an image of a Buddha); the meditator alternately looks at the object and visualizes it, until he or she is able to visualize without looking.

Gedün Lodrö discusses a qualm concerning meditation on the

---

[a] *Meditation on Emptiness*, p. 552; Hopkins' translation of Jam-yang-shay-pa's debate, pp. 553–58 (Jam-yang-shay-pa, *Concentrations,* 66.4–70.2, abridged in Kön-chok-jik-may-wang-po, *Condensed Statement,* 551.4–552.1).

[b] Gedün Lodrö, pp.67, 68.

[c] Ibid., p. 42.

[d] Ibid., p. 68.

breath, which is an internal tangible object (*reg bya, spraṣṭavya*); the question arises, therefore, whether meditation on it uses the body consciousness (*lus kyi rnam par shes pa, kāyavijñāna*), and if so, whether there is a contradiction with the argument that calm abiding cannot be achieved with a sense consciousness. According to Gedün Lodrö, there is no contradiction because (1) the time of the settling down of the winds is not calm abiding itself, when "the sense consciousnesses will cease," but "a phase preparatory to calm abiding during which, indeed, you have to use your body consciousness to know whether you are exhaling or inhaling,"[a] and (2) in the case of meditation on the breath to pacify discursiveness, the nature of the meditation is deduced both from a long tradition of empirical observation that such meditation is "the best way to pacify all coarse minds" and from the fact that in the visualization of the descent of ambrosia, the breath is not the only object of observation; in the visualization of the descent of ambrosia, meditation on the breath is done in conjunction with a visualization in which the afflictive emotions are imagined as being expelled with the exhalation and good qualities, as entering with the inhalation; the afflictive emotions and good qualities "are imagined to be of one entity with" the meditator's breath.[b]

Another piece of evidence cited by Gedün Lodrö to show that calm abiding cannot be achieved with the body consciousness is the feature of the posture in which the tongue is set behind the teeth to prevent the flow of saliva, which the meditator would not notice in deep meditative equipoise "because the coarse sense consciousnesses such as the body consciousness cease during the higher stages of meditative stabilization."[c]

The Ge-luk emphasis on the importance of using an internal object of observation has significant psychological implications. In modern psychological experiments, an external meditation object is useful; for, if the meditators used as subjects in a clinical experiment were asked to visualize an object, the researcher could not be sure that all the meditators were visualizing the same object in the same way. Arthur J. Deikman's 1963 experiment used a blue vase as the object of observation.[d] In all his subjects, Deikman reports a decrease in distraction

---

[a] Ibid., p. 41.

[b] Ibid., p. 75.

[c] Ibid., p. 76.

[d] Arthur J. Deikman, "Experimental Meditation," in Charles T. Tart, ed., *Altered States of Consciousness* (New York: Wiley, 1969), p. 201.

("development of stimulus barriers"), and, in a final experiment in which the vase was absent, all expressed regret at its absence; some also stated that they were able to visualize the vase in its absence, although Deikman had not asked them to do so and did not follow up their reports by asking them to meditate on the visualized vase. One subject reported a sense of merging with the vase when she looked at it.[a]

It is clear from Deikman's experiment that focusing on sense objects can produce a measurable degree of alteration of consciousness, including increased freedom from distraction, but it probably would not produce calm abiding as understood by the Ge-luk-pas. Hopkins, paraphrasing Pa-bong-ka and Jam-yang-shay-pa, gives the general Ge-luk position that "even when non-Buddhists use a pebble or stick as the object, these are only bases of later imagination by the mental consciousness."[b]

How to Choose an Object of Observation

To choose an object of observation, a meditator may "investigate among various objects such as a Buddha image to see what works well"—that is, the meditator may try them out—or "read texts to see what objects of observation are recommended," or "seek the advice of a virtuous spiritual friend, or guide (*dge ba'i bshes gnyen, kalyāṇamitra*)—a lama (*bla ma, guru*) who can identify a suitable object of observation"; although meditators of sharp faculties are able to choose an object of observation by studying the texts and trying out the objects of observation set forth in them, most people need to rely on a teacher.[c]

Ge-luk-pas, however, refute the position that that any object of observation that seems easy or comfortable will do. Rather, the object of observation has to be one that will pacify the mind. Therefore, an object that arouses desire or hatred is not suitable.[d] According to Gedün Lodrö, the erroneous position that any easy or comfortable object of observation is suitable stems from a misinterpretation of a line from Atisha's *Lamp for the Path to Enlightenment,* which Gedün Lodrö interprets in the context of changing the object of observation as, "One

---

[a] Ibid., pp. 204, 206.

[b] *Meditation on Emptiness,* p. 69, citing Pa-bong-ka, *Lectures,* 315b.4 and Jam-yang-shay-pa, *Concentrations,* 89.4–92.3. Jam-yang-shay-pa follows Tsong-kha-pa, *Great Exposition of the Stages of the Path* (Dharamsala: shes rig par khang, no date), 673.2–3.

[c] Gedün Lodrö, pp. 69, 71.

[d] Ibid., pp. 69–71.

should set one's virtuous mind on any *one* object."[a] It can also be understood as an exaggeration of the valid position that for an inexperienced meditator, the cultivation of calm abiding is difficult and that, therefore, the object of observation should not also be difficult.[b]

Meditators who have one of the five predominant afflictive emotions—desire, hatred, obscuration, pride, and discursiveness—must pacify the predominant afflictive emotion by using the specific object of observation that is an antidote to it; they are unable to use any other object of observation successfully until they have done so. The objects of observation that pacify the five predominant afflictive emotions are called objects of observation for purifying behavior (see below, page 92). However, someone whose afflictive emotions are of equal strength or who has few afflictive emotions may use any of the objects of observation set forth in the Ge-luk system.[c] Since the body of a Buddha is considered the best object of observation in this system, it would be seen as the most suitable object of observation for such a person. (See Chapter 6 and especially pages 130ff.)

Changing the Object of Observation

In general, once an object of observation has been chosen, it should not be changed until calm abiding has been attained; as the source for this position, Gedün Lodrö cites the line just discussed, from Atisha's *Lamp for the Path.* He cites Kamalashīla's *Stages of Meditation* to support the position that the meditator *must* change the object of observation *after* the attainment of calm abiding, to consolidate and develop the calm abiding already attained.[d]

Before the attainment of calm abiding, the major exception is a meditator who, upon first choosing an object of observation, failed to recognize a predominant afflictive emotion and chose, for instance, the body of a Buddha. Such a meditator will reach a point at which progress

---

[a] Gedün Lodrö, pp. 69, 146. Atisha, *Lamp for the Path to Enlightenment* (*bodhipathapradīpa, byang chub lam gyi sgron ma*), stanza 40c-d (P 5343, 21.2.8: *dmigs pa gang rung cig la'ang/ yid ni dge la gzhag par bya/*). See also P5344, 337.5.8–38.1.1-2; *A Lamp for the Path and Commentary of Atīśa,* trans. and ann. by Richard Sherburne, S.J. (London: George Allen & Unwin, 1983), pp. 9, 121.

[b] Gedün Lodrö, pp. 70–71.

[c] Gedün Lodrö, pp. 71–75; Kön-chok-jik-may-wang-po, *Condensed Statement,* 558.3–5; *Meditative States,* p. 82; Jam-yang-shay-pa, *Concentrations,* 135.1–4; Tsong-kha-pa, *Great Exposition of the Stages of the Path* (Dharamsala: shes rig par khang, no date), 674.5–676.1, citing Asaṅga's *Grounds of Hearers.*

[d] Gedün Lodrö, p. 146.

becomes impossible: the predominant afflictive emotion arises in the meditator's mind whenever he or she tries to focus on the body of a Buddha. This type of impasse usually occurs at the third mental abiding—that is, at the third of the sequence of nine states of mind through which a meditator progresses in order to achieve calm abiding. At that time, the meditator must change to the object of observation that is the appropriate antidote to the predominant afflictive emotion.[a]

THE CLASSIC LAYOUT

Ge-luk presentations of objects of observation classically begin with the four types of object of observation set forth in the *Sūtra Unraveling the Thought* and explained, with slight differences in interpretation, in Asaṅga's *Grounds of Hearers* and Kamalashīla's *Stages of Meditation*. The four are:

1. Pervasive objects of observation (*khyab pa'i dmigs pa, vyāpyālambana*)
2. Objects of observation for purifying behavior (*spyad pa rnam sbyong gi dmigs pa, caritaviśodanālambana*)
3. Objects of observation for [developing] skill (*mkhas pa'i dmigs pa, mkhas par byed pa'i dmigs pa, kauśalyālambana*)
4. Objects of observation for purifying afflictive emotions (*nyon mongs rnam sbyong gi dmigs pa, kleśaviśodanālambana*)

That these overlapping categories, though classic, are of little practical importance is suggested by Kön-chok-jik-may-wang-po's omission of the complete presentation; he merely refers to "the four, pervasive objects of observation, and so forth."[b]

According to Gedün Lodrö, pervasive objects of observation get their name from their etymology, since "this type pervades all objects of observation"—that is, "all objects are included among them."[c] Objects of observation for purifying behavior "are named for their ability to pacify afflictive emotions temporarily" and are used by meditators who are dominated by one of the five predominant afflictive emotions that prevent the attainment of calm abiding.[d] Objects of observation for developing skill are objects of observation that increase a meditator's

---

[a] Ibid., p. 147.

[b] Kön-chok-jik-may-wang-po, *Condensed Statement*, 557.5.

[c] Gedün Lodrö, pp. 78, 89.

[d] Ibid., p. 78.

skill. Gedün Lodrö explains that *mkhas pa'i dmigs pa* (literally, "objects of skill") is "an abbreviated expression meaning 'to make or bring about skill' (*mkhas par byed pa'i dmigs pa*)." Objects of observation for [developing] skill, such as the twelve-linked dependent-arising, require detailed study; by meditating on them, a meditator becomes skilled in them.[a] Objects of observation for purifying afflictive emotions cause the meditator to separate from the afflictive emotions pertaining to specific cosmological levels—"either the Desire Realm or the upper two realms, the Form and Formless Realms"—or a specific level within the Form or Formless Realms, such as the First Concentration. Unlike the objects of observation for purifying behavior, which pacify specific afflictive emotions that prevent the attainment of calm abiding, objects of observation for purifying afflictive emotions pacify equally all the afflictive emotions of a given level.[b] They are generally explained in the context of the preparations for the first concentration.

The English term "objects of observation for purifying afflictive emotions" requires some comment, since, clearly, these objects of observation do not purify afflictive emotions in the same sense in which objects of observation for purifying behavior purify behavior—that is, by getting rid of impure behaviors; in the case of objects of observation for purifying afflictive emotions, the meditator does not get rid of impure afflictive emotions and end up with pure afflictive emotions. In English, one has to say that both types of object of observation, in different ways, purify the meditator *of* certain afflictive emotions. The Tibetan and Sanskrit words translated as "purifying" (*rnam sbyong, viśodana*) have both meanings; they can take as their direct object both that which is being made pure and the impurities that are being expelled, but in English, one does not "purify" impurities to get rid of them. However, the word "purify" is being used in that sense here to keep the flavor of the Tibetan and Sanskrit terms.

Pervasive Objects of Observation

There are four divisions of pervasive objects of observation:

1 Analytical image (*rnam par rtog pa dang bcas pa'i gzugs brnyan, savikalpikapratibimba*)
2 Non-analytical image (*rnam par mi rtog pa'i gzugs brnyan, nirvikalpakapratibimba*)

---

[a] Ibid., pp. 78–79.
[b] Ibid., p. 79.

3 Observing the limits of phenomena (*dngos po'i mtha' la dmigs pa, vastvantālambana*)
4 Thorough achievement of the purpose (*dgos pa yongs su grub pa, kṛt-yānuṣṭāna*)

It is generally said that the first two are posited from the point of view of the subject and the last two, from that of the object.[a] However, Gedün Lodrö gives a presentation of the third, observing the limits of phenomena, from the point of view of both object and subject.[b] (See page 90.)

The two images. The terms *rnam par rtog pa* (*savikalpaka*) and *rnam par mi rtog pa* (*nirvikalpaka*) are usually translated as "conceptual" and "non-conceptual," respectively. In this context, however, they are translated, respectively, as "analytical" and "non-analytical." There are two explanations of the meaning of "analytical" and "non-analytical," to be discussed below (see pages 88–90).

The term *gzugs brnyan* (*pratibimba*) means image or reflection, such as a reflection in a mirror. According to Kön-chok-jik-may-wang-po, "'image'...refers to the dawning of the object."[c] The present Dalai Lama explains this dawning of the object as, for instance, the visualized image of the body of a Buddha that has been "found" as a result of previous study of an image seen with the eye consciousness: "This image is called a 'reflection', and is the object of observation."[d] Gedün Lodrö explains that these two types of object of observation are called images "because the varieties of objects of observation are not observed nakedly but are perceived by means of an image." He points out that this image is what Dharmakīrti's *Commentary on (Dignāga's) "Compilation of Prime Cognition"* calls a meaning-generality (*don spyi, arthasāmānya*), or generic image.[e]

Hopkins notes that, since all images are conceptual, "conceptual" and "non-conceptual" are interpreted as "analytical" and

---

[a] Gedün Lodrö, p. 81. Kön-chok-jik-may-wang-po, *Condensed Statement,* posits "the two images from the point of view of the observing [consciousness, observing] the limits of phenomena from the point of view of the object observed, and thorough achievement of the purpose from the point of view of the fruit" (Kön-chok-jik-may-wang-po, *Condensed Statement,* 557.5–6).

[b] Gedün Lodrö, pp. 86–87.

[c] Kön-chok-jik-may-wang-po, *Condensed Statement,* 557.6.

[d] *Kindness, Clarity, and Insight,* p. 185

[e] Gedün Lodrö, p. 82.

"non-analytical," respectively.[a] According to the Fifth Dalai Lama:

> It is said indeed that on the occasion of calm abiding non-conceptuality is needed and that the intellect should be stopped. These statements mean that the mind should not spread to thought other than the object of [observation], such as the body of a Buddha. If (in calm abiding) it were necessary to stop all conceptuality, then, since the contemplation of an image of a Tathāgata's body is conceptual, such contemplation would also have to cease, and in that case you would lose your object of [observation].[b]

In the *Sūtra Unraveling the Thought* and Asaṅga's *Grounds of Hearers,* the two images are listed in the order given here.[c] They are explained in terms of analytical and stabilizing meditation. According to Gedün Lodrö, these texts "say that because calm abiding is mainly a case of stabilizing meditation, it is non-analytical, and because special insight is mainly a case of analytical meditation, it is analytical."[d]

Kamalashīla's *Stages of Meditation,* which Gedün Lodrö appears to prefer, lists the non-analytical image first and explains the two images differently. According to Kamalashīla, meditation in the style of a non-analytical image "is so called because it does not analyze the mode of phenomena (their nature or emptiness) but, rather, is a type of calm abiding that takes as its object the varieties (that is, conventional phenomena)," whereas meditation in the style of an analytical image "involves special insight taking to mind (or analyzing) the nature of phenomena"—that is, their emptiness.[e]

Gedün Lodrö, for whom both texts are authoritative, holds that the presentations of Asaṅga and Kamalashīla are not inconsistent. He explains that for Kamalashīla, as for Asaṅga, a non-analytical image is an object of observation for calm abiding and an analytical image is an object of observation for special insight. According to Gedün Lodrö, both presentations are based on the mode of procedure of beginners and the order of achieving calm abiding and special insight, since the former is achieved before the latter. Kamalashīla's presentation accords with this

---

[a] Oral communication.

[b] Fifth Dalai Lama, *Practice of Emptiness: The Perfection of Wisdom Chapter of the Fifth Dalai Lama's "Sacred Word of Mañjuśrī"* (Dharamsala: Library of Tibetan Works and Archives, 1974), p. 18.

[c] Gedün Lodrö, pp. 81, 84–85.

[d] Ibid., p. 84.

[e] Ibid., pp. 81, 82.

mode of procedure in that almost all beginners take a conventional phenomenon as their object of observation for achieving calm abiding and then, when calm abiding has been achieved, can take emptiness as their object of observation for achieving special insight. Asaṅga's presentation also accords with this mode of procedure, since "[w]hether one is observing the mode or the varieties, as a beginner one first mainly practices stabilizing meditation and then, once calm abiding has been achieved, cultivates analytical meditation and thereby achieves special insight."[a]

Observing the limits of phenomena. As was mentioned earlier (page 88), observing the limits of phenomena is usually posited in terms of the object.[b] According to Lati Rinpoche, "'limits of phenomena' refers to the two types, the varieties (*ji snyed pa*) and the mode (*ji lta ba*)"—that is, to conventional phenomena and their emptinesses; phenomena of both types can serve as objects of observation.[c] Thus, this category, in itself, includes all objects of observation.

According to Gedün Lodrö, however, the limit of phenomena "can be posited from the viewpoint of either the object or the subject." Giving what he presents as the Prāsaṅgika position, he explains that, in terms of the object, the limit of phenomena is only the mode:

> The impermanence of sound is not a limit of phenomena. The limit of phenomena is their not existing from their own side, which is the mode of subsistence (*gnas lugs*) of all phenomena whatsoever.[d]

From the viewpoint of the subject, the limit of phenomena is observed at the time of the direct realization of emptiness—presumably, a Bodhisattva's direct realization of emptiness, since Gedün Lodrö states that "the *path* of observing the limits of phenomena is simultaneous with attainment of the first Bodhisattva ground" and, therefore, with attainment of the Mahāyāna path of seeing. Thus, an inferential cognition of emptiness does not observe the limit of phenomena.[e]

Thorough achievement of the purpose. Thorough achievement of the purpose is presented in terms of the fruit, that is to say, the result of meditation. According to Lati Rinpoche,

---

[a] Ibid., p. 85.

[b] Ibid., p. 81.

[c] *Meditative States*, p. 81.

[d] Gedün Lodrö, p. 86.

[e] Ibid., p. 86.

> thorough achievement of the purpose refers not to the object of observation but to the purpose for which one is meditating; this class includes all the fruits of meditative stabilization from liberation up to the omniscience of a Buddha.[a]

Thus, it includes both the final purpose, Buddhahood, and temporary purposes beginning with liberation from cyclic existence.

Gedün Lodrö gives a somewhat different explanation, without stating his source. According to him, "thorough achievement of the purpose" refers only to the final purpose, a Buddha's Nature Body (*ngo bo nyid sku, svabhāvikakāya*). He holds that a Buddha's Nature Body *can* be taken as an object of observation by non-Buddhas for the sake of attaining calm abiding, special insight, and the Bodhisattva grounds, and that a first-ground Bodhisattva, who has directly realized emptiness and, thereby, "has generated the *path* observing the limit of phenomena in his or her own continuum...can take a Nature Body as his or her object of observation and thereby achieve Buddhahood."[b]

How these four pervade all phenomena. As was mentioned earlier (page 86), pervasive objects of observation are so called because "this type pervades" or includes "all objects of observation"[c] According to Kamalashīla's explanation of the two images, the non-analytical image "includes all varieties of conventional phenomena"; therefore, it includes, for example, the objects of observation for purifying behavior. Gedün Lodrö points out that the analytical image, as well as the last two types of pervasive object of observation, "involve emptiness," and that "emptiness is also classified as an object of observation for purifying afflictive emotions."[d]

If one follows Asaṅga's interpretation of the two images, one could probably say that both conventional phenomena and their emptinesses—that is, all phenomena—can be objects of observation of both analytical and stabilizing meditation.

If one understands the limits of phenomena as including both conventional phenomena and their emptinesses (see page 90), one would have to say that it too includes all phenomena. According to the Lo-selling scholar Kensur Yeshey Tupden, it includes the five objects of observation for purifying behavior, the five objects of observation for

---

[a] *Meditative States*, p. 82.

[b] Gedün Lodrö, p. 92 (emphasis added).

[c] Ibid., p. 78.

[d] Ibid., p. 89.

developing skill, and the two objects of observation for purifying afflictive emotions.[a]

OBJECTS OF OBSERVATION FOR PURIFYING BEHAVIOR

As was mentioned earlier (page 86), the objects of observation for purifying behavior temporarily pacify the five predominant afflictive emotions that prevent the attainment of calm abiding. The five predominant afflictive emotions are desire, hatred, obscuration, pride, and discursiveness; their antidotes are, respectively, the unpleasant, love, dependent-arising, the divisions of the constituents, and the exhalation and inhalation of the breath.[b]

In some cases, a meditator is aware of the predominant afflictive emotion outside meditation and can choose the appropriate object of observation before beginning to cultivate calm abiding.[c] In other cases, however, the meditator is unaware of the predominant afflictive emotion or, in Western terms, unconscious. An apparently loving person, for example, may try to meditate on the body of a Buddha and find him- or herself habitually dominated by the thought and image of an enemy instead; such a person has hatred as his or her predominant afflictive emotion. Gedün Lodrö explains that when the meditator withdraws the mind inside in order to cultivate calm abiding, "whatever is strongest in the mind will become manifest," whereas, outside meditation, the predominant afflictive emotion "does not become manifest because the mind is distracted."[d]

In still other cases, the predominant afflictive emotion will not become manifest at all; the meditator experiences only an inability to progress and will have to consult a teacher, who will diagnose the predominant afflictive emotion and assign the appropriate object of observation. As was noted earlier (page 86), problems related to a predominant afflictive emotion usually arise at the time of the third mental abiding; however, Gedün Lodrö notes that occasionally a meditator with an unconscious predominant afflictive emotion may even attain the

[a] Oral commentary.

[b] Kön-chok-jik-may-wang-po merely lists the five, giving no breakdown and mentioning merely "the divisions of the constituents" as the object of observation that counteracts pride, without specifying whether the six or the eighteen constituents are meant (Kön-chok-jik-may-wang-po, *Condensed Statement,* 558.1).

[c] According to Lati Rinpoche, "A meditator knows whether or not a particular affliction is [pre]dominant" (*Meditative States,* p. 82).

[d] Gedün Lodrö, p. 170.

ninth mental abiding and yet be unable to develop the pliancy necessary for the attainment of calm abiding.[a]

To a Western ear, it sounds strange to describe a mental component that is often unconscious as a behavior. Yet the Sanskrit word *carita,* translated into Tibetan as *spyad pa,* includes that meaning, as well as "going, moving, course;...acting, doing, practice,...acts, deeds."[b] It comes from the root *car,* which means "to move oneself, go, walk, move, stir, roam about, wander" and refers not only to humans but also to "animals, water, ships, stars," and so forth; with regard to humans, it also means "to behave, conduct oneself, act, live."[c] The related word *caritra* includes not only the basic meanings of *carita* but also "habit,"[d] and one can, perhaps, think of a predominant afflictive emotion as a mental habit. In Pāli, *carita* occurs in various combinations, with *su-* or *dus-,* in relation to body, speech, and mind (for example, *manoduccarita).*[e] Thus, it is possible to talk about good or bad physical, verbal, or mental behavior. In the context of objects of observation for purifying behavior, what is meant, clearly, is habitual, though not necessarily conscious, mental behavior that prevents the attainment of calm abiding.

The Unpleasant

Gedün Lodrö explains in detail the two major Indian systems of meditation on the unpleasant used in the presentation of the concentrations and formless absorptions—that of Asaṅga's *Grounds of Hearers* and that of Vasubandhu's *Treasury of Manifest Knowledge.*

The presentation of Asaṅga's *Grounds of Hearers.* Asaṅga sets forth five types of meditation on the unpleasant:

1 Meditation on the feeling of suffering
2 Contemplation of what is unpleasant in relation to something else
3 Meditation on the unpleasant which consists of bad activities
4 The unpleasantness of the unsteady, or the unpleasantness of change

[a] Ibid., p. 151.

[b] Monier-Williams, *Sanskrit-English Dictionary,* p. 389, col. 3.

[c] Ibid., p. 389, col. 1.

[d] Ibid., p. 390, col. 1.

[e] T. W. Rhys Davids and William Stede, *Pali-English Dictionary,* p. 521, col. 2. Monier-Williams also gives *sucarita* (p. 1223, col. 1) and *duscarita* (p. 487, col. 1), although not in compounds with *manas.*

5 Contemplation of ugliness[a]

The first, meditation on the feeling of suffering, involves meditation first on the pain experienced in one's own continuum and, later, on the pain experienced by others—not only humans but also hell beings and hungry ghosts.[b]

The second, contemplation of what is unpleasant in relation to something else, is a meditation on relative unpleasantness; the meditator considers that his or her own body is inferior to that of a Superior, since, unlike common beings, a Superior "no longer takes rebirth by the power of [contaminated (*zag bcas, sāsrava*)] actions and afflictive emotions but by the power of uncontaminated (*zag med, anāsrava*) actions." The meditator then goes on to consider the ways in which a Superior's body is inferior to a Buddha's.[c]

The third, meditation on the unpleasant, which consists of bad activities, involves consideration of the unpleasantness of apparently pleasant non-virtuous actions in terms of their karmic consequences.[d]

The fourth, contemplation of the unpleasantness of the unsteady, or the unpleasantness of change, is actually a meditation on coarse and subtle impermanence; the meditator considers that everyone who is born must die and "that the body is disintegrating and approaching closer to death at every moment."[e]

Of the five, the fifth, the contemplation of ugliness, is the most obvious antidote to sense-desire; it is the only type of meditation on the unpleasant mentioned by Lati Rinpoche, who explains it in graphic detail. Although he gives a clear layout of the other four types of meditation on the unpleasant, Gedün Lodrö gives few specifics of the meditation on ugliness; the only type he mentions, briefly, is meditation on the "putrefaction, rotting, gross dismemberment, and so forth" of the meditator's own body. Lati Rinpoche identifies this type as meditation on internal ugliness—that is, the thirty-six impure substances of which the body is composed "from the soles of the feet to the hair on the head, and inside the skin"—and states that this meditation can be applied either to the meditator's own body or to the body of a person

---

[a] See Gedün Lodrö, pp. 93–98; *Meditation on Emptiness*, p. 70; Jam-yang-shay-pa, *Concentrations*, 114.2–5.

[b] Gedün Lodrö, pp. 93–94.

[c] Ibid., p. 95.

[d] Ibid., p. 97.

[e] *Meditative States*, pp. 98–99. Lati Rinpoche gives a detailed presentation of this meditation in the context of preparations having the aspect of the truths (pp. 135–41).

toward whom the meditator feels sexual desire.[a]

Lati Rinpoche also describes graphically the nine divisions of meditation on external ugliness. He gives "the four colors of rotting corpses" as the four objects of observation that serve as antidotes to attachment to color—that is, to the color of the desired person's complexion. The "two antidotes to attachment to shape...the shape of someone's face, for example," are meditation "on that face as though a dog or cat had chewed part of it," and, more grossly, "as though a dog or a cat had ripped off pieces, such as the ears and the nose, and scattered them about." The antidotes to attachment to touch are meditations "on the flesh as eaten by worms but with the bone and skin still intact" and "on the skeleton held together by ligaments." The antidote to attachment to copulation (*bsnyen bkur, upacāra*) is meditation on the desired person as a corpse—"a dead body that does not move."[b]

Although Lati Rinpoche does not discuss the question, Gedün Lodrö finds textual support for an explanation of sense-desire aroused by the mental qualities of the desired person, a common experience not accounted for by either Asaṅga's or Vasubandhu's presentation of meditation on the unpleasant. He describes this as "the desire for another's 'good nature'" even when the person lacks the physical qualities of color and shape generally considered attractive. Here, too, if the meditator follows Asaṅga's system, the antidote is meditation on an unmoving corpse, "since a corpse has neither good nature nor bad." Gedün Lodrö notes that in texts on monastic discipline (*'dul ba, vinaya*) this type of desire is to be understood as desire for copulation, whereas, in the First Dalai Lama's commentary on Chapter 6 of Vasubandhu's *Autocommentary on the "Treasury of Manifest Knowledge"* in the *Path of Liberation,* "it should be understood as good nature."[c]

Reasoning from within his textual tradition, Gedün Lodrö denies the possibility that desire will be replaced by hatred as a result of meditation on ugliness. He asserts that hatred will not arise because the

---

[a] Gedün Lodrö, p. 95; *Meditative States,* pp. 82–83.

[b] *Meditative States,* pp. 83–84. These four are also mentioned briefly in Vasubandhu, *Autocommentary on the "Treasury of Manifest Knowledge,"* 6.9c (P5591, vol. 115, 244.4.1–5; Shastri, vol. 3, p. 865; La Vallée Poussin, 16:4, pp. 148–49; Pruden, vol. 3, p. 917).

[c] Harvey B. Aronson points out that there are two Tibetan translations of the Sanskrit word *upacāra—bsnyen bkur* ("copulation") in Vasubandhu's *Autocommentary on the "Treasury of Manifest Knowledge"* and *rnyed bkur* ("good nature") in the First Dalai Lama's *Path of Liberation.* (*Meditative States,* p. 238 n. 25, citing Harvey B. Aronson, trans. and ed., "The Buddhist Path: A Translation of the Sixth Chapter of the First Dalai Lama's *Path of Liberation,*" *Tibet Journal* 5:4 [1980], pp. 35, 47.)

meditator's motivation is not that which would cause hatred: according to him, the meditator "does not cultivate a sense of a certain person as unpleasant within a sense that this person is an enemy but only with the motivation of overcoming attachment."[a]

The presentation of Vasubandhu's *Treasury of Manifest Knowledge*. The practical instruction on meditation on the skeleton set forth in Vasubandhu's *Treasury of Manifest Knowledge*[b] is a general antidote to all forms of desire; according to Gedün Lodrö, it is the best antidote.[c] This meditation investigates the nature of the body beneath its superficial attractiveness; in a comment on it, the present Dalai Lama remarked, "If I were wearing X-ray glasses, I would see a room full of skeletons as well as a skeleton that is talking from this podium."[d]

It is a three-stage meditation in which considerable dexterity is developed. The three stages are:

1 The yoga of a beginner at mental contemplation (*yid la byed pa las dang po pa'i rnal 'byor, manaskārādikarmika[yoga]*)
2 The yoga of someone who is practiced (*yongs su sbyangs pa byas pa'i rnal 'byor, kṛtaparicaya[yoga]*)
3 The yoga of one whose mental contemplation is perfected (*yid la byed pa yongs su rdzogs pa'i rnal 'byor, atikrāntamanaskāra[yoga]*)

---

[a] Gedün Lodrö, p. 100, in answer to a Western student's question. This question has arisen especially among scholars of women in religion because of the misogyny evident in many monastic presentations of the meditations on ugliness. A comprehensive discussion of the treatment of this question, covering a wide range of Indian and Tibetan Buddhist schools, is beyond the scope of this book. However, Karen Christina Lang's examination of the poems of Theravāda monks and nuns, the *Theragāthā* and *Therīgāthā,* raises interesting possibilities; she suggests that, within "shared values," the monks and nuns express their repudiation of the profane world differently: The monks' poems are misogynistic; they use "androcentric language"—especially "the stock phrase 'Lord Death's snare'" in reference to women—that makes women "the image of the profane world—their bodies the metaphor for all sensual desire," whereas "in the nuns' verses this same phrase is used to stress that the danger of sensual pleasures and of Māra's control holds for both sexes." (Karen Christina Lang, "Lord Death's Snare: Gender-Related Imagery in the Theragāthā and the Therīgāthā," *Journal of Feminist Studies in Religion,* 2:2 [1986], 78.) It may be worth noting that the meditation on the skeleton set forth in Vasubandhu's *Treasury of Manifest Knowledge,* discussed below, can be applied to any desired person and probably could not be considered either sexist or homophobic.

[b] Vasubandhu, *Treasury of Manifest Knowledge,* 6.9d–11a-b and the *Autocommentary* to those verses (P5591, vol. 115, 244.4.7–244.5.7; Shastri, vol. 3, pp. 865–68; La Vallée Poussin, 16:4, pp. 150–51; Pruden, vol. 3, pp. 918–20).

[c] *Meditative States,* p. 238 n. 25, citing Aronson, "The Buddhist Path," p. 34.

[d] *Kindness, Clarity, and Insight,* p. 185.

Gedün Lodrö describes the first, the yoga of a beginner at mental contemplation, in detail; it

> consists of meditating that a piece of skin is removed from the areas between one's eyes, exposing the white bone underneath. One is to think that the piece of skin falls off as if causelessly, adventitiously, and one then directs the mind to that white bone. When the meditator is able to set the mind on that, he or she gradually enlarges the area of bone until the entire body is exposed as just bone. After this, one considers that all the lands and oceans of the world are filled with skeletons. Having succeeded in extending one's scope to include the whole world, one withdraws the observation gradually until one is again observing just one's own body. At that point, one is seeing just one's own body as a skeleton, and one remains in contemplation of this as long as possible.[a]

In the second stage, the yoga of someone who is practiced, the meditator extends the scope of the meditation and withdraws it, as before, and then "continues to withdraw the observation so that only the top half of the skull remains as skeleton"; the meditator then focuses on the top half of the skull as long as possible.[b]

The third stage, the yoga of one whose mental contemplation is perfected, begins by repeating the second. The meditator then withdraws the observation "until only a small area remains between the eyebrows." Gedün Lodrö emphasizes the importance of making this area as small as possible to increase the meditator's stability and dexterity. The meditator then focuses on this small area of bone as long as possible.[c]

Love

Gedün Lodrö explains love as the wish "that sentient beings have either temporary or final happiness"; he distinguishes it from compassion, which is the wish that they be free from suffering.[d]

According to Lati Rinpoche, one cultivates love in meditation by taking friends, persons toward whom one is neutral, and enemies, in that order, as objects of observation, and meditating on those objects of

---

a Gedün Lodrö, pp. 98–99.

b Ibid., p. 99.

c Ibid., p. 99.

d Ibid., p. 102.

observation according to either the method of mental engagement of belief or that of taking to mind. Mental engagement of belief involves seeing the sentient beings who are the objects of observation as having already attained happiness. In the method of taking to mind, the meditator first thinks with regard to those persons, "How nice it would be if they possessed happiness free of suffering!"; then, "May they possess happiness free of suffering!"; and finally, "I will cause them to possess happiness free of suffering!" The first type of meditation is placed in the present, whereas the second is directed toward the future.[a]

Gedün Lodrö also explains the system of Chandrakīrti's *Supplement to (Nāgārjuna's) "Treatise on the Middle"* and its *Autocommentary*, explicitly Mahāyāna texts outside the usual Indian sources for the presentation of calm abiding, special insight, and the concentrations and formless absorptions. Here the meditator "observe[s] sentient beings regardless of whether they are pleasant, unpleasant[, or neutral]" and cultivates three types of love that correspond to the three types of compassion set forth by Chandrakīrti.[b]

The three types of love, in the order in which they are cultivated, are:

1 Love observing mere sentient beings (*sems can tsam la dmigs pa'i byams pa, *sattvālaṃbanā maitri*)
2 Love observing phenomena (*chos la dmigs pa'i byams pa, *dharmālaṃbanā maitri*)
3 Love observing the unapprehendable (*dmigs med la dmigs pa'i byams pa, *anālaṃbanā maitri*)

All three types of love observe sentient beings, and all three have the subjective aspect of wishing that sentient beings have happiness. Gedün Lodrö describes the first type, love observing mere sentient beings, as "our usual type of love"; the meditator does not observe the sentient beings who are the objects of observation as qualified in any way.[c]

The second type, love observing phenomena, observes sentient beings "within the thought that they are disintegrating moment by moment" and, therefore, are impermanent.[d] It also refers to love observing

---

[a] *Meditative States*, p. 84. Gedün Lodrö (pp. 102–103) discusses variations of the method of taking to mind, suitable for some practitioners, in which one initially takes an unpleasant or neutral person as the object of observation.

[b] Gedün Lodrö, pp. 103–104.

[c] Ibid., p. 104.

[d] Ibid., p. 103.

sentient beings "who do not substantially exist in that they are not self-sufficient"; here "observing phenomena" is a contraction of "observation of sentient beings who are designated to mere phenomena."[a]

The third type, love observing the unapprehendable, observes "sentient beings who are empty of inherent existence"; here "observing the unapprehendable" is a contraction of "observation of sentient beings qualified by an absence of true existence."[b]

In the second and third types of love, the meditator first develops the realizations that sentient beings are impermanent and do not exist from their own side, and then, within those realizations, cultivates the wish that sentient beings have happiness.[c]

It is important to understand the distinctions between the cultivation of love as an object of observation for purifying behavior in order to achieve calm abiding, and the cultivation of love in other types of meditation. Gedün Lodrö points out that when love is cultivated as an object of observation for purifying behavior, there is no certainty that love will actually be generated in the meditator's mental continuum. This is because the generation of love is not the goal of this meditation; rather, the goal is that the meditator's predominant afflictive emotion, hatred, be sufficiently pacified to allow him or her to proceed with the cultivation of calm abiding, usually by returning to the original object of observation—the body of a Buddha, for example. The pacification of hatred may occur when the meditator has achieved "the same type of wish for happiness in relation to the enemy that he or she already has in relation to friends"—that is, when some degree of even-mindedness has been achieved but before the generation of love.[d]

Thus, although Chandrakīrti's three types of love, in their original context, are all types of great love, each of which "observes *all* sentient beings,"[e] there is no guarantee that great love will be generated when this type of meditation is used in order to pacify hatred as a predominant afflictive emotion preventing the attainment of calm abiding. The

[a] Tsong-kha-pa, "Illumination of the Thought: An Extensive Explanation of Chandrakīrti's 'Supplement to the Middle Way' " in Tsong-kha-pa, Kensur Lekden, Jeffrey Hopkins, *Compassion in Tibetan Buddhism* (Ithaca, NY: Snow Lion Publications, 1980), p. 121.

[b] Ibid., p. 122; Gedün Lodrö, p. 104.

[c] Gedün Lodrö, p. 104; Tsong-kha-pa, "Illumination of the Thought" in *Compassion in Tibetan Buddhism,* p. 122. See also Guy Newland, *Compassion: A Tibetan Analysis; A Buddhist Monastic Textbook* (London: Wisdom Publications, 1984), pp. 58–61.

[d] Gedün Lodrö, pp. 106–107.

[e] Newland, *Compassion: A Tibetan Analysis,* p. 55.

relationship between the cultivation of love in this context and the great love necessary for the generation of the altruistic mind of enlightenment is indefinite. According to Gedün Lodrö,

> It is possible first to develop calm abiding and then to cultivate the seven cause-and-effect quintessential instructions [for generating the altruistic mind of enlightenment]; it is also possible first to cultivate the seven quintessential instructions and then, when one has generated an altruistic mind of enlightenment at the time of the Mahāyāna path of accumulation, to develop calm abiding.[a]

Dependent-arising

Dependent-arising is the object of observation for meditators whose predominant afflictive emotion is obscuration. Lati Rinpoche presents in this context a basic meditation on phenomena as arising from causes and conditions and "creating their own specific effect." He regards this meditation as an effective method for refuting the existence of a permanent self and, therefore, as "one of the best meditations for eventually generating special insight."[b]

Gedün Lodrö's presentation is more complicated. He distinguishes between obscuration as a predominant afflictive emotion that prevents the attainment of calm abiding and ignorance in general and, further, between two general types of ignorance: (1) that which is obscured regarding the cause and effect of actions and (2) that which is obscured regarding reality (*de kho na nyid, tathatā*). He gives as an example of someone who has the first type of ignorance "an ordinary being who, not knowing the virtues to be adopted and the non-virtues to be discarded, engages in activities such as killing and stealing"; that person's ignorance "specifically...consists of not knowing that happiness arises because of having done virtue and suffering, because of non-virtue." Therefore, the person commits non-virtuous actions. Someone who has the second type of ignorance "accumulates actions that will cause rebirth in one of the pleasant migrations in cyclic existence, perhaps thinking, 'I will take rebirth as a god.'"[c]

---

[a] Gedün Lodrö, p. 106. Immeasurable (*tshad med, apramāṇa*) love is not discussed in the context of the cultivation of calm abiding because, for the generation of immeasurable love, an actual concentration is necessary (see Denma Lochö Rinpoche in Perfections Transcript, p. 84).

[b] *Meditative States*, p. 85.

[c] Gedün Lodrö, p. 73.

Gedün Lodrö identifies a person in whom obscuration is predominant as someone who has the second type of ignorance, ignorance of reality, which also has two types: it "can relate to either the temporary or the ultimate nature of phenomena." According to Gedün Lodrö, a meditator whose predominant afflictive emotion is obscuration is "obscured with regard to the temporary nature of phenomena"—in this case, the presentation of calm abiding. This person's obscuration "is simply a matter of not having studied," and, therefore, "the antidote is to study about calm abiding"—that is, to "study and contemplate books or listen to a teacher."[a]

A more advanced form of this meditation involves application of the four reasonings to what has been learned. The four reasonings are:

1 Reasoning of the performance of function (*bya ba byed pa'i rigs pa, kāryakāraṇayukti*)
2 Reasoning of nature (*chos nyid kyi rigs pa, dharmatāyukti*)
3 Reasoning of dependence (*ltos pa'i rigs pa, apekṣāyukti*)
4 Logical reasoning (*'thad sgrub kyi rigs pa, upapattisādhanayukti*; literally, "the reasoning that establishes correctness")[b]

Each of these reasonings helps to pacify obscuration. As an example of reasoning of the performance of function, Gedün Lodrö mentions examination of "the activity of the eye consciousness," which is "to see forms." Such reasoning "eliminates obscuration with respect to the three—object, agent, and action (*bya byed las gsum*)."[c]

Gedün Lodrö explains reasoning of nature as "an analysis of the nature of things"; as Denma Lochö Rinpoche points out, "'Nature' here refers to the nature of phenomena as it is known in the world."[d] As examples, Gedün Lodrö refers to common definitions, such as those of wind and fire. Such reasoning helps to dispel obscuration because, by extending it, a meditator can learn "the natures of the afflictive emotions to be abandoned and of the various good qualities to be achieved"—especially, "that adventitious things do not have the nature of good qualities and can be eliminated."[e]

Gedün Lodrö's example of reasoning of dependence is an analysis of how "the person does not exist from his or her own side" but "is

[a] Ibid., pp. 73–74, 109.
[b] Ibid., p. 110.
[c] Ibid., p. 110.
[d] Gedün Lodrö, p. 110; *Meditative States*, p. 155.
[e] Gedün Lodrö, p. 110.

designated in dependence on the aggregates." This analysis helps the meditator realize "that the person is not something able to stand by itself."[a] He mentions reasoning establishing that a pot is impermanent as an example of logical reasoning.[b]

Gedün Lodrö's explanation presents some difficulties. Although, as he remarks, there are many "people who have neither heard nor thought about the cultivation of calm abiding yet who desire to cultivate it,"[c] it is not clear how the study of scriptures and textbooks dealing with calm abiding can be interpreted as a meditation on dependent-arising. Moreover, although each of the examples of the four reasonings can be regarded as, in itself, a meditation on dependent-arising, Gedün Lodrö does not directly apply the four reasonings to what a meditator obscured concerning the presentation of calm abiding learns from study.

Gedün Lodrö also mentions a simplified meditation on the twelve-linked dependent-arising as an antidote to obscuration. In this context, it is a meditation on "the coarser form of the order of the twelve-linked dependent-arising, both the forward progression and the reverse one" that makes it possible for the meditator to decide that the second through twelfth members "all derive from ignorance...in this way obscuration can be eliminated or suppressed."[d] The detailed presentation of the twelve-linked dependent-arising, however, is not one of the objects of observation for purifying behavior but an object of observation for developing skill. (See Chapter 6.)

The divisions of the constituents

There are several presentations of meditation on the divisions of the constituents. Lati Rinpoche explains a meditation on the six constituents—earth (*sa, pṛthivi*), water (*chu, āp*), fire (*me, tejas*), wind (*rlung, vāyu*), space (*nam mkha', ākāśa*), and consciousness (*rnam shes, vijñāna*). Since "persons" are designated based on a composite of these six constituents," the meditator identifies these six in his or her continuum.

> The earth constituent is identified as flesh, skin, bone that which is hard. Water is blood, lymph, and so forth. Fire refers to the heat in one's own continuum. Space refers to the empty

---

[a] Ibid, p. 111.
[b] Ibid, p. 111.
[c] Ibid., p. 109.
[d] Ibid., p. 111.

places within the body. Consciousness, in this context, refers to the mind that is connected with this body.[a]

Gedün Lodrö presents a meditation on the eighteen constituents—the six external objects (*yul, viṣaya*), the six sense powers (*dbang po, indriya*), and the six sense consciousnesses:

Six Sense Powers	*Six Objects*	*Six Consciousnesses*
eye sense power	visible forms	eye consciousness
ear sense power	sounds	ear consciousness
nose sense power	odors	nose consciousness
tongue sense power	tastes	tongue consciousness
body sense power	tangible objects	body consciousness
mental sense power	other phenomena	mental consciousness

As is the case with Lati Rinpoche's presentation of six constituents, a composite of these eighteen can be considered as the basis of designation (*gdags gzhi*) of the person.

> The meditator is to contemplate four characteristics in relation to these: (1) the fact that many causes are involved in bringing them about, (2) the place in which the causes were amassed, (3) the person who amassed them, (4) the causes through which the eighteen constituents are enhanced.[b]

There are also several explanations of how meditation on the divisions of the constituents works to break down pride. According to Lati Rinpoche, meditation on the six constituents breaks down pride by fostering "a sense of unpleasantness...with regard to the body."[c] Gedün Lodrö, however, emphasizes the development of an awareness of how little one knows about the mind and body as the meditator analyzes his

---

a *Meditative States*, p. 86.

b Gedün Lodrö, p. 74. Gedün Lodrö also presents a meditation on the aggregates as an antidote to pride; this meditation uses the same method as the meditations on the six and eighteen constituents—namely, the analysis of the person into smaller and smaller parts. In this case, the set of divisions in question is the aggregates. The meditation works by breaking down "the pride that thinks 'I,'" which "is based on the view that the aggregates are a partless whole" (Gedün Lodrö, p. 112). Lati Rinpoche discusses the eighteen constituents in the context of objects of observation for developing skill (*Meditative States*, p. 88).]

c *Meditative States*, p. 86.

or her continuum into smaller and smaller parts.[a] The Fourteenth Dalai Lama also gives this explanation.[b]

[a] Gedün Lodrö, p. 112.

[b] *Kindness, Clarity, and Insight,* p. 185.

6 OBJECTS OF OBSERVATION: II

THE EXHALATION AND INHALATION OF THE BREATH

The exhalation and inhalation of the breath is the object of observation for purifying discursiveness (*rnam rtog, vikalpa*) when it is a predominant afflictive emotion preventing the attainment of calm abiding. Technically, *rnam rtog/vikalpa* is coarse conceptuality; according to Gedün Lodrö, it "is included within mental discomfort" (*yid mi bde, daurmanasya*).[a] In this context, however, the word *rnam rtog/vikalpa* is translated, for practical purposes, as "discursiveness," since it refers to excessive thinking—that is, mental busyness in which, distracted by a constant stream of thought, the meditator is prevented from focusing on the object of observation.

Gedün Lodrö notes the importance of distinguishing among the various degrees of conceptuality: Although, in general, conceptuality is "abandoned by the path of seeing" with the attainment of the nonconceptual exalted wisdom (*rnam par mi rtog pa'i ye shes*) directly realizing emptiness, conceptuality is not completely eliminated until the attainment of Buddhahood:[b] "As one goes higher and higher on the path, the conceptuality to be abandoned becomes more and more subtle."[c] In the context of a beginner's cultivation of calm abiding, conceptuality refers merely to "those factors which hinder calm abiding."[d]

Ge-luk presentations do not explain why the exhalation and inhalation of the breath is considered the best object of observation for "purifying" discursiveness. Simply, it works; the choice seems to be an empirical one, based on a long tradition of Buddhist practice. The governing principle seems to be the one cited earlier in the context of the settling down of the winds, the breath meditation done at the beginning of the session (see pages 78ff.)—namely, that in systems asserting six consciousnesses, different conceptual consciousnesses of a similar type cannot operate simultaneously in the mental continuum of one person. Therefore, meditation on the inhalation and exhalation of the breath is able to *pacify* discursiveness, even though it is "not an actual antidote" to discursiveness[e] and, thus, cannot eradicate it. Meditation on the

---

[a] Gedün Lodrö, pp. 75, 76.

[b] Ibid., p. 77.

[c] Ibid., p. 77.

[d] Ibid., p. 77.

[e] Ibid., p. 75.

exhalation and inhalation of the breath pacifies discursiveness because it causes "all other minds" to "settle down into a neutral (*lung du ma bstan pa, avyākṛta*) state"; from that ethically neutral state, "it becomes easy [for the meditator] to develop a virtuous attitude."[a]

As a basic explanation for beginners, Lati Rinpoche gives a simplified presentation of breath meditation similar to the one Gedün Lodrö gives under the topic "the settling down of the winds"[b] (see page 78). However, Gedün Lodrö presents the settling down of the winds as a three-stage process in which the first two stages are watching and counting, whereas Lati Rinpoche distinguishes between watching and counting according to the faculties of the meditator; according to him, meditators of dull faculties have to count, whereas meditators of sharp faculties are able to watch the breath without counting.[c] Both Gedün Lodrö's and Lati Rinpoche's explanations are intended to serve not only as introductory presentations of the Ge-luk system according to their respective colleges' textbooks but also as practical instruction for beginning meditators.

In his more extensive exposition of objects of observation for purifying behavior, Gedün Lodrö follows Jam-yang-shay-pa in distinguishing between the presentations of the two main Indian sources—Vasubandhu's *Treasury of Manifest Knowledge* and Asaṅga's *Grounds of Hearers*—in addition to the basic presentation for beginners he had already given under "the settling down of the winds."[d] He also follows Jam-yang-shay-pa in regarding both Vasubandhu's and Asaṅga's presentations as internally coherent systems,[e] each of which offers a sequential practical method to the meditator. He discusses Jam-yang-shay-pa's exposition of the presentation of the *Treasury* but not Jam-yang-shay-pa's presentation of the "system" of Asaṅga's *Grounds of Hearers*, which he considered too long and complicated for a semester-long lecture course; he therefore offered, as a substitute, his earlier presentation of "the settling down of the winds."[f]

---

[a] Ibid., p. 40.

[b] Ibid., pp. 34–36.

[c] *Meditative States*, p. 86.

[d] Kön-chok-jik-may-wang-po, in his condensation of Jam-yang-shay-pa's text, omits the presentation of both systems, as well as explanations of the remaining objects of observation.

[e] Gedün Lodrö, p. 112; Jam-yang-shay-pa, *Concentrations*, 115.3 (*nyan sa dang mdzod lugs gnyis*).

[f] Gedün Lodrö also presents an alternative explanation of the "system" of the *Treasury*, refuted by Jam-yang-shay-pa, which I will not discuss here (Gedün Lodrö, pp. 113–14).

The Presentation of Vasubandhu's Treasury of Manifest Knowledge

Vasubandhu introduces the topic of meditation on the exhalation and inhalation of the breath with the statement, "Mindfulness of exhalation and inhalation is wisdom" (*Treasury* 6.12a). The *Autocommentary* to this verse notes that mindfulness is equated with wisdom in this context just as it is in the context of the four mindful establishments (*dran pa nye bar bzhag pa, smṛtyupasthāna*)—namely, "because [wisdom] occurs by generation of the force of [mindfulness]."[a] Expounding this passage further, the First Dalai Lama notes in the *Path of Liberation,* his commentary on Vasubandhu's *Autocommentary on the "Treasury of Manifest Knowledge,"* that mindfulness actually precedes wisdom; wisdom is called mindfulness in this context "because when the strength of mindfulness has been developed, [wisdom] engages the object." In his oral commentary on the *Path of Liberation,* Lati Rinpoche adds that "since wisdom occurs due to the power of mindfulness, the effect—wisdom—is given the name of the cause—mindfulness."[b]

Although Ge-luk scholars make these observations when they direct their attention to Vasubandhu's *Treasury of Manifest Knowledge* and its *Autocommentary* as a topic in its own right, they do not appear to apply this analysis to citations and discussions of the same texts in their presentations of breath meditation in the context of the cultivation of calm abiding, as part of the topic of the concentrations and formless absorptions. What they seem to overlook, especially, is the relationship between the *Treasury* and *Autocommentary* passages just cited and the *Treasury* and *Autocommentary* introduction to the presentation of the four mindful establishments (6.14a–b):

> Having attained meditative stabilization by means of those two [that is, meditation on the unpleasant and mindfulness of the exhalation and inhalation of the breath], in order to achieve special insight
>
> One who has achieved calm abiding
> Should cultivate mindful establishment
> For the sake of attaining special insight.[c]

---

[a] Vasubandhu, *Treasury of Manifest Knowledge* and *Autocommentary on the "Treasury of Manifest Knowledge,"* 6.12a (P5591, vol. 115, 245.1.6; Shastri, part 3, p. 898; La Vallée Poussin, 16:4, p. 153; Pruden, vol. 3, p. 921).

[b] Aronson, "The Buddhist Path," p. 38.

[c] Vasubandhu, *Treasury of Manifest Knowledge*, 6.14a–b (P5591, vol. 115, 245.4.7–8; Sha-

Since Ge-luk-pa scholars typically regard calm abiding as a meditative stabilization and special insight as a wisdom consciousness,[a] juxtaposition of the two passages might have suggested that the types of breath meditation discussed in the *Treasury* (and also in Asaṅga's *Grounds of Hearers*) not only, in their initial stages, serve to pacify discursiveness and calm the mind but can also, in their higher developments, lead to special insight and beyond; for the first passage, with its reference to the four mindful establishments, associates mindfulness and wisdom, and the second passage states that cultivation of the four mindful establishments—preceded, in one mode of practice, by mindfulness of breathing leading to the attainment of calm abiding—leads to the attainment of special insight. But somehow, the juxtaposition was not made.

There may be two reasons for the Ge-luk failure to associate Vasubandhu's and Asaṅga's presentations of the higher stages of breath meditation with special insight. The first reason is that the main Ge-luk presentation of special insight is not drawn from the Indian source texts for the topic of the concentrations and formless absorptions; rather, it is Tsong-kha-pa's Prāsaṅgika-Madhyamaka presentation, based on Chandrakīrti's *Clear Words,* in the *Middling* and *Great Exposition(s) of the Stages of the Path.* The second reason is that practice traditions related to Vasubandhu's or Asaṅga's presentations of breath meditation were probably not transmitted to Tibet.

The practice tradition suggested by the *Treasury* itself—and also by Asaṅga's *Grounds of Hearers*—is one in which mindfulness of breathing becomes a basis for inductive reasoning on such topics as the five aggregates; as a result of such inductive reasoning, the meditator progresses through the Hearer paths of preparation, seeing, and meditation. It seems at least possible that both Vasubandhu and Asaṅga presented their respective versions of such a method, analogous to but different from modern Theravāda insight meditation, and that Ge-luk-pa scholars were unable to reconstruct it in the absence of a practice tradition because of the great difference between this type of inductive

stri, p. 602. See also La Vallée Poussin, vol. 4, p. 158 and Pruden, vol. 3, p. 925. The Tibetan version of the *Autocommentary* is closer to Hsüan Tsang's, as given by La Vallée Poussin and Pruden, than to Shastri's.

[a] Paṇ-chen Sö-nam-drak-pa, "Concentrations," 155b.6–156a.1; Jam-yang-shay-pa (followed by Kön-chok-jik-may-wang-po) gives "meditative stabilization" and "wisdom" as the key terms in the definitions of "calm abiding" and "special insight," respectively (Jam-yang-shay-pa, *Concentrations,* 110.6 and 162.3; Kön-chok-jik-may-wang-po, *Condensed Statement,* 557.3 and 563.6).

meditative reasoning based on observation and the types of meditative reasoning using consequences (*thal 'gyur, prasaṅga*) or syllogisms (*sbyor ba, prayoga*) with which Ge-luk-pas were familiar.[a] Thus, although Ge-luk-pa scholars give detailed interpretations of the systems of breath meditation set forth in Vasubandhu's and Asaṅga's texts, they may not fully account for the higher stages of breath meditation set forth in those texts.

According to the *Treasury* (6.12d and its *Autocommentary*),[b] meditation on the exhalation and inhalation of the breath has six aspects, or stages:

1 counting (*grangs pa, gaṇanā*)
2 following (*rjes su 'gro ba, anugama*)
3 placement (*'jog ba, sthāna*)
4 investigation (*nye bar rtog pa, upalakṣaṇā*)[c]
5 change (*yongs su sgyur ba, vivartanā*)
6 purifying (*yongs su dag pa, pariśuddhi*)

Following the *Autocommentary* closely, Gedün Lodrö explains the first, **counting**, as "the ability to withdraw the mind inside and count the breaths from one to ten single-pointedly without confusing the order."[d]

The second, **following**, involves observation and recognition of where the breath goes in the body; the meditator examines whether the breath fills all or only part of the body. The *Autocommentary* lists some of the places in the body into which the meditator follows the breath—"the throat, the heart, the navel, the kidneys, the thigh, and so on to the two feet," and "out to a distance of a hand and a cubit."[e] Lati Rinpoche seems to explain this as a *method* of breathing—"breathing in all the way to the feet and breathing out to a distance ranging from a fathom or a hand's span, depending on the strength of

---

[a] See *Meditation on Emptiness*, pp. 360–61, 431–32, 443–53—and indeed, the entire work is an extended presentation of the use of reasoning in meditation.

[b] Vasubandhu, *Treasury of Manifest Knowledge* and *Autocommentary*, 6.12d (P5591, vol. 115, 245.2.4–245.3.8; Shastri, part 3, pp. 899–900; La Vallée Poussin, vol. 4, pp. 154–56; Pruden, vol. 3, pp. 922–23).

[c] "Investigation" is an English translation of the Tibetan *nye bar rtog pa;* a more literal translation of the Sanskrit *upalakṣaṇā* would be "characterization."

[d] Gedün Lodrö, p. 115.

[e] Vasubandhu, *Autocommentary on the "Treasury of Manifest Knowledge,"* 6.12d (P5591, vol. 115, 245.3.1–4; Shastri, part 3, pp. 899–900; La Vallée Poussin, vol. 4, p. 154; Pruden, vol. 3, p. 922.

the individual"[a]—rather than as an aspect of *mindfulness* of breathing—that is, as part of the process of *observing* the breath. Gedün Lodrö introduces from Tibetan meditational physiology the notion of analyzing the "many coarse and subtle channels (*rtsa, nāḍi*) through which the breath passes,"[b] which is not found at this point in the *Autocommentary*.

As Gedün Lodrö notes, the third way of meditating on the breath, **placement**, involves examination of "how the breath brings help or harm to the body."[c] Lati Rinpoche, paraphrasing the *Autocommentary*, explains the meditator's method:

> ...one observes the breath abiding like a string for a necklace from the tip of the nose to the bottom of the feet. Then one considers whether this abiding wind is harming or helping the body, or whether it is hot or cold.[d]

Thus, Lati Rinpoche explains placement in terms of observation of the breath, although he had explained following in somewhat different terms.

Gedün Lodrö, developing his earlier reference to analysis of the channels in the body, explains placement as involving the straightening of channels which, up to that time, had been "bent or contracted." According to him,

> The beginning meditator imagines the wind moving through all the coarse and subtle channels of the body and considers if it is helping or harming. Initially this is an aspiration, but with practice unsuitable winds can be stopped and a wind developed through the force of meditation can be directed through the coarse and subtle channels down to the feet. At this time the coarse channels straighten out.[e]

Thus, Gedün Lodrö seems to understand placement as something other than observation; he interprets the *Autocommentary*'s reference to "a [straight] string in a rosary," or necklace, as referring to "a rosary grasped at two ends and pulled taut," and, therefore, as alluding to the process he describes—perhaps because of the implicit analogy between

---

[a] Aronson, "The Buddhist Path," p. 39.

[b] Gedün Lodrö, p. 116.

[c] Ibid., p. 116.

[d] Aronson, "The Buddhist Path," p. 39.

[e] Ibid., p. 40; Gedün Lodrö adds that he does not think the Vaibhāṣhikas' method (as he understands it) affects the subtle channels.

the taut rosary and the straightened channels.[a]

All accounts of the fourth way of meditating on the breath, **investigation**, agree that it differs radically from the first three: whereas the first three involve counting and observation of the breath itself, the fourth involves an inductive analysis, based on observation, that leads to the experiential discovery of the five aggregates. According to the *Autocommentary,* which summarizes the meditator's process of analysis and states its conclusion, "'Not only are there just the winds (*vāyu*); there are the four great elements (*mahābhūta*), along with the [secondary] materiality (*rūpa*) resulting from the great elements [and] the minds and mental factors based on these'; thus [the meditator] investigates [and characterizes] (*upalakṣayati*) the five aggregates."[b]

Gedün Lodrö notes that the first three and the last three meditations on the breath differ in function, but it appears that neither he nor Lati Rinpoche recognizes that the fourth meditation involves experiential discovery through inductive rather than deductive analysis. Rather, Gedün Lodrö suggests that "the first three...are primarily for beginners attempting to achieve or deepen calm abiding," whereas "the last three meditations are primarily used for developing proficiency in the calm abiding one has already achieved or for attaining special insight"; his categories overlap, since he also suggests that "the second and third can also be used by those with calm abiding for cultivating special insight."[c] Summarizing and extending the brief analysis given in the *Autocommentary*, Gedün Lodrö explains that the first "three ways of meditating on the breath all involve meditation on the breath itself, which is a tangible object (*reg bya, spraṣṭavya*)," whereas the fourth involves "putting aside the examination of [breath as] wind" and investigating "what is and is not of the nature of the five aggregates in relation to wind."[d] Lati Rinpoche, who also briefly summarizes the analysis given in the *Autocommentary,* notes that "when considering the breath in the above way, one is investigating its mode of existence."[e] However, he too does not seem to consider the possibility that the meditator discovers the mode of existence of the breath through an investigation begun inductively through mindfulness.

According to the *Autocommentary,* the fifth stage of mindfulness of

[a] Ibid., p. 40.

[b] Vasubandhu, *Autocommentary on the "Treasury of Manifest Knowledge,"* 6.12d (P5591, vol. 115, 245.3.4–8; Shastri, p. 900; La Vallée Poussin, vol. 4, p. 156; Pruden, vol. 3, p. 923).

[c] Aronson, "The Buddhist Path," p. 40.

[d] Gedün Lodrö, pp. 116.

[e] Aronson, "The Buddhist Path," p. 40.

breathing, **change**, involves "modifying the mind that has wind as its object of observation," so that the meditator "practices with respect to higher and higher virtuous roots up to the supreme [mundane] qualities" (*'jig rten pa'i chos kyi mchog, laukikāgryadharma*) of the path of preparation.[a] The *Autocommentary*'s descriptions of the fifth and sixth stages are brief and do not give specific practical instructions or describe the meditator's actual procedure in detail. Thus, the literal wording of the text, especially with regard to the fifth stage, is ambiguous. It can be read to imply that the meditator—who, up to that point, had been observing the breath and, on the basis of that observation, drawing conclusions concerning the aggregates—either changes the object of observation in some way, or attains the four levels of the path of preparation, or both.

Lati Rinpoche's interpretation includes both meanings:

> "Change" involves the transformation of the object of observation from the breath to the paths of preparation. One now observes the heat stage of the path of preparation through to the stage of highest mundane phenomena..., changing the mind into the four levels of the path of preparation.[b]

Similarly, in his interpretation of the sixth stage of mindfulness of breathing, **purification**, Lati Rinpoche states that "one transforms the mind into the paths of seeing and meditation."[c]

Gedün Lodrö, however, emphasizes the change of object of observation, both in his lectures on calm abiding and in his comments on the sixth chapter of the First Dalai Lama's *Path of Liberation.*[d] Although he explains, in the latter context, that observation of the path of preparation by someone who has attained calm abiding can lead to attainment of the heat level of the path of preparation and, subsequently, to attainment of its remaining levels—peak, forbearance, and supreme mundane qualities—he seems to imply that, if a meditator attains the path of preparation during the fifth stage of breath meditation, or the paths of seeing and meditation during the sixth, those attainments are the successful result of having taken those paths as objects of observation: "while one contemplates the paths as objects of observation, one

---

[a] Vasubandhu, *Autocommentary on the "Treasury of Manifest Knowledge,"* 6.12d (P5591, vol. 115, 245.3.6–7; Shastri, p. 600; La Vallée Poussin, vol. 4, p. 156; Pruden, vol. 3, p. 923).

[b] Aronson, "The Buddhist Path," p. 40.

[c] Ibid., p. 42.

[d] Gedün Lodrö, p. 117; Aronson, "The Buddhist Path," pp. 40–41.

is also subjectively cultivating them."[a]

The two contemporary Tibetan commentators, Lati Rinpoche and Gedün Lodrö, explain the first three stages of Vasubandhu's system in practical terms, for the most part, since the first two, especially, are practices a beginning meditator might use to overcome discursiveness, and the third still involves direct observation of the breath, although it also involves drawing conclusions from that observation. However, they do not state that, in the last three, the meditator progresses through the Hearer paths of preparation, seeing, and meditation by using mindfulness of breathing and inductive reasoning based on such mindfulness, even though Vasubandhu's *Treasury of Manifest Knowledge* and its *Autocommentary* explicitly lay out such a correspondence.

Moreover, neither scholar posits a relationship between the attainment of the heat stage of the path of preparation at the beginning of the fifth stage of Vasubandhu's system of breath meditation with the attainment of special insight. Although such a correlation would have been consistent with the synthetic system-building methods of Ge-luk religious scholarship, and although Kön-chok-jik-may-wang-po, in his *Condensed Statement,* twice states the commonly held Ge-luk assertion that the attainment of the heat stage of the path of preparation and the attainment of special insight are simultaneous, he does so only in the context of meditation on emptiness or selflessness as such meditation was understood by Ge-luk-pas.[b] It appears that neither Ge-luk-pa textbook writers nor modern scholars such as Lati Rinpoche and Gedün Lodrö were in a position to conclude that the first moment of the fifth stage of Vasubandhu's system of breath meditation coincides with the attainment of special insight and that, therefore, the first four stages must be a method for cultivating special insight.

THE PRESENTATION OF ASAṄGA'S GROUNDS OF HEARERS

Asaṅga's *Grounds of Hearers* has been, for the most part, unexplored by Western scholarship; an examination of the theories of meditation and practical instructions set forth in it would require a separate study. It

---

[a] Aronson, "The Buddhist Path," p. 41.

[b] Kön-chok-jik-may-wang-po, *Condensed Statement,* 552.2 ("the attainment of the wisdom arisen from meditating on [emptiness], of the special insight on [emptiness], and of the heat [stage of the] Mahāyāna path of preparation are simultaneous") and 575.6 ("a state arisen from meditation which analyzes the object, selflessness; the mental contemplation [arisen from] belief; [and] the heat stage of the Hearer path of preparation...are attained simultaneously").

seems possible, however, that Asaṅga has collected in *Grounds of Hearers* versions of several meditation techniques better known to Westerners from Theravāda texts and modern systems of practice, and that Tibetan commentators, lacking such practice traditions, developed theoretical interpretations based solely on the descriptions in Asaṅga's text. Comparisons with analogous Theravāda presentations suggest that even Asaṅga's accounts of Hearer practices may not have been based entirely on practice traditions.

Although Jam-yang-shay-pa and Gedün Lodrö refer to the "system" of Asaṅga's *Grounds of Hearers,* it is possible that Asaṅga's descriptions of various practices of breath meditation represent neither a single system nor a progressive sequence and that the extreme complexity of Jam-yang-shay-pa's explanation of Asaṅga's presentation may stem from his trying to find internal coherence in a section of Asaṅga's text that may not have been intended to have it. Lacking a Tibetan practice tradition for most of these meditations, Jam-yang-shay-pa seems to have posited or constructed relationships among the headings and subheads of Asaṅga's lists—a hypothetical order of practice that, in some cases, does not agree with what is known about analogous meditations from Theravāda sources.

Jam-yang-shay-pa presents Asaṅga's "system" of meditation on the exhalation and inhalation of the breath under five major headings, all of which represent modes of purification:

1 thorough purification through counting
2 thorough purification through engagement in the aggregates
3 thorough purification through engagement in dependent-arising
4 thorough purification through engagement in the [four] truths
5 thorough purification through sixteen aspects[a]

According to Jam-yang-shay-pa these five modes of purification follow each other sequentially. His description of the first suggests that counting the breaths, in itself, can lead to the attainment of calm abiding, and it is clear from his descriptions and supporting citations from Asaṅga's *Grounds of Hearers* how the second, third, and fourth meditations develop from conclusions reached by the meditator in the preceding meditation as the result of inductive reasoning based on observation.

Thorough purification through counting. In thorough purification through counting—which, despite differences in the methods

[a] Jam-yang-shay-pa, *Concentrations,* 116.1.

presented by the two texts, corresponds to the category "counting" in the system of Vasubandhu's *Treasury of Manifest Knowledge*—the meditator observes and then counts exhalations and inhalations. The exhalation and inhalation can be counted separately, or the two can be counted as a unit. In either case, the meditator counts from one to ten and then backward from ten to one; Jam-yang-shay-pa makes the interesting practical point that the forward and backward sequence must always alternate, since "if [a meditator] counts, for instance, 'one' immediately after 'ten,' [his or her] meditative stabilization becomes disturbed."[a] Jam-yang-shay-pa cites Asaṅga's *Grounds of Hearers* as stating that, by merely counting in this way, a meditator can generate physical and mental pliancy and calm abiding. Thus, it appears that thorough purification through counting can, in itself, lead to the attainment of calm abiding, independently of the other four modes of thorough purification. Jam-yang-shay-pa further notes that, according to Asaṅga, meditators of dull faculties count the breath, whereas those of sharp faculties direct the mind to the breath and watch it.

Thorough purification through engagement in the aggregates. Engagement in the aggregates is done after counting. "Engagement" refers to a process of inductive reasoning, based on previous observation of the breath, in which the meditator, examining mindfulness of the exhalation and inhalation of the breath in terms of the aggregates, thinks:

> The basis of the breath, the body, is form; mindfulness—that is, the mindfulness of the going and coming of the breath—and the experience [of the going and coming of the breath] are feeling; the knowing of all those is discrimination; mindfulness of, attention to, and knowledge of [the going and coming of the breath] are compositional factors; and the mind (*sems, citta*) and intellect (*yid, manas*) at that time are consciousness (*rnam shes, vijñāna*).[b]

"Thorough purification" refers to "abiding many times in having engaged in that."[c]

Although Jam-yang-shay-pa does not use the term "analytical meditation," "engagement" in this context could be described as an analytical meditation if the meaning of "analytical meditation" were

---

[a] Ibid., 116.3–4.

[b] Ibid., 116.6–6.

[c] Ibid., 117.1, with citation from Asaṅga's *Grounds of Hearers.*

extended to include inductive reasoning based on observation in addition to the usual reasoning using syllogisms and consequences.

Thorough purification through engagement in dependent-arising. Jam-yang-shay-pa explains engagement in dependent-arising as a meditation that follows engagement in the aggregates and that involves research into a series of causes; working backward, the meditator traces the cause of the exhalation and inhalation of the breath to ignorance. This meditation, however, differs from both the simplified meditations on dependent-arising suggested, under objects of observation for purifying behavior, for meditators whose predominant afflictive emotion is obscuration, on the one hand, and the detailed presentation of the twelve-linked dependent-arising included among the objects of observation for developing skill, on the other. Specifically, the meditator determines that the body and mind—that is, the physical and mental aggregates, which the meditator had analyzed in the previous stage of the meditation—are the cause of the going and coming of the breath; that the life faculty (*srog gi dbang po, jivitendriya*) is the cause of the body and mind; that former actions, or compositional factors (*sngon gyi las sam 'du byed*),[a] are the cause of the life faculty, and that ignorance is the cause of former actions, or compositional factors. The meditator then reviews the series in forward progression, beginning with ignorance, and concludes:

> By the ceasing of ignorance, compositional factors cease; by the ceasing of [compositional factors], the life faculty ceases; by the ceasing of [the life faculty], the afflicted body and mind cease; by the ceasing of [the afflicted body and mind], the exhalation and inhalation of the breath cease.[b]

Purification, again, is explained as the result of the meditator's having repeated and "abided in" the above meditation many times.[c]

Thorough purification through engagement in the [four] truths. In thorough purification through engagement in the [four] truths, the meditator comes to recognize the relationship between the dependent-arisings analyzed during the previous meditation and the four truths, beginning with **true sufferings** (*sdug bsngal bden pa, duḥkhasatya*). The meditator thinks:

---

[a] Ibid., 117.4. Hopkins has remarked in conversation that "or" (*sam*) is appositive here: these are equivalent, not alternative, terms.

[b] Ibid., 117.5–6.

[c] Ibid., 117.6.

> These dependent-arisings which are the breath, and so forth, are impermanent. Since they are impermanent, they arise and disintegrate. Therefore, they have the qualities of birth, aging, sickness, and death. Since they have the qualities of these four, they are [cases of] suffering and, therefore, are selfless, without independence, and without an owner.[a]

The meditation on the second of the four truths, **true origins** (*kun 'byung bden pa, samudayasatya*), involves the thought, "All those [things] that are the sicknesses and effects of these sufferings arise from the causal condition which is cyclic existence." The meditation on **true cessations** (*'gog pa'i bden pa, nirodhasatya*), the third of the four truths, involves the thought, "The abandonment of cyclic existence, which is the causal condition of suffering, is peaceful and auspiciously high." The meditation on **true paths** (*lam gyi bden pa, mārgasatya*) involves the thought, "Having known and seen in that way, when I abide many times in that way, I will abandon craving."[b] Again, as with the previous "engagements," purification is explained as the result of the meditator's having repeated and "abided in" the above meditations many times.[c]

Jam-yang-shay-pa, citing Asaṅga's *Grounds of Hearers*, explains that at this point the meditator has manifestly realized (*mngon par rtogs pa*)—that is, directly realized (*mngon sum du rtogs pa*)—the four truths; such a meditator "has abandoned the afflictive emotions to be abandoned by [the path of] seeing."[d] Jam-yang-shay-pa implies here that the meditator has attained the path of seeing. However, he has not yet identified an earlier point in these thorough purifications at which the meditator attained the path of preparation, which precedes the path of seeing and which, as was mentioned above (page 113), is attained simultaneously with special insight. Thus, he has not identified the point in these thorough purifications at which the meditator attains special insight, or even acknowledged that they might be a means of attaining it. Nevertheless, since he has identified the end of thorough purification through counting as the point at which the meditator attains calm abiding, the attainment of special insight probably occurs at the end of either thorough purification through engagement in the aggregates or thorough purification through engagement in dependent-arising, both

[a] Ibid., 118.2-3.

[b] Ibid., 118.3–4.

[c] Ibid., 118.5.

[d] Ibid., 118.7–119.2.

of which are the result of reasoning, albeit inductive reasoning based on observation.

Thorough purification through sixteen aspects. Having identified the point at which the meditator attains the path of seeing, Jam-yang-shay-pa, still following Asaṅga closely, asserts that the meditator undertakes the next thorough purification listed—the thorough purification through sixteen aspects—in order to abandon "the mere afflictive emotions to be abandoned by [the path of] meditation."[a] Contrary to the expectations of readers familiar with Ge-luk presentations of the sixteen aspects, or attributes, of the four noble truths—based on Vasubandhu's *Treasury of Manifest Knowledge* (7.13a) and its *Autocommentary*[b]—Jam-yang-shay-pa "unpacks," numbers, and summarizes Asaṅga's presentation of the sixteen aspects referred to in this context as follows:

> ...a yogi who has done the purification through engagement in the truths, in order to purify mainly the afflictive emotions to be purified by [the path of] meditation, views and trains thinking (1) "Exhalation, inhalation," with respect to the exhalation and inhalation of the breath while being mindful [of it], and similarly views, thinking, "Exhalation, inhalation," (2) with respect to exhalation and inhalation as long breaths, (3) with respect to exhalation and inhalation as short breaths, (4) with respect to exhalation and inhalation upon having correctly experienced the entire body, (5) with respect to exhalation and inhalation upon having thoroughly purified the workings (*'du byed*) of the body, (6) with respect to exhalation and inhalation upon having correctly experienced joy, (7) with respect to exhalation and inhalation upon having correctly experienced bliss, (8) with respect to exhalation and inhalation upon having thoroughly purified the workings of the mind, (9) with respect to exhalation and inhalation upon having correctly experienced the mind, (10) with respect to exhalation and inhalation when the mind has thorough and strong joy, (11) with

---

[a] Ibid., 119.2.

[b] Vasubandhu, *Treasury of Manifest Knowledge* and *Autocommentary*, 7.13a (P5591, vol. 115, 262.3.7–263.2.4; Shastri, part 4, pp. 1056–62; La Vallée Poussin 16:5, pp. 30–39; Pruden, vol. 4, pp. 1110–1116). For expositions in English of Ge-luk presentations, see *Meditation on Emptiness*, pp. 285–96; Geshe Lhundup Sopa and Jeffrey Hopkins, *Cutting Through Appearances: Practice and Theory of Tibetan Buddhism* (Ithaca, NY: Snow Lion Publications, 1989), pp. 203–204; Lati Rinpoche in *Meditative States*, pp. 134–43.

> respect to exhalation and inhalation upon having set the mind in meditative stabilization, (12) with respect to exhalation and inhalation upon the mind's being released, (13) with respect to exhalation and inhalation upon viewing impermanence, (14) with respect to exhalation and inhalation upon viewing abandonment, (15) with respect to exhalation and inhalation upon viewing separation from desire, (16) with respect to exhalation and inhalation upon viewing cessation; [thus] there are sixteen [aspects].[a]

To support this way of identifying the sixteen, he cites in abridged form, with an ellipsis (*zhes pa nas*) indicating the middle, a passage from Asaṅga's *Grounds of Hearers* that begins, "What are the sixteen aspects? They are these: (1) When one inhales while being mindful, one trains thinking, 'I am inhaling while being mindful,'" and that ends, "When, viewing cessation, one exhales, one trains thinking, 'I am viewing cessation and exhaling.'"[b] In itself, the abridged citation suggests that, in Jam-yang-shay-pa's opinion, Asaṅga has identified the first item after the question as the first in the list of sixteen; Jam-yang-shay-pa's manner of citing the passage is intended to imply that the first and last items of his own list agree with Asaṅga's first and last items and that, therefore, Jam-yang-shay-pa has also interpreted the rest of the passage correctly.

Comparison with the *Ānāpānasatisutta,* however, and with Buddhaghosa's presentation of mindfulness of breathing in the *Path of Purification,* which is based on it, suggests (1) that thorough purification through sixteen aspects is a method of cultivating the four mindful establishments; (2) that Asaṅga's list, at least according to the Peking edition of *Grounds of Hearers,* agrees, for the most part, with Buddhaghosa's citation of the *Ānāpānasatisutta* and, like it, consists of seventeen items—a general description of mindfulness of breathing followed by the list of sixteen—but that Asaṅga does not explicitly identify the series as a method of cultivating the four mindful establishments; (3) that the passage from Asaṅga's *Grounds of Hearers* may be a citation or paraphrase of an unidentified scripture related to that cited in Buddhaghosa's *Path of Purification;* and (4) that Jam-yang-shay-pa's list differs from the Pāli presentations and Asaṅga's in slight but significant ways that prevent Jam-yang-shay-pa from recognizing the boundaries of the four mindful establishments in his own list of sixteen.

---

[a] Jam-yang-shay-pa, *Concentrations,* 119.5–120.3.

[b] Ibid., 120.3–5; P5537, vol. 110, 78.5.3–79.1.7.

The table on the following page compares Jam-yang-shay-pa's presentation of thorough purification through sixteen aspects, based on his own reading of Asaṅga's *Grounds of Hearers,*[a] with both the Tibetan text of the source passage in the Peking edition of Asaṅga's *Grounds of Hearers*[b] and the *Ānāpānasatisutta* (*Majjhima Nikāya,* 118), as cited by Buddhaghosa as the basis of his presentation of mindfulness of breathing in the *Path of Purification.*[c]

---

[a] Ibid., 119.5–120.3.

[b] P5537, vol. 110, 78.5.3–79.1.7.

[c] *Ānāpānasati-sutta,* in *The Middle Length Sayings* (*Majjhima-Nikāya*), trans. I. B. Horner (Pali Text Society: London: Luzac, 1967), vol. 3, 125–26; Buddhaghosa, *The Path of Purification* (*visuddhimagga*), 8.145; Buddhaghosa, *The Path of Purification,* trans. Ñyāṇamoli [Berkeley and London: Shambhala, 1976], vol. 1, pp. 285–86.

Chart 1: Mindfulness of Breathing in Sixteen Aspects: Three Presentations

Asaṅga's *Grounds of Hearers*	JYSP's *Concentrations*	*Ānāpānasati-sutta*
0. When one inhales while being mindful...when one exhales while being mindful	1. Thinking, "Exhalation, inhalation," with respect to the exhalation and inhalation of the breath while being mindful [of it]	0. Just mindful he breathes in, mindful he breathes out
1. long breaths	2. with respect to...long breaths	**[Contemplation of the body]** 1. long breaths
2. short breaths	3. with respect to...short breaths	2. short breaths
3. upon having correctly experienced the entire body	4. upon...having correctly experienced the entire body	3. experiencing the entire body
4. upon having thoroughly purified the workings of the body	5. upon having thoroughly purified the workings of the body	4. calming the workings of the body
5. upon having correctly experienced joy	6. upon having correctly experienced joy	**[Contemplation of feelings]** 5. experiencing joy
6. upon having correctly experienced bliss	7. upon having correctly experienced bliss,	6. experiencing bliss
7. upon having correctly experienced the workings of the mind		7. experiencing the workings of the mind
8. upon having thoroughly purified the workings of the mind	8. upon having thoroughly purified the workings of the mind	8. calming the workings of the mind
9. upon having correctly experienced the mind	9. upon having correctly experienced the mind	**[Contemplation of the mind]** 9. experiencing the mind
10. when the mind has thorough and strong joy	10. when the mind has thorough and strong joy	10. gladdening the mind
11. upon having set the mind in meditative stabilization	11. upon having set the mind in meditative stabilization	11. stabilizing the mind
12. upon the mind's being released	12. upon the mind's being released	12. releasing the mind
13. upon viewing impermanence	13. upon viewing impermanence	**[Contemplation of mind-objects]** 13. contemplating impermanence
14. upon viewing abandonment	14. upon viewing abandonment	14. contemplating separation from desire
15. upon viewing separation from desire	15. upon viewing separation from desire	15. contemplating cessation
16. upon viewing cessation	16. upon viewing cessation	16. contemplating renunciation

Asaṅga—like Buddhaghosa's Pāli scriptural source, the *Ānāpānasatisutta*—presents a series of seventeen items: a topic head giving the general characteristics of mindfulness of the exhalation and inhalation of the breath and sixteen subheads under it that divide evenly into four, corresponding to the four mindful establishments. The *Ānāpānasatisutta* itself goes on to identify this series of sixteen as a method of cultivating the four mindful establishments.[a] Asaṅga, however, does not identify the series in this way. Moreover, Jam-yang-shay-pa interprets the topic sentence as the first of the sixteen aspects and omits the seventh of Asaṅga's and the *Ānāpānasatisutta*'s series, mindfulness of exhalation and inhalation upon having correctly experienced the workings of the mind. Since Jam-yang-shay-pa's citation gives only the beginning and end of the passage, with an ellipsis in the middle, there is no way of knowing whether he misread Asaṅga or was working from a corrupt text. It is clear from the extensive debates concerning the level of the mental contemplation of individual knowledge of the character, which revolve around the presence or absence of the negative (*ma*), that several versions of the Tibetan translation of Asaṅga's *Grounds of Hearers* existed in Tibet even in Tsong-kha-pa's time and that some of them were textually corrupt.[b] Moreover, Jam-yang-shay-pa's experience with lists in Indian commentaries would have led him to expect that the topic sentence "What are the sixteen aspects? They are these:" would immediately introduce a list consisting of sixteen items and not seventeen items, the first of which is a second topic sentence introducing the actual list of sixteen; if Asaṅga is citing or paraphrasing a scriptural passage similar to the one in the Pāli *Ānāpānasatisutta* instead of giving his own list, he gives no indication that he is doing so. In either case, the result of Jam-yang-shay-pa's misreading of the key passage in Asaṅga's text is that he does not recognize in it a way of cultivating the four mindful establishments and, therefore, is prevented from drawing any conclusions that might have been drawn from such a recognition.

Jam-yang-shay-pa's explanation of the passage also presents problems. According to him, Asaṅga identifies two types of meditators who

---

[a] *Ānāpānasatisutta*, in *The Middle Length Sayings* (*Majjhima-Nikāya*), trans. I. B. Horner, vol. 3, p. 127.

[b] See page 206. The only extant Sanskrit manuscript, discovered in the 1930s, is also corrupt and, moreover, incomplete. (Alex Wayman, *Analysis of the Śrāvakabhūmi Manuscript*, University of California Publications in Classical Philology, vol. 17 [Berkeley and Los Angeles: University of California Press, 1961], p. 1; *Śrāvakabhūmi of Ācārya Asaṅga*, ed. by Karunesha Shukla, Tibetan Sanskrit Works Series, vol. 14 [Patna: K. P. Jayaswal Research Institute, 1973], pp. xx–xxii.)

cultivate the thorough purification through sixteen aspects—(1) "meditators on...[the first three of] the sixteen mindfulnesses of exhalation and inhalation of the breath that are explicitly taught on this occasion" and (2) "meditators who have previously counted the exhalation and inhalation of the breath [before they reach the level of these sixteen practices]."[a] In brief, he identifies the first type of meditator as "necessarily a learner Superior"—that is, someone who has attained the path of seeing but has not yet attained the path of no more learning (*mi slob lam, aśaikṣamārga*), in this case, Foe Destroyerhood, since Asaṅga's text is called *Grounds of Hearers*—and the second type of meditator as "necessarily someone on the path of accumulation and below."[b]

Jam-yang-shay-pa's interpretation appears to be inconsistent with the earlier passage introducing the list of sixteen, in which Jam-yang-shay-pa had identified only the first type of meditator; he begins the earlier passage, "a yogi who has done the purification through engagement in the truths ..., in order to purify mainly the afflictive emotions to be purified by [the path of] meditation, views and trains thinking...."[c] This is the meditator identified earlier (see page 118), who had previously directly realized the four truths and attained the path of seeing and who is undertaking the thorough purification through sixteen aspects on the path of meditation in order to abandon the afflictive emotions to be abandoned on that path; having attained the path of seeing, such a meditator is a learner Superior.

Jam-yang-shay-pa's reason for distinguishing here between these two types of meditators who undertake the thorough purification through sixteen aspects is that

> (1) a meditator on [the sixteen mindfulnesses of exhalation and inhalation of the breath] that are explicitly taught on this occasion is necessarily a learner Superior and, however low he or she may be, must definitely be someone who has entered the path and (2) a meditator who has previously [counted the exhalation and inhalation of the breath] is someone who has not entered the path and, however high he or she may be, is necessarily someone on the path of accumulation and below.[d]

As Hopkins points out, the wording of Jam-yang-shay-pa's reason is

---

[a] Jam-yang-shay-pa, *Concentrations*, 120.5–6.

[b] Ibid., 120.6–7.

[c] Ibid., 118.7–119.2.

[d] Ibid., 120.7–7.

atypical since, once a debate text states that something is *necessarily* (*khyab pa*) the case, it is very unusual to qualify the statement in a manner suggesting that there may be exceptions. Moreover, the terms of the qualification are also odd, since, as Hopkins also points out, there is no doubt that a learner Superior "must definitely be someone who has entered the path." Hopkins suggests that Jam-yang-shay-pa is implicitly making a concession; it is as though he had said, "Even if you do not agree with me that such a meditator is necessarily a learner Superior, at least you have to admit that such a meditator has definitely entered the path." Hopkins also notes that the second part of the reason is done the same way and is also very strange, since someone on the path of accumulation *has* entered the path and cannot be "someone who has not entered the path."[a]

Paraphrasing his citation from Asaṅga, Jam-yang-shay-pa explains that the first type of meditator

> has definitely attained the four mindful establishments and, hence, is someone who has entered the path; not only that: he or she is posited as a person who, having directly realized the four truths, makes effort in order to abandon the remaining thorough enwrapments.[b]

He explains the second type of meditator with reference to the three divisions of the path of accumulation: according to him,

> before entering the path and on the lesser and middling path of accumulation, certain persons who have very great predominant discursiveness purify it in meditation by counting the breath, but since such a fault of discursiveness does not occur on the greater path of accumulation and above, there is no need for meditation on [counting the breath]. This is because in the period of the greater path of accumulation, anyone of any of the three vehicles has necessarily attained calm abiding. This is because, thereby, (a) the attainment, in dependence on calm abiding, of a state arisen from meditation by means of analytical meditation on either of the two selflessnesses, (b) the attainment of such special insight, and (c) the attainment of the path of preparation are simultaneous.[c]

---

a Jeffrey Hopkins in conversation.

b Jam-yang-shay-pa, *Concentrations*, 120.7–121.1.

c Ibid., 121.3–5.

Here, indirectly, he finally identifies the point at which special insight is attained in this type of meditation and implicitly admits that the meditator in question will attain it. However, he does not identify the practice by which *this* meditator attains it. He names the practice his own system identifies as the means of attaining special insight and implies that, in order to have attained special insight, this meditator must have engaged in that practice, but the passage from Asaṅga suggests that a meditator who cultivates the thorough purification through sixteen aspects is not engaged in "analytical meditation on either of the two selflessnesses" as Jam-yang-shay-pa understands it but, rather, in a type of "analytical meditation" consisting of inductive reasoning based on observation.

It is possible that the awkward qualifications in Jam-yang-shay-pa's reasoning may result from some suspicion on Jam-yang-shay-pa's part that the traditions included in his own system did not fully account for the distinctions in Asaṅga's text. According to Buddhaghosa, mindfulness of breathing with sixteen aspects has two benefits: (1) it calms the mind by stopping discursiveness, and (2) it leads to realization of the four mindful establishments and to insight; he remarks also that the first three groups of four are relevant to both serenity and insight, whereas the last applies only to insight.[a] Thus, comparison with Theravāda sources suggests the possibility that Asaṅga's and Jam-yang-shay-pa's two types of meditators may correspond, respectively, to followers of the paths of serenity and bare insight in modern Theravāda practice, and that Jam-yang-shay-pa had no information concerning the type of "analytical meditation" based on observation, described in Theravāda sources, from which the latter is derived and which it isolates as a practice vehicle in its own right.

Conclusion. It is clear that, according to both Vasubandhu and Asaṅga, and according to the Ge-luk-pa textbook writers and scholars discussed here, the early stages of breath meditation can "purify" discursiveness and lead to the attainment of calm abiding. Both Vasubandhu and Asaṅga give practical instructions for this type of meditation, as do Lati Rinpoche and Gedün Lodrö. The status of the later stages of breath meditation is less clear, however. From one point of view, their inclusion among objects of observation for purifying discursiveness may be regarded as yet another instance of the Ge-luk presentation of all objects

[a] Buddhaghosa, *The Path of Purification* (*visuddhimagga*), 8.238–39, 237, citing the *Ānāpānasatisutta*; Buddhaghosa, *The Path of Purification,* trans. Ñyāṇamoli (Berkeley and London: Shambhala, 1976), vol. 1, p. 315.

of observation under the heading "calm abiding" even though—like some of the four types of object of observation in the classic layout derived from Asaṅga, Kamalashīla, and the *Sūtra Unraveling the Thought*—they may be objects of observation for the attainment of special insight or higher stages of the path (see page 81). The presentation of the later stages is complicated, however, by the virtual omission, in the Ge-luk presentations considered here, of any clear identification of the point at which special insight is attained, or even of any acknowledgment that special insight *can* be attained by this type of meditation, despite references to the path of preparation in the Indian sources. This omission may be due to several causes:

1. Limitations imposed by the transmission of the Indian source texts to Tibet without practice traditions based on those texts, and without knowledge of other Buddhist cultures in which such practices existed.
2. Non-application to the topic of the concentrations and formless absorptions of Vasubandhu's equation of mindfulness and wisdom in the *Treasury of Manifest Knowledge* and its *Autocommentary*, as well as his reference to the four mindful establishments as an example—points Ge-luk writers and contemporary scholars discuss when they study the *Treasury* as a topic in its own right; given the nature of Ge-luk system-building, it seems possible that, if they had been able to apply this point to Vasubandhu's presentation of breath meditation, they might have applied it to Asaṅga's as well.
3. Non-recognition of methods of attaining special insight outside the system of Chandrakīrti and, to a lesser extent in the context of the concentrations and formless absorptions, outside those mentioned in the *Sūtra Unraveling the Thought* and Asaṅga's *Grounds of Hearers*—especially a method that relies on inductive reasoning based on observation.

Objects of observation for [developing] skill

The objects of observation for developing skill are: the aggregates, the constituents, the twelve spheres, the twelve-linked dependent-arising, and the appropriate and the inappropriate (*gnas dang gnas ma yin pa, sthānāsthāna*). Meditation on them involves the detailed analysis, in the meditation session, of Manifest Knowledge topics previously studied outside the context of meditation. Although Lati Rinpoche's summary of each topic ends with advice to the meditator to stabilize on what has been understood through analysis and thereby achieve calm abiding,[a] according to Gedün Lodrö, objects of observation for developing skill are in general not used for the attainment of calm abiding but to strengthen and consolidate calm abiding already attained and enable the meditator to begin the cultivation of special insight.[b] Despite Lati Rinpoche's advice concerning the use of these objects of observation to achieve calm abiding, it is clear—from his identification of what skill in each of these objects of observation consists of—that he, like Gedün Lodrö, also regards the objects of observation for developing skill as preparatory to the cultivation of special insight, since all of them, according to his presentation, lead to realization of the non-existence of a partless, independent person and to an understanding of causality.[c]

The topics themselves are discussed at length in the Manifest Knowledge texts—Vasubandhu's *Treasury of Manifest Knowledge* and its *Autocommentary* and Asaṅga's *Summary of Manifest Knowledge*—and in Ge-luk monastic textbooks based on them. Since Ge-luk presentations of these topics are discussed in detail in English in Hopkins' *Meditation on Emptiness,* I will merely sketch them briefly here, mainly from Lati Rinpoche's concise oral presentation.

THE AGGREGATES

Lati Rinpoche explains meditation on the five aggregates in this context as recognition of these five—forms (*gzugs, rūpa*), feelings (*tshor ba, vedanā*), discriminations (*'du shes, saṃjñā*), compositional factors (*'du byed, saṃskāra*), and consciousnesses (*rnam shes, vijñāna*). Skill in the aggregates is the understanding "that there is no partless, independent person apart from these aggregates."[d]

THE CONSTITUENTS

According to Lati Rinpoche, meditation on the constituents in this context involves the analysis in meditation of the eighteen constituents for the sake of acquiring skill in them. The eighteen constituents are the six sense powers—the eye, ear, nose, tongue, body, and mental sense powers—the six consciousnesses corresponding to these sense powers, and the six objects of those consciousnesses. The meditator considers

---

[a] *Meditative States,* pp. 87–90.

[b] Gedün Lodrö, p. 139.

[c] *Meditative States,* pp. 88–90.

[d] Ibid., p. 88.

the relationship of each of these to the other, especially their causes and conditions. Skill in the constituents is attained when the meditator understands "that there is no separate creator of these, such as a substantially existent (*rdzas su yod pa, dravyasat*) self."[a]

THE TWELVE SPHERES

Lati Rinpoche identifies the twelve spheres as the six sense powers and the six sense objects included within the eighteen constituents; he notes that "through rearrangement of these, all phenomena can be included in the twelve [spheres]." The meditator comes to understand that the sense powers and their objects are in the relationship of user and used and that pleasant, painful, and neutral feelings are produced as a result of this use. Again, skill is attained when the meditator realizes that "there is no substantially existent person separate from these."[b]

THE TWELVE-LINKED DEPENDENT-ARISING

According to Lati Rinpoche, skill in dependent-arising involves understanding of the causes and conditions that produce a lifetime in cyclic existence (*'khor ba, saṃsāra*); the fundamental cause is ignorance (*ma rig pa, avidyā*), which is followed by the remaining eleven links—compositional action (*'du byed kyi las, saṃskārakarma*), consciousness (*rnam shes, vijñāna*), name and form (*ming gzugs, nāmarūpa*), spheres (*skye mched, āyatana*), contact (*reg pa, sparśa*), feeling (*tshor ba, vedanā*), attachment (*sred pa, tṛṣṇa*), grasping (*len pa, upādāna*), existence (*srid pa, bhava*), birth (*skye ba, jāti*), and aging and/or death (*rga shi, jarāmaraṇa*). In his more detailed presentation, Gedün Lodrö identifies this as the forward progression and adds that the meditator can also become skilled in the reverse progression and in the various presentations of "how one person cycles in cyclic existence by way of the twelve-linked dependent-arising."[c] According to Lati Rinpoche, skill in dependent-arising occurs when the meditator realizes "that a lifetime in cyclic existence is not produced causelessly and is not produced from discordant causes, such as a permanent deity."[d]

---

[a] *Meditative States*, p. 88. See also Gedün Lodrö, pp. 122–23.

[b] *Meditative States*, p. 89.

[c] Gedün Lodrö, p. 123; he sets these forth in detail. Another detailed presentation in English can be found in *Meditation on Emptiness*, pp. 275–83 and 707–11.

[d] *Meditative States*, p. 89.

THE APPROPRIATE AND THE INAPPROPRIATE

The appropriate and the inappropriate is a meditation on actions and their effects; the topic is seen as an aspect of dependent-arising.[a] According to Lati Rinpoche, "'The appropriate and the inappropriate' means the possible and the impossible."[b] It is appropriate—that is, possible—for birth in a happy transmigration to be caused only by a virtuous action and not by a non-virtuous action, and, similarly, for birth in a bad transmigration to be caused only by a non-virtuous action, and not by a virtuous action. Lati Rinpoche identifies skill in the appropriate and the inappropriate as the realization that "these births are not created by a permanent deity and do not result from the activity of a substantially existent person."[c]

OBJECTS OF OBSERVATION FOR PURIFYING AFFLICTIVE EMOTIONS

Objects of observation for purifying afflictive emotions are used after the attainment of calm abiding by meditators who wish to progress mentally to the next higher level—for example, by a person of the Desire Realm who has attained calm abiding and who wishes to attain an actual meditative absorption of the first concentration, or by someone who wishes to progress from the first concentration (either as an actual absorption or as a rebirth level) to an actual absorption of the second concentration (*bsam gtan gnyis pa, dvitīyadhyāna*). As mentioned in the previous chapter, objects of observation for purifying afflictive emotions pacify equally all the afflictive emotions of a given level. Ge-luk monastic textbooks and oral presentations generally explain them in the context of the preparations for the first concentration (see Chapter 8).

OTHER OBJECTS OF OBSERVATION

In addition to the classification of four types of object of observation originally set forth in the *Sūtra Unraveling the Thought*, Ge-luk commentators explain two other sūtra-system objects of observation—the body of a Buddha and one's own mind. Gedün Lodrö also mentions briefly objects of observation used in tantra but not in the sūtra system; these

---

[a] Ibid., p. 90.

[b] Ibid., p. 92.

[c] Ibid., p. 90.

include meditations in which the meditator, generating him- or herself as a deity, visualizes him- or herself as having a divine body. Also included is the visualization of hand symbols (*phyag mtshan, mudrā*) or of subtle drops (*thig le, bindu*) at important points of the body, such as the center of the heart or at the point between the eyebrows.[a] I will not discuss tantric objects of observation here.

The Body of a Buddha

Ge-luk presentations of meditation on the body of a Buddha are taken from Asaṅga's *Grounds of Hearers;* it is the object of observation considered best by Asaṅga and Tsong-kha-pa and by the Ge-luk textbook writers studied here. The meditation involves visualization of the Buddha Shākyamuni seated on lotus, sun, and moon cushions—and, if the meditator is able to do the full visualization, also on a lion-throne—with his hand in the earth-touching gesture. This image is visualized in the space in front of the meditator, about six feet in front of either the eyes or the navel, depending on the meditator's temperament.[b]

In oral presentations, the body of a Buddha is generally used as an example of an object of observation when no object of observation is specified; it is, so to speak, a "generic object of observation." Moreover, it is the object of observation still generally taught to beginners in practical instruction; Gedün Lodrö describes it as the best sūtra-system object of observation for a beginner.[c] In this opinion, he is following Jam-yang-shay-pa's *Great Exposition of the Concentrations and Formless Absorptions,* which states that the body of a Buddha not only performs the function of other objects of observation by enabling the meditator to achieve meditative stabilization but that each session of meditation on it also increases the meditator's collection of merit (*bsod nams kyi tshogs, puṇyasaṃbhāra*) and, thus, contributes to his or her eventual attainment of Buddhahood.[d]

---

[a] Gedün Lodrö, p. 140.

[b] Gedün Lodrö, pp. 143–44; *Meditative States,* p. 57.

[c] Gedün Lodrö, p. 142.

[d] Jam-yang-shay-pa, *Concentrations,* 135.4–6 (abridged in Kön-chok-jik-may-wang-po, *Condensed Statement,* 558.6). Jam-yang-shay-pa's explanation is a condensation of Tsong-kha-pa's (*Great Exposition of the Stages of the Path* [Dharamsala: shes rig par khang, 1964], 679.2–680.5). See also *Meditative States,* p. 80.

ONE'S OWN MIND

The mind itself is the main object of observation mentioned in the *Sūtra Unraveling the Thought* and, in a citation from that text, is mentioned by Paṇ-chen Sö-nam-drak-pa.[a] Lati Rinpoche describes it as clear (*gsal ba*), a knower (*rig pa, saṃvedana*), and empty (*stong pa, śūnya*).[b] However, instead of recommending this object of observation, Ge-luk oral explanations caution against the errors likely to be incurred in its practice. Lati Rinpoche warns that it is possible to repeat the error of earlier Tibetan meditators who, in his opinion, mistook the calm abiding attained by using this object of observation for the realization of emptiness. Moreover, he states that those meditators mistook the bliss of pliancy for the innate bliss and the calm abiding attained by using this object of observation for "the primordial, innate wisdom-consciousness."[c]

He also warns against the possibility of mistaking the meditational fault of subtle laxity (*bying ba, laya*) for meditative stabilization (*ting nge 'dzin, samādhi*) and cites Sa-kya (*sa skya*) Paṇḍita as having said "that a stupid person who tries to cultivate the Great Seal (*phyag rgya chen po, mahāmudrā*) usually" makes this error and, thereby, "creates the causes for being reborn as an animal."[d] It is not clear that this argument would stand in debate, since an animal rebirth is rebirth in a bad transmigration (*ngan 'gro, durgati*), and rebirth in a bad transmigration is generally held to be caused only by a non-virtuous action, whereas subtle laxity is considered to be either virtuous or, at worst, ethically neutral, but not non-virtuous.[e] At best, Lati Rinpoche's argument seems to be based on the forgetfulness and mental dullness that are the observed consequences of subtle laxity in this lifetime, and their similarity, in Lati Rinpoche's opinion, to the stupidity that is held to be the salient characteristic of animals.[f] Lati Rinpoche seems to be arguing mainly from analogy; what he seems to be saying is that a meditator whose way of meditating leads to forgetfulness and mental dullness comes to resemble an animal mentally and, thus, is in danger of being reborn as one, but he does not establish that such a way of meditating is non-virtuous. These warnings seem to be mainly disguised sectarian polemics against the Nying-ma (*rnying ma*) Great Completeness (*rdzogs chen*) and Ka-gyu

---

[a] Paṇ-chen Sö-nam-drak-pa, "Concentrations," 155b.4.

[b] *Meditative States*, p. 80.

[c] Ibid., p. 81.

[d] Ibid., p. 61.

[e] Ibid., p. 59; Gedün Lodrö, p. 177;.

[f] *Meditative States*, p. 61.

(*bka' rgyud*) Great Seal meditations.

Unlike the other Ge-luk commentators considered here, the present Dalai Lama recommends the mind itself as an object of observation and gives clear directions for meditating on it:

> Another type of meditation involves looking at the mind itself. Try to leave your mind vividly in a natural state, without thinking of what happened in the past or of what you are planning for the future, without generating any conceptuality. Where does it seem that your consciousness is?...
>
> With persistent practice, consciousness may eventually be perceived or felt as an entity of mere luminosity and knowing [the classic textbook definition of a consciousness], to which anything is capable of appearing and which, when appropriate conditions arise, can be generated in the image of whatsoever object. As long as the mind does not encounter the external circumstance of conceptuality, it will abide empty without anything appearing in it, like clear water. Its very entity is that of mere experience. In realizing this nature of the mind, we have for the first time located the object of observation of this internal type of meditation. The best time for practicing this form of meditation is in the morning, in a quiet place, when the mind is very clear and alert.[a]

It is probable that his recommendation, which appears to be based on experience, stems, at least in part, from his strong efforts to overcome Tibetan sectarianism.[b]

Objects of Observation Considered Suitable for Beginners

The objects of observation generally given to beginners are the body of a Buddha and, from among the four main types of object of observation, those for purifying behavior. According to Kön-chok-jik-may-wang-po and Jam-yang-shay-pa—who follows closely, but does not cite, a passage in the calm abiding section of Tsong-kha-pa's *Great Exposition of the Stages of the Path*—meditators who have any of the predominant afflictive emotions *must* use the corresponding object of observation for

---

[a] *Kindness, Clarity, and Insight*, p. 68.

[b] See his "Union of the Old and New Translation Schools," in *Kindness, Clarity, and Insight*, pp. 200–24.

purifying behavior, whereas meditators in whom the five predominant afflictive emotions are of equal strength, or who have few afflictive emotions, are not restricted but may choose any of the objects of observation set forth above.[a] Tsong-kha-pa emphasizes that "It is especially necessary for someone with excessive discursiveness definitely to meditate on the winds [that is, the breath]."[b]

It is evident from the present Dalai Lama's description of the process of meditating on the mind itself that it would be considered a difficult object of observation for most beginners, especially for those with discursiveness, since he instructs the meditator initially to "[T]ry to leave your mind vividly in a natural state...without generating any conceptuality."[c] This is only the first step. Moreover, recognition of the mind as "an entity of mere luminosity and knowing" is just the initial finding of the object of observation;[d] there remains the task of sustaining meditation on it.

Emptiness is also considered a difficult object of observation; beginners who are capable of using it are extremely rare. As Gedün Lodrö explains, in general

> it is necessary to find the object of observation and then, to stabilize on it; here it is difficult even to find the object of observation, much less stabilize on it. One must analyze in order to find it, and for a complete beginner who is analyzing without stability, even the first of the nine mental abidings (*sems gnas, cittasthiti*)[e] is impossible.[f]

Thus, according to Gedün Lodrö, who cites Kamalashīla's *Stages of Meditation,* most meditators achieve calm abiding using a conventional object of observation; they then cultivate special insight observing emptiness. He notes, further, that "when the cultivation of special insight is set forth, it is done only in the context of meditating on emptiness, not on other topics" and that "A person who achieves calm abiding using emptiness as the object of observation and then, still taking emptiness as the object of observation, achieves special insight, has the best type

[a] Kön-chok-jik-may-wang-po, *Condensed Statement,* 558.3–6; Jam-yang-shay-pa, *Concentrations,* 135.1–4; Tsong-kha-pa, *Great Exposition of the Stages of the Path*, 678.4–679.2.

[b] Tsong-kha-pa, *Great Exposition of the Stages of the Path*, 679.1–2.

[c] *Kindness, Clarity, and Insight,* p. 68.

[d] Ibid., p. 68.

[e] The nine mental abidings are the nine mental states through which the meditator passes in order to achieve calm abiding; for a full discussion of them, see pages 155–164.

[f] Gedün Lodrö, p. 141.

of special insight."[a]

Beginners do not use the remaining objects of observation discussed here in order to achieve calm abiding. As was mentioned earlier (see page 127), objects of observation for developing skill are used after the attainment of calm abiding in order to consolidate and enhance the calm abiding already achieved. Objects of observation for purifying afflictive emotions are used during the preparations for the concentrations, when the meditator has already achieved calm abiding and is trying to attain an actual concentration; they are generally explained in the context of the preparations for the first concentration. (See the chart listing the types of object of observation and indicating those suitable for beginners, next page.)

[a] Ibid., p. 142.

Chart 2: Objects of Observation

(Objects of observation in *italics* are considered suitable for beginners.)

THE FOUR TYPES OF OBJECT OF OBSERVATION (from the *Sūtra Unraveling the Thought,* Asaṅga's *Grounds of Hearers,* and Kamalashīla's *Stages of Meditation*)

1 Pervasive objects of observation
- a. Non-analytical image
- b. Analytical image
- c. Observing the limits of phenomena
  - (1) the varieties (conventional phenomena)
  - (2) the mode (their emptiness)
- d. Thorough achievement of the purpose

2 Objects of observation for purifying behavior
- *a. The unpleasant: for persons in whom desire predominates*
- *b. Love: for persons in whom hatred predominates*
- *c. Dependent-arising: for persons in whom obscuration predominates*
- *d. The divisions of the constituents: for persons in whom pride predominates*
- *e. The exhalation and inhalation of the breath: for persons in whom discursiveness predominates*

3 Objects of observation for [developing] skill
- a. The aggregates
- b. The constituents
- c. The twelve sources
- d. The twelve-linked dependent-arising
- e. The appropriate and the inappropriate

4 Objects of observation for purifying afflictive emotions
- a. Those having the aspect of grossness/peacefulness
- b. Those having the aspect of the truths

OTHER OBJECTS OF OBSERVATION

A Buddha's body

One's own mind

OBJECTS OF OBSERVATION USED IN TANTRA

A divine body (visualization of oneself as having a divine body)

Subtle drops

Finding the Object of Observation (Once It Has Been Correctly Chosen)

Once a meditator has chosen a suitable object of observation, he or she has to search for and find it—that is, reach a basic level of proficiency in bringing it to mind at will. This process has two phases. Using the body of a Buddha as an example, Gedün Lodrö identifies the first phase as the ability to visualize "the entire body of a Buddha...in a rough way." The important point, at this stage, is that "the whole figure" must appear; he notes that "Even if what first appears is unclear and without much detail, it is suitable; if only half the image or blackness appears, it is not suitable."[a] The second phase involves working on clarity—increasing the brightness of the visualized image and sharpening the details. Gedün Lodrö emphasizes that it is important for a meditator to develop confidence in his or her ability to visualize the object of observation roughly before attempting to visualize it in detail; if the second phase is begun too soon, the entire visualization may be lost.[b] Explanations along the same lines can probably be worked out for objects of observation that do not require visualization, such as the exhalation and inhalation of the breath or the mind itself.

The completion of the second phase indicates that the meditator has found the object of observation.[c] Having achieved a basic level of proficiency, he or she is ready to confront the faults (*nyes pa, ādīnava*) that prevent the attainment of calm abiding and to progress through the nine mental states that precede calm abiding and lead to its attainment.

---

[a] Ibid., p. 142.
[b] Ibid., p. 143.
[c] Ibid., p. 143.

7 THE CULTIVATION AND ATTAINMENT OF CALM ABIDING

THE CULTIVATION OF CALM ABIDING

Ge-luk presentations of the cultivation of calm abiding involve a synthesis of two systems—that of the five faults and eight antidotes, or applications, from Maitreya's *Differentiation of the Middle and the Extremes,* and that of the nine mental abidings, from Asaṅga's *Grounds of Hearers* and *Summary of Manifest Knowledge* and Maitreya's *Ornament for the Mahāyāna Sūtras.*[a] This synthesis, made by the textual lineage of the Kadam-pa (*dka' gdams pa*) School,[b] is both scholarly and practical. From the point of view of Ge-luk religious scholarship, the synthesis reconciles the two systems. From the practical point of view, it represents a psychology of meditation, derived from the experiences of meditators and teachers of meditation who have noticed that the faults become noticeable and are overcome at specific points in the meditator's gradual progress toward the attainment of calm abiding. According to Gedün Lodrö:

> ...anyone who cultivates the abandonment of the five faults and reliance on the eight antidotes necessarily passes through the nine mental abidings. Similarly, a person wishing to progress through the nine mental abidings can do so only by abandoning the five faults and relying on the eight antidotes.[c]

I will explain the faults and antidotes briefly and then present the nine mental abidings; I will relate the five faults with their respective antidotes, to that mental abiding in which the given fault becomes of overriding concern to the meditator.

THE FIVE FAULTS AND THE EIGHT ANTIDOTES

The five faults are: laziness (*le lo, kausīdya*), forgetting the instruction (*gdam ngag brjed pa, avavādasammoṣa*), [non-identification of] laxity (*bying ba, laya*) and excitement (*rgod pa, auddhatya*), non-application (*'du mi byed pa, anabhisaṃskāra*), and over-application (*'du byed pa,*

[a] Gedün Lodrö, pp. 163–64 (see pages 20ff. above).

[b] Ibid., pp. 193–94 (see pages 20ff. above).

[c] Ibid., p. 164.

abhisaṃskāra)—in this context, overapplication.[a] Laziness has four antidotes: faith (*dad pa, śraddhā*), aspiration (*'dun pa, chanda*), exertion (*rtsol ba, vyāyāma*), and pliancy (*shin sbyangs, praśrabdhi*); they are applied in the order given. The antidote to forgetting the instruction is mindfulness (*dran pa, smṛti*). The antidote to laxity and excitement is introspection (*shes bzhin, samprajanya*). The antidote to non-application is application (*'du byed pa, abhisaṃskāra*), and the antidote to overapplication is the equanimity (*btang snyoms, upekṣā*) that consists of desisting from application.[b] The relationship of the faults and antidotes is summarized in the following chart.

Chart 3: Faults of Meditative Stabilization and Their Antidotes

Faults	*Antidotes*
laziness	faith aspiration exertion pliancy
forgetting the instruction	mindfulness
[non-identification of] laxity and excitement	introspection
non-application	application
application	desisting from application

Laziness

In the context of the cultivation of calm abiding, Lati Rinpoche explains laziness loosely as an absence of the wish to cultivate meditative stabilization continually.[c] Gedün Lodrö defines it more precisely as "a mental factor (*sems byung, caitta*) which, through its own power, causes procrastination with respect to cultivating meditative stabilization."[d]

There are three types of laziness:

1 laziness of neutral activities (*snyoms las kyi le lo*)
2 laziness which is an attachment to bad activities (*bya ba ngan zhen gyi le lo*)

---

a *Meditative States*, p. 52.

b Ibid., p. 53.

c *Meditative States*, p. 55.

d Gedün Lodrö, p. 165.

3 laziness of inadequacy (*sgyid lugs pa'i le lo*—literally, "losing affinity")[a]

The first type is a case of simple procrastination: the practitioner engages in ethically neutral activities such as sleep, conversation, or housework, to put off cultivating calm abiding.[b] Gedün Lodrö remarks that in practice the laziness of neutral activities is the worst type of laziness because the meditator is least likely to recognize it.[c]

The second type involves non-virtuous activities, such as thoughts of hatred toward an enemy.[d]

The third type, laziness of inadequacy, involves the meditator's sense of inferiority in relation to the qualities he or she aspires to attain. Gedün Lodrö gives as an example a person who "take[s] cognizance of a...Bodhisattva's great qualities of mind" and then thinks, "I could not possibly achieve such qualities."[e] He explains:

> The word *sgyid* means "affinity," and *lugs* means "discard"; in other words, because of this type of laziness, one has no sense of affinity with such a high state of mind, as if compatibility or facility with it has been lost. This is the opposite of being able to engage in something fully; it is a case of letting it go altogether. People who have this type of laziness initially want to achieve a Bodhisattva's qualities, and so forth, but when they encounter difficulty in doing so, they give up.[f]

He identifies the laziness of inadequacy as a type of slackness (*zhum pa*), here identified as *yid shi ba'i zhum pa*, meaning "a death of the mind"; that is, "Someone thinks about doing something [virtuous], and then that thought dies."[g]

According to Jam-yang-shay-pa, this explanation of laziness in the context of the cultivation of calm abiding follows the general presentation of laziness: the three types of laziness are explained in this way in relation to the cultivation of meditative stabilization "because it is the case that these three act in this way with respect to most virtues."[h]

---

[a] Ibid., p. 165.
[b] Ibid., p. 166.
[c] Ibid., pp. 166–67.
[d] Ibid., p. 166.
[e] Ibid., p. 166.
[f] Ibid., p. 166.
[g] Ibid., p. 166.
[h] Jam-yang-shay-pa, *Concentrations*, 139.7.

Antidotes to laziness. Because laziness is most dangerous during the early stages of cultivating calm abiding and can prevent the would-be practitioner from even beginning, four of the eight antidotes are antidotes to laziness. As was mentioned earlier (see page 138), the four are **faith**, **aspiration**, **exertion**, and **pliancy**; they are applied in the order given. Thus, the greatest emphasis is placed on the explanation of faith and the methods for cultivating it.

Faith in this context is explained as faith in the good qualities of meditative stabilization.[a] Of the three types of faith—the faith of clarity (*dvang ba, prasāda*), the faith of conviction (*yid ches, abhisaṃpratyaya*), and the faith that is a wish to attain (*'thob 'dod, abhilāṣa*)—faith in this context is the second, the faith of conviction.[b] Lati Rinpoche gives detailed instructions for contemplating the faults of distraction and the advantages of meditative stabilization.[c]

Kön-chok-jik-may-wang-po and Gedün Lodrö both explain **aspiration** in this context as an "aspiration that seeks the good qualities of meditative stabilization."[d] According to Lati Rinpoche, it follows naturally from faith in the value of attaining meditative stabilization.[e]

The third antidote is classically given as **exertion.**[f] According to Lati Rinpoche, exertion follows naturally from aspiration.[g] Exertion here is actually effort, as becomes clear from the Go-mang explanations of the relationship between the two. Kön-chok-jik-may-wang-po defines effort as "that intention which observes and is enthusiastic about a virtuous object of observation."[h] According to Jam-yang-shay-pa, there are four possibilities between exertion and effort:

> namely, that which is exertion but not effort, that which is effort but not exertion, that which is both, and that which is neither because (1) exertion toward a neutral [object], for instance, is the first; (2) that which has enthusiasm toward virtue but does not apply itself is the second; (3) that which has

---

[a] Kön-chok-jik-may-wang-po, *Condensed Statement,* 561.1; Lati Rinpoche in *Meditative States,* pp. 142–43.

[b] Kön-chok-jik-may-wang-po, *Condensed Statement,* 561.1; Gedün Lodrö, pp. 168–69 (Gedün Lodrö explains the third type of faith as a kind of aspiration). See also Hopkins, *Meditation on Emptiness,* pp. 248–50, for a discussion of the three types of faith.

[c] *Meditative States,* pp. 55–56,

[d] Kön-chok-jik-may-wang-po, *Condensed Statement,* 560.7; Gedün Lodrö, pp. 168–69.

[e] *Meditative States,* p. 56.

[f] Jam-yang-shay-pa, *Concentrations,* 146.1–2.

[g] *Meditative States,* p. 56.

[h] Kön-chok-jik-may-wang-po, *Condensed Statement,* 560.5.

> enthusiasm toward virtue and is exertion, for instance, is the third; (4) a consciousness, for instance, is the fourth.[a]

Gedün Lodrö, however, gives three possibilities between exertion and effort:

> Exertion is necessary for effort, but effort is not necessary for exertion because effort is defined as an enthusiasm for virtue, whereas it is possible to have exertion in connection with non-virtue. [b]

Although he would not wish to disagree publicly with his college's textbooks, he probably does not accept "that which has enthusiasm toward virtue but does not apply itself" as being effort.

According to Lati Rinpoche, **pliancy** is the actual antidote to laziness.[c] However, as was mentioned earlier (page 63), pliancy is the physical and mental serviceability that allows a meditator to remain focused on an object of observation without distraction, at will, for as long as he or she wishes. It is attained only with the achievement of calm abiding and, therefore, cannot help the beginning meditator directly. Gedün Lodrö regards pliancy in this context as "a benefit arising from the process of applying the first three antidotes" that "is said to be used as an antidote in the sense that one can reflect on the benefit of having pliancy." However, he regards the first three antidotes to laziness as more important for beginning meditators, up through the third mental abiding.[d] Lati Rinpoche points out, however, that pliancy is directly useful as an antidote to laziness for meditators cultivating special insight and/or the mental contemplation of individual knowledge of the character. Such meditators have already achieved calm abiding and, with it, mental and physical pliancy; for them, therefore, pliancy arises after exertion. "Thus, pliancy, the actual antidote to laziness, is now the way of overcoming laziness."[e]

Forgetting the instruction

To forget the instruction is to lose the object of observation; Lati

---

[a] Jam-yang-shay-pa, *Concentrations,* 146.7–147.2; see also Kön-chok-jik-may-wang-po, *Condensed Statement,* 560.5–6.

[b] Gedün Lodrö, p. 169.

[c] *Meditative States,* p. 55.

[d] Gedün Lodrö, p. 168.

[e] *Meditative States,* p. 97.

Rinpoche explains that, while the meditator is observing the object of observation—for instance, the body of a Buddha—it suddenly disappears.[a] Gedün Lodrö describes forgetfulness more technically, on the basis of Jam-yang-shay-pa's definition, as "an afflicted (*nyon mongs can, kliṣṭa*) mindfulness (*dran pa, smṛti*)" that "has the function of causing distraction" and "is an unserviceability with regard to cultivating meditative stabilization."[b] The object of observation is called an "instruction" (*gdams ngag, avavāda*) here because the meditator has received instruction concerning it from a teacher or a text and also, in the case of a visualized object of observation such as the body of a Buddha, by studying a painting or statue of the object until he or she is able to visualize it.[c]

Forgetting the instruction, or forgetfulness, can be experienced in two different ways. One is that, when the object of observation disappears, everything seems to go dark, so that the meditator is aware of no object of observation at all. The other is that the meditator's mind is distracted to something else, perhaps a desirable sense object. These two ways of losing the object of observation correspond to the two divisions of forgetfulness given by Kön-chok-jik-may-wang-po and Jam-yang-shay-pa—"two in terms of laxity and excitement."[d]

As soon as the object of observation is lost, the meditator must bring it back to mind and again focus on it. Therefore, the antidote to forgetting the instruction is **mindfulness.** Lati Rinpoche explains mindfulness as meaning that the meditator holds the object of observation tightly, "as we might hold a full mug tightly rather than loosely."[e] This explanation, like those of the other textbooks and oral commentaries discussed here, is based on the definition given in the section on mental factors in Asaṅga's *Summary of Manifest Knowledge:*

> What is mindfulness? It is non-forgetfulness of mind with respect to a familiar thing; it has the function of [causing] non-distraction.[f]

---

[a] Ibid., p. 57.

[b] Gedün Lodrö, p. 169. See Jam-yang-shay-pa, *Concentrations,* 139.7–140.1.

[c] See *Meditative States,* p. 57, on the power of hearing.

[d] Kön-chok-jik-may-wang-po, *Condensed Statement,* 559.5; Jam-yang-shay-pa, *Concentrations,* 140.2.

[e] *Meditative States,* p. 57.

[f] Cited in Jam-yang-shay-pa, *Concentrations,* 148.1–2. See also *Meditative States,* p. 58; Gedün Lodrö, p. 169; Walpola Rahula, trans., *Le Compendium de la super-doctrine (philosophie) (Abhidharmasamuccaya) d'Asaṅga* (Paris: École française d'extrême-orient, 1971), p. 8; P 5550, vol. 112, 238.3.8.

Thus, mindfulness is first of all a mental factor, as Jam-yang-shay-pa and Gedün Lodrö state in their definitions.[a] According to Lati Rinpoche's explanation of Asaṅga's definition, mindfulness has three features:

1 The object of observation must be familiar to the meditator, since "[i]t is impossible to be mindful of something that we have not previously seen."
2 The mode of apprehension "must be continuous, without forgetfulness of the aspects of the object."
3 The function of mindfulness "is to cause non-distraction, non-scattering, to other objects."[b]

A simpler explanation of the last two features is that "the meditator must hold on" to the object of observation "tightly, without distraction, and cause only that object to appear to the mind."[c]

[Non-identification of] laxity and excitement

According to contemporary Tibetan scholars, the third fault is given loosely in Maitreya's *Differentiation of the Middle and the Extremes* as laxity and excitement; the antidote is given as introspection.[d] The looseness of the description causes some problems for commentators; there seem to be two lines of interpretation. On the one hand, there are explanations of why "non-identification of" should be bracketed into the name of the fault. On the other hand, the original name is accepted, and there are explanations of why, although introspection is not the actual antidote to laxity and excitement, it is called the antidote. The Go-mang commentators seem to follow the first line and Lati Rinpoche, the second.

Jam-yang-shay-pa and Kön-chok-jik-may-wang-po follow the first line of interpretation when they name the fault as "*non-identification* of laxity and excitement" and give the antidote as "introspection, which quickly recognizes laxity and excitement, as the antidote to laxity and excitement *and non-identification of them*."[e] Lati Rinpoche follows the second line of interpretation when he states that:

---

[a] Jam-yang-shay-pa, *Concentrations,* 148.1; Gedün Lodrö, p. 169.

[b] *Meditative States,* p. 59.

[c] Ibid., p. 59. See also Gedün Lodrö, p. 169.

[d] Cited in Jam-yang-shay-pa, *Concentrations,* 139.5 and 148.4.

[e] Kön-chok-jik-may-wang-po, *Condensed Statement,* 559.3; Jam-yang-shay-pa, *Concentrations,* 138.6, italics added.

> [introspection] is posited as the antidote to laxity and excitement, although it is not the actual antidote, because it identifies laxity and excitement. Introspection is like a spy in wartime. Just as a spy is not an actual combatant but is included within the category of combatants, so introspection, which is like a spy in that it analyzes the mind to see whether laxity or excitement has arisen, is included among the antidotes.[a]

In practice, the meditator uses introspection to inspect the mind for laxity and excitement. Gedün Lodrö explains that the meditator "must inspect from time to time whether or not laxity or excitement has arisen." This is done "within not giving up meditative stabilization"; Gedün Lodrö explains further that

> Once the yogic practitioner has confidence that his or her mind will stay on the object of observation, it is possible to have an inspection that functions simultaneously with observation of the object.[b]

He adds that introspection must be done while the meditation is still going well, "before losing the intensity of meditative stabilization."[c] Lati Rinpoche makes the additional point that introspection should not be used continuously because continuous use of introspection puts the meditator in danger of generating excitement.[d]

Once it is clear that the third fault is [non-identification of] laxity and excitement, and that the antidote is the introspection that identifies them, the next question is, What is introspection supposed to be looking for? What are the laxity and excitement that the meditator is failing to identify?

Laxity

General Description and Definition

The Tibetan word *bying ba,* translated here as "laxity," literally means "sinking."[e] Following the Go-mang textbook writers, Gedün Lodrö

---

[a] *Meditative States,* p. 62.

[b] Gedün Lodrö, p. 186.

[c] Ibid., p. 186.

[d] *Meditative States,* p. 62.

[e] Sarat Chandra Das, *Tibetan-English Dictionary,* p. 924, col. 1. According to Monier-Williams, *laya* literally means "the act of sticking or clinging to"; by extension, it also means "lying down, cowering," "melting, dissolution, disappearance or absorption in,"

defines laxity technically as

> an internal distraction which is a mental factor that destroys the intensity of clarity in [a mind of] meditative stabilization.[a]

As the definition implies, and as Gedün Lodrö explicitly points out, laxity does not occur at all outside meditation. Indeed, it "occurs only when one is fairly advanced in the cultivation of meditative stabilization." Therefore, he emphasizes that it is important for a meditator to study and understand the nature and mode of production of laxity *before* beginning to cultivate calm abiding, for, without such study, the meditator will be unprepared to recognize laxity when it occurs.[b]

Divisions of Laxity

There are two ways of dividing laxity. According to the first, laxity can be either virtuous or neutral; it is not non-virtuous.[c] The other main division of laxity is into two types, coarse and subtle. Lati Rinpoche gives the most basic explanation:

> Coarse laxity is a case of having stability—the ability to stay on the object [of observation]—but not clarity. Subtle laxity is a case of having stability and clarity but not intensity of clarity.[d]

According to Lati Rinpoche's presentation, the object of observation is not lost even in coarse laxity, since the meditator has stability.[e] He explains further that

> "Clarity," here, refers not to the clarity of the object [of observation] but to the clarity of the mind apprehending the object [of observation]. When we do not have clarity, it is as if we have become dark, as if we are in a shadow. Not to have intensity of clarity means that, though we have stability and clarity, the mind's mode of apprehension has become loose with respect to the object [of observation]. If, within that looseness, we become even more stable, this state turns into subtle laxity. When we

---

"extinction, destruction, death," "rest," and "mental inactivity, spiritual indifference" (Monier-Williams, *Sanskrit-English Dictionary,* p. 903, col. 2).

[a] Gedün Lodrö, pp. 176–77. See Jam-yang-shay-pa, *Concentrations,* 140.6–7.

[b] Ibid., p. 176.

[c] Ibid., p. 177; Kön-chok-jik-may-wang-po, *Condensed Statement,* 560.2; Jam-yang-shay-pa, *Concentrations,* 141.3.

[d] *Meditative States,* p. 59.

[e] Ibid., p. 59.

> have intensity of clarity, we have not only stability and clarity but also a sense of tightness of mind with respect to the object [of observation]. The difference is like that between holding a mug loosely and holding it tightly.[a]

Lati Rinpoche especially warns against the danger of subtle laxity, which he describes as "the worst unfavorable circumstance with regard to generating meditative stabilization" because it is difficult for a meditator to distinguish between the two, since both subtle laxity and meditative stabilization have both stability and clarity.[b] He cites Tsong-kha-pa's advice that "in general, we should tend to err to the side of tightness" because in that way "what will be generated will be excitement, and excitement is easier to overcome than laxity."[c] It is also easier to recognize.

In a more complex presentation based on Jam-yang-shay-pa's, Gedün Lodrö divides laxity into virtuous and ethically neutral types and discusses coarse and subtle laxity in terms of four factors:

1 factor of stability (*gnas cha*)
2 factor of subjective clarity (*dvang cha*)
3 factor of clarity (*gsal cha*)—both subject and object have to be clear
4 intensity (*ngar*)[d]

He explains coarse laxity as an ethically neutral state in which the meditator has subjective clarity but in which "there is some fault with the factor of stability." He identifies subtle laxity as virtuous rather than neutral and further divides subtle laxity into two types: coarse subtle and subtle subtle:

> In the coarse form of subtle laxity, one has the first three factors—stability, subjective clarity, and both subjective and objective clarity—but lacks the fourth, intensity. In the subtle form of subtle laxity, one has all four qualities, but there is a slight fault with the factor of stability.[e]

Jam-yang-shay-pa's reason for identifying subtle laxity as virtuous rather than neutral is that, since the object of observation is virtuous,

---

[a] Ibid., pp. 59–60.

[b] Ibid., p. 60.

[c] Ibid., p. 63. Tsong-kha-pa, *Great Exposition of the Stages of the Path* (Dharamsala: shes rig par khang, no date), 692.2–3.

[d] Gedün Lodrö, p. 177.

[e] Ibid., p. 177.

subtle laxity "is associated with faith."[a]

Causes of Laxity

According to Gedün Lodrö, laxity can be produced in three ways:

1 by the mind's being overly withdrawn inside
2 by a lessening of the intensity of meditative stabilization
3 through sleepiness or lethargy.[b]

The first cause of laxity leads in turn to the second—that is, excessive withdrawal of the mind leads to a loss of intensity of clarity. Gedün Lodrö explains the third cause of laxity as being

> like the casting of a shadow. One's mind becomes cloudy, as if something that was illumined had become dark. Sleepiness and lethargy are not causes in the sense of preceding laxity but because, instead of going to sleep, one becomes lax.[c]

Apparently for practical reasons related to the antidotes to laxity, to be discussed below pages 152–153), Lati Rinpoche gives a similar explanation of the causes of laxity: "...lethargy, sleep, and those factors that cause the mind to become dark, like a darkened sky."[d]

Distraction to virtuous objects other than the object of observation also produces subtle laxity. Gedün Lodrö does not list this as a cause of laxity, but he cites a case of it—namely, the arising of love and compassion when one is meditating on the body of a Buddha—as an example of subtle laxity. He describes the apparent virtues as "deceivers" in this context.[e]

Comparison with Lethargy

Discussions of laxity stress the importance of distinguishing it from lethargy, despite the superficial similarities. Laxity and lethargy are mutually exclusive (*'gal ba, viruddha*)—that is, there is nothing that can

---

[a] Jam-yang-shay-pa, *Concentrations,* 141.4.

[b] Gedün Lodrö, p. 175.

[c] Ibid., p. 175.

[d] *Meditative States,* p. 65. Jeffrey Hopkins, in conversation, expressed skepticism concerning this generally accepted explanation of the causes of laxity. He holds that attenuated forms of lethargy are still lethargy, not laxity, and points out that, in explaining why sleepiness and lethargy are held to be causes of laxity, Gedün Lodrö "fudged" the meaning of "cause."

[e] Gedün Lodrö, p. 175.

be cited as being both. Lethargy is an afflictive emotion and, therefore, non-virtuous, whereas laxity, as mentioned earlier (page 145) is either virtuous or neutral but not non-virtuous. Lethargy is a mental and physical heaviness that is included with obscuration (*gti mug, moha*); according to Gedün Lodrö, it "accompanies all root and secondary afflictive emotions," even excitement.[a] Lethargy occurs "either when the mind is withdrawn inside or when the mind is scattered outside," whereas laxity "occurs only when the mind is withdrawn inside in the process of developing meditative stabilization."[b] Gedün Lodrö notes that if someone begins to feel dull while listening to a lecture, that is a case of lethargy, not laxity.[c]

Comparison with Slackness

Gedün Lodrö points out that some Indian texts—including the *Sūtra Unraveling the Thought,* Asaṅga's *Grounds of Hearers,* and Bhāvaviveka's *Heart of the Middle* and *Blaze of Reasoning*—use the term "slackness" (*zhum pa*) more often than "laxity" (*bying ba, laya*); in these texts, the two terms have the same meaning and, according to Gedün Lodrö, most "monastic colleges consider them to be equivalent." Gedün Lodrö follows Jamyang-shay-pa, however, in distinguishing three possibilities between them: "whatever is laxity is necessarily slackness, but whatever is slackness is not necessarily laxity." He identifies three instances of slackness—observing virtuous, non-virtuous, and neutral objects—that are not laxity. The first is the equivalent of the laziness of inadequacy (see page 139). An example of the second is a would-be murder's disheartenment at his or her inability to succeed in committing the murder. An example of the third is a walker's discouragement upon learning that the distance still to be covered is greater than that already covered. The last two types of slackness would not occur in meditation.

Gedün Lodrö observes that

> Laxity necessarily has a factor of non-clarity with respect to the object of observation, but in the three types of slackness, or disheartenment, discussed just above, the object of observation can still remain vivid; indeed, it is because the object is so clear that the person becomes disheartened.

He cites this clarity of the object in some types of slackness as the

---

[a] Ibid., pp. 179–80. See also *Meditative States,* p. 59.

[b] Gedün Lodrö, p. 179.

[c] Ibid., p. 175.

reason for Jam-yang-shay-pa's distinction between laxity and slackness.[a]

Excitement

General Description and Definition

The Tibetan word *rgod pa,* translated here as "excitement" literally means "wildness."[b] Excitement is a non-virtuous mental factor—specifically, a secondary afflictive emotion.[c] It involves "a scattering of the mind to the outside,"[d] toward an object that the excited consciousness regards as attractive, and thereby interrupts the cultivation of calm abiding. Gedün Lodrö defines it as

> a mental factor, included within the class of desire, which—observing its object, an attractive contaminated thing—has the subjective aspect of not being pacified, is a scattering of the mind to the outside, and interrupts the cultivation of meditative stabilization.[e]

Divisions of Excitement

Like laxity, excitement has two forms, coarse and subtle. Coarse excitement involves loss of the object of observation, whereas subtle excitement does not involve such loss. Lati Rinpoche explains that

> If we were meditating on the body of a Buddha and lost the object [of observation]—that is, if the body of a Buddha no longer appeared—and if we became mindful of an object of desire, that state would be coarse excitement.[f]

He explains subtle excitement through a simile:

---

[a] Ibid., pp. 178–79. Gedün Lodrö suggests (p. 179) that both *bying ba* and *zhum pa* may be Tibetan translations of a single Sanskrit term; nevertheless, he explains through reasons why there are three possibilities between them.

[b] Das, *Tibetan-English Dictionary,* p. 302, col. 2. According to Monier-Williams, the Sanskrit *auddhatya* means "arrogance, insolence" and is related to *uddhata,* which literally means "raised (as dust)" and has a range of meanings including "elevated," "arrogant," "excessive," and "stirred up, excited, agitated" (Monier-Williams, *Sanskrit-English Dictionary,* pp. 237, col. 3; 188, col. 3).

[c] Hopkins, *Meditation on Emptiness,* pp. 262, 265.

[d] Gedün Lodrö, p. 181.

[e] Ibid., p. 181.

[f] *Meditative States,* p.61.

> Subtle excitement is commonly explained through the example of water moving under ice; the meditator does not lose the object [of observation], but a corner of the mind has come under the influence of discursiveness, and a pleasing object of desire is about to appear to the mind.[a]

Comparison with Scattering

Excitement is best understood in relation to scattering (*'phro ba*), which Lati Rinpoche explains as "the moving of the mind to external objects."[b] Excitement itself is a case of scattering. Lati Rinpoche notes that "[a]lmost all distractions are cases of the scattering of the mind" and that "[w]hen excitement is mentioned, scattering is implied."[c]

The difference between excitement and scattering is that excitement involves scattering only to objects of desire, whereas scattering involves the mind's moving toward any type of object. There are three possibilities between the two. Whatever is excitement is necessarily a case of scattering, but whatever is a case of scattering is not necessarily excitement: for example, someone cultivating calm abiding might begin to think about an object of hatred, such as an enemy. As both Kön-chok-jik-may-wang-po and Jam-yang-shay-pa point out,

> With respect to scattering, since there is scattering to various [objects], virtuous and non-virtuous, it is not the same as excitement.[d]

According to Lati Rinpoche,

> in the discussion of how to cultivate meditative stabilization, excitement is posited as one of the five faults and scattering is not because, in the cultivation of meditative stabilization, there are more cases of excitement than of scattering.[e]

Jam-yang-shay-pa explains that

> the basis of newly achieving meditative stabilization is only a Desire Realm [basis], and low common beings of the Desire Realm must mainly stop excitement, which is that interruption

---

[a] Ibid., p. 61.

[b] Ibid., p. 61.

[c] Ibid., p. 61.

[d] Kön-chok-jik-may-wang-po, *Condensed Statement*, 560.4; Jam-yang-shay-pa, *Concentrations*, 145.2.

[e] *Meditative States*, p. 61.

> to meditative stabilization which is desire for the five [sense] objects.[a]

Causes of Excitement

Citing Bhāvaviveka's *Blaze of Reasoning,* Gedün Lodrö identifies haughtiness (*rgyags pa, mada*) as a cause of excitement;[b] he defines haughtiness as "a heightening or pumping up of the mind within an attachment to one's own qualities."[c] He suggests that the type of haughtiness most dangerous to a meditator is haughtiness related to one's having accumulated learning. This is especially likely to arise when a learned meditator, as an antidote to laxity, reflects on the meaning of scripture; if such haughtiness occurs, it can lead to excitement.[d]

Non-application [of the antidotes to laxity and excitement]

Jam-yang-shay-pa defines non-application in this context as

> a non-exertion in stopping laxity and excitement even when one sees them.[e]

He gives three divisions, "three [types of] non-exertion due to the three [types of] laziness."[f] Lati Rinpoche describes the effect of non-application metaphorically:

> Not to apply the antidotes to laxity and excitement once the spy of introspection has discovered that laxity and excitement had set in would be like not sending out the troops once the spy had discovered the enemy's oncoming army.[g]

The antidote to non-application is **application**—that is, practical application of specific techniques to counteract laxity and excitement. Thus, this is usually the point at which these techniques are explained.

---

[a] Jam-yang-shay-pa, *Concentrations,* 145.2–3.

[b] Gedün Lodrö, pp. 183, 185.

[c] Ibid., p. 183.

[d] Ibid., pp. 184–85.

[e] Jam-yang-shay-pa, *Concentrations,* 140.4.

[f] Ibid., 140.4.

[g] *Meditative States,* p. 62.

Specific Antidotes to Laxity

Lati Rinpoche gives the antidotes to laxity in an order ranging from subtlest to coarsest. He identifies subtle laxity, which has "stability and clarity but not intensity of clarity," as arising "from weakness in the mode of apprehension of the object [of observation]." The antidote, therefore, is to "tighten the mode of apprehension" without changing the object of observation. This is a subtle and difficult technique, for the meditator has to be careful not to overtighten and thereby generate excitement; Lati Rinpoche compares this technique to the process of tuning a stringed instrument.[a]

If this technique does not work and "laxity is still being generated," the meditator is "at the point of generating coarse laxity." The symptoms are that "it seems as though the mind is falling apart," and the meditator "also [does] not have clarity." Since coarse laxity is caused by the mind's being too withdrawn inside, the corrective is "to enlarge the scope of the object [of observation]," either by making it "brighter, as though it were made of light" or by considering its features in detail.[b]

If this antidote to laxity does not work, coarser methods are needed. The meditator temporarily puts aside the original object of observation and contemplates such invigorating topics as the difficulty of obtaining a human life with leisure (*'byor ba, saṃpad*) and fortune (*dal ba, kṣaṇa*), the good qualities of the Three Jewels, "or the benefits of the altruistic mind of enlightenment."[c] Gedün Lodrö also mentions "causing the meaning of sūtras, and so forth, to appear to the mind."[d] A similar technique, suggested by Lati Rinpoche, is to "engage in meditative practices of giving." A related method is to visualize a "bright object such as the sun or moon";[e] Gedün Lodrö notes in this context that "A well-educated person could meditate on the nature of the mind as clear light (*'od gsal, prabhāsvara*)."[f] These techniques work well—they are "like splashing cold water on one's face," according to Lati Rinpoche—if the meditator is already familiar with the topics and methods.[g]

For beginners who are unable to use such contemplations, Lati Rinpoche suggests that

[a] Ibid., p. 63.
[b] Ibid., p. 64.
[c] Ibid., p. 64.
[d] Gedün Lodrö, p. 176.
[e] *Meditative States*, p. 64; Gedün Lodrö, p. 176.
[f] Gedün Lodrö, p. 176.
[g] *Meditative States*, p. 64.

> it is necessary to rely on quintessential instructions for removing laxity forcefully—that is, for forcing it out of our mental continuum. We should visualize our own mind as a white light, the size of a white pea, at the heart. We can also visualize the mind in the shape of the Tibetan or Sanskrit letter *a* at the heart. Then we should say *phaṭ* loudly and visualize the mind exiting through the top of the head and dissolving in the sky. This is called a mixing of the expanse of space and the mind. It should be done again and again many times....If it does not help, we should stop the session.[a]

Since lethargy and sleep are mentioned among the causes of laxity, Lati Rinpoche suggests measures at this point, when the meditator has had to stop the session, "to overcome these causes"—going "to a cool place or to a high place, a place with a wide view, or...wash[ing] the face with cold water. If we need to rest, we should rest."[b] Despite the qualm raised earlier (see page 147) about lethargy and sleep as causes of laxity, these coarsest of all antidotes are probably mentioned because they work: the meditator can use them and return to the session refreshed.

Jam-yang-shay-pa's textbook presentation of the antidotes to laxity, which is not intended as a practical instruction, mentions two types of antidote in terms of the causes of laxity. Citing Bhāvaviveka's *Heart of the Middle,* he suggests expanding the object of observation as an antidote to the type of laxity that is caused by the mind's being too strongly withdrawn inside, whereas, for the type that "is merely a lowering of the mind's mode of apprehension" and is said to be caused by lethargy and sleep, he follows Kamalashīla's first *Stages of Meditation* in suggesting "heightening the mind and cultivating joy."[c]

SPECIFIC ANTIDOTES TO EXCITEMENT

As was the case with the antidotes to laxity, Lati Rinpoche explains the antidotes to excitement in an order ranging from subtlest to coarsest. Since subtle excitement is "caused by the mind's being a little too tight," the meditator "should loosen the mode of apprehension a little. If loosening the mode of apprehension a little does not help,...coarse

---

[a] Ibid., p. 64. Lati Rinpoche mentions Pa-dam-pa-sang-gyay (*pha dam pa sangs rgyas*, equated by some Tibetan scholars with Bodhidharma) as the source for this practice and advises that "there is no need to have qualms" with regard to it—a remark implying that some Tibetan scholars have qualms (p. 236 n. 12).

[b] Ibid., p. 65.

[c] Jam-yang-shay-pa, *Concentrations,* 144.1–4.

excitement is about to be generated."[a]

Antidotes to coarse excitement "reduce the height of the mind." Meditators

> should leave the object of observation, which here is the body of a Buddha, but should not leave the session. Rather, we should meditate on such topics as death and impermanence and the suffering of cyclic existence in general and of the bad [trans]migrations in particular—topics that cause the mind to be slightly sobered. Thoughts that would cause a wish to leave cyclic existence will help people who are familiar with such contemplation.[b]

As he did with coarse laxity, Lati Rinpoche gives a forceful antidote for overcoming coarse excitement: to "meditate on a black drop at the navel (that is, at the center of the body behind the navel), or [to] concentrate on the inhalation and exhalation of the breath." Again, if these methods do not work, the meditator "should give up the session and rest."[c]

In his brief textbook presentation of antidotes to excitement, Jam-yang-shay-pa again cites Bhāvaviveka's *Heart of the Middle* and Kamalashīla's first *Stages of Meditation* to support his recommendation of "meditation on very sobering [topics] such as impermanence."[d]

Texts and oral presentations do not discuss the circumstances in which a meditator may fail to apply the antidotes, even when he or she knows through introspection that laxity or excitement is present. It is possible to speculate, however, that the primary reason is premature satisfaction with what has already been achieved, especially if the meditator has achieved a fairly high degree of stability. This is suggested by Jam-yang-shay-pa's division of non-application, cited earlier (page 151), into "three [types of] non-exertion due to the three [types of] laziness."

Application, or [over]application

As a fault, application is the unnecessary application of antidotes when no other faults are present. For clarity, we sometimes differentiate in English between correct application of antidotes to overcome faults

---

a *Meditative States,* p. 65.

b Ibid., p. 65.

c Ibid., pp. 65–66. Gedün Lodrö does not discuss specific antidotes to excitement.

d Jam-yang-shay-pa, *Concentrations,* 145.4–7.

and unnecessary application of antidotes by using the English terms "application" and "[over]application," respectively. However, the mental activity involved is the same in both cases; only the context has changed. The application of antidotes becomes a fault when the meditator continues to apply antidotes out of habit and fails to recognize a changed situation in which faults, especially laxity and excitement, are no longer present. As Kön-chok-jik-may-wang-po points out, the application of antidotes to laxity and excitement even in the absence of these faults becomes a distraction that prevents the increase of meditative stabilization.[a]

The antidote to the unnecessary application of antidotes is the equanimity that consists of **desisting from application** (*'du byed btang snyoms*). It is one of three types of equanimity, the other two being neutral feeling (*tshor ba btang snyoms*) and immeasurable equanimity (*btang snyoms tshad med*). Neutral feeling is also known as neither pain nor pleasure (*sdug bsngal ma yin bde ba yang ma yin, aduḥkhāsukha*). Immeasurable equanimity—equanimity directed toward an incalculably large number of sentient beings—requires the attainment of an actual concentration.

[Over]application occurs, and its antidote is applied, late in the cultivation of calm abiding. The fault does not occur until in the eighth of the nine mental abidings, and the antidote, desisting from application, is mutually inclusive with the ninth.[b] As Lati Rinpoche points out, however, "a similitude" of [over]application can occur earlier when the meditation is proceeding well, and at those times the meditator would apply "a similitude" of desisting from application, although the meditator, aware that laxity and excitement will still arise in the future, "would not desist from application altogether."[c]

THE NINE MENTAL ABIDINGS

The nine mental abidings are the nine states of mind through which a meditator progresses, as through grades in a school, to achieve calm abiding. The Sanskrit term, *navākārā cittasthiti,* literally means "nine-aspected mental abiding"; *cittasthiti* is literally a state (*sthiti*) of mind (*citta*), and *navākārā,* "nine-aspected," is a *bahuvrihi* compound that serves as an adjective modifying it. The literal Tibetan translation, *sems gnas pa rnam pa dgu,* is used in Tibetan translations of the Sanskrit texts

---

[a] Kön-chok-jik-may-wang-po, *Condensed Statement,* 560.1.

[b] *Meditative States,* p. 66; Gedün Lodrö, p. 190.

[c] *Meditative States,* p. 66.

that discuss the nine mental abidings and in monastic-textbook citations from those texts.[a] However, the Tibetan term in general use is the simpler *sems gnas dgu*, which means "nine mental abidings."[b]

The nine mental abidings are:

1 Setting the mind (*sems 'jog pa, cittasthāpana*)
2 Continuous setting (*rgyun du 'jog pa, saṃsthāpana*)
3 Resetting (*slan te 'jog pa, avasthāpana*)
4 Close setting (*nye bar 'jog pa, upasthāpana*)
5 Disciplining (*dul bar byed pa, damana*)
6 Pacifying (*zhi bar byed pa, śamana*)
7 Thorough pacifying (*nye bar zhi bar byed pa, vyupaśamana*)
8 Making one-pointed (*rtse gcig tu byed pa, ekotīkaraṇa*)
9 Setting in equipoise (*mnyam par 'jog pa, samādhāna*)

The nine mental abidings are presented in conjunction with two related sets of terms—the six powers (*stobs, bala*) and the four mental engagements. The six powers—the six capacities a meditator needs in order to attain calm abiding—are:

1 hearing (*thos pa, śruta*)
2 thinking (*bsam pa, cintā*)
3 mindfulness (*dran pa, smṛti*)
4 introspection (*shes bzhin, samprajanya*)
5 effort (*brtson 'grus, vīrya*)
6 familiarity (*yongs su 'dris pa, paricaya*)

They are developed in that order as a meditator progresses through the nine mental abidings; I will discuss them as they occur.

The four mental engagements[c] are the four ways in which the

---

[a] Jam-yang-shay-pa, *Concentrations*, 152.3, citing Asaṅga's *Grounds of Hearers*.

[b] For a discussion of the etymology of "mental abiding" (*sems gnas, cittasthiti*), see page 65, where it is discussed in relation to the etymology of "calm abiding" (*zhi gnas, śamatha*).

[c] Jam-yang-shay-pa explains that *yid la byed pa* (*manaskāra*) has two different meanings. In the context of the four mental engagements, *manaskāra* is posited as "the mental factor of mental engagement (*sems byung yid byed*)," whereas, in the context of the seven mental contemplations (or eight mental contemplations, from calm abiding, which is the mental contemplation of a mere beginner, up through the mental contemplation that is the fruit of final training), *manaskāra* (literally, "taking to mind") "is posited as 'contemplation' (*sems par byed pa*)" Jam-yang shay pa, *Concentrations*, 232.3–5, citing Asaṅga's *Grounds of Hearers* and the *Sūtra Unraveling the Thought*. These two meanings are translated, respectively, by the English terms "mental engagement" and "mental contemplation."

meditator's mind relates to the object of observation; they include the nine mental abidings. The four mental engagements are:

1 forcible engagement (*sgrim ste 'jug pa, balavāhana*)
2 interrupted engagement (*bar du chad cing 'jug pa, sacchidravāhana*)
3 uninterrupted engagement (*chad pa med par 'jug pa, niśchidravāhana*)
4 spontaneous engagement (*lhun grub tu 'jug pa, anābhogavāhana*)

In forcible engagement, operative during the first two mental abidings, the meditator forcibly tightens the mind to direct it toward and hold it on the object of observation. The third through seventh mental abidings are characterized by interrupted engagement; Gedün Lodrö notes that "During these mental abidings, the mind is sometimes able to stay on its object of observation and sometimes not." The eighth mental abiding is marked by uninterrupted engagement, in which "the mind stays on its object of observation without being interrupted by laxity and excitement." Spontaneous engagement characterizes the ninth mental abiding

> because the ninth mental abiding does not depend on the exertion that observes whether laxity or excitement has arisen: the mind is one-pointedly engaged with the object of observation and is able to operate according to the meditator's own intention.[a]

The following chart sets forth the relationship of the three sets of terms.

[a] Gedün Lodrö, p. 192.

Chart 4: States and Factors in Achieving Calm Abiding

(Read from bottom to top.)

Six Powers	*Nine Mental Abidings*	*Four Mental Engagements*
familiarity	9. Setting in equipoise	spontaneous engagement
	8. Making one-pointed	uninterrupted engagement
effort	7. Thorough pacifying	interrupted engagement
	6. Pacifying	
introspection	5. Disciplining	
	4. Close setting	
mindfulness	3. Resetting	
thinking	2. Continuous setting	forcible engagement
hearing	1. Setting the mind	

The first mental abiding: Setting the mind

The first mental abiding marks the meditator's first attempts to withdraw the mind from external objects and set it on an internal object of observation. This is very hard to do; the mind is *off* the object of observation much more than it is *on* it. As Gedün Lodrö remarked, the meditator is not so much setting the mind on the object as forcibly putting it there.[a] The mind wanders easily to external objects, and there is a great deal of discursiveness. The meditator experiences much more distraction than usual—not because of an increase in distraction but because distraction has been identified for the first time.[b]

At this point, the meditator has the **power of hearing** because of having heard about and chosen the object of observation through a teacher's instruction; the reading of texts that explain the object of observation is also included in the meaning of "hearing." Even looking at a painting or statue of a Buddha in preparation for visualizing is included in "hearing," since this is done on the advice of a teacher.[c]

According to Lati Rinpoche,

> the measure of having finished the first mental abiding is that the mind stays on the object [of observation] for as long as it would take to count twenty-one breaths; however, it is easier to count the breath to twenty-one than to stay on another object

---

[a] Gedün Lodrö, p. 191.

[b] Ibid., p. 164.

[c] *Meditative States*, p. 57.

> [of observation] for the same length of time.[a]

Thus, with an object of observation other than the breath, it takes longer to complete the first mental abiding. Gedün Lodrö notes that "One can pass to the second mental abiding only within the functioning of this continuum of setting the mind"—that is, during the same session.[b]

The main faults during the first mental abiding are laziness and forgetfulness. Although the other faults also occur, they are less noticeable because laziness and forgetfulness are much stronger. According to Gedün Lodrö, it is best, during the first mental abiding—indeed, during the first three mental abidings—to concentrate on overcoming laziness and forgetfulness by applying the antidotes to them.[c]

The second mental abiding: Continuous setting

During the second mental abiding, continuous setting, the mind is able to remain longer on the object of observation. Gedün Lodrö notes that "one is able to lengthen a little the continuum of observing the object of observation."[d] According to Lati Rinpoche,

> at this point a meditator would be able to stay on the object [of observation] for as long as it would take to go around the rosary once reciting the mantra *oṃ maṇi padme hūṃ* [the mantra of the Bodhisattva Avalokiteshvara]; at the correct speed, the recitation would take about a minute and a half.[e]

Lati Rinpoche and Gedün Lodrö agree that, during the second mental abiding, the meditator's experience is that there are times during which thought is resting.[f] This means that there are noticeable periods of time during which the mind is set only on the object of observation, that at other times there is distraction, and that the meditator is able to distinguish clearly between these two states.

During the second mental abiding, the meditator has the **power of thinking** because he or she "again and again contemplates the object

---

[a] Ibid., p. 67.

[b] Gedün Lodrö, p. 164.

[c] Ibid., p. 165.

[d] *Meditative States*, p. 67; Gedün Lodrö, p. 165.

[e] *Meditative States*, p. 67.

[f] *Meditative States*, p. 67; Gedün Lodrö, p. 165.

[of observation]"[a] and thinks about the teacher's instructions concerning it. In the second mental abiding, as in the first, the main faults are laziness and forgetting the instruction.[b]

The third mental abiding: Resetting

The third mental abiding is called "resetting" because, at this point, the meditator is able to recognize distraction as soon as it occurs and immediately place the mind back on the object of observation. Moreover, the meditator is able to focus on the object of observation for a longer period of time than in the second mental abiding.[c]

In the third mental abiding, the meditator has the **power of mindfulness;** Lati Rinpoche explains that as a result of the strong mindfulness applied during the first two mental abidings, the meditator has the power of mindfulness in the third. As in the first two mental abidings, the main faults are laziness and forgetfulness.[d]

As was noted earlier (see page 86), the third mental abiding is the point at which predominant afflictive emotions often impede progress, even if they were not manifest earlier. Sometimes they impede progress at this time even without becoming manifest. Gedün Lodrö describes a frequently occurring situation in which the meditator cannot overcome laziness and forgetfulness despite reliance on the antidotes to them. At this point, he says, the meditator

> must analyze the situation. There are many such cases in which meditators cannot conquer the difficulties and cannot go on. A very sharp person can do his or her own analysis at this time. Otherwise, as in the Ka-gyu tradition, you offer your realization (*rtogs ba phul ba*) to your teacher—that is, you tell him or her about your meditation. Your teacher will then tell you what to do. The practice of offering one's realization to a spiritual guide comes at this point in the nine mental abidings.[e]

The fourth mental abiding: Close setting

As Lati Rinpoche explains, "the fourth mental abiding is called close setting because the meditator has become more familiar with the

---

[a] *Meditative States*, p. 68.

[b] Gedün Lodrö, p. 165.

[c] *Meditative States*, p. 68; Gedün Lodrö, p. 169.

[d] *Meditative States*, p. 69.

[e] Gedün Lodrö, p.170.

object [of observation]—closer to it and better able to set the mind on it continuously."[a] The main feature of the fourth mental abiding is that the meditator does not lose the object of observation at all during the fourth and subsequent mental abidings. Thus, the meditator no longer has coarse excitement or the coarser form of coarse laxity. There is still subtle excitement, however, and since, for the first time, the mind is strongly withdrawn inside, there is danger of laxity.[b] The fourth mental abiding is characterized by very strong mindfulness; the power of mindfulness has now matured.[c]

The fifth mental abiding: Disciplining

The most obvious feature of the fifth mental abiding is the great danger of subtle laxity. This danger occurs because the mind was strongly withdrawn during the fourth mental abiding and because one of the causes of laxity is excessive withdrawal of the mind. Therefore, it is necessary to apply the antidotes to laxity to heighten and revivify the mind. Through doing so, the meditator overcomes dislike for meditative stabilization and experiences its good qualities. Because the mind thereby becomes disciplined, the fifth mental abiding is called disciplining. At this point, through the meditator's earlier exercise of introspection, the **power of introspection** is generated.[d] The meditator passes from the fifth mental abiding to the sixth in the same session.[e]

The sixth mental abiding: Pacifying

The sixth mental abiding is called pacifying because all dislike for meditative stabilization has been overcome, so that the mind is pacified. During the sixth mental abiding, there is strong danger of subtle excitement because the meditator has overcorrected the subtle laxity of the fifth and, thereby, excessively heightened and revivified the mind. Indeed, according to Lati Rinpoche, this danger of subtle excitement marks the passage from the fifth mental abiding to the sixth. In the sixth mental abiding, however, the power of introspection is fully developed; thus, the meditator can easily inspect for laxity and

---

[a] *Meditative States*, p. 69.

[b] *Meditative States*, p. 69; Gedün Lodrö p. 174.

[c] *Meditative States*, p. 69; Gedün Lodrö p. 174.

[d] *Meditative States*, p. 69; Gedün Lodrö p. 180.

[e] Gedün Lodrö, p. 181.

excitement.[a]

The seventh mental abiding: Thorough pacifying

According to Lati Rinpoche, the seventh mental abiding is called thorough pacifying because the meditator's progress in cultivating calm abiding has begun to affect the time outside the meditation session; even though desire and secondary afflictive emotions still arise between sessions, the practitioner can apply an antidote to any afflictive emotion that arises or suppress it simply by not getting involved with it. Thus, the mind is more deeply pacified than it had been during the sixth mental abiding, which was called pacifying.[b]

In the seventh mental abiding, the meditator has generated the **power of effort.** According to Gedün Lodrö, effort included within the power of effort has six qualities that "are not qualities of effort in general but must be present in the power of effort discussed here":

1 intense application (*gus sbyor*)—that is, "a sense of intentness with regard to the qualities of meditative stabilization"
2 continuous application (*rtag sbyor*)—"that one continuously applies oneself to the task of cultivating meditative stabilization; one does not just do it sometimes"
3 causally concordant application (*rgyu mthun pa'i sbyor ba*)—"a single continuum of effort"; namely, that the meditator's progress, from the beginning of the task, "flows from the same stream of effort"
4 effort arising from application (*sbyor ba las byung ba'i brtson grus*)—"effort generated from application in this lifetime," not in past lifetimes[c]
5 undisturbed effort (*mi 'thugs pa'i brtson grus*)—"that effort which is not disturbed by hardships such as heat"
6 insatiable effort (*chog ma shes pa'i brtson grus*)—"that effort which is motivated by one's not being satisfied with what has been accomplished up to now."[d]

In the seventh mental abiding, there is very little danger that laxity and excitement will arise; if they do, they are easily suppressed.[e] Lati Rinpoche compares them to an enemy that has been weakened; a

---

a *Meditative States,* p. 70; Gedün Lodrö, p. 180.

b *Meditative States,* p. 71.

c Gedün Lodrö, p. 189.

d Ibid., p. 189.

e Gedün Lodrö, p. 188; *Meditative States,* p. 71.

general would have to maintain his defenses and send out spies against a weakened enemy but would not have to fight. Similarly, the meditator still has to use introspection but can stop subtle laxity or subtle excitement simply and directly, without using the antidotes applied earlier.[a]

Although the fault of laziness can arise through the sixth mental abiding, scholars disagree concerning the possibility of its arising during the seventh. Gedün Lodrö points out that "There is no clear explanation of the boundary."[b] Lati Rinpoche is of the opinion that it can probably still occur;[c] his reason may be that in the seventh mental abiding the faults of laxity and excitement are still present, however minimally. According to Gedün Lodrö, however, laziness cannot arise during the seventh mental abiding because the meditator has "fulfilled the powers of mindfulness and introspection" and has also generated the power of effort, which is incompatible with laziness. Gedün Lodrö notes also that "if one were to generate laziness, this would mean that one could not notice it with mindfulness."[d]

The eighth mental abiding: Making one-pointed

According to Lati Rinpoche, "the difference between the seventh and eighth mental abidings is that between the presence and absence of laxity and excitement." During the eighth mental abiding, the meditator has to rely on only a little effort at introspection at the beginning of the session; thereafter, laxity and excitement do not arise and the meditator remains one-pointedly on the object of observation. Therefore, the eighth mental abiding is called making one-pointed.[e]

In the eighth mental abiding, the power of effort is fulfilled.[f] According to Lati Rinpoche, it is at this point that the fault of overapplication can arise[g]—presumably because the meditator does not yet recognize that, after the initial application of effort, laxity and excitement no longer arise. The antidote is desisting from application.[h] According to Gedün Lodrö, the meditator passes from the eighth to the ninth mental

---

[a] *Meditative States*, p. 71.
[b] Gedün Lodrö, p. 189.
[c] *Meditative States*, p. 71.
[d] Gedün Lodrö, p. 189.
[e] *Meditative States*, pp. 71–72.
[f] Ibid., p. 72; Gedün Lodrö, p. 190.
[g] *Meditative States*, p. 72.
[h] Ibid., p. 72.

abiding in one session.

The ninth mental abiding: Setting in equipoise

The ninth mental abiding is the highest mind of the Desire Realm[a] and is very much like calm abiding. It has stability, clarity, and spontaneity; the meditation flows naturally.[b] The meditator has achieved the **power of familiarity.**[c] Laxity and excitement are not present; the meditator has no need to apply antidotes and refrains from applying them unnecessarily. Thus, according to Gedün Lodrö,

> Desisting from application [the antidote to overapplication] is equivalent with the ninth mental abiding. It is through the functioning of such desisting that one is spontaneously able to maintain the continuum of meditative stabilization in the ninth mental abiding.[d]

As Gedün Lodrö notes,

> Persons who have attained the meditative stabilization of the ninth mind of the Desire Realm (*'dod sems dgu pa'i ting nge 'dzin*)—that is, the ninth mental abiding—know from their own experience that they will be attaining calm abiding.[e]

However, the ninth mental abiding is not calm abiding itself because it does not have special pliancy, which is attained *after* the ninth mental abiding.

The Attainment of Calm Abiding

The special pliancy that accompanies calm abiding must be distinguished from mere pliancy. As Denma Lochö Rinpoche points out, there is a mental factor of mere pliancy that "is included among the eleven

---

[a] Although the terms "ninth mind of the Desire Realm" and "ninth mental abiding of the Desire Realm" do not occur in discussions of the nine mental abidings, they are implied by the assertion that calm abiding is the lowest mind of the Form Realm and are used explicitly in discussions of the preparations for the first concentration. Jam-yang-shay-pa, for example, gives "the ninth mental abiding of the Desire Realm" as an illustration of a mental contemplation of a beginner at mental contemplation. (Jam-yang-shay-pa, *Concentrations,* 227.1–2.)

[b] *Meditative States,* p. 72; Gedün Lodrö, p. 190; Jam-yang-shay-pa, *Concentrations,* 154.1–2.

[c] *Meditative States,* p. 72; Gedün Lodrö, p. 190.

[d] Gedün Lodrö, p. 190.

[e] Ibid., p. 209.

virtuous mental factors" and "accompanies all virtuous minds." This mental factor of mere pliancy "is that which provides a serviceability such that the mind can be directed to a virtuous object; it is merely that." The special pliancy that is attained with calm abiding is far greater in scope. It is "a case of serviceability such that the mind can be directed to *any* virtuous object *as much as one likes*."[a]

The four key terms that occur in discussions of pliancy are: mental pliancy, physical pliancy, the bliss of physical pliancy, and the bliss of mental pliancy.[b] The discussion that follows is based mainly on Gedün Lodrö's presentation, which reflects not only his college's textbook but, more unusually, his own interpretation of Asaṅga's *Grounds of Hearers.*

STAGES IN THE DEVELOPMENT OF SPECIAL PLIANCY

As is the case with the meditator's mode of progress in overcoming the five faults by way of the eight antidotes, the development of special pliancy involves finding equilibrium through the correction of excess. Thus, special pliancy is developed in stages, with mental pliancy, physical pliancy, the bliss of physical pliancy, and the bliss of mental pliancy occurring in that order. The development of mental pliancy is preceded by what Gedün Lodrö calls the omen of pliancy (*shin sbyangs skye ba'i snga bltas*).[c] The meditator easily recognizes this omen, a "sense that the brain is heavy in comparison to the body," as an indication that he or she is about to attain mental pliancy.[d]

According to Gedün Lodrö, Jam-yang-shay-pa, and the Fifth Dalai Lama's stages-of-the-path text, the *Sacred Word of Mañjushrī*,[e] the ninth mental abiding is accompanied by a subtle, or non-manifest, pliancy that is a precursor to the special pliancy that accompanies calm abiding. Gedün Lodrö identifies this subtle pliancy as one of two that are mentioned in Asaṅga's *Grounds of Hearers* and cited but not explained in Tibetan commentaries. The two are (1) the pliancy difficult to analyze (*brtags par dka' ba'i shin sbyangs*), or subtle pliancy (*phra ba'i shin sbyangs*), and (2) the pliancy easy to analyze (*brtags par sla ba'i shin sbyangs*), or coarse pliancy (*rags pa'i shin sbyangs*)—which are listed in the order of generation. According to Gedün Lodrö,

---

[a] Denma Lochö Rinpoche in *Meditative States*, p. 174; italics added.

[b] *Meditative States*, p. 73; Gedün Lodrö, p. 209.

[c] Gedün Lodrö, p. 218.

[d] Ibid., p. 209.

[e] Gedün Lodrö, pp. 215–18; Jam-yang-shay-pa, *Concentrations*, 157.2; Fifth Dalai Lama, *Sacred Word of Mañjushrī*, 180.3-4.

> "Subtle pliancy" refers to a non-manifest, or non-obvious, generation of mental and physical pliancy in yogic practitioners who have the ninth mental abiding at the time when they again enter into meditative stabilization. They are not able to identify the presence of that pliancy, but it is present.[a]

Gedün Lodrö notes that, when a meditator who has attained the ninth mental abiding again enters into meditative stabilization, subtle pliancy and meditative stabilization mutually assist each other until "in the manner of a substantial cause (*nyer len, upādāna*),[b] the subtle pliancy induces the pliancy easy to analyze—that is, the coarse pliancy....[T]he cooperative condition is the meditative stabilization of the ninth mind of the Desire Realm." At this point, "the omen of pliancy appears,"[c] and the meditator experiences the stages of generation of the pliancies discussed below (pages 167–171).

Jam-yang-shay-pa cites virtually without comment, apparently as a definitive account, the Fifth Dalai Lama's summary of the stages between the end of the ninth mental abiding and the attainment of calm abiding:

> From the increase higher of that subtle factor of pliancy, finally, having pacified assumptions of bad states unsuitable for exercising whatever virtue one wishes—[that is, states] in the class of afflictive emotions—one generates mental pliancy. By the force of that, a wind of serviceability moves in the body, whereby, having separated from assumptions of bad physical states, one generates a [physical] pliancy in which the body is light as wool. In dependence upon that, one generates a great sense of physical bliss. By the force of that, one generates a bliss of mental pliancy which is a feeling of mental bliss. Moreover, when a feverish mental joy arises upon just having generated physical pliancy, one has not attained calm abiding [even] slightly, but, when that joy has abated a little, one attains an immovable pliancy, concordant with meditative stabilization, in which the mind remains vividly on the object of observation and, simultaneously, one achieves calm abiding.[d]

---

[a] Gedün Lodrö, p. 214.

[b] Gedün Lodrö notes (p. 215) that Asaṅga's "text says only *len pa'i tshul gyis,* but this means *nyer len pa'i tshul gyis.*"

[c] Ibid., p. 215.

[d] Jam-yang-shay-pa, *Concentrations,* 157.2–5. Fifth Dalai Lama, *Sacred Word of Mañjushrī* (*'jam pa'i dbyangs kyi zhal lung*), 180.5–181.3.

According to Gedün Lodrö, the stages of generation of the pliancies are followed by stages in which some of those pliancies, or their coarser forms, cease. He notes that "this is very important and is often not explained in the texts."[a] The explanation appears to be largely his; although the stages of cessation of the pliancies can be inferred from Jam-yang-shay-pa's citation of the Fifth Dalai Lama's discussion of the pliancies, neither the Fifth Dalai Lama nor Jam-yang-shay-pa spells them out explicitly. The following discussion explains the stages of generation and cessation of the pliancies.[b]

(a) **The omen of pliancy.** According to Gedün Lodrö, the stages of generation are preceded by the omen of pliancy mentioned above (page 166)—the "sense that the brain is heavy in comparison to the body."[c]

(1) **Mental pliancy.** Gedün Lodrö describes mental pliancy as "a factor of lightness" that "joyfully and happily engages its object of observation unimpededly" and removes bad mental states (technically, assumptions of bad mental states [*sems kyi gnas ngan len*]), which "are factors that interrupt unimpeded setting [of the mind] on the object of observation, as well as those that interrupt the abandonment of afflictive emotions." Bad mental states are consciousnesses; mental pliancy is a mental factor.[d]

(2) **Physical pliancy.** The attainment of mental pliancy causes a wind of physical pliancy to pervade the meditator's body; this wind of physical pliancy overcomes bad physical states, which Gedün Lodrö explains as "factor[s] of heaviness that [bring] about bodily fatigue." The meditator then attains physical pliancy. Physical pliancy "removes physical tiredness" and enables the body to "be used for whatever virtuous purpose one wishes, without any sense of hardship"; the meditator's body feels "light, like cotton."[e]

Denma Lochö Rinpoche gives a similar summary of the movements of winds that bring about physical pliancy; he also adds, in this context, an important warning for the practitioner:

> In brief, when the meditation is going well, the unfavorable winds no longer move and the favorable

[a] Gedün Lodrö, p. 200.

[b] The main headings of the list are adapted from Gedün Lodrö, p. 209.

[c] Ibid., p. 209.

[d] Ibid., pp. 201, 203, 204.

[e] Gedün Lodrö, p. 205; Lati Rinpoche in *Meditative States*, p. 73.

ones do.

However, if the mode of meditation is not correct and if one forces the meditation, it is possible to create great discomfort in body and mind and to cause a disease called the life-wind disease. This type of fault occurs when we actually do not have stability but think that we have it and when we actually have not overcome laxity and excitement but think that we have and then [as a result of these wrong discriminations] force the meditation. Therefore, it is extremely important to eliminate laxity and excitement.[a]

Gedün Lodrö notes that physical pliancy is "a special tangible object." Thus, it is a form; both "bad physical states and physical pliancy are forms." However, he explains further that physical pliancy "is not an ordinary form but a form generated by meditative stabilization; it is a special touch generated by meditative stabilization."[b]

(3) **The bliss of physical pliancy and (4) the bliss of mental pliancy.** Physical pliancy is followed by the bliss of physical pliancy; because of the connection between mind and body,[c] this is followed immediately by the bliss of mental pliancy. According to Gedün Lodrö, both are feelings.[d] Gedün Lodrö notes that

> The bliss of physical pliancy occurs when the mental factors of feeling that accompany sense consciousnesses are blissful. The blisses of mental pliancy are the mental factors of blissful feelings associated with mental consciousnesses.[e]

Both are special—not ordinary—feelings, since they are induced not by such causes as heat and cold, like "ordinary pleasures," but "by the force of the generation of mental and physical pliancy."[f]

---

[a] Denma Lochö Rinpoche in *Meditative States,* p. 175.

[b] Gedün Lodrö, pp. 204, 205; see also Lati Rinpoche in *Meditative States,* p. 73.

[c] Gedün Lodrö, p. 210.

[d] Ibid., p. 208. Lati Rinpoche, however, explains the bliss of physical pliancy as "a very blissful object of touch." (*Meditative States,* p. 73)

[e] Gedün Lodrö, p. 206. Gedün Lodrö notes further that the upper and lower schools of tenets explain the bliss of physical pliancy differently: "According to the upper schools of tenets [Chittamātra and Madhyamaka], a bliss of physical pliancy is solely a blissful feeling that accompanies the body consciousness," whereas, according to Vasubandhu's *Treasury of Manifest Knowledge*, "blissful feelings that are blisses of physical pliancy" can accompany all the sense consciousnesses (ibid., p. 206).

[f] Ibid., p. 208.

According to Lati Rinpoche, the bliss of mental pliancy is marked by "a sense that the body has melted into the object of observation"; the meditator has "no sense of other objects." Moreover, "[t]he mind is very joyous, almost as though it can no longer stay on the object of observation"; Lati Rinpoche describes this state as one of "almost feverish joy."[a] It is a state of excessive joy that must be moderated before the meditator can attain calm abiding.

(5) **Cessation of coarse physical pliancy and (6) cessation of the blisses of physical and mental pliancy and (7) attainment of calm abiding.** Lati Rinpoche does not mention stages of cessation, but they are implied in his mention of the diminution of feverish joy. Coarse physical pliancy, the bliss of physical pliancy, and the coarseness of the bliss of mental pliancy cease, in that order. Mental pliancy, a subtle physical pliancy, and a subtle bliss of mental pliancy do not cease; these constitute the special pliancy that is attained with calm abiding. The meditator's initial generation of mental pliancy, which does *not* cease, becomes, as Lati Rinpoche says, "an "immovable mental pliancy" that "accords with meditative stabilization and involves complete stability with respect to the object [of observation]. At that point, the meditator has attained calm abiding."[b]

Chart 5: Stages of the Generation and Cessation of the Pliancies

	Stages of Generation
1	mental pliancy
2	physical pliancy
3	bliss of physical pliancy
4	bliss of mental pliancy
	Stages of Cessation
5	coarse physical pliancy
6	bliss of physical pliancy*
7	coarseness of the bliss of mental pliancy
8	*Calm Abiding*

* When coarse physical pliancy ceases, then the bliss of physical pliancy, which is caused by it, must also cease.

[a] *Meditative States*, pp. 73–74.

[b] Ibid., p. 74.

Chart 6: Stages of the Generation and Cessation of the Pliancies
(rearranged to show correspondence)

Stages of Generation	*Stages of Cessation*
1 mental pliancy	
2 physical pliancy	5 coarse physical pliancy
3 bliss of physical pliancy	6 bliss of physical pliancy*
4 bliss of mental pliancy	7 coarseness of the bliss of mental pliancy
8 Calm Abiding	

* When coarse physical pliancy ceases, then the bliss of physical pliancy, which is caused by it, must also cease.

SIGNS OF CALM ABIDING

With calm abiding, the meditator acquires qualities known as the signs of having attained calm abiding. According to Lati Rinpoche's summary:

> The attainment of pliancy is one of them. Another is that, during [meditative] equipoise, there is a sense of appearances vanishing and of the mind fusing with space itself. The mind is like a mountain, able to abide firmly and steadily on its object [of observation]. A sound produced near such a meditator, whether of a train going by or of a cannon, would not affect him or her at all. The meditator has great clarity and feels as though he or she could count the particles in a wall. Further, having risen from meditative stabilization, the meditator retains some portion of pliancy, or mental and physical serviceability. Pliancy and meditative stabilization enhance each other, so that sleep can be mixed with meditative stabilization. Upon rising from [meditative] equipoise, the meditator has a sense of achieving a new body. [Afflictive emotions] are generated to a lesser degree, are weaker, and disappear of their own accord. The meditator is free of the five obstructions (*sgrib pa, āvaraṇa*) we ordinarily have—aspiration to attributes of the Desire Realm (*'dod pa la 'dun pa, kāmacchanda*); harmfulness (*gnod sems, vyāpāda*); lethargy and sleep (*rmugs pa dang gnyid, styānamiddha*); excitement and contrition (*rgod pa dang 'gyod pa, auddhatyakaukṛtya*); and doubt (*the tshom, vicikitsā*).[a]

---

[a] Ibid., p. 74.

In his more detailed presentation, Gedün Lodrö analyzes the meaning of these and other signs of having attained calm abiding, which he gives as:

1 the increase of meditative stabilization due to pliancy
2 the vanishing of all coarse appearances
3 the stoppage of the sense consciousnesses
4 the stoppage of the manifest coarse afflictive emotions
5 the turning of sleep into meditative stabilization
6 the sense, on rising, of having adventitiously acquired a body
7 the dawning of many pure appearances[a]

1 **The increase of meditative stabilization due to pliancy.** As Lati Rinpoche points out, the achievement of pliancy is, in itself, a sign of the attainment of calm abiding.[b] The result of the attainment of pliancy, as Gedün Lodrö notes further, "is the increase of meditative stabilization, which is due to the fact that pliancy and meditative stabilization assist each other."[c]

2 **The vanishing of all coarse appearances.** Gedün Lodrö notes that, although source texts speak of the vanishing of coarse appearances, they "do not specify clearly just which coarse appearances have vanished."[d] Thus, it is necessary to decide through inference. Among the possibilities are coarse appearances to the sense consciousnesses and manifest coarse afflictive emotions. Both of these cease; they are discussed under separate headings below (see page 172). According to Gedün Lodrö, the coarse appearances referred to here are those of the coarser forms of the manifest operative consciousnesses (*'jug shes*)—so called "because they operate on the six types of object."[e]

"Coarse" is a relative term; consciousnesses are considered coarse in relation to others that are considered subtle, and the subtle ones are further subdivided. Gedün Lodrö admits that the word "coarse" is ambiguous; it can mean "manifest," or it can be used pejoratively. He uses it in the latter way when he says that stoppage of the coarse operative consciousnesses "occurs only through the attainment of the supramundane paths, and it occurs at the time of

---

a Gedün Lodrö, pp. 235–55.
b *Meditative States*, p. 74.
c Gedün Lodrö, p. 235.
d Ibid., p. 236.
e Ibid., p. 236.

an exalted wisdom of meditative equipoise (*mnyam bzhag ye shes, samāhitajñāna*);" he admits, however, that if one understands "coarse" to mean "manifest," one would have to consider the exalted wisdom of meditative equipoise—or the mind of calm abiding—as a coarse operative consciousness.[a]

Stoppage of the subtle operative consciousnesses occurs only in Highest Yoga Tantra.[b]

3 **The stoppage of the sense consciousnesses.** The placement of the tongue behind the teeth, as part of the meditation posture, is cited as evidence that the sense consciousnesses stop during calm abiding. This is done to prevent the excessive flow of saliva, which the meditator would not notice once calm abiding had been attained. The failure to notice the excessive flow of saliva during calm abiding establishes that the body consciousness has stopped.[c] From the stoppage of the body consciousness, the stoppage of the remaining sense consciousnesses is inferred.

The stoppage of the sense consciousnesses during calm abiding was mentioned earlier (see page 82) as the reason for using a mental object rather than a sense object as the object of observation for cultivating calm abiding. Obviously, a sense object could no longer be observed once the sense consciousnesses had stopped; therefore, the meditator trains from the beginning in the use of a mental object as the object of observation.

4 **The stoppage of the manifest coarse afflictive emotions.** For a meditator who has attained calm abiding, the manifest coarse afflictive emotions stop during the meditation session itself and also, as Gedün Lodrö notes, "in states subsequent to meditative equipoise, when the functioning of the meditative stabilization has ceased." The type of stoppage referred to here is a temporary suppression of afflictive emotions, not their abandonment from the root, which occurs only with the attainment of a supramundane path.[d]

5 **The turning of sleep into meditative stabilization.** For a meditator who has attained calm abiding, sleep can turn into meditative stabilization because both involve the withdrawal of the mind inside. Sleep involves the powerless withdrawal of the mind,[e] whereas the

---

a Ibid., pp. 244–45.

b Ibid., p. 245.

c Ibid., p. 237.

d Ibid., pp. 238–39.

e Hopkins gives the definition of sleep as "a powerless withdrawal inside of the en-

cultivation of meditative stabilization requires deliberate, controlled withdrawal of the mind. According to Gedün Lodrö, "A person who has attained calm abiding is so familiar with meditative stabilization that when he or she withdraws the mind inside, his or her sleep becomes of the entity of meditative stabilization."[a]

This does not mean, however, that sleep becomes calm abiding. Gedün Lodrö explains that the sleep of a person who has attained calm abiding is a meditative stabilization but not a calm abiding; calm abiding is a state arisen from meditation, whereas, as Gedün Lodrö remarks, "One does not meditatively cultivate sleep."[b] Moreover, as a changeable mental factor,[c] sleep can be virtuous, nonvirtuous, or ethically neutral, depending upon a person's motivation before going to sleep. A person who has attained calm abiding has a virtuous motivation—namely, a state arisen from meditation. This virtuous motivation is so strong that, according to Gedün Lodrö, "it affects any type of behavior. Thus, whenever [a person who has attained calm abiding] withdraws the mind, his or her mind becomes of an entity of meditative stabilization."[d] However, this entity of meditative stabilization (*ting nge 'dzin, samādhi*) "is just the stabilization (*ting nge 'dzin, samādhi*) factor that accompanies a virtuous mind and is not a state arisen from meditation."[e] Therefore, it cannot be a calm abiding. Nevertheless, because the virtuous mind in question is that of a person who has attained calm abiding, the stabilization factor that accompanies that mind, even in sleep, is a *meditative* stabilization. Thus, his or her sleep turns into meditative stabilization.

6 **The sense, on rising, of having adventitiously acquired a body.** Upon rising from meditative equipoise, a meditator feels as though he or she has acquired a new gross body that is not continuous with the old one. This is a sense of discomfort; the "new" body feels awkward and unwieldy, as one might feel just after getting out of a swimming pool. According to Gedün Lodrö, the meditator's sense of having acquired a new body is not explained in any Indian or Tibetan commentary; he suggests that it happens for the same reasons,

---

gagement by sense consciousnesses in objects." Hopkins, *Meditation on Emptiness,* p. 266.

[a] Gedün Lodrö, p. 248.

[b] Ibid., p. 249.

[c] Hopkins, *Meditation on Emptiness,* p. 266.

[d] Gedün Lodrö, p. 248.

[e] Ibid., p. 249.

and in the same manner, that sleep turns into meditative stabilization.

When sleep turns into meditative stabilization, the only manifest consciousness is that of sleep, but the person experiences unimpededness.

> When one awakens, the sense consciousnesses become manifest, at which time the places where the sense consciousnesses reside also become manifest. The person then has a sense of acquiring a new body and feels that it is not just the body that he or she had formerly. This happens because, when the mind becomes of the entity of meditative stabilization in sleep, it is as though the body has ceased or has become of the entity of consciousness.[a]

Similarly, in the meditation session, a person who has attained pliancy experiences unimpededness; it is said that such a person can walk through walls.

> While that person is moving about unimpededly, the body is unimpeded, just as the mind is. To that person's sense of appearance, no gross body appears.[b]

When the meditator returns to a more ordinary type of consciousness, the sense consciousnesses reappear, and the person experiences impededness, with all its discomforts. Because of the freedom experienced during the unimpeded state, the return of the sense consciousnesses and of impededness is experienced not as the return of something familiar that existed earlier, before the meditation session, but as the acquisition of a new gross body.

7 **The dawning of many pure appearances.** As Gedün Lodrö points out, it is necessary to analyze the types of pure appearance to determine which are signs of calm abiding. He distinguishes among three types:[c]

> 1 The occurrence of unusual appearances "through the force of winds' entering into channels in which they usually do not course." These appearances are of various sorts, good and bad; some of them occur as hallucinations. Although

---

[a] Ibid., p. 251.

[b] Ibid., p. 251.

[c] Ibid., pp. 252–53.

some appearances of this type can be pure, people who experience them need not have cultivated calm abiding. They are not the type identified as a sign of calm abiding.[a]

2 The dawning to the mind of meditative visions (*bsgoms pa'i nyams yid la 'char ba*). This is the type of vision that appears to a person who has attained calm abiding; according to Gedün Lodrö, "such an appearance would be due to the force of [the meditator]'s familiarity with meditative stabilization" but can occur either during the session or outside it. Gedün Lodrö gives as an example the spontaneous appearance of a Buddha field to a person who has attained calm abiding. He describes these visions as "innate and like our usual appearances." Nevertheless, "they would start to disappear upon analysis, whereas, without too much attention, they are very clear."[b]

Such visions can also appear in a weaker form to people who have not attained calm abiding. If the person has been cultivating calm abiding in this lifetime, the visions are due to that cultivation; if the person has not been cultivating calm abiding in this lifetime, they are due to cultivation in a former lifetime.

3 The perception of pure appearances by a sense consciousness. This is often referred to as "seeing the face of a deity," but the phrase means that the practitioner sees the deity, not just the face. An example of this type would be the practitioner's directly seeing the goddess Sarasvatī. According to Gedün Lodrö, this type of vision "is probably stronger than the other two" and can be analyzed.[c]

Gedün Lodrö also mentions extraordinary capacities said to be possessed by meditators who have attained calm abiding. These include "a special type of body" and "special abilities such as the capacity to fly" and to "pass unimpededly through a wall."[d] The meditator develops these capacities through the force of having cultivated meditative stabilization—in particular, through having acquired physical pliancy. Gedün Lodrö explains that the meditator's body is initially obstructive and, through the attainment of calm abiding, becomes unimpeded:

---

[a] Ibid., p. 252.

[b] Ibid., pp. 252–53.

[c] Ibid., p. 253.

[d] Ibid., pp. 227, 235.

> Through the power of having cultivated meditative stabilization, the practitioner has made a form that is equal to the space of, and occupies the same area as, his or her obstructive body....The form generated by meditative stabilization is also called a mental body (*yid lus*)....It is not a body that has external matter as its basis of formation; rather, it is a form generated by internal meditative stabilization. Thus, there is no reason for it to be obstructed or impeded. Moreover, once it is generated by meditative stabilization, it must be like a consciousness. It pervades and is equal with the body, its entity being undifferentiable from the body's own.[a]

Because the meditator's extraordinary capacities occur through the power of meditative stabilization, there is no need for concern that passing through a wall, for instance, would cause his or her clothes to be left behind, or "that the yogic practitioner's brain would remain on the other side of the wall as, indeed, pliancy is not generated in the brain." Gedün Lodrö explains that "because [the body of a meditator who has attained calm abiding] is a form generated by meditative stabilization there must not be any such fault."[b]

STATES ATTAINED SIMULTANEOUSLY WITH CALM ABIDING

A meditator who attains calm abiding simultaneously attains several states that are mutually inclusive with it. They are:

1 **A mind included within the Form Realm.** It is important to distinguish between a mind of the Form Realm and a Form Realm rebirth. Although the *mind* of calm abiding is included within the Form Realm, calm abiding is not a Form Realm rebirth state and cannot cause rebirth in the Form Realm; a human or Desire Realm god who attains calm abiding will not be reborn there. The lowest rebirth state in the Form Realm is the First Concentration, and only the attainment of an actual first concentration will cause rebirth there.

2 **The mental contemplation of a mere beginner** (*las dang po pa tsam gyi yid byed*)—the first of the seven preparations for the first concentration.

3 The preparation known as **the not-unable** (*mi lcog med, anāgamya*), so called because it is able to "serve as the mental basis for path

---

[a] Ibid., p. 227.

[b] Ibid., pp. 232, 228.

consciousnesses that are the antidotes to all afflictions of the three realms."[a]

These three states point toward meditative attainments that come after calm abiding. Despite the fact that practitioners can attain it only after passing through the nine mental abidings and the stages of generation and cessation of the pliancies, and despite the extraordinary qualities associated with it, calm abiding is seen, finally, not as an end in itself but as the lowest of the states that follow it.

After the attainment of calm abiding, a meditator who wishes to progress further must develop the capacity to analyze on the basis of calm abiding. In order to do so, he or she undergoes a period of preparatory training (*ngon 'gro'i sbyor ba*) to strengthen and consolidate the calm abiding already attained, since it is still new and easily disturbed. As Gedün Lodrö points out, it "must be developed to such a degree that it cannot be ruined by analysis (*dpyod pa, vicāra*). Not only that; it must be able to advance as the analysis advances."[b] When the meditator has developed this capacity, he or she is ready to begin cultivation of either a mundane or a supramundane path.

Issues Raised by Ge-luk Presentations of Calm Abiding

Ge-luk presentations of calm abiding strongly emphasize the importance of pliancy and intensity of clarity as distinguishing features of calm abiding. From Kön-chok-jik-may-wang-po's definition of calm abiding as "a meditative stabilization, arisen from meditation, which is conjoined with special pliancy," and from Jam-yang-shay-pa's gloss of "special" as "completely qualified,"[c] it is apparent that, according to their system, the presence or absence of pliancy serves as a criterion to distinguish between calm abiding and other, similar, states—especially, the ninth mental abiding; despite Kön-chok-jik-may-wang-po's glowing definition of the latter as "the ninth meditative stabilization, which is the self-flowing dawning of meditative stabilization without reliance on striving and exertion,"[d] it is not considered to be calm abiding

[a] Hopkins, *Meditation on Emptiness*, p. 87. For discussions of these three states, see also *Meditative States*, pp. 74, 93, 152; Gedün Lodrö, pp. 212, 308, 377.

[b] Gedün Lodrö, p. 278. For a discussion of the four aspects of preparatory training, see pages 183ff. and Gedün Lodrö, pp. 273–83.

[c] Kön-chok-jik-may-wang-po, *Condensed Statement*, 557.3; Jam-yang-shay-pa, *Concentrations*, 110.6. For a discussion of this definition, see page 63, above.

[d] Kön-chok-jik-may-wang-po, *Condensed Statement*, 562.6. Jam-yang-shay-pa's fuller definition of the ninth mental abiding as

because it does not have special pliancy.

The issue of intensity of clarity is raised in an important debate in which Jam-yang-shay-pa and Kön-chok-jik-may-wang-po refute definitions of calm abiding and special insight that turn on this point. The opponent's position is that

> the non-existence of intensity in the factor of clarity in a non-scattering mind is calm abiding, and the existence of that [intensity in the factor of clarity in a non-scattering mind] is special insight.[a]

Although Kön-chok-jik-may-wang-po identifies the opponent merely in the usual minimal way as "someone" (*kha cig*), Jam-yang-shay-pa's version of the debate identifies this position as that "of many Tibetans."

To refute this position, Kön-chok-jik-may-wang-po cites a sūtra source. The type of citation, in itself, suggests that the opponent is not a Ge-luk-pa, since, according to Gedün Lodrö, a debater is allowed to cite only texts accepted by both parties. Thus, if the opponent is not a Ge-luk-pa, Kön-chok-jik-may-wang-po cannot cite Tsong-kha-pa or other Ge-luk-pa writers. It would also be correct for him to cite Indian commentaries,[b] and Jam-yang-shay-pa, in his more extensive version of this debate, cites passages from Maitreya's *Ornament for the Mahāyāna Sūtras,* Asaṅga's *Grounds of Bodhisattvas,* and Kamalashīla's *Middling Stages of Meditation.*[c]

The scriptural passage cited by both Jam-yang-shay-pa and Kön-chok-jik-may-wang-po is from the *Cloud of Jewels Sūtra* (*ratnamegha, dkon mchog sprin gyi mdo*): "Calm abiding is a one-pointed mind. Special insight is correct individual analysis."[d] Thus, in its discussion of the definition of special insight, this debate also touches on the question of the role of analysis. Nevertheless, the role of analysis is not the main issue

---

> the ninth meditative stabilization, in which, through familiarization with that meditative stabilization no matter what circumstance arises, meditative stabilization dawns of its own accord without dependence on the striving and exertion of being mindful of antidotes and hence does not involve the workings of conceptuality (Jam-yang-shay-pa, *Concentrations,* 154.2–3)

is more consistent with the technical terms used in his previous definitions of the first eight mental abidings.

[a] Kön-chok-jik-may-wang-po, *Condensed Statement*, 548.5.

[b] Gedün Lodrö, pp. 385–86.

[c] Jam-yang-shay-pa, *Concentrations,* 50.4–51.2.

[d] Kön-chok-jik-may-wang-po, *Condensed Statement,* 548.6; Jam-yang-shay-pa, *Concentrations,* 50.1.

in that part of the debate which concerns calm abiding. Thus, Kön-chok-jik-may-wang-po's version of the debate returns to the discussion of calm abiding and concludes with the Ge-luk position that

> all meditative stabilizations that are free of laxity and excitement necessarily have both abiding in a one-pointed mind and intensity of clarity. This is because all meditative stabilizations that are free of laxity have intensity of clarity and all meditative stabilizations that are free of excitement have the factor of stability.[a]

The next debate refutes a definition of calm abiding as "a steady meditative stabilization in which the prominence of laxity and excitement has been broken and the mind is one-pointed."[b] For, a meditative stabilization free of laxity and excitement is not calm abiding because it lacks special pliancy; it is only a meditative stabilization of the ninth mental abiding that precedes the attainment of calm abiding. Although Kön-chok-jik-may-wang-po's citation from Tsong-kha-pa suggests that the specific opponent here is a Ge-luk-pa, this debate follows from and clarifies the preceding one.

Although the question of the role of analysis in meditation, especially in meditation on emptiness, would seem to concern mainly the cultivation of special insight, it is relevant to the cultivation of calm abiding as well. As was mentioned earlier (page 82), Kön-chok-jik-may-wang-po and Jam-yang-shay-pa emphasize that "meditation on emptiness is not the same as withdrawing from conceptuality."[c] Jam-yang-shay-pa's extensive debate on the question refutes increasingly refined versions of the position that not applying the mind to anything is meditation on emptiness and that the achievement of such a state "is the measure of having achieved special insight realizing selflessness," a position Jam-yang-shay-pa equates with that attributed to the Chinese representative at the Council of Lhasa.[d] In his condensation of Jam-yang-shay-pa's text, Kön-chok-jik-may-wang-po includes the final argument of this debate. The opponent has already admitted that reasoning does have a place in meditation on emptiness; the problem is to

---

[a] Kön-chok-jik-may-wang-po, *Condensed Statement,* 549.2–3.

[b] Ibid., 549.3.

[c] *Meditation on Emptiness,* p. 552; Hopkins' translation of Jam-yang-shay-pa's debate, pp. 553–58 (Jam-yang-shay-pa, *Concentrations,* 66.4–70.2; abridged by Kön-chok-jik-may-wang-po, *Condensed Statement,* 551.4–552.1).

[d] *Meditation on Emptiness,* pp. 553, 555. Jam-yang-shay-pa, *Concentrations,* 68.1. For the Council of Lhasa, see page 22, above.

determine what that place is. The debate establishes as the author's own system the position that, once the view of emptiness has been established by reasoning,

> setting [the mind] non-analytically...is the mode of cultivating the calm abiding and meditative stabilization realizing emptiness. This is because it is stabilizing meditation realizing emptiness,

whereas the opponent had thought it was special insight realizing emptiness. Similarly, the debate establishes that

> analytical meditation realizing emptiness is the cultivation of wisdom [realizing emptiness] and the cultivation of special insight [realizing emptiness].[a]

Although it is not clear that the opponent here is a Nying-ma-pa, Hopkins remarks that these debates contain the germ of the Ge-luk deprecation of the Nying-ma position on the view of emptiness, and of the Nying-ma Great Completeness as a weak form of special insight.[b]

The Fourteenth Dalai Lama, observing that both traditions have produced equally great practitioners, tries to reconcile the two positions in his "Union of the Old and New Translation Schools." In effect, he bypasses the debates found in Jam-yang-shay-pa's and Kön-chok-jik-may-wang-po's texts, which take place in a sūtra-system context, by placing the Great Completeness in the context of Highest Yoga Tantra and comparing it, not with Ge-luk sūtra-system presentations of calm abiding and special insight and of the view of emptiness, but with Ge-luk presentations of Highest Yoga Tantra.[c] The present Dalai Lama's mode of procedure may be considered an extension to methodology of the principle, mentioned earlier, that a debater may cite only texts accepted by both parties. For a Ge-luk-pa to apply a sūtra-system critique to a Nying-ma discussion of calm abiding might be said to contradict that principle, since, as David Germano points out, Ge-luk-pas, in their textbooks, maintain a clear distinction between sūtra and tantra,

---

[a] Kön-chok-jik-may-wang-po, *Condensed Statement,* 551.6; Jam-yang-shay-pa, *Concentrations,* 69.7–70.2; see *Meditation on Emptiness,* p. 557.

[b] Jeffrey Hopkins in conversation. (It is possible that these debates may also be directed against the Ka-gyu Mahāmudrā [*phyag rgya chen po*], discussion of which is beyond the scope of this work.)

[c] The Fourteenth Dalai Lama Tenzin Gyatso, "Union of the Old and New Translation Schools," in *Kindness, Clarity, and Insight,* trans. and ed. by Jeffrey Hopkins (Ithaca, NY: Snow Lion Publications, 1984), pp. 200–224.

whereas Long-chen-pa and his followers, in *their* scholastic works, tend to "eliminate the boundary between" them. Moreover, according to Germano, although Nying-ma scholastic texts frequently use the terms "calm abiding" and "special insight," they do not present the cultivation and attainment of calm abiding using classic sūtra-system categories such as the nine mental abidings, the five faults and the eight antidotes, and so forth. Germano also points out that Nying-ma texts use the term "calm abiding" in both a positive and a negative sense—in a positive sense as a quiet, stable state to be attained and in a negative sense as a passive state to be transcended; at its worst, it seems to be similar to what Ge-luk-pas call subtle laxity [a] It is not impossible that, for the sake of polemic, a passage using the term "calm abiding" in a pejorative sense was quoted or summarized out of context and then refuted as though it described its author's understanding of calm abiding in a positive sense. Full discussion of the polemic from both sides is beyond the scope of this study. The polemic is important here mainly for its indication of the Ge-luk-pa emphasis on the importance of pliancy and intensity of clarity as the features that distinguish their interpretation of calm abiding from those of other traditions of Tibetan Buddhism.

---

[a] David Germano in conversation, May 1993.

8 THE PREPARATIONS FOR THE CONCENTRATIONS AND FORMLESS ABSORPTIONS

After the attainment of calm abiding, the meditator does not proceed immediately to the cultivation of special insight and/or the second preparation for the first concentration—that is, the mental contemplation of individual knowledge of the character. Such cultivation requires analysis based on calm abiding, but a newly attained calm abiding is not yet strong enough to serve as a basis for analysis; the meditator is not yet accustomed to physical and mental pliancy. Therefore, the meditator must take the time to strengthen and consolidate the attainment of calm abiding so that it will not be disturbed when he or she begins to analyze. Gedün Lodrö emphasizes that

> Calm abiding must be developed to such a degree that it cannot be ruined by analysis. Not only that; it must be able to advance as the analysis advances.[a]

THE FOUR ATTRIBUTES OF PREPARATORY TRAINING

Since Jam-yang-shay-pa does not discuss the topic, Gedün Lodrö—apparently from his own readings of Asaṅga's *Grounds of Hearers*—presents four attributes of preparatory training (*sngon 'gro'i sbyor ba'i khyad par bzhi*) that calm abiding must have before the meditator is ready to cultivate special insight or the mental contemplation of individual knowledge of the character. He states, further, that "It is necessary, according to Asaṅga's *Grounds of Hearers*, to 'pass days and nights'—that is, a great deal of time—in this endeavor."[b] Gedün Lodrö notes that "Although Asaṅga's *Grounds of Hearers* does not designate them as preparatory trainings, it sets them forth at this point as attributes which must be developed...if one is going to attain special insight...."[c]

---

a Gedün Lodrö, p. 278.

b Ibid., p. 273.

c Ibid., p. 278.

Chart 7: The Four Attributes of Preparatory Training[a]

1 first attribute:
  a advancing the entity
  b increase
  c breadth
2 second attribute:
  a tightness
  b steadiness
  c hardness
3 third attribute: aspiration toward a true object of observation and engagement in it
4 fourth attribute: skill in the causes of calm abiding and special insight

The first attribute "has three aspects: advancing the entity (*ngo bo 'phel ba*), increase (*rgyas pa*), and breadth (*yangs pa*)." These refer, respectively, to continuation even in the face of interruption, strength, and "the capacity for engaging in many objects of observation" instead of being restricted to the single object of observation that had been used for the achievement of calm abiding.[b]

The second attribute also has three attributes: tightness (*dam pa*), steadiness (*brtan pa*), and hardness (*sra ba*). Gedün Lodrö explains tightness as referring "to the object of observation and the subject, the mind of calm abiding, being stuck together such that they cannot be separated," like things that have been tied together well. He explains steadiness as referring "to the fact that the mind [at this point] cannot easily come to have an unfavorable state" and hardness as indicating "that this is not a meditation whose capacities have not been fulfilled but one that is developed."[c] Gedün Lodrö does not suggest an image to illustrate these qualities of hardness, but some possibilities are gelatin that has hardened in a mold or clay pottery that has been fired.

The third attribute is called aspiration toward a true [or correct] object of observation and engagement in it (*yang dag pa'i dmigs pa la mos pa dang de la 'jug par 'gyur ba*). Gedün Lodrö explains that, in this context, *mos pa* means "aspiration" or "wish," although in other contexts it can mean "belief" or even "pretense," as when a meditator visualizes an area as being filled with water when it is not. A true or correct object

---

[a] Ibid., pp. 273–74.
[b] Ibid., p. 274.
[c] Ibid., p. 275.

of observation, in this context, can be any exalted object of observation; Gedün Lodrö notes that "It could be a phenomenon other than the profound emptiness, such as an exalted knower of all aspects." It is generally an object of observation that had previously been too subtle for the meditator, even after he or she had acquired facility with a broad range of objects of observation. By the time the meditator has the third attribute of preparatory training, he or she not only aspires to meditate on that object of observation but can actually do so.[a]

The fourth attribute is called skill in the causes of calm abiding and special insight (*zhi gnas dang lhag mthong gi mtshan ma la mkhas pa*); Gedün Lodrö notes that, although the word *mtshan ma* sometimes means "sign," "its only meaning here is 'cause.'"[b] This attribute is the most complex of the four and has many subdivisions.

Chart 8: The Fourth Attribute of Preparatory Training: Skill in the Causes of Calm Abiding and Special Insight

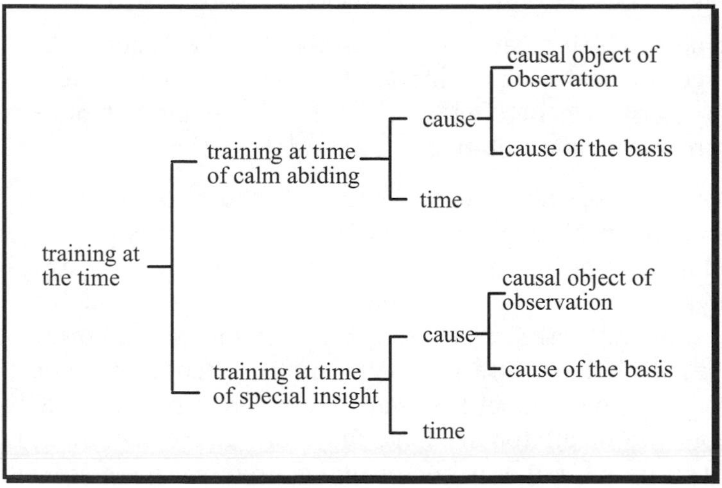

According to Gedün Lodrö, the term "training at the time" (*dus kyi sbyor ba*) "refers to the ability to do whatever is necessary for a particular practice at that time" and "applies to both calm abiding and special

[a] Ibid., pp. 275–76.

[b] Ibid., pp. 276–77.

insight."[a] He does not discuss training at the time of special insight. Training at the time of calm abiding has two main subdivisions: the cause of calm abiding and the time of calm abiding. The cause of calm abiding has two further subdivisions, the causal object of observation (*dmigs pa'i mtshan ma*) and the cause of the basis (*gzhi'i mtshan ma*).[b]

Gedün Lodrö explains the causal object of observation as "the main object of observation itself." It "is a cause in the sense that in dependence on it the mind becomes pacified"; however, it "is an imputed but not an actual cause of the pacification of the mind."[c] He explains "basis," in the term "cause of the basis," as the purification, or advance, of calm abiding. Since the purification of calm abiding "is attained when one achieves the meditative stabilization that is a union of calm abiding and special insight," the *cause* of the basis is *training* in special insight.[d]

The other main division of the topic of training at the time of calm abiding is time. According to Gedün Lodrö, time, in this context, "refers to the ability to engage immediately in the object of observation either when excitement arises or when one has a sense that it is about to arise."[e] He explains that, in the cultivation of special insight,

> If excitement is being generated or is about to be generated, one engages in stabilizing meditation to prevent it. If one feels that laxity is being generated or is about to be generated, one engages in analytical meditation as an antidote to that.[f]

Lati Rinpoche, who does not discuss the four attributes of preparatory training, mentions in his explanation of the mental contemplation of individual knowledge of the character that, in the cultivation of special insight, analytical and stabilizing meditation are used as antidotes to laxity and excitement, respectively.[g] Gedün Lodrö points out, however, that since the cultivation of special insight and the mental contemplation of individual knowledge of the character involves mainly analytical meditation, the meditator needs to find out, before beginning to cultivate either special insight or the mental contemplation of individual knowledge of the character, whether he or she is able to do the requisite analytical meditation. In response to qualms concerning the

---

[a] Ibid., p. 276.
[b] Ibid., p. 277.
[c] Ibid., p. 277.
[d] Ibid., p. 277, italics added.
[e] Ibid., p. 278.
[f] Ibid., p. 279.
[g] Lati Rinpoche in *Meditative States*, pp. 97–98.

degree of proficiency required at this stage, he emphasizes again that he is

> talking about the period between the attainment of the first preparation, calm abiding, which is a mental contemplation, and actually beginning to work at the second. This is the preparatory training for *beginning to work at* the second preparation, the mental contemplation of thorough knowledge of the character.[a]

Special Insight in the Topic of the Concentrations and Formless Absorptions

Both textbooks on the concentrations and formless absorptions and modern scholars giving oral commentary on the textbooks seem reluctant to discuss special insight in relation to that topic. In monastic textbooks, the presentation of calm abiding is followed by a brief presentation of special insight.[b] However, modern Ge-luk-pa scholars tend not to discuss the topic of special insight as such but, rather, prefer to assimilate it to the discussion of the mental contemplation of individual knowledge of the character because of the similarity in the mode of cultivation. Lati Rinpoche describes his method of presentation as follows:

> After achieving calm abiding, we can cultivate the concentrations and formless absorptions; I will explain how to develop them. It is customary, at this point, to insert an explanation of the cultivation of special insight. However, since the mode of cultivating the preparations for the concentrations and formless absorptions and the mode of cultivating special insight are similar, I will discuss them together.[c]

Gedün Lodrö proceeds in a similar manner. Although part two of his presentation is called "Special Insight," he too discusses the seven mental contemplations as "The Mundane Path of Special Insight."[d] He does not cite the brief discussion of special insight included in his college's

---

[a] Gedün Lodrö, p. 281.

[b] Kön-chok-jik-may-wang-po, *Condensed Statement,* 563.6–565.1; Jam-yang-shay-pa, *Concentrations,* 162.1–172.7; Paṇ-chen Sö-nam-drak-pa, "Concentrations," 156a.5–157a.1 (see *Meditative States,* pp. 175–78).

[c] *Meditative States,* p. 92.

[d] Gedün Lodrö, pp. 299–312.

textbook on the concentrations and formless absorptions, Jam-yang-shay-pa's *Great Exposition of the Concentrations and Formless Absorptions,* although he follows Jam-yang-shay-pa closely elsewhere.

Even Jam-yang-shay-pa's short presentation of special insight may indicate some reluctance to discuss the topic. In a departure from his usual style, his exposition of his own system relies largely on unexplained citations from Asaṅga's *Grounds of Hearers* and the *Sūtra Unraveling the Thought,* although he usually explains citations from Indian sources in detail, even in the exposition of his own system, through both phrase-by-phrase analysis and debate. His exposition of this topic, however, seems merely obligatory and not an integral part of his larger presentation of the concentrations and formless absorptions.

One possible reason for the apparent reluctance of Ge-luk-pa scholars to discuss the presentations of special insight included in textbooks on the topic of the concentrations and formless absorptions may be that these presentations do not represent the main Ge-luk presentation of special insight. The discussions in Jam-yang-shay-pa's and Kön-chok-jik-may-wang-po's textbooks on the concentrations and formless absorptions are based on Indian source texts for *that* topic—mainly, on Asaṅga's *Grounds of Hearers* and the *Sūtra Unraveling the Thought*—whereas the main line of Ge-luk presentations of special insight is based on Chandrakīrti's *Clear Words,* as elaborated in the various versions of Tsong-kha-pa's *Stages of the Path.*[a]

Paṇ-chen Sö-nam-drak-pa's treatment of special insight may reflect this discrepancy. He cites the *Sūtra Unraveling the Thought* to explain the relationship of special insight to analytical meditation, but he also cites Tsong-kha-pa's and two Ka-dam-pa stages-of-the-path texts to determine when a union of calm abiding and special insight occurs. Thus, he uses Indian and Tibetan sources for both topics; however, he does not cite Asaṅga's *Grounds of Hearers.* Moreover, he limits his discussion to a few specific technical problems, without discussing the objects of observation or mode of cultivation of special insight.

I will follow the method of the Tibetan oral commentaries discussed here below and proceed directly to the discussion of the preparations and the mundane path of special insight.

---

[a] Discussion of Tsong-kha-pa's presentation of special insight is beyond the scope of this work. Thorough explanations in English may be found in Jeffrey Hopkins, *Meditation on Emptiness* (London: Wisdom Publications, 1983) and *Emptiness Yoga: The Middle Way Consequence School* (Ithaca, NY: Snow Lion Publications, 1987) and in Elizabeth Napper, *Dependent-Arising and Emptiness* (Boston and London: Wisdom Publications, 1989).

The Preparations

Of all the topics related to the concentrations and formless absorptions, that of the preparations is probably the least known to Western scholarship. It deals with the process by which a meditator who has attained calm abiding progresses from a given level to the next higher one—for instance, from the highest mind of the Desire Realm to an actual absorption of the first concentration or from an actual absorption of the first concentration to an actual absorption of the second concentration. To attain the next-higher level, the meditator must separate, at least temporarily, from attachment to the afflictive emotions pertaining to the lower level—that is, the level he or she wishes to advance beyond. Denma Lochö Rinpoche explains preparations, in general, as

> techniques for separating from desires with respect to the lower level, from which the meditator has not yet separated. When, in dependence upon cultivating the preparations, the meditator separates from desire with respect to that lower level, he or she has attained the actual meditative absorption.[a]

He defines a preparation for a concentration as "a mental contemplation included within a training for an actual meditative absorption of a concentration, which is its fruit."[b] Jam-yang-shay-pa and Kön-chok-jik-may-wang-po similarly define a preparation for a concentration as "a mental contemplation that is a training for entering into an actual absorption of a concentration."[c] Paṇ-chen Sö-nam-drak-pa defines a preparation as

> a virtuous knower that is included in the levels of preparation and of concentrations that serve as techniques for attaining an actual absorption of the first concentration, which is its object of attainment.[d]

This definition includes the additional information that a preparation is a consciousness (a "knower") and that it is virtuous rather than non-virtuous or ethically neutral, but it does not consider the relationship between preparation and mental contemplation.

---

[a] *Meditative States,* p. 147.

[b] Ibid., p. 147.

[c] Jam-yang-shay-pa, *Concentrations,* 226.2; Kön-chok-jik-may-wang-po, *Condensed Statement,* 570.3.

[d] Paṇ-chen Sö-nam-drak-pa, "Concentrations," 152a.5–6 (see *Meditative States,* p. 153).

Both Vasubandhu and Asaṅga refer to preparations. By "preparation" Vasubandhu's *Treasury of Manifest Knowledge* and its *Autocommentary* seem to mean merely an undifferentiated period of transition between each level and the next higher one. Thus, Vasubandhu speaks of eight preparations, one for each of the concentrations and formless absorptions.[a] Asaṅga, however, delineates the steps of the meditator's progress by dividing each of these periods into several stages, known as mental contemplations.

Ge-luk-pa writers on the topic combine the presentations of Vasubandhu and Asaṅga into a single system. Tsong-kha-pa and the textbook writers who follow him exemplify the Ge-luk concern for reconciling what Ge-luk-pas regard as the two Manifest Knowledges, Hīnayāna and Mahāyāna—respectively, Vasubandhu's *Treasury of Manifest Knowledge* and Asaṅga's *Summary of Manifest Knowledge,* the details of the latter being filled out by Asaṅga's *Grounds of Hearers.* The resulting synthesis is an example of Ge-luk-pa system-building at its strongest, especially since the two Manifest Knowledge presentations usually are not merely conflated; in his *Notes on the Concentrations and Formless Absorptions*, Tsong-kha-pa consistently differentiates and compares Vasubandhu's and Asaṅga's presentations of major points. In general, when the two Manifest Knowledges differ, preference is given to Asaṅga's version—but usually only after comparison with Vasubandhu's.

Types of Preparation and the Mundane and Supramundane Paths

Calm abiding itself is the first preparation, which is known as the mental contemplation of a mere beginner. The remaining preparations are of two types—those having the aspect of grossness/peacefulness (*zhi rags rnam can*) and those having the aspect of the truths (*bden pa rnam can*). According to Lati Rinpoche, the preparations having the aspect of the truths can have the aspect of either the four truths or the two truths; Kön-chok-jik-may-wang-po defines a supramundane (*'jig rten las 'das pa, lokottara*) preparation for the first concentration as "a preparation for the first concentration included within that which has the aspect of any of the selflessnesses or the attributes of the four truths."[b] These two types of preparation correspond to the two subdivisions of

---

[a] Vasubandhu, *Treasury of Manifest Knowledge,* 8.22a–b (P5591, vol. 115, 274.5.2; Shastri, part 4, p. 1161; La Vallée Poussin, 16:5, p. 178; Pruden, vol. 4, p. 1253).

[b] *Meditative States,* p. 134; Kön-chok-jik-may-wang-po, *Condensed Statement,* 573.6.

objects of observation for purifying afflictive emotions, which are used at this point in the cultivation of the concentrations and formless absorptions.

There is an obvious relationship between the two types of preparation and the two types of path—the mundane path and the supramundane path. As will be mentioned later (pages 273ff.), the mundane path leads to rebirth in high meditative states within cyclic existence, whereas the supramundane path leads to liberation (*thar pa, vimokṣa*) from cyclic existence. According to Gedün Lodrö, a meditator who wishes to progress beyond calm abiding must do so by means of either a mundane path or a supramundane path. Citing Asaṅga's *Grounds of Hearers,* he emphasizes that "there is no third category of path."[a] In general, the mundane path is related to the preparations having the aspect of grossness/peacefulness, whereas the supramundane path is related to the preparations having the aspect of the truths. In monastic textbooks, the preparations having the aspect of grossness/peacefulness are sometimes called mundane preparations, whereas those having the aspect of the truths are sometimes called supramundane preparations. Kön-chok-jik-may-wang-po's text includes definitions of a mundane preparation for the first concentration and of a supramundane preparation for the first concentration (see below page 201). However, the correlation between type of path and type of preparation is not definite. Although persons on a mundane path always use mundane preparations, persons on a supramundane path do not necessarily use supramundane preparations; certain types of persons on a supramundane path may use mundane preparations.

The presentation of the mundane and supramundane paths is related to traditional cosmology—specifically, as Gedün Lodrö points out, to the presentation of the three realms and the nine levels[b] (see chart next page).

---

[a] Gedün Lodrö, p. 272.

[b] Ibid., pp. 271–72.

Chart 9: Cyclic Existence: The Three Realms and Nine Levels

(from the highest levels to the lowest)

III. Formless Realm (*gzugs med khams, ārūpyadhātu*)
- 9 Peak of Cyclic Existence (*srid rtse, bhavāgra*)
- 8 Nothingness (*ci yang med, ākiṃcaya*)
- 7 Limitless Consciousness (*rnam shes mtha' yas, vijñānānantya*)
- 6 Limitless Space (*nam mkha' mtha' yas, ākāśānantya*)

II. Form Realm (*gzugs khams, rūpadhātu*)
- 5 Fourth Concentration (*bsam gtan bzhi pa, caturthadhyāna*)
- 4 Third Concentration (*bsam gtan gsum pa, tritīyadhyāna*)
- 3 Second Concentration (*bsam gtan gnyis pa, dvitīyadhyāna*)
- 2 First Concentration (*bsam gtan dang po, prathamadhyāna*)

I. 1 Desire Realm (*'dod khams, kāmadhātu*)
- Gods of the Desire Realm (*'dod khams kyi lha, kāmadhātudeva*)
  - Those Who Make Use of Others' Emanations (*gzhan 'phrul dbang byed, paranirmitavaśavartin*)
  - Those Who Enjoy Emanation (*'phrul dga', nirmāṇarati*)
  - Joyous Land (*dga' ldan, tuṣita*)
  - Land Without Combat (*'thab bral, yāma*)
  - Heaven of Thirty-Three (*sum cu rtsa gsum, trayastriṃśa*)
  - Four Great Royal Lineages (*rgyal chen rigs bzhi, cāturmahārājakāyika*)
- Demigods (*lha ma yin, asura*)
- Humans (*mi, manuýya*)
- Animals (*dud 'gro, tiryañc*)
- Hungry ghosts (*yi dvags, preta*)
- Hell-beings (*dmyal ba, nāraka*)

Each of the nine levels has cycles of afflictive emotions pertaining to it. There are three main divisions for each level—great (*chen po, adhimātra*), middling (*'bring, madhya*), and small (*chung ngu, mṛdu*)—each of which is subdivided into three by degrees. Thus, each of the nine levels has nine degrees of afflictive emotions pertaining to it—(1) the great of the great (*chen po'i chen po, adhimātrādhimatra*), (2) the middling of the great (*chen po'i 'bring, adhimātramadhya*), and (3) the small of the great (*chen po'i chung ngu, adhimātramṛdu*); (4) the great of the middling (*'bring gi chen po, madhyādhimātra*), (5) the middling of the middling (*'bring gi 'bring, madhyamadhya*), and (6) the small of the middling (*'bring gi chung ngu, madhyamṛdu*); (7) the great of the small (*chung ngu'i chen po, mṛdvadhimātra*), (8) the middling of the small (*chung ngu'i 'bring, mṛdumadhya*), and (9) the small of the small (*chung ngu'i chung ngu*, *mṛdumṛdu*)[a]—making eighty-one in all. (See the chart below.)

Chart 10: Afflictive Emotions to be Abandoned, in Terms of the Three Realms and Nine Levels

(Read from bottom to top.)

afflictive emotions pertaining to the Formless Realm	Peak of Cyclic Existence (ninth level)		73-81
	Nothingness (eighth level)		64-72
	Infinite Consciousness (seventh level)		55-63
	Infinite Space (sixth level)		46-54
afflictive emotions pertaining to the Form Realm	Fourth Concentration (fifth level)		37-45
	Third Concentration (fourth level)		28-36
	Second Concentration (third level)		19-27
	First Concentration (second level)		10-18
afflictive emotions pertaining to the Desire Realm (first level)	small	small of the small	9
		middling of the small	8
		great of the small	7
	middling	small of the middling	6
		middling of the middling	5
		great of the middling	4
	great	small of the great	3
		middling of the great	2
		great of the great	1

All nine cycles of afflictive emotions pertaining to a given level must be overcome before a meditator can attain the meditative absorption of the next-higher level. In general, they are overcome by the preparations for the higher level. (The notable exception is the Foe Destroyer who proceeds by simultaneously abandoning the great of the great afflictive emotions of all levels, then the middling of the great

[a] *Meditative States*, p. 102.

afflictive emotions of all levels, then the small of the great afflictive emotions of all levels, and so forth.

How these are overcome is a major factor in determining whether a meditator's path is mundane or supramundane. Gedün Lodrö explains clearly the three major terms used by Indian source texts and Tibetan commentators to identify the ways of overcoming afflictive emotions—suppression (*nyams smad*), separation from attachment (*chags bral, kāmād virakta*), and abandonment (*spangs pa, prahāṇa*) from the root. In the suppression of afflictive emotions—whether by a mind of calm abiding or, more forcefully, by mundane special insight—coarse afflictive emotions are not manifest; they "also do not become manifest in states subsequent to meditative equipoise, when the functioning of the meditative stabilization has ceased." Nevertheless, they can easily become manifest at a later time.[a]

Separation from attachment to the afflictive emotions of a given level is achieved "through the fourth, fifth, and seventh of the seven preparations" for the next-higher level. Gedün Lodrö points out that

> Like suppression of the afflictive emotions through calm abiding, such separation is to be distinguished from the abandonment from the root that is achieved through a supramundane path; even when one attains such separation from attachment, one is still ready to generate the afflictive emotions. Nevertheless, there is a great difference between suppression of an afflictive emotion through calm abiding and separation from attachment by way of a mundane path. In the latter case, one attains a situation in which, temporarily, the afflictive emotions cannot be generated. A mundane path has an uninterrupted path and a path of release—a true cessation of afflictive emotions, temporarily.[b]

Gedün Lodrö notes that the abandonment of afflictive emotions from the root

> involves a person's first identifying the *root* of these afflictive emotions to be the ignorance that is the conception of true existence. Then, in dependence on calm abiding, meditating on the four noble truths, and generating a supramundane path, one eliminates that very ignorance.[c]

---

[a] Gedün Lodrö, pp. 238–39.

[b] Ibid., p. 239.

[c] Ibid., p. 80.

Thus, the generation of a supramundane path depends on a direct realization of emptiness at the time of the path of seeing.[a]

Summarizing the relationship between the mundane and supramundane paths, on the one hand, and the three realms and nine levels, on the other, Gedün Lodrö observes that, in dependence upon a mundane path, it is possible "to separate temporarily from attachment to afflictive emotions pertaining to the Nothingness level—that is, the eighth level—and below."[b] Because a mundane path does not lead to liberation from cyclic existence, however, it cannot separate from attachment, even temporarily, to afflictive emotions pertaining to the ninth level, the Peak of Cyclic Existence. According to Paṇ-chen Sö-nam-drak-pa, this is because there is no mundane level above the Peak of Cyclic Existence.[c] Gedün Lodrö emphasizes that "[s]omeone who wishes to get rid of the afflictive emotions pertaining to the Peak of Cyclic Existence must definitely depend on a supramundane path."[d] As was pointed out in relation to the physical basis of the concentrations and formless absorptions (page 47), a mind of the level of the Peak of Cyclic Existence also cannot be used as a mental basis for overcoming afflictive emotions pertaining to its own level, even by a supramundane path; thus, a Hīnayāna Superior born at the level of the Peak of Cyclic Existence uses a mind of the level below, that of Nothingness, as a mental basis for attaining the status of Foe Destroyer.

Preparations for the First Concentration

Ge-luk-pa textbook-writers and scholars generally begin their explanation of the preparations with a detailed presentation of the preparations for the first concentration, for the most part in terms of those having the aspect of grossness/peacefulness, as an example of the mode of procedure—not because that is the preferred mode of procedure but because the presentation of the preparations having the aspect of grossness/peacefulness is more straightforward than that of the preparations having the aspect of the truths, which intersect in complicated ways with the five Buddhist paths—the paths of accumulation, preparation, seeing, meditation, and no more learning. Each of the

---

[a] *Meditation on Emptiness*, p. 86.

[b] Gedün Lodrö, p. 272.

[c] Paṇ-chen Sö-nam-drak-pa, "Concentrations," 158b.5–6 (see *Meditative States*, p. 186). Paṇ-chen Sö-nam-drak-pa discusses this question in relation to the types of meditative absorption.

[d] Gedün Lodrö, p. 272.

remaining meditative absorptions, from the second concentration through the peak of cyclic existence, has a similar set of preparations; Asaṅga and Tibetan commentators tend to summarize them and to discuss mainly the ways in which they differ from each other and from the preparations for the first concentration. Citing Asaṅga's *Summary of Manifest Knowledge* as his source, Paṇ-chen Sö-nam-drak-pa states:

> According to the explanation concerning the preparations for the first concentration, so, too, [is the explanation of] the remaining preparations until the peak of cyclic existence.[a]

The seven preparations, in order of cultivation, are:

1 mental contemplation of a mere beginner (*las dang po pa tsam gyi yid byed*)
2 mental contemplation of individual knowledge of the character (*mtshan nyid so sor rig pa'i yid byed, lakṣaṇapratisaṃvedīmanaskāra;* also known as thorough knowledge of the character [*mtshan nyid rab tu rig pa*])
3 mental contemplation arisen from belief (*mos pa las byung ba'i yid byed, adhimokṣikamanaskāra*)
4 mental contemplation of thorough isolation (*rab tu dben pa'i yid byed, prāvivekyamanaskāra*)
5 mental contemplation of joy-withdrawal (*dga' ba sdud pa'i yid byed, ratisaṃgrāhakamanaskāra*)
6 mental contemplation of analysis (*dpyod pa yid byed, mīmāṃsāmanaskāra*)
7 mental contemplation of final training (*sbyor mtha'i yid byed, prayoganiṣṭhamanaskāra*)

This list of seven preparations is derived from Asaṅga's list of seven mental contemplations, the first six of which he identifies as preparations.[b] **The seven mental contemplations**, in order of cultivation, are:

1 mental contemplation of individual knowledge of the character (*mtshan nyid so sor rig pa'i yid byed, lakṣaṇapratisaṃvedīmanaskāra;* also known as thorough knowledge of the character [*mtshan nyid rab tu rig pa*])
2 mental contemplation arisen from belief (*mos pa las byung ba'i yid byed, adhimokṣikamanaskāra*)

---

[a] Paṇ-chen Sö-nam-drak-pa, "Concentrations," 154a.2 (see *Meditative States*, p. 162).
[b] Gedün Lodrö, pp. 299–300, 304.

3 mental contemplation of thorough isolation (*rab tu dben pa'i yid byed, prāvivekyamanaskāra*)
4 mental contemplation of joy-withdrawal (*dga' ba sdud pai' yid byed, ratisaṃgrāhakamanaskāra*)
5 mental contemplation of analysis (*dpyod pa yid byed, mīmāṃsāmanaskāra*)
6 mental contemplation of final training (*sbyor mtha'i yid byed, prayoganiṣṭhamanaskāra*)
7 mental contemplation that is the fruit of final training (*sbyor mtha'i 'bras bu'i yid byed, prayoganiṣṭhaphalamanaskāra*).[a]

Asaṅga's list of mental contemplations overlaps the list of seven preparations but is not identical with it, since it does not include the mental contemplation of a mere beginner—that is, calm abiding—and contains, as its final item, the mental contemplation that is the fruit of final training, which is a mental contemplation but not a preparation; it is an actual absorption. The following chart shows the relationship between the two lists:

Chart 11: Relationship between the Seven Preparations and the Seven Mental Contemplations

Seven Preparations	*Seven Mental Contemplations*
1 mental contemplation of a mere beginner	
2 mental contemplation of individual knowledge of the character	1 mental contemplation of individual knowledge of the character
3 mental contemplation arisen from belief	2 mental contemplation arisen from belief
4 mental contemplation of thorough isolation	3 mental contemplation of thorough isolation
5 mental contemplation of joy-withdrawal	4 mental contemplation of joy-withdrawal
6 mental contemplation of analysis	5 mental contemplation of analysis
7 mental contemplation of final training	6 mental contemplation of final training
	7 mental contemplation that is the fruit of final training

Gedün Lodrö notes that "In Tibetan commentaries a designation of eight mental contemplations is also used." It reflects the relationship shown in the above chart and consists of Asaṅga's list of seven mental contemplations preceded by the mental contemplation of a mere

[a] Ibid., p. 300.

beginner.[a]

Calm abiding as a preparation

As the chart of preparations indicates, calm abiding, when it is considered as the first of the preparations, is called the mental contemplation of a mere beginner. It is discussed in the context of three beginner mental contemplations, unrelated to the list of seven. Gedün Lodrö lists the three as:

1 a beginner at mental contemplation, *or, as an exception*, a beginning mental contemplation (*yid la byed pa las dang po pa, manaskārādikarmika*). (The word "beginner" (*las dang po pa, ādikarmika*) usually refers to a person, but it does not necessarily refer to a person in this context.)
2 a mental contemplation of a mere beginner
3 the mental contemplation of a beginner at purifying afflictive emotions (*nyon mongs rnam par sbyong ba'i las dang po pa'i yid byed, kleśaviśuddhyādikarmikamanaskāra*)[b]

Following Jam-yang-shay-pa, Gedün Lodrö posits the first, a beginner at mental contemplation, as ranging from the attainment of the ninth mental abiding "up to but not including calm abiding." He posits the second, a mental contemplation of a mere beginner, as ranging "from the attainment of calm abiding up to but not including the attainment of the mental contemplation of individual knowledge of the character." He posits the third, the mental contemplation of a beginner at purifying afflictive emotions, as ranging "only over the mental contemplation of individual knowledge of the character."[c]

Still following Jam-yang-shay-pa, Gedün Lodrö points out that the "mental contemplation" referred to in the term "a beginner at mental contemplation" is calm abiding and that the ninth mind of the Desire Realm (that is, the ninth mental abiding) is called a *beginner* at mental contemplation (that is, calm abiding) because calm abiding has not yet been attained.[d] Moreover, in the context of the discussion of pliancy and the attainment of calm abiding, he gives another reason the ninth mental abiding is called a beginner at mental contemplation: it is so

---

[a] Ibid., p. 309.

[b] Ibid., p. 307.

[c] Ibid., p. 308; Jam-yang-shay-pa, *Concentrations,* 226.7–3; see also Kön-chok-jik-may-wang-po, *Condensed Statement,* 570.5–6.

[d] Gedün Lodrö, p. 308.

called because calm abiding "is a continuation of the earlier meditative stabilization of the ninth mental abiding."[a]

Since Asaṅga identifies only six of the seven mental contemplations as preparations, his identification in this context of calm abiding as a mental contemplation is the key to Ge-luk reasoning establishing that calm abiding is the first of the preparations. This reasoning, based on textual premises of internal religious scholarship, involves a comparison of discrete passages of Asaṅga's text and the use of them to construct a coherent system claiming Asaṅga as its source. Gedün Lodrö suggests why this type of reasoning is needed, as well as its direction:

> Are there no more preparations than these six? It is not that there are no more, for before these there is another preparatory mental contemplation, that of a mere beginner—that is, calm abiding. This, however, is not explicitly mentioned as a preparatory mental contemplation in Asaṅga's *Grounds of Hearers*. It is not mentioned in any of these counts of mental contemplations, but it can be established by reasoning that simultaneous with the attainment of calm abiding is the attainment of a preparatory mental contemplation. Therefore, before one can attain the mental contemplation of individual knowledge of the character, one must attain calm abiding. Thus, there are seven preparatory mental contemplations.[b]

He explains further that calm abiding is called the mental contemplation of a *mere* beginner because it is the initial step in the process of purifying afflictive emotions:

> ...any actual path that can serve as an antidote to afflictive emotions begins with the mental contemplation of thorough isolation, and its direct inducer is special insight, the mental contemplation arisen from belief. Thus, the beginning work on it comes at the mental contemplation of individual knowledge of the character [which is the cultivation of special insight]. Since calm abiding is achieved before that, calm abiding is called the mental contemplation of a mere beginner. Therefore, this term means that calm abiding is a mental contemplation of a person who is a mere beginner at purifying afflictive

---

[a] Ibid., p. 212.

[b] Ibid., p. 304.

emotions.[a]

He also explains Asaṅga's reasons for omitting calm abiding from the list of preparations and, thereby, defends Asaṅga against a possible charge of internal inconsistency.

> Nevertheless, Asaṅga's *Grounds of Hearers* mentions six preparatory mental contemplations, although there are seven, because the attainment of the mental contemplation of a beginner at purifying afflictive emotions begins with attainment of the mental contemplation of individual knowledge of the character. Here "purification" refers, at minimum, to the beginning of the antidotal process of analysis that views the lower level as gross. It is said that, although the mental contemplation of individual knowledge of the character is not the beginning of the preparations, the mental contemplations which purify afflictive emotions begin with individual knowledge of the character, in the process of cultivating special insight. This is why Asaṅga posits six preparatory mental contemplations. The analysis of this is found in Tsong-kha-pa's *Great Exposition of the Stages of the Path*.[b]

The mental contemplation of individual knowledge of the character

Paṇ-chen Sö-nam-drak-pa and Denma Lochö Rinpoche describe the mental contemplation of individual knowledge of the character as "a technique for achieving special insight."[c] Special insight here can refer either to actual special insight or to a mundane special insight that is a facsimile of actual special insight. Special insight of whichever type is attained simultaneously with the next preparation, the mental contemplation arisen from belief. Like all the preparations except the first and sixth—that is, the mental contemplation of a mere beginner, or calm abiding, and the mental contemplation of analysis—the mental contemplation of individual knowledge of the character can have either the aspect of grossness/peacefulness or the aspect of the truths. Textbooks and oral commentators discuss mainly the type having the aspect of grossness/peacefulness, as an example of the mode of

---

[a] Ibid., p. 308.

[b] Ibid., pp. 304–305.

[c] Paṇ-chen Sö-nam-drak-pa, "Concentrations," 153a.1–2 (see *Meditative States*, p. 154).

procedure.

Etymology and definition. According to both Lati Rinpoche and Jam-yang-shay-pa, the mental contemplation of individual knowledge of the character is so called because it reflects individually on the lower level as gross and the upper level as peaceful "or on the general character (*spyi'i mtshan nyid, sāmānyalakṣaṇa*) and the specific character (*rang gi mtshan nyid, svalakṣaṇa*) of these levels."[a] Adapting the abridged definitions Jam-yang-shay-pa suggests for use in debate, Gedün Lodrö defines the mental contemplation of individual knowledge of the character as "a mental contemplation of a beginner at purifying afflictive emotions."[b] This is a general definition that applies to both types of mental contemplation of individual knowledge of the character—that having the aspect of grossness/peacefulness and that having the aspect of the truths.

Kön-chok-jik-may-wang-po and Jam-yang-shay-pa give more specific definitions to explain one type of mental contemplation of individual knowledge of the character—a mental contemplation of individual knowledge of the character that is a mundane preparation for the first concentration. Kön-chok-jik-may-wang-po defines it as:

> a taking to mind by a beginner at purifying afflictive emotions which is mainly analysis having individually distinguished the Desire Realm as faulty and the First Concentration as having good qualities, and so forth, in dependence upon calm abiding.[c]

This is Kön-chok-jik-may-wang-po's abridgment of Jam-yang-shay-pa's more combative definition:

> a taking to mind by a beginner at purifying afflictive emotions which is mainly analysis having individually distinguished the Desire Realm as faulty and the First Concentration as having good qualities, and so forth, in dependence upon calm abiding,

---

[a] *Meditative States*, p. 93. This is also Jam-yang-shay-pa's etymology (Jam-yang-shay-pa, *Concentrations*, 231.6–7).

[b] Gedün Lodrö, p. 328. The definitions Jam-yang-shay-pa offers for use in debate are "a preparation for the first concentration in the continuum of a beginner at purifying afflictive emotions which is mainly analytical meditation in order to attain special insight after achieving calm abiding" and "a preparation for the first concentration that is the initial activity toward purifying afflictive emotions" (Jam-yang-shay-pa, *Concentrations*, 232.6–233.1). For a more informative definition by Jam-yang-shay-pa, see below, page 201. Definitions intended primarily for use in debate tend to be minimalist; they are designed to be proof against attack rather than to give information.

[c] Kön-chok-jik-may-wang-po, *Condensed Statement*, 571.2.

which is of a level of equipoise.[a]

By including the phrase "which is of a level of equipoise," Jam-yang-shay-pa alludes to the controversial question of the level of the mental contemplation of individual knowledge of the character. Although everyone agrees that calm abiding is "of a level of equipoise," not everyone agrees that the mental contemplation of individual knowledge of the character is of that level; indeed, Jam-yang-shay-pa himself holds that it is not (see below, page 206). This is a most hotly debated issue concerning the mental contemplation of individual knowledge of the character; it will be discussed below (see pages 206–211).

The mode of analysis of grossness/peacefulness. The mode of analysis used in the preparations having the aspect of grossness/peacefulness (*zhi rags rnam can gyi nyer bsdogs*[b]) involves viewing the lower level—the meditator's current level, which he or she is trying to leave—as gross in comparison to the next-higher level, which the meditator is trying to attain; the meditator first views the lower level as gross and then views the upper level as peaceful. For a meditator who is trying to attain an actual first concentration, the two levels are, respectively, the Desire Realm and the First Concentration. For a meditator who is trying to attain an actual second concentration—whether that meditator is a human or god born in the Desire Realm who has attained an actual first concentration or a Form Realm being born in the First Concentration—the two levels are, respectively, the First Concentration and the Second Concentration.

Kön-chok-jik-may-wang-po's and Jam-yang-shay-pa's definitions of a mental contemplation of individual knowledge of the character that is a mundane preparation for the first concentration include a brief description of the mode of analysis of grossness/peacefulness in the phrase "having individually distinguished the Desire Realm as faulty and the First Concentration as having good qualities".[c]

Lati Rinpoche gives a graphic description of the faults of the Desire

---

[a] Jam-yang-shay-pa, *Concentrations,* 227.5–6.

[b] Literally, "peacefulness/grossness," for reasons of euphony in Tibetan and Sanskrit (**śāntaudārika*). However, *zhi rags* is translated here as "grossness/peacefulness" to reflect the order of cultivation, as well as Jam-yang-shay-pa's position that grossness/peacefulness does not mean grossness *and* peacefulness because the two cannot occur simultaneously (see below, page 219).

[c] Kön-chok-jik-may-wang-po, *Condensed Statement,* 571.2; Jam-yang-shay-pa, *Concentrations,* 227.5.

Realm in terms of its beings and environment.[a] Physically, despite the variations in beauty we perceive among the people and animals of the Desire Realm, the sentient beings of the Desire Realm are uniformly ugly compared to those of the First Concentration. Mentally, they are ill-natured; they quarrel and make war; they are subject to all the afflictive emotions and commit all of the ten non-virtues. Moreover, they undergo great suffering. They experience the sufferings of birth, aging, sickness, and death, as well as those of the eight worldly concerns (*'jig rten chos brgyad, aṣṭalokadharma*)—happiness (*bde ba, sukha*) and suffering (*sdug bsngal, duḥkha*), gain (*rnyed pa, lābha*) and loss (*ma rnyed pa, alābha*), praise (*bstod pa, praśaṃsa*) and blame (*smad pa, nindā*), fame (*snyan grags, yaśas*) and disgrace (*ma snyan grags, ayaśas*).[b] Unlike beings of the First Concentration, they have to sleep. They have a short lifespan; they are nourished by impure substances, and in digesting these, excrete impure substances that do not exist in the First Concentration. The environment of the Desire Realm is also faulty: "the lumpy landscape we have, with its mountains and valleys; it is a land of ordinary stones and earth, of thorns, cesspools, and harmful places."[c]

Lati Rinpoche describes the First Concentration as peaceful, by contrast, "in the sense of not having these faults."[d] Lati Rinpoche describes the beings of the First Concentration as peaceful by nature: they do not fight or quarrel. Mentally, they are free of such afflictive emotions as hatred (*zhe sdang, dveṣa*), resentment (*'khon 'dzin, upanāha*), belligerence (*khro ba, krodha*), jealousy (*phrag dog, irṣyā*), miserliness (*ser sna, mātsarya*), and non-shame (*ngo tsha med pa, āhrikya*). They do not commit the non-virtues of body and speech, and they commit the mental non-virtues—covetousness (*brnab sems, abhidhyā*), harmfulness (*gnod sems, vyāpāda*), and wrong views (*log lta, mithyādṛṣṭi*)—to a lesser degree and in a subtler manner than beings of the Desire Realm. They also do not suffer as much as beings of the Desire Realm, and they have a long lifespan and pure resources. The environment consists of houses that are called inestimable mansions (*gzhal med khang, *amātragṛha*) because they are made of precious substances that are priceless, and of land that is also made of precious substances.

Gedün Lodrö takes a more textual approach. Breaking down a key passage of Asaṅga's *Grounds of Hearers,* he identifies five faults related to

---

[a] Lati Rinpoche in *Meditative States,* pp. 93–95.

[b] Ibid., p. 231 n. 3.

[c] Ibid., p. 95.

[d] Ibid., pp. 95–96.

the Desire Realm (*'dod pa la brten pa'i nye dmigs lnga*), with their subdivisions, as indicated in the following list:

Chart 12: The Five Faults Related to the Desire Realm

First fault

- *a.* Desire Realm beings are of little import (*'dod pa rnams ni gnog chung ba*).
- *b.* They have many sufferings (*sdug bsngal mang ba*).
- *c.* They have many faulty objects of observation (*nyes dmigs mang ba*).

Second fault

- *a.* When one depends on phenomena of the Desire Realm, one does not experience auspiciousness (*'dod pa rnams la brten pa na ngoms mi myong*).
- *b.* When one depends on phenomena of the Desire Realm, one does not know satisfaction (*'dod pa rnams la chog mi shes*).
    - (1) not knowing satisfaction (*chog mi shes*)
    - (2) having great desire (*'dod chen can*)
- *c.* With respect to Desire Realm phenomena, there is no end that satisfies the heart (*'dod pa rnams la snying tshim pa'i mtha' med pa*).

Third fault

- *a.* Excellent ones (*dam pa rnam*),
- *b.* Those who have become elevated (*yang dag par song ba*), and
- *c.* Excellent beings deride the Desire Realm on many counts (*skyes bu dam pa rnams kyis rnam grangs du ma'i sgo nas smad pa*).

Fourth fault: When one depends on [phenomena of] the Desire Realm, one will accumulate [one of the nine] thorough enwrapments (*'dod pa rnams la brten pa na kun tu sbyor ba rnams nye bar gsog par 'gyur ba*).

Fifth fault: When one depends on [phenomena of] the Desire Realm, there is not the least sinful non-virtue that one will not do (*'dod pa la brten pa na sdig pa mi dge ba mi bya ba cung zad kyang med pa*).[a]

The nine thorough enwrapments mentioned in the fourth fault are:

1 thorough enwrapment of desire (*'dod chags kyi kun sbyor, *rāga-saṃyojana*)

[a] Gedün Lodrö, pp. 330–31.

2 thorough enwrapment of anger (*khong khro'i kun sbyor, *pratigha-saṃyojana*)
3 thorough enwrapment of pride (*nga rgyal gyi kun sbyor, *mānasaṃyojana*)
4 thorough enwrapment of doubt (*the tshom gyi kun sbyor, *vicikitsā-saṃyojana*)
5 thorough enwrapment of ignorance (*ma rig pa'i kun sbyor, *avidyā-saṃyojana*)
6 thorough enwrapment of [bad] view (*lta ba'i kun sbyor, *dṛṣṭi-saṃyojana*), view of the transitory collection [as real I and mine] (*'jig tshogs la lta ba, satkāyadṛṣṭi*), view holding to an extreme (*mthar 'dzin pa'i lta ba, antagrāhadṛṣṭi*), and wrong view (*log lta, mithyādṛṣṭi*)
7 thorough enwrapment of misapprehension of the supreme (*lta ba mchog 'dzin gyi kun sbyor, *dṛṣṭiparāmarśasaṃyojana*), conception of a [bad] view as supreme (*lta ba mchog 'dzin, dṛṣṭiparāmarśa*), and conception of ethics and systems of behavior as supreme (*tshul khrims dang brdul zhugs mchog 'dzin, śīlavrataparāmarśa*)
8 thorough enwrapment of jealousy (*phrag dog gi kun sbyor, *irṣyā-saṃyojana*)
9 thorough enwrapment of miserliness (*ser sna'i kun sbyor, *mātsarya-saṃyojana*)[a]

Gedün Lodrö notes that "The eighth and ninth, jealousy and miserliness, are chosen out of the long list of twenty secondary afflictive emotions because they are the two chief factors opposing altruism."[b]

The six investigations and the four reasonings. The formal way of meditating on the faults of the Desire Realm and the good qualities of the First Concentration is by way of the six investigations (*rtog pa, vitarka*)—of meaning (*don, artha*), things (*dngos po, vastu*), character (*mtshan nyid, lakṣaṇa*), class (*phyogs, pakṣa*), time (*dus, kāla*), and reasoning (*rigs pa, yukti*). The last consists of the four reasonings, which Denma Lochö Rinpoche gives as

1 reasoning of dependence (*ltos pa'i rigs pa, apekṣāyukti*) in terms of cause
2 reasoning of the performance of function (*bya ba byed pa'i rigs pa, kāryakāraṇayukti*)
3 logical reasoning (*'thad sgrub kyi rigs pa, upapattisādhanayukti*)

---

[a] Ibid., pp. 334–35.
[b] Ibid., p. 335.

4 reasoning of nature (*chos nyid kyi rigs pa, dharmatāyukti*)[a]

According to Denma Lochö Rinpoche, "The last refers to the nature of phenomena as it is known in the world."[b] He notes that

> For the most part, the viewing of the Desire Realm as gross and of the First concentration as peaceful would be included within the investigation of meaning, but there are also opportunities for the other types of investigation to take place.[c]

Level. The question of the level of the mental contemplation of individual knowledge of the character, especially as a preparation for the first concentration, has generated a great deal of controversy among Ge-luk-pa scholars. The discussion concerns whether that mental contemplation is of a level of meditative equipoise or of a level of non-equipoise. "Meditative equipoise" here refers to calm abiding, in which the meditator focuses one-pointedly on the object of observation and does not engage in analysis. In the mental contemplation of individual knowledge of the character, however, the meditator *is* engaged in analysis. Thus, the question under discussion is whether the mind of the mental contemplation of individual knowledge of the character remains of the same level as the calm abiding previously attained—that is, a mind of the Form Realm—or whether it is a mind of the Desire Realm. According to Gedün Lodrö, the level in which the mental contemplation of individual knowledge of the character is included is "probably the most important topic with respect to" that mental contemplation.[d]

Paṇ-chen Sö-nam-drak-pa, whose texts are followed by Lo-sel-ling College, holds that the mental contemplation of individual knowledge of the character is of a level of meditative equipoise, whereas the textbook-writers for Go-mang College—Jam-yang-shay-pa and Kön-chok-jik-may-wang-po—hold that it is of a level of non-equipoise.[e] Both

---

[a] *Meditative States,* p. 155. Gedün Lodrö gives the order somewhat differently as (1) reasoning of the performance of function, which he interprets literally as that which "eliminates obscuration with respect to the three—object, agent, and action"; (2) reasoning of nature; (3) reasoning of dependence, and (4) logical reasoning—"literally, 'the reasoning that establishes correctness'" (Gedün Lodrö, pp. 110, 111). Lati Rinpoche refers to the four reasonings without listing them; he says he has "combined them in order to make them easier to comprehend" (*Meditative States,* p. 96).

[b] *Meditative States,* p. 155.

[c] Ibid., p. 157.

[d] Gedün Lodrö, p. 339.

[e] Jam-yang-shay-pa, *Concentrations,* 203.4–214.2; Kön-chok-jik-may-wang-po, *Condensed*

opinions are based on a passage in Asaṅga's *Grounds of Hearers* for which two variant textual readings exist—one with and one without the negative "non-" (*ma*). According to Paṇ-chen Sö-nam-drak-pa, the negative is a textual corruption; he cites a passage from Yashomitra's *Commentary on (Asaṅga's) "Summary of Manifest Knowledge"*—"By means of mental contemplations that are of a level of meditative equipoise one views the Desire Realm as faulty"—to support his position.[a]

Both camps agree that the mental contemplation of individual knowledge of the character is a mixture of hearing and thinking.[b] Lati Rinpoche, who does not discuss the question of the level of individual knowledge of the character, notes that "At this point, the meditator is mainly analyzing through mental states arisen from hearing and...thinking."[c] Indeed, the term "a mixture of hearing and thinking" occurs later in the Yashomitra passage Paṇ-chen Sö-nam-drak-pa cites to support his position that the mental contemplation of individual knowledge of the character is of a level of meditative equipoise; it also occurs in Asaṅga's *Grounds of Hearers*.[d] Jam-yang-shay-pa, however, refutes Paṇ-chen Sö-nam-drak-pa's position—which he summarizes, together with Paṇ-chen Sö-nam-drak-pa's Indian source citations—by arguing that a mind that is a mixture of hearing and thinking must necessarily be of a level of non-equipoise—that is, a Desire Realm Mind—and that, therefore, the mental contemplation of individual knowledge of the character cannot be of a level of meditative equipoise. This is the decisive reason Kön-chok-jik-may-wang-po selects from Jam-yang-shay-pa's extensive series of debates on the topic.

Paṇ-chen Sö-nam-drak-pa's position follows what Gedün Lodrö calls the "main interpretation" given by Tsong-kha-pa's *Great Exposition of the Stages of the Path* and other Tibetan commentators, including "Ba-trül Chö-kyi-gyel-tsen[e]...as well as Gyel-tsap,[f] Kay-drup,[g] and many monastic textbooks"; he notes that, indeed, "almost all monastic textbooks follow this position, not just one or two, but most."[h] Gedün Lodrö also

---

Statement, 568.2–569.1.

[a] Paṇ-chen Sö-nam-drak-pa, "Concentrations," 152a.2–3; *Meditative States*, p. 150.

[b] For an extended discussion of "hearing," "thinking," and "meditating," see page 12.

[c] *Meditative States*, p. 93.

[d] P5537, vol. 110, p. 116.3.7.

[e] Probably Ba-so Chö-kyi-gyel-tsen (*ba so chos kyi rgyal mtshan*, 1402–1473); Gedün Lodrö, p. 340.

[f] *rgyal tshab dar ma rin chen*, 1364–1432; ibid., p. 340..

[g] *mkhas grub dge legs dpal bzang*, 1385–1438; ibid., p. 340..

[h] Ibid., pp. 340–41.

admits that, in the key passage from Asaṅga's *Grounds of Hearers,* the reading without the negative, according to which the mental contemplation of individual knowledge of the character is of a level of meditative equipoise, is the correct one.

The discussion is complicated, however, by the fact that Tsong-kha-pa's views on the level of mental contemplation of individual knowledge of the character changed over the course of his life. Although his *Great Exposition of the Stages of the Path* asserts that the mental contemplation of individual knowledge of the character is of a level of meditative equipoise, his early Perfection of Wisdom commentary, the *Golden Rosary of Eloquence,* and his late *Notes on the Concentrations and Formless Absorptions* hold that it is of a level of non-equipoise. The Go-mang textbook writers base their significant minority opinion on these two works.

In the *Golden Rosary of Eloquence,* according to Gedün Lodrö, Tsong-kha-pa "us[ed] the reading from the 'corrupt' text, which has the negative."[a] In *Notes on the Concentrations and Formless Absorptions,* Tsong-kha-pa states unequivocally that the mental contemplation of individual (or thorough) knowledge of the character that is a preparation for the first concentration "is included within the level of the Desire Realm."[b] It is in this late text, according to Gedün Lodrö, that Tsong-kha-pa offers a reasoned position that is intended to stand on its own, without reference to the textual status of the passage in Asaṅga's source text.[c]

His argument rests on the relationship between states arisen from hearing, thinking, and meditating, on the one hand, and Buddhist cosmology, as set forth in Vasubandhu's *Autocommentary on the "Treasury of Manifest Knowledge"* on the other. According to Gedün Lodrö's summary of the Manifest Knowledge position:

1 There are states arisen from hearing and states arisen from thinking included within the level of the Desire Realm.
2 There are states arisen from hearing and states arisen from meditation included within the Form Realm; there is no state arisen from thinking included within the Form Realm.
3 There are only states arisen from meditation included within the levels of the Formless Realm.[d]

---

[a] Ibid., p. 341.

[b] Tsong-kha-pa, *Notes,* 4.1.

[c] Gedün Lodrö, pp. 341, 346.

[d] Ibid., p. 339; Jam-yang-shay-pa, *Concentrations,* 214.2–7, 247.5–6, citing Tsong-kha-pa's *Golden Rosary of Eloquence* and Yashomitra's *Commentary on (Vasubandhu's) "Treasury of*

From this presentation, according to the Go-mang textbook writers, Tsong-kha-pa concludes that the level of the mental contemplation of individual knowledge of the character depends on the life-basis of the meditator—that is, on the cosmological level into which the meditator is born. The mental contemplation of individual knowledge of the character that is a preparation for the first concentration is always cultivated by a being born in the Desire Realm, is a mixture of hearing and thinking, and is always included within the level of the Desire Realm. As a preparation for the second concentration, the mental contemplation of individual knowledge of the character can be cultivated either by a Desire Realm being or by a being born in the First Concentration. If it is cultivated by a Desire Realm being, it is included within the level of the Desire Realm. However, if it is cultivated by a being born in the First Concentration, it is included within the level of the Form Realm. The same reasoning is applied to the remaining concentrations and formless absorptions.[a]

Paṇ-chen Sö-nam-drak-pa does not discuss the manner in which Form and Formless Realm beings cultivate the mental contemplation of individual knowledge of the character. He merely states the Manifest Knowledge position that

> on the levels of the upper realms [that is, the Form and Formless Realms] there are no states risen from thinking and, in the Formless Realm, no states arisen from hearing, therefore, in the upper realms [that is, the Form and Formless Realms], when one begins to think, one goes into meditative stabilization without time for thinking.[b]

He concludes, therefore, that

> In accordance with [the explanation from the Manifest Knowledges], when one meditates from within a basis of the Formless Realm, there is neither hearing nor thinking in the first mental contemplation [that is, individual knowledge of the character], and when one meditates from within a basis of the

Manifest Knowledge" (*abhidharmakośaṭīkā, chos mngon pa'i 'grel bshad*). Jam-yang-shay-pa's discussion is abridged in Kön-chok-jik-may-wang-po, *Condensed Statement,* 569.1–3. Paṇ-chen Sö-nam-drak-pa, "Concentrations," 154a.2–4 (see also *Meditative States,* p. 163) presents a position refuted by Jam-yang-shay-pa. See also Tsong-kha-pa, *Notes,* 6.3–4.

[a] Gedün Lodrö, p. 341.

[b] Paṇ-chen Sö-nam-drak-pa, "Concentrations," 154a.2–4 (see also *Meditative States,* p. 163).

Form Realm, there are no states arisen from thinking.[a]

According to Denma Lochö Rinpoche, "'In accordance with [the explanation from the Manifest Knowledges]' implies that according to the Madhyamaka system there is room for analysis whether there could be states arisen from hearing or thinking in the Form and Formless Realms."[b] Paṇ-chen Sö-nam-drak-pa, however, does not develop a Madhyamaka interpretation.

Jam-yang-shay-pa, on the other hand, considers the process by which beings born in the Form and Formless Realms cultivate the mental contemplation of individual knowledge of the character as a preparation for actual absorptions of higher Form and Formless Realm levels; he questions whether it is possible to analyze a lower level as gross and an upper level as peaceful in the absence of hearing and thinking and of states arisen from them. He points out that literal acceptance of the Manifest Knowledge position is based on the assumption that "whatever is a state arisen from hearing must be a state arisen from hearing at that time and in that life."[c] In his summary of Jam-yang-shay-pa's argument, Kön-chok-jik-may-wang-po establishes that Form Realm beings can have states arisen from hearing and thinking because they have clairvoyance and, thus, "can easily achieve [states arisen from] hearing and thinking."[d] He establishes that Formless Realm beings can have states arisen from hearing and thinking because of hearing and thinking done in a former lifetime:

> in the [Formless Realm], there are both states arisen from hearing that think about the meaning of that concerning which, although one had heard it in a former lifetime, one did not gain ascertainment and also states arisen from thinking about that concerning which one gained ascertainment.[e]

Jam-yang-shay-pa raises these questions in his Refutation section. In his exposition of his own system concerning the preparations, however, he gives, without comment, a straightforward presentation of the standard Manifest Knowledge position concerning the status of states arisen from hearing and thinking in the upper realms. Apparently, it was a tradition he did not feel entirely free to refute.

---

[a] Ibid., 154a.3–4 (see also *Meditative States*, p. 163).

[b] *Meditative States*, p. 163.

[c] Jam-yang-shay-pa, *Concentrations*, 215.2.

[d] Kön-chok-jik-may-wang-po, *Condensed Statement*, 569.2–3.

[e] Ibid., 569.3.

Denma Lochö Rinpoche's oral comments on Paṇ-chen Sö-nam-drak-pa's text suggest that some non–Go-mang scholars seem to be at least partly drawn to the Go-mang position. Without refuting his own textbook or agreeing with Jam-yang-shay-pa's position, Denma Lochö Rinpoche refers to Jam-yang-shay-pa's text and suggests, as an apparent compromise, that

> even according to the Madhyamaka system, the mental contemplation of individual knowledge of the character would not be a mixture of hearing and thinking in the Form and Formless Realms. This is because the positing of a mixture of hearing and thinking relates only to the viewing of a lower level as gross and an upper level as peaceful, and in the Form and Formless Realms the mind would naturally flow into meditative stabilization with regard to viewing a lower and an upper level in this way. Still, there would have to be states arisen from hearing and thinking for meditation on the four truths or on any of the profound Mahāyāna doctrines to take place in the Form Realm.[a]

Although he does not endorse Jam-yang-shay-pa's position concerning the mental contemplation of individual knowledge of the character having the aspect of grossness/peacefulness, he seems to be willing to apply it, by analogy, to the mental contemplation of individual knowledge of the character having the aspect of the truths.

Mental basis. Although Paṇ-chen Sö-nam-drak-pa and Lati Rinpoche do not explicitly discuss the topic of the mental basis of individual knowledge of the character, it would probably be correct to say that there is general agreement that the mental basis of that mental contemplation is the calm abiding already attained, although Gedün Lodrö introduces an important qualification of this position. According to Go-mang textbook writers and commentators, the mental basis of the mental contemplation of individual knowledge of the character is a hidden (*lkog gyur, parokṣa*), or *subliminal,* calm abiding; the position that a subliminal consciousness can exist simultaneously with another, manifest, consciousness is unique to Go-mang.[b] With regard to the mental contemplation of individual knowledge of the character that is a preparation for the first concentration, the Go-mang writers and commentators base their position on a phrase from Tsong-kha-pa's *Great Exposition of the Stages of the Path*—"Within the state of the non-deterioration of a

---

[a] *Meditative States,* p. 163.

[b] Jeffrey Hopkins in conversation.

calm abiding that observes any of the varieties of phenomena..."[a]

Gedün Lodrö asks, with regard to the mental contemplation of individual knowledge of the character, whether analysis is "done from within the state of calm abiding" or whether calm abiding is "left when analysis is done"—that is, whether the analysis is done "within the state of dwelling in calm abiding." His opinion is that the latter is the case and that "the state of dwelling in calm abiding" implies that, for a meditator at the level of individual knowledge of the character, "a mind of strong analysis...must initially be manifest," whereas, if the analysis "were done within the state of the meditative equipoise of calm abiding, it would be necessary that the meditative equipoise be manifest."[b] Moreover, he argues, both cannot be manifest simultaneously because both the mental contemplation of individual knowledge of the character and the meditative equipoise of calm abiding are main minds rather than mental factors; if they were mental factors accompanying a single main mind, it would be possible for them to manifest simultaneously, but since they are main minds, only one of them can be manifest at any given time. Therefore, Gedün Lodrö argues,

> The previously attained mind of calm abiding becomes slightly hidden—that is, slightly subliminal. It serves as a concomitant (*grogs, sahāya*) of the analysis; it does not serve as the actual mental basis for the analysis. However, when the mental contemplation of individual knowledge of the character turns into an entity of special insight, the meditative stabilization which accompanies it turns into a calm abiding; therefore, the earlier calm abiding serves as a mental basis in the sense of being a means of attainment.[c]

It appears that the acceptance of the possibility of subliminal consciousnesses also affects the Go-mang position concerning the level of individual knowledge of the character and allows Go-mang scholars to maintain that the mental contemplation of individual knowledge of the character is of a level of non-equipoise—that is, included within the level of the Desire Realm. If they held that the previously attained calm abiding is always manifest, even when a meditator is doing the analysis required for the mental contemplation of individual knowledge of the character, it would be harder to argue that the mental contemplation

---

a Gedün Lodrö, p. 347; Jam-yang-shay-pa, *Concentrations,* 212.6.

b Gedün Lodrö, p. 315.

c Ibid., p. 316.

of individual knowledge of the character that is a preparation for the first concentration is included within the level of the Desire Realm.

The mode of procedure. The mode of procedure of individual knowledge of the character refers to the cultivation of special insight, whether actual or mundane. According to Lati Rinpoche, the meditator passes "through nine states *exactly like* the nine mental abidings that lead to calm abiding" (italics added); in the cultivation of mundane special insight, "there are two objects of observation—the Desire Realm and the First Concentration."[a] Lati Rinpoche explains that the meditator "has to cultivate the nine mental abidings *within analytical meditation,* in dependence upon the calm abiding already achieved."[b] He presents the cultivation of special insight in a form similar to his presentation of the cultivation of calm abiding, using the terminology of the nine mental abidings, the five faults and eight antidotes, the six powers, and the four mental engagements.[c] According to Gedün Lodrö, however, the terminology of the four mental engagements is used in relation to special insight in a different sense from the way it is used in relation to calm abiding; moreover, the terminology of the nine mental abidings is not used in relation to special insight, although "[i]f you want to designate them as being present at that time, it is suitable to do so."[d]

For both Lati Rinpoche and Gedün Lodrö, the main difference between the modes of cultivation of calm abiding and special insight is in the techniques used as antidotes to laxity and excitement. Instead of applying the antidotes used during the cultivation of calm abiding—such techniques, for instance, as meditating on a bright object or on invigorating topics such as leisure and fortune as antidotes to laxity or meditating on sobering topics such as death and impermanence as antidotes to excitement (see pages 153ff.)—the meditator cultivating special insight alternates between analytical and stabilizing meditation, using analytical meditation as an antidote to laxity and stabilizing meditation as an antidote to excitement. Gedün Lodrö discusses this method both in relation to the fourth of the four attributes of preparatory training and in relation to the mental contemplation of individual knowledge of the character.[e]

---

[a] *Meditative States,* p. 93.

[b] Ibid., p. 96.

[c] Ibid., pp. 96–101.

[d] Gedün Lodrö, pp. 230–31.

[e] *Meditative States,* pp. 99–100; Gedün Lodrö, pp. 279, 317.

According to Gedün Lodrö, states arisen from meditation are of two types: realizational consciousnesses that are states arisen from stabilizing meditation (*'jog sgom gyi sgom byung gi rtogs pa*), which are achieved with calm abiding, and realizational consciousnesses that are states arisen from analytical meditation (*dpyad sgom gyi sgom byung gi rtogs pa*), which are achieved only with the attainment of special insight.[a] Gedün Lodrö points out that, when analytical meditation is done before the achievement of special insight,

> [t]hose occasions of analysis are minds of analytical meditation but not realizational consciousnesses that are states arisen from meditation....The reason for cultivating analysis at this time of the mental contemplation of individual knowledge of the character is to develop experience that is a state arisen from meditation with regard to analytical meditation [b]

With the gaining of that experience, the meditator attains special insight, a union of calm abiding and special insight, and, simultaneously, the mental contemplation arisen from belief.

The mental contemplation arisen from belief

According to Lati Rinpoche,

> [t]he mental contemplation arisen from belief is so called because, during the mental contemplation of individual knowledge of the character, the meditator reflected on the grossness of the Desire Realm and the peacefulness of the First Concentration through mental abidings arisen from hearing and thinking and believed them to be that way. Since this state arises through the power of such belief, it is called the mental contemplation arisen from belief.[c]

His etymology is close to Tsong-kha-pa's:

> By reason of being the mental contemplation which arises in dependence upon having believed in the grossness and peacefulness [of the Desire Realm and the First Concentration, respectively] through hearing and thinking in the context of [the mental contemplation of] thorough knowledge of the

---

[a] Gedün Lodrö, p. 316.

[b] Ibid., p. 317.

[c] *Meditative States*, p. 101.

> character, it is called [the mental contemplation arisen from belief].[a]

Jam-yang-shay-pa's slightly different etymology emphasizes the union of calm abiding and special insight that characterizes the mental contemplation arisen from belief:

> having passed beyond alternating (*res 'jog*) hearing and thinking with respect to that object, it—in terms of having the two, calm abiding and special insight, in one [union] or of having gained ascertainment with respect to that object—meditates in that way and other objects of observation do not interfere[b]

"that object" being, here, the Desire Realm and the First Concentration. Jam-yang-shay-pa also mentions the role of belief during the mental contemplation arisen from belief itself, since it generates the preparation that follows, the mental contemplation of thorough isolation, "by way of forceful belief in the union of calm abiding and special insight such that [one] is not captivated by anything else."[c]

Although the mental contemplation arisen from belief does not, itself, purify afflictive emotions, it is considered a mental contemplation that purifies afflictive emotions because, as Gedün Lodrö explains,

> [e]ven though the mental contemplation arisen from belief is not an actual antidote, it is the actual inducer of an antidote; it is the uncommon direct cause of an antidotal mental contemplation. For this reason, it is posited as a purifier.[d]

According to Paṇ-chen Sö-nam-drak-pa, the mental contemplation arisen from belief is a beginner at purifying afflictive emotions.[e] Gedün Lodrö, however, follows Jam-yang-shay-pa in limiting the term "beginner at purifying afflictive emotions" to the mental contemplation of individual knowledge of the character.[f] Nevertheless, because the mental contemplation arisen from belief induces the first mental contemplation that is an actual antidote, Lati Rinpoche asserts that "[a]t this

---

[a] Tsong-kha-pa, *Notes,* 4.2–3.

[b] Jam-yang-shay-pa, *Concentrations,* 231.7–232.1.

[c] Ibid., 236.6.

[d] Gedün Lodrö, pp. 311–12.

[e] Paṇ-chen Sö-nam-drak-pa, "Concentrations," 152b.2 (see also *Meditative States,* p. 153).

[f] Gedün Lodrö p. 308; Jam-yang-shay-pa, *Concentrations,* 227.2; Kön-chok-jik-may-wang-po, *Condensed Statement,* 570.6.

point, a practitioner has attained the capacity to abandon" the great afflictive emotions pertaining to the Desire Realm.[a] The meditator begins to overcome them with the next preparation, the mental contemplation of thorough isolation.

The mental contemplation of thorough isolation

According to Lati Rinpoche, the mental contemplation of thorough isolation that is a preparation for the first concentration is so called "because it is the meditator's initial isolation" from afflictive emotions pertaining to the Desire Realm.[b] Jam-yang-shay-pa, in an etymology that covers mental contemplations of thorough isolation that are preparations for any level, both those having the aspect of grossness/peacefulness and those having the aspect of the truths, similarly explains the name of this mental contemplation as referring to the fact that "in terms of either overcoming the seeds or suppression, it has separated from the great obstructions" pertaining to the lower level;[c] the type having the aspect of grossness/peacefulness merely suppresses the great afflictive emotions, whereas that having the aspect of the truths overcomes the seeds. His specific definition of a "mental contemplation of thorough isolation which is a mundane preparation for the first concentration" as

> the second taking to mind purifying afflictive emotions, which abides in the type of causing the mere suppression (*nyams smad*) of any of the three cycles of the corresponding great coarse afflictive emotions pertaining to the Desire Realm in terms of viewing the lower or upper level as either faulty or having good qualities, [respectively][d]

underscores both the overcoming of the great afflictive emotions pertaining to the lower level that characterizes all forms of this mental contemplation and the distinction between mere suppression and actual abandonment that differentiates the mundane and supramundane forms of it.

The mental contemplation of thorough isolation has three divisions: uninterrupted paths (*bar chad med lam, ānantaryamārga*), paths of

---

[a] *Meditative States*, p. 102.

[b] Ibid., p. 102. His etymology closely follows the one in Tsong-kha-pa, *Notes*, 4.4.

[c] Jam-yang-shay-pa, *Concentrations*, 232.1

[d] Ibid., 228.3–4, summarized in Kön-chok-jik-may-wang-po, *Condensed Statement*, 571.5–6.

release (*rnam grol lam, vimuktimārga*), and a type that is neither of these. Of the three, the uninterrupted path is the consciousness that acts as an actual antidote to afflictive emotions and overcomes them. The path of release, according to Lati Rinpoche, is a "state of having been freed" from the afflictive emotions overcome by the preceding uninterrupted path. The type that is neither occurs when the meditator has completed a path of release and "is trying to achieve the capacity to reach the next uninterrupted path."[a] A mental contemplation of thorough isolation contains three uninterrupted paths, each of which is followed by a path of release and a period that is neither. In the case of a mental contemplation of thorough isolation that is a preparation for the first concentration, the first uninterrupted path overcomes the great of the great afflictive emotions pertaining to the Desire Realm; the second overcomes the middling of the great, and the third overcomes the small of the great.[b] (See chart next page.)

---

[a] *Meditative States*, pp. 102, 110.

[b] *Meditative States*, p. 111.

Chart 13: Preparations for the First Concentration

(Read from bottom to top.)

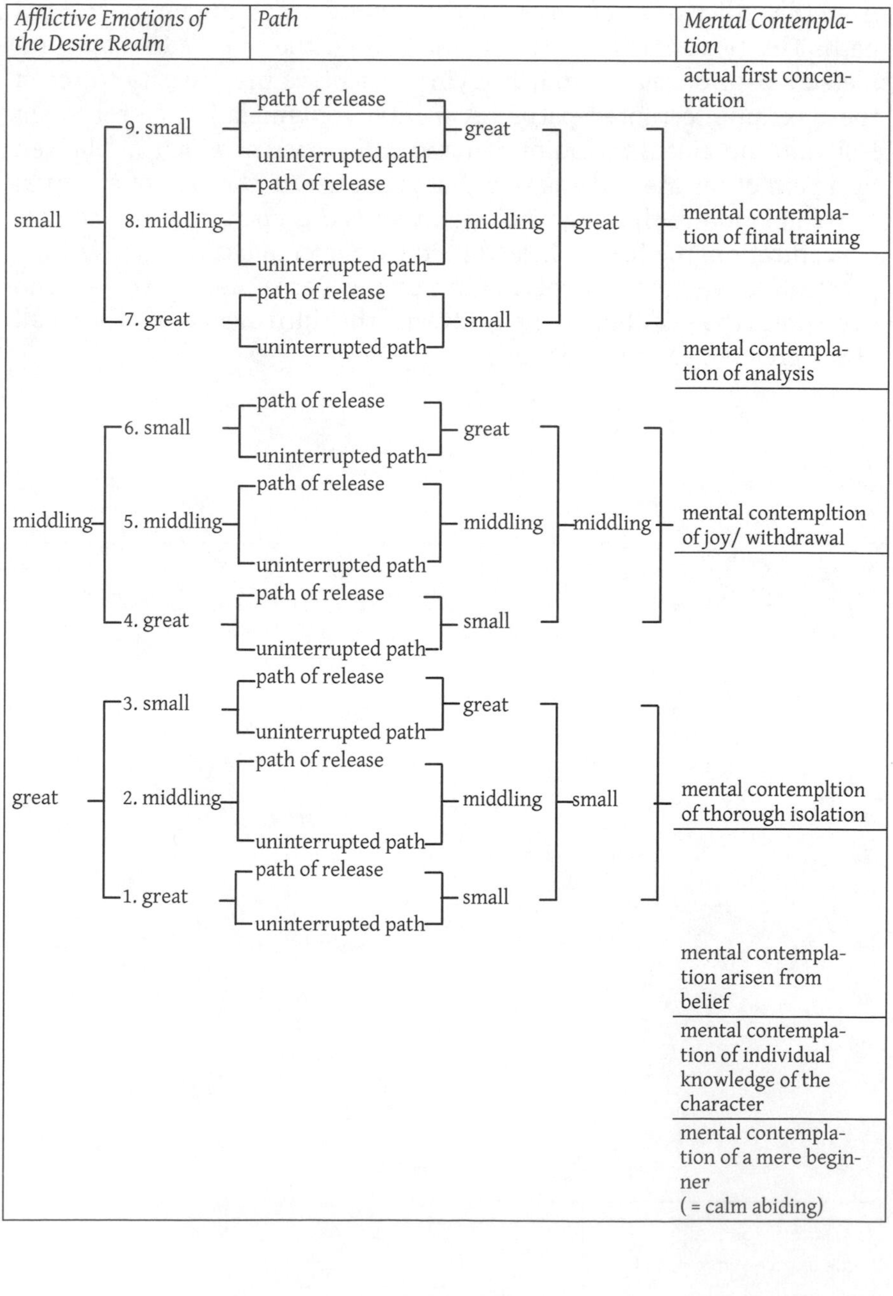

Afflictive Emotions of the Desire Realm
Path
Mental Contemplation
actual first concentration
path of release
9. small
great
uninterrupted path
path of release
small
8. middling
middling
great
mental contemplation of final training
uninterrupted path
path of release
7. great
small
uninterrupted path
mental contemplation of analysis
path of release
6. small
great
uninterrupted path
path of release
middling
5. middling
middling
middling
mental contempltion of joy/ withdrawal
uninterrupted path
path of release
4. great
small
uninterrupted path
path of release
3. small
great
uninterrupted path
path of release
great
2. middling
middling
small
mental contempltion of thorough isolation
uninterrupted path
path of release
1. great
small
uninterrupted path
mental contemplation arisen from belief
mental contemplation of individual knowledge of the character
mental contemplation of a mere beginner
(= calm abiding)

It is in terms of the uninterrupted path that the mental contemplation of thorough isolation is defined. In Jam-yang-shay-pa's definition (page 377), the phrase "which abides in the type" implies that there are exceptions, that the definition does not cover all instances. The type that is neither an uninterrupted path nor a path of release is an obvious exception, since it does not suppress afflictive emotions. There is also some question whether the path of release fulfills the definition, since it does not *cause* the suppression of afflictive emotions but, rather, is a state of *having* suppressed them.

Lati Rinpoche notes that, beginning with the mental contemplation of thorough isolation, the analysis of grossness/peacefulness becomes condensed. Instead of using the six investigations, as in the mental contemplation of individual knowledge of the character and that arisen from belief, the meditator now views the Desire Realm as gross in nature and in number—that is, as being naturally faulty in many ways. The meditator then views the First Concentration as peaceful.[a] This condensation is possible because, in mental contemplations of thorough isolation having the aspect of grossness/peacefulness, the uninterrupted paths have the aspect of grossness—that is, view the lower level as gross—and the paths of release have the aspect of peacefulness—that is, view the upper level as peaceful. Jam-yang-shay-pa develops this point in an extended debate seeking to prove, on the basis of both textual sources and psychological principles derived from reasoning, that grossness/peacefulness does not mean grossness *and* peacefulness because the two aspects cannot occur simultaneously. He argues that

> the mundane uninterrupted paths have the aspect of grossness and [the mundane] paths of release have the aspect of peacefulness (1) because such is explained in the root text [Tsong-kha-pa's *Notes on the Concentrations and Formless Absorptions*] and in Vasubandhu's *Autocommentary on the "Treasury of Manifest Knowledge"*; (2) because it is explained in Asaṅga's *Grounds of Hearers* also that, having first viewed [the lower level] as gross, one meditates after that on [the upper level] as peaceful, and (3) because attachment to the lower level is abandoned if one has viewed [the lower level] as faulty but cannot be abandoned merely by viewing the upper level as peaceful or as having good qualities. This is because simultaneous engaging in

[a] *Meditative States*, p. 110.

> attachment to the lower and upper [levels] occurs but [consideration of something] as the two, pleasant and unpleasant, does not occur [simultaneously].[a]

The mental contemplation of joy-withdrawal

The final period of the mental contemplation of thorough isolation that is neither an uninterrupted path nor a path of release leads to another uninterrupted path—the first uninterrupted path of the mental contemplation of joy-withdrawal. This mental contemplation overcomes the middling afflictive emotions pertaining to the lower level—here, the Desire Realm.

The name of this mental contemplation, as understood by Tibetan commentators, literally means "joy-withdrawal"; that is the translation used here because the relationship between these two terms is matter for debate. In his translation of Asaṅga's *Summary of Manifest Knowledge*, Walpola Rahula, without citing any commentarial tradition, mistranslates the Sanskrit name, *ratisaṃgrāhakamanaskāra*, as "l'attention [his translation of *manaskāra*] qui favorise le contentement."[b] Tibetan interpreters, by contrast, translate *saṃgrāhaka* as *sdud pa* ("withdrawal"). Although they do not analyze the grammatical structure of the compound, they appear to understand it as similar to a *dvanda* compound, but one in which the relationship between the two elements is "or" rather than "and." According to Lati Rinpoche, the two terms of the compound are given in reverse order for the sake of euphony; the correct order—that is, the order in which the two elements of the compound occur in practice—is withdrawal-joy.[c] He goes on to explain the name of this mental contemplation in relation to its structure:

> "Withdrawal" refers to the uninterrupted paths and is so called because the practitioner is observing the Desire Realm and turning away from attachment to it; the mind becomes withdrawn from coarser objects of observation. The paths of release

---

[a] Jam-yang-shay-pa, *Concentrations,* 231.3–6. Jam-yang-shay-pa, atypically, does not support his assertion by citing specific passages from Tsong-kha-pa's *Notes* (the "root text") and the *Autocommentary on [Vasubandhu's] "Treasury of Manifest Knowledge,"* and I have not been able to find any passages that *explicitly* assert a correspondence between uninterrupted paths and the aspect of grossness, on the one hand, and paths of release and the aspect of peacefulness, on the other.

[b] Rahula, trans., *Le Compendium de la super-doctrine (philosophie) (Abhidharmasamuccaya d'Asaṅga)*, p. 112.

[c] *Meditative States,* p. 112.

> of this preparation are called "joy" because the practitioner has become freed from the middling [afflictive emotions] with respect to the Desire Realm.[a]

In his etymology of the mental contemplation of joy-withdrawal, Tsong-kha-pa refers to "enhancement in body and mind by way of a small [degree of] joy and bliss, included within the level of the first concentration, which are produced from isolation."[b] Paṇ-chen Sö-nam-drak-pa explains that from this point on, the meditator "is touched to some extent by joy and bliss, the benefit branches [of the first concentration]."[c]

Jam-yang-shay-pa explains in detail, through citations of the relevant passages in Asaṅga's *Grounds of Hearers,* that it is incorrect to call a mental contemplation which is an actual antidote to any of the middling coarse afflictive emotions pertaining to the level below—that is, an uninterrupted path of this mental contemplation—a mental contemplation of joy-withdrawal because the uninterrupted path "engages its object of observation by way of the aspect of either defect or discouragement"; moreover, "withdrawal" means discouragement, "since it is...explained frequently that, when one becomes discouraged, the mind withdraws inside."[d] Thus, the uninterrupted path is only a mental contemplation of discouragement, or withdrawal. He also explains, by referring to Asaṅga's designation of joy-withdrawal as a thoroughly clear mental contemplation in the division of mental contemplations into four (see below, page 231) and by citing Asaṅga's enumeration of objects of joy for Buddhists and non-Buddhists, that mental contemplations of joy engage their objects of observation by way of joy; he implies—although he does not spell it out—that the mental contemplations of joy are the paths of release of this mental contemplation. He also argues that joy and withdrawal cannot occur simultaneously because feelings of joy and discouragement cannot arise in a single consciousness at the same time. Thus, since withdrawal and joy cannot occur simultaneously, there is an either/or relationship between them.[e] When Jam-yang-shay-pa defines the mental contemplation of joy-withdrawal in the exposition of his own system, he underscores this

---

[a] Ibid., p. 113.

[b] Tsong-kha-pa, *Notes,* 4.5–6.

[c] Paṇ-chen Sö-nam-drak-pa, "Concentrations," 153a.6 (see also *Meditative States,* p. 159).

[d] Jam-yang-shay-pa, *Concentrations,* 217.4, 218.5.

[e] Ibid., 217.2–219.2.

point by giving the definiendum as "the mental contemplation of either joy or withdrawal" (*dga' sdud ci rigs kyi yid byed*)—a gloss giving his own interpretation of the standard term.[a] His etymology also underscores the mutual exclusiveness of joy and withdrawal:

> (a) because it purifies the mind by the faith of wishing [to attain] or conviction...[the fifth preparation] is posited as joy; (b) because, having reversed adherence to [the middling obstructions] or withdrawn the mind from any of the coarse afflictive emotions, it is directed toward the object of observation, [the fifth also] is posited as withdrawal.[b]

Jam-yang-shay-pa's etymology does not mention the relationship between the joy of joy-withdrawal and the joy that is a branch of the first concentration and, thus, appears to differ somewhat in emphasis from that of Tsong-kha-pa's root text.

Like the mental contemplation of thorough isolation, the mental contemplation of joy-withdrawal has three uninterrupted paths, which overcome, respectively, the great of the middling, middling of the middling, and small of the middling coarse afflictive emotions pertaining to the Desire Realm. It also has three paths of release and three periods that are neither, which occur when the meditator has experienced a path of release and is working to attain the next uninterrupted path. Joy-withdrawal is also similar to thorough isolation in that the meditator uses a condensed analysis of grossness/peacefulness according to nature and number.[c] (See chart, page 218.)

The mental contemplation of analysis

With the final path of release of the mental contemplation of joy-withdrawal, the meditator has overcome six of the nine cycles of afflictive emotions pertaining to the Desire Realm and, therefore, thinks he or she has overcome all of them.[d] Without further analysis, meditators at this point are likely to overestimate their degree of attainment. As Gedün Lodrö points out, "Because most of the manifest coarse afflictive emotions have been suppressed, yogis even think that they have become like Foe Destroyers—as though all afflictive emotions have been

---

[a] Ibid., 229.1.

[b] Ibid., 232.1–2.

[c] *Meditative States*, p. 113.

[d] *Meditative States*, p. 113.

overcome."[a] Therefore, analysis is necessary to see whether that is the case. This analysis differs from that used during the preparatory mental contemplations beginning with individual knowledge of the character, for, as Kön-chok-jik-may-wang-po notes, the mental contemplation of analysis does not have either the aspect of grossness/peacefulness or the aspect of the truths.[b] Rather, the meditator "tests himself or herself" by taking to mind, or visualizing, a Desire Realm object that had previously caused an afflictive emotion—desire or hatred—to be generated.[c] Denma Lochö Rinpoche notes that "[a]lthough, at that time, desire or hatred would not be generated strongly, nevertheless because of habit, a slight degree of desire or hatred would be generated." Therefore, the meditator concludes that all the Desire Realm afflictive emotions have not been overcome and that further cultivation is necessary.[d]

Because the mental contemplation of analysis is concerned with self-testing and does not overcome any afflictive emotions, it has, as Lati Rinpoche notes, "neither uninterrupted paths nor paths of release."[e] Gedün Lodrö points out, however, that although the mental contemplation of analysis is not an actual purifier of afflictive emotions, it is called a purifier of afflictive emotions because it "directly induces the mental contemplation of final training."[f]

Although only a single mental contemplation of analysis is listed in classifications of preparatory mental contemplations, the term "mental contemplation of analysis" does not refer to a single period of time. Rather, as Kön-chok-jik-may-wang-po and Jam-yang-shay-pa point out in their discussions of the boundaries of the mental contemplation of analysis, there are three similar periods of analysis—one after the last path of release of the mental contemplation of joy-withdrawal, when the small of the middling afflictive emotions pertaining to the Desire Realm have been overcome; a second after the first path of release of the mental contemplation of final training, when the great of the small afflictive emotions pertaining to the Desire Realm have been overcome; and a third after the second path of release of the mental contemplation of final training, when the middling of the small afflictive

[a] Gedün Lodrö, p. 301.

[b] Kön-chok-jik-may-wang-po, *Condensed Statement*, 567.5–6, corresponding to Jam-yang-shay-pa, *Concentrations*, 191.2.

[c] *Meditative States*, p. 114.

[d] Ibid., pp. 159, 114.

[e] Ibid., p. 114.

[f] Gedün Lodrö, p. 312.

emotions pertaining to the Desire Realm have been overcome.[a]

The mental contemplation of final training

The mental contemplation of final training overcomes the small afflictive emotions pertaining to the Desire Realm. According to Lati Rinpoche, it "is so called because it is the last of the preparations and because it is a training."[b] Continuing the condensed cultivation of grossness/peacefulness, the meditator views the Desire Realm as gross and the First Concentration as peaceful "in nature and in number."[c]

Like the mental contemplations of thorough isolation and joy-withdrawal, the mental contemplation of final training has three uninterrupted paths. The first overcomes the great of the small afflictive emotions pertaining to the Desire Realm; the second overcomes the middling of the small afflictive emotions pertaining to the Desire Realm, and the third overcomes the small of the small afflictive emotions pertaining to the Desire Realm. Each of these uninterrupted paths is followed by a path of release, but only the first two paths of release are part of the mental contemplation of final training. As was noted earlier, the first two paths of release are followed by periods of analysis to see whether all the afflictive emotions pertaining to the Desire Realm have been overcome. Each of these periods of analysis is a mental contemplation of analysis.

There is also a mental contemplation of final training that is neither an uninterrupted path nor a path of release.[d] As in the mental contemplations of thorough isolation and joy-withdrawal, the type that is neither occurs when the meditator has experienced a path of release and is cultivating the next uninterrupted path; it is to be distinguished from the mental contemplations of analysis that immediately follow the paths of release of this mental contemplation and lead the meditator to conclude that further cultivation is necessary.

---

[a] Kön-chok-jik-may-wang-po, *Condensed Statement,* 572.6–573.2, from Jam-yang-shay-pa, *Concentrations,* 229.6–230.1.

[b] *Meditative States,* p. 115. Jam-yang-shay-pa gives a similar etymology: the mental contemplation of final training is so called "because of being the last cycle of training—[that is, of training] in antidotes and abandoning [afflictive emotions]—for an actual [absorption], or the last cycle of the three cycles of preparations for an actual [absorption]" (Jam-yang-shay-pa, *Concentrations,* 232.2–3).

[c] *Meditative States,* p. 114.

[d] Kön-chok-jik-may-wang-po, *Condensed Statement,* 573.3–4, from Jam-yang-shay-pa, *Concentrations,* 230.4.

The mental contemplation that is the fruit of final training

There is, indeed, a path of release that follows the last uninterrupted path of the mental contemplation of final training. This path of release, however, is not a mental contemplation of final training but the mental contemplation that is the fruit of final training, the last of Asaṅga's seven mental contemplations. Although the question is complicated, most commentators hold that the mental contemplation that is the fruit of final training is not a preparation but an actual absorption of the first concentration.[a] According to Jam-yang-shay-pa, this mental contemplation is called the fruit of final training "because of being the fruit of [the three cycles of antidotes] and release from [the three cycles of objects of abandonment] and a factor which is an actual [absorption]."[b] He and Kön-chok-jik-may-wang-po also give the five divisions of the mental contemplation that is the fruit of final training as investigation (*rtog pa, vitarka*), analysis (*dpyod pa, vicāra*), joy (*dga' ba, prīti*), bliss (*bde ba, sukha*), and meditative stabilization (*ting nge 'dzin, samādhi*)[c]—that is to say, as the five branches of the first concentration. Their definitions of this mental contemplation, however, include the qualification "which abides in the type." Kön-chok-jik-may-wang-po defines a mundane mental contemplation that is the fruit of final training for the first concentration as "an actual absorption of the first concentration which abides in the type of the path of release induced by the ninth mundane uninterrupted path."[d] (See chart, page 218.)

---

[a] *Meditative States,* p. 115.

[b] Jam-yang-shay-pa, *Concentrations,* 232.3.

[c] Kön-chok-jik-may-wang-po, *Condensed Statement,* 573.5; Jam-yang-shay-pa, *Concentrations,* 230.7.

[d] Kön-chok-jik-may-wang-po, *Condensed Statement,* 573.4–5. Jam-yang-shay-pa's full definition of a mundane mental contemplation that is the fruit of final training for the first concentration is "an actual absorption of the first concentration which abides in the type of the path of release that is the ninth [path of release], induced by the mundane uninterrupted path which causes the mere suppression of the ninth of the coarse afflictions pertaining to the Desire Realm in dependence upon such [a union of] calm abiding and special insight having the aspects of grossness/peacefulness," although his short definition intended for debate—"an actual first concentration included within the path of release of the ninth preparation for the first concentration"—changes the definiendum to "an absorption that is the fruit of final training for the first concentration" and omits the qualification (Jam-yang-shay-pa, *Concentrations,* 230.6–7 and 233.2–3).

The ninth path of release and the feeling accompanying the preparations. Ge-luk interpretations of the status of the ninth path of release are closely related to the question of the feeling accompanying the preparations. Discussion of this issue, in turn, is derived from the Tibetan commentators' understanding of the Indian schools of tenets and the distinctions between the so-called Mahāyāna and Hīnayāna Manifest Knowledge positions. Nevertheless, it must be admitted that here Ge-luk-pa commentators, beginning with Tsong-kha-pa, unconsciously conflate the two to some extent, even while attempting to distinguish between them, for, although, in the *Treasury of Manifest Knowledge* and *Autocommentary,* Vasubandhu indeed discusses a ninth, final, path of release,[a] he does so in the context of the abandonment of the ninth level of afflictive emotions pertaining to a given level, not in relation to the mental contemplations set forth by Asaṅga. Gedün Lodrö comments on this discussion:

> The various tenet systems have different answers to the question whether this path of release is an actual first concentration, but there is no complication concerning its being the seventh mental contemplation. Everyone agrees that when one has the final path of release, one has attained the first concentration, but there is a great deal of complication regarding whether or not that final path of release itself is a first concentration.[b]

The presentation is a general one concerned not only with the preparations for the first concentration but also with those for higher absorptions, although the topic is discussed under the general heading of preparations for the first concentration. Assumed in this discussion is knowledge of information concerning the actual absorptions, given later in presentations of the concentrations and formless absorptions—namely, that both the first and second concentrations have joy and bliss as branches, that the third concentration has bliss but not joy, and that the fourth concentration and the formless absorptions have the feeling of equanimity, also known as neutral feeling (*sdug bsngal ma yin bde ba yang ma yin, aduḥkhāsukha;* see page 253).

Tsong-kha-pa states unequivocally in his *Notes on the Concentrations and Formless Absorptions* that "in the system of Asaṅga's *Summary of*

---

[a] Vasubandhu, *Treasury of Manifest Knowledge,* 6.48a–c (P5591, vol. 115, 253.2.4, 6; Shastri, part 3, p. 976; La Vallée Poussin 16:3, pp. 237–38; Pruden, vol. 3, pp. 988–89).

[b] Gedün Lodrö, p. 303.

Manifest Knowledge the ninth path of release, which is released from the ninth [cycle] of afflictive emotions pertaining to the lower level, is necessarily generated as the entity of an actual absorption of the upper level."[a] Although he does not give reasons here, this is because, in Asaṅga's system, which is the one generally accepted by Ge-luk-pa commentators, the feeling of the preparations is bliss, as is apparent from the previous discussion of the mental contemplation of joy-withdrawal (see page 237).

Discussion arises concerning what Tsong-kha-pa calls "the system of Vasubandhu's *Treasury of Manifest Knowledge*," in which the status of the last path of release depends on the feeling of the absorption being cultivated and the sharpness or dullness of the meditator's faculties. Tsong-kha-pa explains that

> In the system of Vasubandhu's *Treasury of Manifest Knowledge*, there are cases of generating the path of release which is released from the ninth [cycle of] afflictive emotions pertaining to the Desire Realm and the ninth paths of release which are released from the ninth [cycles of] afflictive emotions pertaining to the First, Second, and Third Concentrations as entities of either an actual absorption or a preparation. From the Fourth Concentration through the Peak of Cyclic Existence, the ninth paths of release that are released from the ninth [cycles of] afflictive-emotions-to-be-abandoned-by-meditation of their own lower level are necessarily generated as the entities of actual absorptions of [their respective upper levels]. The *Treasury* also gives a reason for asserting such—[namely,] that in general the feeling of the preparations is necessarily equanimity. The feelings of the actual absorptions of the two—the first and second concentrations—have mental bliss (*yid bde*) and the feeling of the actual absorption of the third concentration has the feeling of mental bliss (*tshor ba sems bde*), and therefore, because there are faculties of feeling of dissimilar type, it is difficult to shift faculties [of feeling from equanimity to bliss]; therefore, such [namely, that in the system of Vasubandhu's *Treasury of Manifest Knowledge*, the ninth paths of release that are released from afflictive emotions pertaining to the Desire Realm and to the First, Second, and Third Concentrations may be generated as entities of either an actual absorption or a preparation] is presented.

---

[a] Tsong-kha-pa, *Notes*, 5.3–4.

> Since the feeling of the actual absorptions of the fourth concentration and above is necessarily equanimity, therefore, because the faculties of feeling do not differ in type, it is easy to shift faculties; therefore, such [namely that in the system of Vasubandhu's *Treasury of Manifest Knowledge*, from the Fourth Concentration through the Peak of Cyclic Existence, the ninth paths of release are necessarily generated as actual absorptions] is presented. Accordingly, [in both systems] the nine uninterrupted paths that abandon the nine [cycles of] afflictive-emotions-to-be-abandoned-by-meditation of the lower level and the first eight paths of release of those [uninterrupted paths] are necessarily preparations.[a]

Jam-yang-shay-pa spells out Tsong-kha-pa's implication that, according to the system of the *Treasury*, the ninth path of release generated during the cultivation of the first, second, and third concentrations is experienced as a preparation by meditators of dull faculties, for whom the shift of feeling is difficult, and as an actual absorption by meditators of sharp faculties, for whom the shift of feeling is easy.[b]

A further complication in Ge-luk-pa interpretations of the system of the *Treasury* is Jam-yang-shay-pa's difference with Paṇ-chen Sö-nam-drak-pa concerning the meaning of a key citation from the *Treasury*, which Paṇ-chen Sö-nam-drak-pa cites as evidence that the mental contemplation that is the fruit of final training is necessarily always an actual absorption rather than a preparation:

> That concentration which has conquered over the three levels
> Or [is] the path of release at the end of the preparations
> Is not among the preparations for the higher [concentrations and formless absorptions].[c]

According to Paṇ-chen Sö-nam-drak-pa, who cites only the first two lines, the "concentration" of the first line is the fourth concentration, and the three levels over which it has conquered are the first, second, and third concentrations. Explaining Paṇ-chen Sö-nam-drak-pa's position, Denma Lochö Rinpoche asserts that "[t]his concentration *is* a

---

a Ibid., 5.4–6.2.

b Jam-yang-shay-pa, *Concentrations,* 252.2.–253.4.

c Vasubandhu, *Treasury of Manifest Knowledge,* 6.48a–c (P5591, vol. 115, 253.2.4, 6; Shastri, part 3, p. 976; La Vallée Poussin 16:3, pp. 237–38; Pruden, vol. 3, pp. 988–89), cited in Paṇ-chen Sö-nam-drak-pa, "Concentrations," 152b.4–5; Kön-chok-jik-may-wang-po, *Condensed Statement,* 577.1; and Jam-yang-shay-pa, *Concentrations,* 252.7. See also *Meditative States,* pp. 153 and 242 n. 11.

mental contemplation that is the fruit of final training" and that therefore, by analogy, "'the path of release at the end of the preparations' is also a mental contemplation that is the fruit of final training."[a]

According to Jam-yang-shay-pa, whose position appears to reflect that of Tsong-kha-pa's *Notes*, the "concentration" of the first line is the third concentration, which has conquered over the first three of the nine levels—the Desire Realm and the First and Second Concentrations. The "higher [concentrations and formless absorptions]" of the third line are the fourth concentration and the formless absorptions. To support his interpretation, Jam-yang-shay-pa cites Vasubandhu's *Autocommentary* to the first two lines of this verse:

> The levels of birth are nine in all: the Desire Realm and the eight concentrations and formless absorptions. With respect to that which has conquered over three levels by separation from attachment to [levels] up to two concentrations, it is generated as the last path of release, as either a preparation or an actual absorption.[b]

Since both Paṇ-chen Sö-nam-drak-pa and Jam-yang-shay-pa would agree that the mental contemplation that is the fruit of final training is generated as an actual absorption according to the dominant, generally accepted system—namely, Asaṅga's—the point of Jam-yang-shay-pa's argument seems to be that Paṇ-chen Sö-nam-drak-pa fails to distinguish between the two Manifest Knowledge systems and, as a result of this failure, misreads the *Treasury* to support a position that occurs only in Asaṅga's system and not in that of the *Treasury*.

OTHER WAYS OF GROUPING THE SEVEN MENTAL CONTEMPLATIONS

To demonstrate that Asaṅga's seven mental contemplations are both necessary and sufficient for the attainment of the first concentration, Tsong-kha-pa divides the seven into three groups: three in terms of cause, three in terms of entity, and one in terms of effect. This grouping is discussed in Tsong-kha-pa's *Notes* and in Jam-yang-shay-pa's and Kön-chok-jik-may-wang-po's textbooks on the concentrations and formless absorptions under the heading "ascertainment of the

---

[a] *Meditative States*, pp. 153–54.

[b] Vasubandhu, *Autocommentary on the "Treasury of Manifest Knowledge,"* 6:48a–b (P5591, vol. 115, 253.2.4; Shastri, part 3, p. 976; La Vallée Poussin 16:3, p. 237; Pruden, vol. 3, pp. 988–89).

number."[a] Jam-yang-shay-pa adds that these seven are necessary "in order to bring about the attainment of an actual first concentration in dependence upon the mental contemplation of a beginner, calm abiding"—that is, in dependence upon the first preparation, which is not included in Asaṅga's list of seven mental contemplations.[b]

The three in terms of cause are the mental contemplation of individual knowledge of the character, the mental contemplation arisen from belief, and the mental contemplation of analysis. The three in terms of entity are the mental contemplations of thorough isolation, joy-withdrawal, and final training. The one in terms of effect is the mental contemplation that is the fruit of final training.[c] Tsong-kha-pa points out that this grouping applies only to the mental contemplations having the aspect of grossness/peacefulness.[d]

Tsong-kha-pa explains that, of the three in terms of cause, the first two—the mental contemplation of individual knowledge of the character and the mental contemplation arisen from belief—are causes in the sense of generating what has not been generated, whereas the third—the mental contemplation of analysis—is a cause in the sense of enhancing what has already been generated.[e] According to Gedün Lodrö, the texts do not state why the first two mental contemplations are posited in terms of generating what has not been generated because the reason is obvious: afflictive emotions pertaining to the lower level are not actually overcome until the mental contemplation of thorough isolation, for which the first two mental contemplations prepare. The mental contemplation of analysis is posited in terms of enhancing what has already been generated because six of the nine cycles of afflictive emotions pertaining to the lower level have already been overcome, and the analysis done during this mental contemplation causes the meditator to make further effort to overcome the remaining three.[f]

Jam-yang-shay-pa and Kön-chok-jik-may-wang-po elaborate "entity" as referring to "the entities of the paths that abandon the afflictive emotions pertaining to the Desire Realm."[g] Gedün Lodrö points out that

---

[a] Tsong-kha-pa, *Notes*, 2.2; Jam-yang-shay-pa, *Concentrations*, 235.7; Kön-chok-jik-may-wang-po, *Condensed Statement*, 574.4

[b] Jam-yang-shay-pa, *Concentrations*, 235.7–236.1.

[c] Tsong-kha-pa, *Notes*, 2.3–3.3; Gedün Lodrö, p. 300.

[d] Tsong-kha-pa, *Notes*, 3.3.

[e] Ibid., 2.4–3.1.

[f] Gedün Lodrö, pp. 300–301.

[g] Kön-chok-jik-may-wang-po, *Condensed Statement*, 574.6; Jam-yang-shay-pa, *Concentrations*, 237.7.

the three in terms of entity "are posited in terms of entity in the sense of being the entity of an antidote; they are the actual antidotal mental contemplations," each of which has uninterrupted paths and paths of release.[a] As was mentioned earlier, the mental contemplation of thorough isolation overcomes the three cycles of great afflictive emotions pertaining to the lower level; the mental contemplation of joy-withdrawal overcomes the three cycles of middling afflictive emotions, and the mental contemplation of final training overcomes the three cycles of small afflictive emotions (see chart, page 218).

The one in terms of effect is the mental contemplation that is the fruit of final training,[b] which, according to Jam-yang-shay-pa, is posited "in terms of experiencing the fruit of having abandoned the afflictive emotions by way of the previous [mental contemplations]."[c]

Asaṅga's *Grounds of Hearers* also mentions groupings of six and of four mental contemplations, which, according to Jam-yang-shay-pa, are included in each other.[d] The six are the first six of the seven, excluding the mental contemplation that is the fruit of final training—that is, the six which are preparations. The four mental contemplations, together with those of the six mental contemplations that are included in them, are as follows:

concordant mental contemplation (*rjes su mthun pa las byung ba'i yid byed*)
- the mental contemplation of individual knowledge of the character
- the mental contemplation arisen from belief

antidotal mental contemplation (*gnyen po yid la byed pa*)
- the mental contemplation of thorough isolation
- the mental contemplation of final training
- the mental contemplation of withdrawal—that is, the uninterrupted paths—from within joy-withdrawal

thoroughly clear mental contemplation (*rab tu dvang ba yid la byed pa*)
- the mental contemplation of joy—that is, the paths of release—from within joy-withdrawal

mental contemplation of individual investigation (*so sor rtog pa yid la byed pa*)

---

[a] Gedün Lodrö, p. 302.

[b] Jam-yang-shay-pa, *Concentrations,* 239.3; Kön-chok-jik-may-wang-po, *Condensed Statement,* 574.6–575.1; Gedün Lodrö, p. 300.

[c] Jam-yang-shay-pa, *Concentrations,* 239.3.

[d] Ibid., 240.2.

the mental contemplation of analysis[a]

According to Gedün Lodrö, the mental contemplation of individual knowledge of the character and that arisen from belief are included within the concordant mental contemplation because they are concordant with, or similar to, the actual antidotes, which begin with the mental contemplation of thorough isolation.[b] Jam-yang-shay-pa notes that their concordance with the actual antidotes consists in their "having the aspect of uprooting" attraction to the lower level.[c]

Gedün Lodrö points out that the three antidotal mental contemplations are classified as such "for the same reasons that they are considered to be in the category of those posited in terms of entity—namely, that they are actual entities of the antidote; they themselves are actual antidotes."[d]

According to Gedün Lodrö, neither Asaṅga's *Grounds of Hearers* nor Tibetan commentators explain why the mental contemplation of joy-withdrawal is classified as a thoroughly clear mental contemplation. He suggests, however, that

> according to some of the upper tenet systems' views on Manifest Knowledge, it is thought that, with the attainment of the mental contemplation of joy-withdrawal, one initially attains the feeling of bliss that accompanies a preparation. When that is attained, a sense of great clarity is generated in the meditator's mind. This is a far greater sense of clarity than one has with calm abiding. In calm abiding, there is clarity with respect to the object of observation, but one has not abandoned any of the afflictive emotions, whereas here, internally, one is clarified, or purified, of afflictive emotions.[e]

He observes that "It is easy to understand why the mental contemplation of analysis is called the mental contemplation of individual investigation."[f]

---

[a] Gedün Lodrö, p. 305; Jam-yang-shay-pa, *Concentrations*, 240.2–5. The distinction between the paths of withdrawal and of joy of the mental contemplation of joy-withdrawal and their assignment to separate categories are Jam-yang-shay-pa's; Gedün Lodrö merely includes the mental contemplation of joy-withdrawal under both thoroughly clear mental contemplation and antidotal mental contemplation.

[b] Gedün Lodrö, p. 306.

[c] Jam-yang-shay-pa, *Concentrations*, 240.3.

[d] Gedün Lodrö, p. 306.

[e] Ibid., p. 306.

[f] Ibid., p. 307.

Which Persons Proceed by Which Path

Hearers have two ways of abandoning the eighty-one cycles of afflictive emotions of cyclic existence. They may proceed either gradually or simultaneously—that is, they may either abandon the eighty-one cycles of afflictive emotions one by one or simultaneously abandon the great of the great afflictive emotions of all nine levels, then the great of the middling afflictive emotions, and so on, until they have abandoned the small of the small afflictive emotions of all nine levels.[a] According to Lati Rinpoche, Hearers who proceed gradually use the preparations having the aspect of grossness/peacefulness on the path of accumulation, attain an actual first concentration, and then realize the truths and attain the path of seeing. Hearers who proceed simultaneously, however, use preparations for the first concentration having the aspect of the truths and attain the five Buddhist paths before attaining an actual first concentration. They "cultivate the mental contemplation of individual knowledge of the character at the time of the path of accumulation," attain the path of preparation simultaneously with the mental contemplation arisen from belief, attain the path of seeing at the time of the mental contemplation of thorough isolation, and attain the mental contemplations of joy-withdrawal, analysis, and final training during the path of meditation.[b] They become Approachers to Foe Destroyer (*dgra bcom zhugs pa, arhattvapratipannaka*) and Abiders in the Fruit of Foe Destroyer (*dgra bcom 'bras gnas, arhattvaphalasthita*) without attaining an actual first concentration and are, therefore, known as Unadorned Foe Destroyers (*dgra bcom rgyan med*).[c]

According to both Lati Rinpoche and Denma Lochö Rinpoche, Bodhisattvas use the preparations having the aspect of grossness/peacefulness, although "they take emptiness as their object [of observation] during the actual absorptions." Denma Lochö Rinpoche notes, however, that Bodhisattvas cultivate the preparations having the aspect of grossness/peacefulness "not within the context of meditating

---

[a] *Meditative States*, pp. 144, 165.

[b] Ibid., p. 144. See also Jam-yang-shay-pa, *Concentrations*, 245.2–246.3.

[c] Denma Lochö Rinpoche in *Meditative States*, p. 166. For discussions of the Eight Approachers and Abiders—Approachers to and Abiders in the Fruit of Stream Enterer (*rgyun zhugs, śrotāpanna*), Once Returner (*phyir 'ong, sakṛdāgāmin*), Non-Returner (*phyir mi 'ong, anāgāmin*), and Foe Destroyer (*dgra bcom pa, arhan*)—see Geshe Lhundup Sopa and Jeffrey Hopkins, *Cutting Through Appearances: Practice and Theory of Tibetan Buddhism* (Ithaca, NY: Snow Lion Publications, 1989), pp. 212–14; *Meditation on Emptiness*, pp. 106–108; and *Meditative States*, pp. 165–66.

on emptiness but within that of the altruistic aspiration to enlightenment." They attain an actual concentration on the path of accumulation; according to Denma Lochö Rinpoche, "they cultivate all the concentrations by the time of the path of preparation," although "it is not definite when they cultivate the formless absorptions."[a]

Denma Lochö Rinpoche points out that

> Bodhisattvas and those Hearers who use [the preparations having the aspect of grossness/peacefulness]...would not think of any rebirth state as truly peaceful. They consider all cyclic existence to be like a garbage heap; however, some places in a garbage heap are less dirty than others, and in that sense Bodhisattvas and Hearers view the upper level as peaceful.[b]

He also suggests that they may use another method of cultivating the preparations having the aspect of grossness/peacefulness. Instead of viewing the lower and upper rebirth states as gross or peaceful, respectively, they view the lower and upper actual meditative absorptions of the concentrations "as gross or peaceful in terms of their branches"—that is, in terms of the mental factors associated with them.[c] (For a discussion of the branches of the concentrations, see pages 251ff., below.)

Instead of discussing the modes of procedure of Hearers and Bodhisattvas, Gedün Lodrö relies on Asaṅga's *Grounds of Hearers* to identify four categories of persons who proceed by a mundane path:

1 Non-Buddhists, known as Outsiders (*phyi rol pa*)
2 Buddhists of dull faculties (*dbang rdul gyi nang pa*)
3 Buddhists of sharp faculties whose virtuous roots are not thoroughly ripened (*dbang rnon gyi dge rtsa yongs su ma smin pa*)
4 Bodhisattvas who are one lifetime away from achieving Buddhahood (*skye ba gcig gis thogs pa'i byang chub sems dpa'*)[d]

Non-Buddhists who have achieved calm abiding can proceed only by a mundane path. In an explanation that asserts the superiority of

---

[a] *Meditative States,* pp. 144, 202–204.

[b] Ibid., p. 203.

[c] Ibid., p. 203. Although Denma Lochö Rinpoche gives no evidence of familiarity with Theravāda presentations of the concentrations and formless absorptions, it is interesting to note that this is also the method of progressing to the next-higher level according to Buddhaghosa's *Path of Purification (visuddhimagga),* IV.138, IV.152, IV.185 (Buddhaghosa, *The Path of Purification (visuddhimagga),* trans. Bhikkhu Ñyāṇamoli [Berkeley & London: Shambhala, 1976], vol. 1, pp. 161, 154, 171.

[d] Gedün Lodrö, pp. 285–86.

Buddhist teachings while acknowledging the considerable achievements of non-Buddhist meditators, Gedün Lodrö notes that they "do not accept the four noble truths and their sixteen attributes" and, therefore, cannot even begin "to achieve a path which has as its aspect realization of the truths."[a] Nevertheless, they are presented as proficient meditators who are capable of achieving the highest meditative states within cyclic existence and "the first five of the six clairvoyances," which are attained in dependence upon an actual concentration.[b]

Gedün Lodrö identifies **Buddhists of dull faculties** as those who "have attained calm abiding but are unable to achieve a special insight observing any of the four noble truths" or "a coarse or subtle selflessness" because they are troubled by afflictive emotions pertaining to levels of cyclic existence up to that of Nothingness.[c]

According to Gedün Lodrö, the category **Buddhists of sharp faculties whose virtuous roots are not thoroughly ripened** is listed in Asaṅga's *Grounds of Hearers* without explanation;

> however, Tsong-kha-pa's *Exposition of the Stages of the Path* identifies persons of this type as those who, although they have understood emptiness, have not ripened the virtuous roots needed for *directly* realizing emptiness.[d]

Since they have sharp faculties, they have realized emptiness conceptually, even if they have not yet entered a path. Nevertheless, they are not yet ready to realize emptiness directly and, therefore, cannot separate from afflictive emotions pertaining to the Desire Realm by means of a supramundane path, since this depends on a direct realization of emptiness. Thus, they must use a mundane path to separate from those afflictive emotions.

Gedün Lodrö explains that **Bodhisattvas who are one lifetime away from achieving Buddhahood** will have "one lifetime between their present life and the attainment of Buddhahood."[e] Since Asaṅga did not specify the system to which he was referring in setting forth this category, Gedün Lodrö discusses the status of such persons in both the Mahāyāna sūtra system and the system of Vasubandhu's *Treasury of*

[a] Ibid., p. 286.
[b] Ibid., p. 286.
[c] Gedün Lodrö, p. 289.
[d] Ibid., p. 289; italics added.
[e] Ibid., p. 291.

Manifest Knowledge and suggests, on the basis of a passage from the *Treasury* referring to "the Teacher Shākyamuni Buddha or a rhinoceroslike Solitary Realizer (*bse ru lta bu rang sangs rgyas, khaḍgaviṣāṇakalpapratyekabuddha*),"[a] that Asaṅga is referring, not to the Mahāyāna sūtra system, as one might expect, but, rather, to the system of Vasubandhu's *Treasury of Manifest Knowledge.*

In the Mahāyāna sūtra system, a person one lifetime away from achieving Buddhahood would be an eighth-, ninth-, or tenth-ground Bodhisattva—probably, in Gedün Lodrö's opinion, the last.[b] He does not state his reason for ruling out high-ground Bodhisattvas as the persons to whom Asaṅga is referring in the fourth category. However, Lati Rinpoche and Denma Lochö Rinpoche give the generally accepted Ge-luk presentation of the Mahāyāna sūtra system, according to which Bodhisattvas "achieve an actual concentration on the path of accumulation" and attain "all the concentrations by the time of the path of preparation"—that is, before achieving even the first Bodhisattva ground, which coincides with the initial direct realization of emptiness at the time of the path of seeing. Thus, a tenth-ground Bodhisattva would have achieved all the concentrations many lifetimes earlier. Both Lati Rinpoche and Denma Lochö Rinpoche explicitly state that Mahāyāna sūtra-system Bodhisattvas use mundane preparations to separate from attachment to afflictive emotions pertaining to the Desire Realm.[c] Since, according to the Mahāyāna sūtra-system, Bodhisattvas must belong in Asaṅga's third category, Gedün Lodrö suggests that in this context Asaṅga is referring to a system other than his own.

In the system of Vasubandhu's *Treasury of Manifest Knowledge*, however, a person one lifetime away from achieving Buddhahood would be a Bodhisattva on the path of accumulation who "in the next lifetime, passes from the path of preparation right through to the [path of no more learning] in one meditative session. This is done in dependence on a final (*rab mtha'*) fourth concentration." Gedün Lodrö explains that "during the path of accumulation such practitioners separate from attachment to the afflictive emotions pertaining to the Desire Realm...in dependence on a mundane path."[d]

Buddhists of sharp faculties whose virtuous roots *are* thoroughly

---

[a] Vasubandhu, *Treasury of Manifest Knowledge* and *Autocommentary on the "Treasury of Manifest Knowledge,"* 6.24a–cb (P5591, vol. 115, 247.3.7–8; Shastri, part 3, p. 920; La Vallée Poussin, 16:4, p. 177; Pruden, vol. 3, p. 941).

[b] Ibid., pp. 291, 292.

[c] *Meditative States,* pp. 144, 204.

[d] Gedün Lodrö, p. 293.

ripened for the direct realization of emptiness during the cultivation of an actual first concentration are not included in these four and are not discussed by Gedün Lodrö; they are probably Hearers who proceed simultaneously, who separate from attachment in dependence on supramundane preparations having the aspect of the truths.

The type of mundane path used by persons of the third and fourth types. Gedün Lodrö argues that, although persons of the first two types separate from attachment to the lower level in dependence upon a mundane path having the aspect of grossness/peacefulness, persons of the third and fourth types do not. Rather, "they separate from attachment in dependence on a path of realizing selflessness," since "they have already realized the four noble truths." However, they have not realized the four noble truths directly; their realization is only conceptual. Thus, according to Gedün Lodrö, "The word 'mundane' here refers to the path of a common being as opposed to that of a Superior."[a] Although the suggested methods differ, Gedün Lodrö, like Denma Lochö Rinpoche, suggests an alternative method of cultivating a mundane path; both scholars also point out that persons who use these alternative methods would not view the upper level as truly peaceful. Gedün Lodrö remarks that "by viewing selflessness in dependence on a common being's path," a person of the third or fourth type "is able to undermine the ignorance which serves as the basis of both the lower and upper levels. Such a person is really seeing both the lower and upper levels as gross."[b]

PREPARATIONS FOR THE REMAINING CONCENTRATIONS AND FORMLESS ABSORPTIONS

In general, as was mentioned earlier (see page 195), the preparations for the remaining concentrations and formless absorptions are similar to those for the first concentration. However, there are significant differences. One concerns the feeling of the mental contemplation of joy-withdrawal, which is the same as the feeling of the meditative absorption for which it is a preparation. (This point depends on the presentation of the branches of the concentrations, pages 251ff.) As a preparation for the first two concentrations, which have joy and bliss as branches, the mental contemplation of joy-withdrawal has the feelings of joy and bliss, as was mentioned earlier (see page 221). The third

[a] Ibid., p. 294.

[b] Ibid., p. 295.

concentration, however, has bliss but not joy; therefore, the mental contemplation of joy-withdrawal which is a preparation for the third concentration also has the feeling of bliss without joy. Since the fourth concentration and the formless absorptions have neutral feeling rather than bliss, Paṇ-chen Sö-nam-drak-pa, following Tsong-kha-pa's *Notes,* asserts that "the meaning of 'the mental contemplation of joy-withdrawal' [as a preparation for those levels] is to be taken as just seeing the abandonment [of the afflictive emotions of the level below] as a good quality."[a] According to Jam-yang-shay-pa, seeing the abandonment of afflictive emotions as a good quality is to be understood as faith.[b]

The other major difference is that, although an actual first concentration must be attained by means of the preparations, that is not necessarily the case for an actual second concentration and the remaining concentrations and formless absorptions, since Foe Destroyers who proceed simultaneously constitute a significant exception. Jam-yang-shay-pa and Kön-chok-jik-may-wang-po point out that simultaneous Foe Destroyers need not attain the remaining meditative absorptions by means of the preparations; having attained an actual first concentration by means of the preparations, they can then, successively, "enter into any absorption they wish." According to Jam-yang-shay-pa, they are able to do so "because the preparations conquer the afflictive emotions pertaining to the lower [level], but [a simultaneous Foe Destroyer] has already conquered those [afflictive emotions]."[c] Despite this significant exception, however, the Ge-luk presentations of the preparations for the concentrations and formless absorptions stand as a developed gradualist approach to the process of progressing from one meditative level to the next.

---

[a] Paṇ-chen Sö-nam-drak-pa, "Concentrations," 154a.4–5, following Tsong-kha-pa, *Notes,* 6.4–5, and *Meditative States,* p. 164.

[b] Jam-yang-shay-pa, *Concentrations,* 248.3.

[c] Ibid., 234.3–235.2, 246.7–247.3. See also Kön-chok-jik-may-wang-po, *Condensed Statement,* 574.2–4, 576.2.

9 THE MEDITATIVE ABSORPTIONS OF THE CONCENTRATIONS AND FORMLESS ABSORPTIONS

Since the final mental contemplation of each set of seven, the mental contemplation that is the fruit of final training, is not a preparation but an actual meditative absorption of the next-higher level, the next topic after that of the preparations is that of the meditative absorptions of the concentrations and formless absorptions. This presentation of the meditative absorptions will be brief, since the material is fairly well known from translations of Manifest Knowledge texts, especially Vasubandhu's *Treasury of Manifest Knowledge*, one of the main Indian sources for the Ge-luk presentations discussed here. It is also well known from the similar Theravāda presentation in Buddhaghosa's *Path of Purification.*

The discussions of the meditative absorptions in Tsong-kha-pa's *Notes on the Concentrations and Formless Absorptions* and Ge-luk monastic textbooks based on it mainly cite Vasubandhu's *Treasury* but also refer to what they call the system of Asaṅga's *Summary of Manifest Knowledge.* Their sources for this system include the brief presentation of the meditative absorptions in that text itself, available in Walpola Rahula's French translation,[a] and, for the branches of the concentrations, key passages from Asaṅga's *Compendium of Ascertainments.* As is usually the case in Ge-luk presentations of the concentrations and formless absorptions, when the two Indian Manifest Knowledge systems differ, each is explained clearly and preference is given to Asaṅga's. Thus, Ge-luk presentations of the meditative absorptions represent a careful synthesis of Vasubandhu's and Asaṅga's positions.

There are several points of difference between both Vasubandhu's and Asaṅga's presentations, on the one hand, and Theravāda presentations, on the other, as well as between Theravāda and Ge-luk presentations. One important difference is that, instead of regarding the meditative absorptions of the concentrations as being primarily calm abiding, as the Theravādins do, the Ge-luk-pas follow the *Treasury* in regarding the meditative absorptions of the concentrations as a balance of

---

[a] Walpola Rahula, trans., *Le Compendium de la super-doctrine (philosophie) (Abhidharmasamuccaya) d'Asaṅga* (Paris: École française d'extrême-orient, 1971); and *Abhidharmasamuccaya: The Compendium of the Higher Teaching (Philosophy) by Asaṅga*, trans. Sara Boin-Webb, (Fremont, Calif.: Asian Humanities Press, 2001).

calm abiding and special insight. This difference has bearing on the Theravāda interpretation of investigation and analysis as branches of the first concentration, which differs significantly from the Vaibhāṣhika and Sautrāntika positions discussed by Ge-luk scholars (see page 255, note c). Other points of difference are interesting but minor; I will not discuss them here.

General Comparison of Concentrations and Formless Absorptions

Comparing the general characteristics of concentrations and formless absorptions, Lati Rinpoche notes that they differ in the way the meditator progresses into them—a point discussed in detail in Tsong-kha-pa's *Notes* and monastic textbooks based on it. Paraphrasing Tsong-kha-pa's root text without citing it, Lati Rinpoche also remarks that

> In the four concentrations, the main meditative activity is that of analytical meditation; in the formless absorptions, however, the main meditative activity is that of stabilizing meditation. The sign of having attained any of the actual four concentrations is the sense that the body is sinking under the ground, whereas the sign of having attained any of the four formless absorptions is the sense that the body is flying off into space.[a]

It is clear, given the high value Ge-luk-pas place on analytical meditation, that preference is being given to the concentrations; indeed, whereas the *Autocommentary on the "Treasury"* describes the concentrations as being a balance of calm abiding and special insight,[b] Lati Rinpoche tips the balance toward analytical meditation. Gedün Lodrö remarks that, in the formless absorptions, the meditator "is as though dissolved into the factor of calm abiding. The meaning of calm abiding's being too predominant is probably that the mind is not very clear."[c]

Divisions: Types of Meditative Absorption

There are several types of meditative absorption that are common to both concentrations and formless absorptions. Kön-chok-jik-may-

---

[a] *Meditative States*, p. 129; Tsong-kha-pa, *Notes*, 18.3–4.

[b] Vasubandhu, *Autocommentary on the "Treasury of Manifest Knowledge,"* 8.1e (P5591, vol. 115, 270.4.3; Shastri, part 4, p. 1126; La Vallée Poussin, 16:5, p. 131; Pruden, vol. 4, p. 1218).

[c] Gedün Lodrö, p. 380.

wang-po has classified these divisions according to type; his classification includes:

1 A division in terms of cause and effect into causal (*rgyu, kāraṇa*) and resultant-birth (*'bras bu skye ba, kārya*; in Tibetan, literally "effect birth," birth which is an effect) meditative absorptions
2 A division in terms of substantial entity into pure, uncontaminated, and afflicted meditative absorptions
3 A third category of divisions, "in terms of objects of observation and subjective aspects," that comprises the first two of the previous set, described from a different point of view. The pure actual meditative absorptions are listed as "pure mundane virtues" and the uncontaminated actual meditative absorptions, as "uncontaminated [concentrations] having the aspect of the truths."[a]

THE DIVISION INTO CAUSAL AND RESULTANT-BIRTH MEDITATIVE ABSORPTIONS

The frequently used term "actual meditative absorption"—literally "actual-basis meditative absorption" in Tibetan and "root meditative absorption" in Sanskrit—refers to meditative absorptions cultivated and attained in a given lifetime. However, actual meditative absorption and causal meditative absorption are not mutually inclusive, since an actual meditative absorption does not automatically cause rebirth in the corresponding level of cyclic existence; this difference between types of actual meditative absorption is the basis of the distinction between pure and uncontaminated meditative absorptions (see pages 243–248). Paṇ-chen Sö-nam-drak-pa emphasizes this distinction by defining a casual meditative absorption of a concentration or formless absorption as an actual meditative absorption of its specific type that "is included within cyclic existence and is a producer of a true suffering, its effect."[b]

Kön-chok-jik-may-wang-po makes clear in his definitions of an actual meditative absorption of a concentration, of an actual meditative absorption of a formless absorption, and of the corresponding causal meditative absorptions, that an actual meditative absorption is a *consciousness*. He distinguishes between the actual and causal meditative absorptions of concentrations and those of formless absorptions

---

[a] Kön-chok-jik-may-wang-po, *Condensed Statement*, 582.6–583.3.

[b] Paṇ-chen Sö-nam-drak-pa, "Concentrations," 157a.2–3 and 157b.4–5 (see also *Meditative States*, pp. 178, 181.).

according to their mode of progressing to the next-higher level.[a]

Paṇ-chen Sö-nam-drak-pa defines a concentration that is a resultant birth as

> that which is included within either a fruitional effect (*rnam smin gyi 'bras bu, vipākaphala*) or a causally concordant effect (*rgyu mthun gyi 'bras bu, niṣyandaphala*) of having cultivated, in another birth, a concentration that is a causal absorption.[b]

His definition of a formless absorption that is a resultant birth is similar. Kön-chok-jik-may-wang-po adds possessional effect (*bdag 'bras, adhipatiphala*) to the types of effect included.[c] He explains fruitional effects as "the appropriative aggregates in the continuum of" a being of the level in question—either in the Form Realm or the Formless Realm. For Form Realm beings, he explains possessional effects as those of the environment—"an inestimable mansion, and so forth."[d] He explains causally concordant effects as "the actual meditative absorptions, and so forth, of the four concentrations attained by birth, in the continuum of [a Form Realm being]."[e]

Kön-chok-jik-may-wang-po defines a resultant-birth concentration as "a contaminated [phenomenon] included within" any of the above-mentioned effects. In general, a contaminated phenomenon is one that either is or produces a rebirth within cyclic existence. Paṇ-chen Sö-nam-drak-pa refers to contaminated phenomena, without using the term, in the second part of his definitions of an actual concentration that is a causal meditative absorption and an actual formless absorption that is a causal meditative absorption, as "that which is included within cyclic existence and is a producer of a true suffering, its effect." Gedün Lodrö explains that

> With a contaminated absorption, there would be a temporary factor of having separated from attachment to some afflictive emotion....Whatever is a causal absorption is necessarily a contaminated absorption; this is the only one that will produce a rebirth in the respective absorption. Whatever is a resultant-birth absorption is necessarily contaminated; both the casual

[a] Kön-chok-jik-may-wang-po, *Condensed Statement,* 582.5, 588.2–4, 585.3–4.

[b] Paṇ-chen Sö-nam-drak-pa, "Concentrations," 157b.2–3 (see also *Meditative States,* p. 180).

[c] Kön-chok-jik-may-wang-po, *Condensed Statement,* 585.5.

[d] Ibid., 585.6.

[e] Ibid., 585.6–586.1.

absorption and resultant-birth absorption of any level are necessarily contaminated.[a]

Kön-chok-jik-may-wang-po does not define a resultant-birth formless absorption. Presumably, it would include the characteristics of the causal meditative absorption as a causally concordant effect. With regard to the term "fruitional effect" in Paṇ-chen Sö-nam-drak-pa's definition, Denma Lochö Rinpoche explains that, since a Formless Realm being does not have a form aggregate, or body, "fruitional effect" in the Formless Realm refers to the four mental aggregates, which are "the bases of designation of a Formless Realm being" and "are called the aggregates that are the basis of name" (in name and form [*ming gzugs, nāmarūpa*], the fourth link of the twelve-linked dependent-arising).[b] It is not clear what possessional effects, if any, would be included in a resultant-birth formless absorption.

THE DIVISION INTO PURE, UNCONTAMINATED, AND AFFLICTED MEDITATIVE ABSORPTIONS

Pure meditative absorptions

Elaborating on Paṇ-chen Sö-nam-drak-pa's definition,[c] Lati Rinpoche explains a pure meditative absorption as one in which the meditator has separated from the afflictive emotions of the level below and is also free of the afflictive emotions pertaining to the level of the meditative absorption itself. In a pure actual meditative absorption of the first concentration, for example, the meditator has separated from the afflictive emotions pertaining to the Desire Realm and is also free of the afflictive emotions pertaining to the First Concentration.[d] Pure meditative absorptions are mundane and contaminated.

As divisions of pure meditative absorptions, Lati Rinpoche, Paṇ-chen Sö-nam-drak-pa, and Kön-chok-jik-may-wang-po discuss the four types set forth in Vasubandhu's *Treasury of Manifest Knowledge* and *Auto-commentary* (8.17)—namely, those

1 concordant with degeneration (*nyams pa cha mthun, hānabhāgīya*)
2 concordant with abiding (*gnas pa cha mthun, sthitibhāgīya*)

---

[a] Gedün Lodrö, p. 353.

[b] *Meditative States*, p. 182.

[c] Paṇ-chen Sö-nam-drak-pa, "Concentrations," 158a.3–4 (see also *Meditative States*, p. 183).

[d] *Meditative States*, p. 120.

3 concordant with enhancement (*khyad par cha mthun, viśeṣabhāgīya*)
4 concordant with definite differentiation (*nges 'byed cha mthun, nirvedhabhāgīya*)[a]

All four are defined in terms of their tendencies—that is, in terms of the type of meditative absorption likely to be generated in the next moment or period of meditation. Kön-chok-jik-may-wang-po and Paṇ-chen Sö-nam-drak-pa give almost identical definitions. I will cite only Kön-chok-jik-may-wang-po's here.[b]

Kön-chok-jik-may-wang-po defines a pure meditative absorption concordant with degeneration as one "concordant with the generation of an afflictive emotion of its own or a lower level immediately after itself."[c] In his commentary on Paṇ-chen Sö-nam-drak-pa's definition, Denma Lochö Rinpoche notes that "'[i]mmediately after itself' refers to the next moment or period; if it referred to an indefinite future time, any of the pure actual meditative absorptions...could be concordant with degeneration."[d]

Kön-chok-jik-may-wang-po defines a pure meditative absorption concordant with abiding as one "that induces another pure [actual meditative absorption] of the same level as itself immediately after itself."[e] It is a continuation of that which preceded it; Denma Lochö Rinpoche explains that "[s]uch an absorption is called concordant with abiding because that very meditative absorption continues to remain." However, he points out that, in this case, "immediately after itself" does not refer to the next moment:

> It is not a case of one moment of [a given] meditative absorption...inducing a second, similar moment. The inducing of a second moment similar to the first is common to products in general and is not what is being referred to here. Rather, a period of meditation comes to a close and induces another pure meditative absorption of the same level.[f]

Kön-chok-jik-may-wang-po defines a pure meditative absorption

---

[a] Vasubandhu, *Treasury of Manifest Knowledge* and *Autocommentary*, 8.17 (P5591, vol. 115, 274.1.4–5; Shastri, part 4, p. 1156; La Vallée Poussin, 16:5, p. 172; Pruden, vol. 4, p. 1247).

[b] For Paṇ-chen Sö-nam-drak-pa's definitions, see Paṇ-chen Sö-nam-drak-pa, "Concentrations," 158a.5–158b.3; *Meditative States*, pp. 182–85.

[c] Kön-chok-jik-may-wang-po, *Condensed Statement*, 587.3–4.

[d] *Meditative States*, p. 184.

[e] Kön-chok-jik-may-wang-po, *Condensed Statement*, 587.4–5.

[f] *Meditative States*, pp. 185–86.

concordant with enhancement as one "that induces a pure actual meditative absorption of a higher level than itself immediately after itself" and notes that "The peak of cyclic existence does not have a type concordant with enhancement."[a] Paṇ-chen Sö-nam-drak-pa explains that this is "because above the peak of cyclic existence there is no other mundane level."[b]

Kön-chok-jik-may-wang-po defines a pure meditative absorption concordant with definite differentiation as one "immediately after which an uncontaminated path is manifestly generated."[c] An uncontaminated path, here, is a supramundane path—specifically, the path of seeing, which, according to Vasubandhu's *Autocommentary on the "Treasury of Manifest Knowledge"* (6.20), is called the path of definite differentiation because "by means of it there is abandonment of doubt through differentiating the truths, ranging from 'This is suffering' through 'This is the path.'"[d] Denma Lochö Rinpoche notes in this connection that "[t]he path of preparation is called a partial concordance with definite differentiation because it induces the path of seeing."[e]

Paṇ-chen Sö-nam-drak-pa also suggests that "[a]ccording to the upper and lower Manifest Knowledges, there is also no actual meditative absorption of the peak of cyclic existence that is concordant with definite differentiation because there is no uncontaminated actual absorption of the peak of cyclic existence."[f] He elaborates on this reason:

> that which is unclear in its object of observation and subjective aspect cannot be a basis of a very clear supramundane path. [This is so] because a Hearer Superior who has attained an actual meditative absorption of the peak of cyclic existence actualizes the supramundane path that is his object of attainment on the basis of a mind of [the level of] nothingness.[g]

To establish the last point, he cites Vasubandhu's *Treasury of Manifest Knowledge:*

---

[a] Kön-chok-jik-may-wang-po, *Condensed Statement,* 587.5–6.

[b] Paṇ-chen Sö-nam-drak-pa, "Concentrations," 158b.4–5; *Meditative States,* p. 186.

[c] Kön-chok-jik-may-wang-po, *Condensed Statement,* 587.6–588.1.

[d] Vasubandhu, *Treasury of Manifest Knowledge* and *Autocommentary,* 6.20a (P5591, vol. 115, 246.5.3; Shastri, part 3, p. 914; La Vallée Poussin, 16:4, p. 169; Pruden, vol. 3, p. 935); cited in *Meditative States,* p. 245 n. 2.

[e] *Meditative States,* p. 185.

[f] Paṇ-chen Sö-nam-drak-pa, "Concentrations," 158b.5; *Meditative States,* p. 186.

[g] Paṇ-chen Sö-nam-drak-pa, "Concentrations," 158b.6–159a.1; *Meditative States,* p. 186.

A Superior at the peak of cyclic existence, having actualized nothingness,
Consumes contamination [8.20a–b].[a]

This line of argument appears at first glance to be a direct contradiction of Tsong-kha-pa's statement, in his *Notes*, that "the actual meditative absorption of the peak of cyclic existence has three [types], excluding that concordant with enhancement."[b] However, it is probably only a qualification of Tsong-kha-pa's statement, since, according to Denma Lochö Rinpoche, "according to the upper and lower Manifest Knowledges" implies that "according to the Madhyamaka system, there is room for analysis."[c]

Uncontaminated meditative absorptions

Tsong-kha-pa explains uncontaminated meditative absorptions as "meditative absorptions of the concentrations and formless absorptions that are generated as the entity of a supramundane path."[d] He notes that, unlike pure meditative absorptions, they are "not capable of being made afflicted."[e]

Distinguishing between actual meditative absorptions and preparations, Paṇ-chen Sö-nam-drak-pa points out that "[i]t is not necessary for the actual concentrations and formless absorptions to separate from desire for the levels below them because the preparations do the separating." He goes on to explain that contaminated—that is, pure—and uncontaminated actual meditative absorptions differ from each other in their capacity to "act as antidotes to [the afflictive emotions of] their own and higher levels." Only uncontaminated actual meditative absorptions have this capacity.[f]

Paṇ-chen Sö-nam-drak-pa further distinguishes among preparations, contaminated actual meditative absorptions, and uncontaminated actual meditative absorptions as "paths that, respectively, separate from desire, abide blissfully in this lifetime, and thoroughly

---

[a] Vasubandhu, *Treasury of Manifest Knowledge*, 8.20a–b (P5591, vol. 115, 274.3.8; Shastri, part 4, pp. 1158–59; La Vallée Poussin, 16:5, p. 175; Pruden, vol. 4, p. 1251); cited in Paṇ-chen Sö-nam-drak-pa, "Concentrations," 159a.1; *Meditative States*, p. 186.

[b] Tsong-kha-pa, *Notes*, 9.1–2.

[c] *Meditative States*, pp. 246 n. 3, 163, 246.

[d] Tsong-kha-pa, *Notes*, 9.4.

[e] Ibid., 7.4.

[f] Paṇ-chen Sö-nam-drak-pa, "Concentrations," 159a.3–5; *Meditative States*, p. 187.

achieve good qualities."[a] Denma Lochö Rinpoche explains that the preparations are called paths that separate from desire because they separate from desire for the level below; contaminated actual meditative absorptions are called paths that abide blissfully in this lifetime because a meditator who has attained them "can in this lifetime, without suffering or mental discomfort (*yid mi bde, daurmanasya*), set in [meditative] equipoise according to his or her wish." (He notes that "'[b]lissfully' cannot refer to the feeling of bliss because in the fourth concentration and the formless absorptions there is no feeling of bliss.") Uncontaminated actual meditative absorptions are called paths that thoroughly achieve good qualities because "in dependence upon [them], it is possible to achieve true cessations."[b]

Kön-chok-jik-may-wang-po distinguishes between two types of uncontaminated meditative absorption: "a contaminated, conceptual type and an uncontaminated type free from conceptuality."[c] He does not identify the persons who attain these two types of meditative absorption. However, Gedün Lodrö's discussion of persons who proceed by the mundane path, in the context of the preparations (see Chapter 8), may be relevant to actual meditative absorptions as well. Citing Asaṅga's *Grounds of Hearers,* he identifies four types of person who proceed by the mundane path (as cited above):

1 Non-Buddhists, known as Outsiders
2 Buddhists of dull faculties
3 Buddhists of sharp faculties whose virtuous roots are not thoroughly ripened
4 Bodhisattvas who are one lifetime away from achieving Buddhahood[d]

He suggests that persons of the last two types have achieved a conceptual, but not a direct, realization of selflessness and that, therefore, although such persons "separate from attachment in dependence on a path of realizing selflessness," the preparations they use are mundane insofar as they are in the continuum "of a common being as opposed to that of a Superior."[e] It is likely that uncontaminated actual meditative absorptions of the contaminated, conceptual type also involve a

---

[a] Paṇ-chen Sö-nam-drak-pa, "Concentrations," 159a.5–6; and *Meditative States,* p. 188.

[b] *Meditative States,* p. 188.

[c] Kön-chok-jik-may-wang-po, *Condensed Statement,* 588.1.

[d] Gedün Lodrö, pp. 285–86.

[e] Ibid., p. 294.

conceptual realization of selflessness and may be actual meditative absorptions in the continuum of a common being—in this case, a Buddhist on the path of accumulation or preparation—that are capable of serving as a mental basis of a supramundane path.[a]

Afflicted meditative absorptions

An afflicted meditative absorption, generally speaking, begins as a pure meditative absorption, which then becomes spoiled by afflictive emotions of its own level—that is to say, not by afflictive emotions of the level below, from which the meditator has separated by means of the preparations. Denma Lochö Rinpoche explains that

> An afflicted meditative absorption is not something that is both a meditative absorption and afflicted, as it would appear to be. Rather, in the first period, there is a meditative absorption, but in the second period, it becomes associated with an [afflictive emotion], whereby it becomes [ethically] neutral (*lung du ma bstan pa, avyākṛta*), whereas whatever is a meditative absorption is necessarily virtuous.[b]

Therefore, he remarks that the discussion of afflicted meditative absorptions "is relevant to [that of] pure meditative absorptions concordant with degeneration."[c] However, since the afflictive emotions in question are not those of the level below, an afflicted meditative absorption is also not considered to be non-virtuous.

According to Kön-chok-jik-may-wang-po, an afflicted meditative absorption "has come to be in similar association with any of [the four]—craving, [bad] view, pride, or ignorance—which are neutral."[d] Paṇ-chen Sö-nam-drak-pa gives the same list.[e] Both follow Tsong-kha-pa, who notes that

> The two, the western Vaibhāṣhikas and Asaṅga's *Summary of Manifest Knowledge*, agree in considering the afflicted meditative

---

[a] Lati Rinpoche's explanation of uncontaminated meditative absorptions as "in brief...those used by Superiors as a mental basis for their path consciousnesses" (*Meditative States*, p. 120) does not appear to include Kön-chok-jik-may-wang-po's "contaminated, conceptual type" (see page 247).

[b] *Meditative States*, p. 189.

[c] Ibid., p. 189; for pure meditative absorptions concordant with degeneration, see above, page 244.

[d] Kön-chok-jik-may-wang-po, *Condensed Statement*, 586.2.

[e] Paṇ-chen Sö-nam-drak-pa, "Concentrations," 159b.1–2.

> absorptions to be fourfold in terms of predominant attachment, and so forth. The Kashmīri Vaibhāṣhikas assert [afflicted meditative absorptions] only in terms of predominant attachment,[a]

and cite Asaṅga's *Summary of Manifest Knowledge*—as well as Vasubandhu's *Treasury of Manifest Knowledge* (5.21 and 8.6a) for the two Vaibhāṣhika positions.[b] Tsong-kha-pa points out that the meditative absorptions of the concentrations and formless absorptions cannot be made afflicted by anger "because someone having a basis of an upper realm does not have anger,"[c] which is an afflictive emotion of the Desire Realm.

Tsong-kha-pa, without citing his source, lists the afflictive emotions by which pure meditative absorptions are made afflicted as "attachment to an upper realm, pride, doubt, and [bad] view" and explains that doubt implies ignorance because

> [t]he faculty of ignorance makes [meditative absorptions] have the affliction of doubt. Hence, there is also an explanation that the two, doubt and ignorance, operate together.[d]

Lati Rinpoche, apparently combining Tsong-kha-pa's and Paṇ-chen Sö-nam-drak-pa's presentations, lists five afflictive emotions that can pollute meditative absorptions: attachment, bad view, pride, ignorance, and doubt.[e]

Lati Rinpoche elaborates on Tsong-kha-pa's and Paṇ-chen Sö-nam-drak-pa's presentations to explain the mental processes by which pure meditative absorptions become afflicted. Using the first concentration as an example, he explains that it

---

[a] Tsong-kha-pa, *Notes,* 8.5–6. *nyi 'og bye brag tu mra ba* and *nyi 'og ma* (*aparāntika*) are translated here as "western Vaibhāṣhikas," adapting Pruden's usage in volume 4 of *Abhidharmakośabhāṣyam* (see, for example, p. 1136, which contrasts a position of "the Vaibhāṣikas of the West" with a position of "the Vaibhāṣikas of Kaśmīr"). See also Das, *Tibetan-English Dictionary*, p. 481.

[b] Paṇ-chen Sö-nam-drak-pa, "Concentrations," 159b.2–3; Kön-chok-jik-may-wang-po, *Condensed Statement,* 587.1–2. Asaṅga, *Summary of Manifest Knowledge,* P5550, vol. 112, 261.1.1–2; Rahula, trans., *Le Compendium de la super-doctrine,* p. 110. Vasubandhu, *Treasury of Manifest Knowledge,* 5.21, 8.6a (P5591, vol. 115, 227.1.1–2 and 271.5.2–3; Shastri, part 3, pp. 795–96 and part 4, p. 1139; La Vallée Poussin, 16:4, pp. 42–43 and 16:5, p. 144; Pruden, vol. 3, p. 799, vol. 4, p. 1228).

[c] Tsong-kha-pa, *Notes,* 7.4–5.

[d] Ibid., 7.5–6.

[e] *Meditative States,* p. 120.

> can become polluted by attachment with respect to the First Concentration—that is, by attachment to the bliss of the first concentration. The meditator experiences its taste and becomes attached to it, and through that attachment the first concentration becomes afflicted.[a]

Since, as Denma Lochö Rinpoche remarked, the fourth concentration and the formless absorptions do not have bliss,[b] attachment to those meditative absorptions would have to mean attachment to their good qualities.

Lati Rinpoche explains that the first concentration can be polluted by a mistaken view if the meditator draws a mistaken conclusion from the clairvoyance attained in dependence upon the first concentration. If the meditator "sees his or her past and future lifetimes and assumes that the self is permanent," the first concentration becomes afflicted by a bad view. The first concentration can be polluted by pride if the meditator "becomes puffed up" and thinks he or she is the only person who has ever been capable of attaining that meditative absorption.

Apparently elaborating on Tsong-kha-pa's statement that "[i]gnorance and doubt are explained together," Lati Rinpoche explains that

> [t]hrough the power of ignorance, the meditator generates doubt wondering whether the first concentration itself is a path of liberation. Since the first concentration is not a path of liberation, this doubt is mistaken and is a means by which the first concentration becomes afflicted.[c]

Afflicted meditative absorptions are not considered to be fully qualified meditative absorptions; they are called meditative absorptions only by analogy, because they are continuations of pure meditative absorptions. To establish this point, Paṇ-chen Sö-nam-drak-pa cites Vasubandhu's *Autocommentary on the "Treasury of Manifest Knowledge"* (8.1e): "[this is a case] of designating that which is only of a type similar to [a concentration] with the name ["concentration"], as is the case, for example, with a rotten seed."[d]

---

[a] Ibid., p. 121.

[b] Ibid., p. 188.

[c] Ibid., p. 121.

[d] Paṇ-chen Sö-nam-drak-pa, "Concentrations," 159b.6–160a.1 and *Meditative States*, p. 190, citing Vasubandhu's *Autocommentary on the "Treasury of Manifest Knowledge"* 8.1e (P5591, vol. 115, 270.4.4–5; Shastri, part 4, p. 1128; La Vallée Poussin, 16:5, p. 131; Pru-

THE FOUR CONCENTRATIONS

Kön-chok-jik-may-wang-po defines an actual meditative absorption of a concentration as

> a consciousness that is either a meditative stabilization posited from the point of view of possessing antidotal, benefit, and basis branches or that possessing similar association with it.[a]

Paṇ-chen Sö-nam-drak-pa defines it as

> a virtuous knower that is included within the level of a concentration and that has passed beyond the level below it by way of its branches.[b]

It is clear from these definitions that an actual meditative absorption of a concentration is a consciousness—"knower" (*rig pa, saṃvedana*) being synonymous with consciousness (*shes pa*). By specifying that this knower is "virtuous," Paṇ-chen Sö-nam-drak-pa excludes afflicted meditative absorptions, which, as was mentioned earlier (see page 248), are neutral rather than virtuous. The two definitions also make clear that an actual meditative absorption of a concentration is distinguished (a) by possessing branches (Kön-chok-jik-may-wang-po) and (b) by passing beyond the level below by means of its branches.

Although the term "branch" (*yan lag, aṅga*) in this context is not defined in the sources discussed here, it is clear from Kön-chok-jik-may-wang-po's entire discussion of the individual branches[c] that the branches are mental factors. Tsong-kha-pa points out in his *Notes* that the branches of the concentrations are posited as consisting of a specific number—five in the first concentration, four in the second, five in the third, and four in the fourth, giving a total of eighteen—"in terms of including the main [branches]" and that the main branches are posited in terms of being included as antidotal, benefit, and basis branches. However,

> [t]he branches of the actual [meditative absorptions] of the concentrations are not definite as these [that is, limited to these] because there are many [branches of] actual meditative absorptions of concentrations which are not any of these

den, vol. 4, p. 1218).

[a] Kön-chok-jik-may-wang-po, *Condensed Statement*, 582.5.

[b] Paṇ-chen Sö-nam-drak-pa, "Concentrations," 157a.1–2; *Meditative States*, p. 178.

[c] Kön-chok-jik-may-wang-po, *Condensed Statement*, 596.1–602.3.

branches.[a]

Therefore, it may be said that the branches of the concentrations are those mental factors that serve to characterize each of the four concentrations and distinguish them from each other, in terms of antidote, benefit, and basis. The branches are listed in Vasubandhu's *Treasury of Manifest Knowledge* and *Autocommentary*, as well as in Asaṅga's *Summary of Manifest Knowledge.* Paṇ-chen Sö-nam-drak-pa cites Asaṅga's *Summary of Manifest Knowledge* as the source of the division into antidotal, benefit, and basis branches.[b]

Paṇ-chen Sö-nam-drak-pa explains an antidotal branch as "that which abandons harm," a benefit branch as "that which achieves help," and the basis branch—meditative stabilization in all four concentrations—as one-pointedness.[c] The term "antidotal branch" presents a problem, however, since the actual antidotes to the afflictive emotions of the level below are the uninterrupted paths of the preparations. Following a passage in Tsong-kha-pa's *Golden Rosary*, which Kön-chok-jik-may-wang-po cites, the texts and scholars considered here agree with Kön-chok-jik-may-wang-po's position that

> in the actual meditative absorption the so-called antidotal branches are not [antidotes] that abandon that which has not been abandoned; rather, the meaning is that they merely lengthen the distance from the afflictive emotions, and so forth, of the level below.[d]

Meditative stabilization is posited as the basis branch, according to Lati Rinpoche, because the antidotal and benefit branches "exist in dependence on meditative stabilization; it is the basis, or source, of the

---

[a] Tsong-kha-pa, *Notes,* 14.1–3. See also Lati Rinpoche in *Meditative States,* p. 118.

[b] Vasubandhu, *Treasury of Manifest Knowledge* and *Autocommentary*, 8.7–8 (P5591, vol. 115, 271.5.6–272.1.5; Shastri, part 4, p. 1140; La Vallée Poussin, 16:5, p. 147; Pruden, vol. 4, p. 1229); Asaṅga, *Summary of Manifest Knowledge,* P5550, vol. 112, 261.2.1–2; Rahula, trans., *Le Compendium de la super-doctrine*, p. 111. Paṇ-chen Sö-nam-drak-pa, "Concentrations," 163a.2.

[c] Paṇ-chen Sö-nam-drak-pa, "Concentrations," 163a.1.

[d] Kön-chok-jik-may-wang-po, *Condensed Statement,* 592.4. Cf. Lati Rinpoche in *Meditative States,* p. 116. Although Paṇ-chen Sö-nam-drak-pa does not explicitly discuss the question of antidotal branches, he remarks that "[i]t is not necessary for the actual concentrations and formless absorptions to separate from desire for the levels below them because the preparations do the separating" (Paṇ-chen Sö-nam-drak-pa, "Concentrations," 159a.3–4; see also *Meditative States,* p. 187).

antidotes and benefits."[a]

The first concentration has five branches: investigation (*rtog pa, vitarka*), analysis (*dpyod pa, vicāra*), joy (*dga' ba, prīti*), bliss (*bde ba, sukha*), and meditative stabilization (*ting nge 'dzin, samādhi*). The second has four: internal clarity (*nang rab tu dvang ba, adhyātmasamprasāda*), joy, bliss, and meditative stabilization. The third has five: mindfulness (*dran pa, smṛti*), introspection (*shes bzhin, saṃprajanya*), the compositional factor of equanimity (*btang snyoms, upekṣā*), bliss, and meditative stabilization. The fourth has four: mindfulness, the compositional factor of equanimity (*btang snyoms, upekṣā*), neutral feeling (*btang snyoms, upekṣā; sdug bsngal ma yin bde ba yang ma yin, aduḥkhāsukhavedanā*), and meditative stabilization. The table below shows how these are classified as antidotal, benefit, and basis branches.

Chart 14: Branches of the Concentrations

(Read from bottom to top.)

Concentration	Antidote	Benefit	Basis
Fourth Concentration	mindfulness equanimity	neutral feeling	meditative stabilization
Third Concentration	mindfulness introspection equanimity	bliss	meditative stabilization
Second Concentration	internal clarity	joy bliss	meditative stabilization
First Concentration Special	analysis	neutral feeling	meditative stabilization
Mere	investigation analysis	joy bliss	meditative stabilization

Progressing by way of the branches means giving up those branches considered to be inferior from the point of view of the level the meditator is trying to attain. Although the inferior branches are given up in any case, no matter which preparations are used, when the next-higher level is attained, the branches themselves can be made the focus of meditation during the preparations, and the inferior ones can be given up deliberately. This is the mode of progress mentioned in Buddhaghosa's *Path of Purification,* where it is called "mastery in reviewing" (Pāli, *paccavekkhaṇvasi*).[b] Denma Lochö Rinpoche suggests that, for Bodhisattvas and Hearers who proceed gradually, it is another way of doing

[a] *Meditative States,* p. 118. I have found no explanation of why the benefit branches are so called—perhaps because the reason was considered obvious.

[b] Buddhaghosa, *The Path of Purification,* trans. Ñyāṇamoli, vol. 1, pp. 161, 165, 171.

the preparations having the aspect of grossness/peacefulness, since, although Bodhisattvas and Hearers who proceed gradually do the preparations having the aspect of grossness/peacefulness, they "would not think of any rebirth state as truly peaceful" but instead "consider all cyclic existence to be like a garbage heap" in which "some places...are less dirty than others":

> Instead of viewing the lower and upper rebirth states as gross and peaceful, respectively, the meditator views the actual meditative absorptions as gross or peaceful in terms of their branches. Thus, to progress from the first concentration to the second, the meditator would think...that the first concentration has investigation and analysis, whereas the second concentration is free of them. The mode of procedure for the remaining concentrations is similar.[a]

THE FIRST CONCENTRATION

The first concentration has two types—a mere first concentration (*bsam gtan dang po'i dngos gzhi'i snyoms 'jug tsam po ba*) and a special first concentration (*bsam gtan dang po'i dngos gzhi'i snyoms 'jug khyad par can*). The mere first concentration, which is the general type, has investigation and analysis as its antidotal branches, joy and bliss as its benefit branches, and meditative stabilization as the basis branch. The special first concentration differs from the mere first concentration in having only analysis as the antidotal branch and neutral feeling, rather than joy and bliss, as the benefit branch. (See chart, page 253.)

Investigation and analysis. Kön-chok-jik-may-wang-po points out that the four schools of tenets have different explanations of investigation and analysis. The Vaibhāṣhikas explain investigation as a mental factor that acts coarsely and analysis, as a mental factor that acts finely, "whereupon they assert that [investigation and analysis] occur as concomitants of a single mind," whereas the Sautrāntikas explain investigation and analysis "as coarse and fine awarenesses that motivate speech expressing[, respectively,] the entity and features of an object, whereupon they assert that these do not arise as concomitants of a single mind." Kön-chok-jik-may-wang-po cites Vasubandhu's *Treasury of Manifest Knowledge* (2.33) as his source for the Vaibhāṣhika position and Vasubandhu's *Autocommentary on the "Treasury of Manifest Knowledge"*

---

[a] *Meditative States*, pp. 203 and 247 n. 18.

(2.33) as his source for the Sautrāntika position. He states that "the Chittamātrins and those above"—that is, the Mādhyamikas—"posit those two [investigation and analysis] from the point of view of coarse and fine engagement in their objects and coarse and fine functioning" because each depends, for its manner of engaging in its object, "upon either intention or wisdom."[a] Citing as his source Yashomitra's *Commentary on (Asaṅga's) "Summary of Manifest Knowledge"* he explains that "when the object has not been settled, one relies mainly on intention, and when it has been settled, one relies mainly on wisdom."[b] Kön-chok-jik-may-wang-po's own definitions follow the position of "the Chittamātrins and those above." His method is to proceed from the general to the specific—that is, to define investigation and analysis as changeable mental factors and then make the definitions specific to the first concentration.[c]

Joy and bliss. As with investigation and analysis, Tsong-kha-pa and the writers who follow him distinguish among the assertions of the lower and higher schools of tenets concerning joy and bliss. According to Tsong-kha-pa's summary of the Vaibhāṣhika position, the bliss of the first concentration "is the bliss that is the mental factor of pliancy," whereas "joy is the feeling of mental bliss (*tshor ba yid bde*)." Paṇ-chen Sö-nam-drak-pa cites the *Treasury* [8.9b, 8.9c–d] as the source of the Vaibhāṣhika position.[d] Asaṅga's system is also concisely summarized by Tsong-kha-pa:

> ...the single mental factor that is generated in the sphere of one

---

[a] Kön-chok-jik-may-wang-po, *Condensed Statement,* 594.1–595.5; 603.6–604.1. See also Tsong-kha-pa, *Notes,* 10.7–11.3. Vasubandhu, *Treasury of Manifest Knowledge* and *Autocommentary,* 2.33 (P5591, vol. 115, 147.3.3 and 147.3.5; Shastri, part 1, pp. 204–207; La Vallée Poussin, 16:1, pp. 173, 175–76; Pruden, vol. 1, pp. 202–204).

[b] Kön-chok-jik-may-wang-po, *Condensed Statement,* 596.3–4.

[c] Ibid., 596.1–2, 596.5, 596.6–597.1, 597.2–3. Paṇ-chen Sö-nam-drak-pa's explanation of investigation and analysis is similar to, but less detailed than, Kön-chok-jik-may-wang-po's (Paṇ-chen Sö-nam-drak-pa, "Concentrations," 160b.3–4; see also *Meditative States,* p. 193).

The Theravādins assert, apparently as a corollary of their position that the first concentration is pure calm (Pāli, *samatha*), without analysis, that *vitakka* and *vicāra* cannot be understood literally as investigation and analysis but must be reinterpreted as initial application of mind and sustained application of mind, respectively.

[d] Tsong-kha-pa, *Notes,* 11.2–4; Paṇ-chen Sö-nam-drak-pa, "Concentrations," 160b.4–5; see also Kön-chok-jik-may-wang-po, *Condensed Statement,* 594.6–595.5, 597.4–599.1. Vasubandhu, *Treasury of Manifest Knowledge,* 8.9b, 8.9c–d (P5591, vol. 115, 272.2.2, 272.5.6; Shastri, part 4, pp. 1151–58; La Vallée Poussin, 16:5, pp. 150, 158–60; Pruden, vol. 4, pp. 1231, 1237).

main mental consciousness and experiences refreshment [is posited as] bliss from the point of view of its helping the body—that is, the sense powers together with their bases—[and it is posited as] joy from the point of view of its refreshing mental bliss (*yid bde*), together with its sphere. It is posited as those two from the point of view of [its having] different functions, but they do not have different substantial entities; this is explained in [Yashomitra's] *Commentary on (Asaṅga's) "Summary of Manifest Knowledge."*[a]

The mere and special first concentrations. Although the two types of first concentration differ with regard to both their antidotal and benefit branches, the distinction between them is explained mainly in terms of a difference in the degree of subtlety of investigation and analysis, the antidotal branches of the mere first concentration. Because investigation is considered to be coarser than analysis, the texts and scholars considered here agree that it is possible to separate from one of the antidotal branches without changing level. However, because the second, third, and fourth concentrations do not have any branch that is coarser than the others of its level, they have no variations in type.[b]

None of the texts and scholars considered here explain why the special first concentration has neutral feeling rather than joy and bliss as a benefit branch.

THE SECOND CONCENTRATION

The second concentration has internal clarity as the antidotal branch, joy and bliss as the benefit branches, and meditative stabilization as the basis branch. Since the explanations of the joy, bliss, and meditative stabilization of the second concentration are similar to those of the first, the discussion of the branches mainly concerns internal clarity. As an antidotal branch, internal clarity has the function of causing the meditator to be further separated from the discarded branches of the level below—in this case, investigation and analysis. According to Tsong-kha-pa's *Notes*, "The meaning of internal clarity is that it has thoroughly pacified the distraction of the investigation and analysis of

---

[a] Tsong-kha-pa, *Notes*, 11.4–5. See also Paṇ-chen Sö-nam-drak-pa, "Concentrations," 160b.5–161a.4 and Kön-chok-jik-may-wang-po, *Condensed Statement*, 597.4–599.1.

[b] Tsong-kha-pa, *Notes*, 11.7–12.2; Paṇ-chen Sö-nam-drak-pa, "Concentrations," 157a.5–157b.1; Kön-chok-jik-may-wang-po, *Condensed Statement*, 584.3–4. See also Lati Rinpoche in *Meditative States*, p. 120.

the first concentration, which disturbed [the meditator's] continuum."[a] Concerning the nature of internal clarity, Vasubandhu's and Asaṅga's systems differ. The *Treasury* identifies internal clarity as faith—in particular, according to Paṇ-chen Sö-nam-drak-pa, as "the faith of the conviction that one has emerged from the first concentration, in accordance with the statement, 'Internal clarity is faith.'"[b] According to Asaṅga, however, internal clarity consists of mindfulness, introspection, and the compositional factor of equanimity—the antidotal branches of the third concentration—which are not called by their own names in the second concentration because the second concentration still has as its benefit branch joy, which is given up when the meditator progresses from the second to the third concentration. Tsong-kha-pa states this position in his *Notes*, citing Asaṅga's *Compendium of Ascertainments*.[c] In his sixth debate on the branches of the concentrations, Kön-chok-jik-may-wang-po identifies Vasubandhu's position as incorrect and Asaṅga's as correct; in his later discussion of mindfulness, introspection, and equanimity, he cites the more detailed discussion in Tsong-kha-pa's *Golden Rosary of Eloquence*.[d]

THE THIRD CONCENTRATION

The third concentration has mindfulness, introspection, and equanimity as its antidotal branches, bliss as its benefit branch, and meditative stabilization as its basis branch. The bliss that is the benefit branch of the third concentration is characterized by the absence of the joy of the second concentration. The antidotal branches—mindfulness, introspection, and the compositional factor of equanimity—are also explained in relation to the absence of the joy of the second concentration, as well as the investigation and analysis of the first. Thus, according to Paṇ-chen Sö-nam-drak-pa,

---

[a] Tsong-kha-pa, *Notes*, 12.4.

[b] Paṇ-chen Sö-nam-drak-pa, "Concentrations," 161a.5–6, citing Vasubandhu, *Treasury of Manifest Knowledge*, 8.9c (P5591, vol. 115, 272.1.8; Shastri, part 4, p. 1148; La Vallée Poussin, 16:5, p. 158; Pruden, vol. 4, p. 1236); see also Tsong-kha-pa, *Notes*, 12.4–5.

[c] Tsong-kha-pa, *Notes*, 12.4–5.

[d] Kön-chok-jik-may-wang-po, *Condensed Statement*, 595.5–6 and 601.3–5.

According to Kön-chok-jik-may-wang-po, mindfulness, introspection, and the compositional factor of equanimity are also present in the first concentration but are not named as branches because "there is strong fluctuation due to investigation and analysis and [those three] are not predominant like other branches." Here too he cites Tsong-kha-pa's *Golden Rosary of Eloquence* as his source (ibid., 601.2–3).

> The bliss that is a branch of the third concentration is a faculty of blissful feeling which is devoid of joy. Mindfulness is that which holds on to the object of observation and in which the entanglements of joy have ceased, and introspection watches whether one has or does not have a holding on to the object of observation in which the entanglements of joy have ceased. Equanimity, because of being free of the faults of investigation, analysis, and joy, is an absence of imbalance due to those three.[a]

THE FOURTH CONCENTRATION

The fourth concentration has mindfulness and the compositional factor of equanimity as the antidotal branches, neutral feeling as the benefit branch, and meditative stabilization as the basis branch. According to Paṇ-chen Sö-nam-drak-pa, the mindfulness and equanimity of the fourth concentration "are called completely pure because they have separated from the eight faults of concentration."[b] The eight faults (*skyon, apakṣāla*) of concentration are:

investigation (*rtog pa, vitarka*)
analysis (*dpyod pa, vicāra*)
inhalation (*dbugs rngub pa, śvāsa*)
exhalation (*dbugs 'byung pa, praśvāsa*)
the feeling of pleasure (*bde ba, sukha*)
the feeling of pain (*sdug bsngal, duḥkha*)
the feeling of mental discomfort (*yid mi bde, daurmanasya*)
the feeling of mental bliss (*yid bde, saumanasya*)[c]

These eight faults are described as "faults of fluctuation"[d]; since the

---

[a] Paṇ-chen Sö-nam-drak-pa, "Concentrations," 161b.3–5; see also Kön-chok-jik-may-wang-po, *Condensed Statement*, 599.5–600.3.

[b] Paṇ-chen Sö-nam-drak-pa, "Concentrations," 162a.4–5; see also Kön-chok-jik-may-wang-po, *Condensed Statement*, 585.2–3, 600.3–5; Tsong-kha-pa, *Notes*, 10.2, 13.4.

According to Lati Rinpoche (*Meditative States*, p. 127), the benefit branch, neutral feeling, is also called "thoroughly pure." Although it is not so called in the other sources considered here, Tsong-kha-pa's *Notes*, 13.5, describes it as "a release from the eight faults of concentration which is an experience of neutral [feeling]"; it is possible that, in that sense, the benefit branch of the fourth concentration may also be called completely pure.

[c] Paṇ-chen Sö-nam-drak-pa, "Concentrations," 162a.5–6; *Meditative States*, pp. 127, 197.

[d] Paṇ-chen Sö-nam-drak-pa, "Concentrations," 162a.6; Kön-chok-jik-may-wang-po, *Condensed Statement*, 591.2–5, 600.4–5, 602.1–3.

fourth concentration is free of them, it is described as unfluctuating.[a] However, Tsong-kha-pa and his followers point out that investigation, analysis, joy, and bliss are faults only in relation to the fourth concentration, not in relation to their own level.[b]

It is generally explained that introspection is not named as a branch of the fourth concentration because the fourth concentration is free of the eight faults; therefore, the meditator has no need to inspect for them. Kön-chok-jik-may-wang-po also relates the non-mention of introspection as a branch to the thorough purity of the mindfulness and equanimity that are the antidotal branches of the fourth concentration:

> since one has separated from all faults of fluctuation at that time, the two [mindfulness and equanimity] are not only mentioned by their own names but are indicated by the term "completely pure," and since, here, there is no need for watchfulness out of qualms of distraction due to those faults, introspection is not posited as a branch. This is because Vasubandhu's *Treasury of Manifest Knowledge* (8.11a–b) says, "The fourth is unfluctuating."[c]

---

[a] Paṇ-chen Sö-nam-drak-pa, "Concentrations," 162a.5, and Kön-chok-jik-may-wang-po, *Condensed Statement,* 581.5–6 and 602.1–3, and Denma Lochö Rinpoche in *Meditative States,* p. 197. Both cite Vasubandhu's *Treasury of Manifest Knowledge,* 8.11a–b: "Because of being released from the eight faults, the fourth is unfluctuating" (P5591, vol. 115, 273.1.5–6; Shastri, part 4, p. 1150; La Vallée Poussin, 16:5, p. 161; Pruden, vol. 4, p. 1239).

[b] Tsong-kha-pa, *Notes,* 13.7–14.1; Paṇ-chen Sö-nam-drak-pa, "Concentrations," 162a.6–162b.3 and *Meditative States,* pp. 197–98, citing Asaṅga's *Compendium of Ascertainments*; Kön-chok-jik-may-wang-po, *Condensed Statement,* 600.6–601.2.

[c] Kön-chok-jik-may-wang-po, *Condensed Statement,* 602.1–3; see also Tsong-kha-pa, *Notes,* 13.6–7; Lati Rinpoche in *Meditative States,* p. 127; Vasubandhu, *Treasury of Manifest Knowledge,* 8.11a–b (P5591, vol. 115, 273.1.5–6; Shastri, part 4, p. 1150; La Vallée Poussin, 16:5, p. 161; Pruden, vol. 4, p. 1239). Although Tsong-kha-pa's *Notes* refers to inspecting for laxity and excitement with regard to both the introspection of the third concentration (12.6) and the non-mention of introspection as a branch of the fourth (13.6), Kön-chok-jik-may-wang-po's explanations of the introspection of the third concentration as "a wisdom consciousness that inspects whether one abides in that mindfulness which apprehends either the object of observation or the subjective aspect of stopping the entanglement of joy" (600.1–2) and of the non-mention of introspection as a branch of the fourth as a result of the absence of the faults of fluctuation appear to make more sense.

Comparison of the Concentrations

On the basis of a passage from Asaṅga's *Compendium of Ascertainments*,[a] the concentrations are compared in terms of the completion of meditative stabilization, the completion of help (*phan 'dogs pa*, synonymous with benefit [*phan yon, anuśaṃsa*]), and the completion of thorough purity (*yongs su dag pa, pariśuddhi*). The comparison answers the unstated question, "How is each concentration superior to the level below it?"

Kön-chok-jik-may-wang-po explains that the first two concentrations "differ in the completeness of the strength of meditative stabilization" because the first concentration has "investigation and analysis [which] cause the mind to fluctuate," whereas the second concentration is free of them; therefore, meditative stabilization is said to be complete in the second concentration. The second and third concentrations "differ in the completeness of the strength of help" because the second concentration

> is polluted by the fault of joy,...[whereas], at the time of the third concentration, since one has separated from the three entanglements of investigation, analysis, and joy, the strength of the three—the compositional factor of equanimity, mindfulness, and introspection—is complete.[b]

Therefore, the strength of help is said to be complete in the third concentration.

The term "thorough purity" refers here to "purification of the faults of fluctuation." The third and fourth concentrations differ in the completeness of thorough purity because "in the fourth concentration, since one has become purified of the eight faults, there is completion of entirely pure equanimity and mindfulness."[c]

The Four Formless Absorptions

The formless absorptions are discussed only briefly in the texts considered here; they are not a major topic and, indeed, are considered inferior to the concentrations because they are mainly calm abiding, without analysis (see page 240). According to Kön-chok-jik-may-wang-po's etymology, the formless absorptions are called formless because "the discrimination of form has been destroyed or because there is not the

---

[a] Cited in Paṇ-chen Sö-nam-drak-pa, "Concentrations," 162b.3–6.

[b] Kön-chok-jik-may-wang-po, *Condensed Statement*, 590.6–591.2

[c] Ibid., 591.2, 591.5.

least form."[a] This etymology includes both the actual meditative absorptions and the resultant-birth meditative absorptions of the formless absorptions. In the former, the meditator may be a Desire or Form Realm being; such a meditator has a form aggregate—that is, a body—but "the discrimination of form has been destroyed." In a resultant-birth meditative absorption of a formless absorption, the meditator is a Formless Realm being who possesses in his or her continuum the meditative absorption of the rebirth level (and may or may not have attained an actual formless absorption of a higher level). Such a meditator not only lacks the discrimination of form but also does not have a form aggregate; "there is not the least form" in the Formless Realm.

Kön-chok-jik-may-wang-po gives a detailed definition of an actual meditative absorption of a formless absorption:

> an actual meditative absorption of an upper [level], having the type of being posited from the point of view of its object of observation and subjective aspect without having branches, which arises from having familiarized oneself again and again, mainly by way of calm abiding, with any of the discriminations of space, and so forth, upon having viewed as coarse any of the discriminations of form, space, consciousness, and nothingness for one's awareness at the time of training.[b]

This definition includes both the nature and the mode of cultivation of such a meditative absorption. Kön-chok-jik-may-wang-po derives the absence of branches in the formless absorptions both from textual tradition and from the mode of cultivation. He notes that branches of formless absorptions are not mentioned "in any sūtra or [commentarial] treatise (*bstan bcos, śāstra*)" and also that

> when the meditative absorptions of the formless absorptions are newly achieved, one enters [into meditative absorption] by way of the later object of observation and subjective aspect upon leaving the discrimination of the previous object of observation.[c]

This means, in general, that the meditator views the previous object of observation as gross and the object of observation of the level to be attained as peaceful. This process, however, is described in the definition

a Ibid., 588.4–5.

b Ibid., 588.2–4.

c Ibid., 589.5–6.

as being done "for one's awareness at the time of training"[a]—that is, during the preparations having the *aspect* of grossness/peacefulness. Kön-chok-jik-may-wang-po seems to be alluding here, without discussing the point, to the distinction between object of observation and subjective aspect. Technically, the object of observation for all the formless absorptions is what Tsong-kha-pa calls "the coarse aggregates that are the basis of the name"—that is, in Lati Rinpoche's paraphrase, the meditator's mental aggregates—whereas the discriminations that space is limitless, consciousness is limitless, and so forth, actually constitute the subjective aspect of the formless absorptions.[b]

Kön-chok-jik-may-wang-po himself points out that the qualifications in his definitions of formless absorptions, such as "*having the type of being posited from the point of view of* its object of observation and subjective aspect" in the definition of an actual meditative absorption of a formless absorption cited above (page 241), includes formless absorptions having the aspect of the truths.[c]

The four formless absorptions are limitless space, limitless consciousness, nothingness, and the peak of cyclic existence. The last is also known as without discrimination and without non-discrimination (*'du shes med 'du shes med min, naivasaṃjñānāsaṃjñā*).

Limitless space. To attain an actual meditative absorption of limitless space, a meditator who has attained the fourth concentration, the highest level of the Form Realm, thinks of that level as gross and thinks of limitless space as peaceful. Repeatedly thinking, "Space is limitless," the meditator stabilizes on that thought and attains an actual meditative absorption of limitless space. Only space appears to the meditator's mind; forms no longer appear. The meditator does not perceive obstruction, as of walls, or variety, as of groves and colors.[d] Lati Rinpoche points out, however, that the meditator is cultivating the non-appearance of forms but "is not meditating that they do not exist."[e]

Limitless consciousness. To attain an actual meditative absorption of limitless consciousness, a meditator who has attained the meditative absorption of limitless space thinks of that level as gross and of the discrimination that consciousness is limitless as peaceful. Stabilizing on

---

[a] Ibid., 588.2.

[b] Tsong-kha-pa, *Notes,* 16.2; Lati Rinpoche in *Meditative States,* p. 130.

[c] Kön-chok-jik-may-wang-po, *Condensed Statement,* 588.3–4, italics mine; 589.4.

[d] Tsong-kha-pa, *Notes,* 15.7–16.3; Lati Rinpoche in *Meditative States,* pp. 129–30.

[e] Lati Rinpoche in *Meditative States,* p. 130.

that thought, the meditator attains an actual meditative absorption of limitless consciousness.[a]

Nothingness. To attain an actual meditative absorption of nothingness, a meditator who has attained the meditative absorption of limitless consciousness thinks of that level as gross and of the level of nothingness as peaceful.[b] According to Tsong-kha-pa, the meditator stabilizes on the thought, "There is not even any object of observation that has form or is formless."[c]

The peak of cyclic existence. To attain an actual meditative absorption of the peak of cyclic existence—that is, a meditative absorption without discrimination and without non-discrimination—a meditator who has attained the meditative absorption of nothingness thinks of that level as gross and of the discrimination "coarse discrimination does not exist; subtle discrimination is not non-existent" as peaceful.[d] Lati Rinpoche explains:

> "Coarse discrimination does not exist" means that the gross, or coarse, discrimination called nothingness which the meditator is now viewing does not exist; in other words, the meditator lets it go, and subtle discrimination is left.[e]

The meditative absorption of the peak of cyclic existence lacks some of the types of the other meditative absorptions. It does not have a type concordant with enhancement because there is no higher mundane level, and according to the Manifest Knowledge systems, it also does not have an uncontaminated type, since the mind of the peak of cyclic existence is thought to be weak and unclear (see page 245).

Conclusion

In a Buddhist system, whether Hīnayāna or Mahāyāna, the meditative absorptions are important insofar as they serve as either path consciousnesses or mental bases of path consciousnesses. Much of the topic of mental bases (see Chapter 3) is concerned with this question, and echoes of it occur in the presentations of the absorptions themselves—for instance, in the discussions of pure meditative absorptions

---

[a] Tsong-kha-pa, *Notes,* 16.3–5; Lati Rinpoche in *Meditative States,* p. 131.

[b] Tsong-kha-pa, *Notes,* 16.5–17.1; Lati Rinpoche in *Meditative States,* p. 131.

[c] Tsong-kha-pa, *Notes,* 16.7.

[d] Tsong-kha-pa, *Notes,* 17.2; Lati Rinpoche in *Meditative States,* p. 132.

[e] Lati Rinpoche in *Meditative States,* p. 132.

concordant with definite differentiation and of uncontaminated meditative absorptions. Critiques of the meditative absorption of the peak of cyclic existence—which, according to the Manifest Knowledge position, does not have a type concordant with definite differentiation—especially reflect this concern.

According to Gedün Lodrö, "most persons attain the path of seeing using the fourth concentration as their mental basis."[a] Although "[t]here are Hīnayānists who use the not-unable preparation as a mental basis for the path of seeing—specifically, Stream Enterers who proceed in a simultaneous (*gcig car, sakṛt*) manner," this is only because they

> will not attain the first concentration; they have nothing better than the not-unable. However, those on the Mahāyāna path of preparation attain all four concentrations; thus, of course, those persons would use a better type of mind as the basis—specifically, the fourth concentration. There is nothing better than using the fourth concentration as a basis for the path of seeing.[b]

Gedün Lodrö explains that an actual fourth concentration provides the best mental basis for the path of seeing—the initial direct realization of emptiness—because it is free of the eight faults of fluctuation (see page 258) and also because it is "an equal combination of calm abiding and special insight."[c]

A more advanced Bodhisattva, Gedün Lodrö points out, has developed greater dexterity in meditation and, therefore, no longer needs to use the fourth concentration as the mental basis of uncontaminated paths: "Any of the other absorptions or even a mind of the Desire Realm can serve as the mental basis."[d] Thus, cultivation of the meditative absorptions is important for a Bodhisattva's own development of dexterity. Cultivation of the meditative absorptions is also considered to be important for a Bodhisattva's development of the ability to help others; thus, the topic of the Perfections provides a context in which the concentrations and formless absorptions can be studied as part of a Bodhisattva's practice (see pages 291ff.).

As will be discussed below (pages 300ff.), the concentrations and

[a] Gedün Lodrö, p. 324.

[b] Ibid., p. 377.

[c] Ibid., p. 324.

[d] Ibid., p. 325.

formless absorptions are studied in the Ge-luk tradition, even though they are not practiced, partly because of their place in the biography of Shākyamuni Buddha; intense study of the characteristics of the meditative absorptions of the concentrations and formless absorptions enables Ge-luk-pa scholars to develop a sense of connection to Shākyamuni Buddha even without cultivation of the absorptions themselves. They are also studied because of their relationship to Buddhist cosmology. Primarily, however, the topic of the concentrations and formless absorptions is studied because it presents an ideal model of Buddhist practice—mainly the practice of Bodhisattvas according to the sūtra system, but also that of Hearers and Solitary Realizers. It also provides a Buddhist model of Indian non-Buddhist practice that presents a case for the superiority of Buddhist goals and methods while acknowledging and respecting the skill and high attainments of non-Buddhist meditators.

Since the model is of types of meditation practiced in an ideal Buddhist past, and since the meditative absorptions themselves are not cultivated in Tibet, the chief means of connecting with the model is through study. As was pointed out earlier (pages 16ff.), the texts translated here are scholarly works developed within a religious system. Moreover, the texts themselves are objects of intense study. Like traditional Jewish Talmud scholars, Ge-luk-pa scholar-monastics live in a religious culture willing to support a class of people who devote their time to religious scholarship and for whom study is a form of practice. By studying the texts thoroughly with teachers, memorizing them, and debating their fine points, Ge-luk-pa scholar-monastics immerse themselves in the model, and absorb its values.

PART TWO:
COMPARISONS

10 THE CONCENTRATIONS AND FORMLESS ABSORPTIONS IN THE LIFE OF SHĀKYAMUNI BUDDHA

The life of Shākyamuni Buddha is best known to Westerners from the Theravāda discourses. Although modern Tibetan teachers seldom refer to it, it is also known to Tibetans, mainly from the *History of Buddhism* of Bu-tön, as well as from Ashvaghoṣha's *Buddha's Deeds*. According to Obermiller, Bu-tön's account of the first eleven of the twelve deeds of a Buddha "represents a summary of the *Lalita-vistara-sūtra* [*rgya cher rol pa'i mdo, Extensive Sport Sūtra*] and contains numerous verses from it."[a] His account of the *parinirvāṇa* "is taken from the *Vinaya-kṣudraka*"[b] (*'dul ba phran tshegs, Minutiae of Discipline*).

The Theravāda discourses and the *Extensive Sport Sūtra* agree on the main episodes of Shākyamuni Buddha's life up to his enlightenment, although the latter is much more elaborate. Thus, both contain versions of a childhood experience of concentration. According to the *Middle Length Sayings*, it occurred during an annual plowing ritual; while his father was plowing, the future Buddha sat under a tree and entered a meditative absorption of the first concentration.[c] He remembered this experience at the end of his period of fruitless asceticism and, after giving up asceticism, used it as a basis of further attainment.[d] In Bu-tön's summary of the *Extensive Sport Sūtra*, the episode occurs in the palace garden, and the future Buddha attains all four concentrations. In the *Extensive Sport Sūtra*, however, the episode serves only to illustrate his precocity, and there is no further reference to it.[e]

Ashvaghoṣha's *Buddha's Deeds* places the episode later, just before the future Buddha meets the ascetic and decides to leave home, but in other respects his account resembles the Theravāda one. In both, the future Buddha attains only the first concentration, and he remembers and uses the experience later. In both, too, the experience is associated

---

[a] Bu-ston, *History of Buddhism*, Part 2: *The History of Buddhism in India and Tibet*, trans. by E. Obermiller (Heidelberg: Harrasowitz, 1932), p. 3.

[b] Ibid., p. 3.

[c] *The Collection of the Middle Length Sayings*, trans. I. B. Horner, Pali Text Society Translation Series, no. 29; first pub. 1954 (London: Luzac, 1967), vol. 1, p. 301; *Majjhima Nikāya*, 1.246–47.

[d] Idem.

[e] Bu-ston, *History of Buddhism*, Part 2, p. 15.

with a scene of plowing, although in *Buddha's Deeds* the future Buddha's father is no longer a participant. Ashvaghoṣha, however, adds a description of the future Buddha's response to the scene—recognition of impermanence and compassion for the suffering of the insects killed by the plow and of the plowmen and their oxen—which provides a motivation for his decision to meditate.[a]

All three accounts agree that the future Buddha learned the formless absorption of nothingness from Āḷāra the Kāḷāma and the formless absorption without discrimination and without non-discrimination from Udraka (Pāli, *uddaka*) the son of Rāma, and that he found both wanting.[b] All three accounts also agree that Shākyamuni Buddha entered the meditative absorptions of the four concentrations just before his enlightenment. Theravāda sources and Bu-tön's summary of the *Extensive Sport Sūtra* agree that he achieved enlightenment on the basis of the fourth concentration, but Ashvaghoṣha does not specify the fourth as the basis.[c]

According to the Theravāda tradition, the four concentrations were an important part of Shākyamuni Buddha's own practice even after his enlightenment.[d] They were also an important part of his teaching. As Gunaratana points out, they "are invariably included in the complete course of training laid down for disciples."[e] Bu-tön, however, does not refer to the concentrations and formless absorptions at all between Shākyamuni Buddha's enlightenment and his *parinirvāṇa.* Instead, following the *Sūtra Unraveling the Thought,* he sets forth three turnings of the wheel of doctrine (*chos kyi 'khor lo bskor ba, dharmacakrapravartana*). The first is that of the Hearer Vehicle (*nyan thos kyi theg pa, śrāvakayāna*). The second and third turnings of the wheel of doctrine are Mahāyāna teachings; they include, respectively, the Perfection of Wisdom Sūtras and the *Sūtra Unraveling the Thought* itself[f] and correspond,

---

[a] Ashvaghoṣha, *Buddha's Deeds* (*buddhacaritranāmamahākavya, sangs rgyas kyi spyod pa shes bya ba'i snyan ngag chen po*), P5356, vol. 129, 130.3.8–130.5.4. *The Buddhacarita; or, Acts of the Buddha,* ed. and trans. E. H. Johnston, first pub. 1936 (Delhi: Oriental Books Reprint Corp., 1972), vol. 1, 5.4–15, pp. 45–47; vol. 2, pp. 62–64.

[b] *Middle Length Sayings,* vol. 1, pp. 207–10; *Majjhima Nikāya,* 1.164–67. Bu-ston, *History of Buddhism,* Part 2, pp. 31–32. Ashvaghoṣha, *Buddha's Deeds,* P5356, vol. 129, 143.1.5–144.4.3; Johnston, vol. 1, 12.1–88, pp. 128–39; vol. 2, pp. 166–82.

[c] *Middle Length Sayings,* vol. 1, p. 28; *Majjhima Nikāya,* 1.22. Bu-ston, *History of Buddhism,* Part 2, p. 38. Ashvaghoṣha, *Buddha's Deeds,* P5356, Vol.129, 147.1.7–147.2.1; Johnston, vol. 1, 14.1–2, p. 157; vol. 2, p. 203.

[d] Henepola Gunaratana, *Path of Serenity and Insight,* p. 6, citing *Dīgha Nikāya,* 2.131–32.

[e] Ibid., p. 6, citing *Dīgha Nikāya,* 1.47–86 and *Majjhima Nikāya,* 1.175–84, 256–80.

[f] Bu-ston, *History of Buddhism,* Part 2, p. 48–56; *Saṃdhinirmocana Sūtra: L'Explication des*

respectively, to the Madhyamaka and Chittamātra systems in Ge-luk presentations of schools of tenets. For the first turning of the wheel of doctrine, Bu-tön follows the narrative of the *Extensive Sport Sūtra,* which agrees in its main outline with Theravāda accounts, but he presents no further teaching of that vehicle in which the concentrations and formless absorptions might figure.[a]

All three accounts agree that before his *parinirvāṇa* Shākyamuni Buddha entered the meditative absorptions of the four concentrations and the four formless absorptions and the meditative absorption of cessation in direct and reverse order—ascending from an actual meditative absorption of the first concentration through an actual absorption of the peak of cyclic existence to that of cessation, and descending from a meditative absorption of cessation through the meditative absorptions of the peak of cyclic existence, nothingness, limitless consciousness, and limitless space, and the meditative absorptions of the fourth, third, second, and first concentrations—and that he then again entered the meditative absorptions of the first, second, third, and fourth concentrations and passed into *parinirvāṇa* from the fourth concentration.[b]

Elements of this account have been retained in the Ge-luk presentations of the concentrations and formless absorptions. Cultivation of the four concentrations and the four formless absorptions and the meditative absorption of cessation in ascending and descending order mentioned as an essential practice of Bodhisattvas—especially in descending order, in which the nine meditative absorptions are alternated with Desire Realm minds for the sake of dexterity in meditative stabilization.[c] The tradition also developed that the fourth concentration is the best mental basis for other attainments—including, according to Gedün Lodrö, direct realization of emptiness at the time of the Mahāyāna path of seeing.[d]

---

mystères, ed. and trans. Étienne Lamotte (Louvain: Bureaux du Recueil, Bibliothèque de l'Université, 1935), pp. 85–86, 206–207.

[a] Bu-ston, *History of Buddhism,* Part 2, p. 46.

[b] Bu-ston, *History of Buddhism,* Part 2, p. 61. Gunaratana, *Path of Serenity and Insight,* p. 6, citing *Dīgha Nikāya,* 1.68–83. Ashvaghoṣha, *Buddha's Deeds,* P5356, Vol. 129, 167.2.3–7.

[c] Jam-yang-shay-pa, *Concentrations,* 210.2–211.1, citing Tsong-kha-pa's *Golden Rosary of Eloquence* and Gyel-tsap's *Explanation of (Maitreya's) "Ornament for Clear Realization," Ornament for the Essence.*

[d] Gedün Lodrö, pp. 377–81.

11 THE RELATIONSHIP OF THE CONCENTRATIONS AND FORMLESS ABSORPTIONS TO TRADITIONAL BUDDHIST COSMOLOGY

Since the actual meditative absorptions of the concentrations and formless absorptions—that is, the absorptions attained in a single lifetime as the result of cultivation[a]—are traditionally held to have corresponding levels of rebirth of which they are the cause, the concentrations and formless absorptions are important not only as a system of meditation but also because of their relationship to traditional Buddhist cosmology. Buddhist scholars have studied this relationship from two points of view, both concerned with action, or karma. The first point of view places those rebirth states in the structure of the cosmology, which, in turn, provides a general map of cyclic existence and of the physical and mental states possible within it. This is the approach of Chapter 3 of Vasubandhu's *Treasury of Manifest Knowledge* and its *Autocommentary*—for Tibetans of all schools, the major Indian source for the map of cyclic existence. Chapter 4, a detailed discussion of the topic of karma, amplifies the general map in Chapter 3 by applying many of its technical points to specific realms and levels of cyclic existence. The second point of view, which presupposes the first, examines the qualities of the sentient beings in the various realms and levels of cyclic existence in order to distinguish between those who are capable of cultivating and attaining the concentrations and formless absorptions and those who are not. It is from this second point of view that Ge-luk monastic textbooks set forth the topic of the physical bases of the concentrations and formless absorptions (discussed in detail in Chapter 2).

The relationship between the actual meditative absorptions and the corresponding levels of rebirth is perhaps the most important reason for the continued study of the system in Buddhist cultures, and knowledge of it is assumed by both Ge-luk-pas and Theravādins. Although the relationship between the actual absorptions of the concentrations and formless absorptions and traditional Buddhist cosmology

[a] The actual absorptions that immediately concern us are those attained by humans, but actual absorptions can also be attained by beings of the Form and Formless Realms. A being born in the First Concentration, for example, can cultivate and attain an actual absorption of the second concentration.

is not explained in the Ge-luk monastic textbooks considered here, knowledge of it is obviously taken for granted—for example, in debates about whether beings of the Form and Formless Realms—that is, beings born in the rebirth states corresponding to the four concentrations and the four formless absorptions, respectively—have states arisen from thinking and whether beings of the Formless Realm have states arisen from hearing.[a]

Lati Rinpoche, however, makes the relationship explicit in his oral exposition of the concentrations and formless absorptions. He begins with a map, as it were, of cyclic existence, from the hells—which he describes vividly—to the Peak of Cyclic Existence. He gives two reasons for providing this map. One of them could apply to any presentation of cyclic existence by any Tibetan teacher in almost any context: since we are people who will die and be reborn, it is important for us to know the various types of rebirth and their causes.[b]

The purpose of such presentations is usually ethical: it is assumed that if listeners know what types of action cause the various types of rebirth, they will try to modify their conduct accordingly so that, at the very least, they may avoid rebirth in bad transmigrations and attain rebirth in happy transmigrations. According to presentations of the topic of Grounds and Paths (*sa lam, bhūmimārga*), engagement in religious practice in order to avoid rebirth in bad transmigrations and attain rebirth in happy transmigrations is the level of the special being of small capacity (*skyes bu chung ngu khyad par can*), the lowest of the three types of religious practitioner. It is assumed to be the level of most people who listen to Buddhist teachings, whereas those of middling capacity (*skyes bu 'bring*) and, especially, those of great capacity (*skyes bu chen po*)—respectively, those who wish to attain freedom from cyclic existence for their own sakes and those who wish to attain Buddhahood for the sake of all sentient beings—are held to be few

---

[a] See page 207 for discussion of these debates in the context of the preparations for the concentrations. Paṇ-chen Sö-nam-drak-pa ("Concentrations," 154a.2–4) presents the basic position of the Mahāyāna Manifest Knowledge, whereas Kön-chok-jik-may-wang-po's debate (569.1–3) represents what Go-mang textbook writers consider to be the Prāsaṅgika-Madhyamaka position. His debate is a condensation of Jam-yang-shay-pa's development of this position in the debates of the "Refutation" section of his presentation of the preparations for the concentrations. Jam-yang-shay-pa, however, also presents the basic Manifest Knowledge position, identified as such, in the section giving his own system (*rang lugs;* Jam-yang-shay-pa, *Concentrations*, 214.2–7, 247.5–6).

[b] *Meditative States*, p. 23.

indeed.[a] Therefore, Lati Rinpoche describes the Desire Realm, especially the bad transmigrations, in far greater detail than is strictly necessary for a presentation of the concentrations and formless absorptions. For the benefit of his Western classroom audience, he adds that "those who do not believe that there is any rebirth will understand the many different types of lives other than our own."[b]

The other reason, however—the correspondence between mental state and rebirth level—is more important for the presentation of the concentrations and formless absorptions. Because of this correspondence, Lati Rinpoche explains, the map of cyclic existence is the context in which the concentrations and formless absorptions must be presented:

> Just as to drive a car or a train one needs a place to drive it—the road or the railroad tracks have to be laid out—and just as to engage in a sport one needs a smooth playing field, so, to explain the form and formless meditative absorptions, we must first explain the three realms and the nine levels [that is, cyclic existence].[c]

The correspondence can also be explained conversely—the presentation of the concentrations and formless absorptions is needed to explain the mental states possible within cyclic existence—although Lati Rinpoche does not do so explicitly. Thus, although Tibetans do not cultivate the concentrations and formless absorptions, the map of cyclic existence that is their context—that is, the three realms and the nine levels—continues to provide a mental cosmology; it shows the range of mental states within cyclic existence, from those of the non-virtuous (*mi dge ba, akuśala*) actions held to cause rebirth in the hells to the actual absorption without discrimination and without non-discrimination held to cause rebirth in the Peak of Cyclic Existence. It also serves as a way of distinguishing between meditative states within cyclic existence and those that lead to liberation from it—that is, between the mundane path and the supramundane path.

---

[a] "Grounds and Paths: Lectures by Denma Lochö Rinpoche on Kön-chok-jik-may-wang-po's *A Presentation of the Grounds and Paths: An Ornament Beautifying the Three Vehicles*" (unpublished transcript), pp. 4–12. Kön-chok-jik-may-wang-po, *Presentation of the Grounds and Paths*, 422.1–424.3. Jules Brooks Levinson, "The Process of Liberation and Enlightenment in the Buddhism of Tibet" (M.A. thesis, University of Virginia, 1983), pp. 12–17.

[b] *Meditative States*, p. 23.

[c] Ibid., p. 23.

THE THREE REALMS AND THE NINE LEVELS

Lati Rinpoche presents cyclic existence in terms of the three realms and the nine levels. The three realms are the Desire Realm, the Form Realm, and the Formless Realm. Humans live in the Desire Realm—together with hell beings, hungry ghosts, animals, demigods,[a] and the six types of gods of the Desire Realm. Form and Formless Realm beings are also gods. (Gods are sentient beings, and although they live for aeons, they die and are reborn elsewhere in cyclic existence when the force of the action that caused them to be reborn as gods has been exhausted.) The transmigrations of hell beings, hungry ghosts, and animals are the three bad transmigrations. Those of humans, demigods, and gods are the three happy transmigrations.

The Form and Formless Realms have four divisions each, corresponding to the actual absorptions that cause rebirth in them. Thus, the divisions of the Form Realm are called the First Concentration, the Second Concentration, the Third Concentration, and the Fourth Concentration; the divisions of the Formless Realm are called Limitless Space, Limitless Consciousness, Nothingness, and the Peak of Cyclic Existence. The Desire Realm and the eight divisions of the Form and Formless Realms constitute the nine levels. Lati Rinpoche explains:

> In the division of cyclic existence into nine levels, the Desire Realm is the first level. The First Concentration is the second level, the Third Concentration is the third level, and the Fourth Concentration is the fifth level. The four formless states are the sixth through ninth levels.[b]

(See chart, page 192.)

---

[a] Vasubandhu's *Treasury of Manifest Knowledge* and its *Autocommentary* list only five transmigrations, whereas Tibetan cosmologies include a sixth, that of demigods. Demigods are also included in Theravāda cosmologies (La Vallée Poussin cites Buddhaghosa, *Atthasālinī*, 62 [Louis de La Vallée Poussin, trans. and ed., *L'abhidharmakośa de Vasubandhu, Mélanges Chinois et Bouddhiques* (16:2 reprinted 1971), p. 1]). For Tibetan descriptions of demigods, the main source seems to be stanza 102 of Nāgārjuna's *Friendly Letter* (*suhṛllekha, bshes pa'i spring yig*), which describes them in the context of a vivid depiction of the sufferings of cyclic existence (Nāgārjuna, *Friendly Letter* [*suhṛllekha, bshes pa'i spring yig*], P 5409, vol. 103; Lozang Jamspal, Ven. Ngawang Samten Chophel, and Peter Della Santina, *Nāgārjuna's Letter to King Gautamiputra* [Delhi: Motilal Banarsidass, 1978], pp. xv, 53, 105 [Tibetan text]). Nāgārjuna's *Friendly Letter* influenced the Ge-luk stages-of-the-path tradition, as well as the more technical discussions of cosmology in Ge-luk monastic textbooks.

[b] *Meditative States*, p. 46.

The Form Realm has further subdivisions, but the Formless Realm does not. The First, Second, and Third Concentrations have three subdivisions each, corresponding to the level of attainment of the actual absorption, which has lesser, middling, and greater types. According to Lati Rinpoche,

> these are posited from the point of view of the meditator's mode of application, or effort, and are combinations of intensity and continuity. The lesser form of meditative absorption is that of a person whose meditation is neither intense nor continual. The middling form is that of a person who meditates either intensely but not continually or continually but not intensely. The greater is that of a person who meditates both intensely and continually.[a]

Meditators who have attained a lesser actual absorption of the first, second, or third concentration are reborn in the lowest level of the First, Second, or Third Concentration; those who have attained the middling type are reborn in the corresponding middle level, and those who have attained the greater type are reborn in the corresponding highest level.

The three levels of the First Concentration take their names from the god Brahmā, who is the chief figure of the First Concentration. They are called, from lowest to highest, Brahmā Type (*tshangs ris, brahmakāyika*), In Front of Brahmā (*tshangs mdun, brahmapurohita*), and Great Brahmā (*tshangs chen, mahābrahmaṇa*).[b]

Because the bodies of beings born in the Second Concentration emit varying degrees of light, the three levels of the Second Concentration, from lowest to highest, are called Little Light (*'od chung, parīttābhā*), Limitless Light (*tshad med 'od, apramāṇābhā*), and Bright Light (*'od gsal, ābhāsvara*).[c]

According to Lati Rinpoche, the three levels of the Third Concentration are called Little Bliss (*bde chung, parīttaśuba*), Limitless Bliss (*tshad med bde, apramāṇaśuba*), and Vast Bliss (*bde rgyas, śubakṛtsna*) because of the degree of bliss experienced by the beings born there.[d] Paṇchen Sö-nam-drak-pa, however, gives these three as Little Virtue (*dge*

---

[a] Ibid., p. 42.
[b] Ibid., p. 41.
[c] Ibid., p. 42.
[d] Ibid., p. 43.

chung), Limitless Virtue (*tshad med dge*), and Vast Virtue (*dge rgyas*).[a] The Sanskrit can support either translation, since *śuba* is synonymous with *kuśala,* which, according to Nga-wang-pel-den's (*ngag dbang dpal ldan*, born 1797) *Annotations,* can be translated as either "bliss" (*bde ba*) or "virtue" (*dge ba*).[b]

The Fourth Concentration has eight subdivisions—what Lati Rinpoche calls "the usual three," and the Five Pure Places (*gnas gtsang lnga, pañcaśuddhāvāsakāyika*); although he calls them "the usual three," Lati Rinpoche does not mention any correspondence in the Fourth Concentration between the level of the causal absorption and the level of resultant birth.[c] "The usual three" levels of the Fourth Concentration, together with the nine levels of the First, Second, and Third Concentrations, are called Lands of Common Beings because they are lands in which common beings are born, although, as Lati Rinpoche notes, Superiors can also be born there. (Superiors (*'phags pa, ārya*) are persons on the path of seeing, the path of meditation, or the path of no more learning of any of the three vehicles—Hearer, Solitary Realizer, and Bodhisattva.) Only Superiors are born in the Five Pure Places.

The three lands that are levels of common beings are called Cloudless (*sprin med, anabhraka*), Born from Merit (*bsod nams skyes, puṇyaprasava*), and Great Fruit (*'bras bu che, bṛhatphala*).[d] One type of being in Great Fruit is called a god of no discrimination. Except for slight discrimination at birth and at the point of death, such beings pass aeons in a state very much like dreamless sleep. According to Lati Rinpoche, "beings are reborn in this region as a result of cultivating a meditative absorption lacking discrimination (*'du shes med pa'i snyoms 'jug, asaṃjñisamāpatti*)."[e] This is considered neither a useful absorption to cultivate nor a good state in which to be reborn, since gods of no discrimination are incapable of analysis and, therefore, of engaging in new cultivation of the concentrations and formless absorptions.[f] Therefore, although they have been reborn in a high level of the Form Realm, they

---

a Paṇ-chen Sö-nam-drak-pa, "Concentrations," 164b.1.

b *Meditative States,* p. 232 n. 5. Nga-wang-pel-den, *Annotations*, section on beings and realms, p. 88a.4.

c According to Gunaratana (*Path of Serenity and Insight*, p. 141), the Theravādins recognize only seven levels in the Fourth Concentration—two levels of common beings and the Five Pure Places—and state explicitly that there is no relationship between the quality of the causal absorption and the level of rebirth.

d *Meditative States*, p. 43; *vṛhatphala* in *Mahāvyutpatti* 3100 (thanks to Karen Lang).

e Ibid., p. 43..

f Ibid., p. 49.

can only fall from that state; they can neither cultivate absorptions that would cause them to be reborn higher in cyclic existence nor seek liberation from it.

The Five Pure Places are called Not Great (*mi che ba, avṛha*), Without Pain (*mi gdung ba, atapas*), Excellent Appearance (*gya nom snang ba, sudṛśa*), Great Perception (*shin tu mthong ba, sudarśana*), and Not Low (*'og min, akaniṣṭha*). Superiors are born in them through alternating uncontaminated and contaminated concentrations. Lati Rinpoche explains:

> In the first moment, a yogi who is practicing alternating concentrations cultivates an uncontaminated fourth concentration; in the second moment, the yogi cultivates a contaminated type, and in the third moment, an uncontaminated type. It is very difficult to alternate concentrations in this way. Therefore, a person who can do only these three has to leave the meditation after three moments.
>
> This cultivation serves as a cause of rebirth in Not Great. A series of six alternating concentrations causes a person to be reborn in Without Pain. Cultivation of alternating concentrations for nine moments causes rebirth in Auspicious Appearance; cultivation for twelve moments causes rebirth in Great Perception, and cultivation for fifteen moments causes rebirth in Not Low.
>
> Only Superiors are able to cultivate these meditations; common beings are not. For those people who have not attained freedom from cyclic existence, the usual reason for cultivating these alternating concentrations is to be reborn in these lands, and for people who have overcome the afflictive emotions and attained freedom from cyclic existence, the reason is to increase still further their distance from the afflictive emotions in order to experience bliss in this very life.[a]

At the higher levels of cyclic existence, not only the meditative states but the beings themselves become more rarefied. The environment also becomes more rarefied, to the point of disappearance. According to Lati Rinpoche,

> the Form Realm is so called because the gods of the Form Realm are free of the type of desire that beings have in the Desire Realm, but they still have desire for, or attachment to, visible form—that is, colour and shape—as well as sounds and objects

---

[a] Ibid., p. 44.

> of touch. However, there are no odours or tastes in the Form Realm.[a]

Form Realm beings have all five aggregates, including the form aggregate. Thus, they have bodies and, as Lati Rinpoche remarks, can "see and talk to each other," but there are no day and night in the Form Realm, and the beings do not sleep.[b] They are said to live in an environment made of precious substances, and their houses are called inestimable mansions.[c] Formless Realm beings have only the four mental aggregates. They do not have the form aggregate and, therefore, do not have bodies. According to Lati Rinpoche, "there is no case of one being seeing another; there is no conversation."[d]

Although the traditional cosmology—the map of cyclic existence—is taken literally, it is also, to some extent, understood as a mental cosmology. The Formless Realm is not a place; as Denma Lochö Rinpoche explains:

> although we refer to the Formless Realm as though it were a place, one does not have to go anywhere at death to be reborn there. In the very place of death, the practitioner manifests that equipoise.[e]

Moreover, Tibetan teachers seem to have two ways of understanding the hells. When pressed by Westerners, especially by those who wish to interpret the hells as purely mental states, they insist that the presentation of the hells is to be taken literally: the hells are really places, as are all the levels of cyclic existence except those of the Formless Realm. But they also understand the hells as part of a mental cosmology. At the end of his presentation of the hells, Lati Rinpoche says:

> In order for the hells to appear to your minds, I have explained them as if they were beneath the earth, one on top of the other. However, for someone who commits a great non-virtue, a hot hell or a cold hell, in accordance with the action, appears right in the place of death; at that very point, the whole area is produced. We should not consider the hot and cold hells to be places like Europe, to which one would have to travel.[f]

---

[a] Ibid., p. 41.
[b] Ibid., p. 47.
[c] Ibid., p. 96.
[d] Ibid., p. 47.
[e] Ibid., p. 202.
[f] Ibid., p. 33.

The causes of rebirth in the bad transmigrations are non-virtuous actions. The causes of rebirth in the happy transmigrations are virtuous actions, which are of two types—meritorious (*bsod nams, puṇya*) and unfluctuating (*mi g.yo ba, āniñjya*). Meritorious actions are those that cause rebirth as humans or as gods of the Desire Realm. Unfluctuating actions are those that cause rebirth in the Form and Formless Realms—the actual absorptions of the concentrations and formless absorptions. "Thus," Lati Rinpoche comments, "from the point of view of taking rebirth in cyclic existence, these eight concentrations and formless absorptions are the best possible actions."[a] But his comment raises the question of motivation: does the practitioner seek rebirth in cyclic existence or liberation from it?

The correspondence posited between traditional Buddhist cosmology and the actual absorptions of the concentrations and formless absorptions may be regarded as an interpretation of both the cosmology and the meditative absorptions of the concentrations and formless absorptions, since it raises the possibility that directing the mind inward is not in itself a guarantee of liberation; even if extremely subtle states are reached, they may lead, not to liberation, but only to subtle states of suffering—that is, to rebirth in high levels within cyclic existence.

THE MUNDANE AND SUPRAMUNDANE PATHS

This possibility is raised by the distinction between two ways of cultivating the concentrations and formless absorptions—one that leads to liberation and another that does not. The former is known as a supramundane path; the latter, as a mundane path. This distinction is common to both Ge-luk-pas and Theravādins, although they develop it very differently. Since the Theravāda presentation is better known, it may be useful to give the main points of both systems in order to distinguish the Ge-luk presentation from it.

In neither case does the distinction between supramundane and mundane paths in the same system imply that the meditations of the mundane path are performed incorrectly. The mundane path is not an error in meditation that prevents progress, like the five faults listed in the Ge-luk presentation of calm abiding (see pages 137ff.), nor is it incorrect in the manner of afflicted concentrations (see page 248). Like meditations of the supramundane path, meditations of the mundane path must be performed correctly for their goals to be reached;

[a] Ibid., p. 47.

meditators cannot progress on either path if, for example, they are disturbed by laxity or excitement. The difference between the two paths is determined by the meditator's motivation, goal, and choice of object of observation. Therefore, the distinction between the mundane and supramundane path forces examination of these.

The Ge-luk-pas and Theravādins share several basic assumptions. They understand the term "supramundane" similarly. The Tibetan *'jig rten las 'das pa,* "passed beyond the world," is a translation and interpretation of the Sanskrit *lokottara*—"beyond the world" (*loka*). Theravādins accept a similar interpretation of the Pāli *lokuttara;* according to Gunaratana,

> The *Aṭṭhasālinī* explains the word *lokuttara*...as meaning "it crosses over the world, it transcends the world, it stands having surmounted and overcome the world."[a]

Ge-luk-pas and Theravādins also agree that, since the mundane path merely suppresses the afflictive emotions, it leads only to rebirth in cyclic existence, whereas the supramundane path eradicates the afflictive emotions and, therefore, leads to liberation from cyclic existence. Lati Rinpoche compares the mundane path to medicine that controls the symptoms of a chronic illness without curing it;[b] according to Gunaratana, the *Aṭṭhasālinī* compares the supramundane path to the demolition of a wall—the wall representing the rebirths built by the virtuous actions of the mundane path.[c]

Ge-luk-pas and Theravādins both distinguish between the mundane and supramundane paths in terms of their objects of observation. For the Theravādins, that *is* the distinction, and it is unambiguous: the object of a supramundane path is nirvāṇa (Pāli, *nibbāna; mya ngan las 'das pa, nirvāṇa*), which the Theravādins regard as an object of knowledge (Pāli, *ñeyya; shes bya, jñeya*);[d] any other object of knowledge is the object of observation of a mundane path.

Anuruddha's *Manual of Abhidhamma* (*abhidhammattha sangaha*) explains that *nibbāna*

> is termed supramundane, and is to be realized by the wisdom of the Four Paths. It becomes an object to the Paths and Fruits, and is called Nibbāna because it is a departure (*ni*) from

---

[a] Gunaratana, *Path of Serenity and Insight*, p. 177.

[b] *Meditative States*, pp. 121–22. Gunaratana, *Path of Serenity and Insight*, pp. 177, 211, 213.

[c] Gunaratana, *Path of Serenity and Insight*, p. 177.

[d] Harvey Aronson, lectures and conversations.

cord-like (*vāna*) craving.[a]

Buddhaghosa's *Path of Purification* gives a more elaborate version of this etymology:

> It is called *nibbāna* (*extinction*) because it has gone away from (*nikkhanta*), has escaped from (*nissata*), is dissociated from, craving, which has acquired in common usage the name "fastening (*vāna*)"...[b]

This is what Harvey Aronson calls an exegetical etymology[c] and what Tibetans would call, in Hopkins' translation, a contextual etymology (*nges tshig, nirukti*). In his note to this passage, Ñyāṇamoli comments:

> Modern etymology derives the word "*nibbāna* (Skt. *nirvāṇa*)" from the negative prefix *nir* plus the root *vā* (to blow). The original literal meaning was probably "extinction" of a fire by ceasing to blow on it with bellows (a smith's fire for example). It seems to have been extended to extinction of fire by any means, for example, the going out of a lamp's flame (*nibbāyati*—M. iii, 245). By analogy it was extended to the extinction of greed, etc., in the Arahant, with the resultant extinction of the five-aggregate process on the Arahant's death....[d]

Ge-luk-pas and Theravādins also agree that "nirvāṇa is peace"; according to Ge-luk presentations of Buddhist tenet systems, "nirvāṇa is peace" is the fourth of the four seals (*phyag rgya, mudrā*) propounded by all Buddhist systems.[e] Thus, although Theravāda is not among the tenet

---

[a] Nārada Mahā Thera, ed. and trans., *A Manual of Abhidhamma, Being "Abhidhammattha Sangaha" of Bhadanta Anuruddhācariya* (Kandy, Sri Lanka: Buddhist Publication Society, 1975), p. 315. Cited hereafter as *Manual of Abhidhamma*.

[b] *Path of Purification*, 8.247, under the heading "Recollection of Peace" (Buddhaghosa, *The Path of Purification (visuddhimagga)*, trans. Ñyāṇamoli [Berkeley and London: Shambhala, 1976], vol. 1, p. 319).

[c] In lectures and conversation.

[d] *Path of Purification*, vol. 1, p. 319, n. 72. The Tibetan translation of *nirvāṇa* uses a different etymology. The Tibetan *myang ngan las 'das pa* means "passed beyond sorrow." According to Jeffrey Hopkins, "'Sorrow' is here identified as the afflictive emotions, the principal of which [according to the Prāsaṅgikas] is the conception that things inherently or naturally exist" (Jeffrey Hopkins, *Meditation on Emptiness* [London: Wisdom Publications, 1983], p. 337.)

[e] *Meditation on Emptiness*, p. 336; Kön-chok-jik-may-wang-po, *Precious Garland of Tenets*, in Geshe Lhundup Sopa and Jeffrey Hopkins, *Cutting Through Appearances: Practice and Theory of Tibetan Buddhism*, 2nd ed. (Ithaca, NY: Snow Lion Publications, 1989), pp. 176–77.

systems presented by the Ge-luk-pas, Theravādins also assert this; the *Path of Purification* states that *nibbāna* "has peace as its characteristic."[a]

The Theravādins also agree with the tenet systems presented by the Ge-luk-pas that nirvāṇa is to be equated with the third noble truth (Pāli, *ariyasacca; 'phags pa'i bden pa, āryasatya*), cessation (*'gog pa;* Pāli and Skt., *nirodha*), although the details of the presentations differ. According to the *Path of Purification*, "it is *nibbāna* that is called the noble truth of the cessation of suffering."[b] Presenting the Prāsaṅgika-Madhyamaka position, which Ge-luk-pas regard as the highest, Hopkins notes that nirvāṇas are the ultimate of true cessations (or truths of cessation; *'gog pa'i bden pa, nirodhasatya*)[c] and that

> All Foe Destroyers—whether Hearers, Solitary Realizers, or Buddhas—have attained a nirvāṇa that is an utter cessation of the afflictions.[d]

However, there are true cessations that precede nirvāṇas; "these," he notes,

> are the individually enumerated cessations that are states of having abandoned obstructions [*sgrib pa, āvaraṇa*] and correspond to the uninterrupted paths [*bar chad med lam, ānantaryamārga*] causing their attainment.[e]

He also points out that of the three objects of refuge (*skyabs, saraṇa*)—Buddha (*sangs rgyas, buddha*), Doctrine (*chos, dharma*), and Spiritual Community (*dge 'dun, saṃgha*)—the actual object of refuge is the Doctrine, "principally in the sense of the true cessation of all afflictive emotions, or nirvāṇa."[f]

The type of nirvāṇa that Theravādins regard as an object of knowledge to be cognized in meditation is not the nirvāṇa without remainder (Pāli, *anupādisesanibbāna*) that is achieved at the death of a Buddha or Worthy One (Pāli, *arahant*),[g] but nirvāṇa with remainder (Pāli,

---

[a] *Path of Purification*, 16.66, vol. 2, p. 578; see also 8.245–48, vol. 1, pp. 317–20, under the heading "Recollection of Peace"; and *Manual of Abhidhamma*, p. 315, and Nārada commentary, p. 318.

[b] *Path of Purification*, 16.65, vol. 2, p. 577.

[c] *Meditation on Emptiness*, p. 288.

[d] Ibid., p. 288.

[e] Ibid., p. 288.

[f] Sopa and Hopkins, *Cutting Through Appearances*, p. 20.

[g] The Pāli *arahant* is being translated here as "Worthy One" to accord with the main etymology used by Theravādins (*The Pali Text Society's Pali-English Dictionary*, ed. T. W.

saupādisesanibbāna), the "remainder" being the body; since, from the subjective side, the realization of nirvāṇa involves the giving up of certain types of craving, the remainder, for Superiors (Pāli, *ariya*) below the level of Worthy One, also includes the remnants of past clinging.[a]

In brief, the initial realization of nirvāṇa occurs when the practitioner has experienced the suffering of conditioning (Pāli, *saṅkhāra-dukkha; 'du byed kyi sdug bsngal, saṃskāraduhkhatā*) and has come to see that all conditioned phenomena are impermanent (Pāli, *anicca; mi rtag pa, anitya*), suffering (Pāli, *dukkha; sdug bsngal, duhkha*), and selfless (Pāli, *anatta; bdag med pa, anātmaka*). At that point, the practitioner takes as object the peaceful condition that is the opposite of suffering and generates a path (Pāli, *magga*) consciousness—a consciousness that cognizes nirvāṇa. At the time of cognition of nirvāṇa, there are no sensations and no discursive thoughts; the mind is thoroughly absorbed in its object. However, the consciousness and the object can be distinguished later; this fact is adduced as evidence that nirvāṇa "exists as a subtle object of mind," as does the giving up of craving that precedes the realization of nirvāṇa.[b]

There are four path consciousnesses, each with its respective fruit. In ascending order, they are those of Stream Enterers (Pāli, *sotāpanna; rgyun zhugs, śrotāpanna*), Once Returners (Pāli, *sakidāgāmin; phyir 'ong, sakṛdāgāmin*), Non-Returners (Pāli, *anāgāmin; phyir mi 'ong, anāgāmin*), and Worthy Ones. Someone who has experienced at least the first path consciousness—that is, someone who has cognized nirvāṇa at least once—is a Superior; thus, there are four types of Superior. Each path consciousness involves a new and deeper cognition of nirvāṇa.[c]

The Ge-luk-pas present the distinction between the mundane and supramundane paths in two ways: in terms of the object realized and in terms of the preparations; the preparations are the meditations by which the practitioner progresses from his or her present level to the

Rhys Davids and William Stede, first pub. 1921 [London: Pali Text Society; Routledge & Kegan Paul, 1972], pp. 76, 77; *Manual of Abhidhamma*, pp. 426, 432; Harvey Aronson, discussions). *Arhat* or *arhan* (*dgra bcom pa*) is translated as "Foe Destroyer" in Tibetan contexts "to accord with the usual Tibetan translation." For a full explanation of this translation, see *Meditation on Emptiness*, pp. 871–73 n. 553. Both etymologies appear in the *Path of Purification*, along with three others, under the heading "Recollection of the Enlightened One" (7.2, vol. 1, p. 206). In this context, all five etymologies can probably be regarded as what Aronson calls "exegetical etymologies."

[a] Harvey Aronson, lectures; *Manual of Abhidhamma*, Nārada commentary, p. 319.

[b] Harvey Aronson, lectures.

[c] Ibid.

next higher one. For Ge-luk-pas, as for Theravādins, the basic distinction is in terms of the object. No single object is identified, however, because Ge-luk monastic education includes the systematic study of four Buddhist schools of tenets—two Hīnayāna and two Mahāyāna—with their subdivisions, and each of these schools identifies the object differently. In ascending order, the four schools of tenets are Vaibhāṣhika, Sautrāntika, Chittamātra, and Madhyamaka. Moreover, the Mahāyāna schools offer presentations of the paths of both Hīnayānists and Mahāyānists.

The concentrations and formless absorptions are studied as part of the topic of the Perfections (see next chapter). Therefore, although the Ge-luk-pas themselves hold Prāsaṅgika-Madhyamaka tenets, they present this topic, as well as the related topic of Grounds and Paths, according to the tenets of the Yogāchāra-Svātantrika-Madhyamaka (*rnal 'byor spyod pa'i dbu ma rang rgyud pa*) school, which they consider to be the system of Maitreya's *Ornament for Clear Realization;* their presentation of the phase of study called the Perfections is based on this text and its commentaries. The Yogāchāra-Svātantrika-Madhyamaka school posits different objects for Hearers, Solitary Realizers, and Bodhisattvas—the selflessness of persons for Hearers, the non-difference of entity between subject and object for Solitary Realizers, and non–true existence for Bodhisattvas. Since a supramundane path is possible for all three, the minimum requirement is distinguished in terms of the object of Hearers—the selflessness of persons. Kön-chok-jik-may-wang-po does not explicitly state this minimum requirement in his work on the concentrations and formless absorptions, but Paṇ-chen Sö-nam-drak-pa does.[a]

According to the Prāsaṅgikas, realization of the absence of inherent existence is necessary even for liberation from cyclic existence; realization of *only* the selflessness of persons or the non-difference of entity between subject and object does not lead to liberation. Therefore, the object for all three—Hearers, Solitary Realizers, and Bodhisattvas—is the absence of inherent existence.[b] Tsong-kha-pa develops this position in his *Illumination of the Thought: An Extensive Explanation of Chandrakīrti's "Supplement to (Nāgārjuna's) 'Treatise on the Middle.'"* According to Tsong-kha-pa,

---

[a] Paṇ-chen Sö-nam-drak-pa, "Concentrations," 153b.6–154a.1, and *Meditative States*, pp. 160, 162.

[b] *Meditation on Emptiness*, pp. 297–302; chart, p. 298.

> If you lack cognition of suchness, you will conceive the aggregates, such as forms, to exist truly. Your mind will thereby err, and you will consequently not cognize a fully qualified selflessness of persons. This is because you will not have overcome belief in the referent object of a mind misapprehending true existence in the aggregates that are themselves the bases of designating a self or person.[a]

As Tsong-kha-pa points out, the position that Hearers and Solitary Realizers have coarser objects involves the absurdity of considering Hearer and Solitary Realizer Superiors to be like meditators on a mundane path having the aspects of grossness/peacefulness.[b]

Tsong-kha-pa also points out that a similar qualification is necessary with regard to the path having the aspect of the four truths if it is to be regarded as a supramundane path and that Prāsaṅgikas must so qualify it and so regard it to avoid an infraction of the Bodhisattva vow, which prohibits disparagement of Hīnayāna paths as paths to liberation. He demonstrates through scriptural citation that, although "the seeds of the afflictive emotions cannot be abandoned through a path of *only* the sixteen attributes of the four noble truths, impermanence and so forth," Hīnayāna paths are not limited to such but must involve "see[ing] the absence of inherent existence of the four truths."[c]

The distinction in terms of the preparations further clarifies the relationship between the concentrations and formless absorptions and traditional Buddhist cosmology. The preparations are of two types, mundane and supramundane. Mundane preparations are those having the aspects of grossness/peacefulness. They involve viewing the lower level—that is, the level the meditator is leaving—as gross and the upper level—the level he or she wishes to attain—as peaceful. In general, this is done in terms of the rebirth level; for example, someone cultivating the mundane preparations for an actual first concentration would view the Desire Realm as gross and the First Concentration as peaceful (see pages 202ff. for an explanation of how this is done). Supramundane preparations are those having the aspect of the truths; they usually

---

[a] Tsong-kha-pa, *Illumination of the Thought: An Extensive Explanation of Chandrakīrti's "Supplement to (Nāgārjuna's) 'Treatise on the Middle,'"* in Jeffrey Hopkins, ed. and trans., *Compassion in Tibetan Buddhism* (Valois, N.Y.: Gabriel/Snow Lion Publications, 1980), p. 151.

[b] Ibid., p. 151.

[c] Ibid., pp. 163–64, italics added.

involve meditation on the sixteen attributes of the four noble truths.[a] Nevertheless, use of the mundane preparations does not necessarily imply that the person using them is not seeking liberation from cyclic existence.

Both Ge-luk-pas and Theravādins present ways in which mundane meditations can be used toward supramundane ends. For the Theravādins, this involves emergence from a mundane concentration (Pāli, *jhāna*),[b] which is then used as a basis for insight (Pāli, *vipassanā*) meditation; the practitioner observes its factors (or branches; Pāli, *aṅga; yan lag, aṅga*) as impermanent, suffering, and selfless and attains a path consciousness that is momentary (Pāli, *khaṇika; skad cig ma, kṣaṇika*) but of the same level as the preceding concentration, with the appropriate accompanying factors.[c] The concentrations themselves, however, cannot be used on the supramundane path because, according to the Theravādins, they are a heightened form of calm (Pāli, *samatha*), without analysis; therefore, they cannot be used for insight meditation but can only serve as a basis for it.

According to the Ge-luk-pas, the preparations having the aspects of grossness/peacefulness can be used by practitioners having supramundane goals in order to attain the next higher level; the meditator then changes to a supramundane object when that level is attained. According to Lati Rinpoche, this method is used by Hearers who proceed gradually and by Bodhisattvas, whereas Hearers of simultaneous abandonment use the preparations having the aspect of the truths.[d]

---

[a] According to Lati Rinpoche, they can also have the aspect of the two truths. He did not explain these, however (*Meditative States*, p. 134).

[b] In discussions of Theravāda meditation, the usual translation conventions are "concentration" for *samādhi*, "calm" or "serenity" for *samatha*, "insight" for *vipassanā*, "absorption" for *jhāna*, and "attainment" for *samāpatti*, whereas, in translating and discussing the Ge-luk presentation, I am using "meditative stabilization" for *ting nge 'dzin* (*samādhi*), "calm abiding" for *zhi gnas* (*śamatha*), "special insight" for *lhag mthong* (*vipaśyanā*), "concentration" for *bsam gtan* (*dhyāna*), and "absorption" for *snyoms 'jug* (*samāpatti*). To avoid confusion, I am keeping the same terms whenever possible. Thus, I am using "meditative stabilization" for *samādhi* in both systems, "concentration" for both *jhāna* and *dhyāna*, and "absorption" for *samāpatti* in both systems. However, I am using "calm" for Pāli *samatha* because *samatha* is *not* the equivalent of *zhi gnas;* according to Harvey Aronson (in conversation), the equivalent in Theravāda of *zhi gnas* is *upacāra*, or "access [concentration, or meditative stabilization]." I am also following convention in translating *vipassanā* as "insight" rather than "special insight."

[c] Gunaratana, *Path of Serenity and Insight*, pp. 177, 175; the level of the path consciousness in relation to the preceding concentration is debated by Theravāda commentators, but the consensus seems to be that they are of the same level (ibid., pp. 182–84).

[d] *Meditative States*, p. 144.

CONCLUSION

In brief, comparison of Ge-luk and Theravāda presentations of the relationship between the concentrations and formless absorptions and traditional Buddhist cosmology makes it possible to distinguish between shared Buddhist assumptions and points unique to each. Among the shared assumptions are the traditional cosmology itself and, against the background of the cosmology, the distinction between two ways of cultivating the concentrations and formless absorptions, one that does not lead to liberation from cyclic existence and another that does. In a terminology shared by both traditions, these are known, respectively, as the mundane and supramundane paths. The two traditions differ in the way they explain the mundane and supramundane paths. For the Theravādins, there is one deciding factor, the object of observation: the object of observation of a supramundane path is always nirvāṇa. For the Ge-luk-pas, there are two factors that differentiate the mundane and supramundane paths: the object of observation and the preparations—how the meditator proceeds to the next-higher meditative absorption. Ge-luk-pa explanations of the object of observation of a supramundane path are more complex than those in Theravāda because the Ge-luk-pas, unlike the Theravādins, recognize more than one school of Buddhist tenets and distinguish among their ways of identifying the object of observation of a supramundane path. The presentation of the preparations, derived from Asaṅga, is a Ge-luk-pa development discussed in detail in Chapter 8.

12 THE CONCENTRATIONS AND FORMLESS ABSORPTIONS IN GE-LUK MONASTIC EDUCATION

The concentrations and formless absorptions are studied in the Ge-luk monastic universities as part of the topic of the Perfections. This topic does not center on the Perfection of Wisdom Sūtras themselves but on the eight categories and seventy topics derived from them and set forth in Maitreya's *Ornament for Clear Realization*. These are studied through monastic textbooks based on Haribhadra's two commentaries on the *Ornament for Clear Realization*—the *Illumination of (Maitreya's) "Ornament for Clear Realization"* and the *Clear Meaning*. As Hopkins remarks, the writers of the Ge-luk textbooks on the Perfections rely mainly on the *Clear Meaning*

> because it is (1) short, (2) clear, and (3) a commentary on all three of the Perfection of Wisdom Sūtras that were Maitreya's sources—the eight-thousand-stanza, twenty-five-thousand-stanza, and one-hundred-thousand-stanza sūtras.[a]

The textbook writers have clarified the commentaries by establishing definitions for the categories and topics and for related terms—definitions by which opinions can be tested. They also established divisions, boundaries, and mutually inclusive categories and topics.

The order of the categories and topics of the Perfections presents many problems. Unlike the path structure set forth in the related topic of Grounds and Paths, the eight categories and seventy topics are not presented chronologically from the point of view of the practitioner. Rather, as Obermiller points out, they are presented in the order in which they occur in the Perfection of Wisdom Sūtras; thus, "the same subjects" are "discussed over and over again at different places and from different points of view."[b] Moreover, the relationship of the categories to each other and of the topics to the categories varies and is not always clear. There is a considerable degree of overlapping among the categories themselves and among the topics, especially since the topics

---

[a] Denma Lochö Rinpoche and Jeffrey Hopkins, "The Seventy Topics" (unpublished transcript), p. 22. Cited hereafter as Perfections Transcript.

[b] E. Obermiller, "The Doctrine of Prajñā-pāramitā as exposed in the Abhisamayālaṃkāra of Maitreya," *Acta Orientalia* 9 (1932), p. 61.

are not necessarily divisions of their categories[a] but are said in the textbooks to "illustrate" or "characterize" them—although the textbooks do not always indicate the mode of illustration or characterization.[b] Since, according to the textbook writers, many of the categories and topics are mutually inclusive, the mutually inclusive terms given in the textbooks provide a means of cross-referencing occurrences, not only of the same subject under various names, but also of separate but related subjects.

According to Denma Lochö Rinpoche, the eight categories—exalted knower of all aspects (*rnam pa thams cad mkhyen pa nyid, rnam mkhyen, sarvākārajñatā*), knower of paths (*lam shes, mārgajñatā*), knower of bases (*gzhi shes, vastujñāna = thams cad shes pa nyid, sarvajñatā*), complete training in the aspects (*rnam rdzogs sbyor ba = rnam kun mngon par rdzogs par rtogs pa, sarvākārābhisaṃbhodha*), peak training (*rtse sbyor, mūrdhaprayoga*), serial training (*mthar gyis sbyor ba, anupūrvaprayoga*), momentary training (*skad cig ma'i sbyor ba, kṣaṇikaprayoga*), and Truth Body, the fruit (*'bras bu chos sku, *phaladharmakāya*)—can be viewed as following the traditional Buddhist "mode of explanation...by way of presenting the bases (*gzhi, vastu*), paths (*lam, mārga*), and fruits (*'bras pu, phala*)."[c] In general, the first three categories, known collectively as the three exalted knowers, correspond to the basis; the next four correspond to the path, and the last, to the fruit, since an exalted knower of all aspects is the omniscient consciousness of a Buddha and is mutually inclusive with the Wisdom Truth Body (*ye shes chos sku, jñānadharmakāya*) and thus, although it is included in the presentation of the basis, it is also mutually inclusive with the fruit. However, it "is said to be set forth first in order to generate enthusiasm."[d] The concentrations and formless absorptions are discussed in this category.

It may be useful to examine the context of the Ge-luk discussions of the concentrations and formless absorptions in detail in order to see how the textbooks on the Perfections present them as a practice of Bodhisattvas. They are the second division of achieving engagement, the eighth of the ten topics of an exalted knower of all aspects.[e] Although the divisions of achieving engagement are merely listed briefly,

---

[a] Perfections Transcript, p. 102.
[b] Ibid., p. 8.
[c] Ibid., p. 275.
[d] Ibid., p. 224.
[e] Ibid., p. 224.

without comment, in the *Ornament for Clear Realization,*[a] Jam-yang-shay-pa gives the second division as "that [achieving engagement] which is *a Bodhisattva's* engagement in the concentrations and formless absorptions,"[b] or, in Denma Lochö Rinpoche's paraphrase,

> engaging in the activities of practicing the concentrations and formless absorptions *motivated by the precious mind of enlightenment (byang chub kyi sems, bodhicitta),*[c]

thereby spelling out the Mahāyāna motivation necessary in this context. Thus, Jam-yang-shay-pa clearly indicates that the concentrations and formless absorptions will be treated in the context of the Perfections as a Mahāyāna practice. (Paṇ-chen Sö-nam-drak-pa's section on the concentrations and formless absorptions occurs at this same point in his Perfections textbook, the *General Meaning of (Maitreya's) "Ornament for Clear Realization."*[d] However, Jam-yang-shay-pa's extended treatment, the *Great Exposition of the Concentrations and Formless Absorptions,* is not part of either the *Eloquent Presentation of the Eight Categories and Seventy Topics* or his longer Perfections textbook, the *Final Analysis of the Perfections,* but is a separate work, as is Kön-chok-jik-may-wang-po's *Condensed Statement of (Jam-yang-shay-pa's) "Great Exposition of the Concentrations and Formless Absorptions."*

The last four topics of an exalted knower of all aspects—achieving armor (*go sgrub, saṃnāhapratipatti*), achieving engagement (*'jug sgrub, prasthānapratipatti*), achieving the collections (*tshogs sgrub, saṃbhārapratipatti*), and achieving definite emergence (*nges 'byung sgrub pa, niryāṇapratipatti*)—are the four divisions of "achieving" (*sgrub pa, pratipatti*), and "achieving," in the context of the Perfections, is specified as a *Mahāyāna* achieving, which Jam-yang-shay-pa defines as "an activity of achieving the two aims for the sake of unsurpassed enlightenment in dependence upon a Mahāyāna mind generation."[e] Denma

---

[a] Maitreya, "Ornament for Clear Realization," verses 44–45, Jeffrey Hopkins, trans. and comp., "Topics of Enlightenment" (unpublished compilation from various monastic textbooks on the Perfections), p. 24, and Edward Conze, trans., *Abhisamayālaṃkāra* (Rome: Istituto Italiano per il Medio ed Estremo Oriente, 1954), pp. 20–21.

[b] *byang sems kyi bsam gtan gzugs med la 'jug pa'i de.* Jam-yang-shay-pa, *Eloquent Presentation of the Eight Categories and Seventy Topics, The Sacred Word of the Guru Ajita,* 127.2; cited hereafter as Jam-yang-shay-pa, *Seventy Topics;* italics mine.

[c] Perfections Transcript, p. 83; italics mine.

[d] Paṇ-chen Sö-nam-drak-pa, *General Meaning of (Maitreya's) "Ornament for Clear Realization,"* pp. 150a.6–150b.4.

[e] Jam-yang-shay-pa, *Seventy Topics,* quoted in Perfections Transcript, p. 78.

Lochö Rinpoche comments:

> Saying that this achieving arises in dependence on a Mahāyāna mind generation indicates that the altruistic mind of enlightenment is its root...."The two aims" refers to the Truth Body (*chos sku, dharmakāya*), which is the fulfillment of one's own welfare, and the Form Body (*gzugs sku, rūpakāya*), which is the fulfillment of others' welfare. Activities involved in achieving these are called Mahāyāna achievings.[a]

The four divisions of "Mahāyāna achieving" connect the major categories of the Perfections by presenting facets of the path as they relate to the basis and fruit. However, "Mahāyāna achieving" and "achieving armor" are mutually inclusive—a fact that calls the nature of the divisions of "achieving" into question. They are also mutually inclusive with many of the key terms of the Perfections, including "path perfection of wisdom" (*lam sher phyin, mārgaprajñāpāramitā*), "Bodhisattva path" (*byang sems kyi lam*), and "Bodhisattva's yoga" (*sems pa'i rnal 'byor*).[b]

Nevertheless, the relationship of the four achievings is most easily understood sequentially. Denma Lochö Rinpoche explains it through a simile of war. Achieving armor, which refers to the six perfections, is like putting on armor before a battle. Achieving engagement is like entering into battle and using weapons. Achieving the collections is like the Bodhisattva's army, "a whole collection of soldiers," and refers to the collections of merit and wisdom. It is like the ability to defeat the enemy.[c] Achieving definite emergence is the yoga of a Bodhisattva on the eighth, ninth, or tenth ground; it "definitely issues forth an exalted knower of the aspects" because, on those grounds, "the manifest form of the conception of true existence...has been completely overcome."[d]

The first of the achievings, achieving armor, is concerned especially with "the wisdom of how to practice all six perfections within each of the six perfections."[e] Although the fifth of the six perfections is the perfection of concentration, achieving armor deals mainly with the practice of the six perfections outside meditation.

---

[a] Perfections Transcript, p. 78.

[b] The full list of synonyms is given under the fourth category, complete training in the aspects. (Perfections Transcript, p. 165)

[c] Perfections Transcript, p. 80.

[d] Jam-yang-shay-pa, *Seventy Topics,* and Denma Lochö Rinpoche's comment, Perfections Transcript, p. 88.

[e] Jam-yang-shay-pa, *Seventy Topics,* quoted in Perfections Transcript, p. 79.

The second of the achievings, achieving engagement, is defined as:

> an activity of engaging in any of the Mahāyāna causes and effects mainly from the approach of states arisen from meditation (*sgom byung, bhāvanāmayī*).[a]

Thus, the difference between the first two achievings is that the first includes mainly states arisen from hearing and arisen from thinking, whereas the second deals entirely with the Bodhisattva's practice of meditation, and within that, mainly with states arisen from meditation.[b] The main discussion of the concentrations and formless absorptions occurs here, as the first division of achieving engagement.

The concentrations and formless absorptions, or topics related to them, are also mentioned elsewhere in the presentation of the four achievings. The second division of achieving engagement, "engaging in the six perfections of giving, and so forth,"[c] concerns the practice of the six perfections *in meditation.* Although neither the textbooks nor Denma Lochö Rinpoche's oral commentary discusses this, the *Twenty-five Thousand Stanza Perfection of Wisdom Sūtra* at this point states that a Bodhisattva who engages in the concentrations and formless absorptions in relation to the perfection of concentration does not apprehend the concentrations and formless absorptions [as truly existent].[d]

The third of the achievings, achieving the collections, also includes divisions—in this case, collections—related to the concentrations. Among the collections of the six perfections, each of which is a division of the topic of achieving the collections, is the collection of concentration. This is followed by the collection of calm abiding, the collection of special insight, and the collection of a union of calm abiding and special

---

[a] Ibid., p. 83.

[b] The qualifying word "mainly" may be included in the definition because presentations of the concentrations and formless absorptions include discussion of the second preparation for a concentration or formless absorption, the mental contemplation of individual knowledge of the character (*mtshan nyid so sor rig pa'i yid byed, lakṣaṇapratisaṃvedīmanaskāra*), which many Tibetan scholars consider to be a mind of the Desire Realm even though the practitioner has already attained calm abiding, which *is* a state arisen from meditation. There is a great deal of debate on this question. (Paṇ-chen Sö-nam-drak-pa, "Concentrations," 151b.5–152a.4; Kön-chok-jik-may-wang-po, *Condensed Statement*, 568.2–569.1) See discussion pages 206–211 above. See also *Meditative States*, pp. 150–52 for Denma Lochö Rinpoche's oral commentary on Paṇ-chen Sö-nam-drak-pa's debate.

[c] Jam-yang-shay-pa, *Seventy Topics*, quoted in Perfections Transcript, p. 84.

[d] P731, vol. 18. See *The Large Sūtra on Perfect Wisdom*, Edward Conze, trans. (Berkeley: University of California Press), p. 132.

insight; all three—calm abiding, special insight, and a union of calm abiding and special insight—are discussed in presentations of the concentrations and formless absorptions.

Elsewhere in the Perfections textbooks, the four concentrations are also mentioned as a division of the topic of object of observation—that is, "object of observation of a Mahāyāna practice,"[a] the fifth topic of an exalted knower of all aspects—but they are not discussed there. Moreover, the concentrations referred to there are not the four concentrations in general but only "the four supramundane concentrations in the mental continua of Superiors."[b]

Presentations of the Perfections, from the sūtras through the Tibetan monastic textbooks, distinguish between the way in which Hīnayānists engage in primarily Hīnayāna practices (including the concentrations and formless absorptions) and the way in which Mahāyānists engage in them. The *Twenty-five Thousand Stanza Perfection of Wisdom Sūtra,* at the point of the topic of achieving engagement, identifies the distinguishing feature of the Bodhisattva's engagement in Hīnayāna practices as his or her dedication of the merit of the practice to the achievement of complete, perfect enlightenment for the sake of all sentient beings. In other respects, such as the description of the branches of the concentrations, the account in the *Twenty-five Thousand Stanza Perfection of Wisdom Sūtra* of how Bodhisattvas practice the concentrations and formless absorptions[c] is based on, and takes for granted, descriptions such as the following, from the Theravāda discourses (and is closer to the Theravāda version than to that of Vasubandhu's *Treasury of Manifest Knowledge*):

> Here, bhikkhus, a bhikkhu, quite secluded from sense pleasures, secluded from unwholesome states of mind, enters and dwells in the first *jhāna,* which is accompanied by applied thought [Pāli, *vitakka*] and sustained thought [Pāli, *vicāra*] with rapture [Pāli, *pīti*] and happiness [Pāli, *sukha*] born of seclusion [Pāli, *vivekaja*].
>
> With the subsiding of applied thought and sustained thought he enters and dwells in the second *jhāna,* which has internal confidence [Pāli, *ajjhattaṃ sampasādanaṃ*] and unification of mind [Pāli, *cetaso ekodibhāvaṃ*], is without applied thought and sustained thought, and is filled with rapture and

---

[a] Jam-yang-shay-pa, *Seventy Topics,* quoted in Perfections Transcript, p. 74.

[b] Ibid., p. 76.

[c] P731, vol. 18. See *The Large Sūtra on Perfect Wisdom,* pp. 131–32.

happiness born of concentration.

With the fading away of rapture, he dwells in equanimity [Pāli, *upekkha;* with] mindful[ness, Pāli, *sati*] and discern[ment, Pāli, *sampajañña*], and he experiences in his own person the happiness of which the noble ones say: 'Happily lives he who is equanimous and mindful'—thus he enters and dwells in the third *jhāna.*

With the abandoning of pleasure and pain, and with the previous disappearance of joy and grief, he enters and dwells in the fourth *jhāna,* which has neither-pain-nor-pleasure [Pāli, *adukkhamasukha*] and has purity of mindfulness due to equanimity [Pāli, *upekkhāsatipārisuddhi*].[a]

As Gunaratana points out, such descriptions are common: the four concentrations "appear repeatedly in the suttas described by a stock formula showing their process of attainment."[b] The descriptions list the mental factors or branches that distinguish each concentration and show how the practitioner proceeds from each concentration to the next higher one by means of those factors. Such accounts are taken for granted in the Perfection of Wisdom Sūtras. The sūtra is mainly concerned with going on from the basic description to show what in the practice of the concentrations and formless absorptions is specific to Bodhisattvas. Jam-yang-shay-pa's specification that Bodhisattvas practice the concentrations and formless absorptions "motivated by the precious mind of enlightenment" (see page 293), is in this tradition.

The Three Exalted Knowers

Although not directly related to the concentrations and formless absorptions, the Ge-luk presentation of the three exalted knowers is important in showing, at least in theory, how Mahāyānists can practice Hīnayāna paths *as Mahāyānists.* They can do so in two ways. On the one hand, through their motivation and choice of object, they can incorporate such practices into the Bodhisattva path to further their own attainment of Buddhahood and, on the other, they can know Hīnayāna paths in order to be able, even as Bodhisattvas, to help other sentient beings who need to know such paths; for, as Denma Lochö Rinpoche indicated, "a Bodhisattva must effect the aims of all three types of

---

[a] *Dīgha Nikāya,* 2:314–15; *Majjhima Nikāya,* 1:182, trans. in Gunaratana, *Path of Serenity and Insight,* p. 4. Pāli added.

[b] Gunaratana, *Path of Serenity and Insight,* p. 4.

trainees."[a] (The three types of trainees are the two Hīnayāna types—Hearers and Solitary Realizers—and Bodhisattvas.)

All three exalted knowers exist in the mental continuum of a Buddha, but their lower boundaries differ, and it is the lower boundary that clarifies the distinctions among them. An exalted knower of all aspects is the omniscient consciousness of a Buddha and occurs only on the Buddha ground. The lower boundary of a knower of paths is the Mahāyāna path of seeing. Thus, a knower of paths is a Mahāyāna Superior's consciousness; it knows both Mahāyāna and Hīnayāna paths. A knower of bases—that is, of phenomena—"is included in a Hīnayāna *type* of realizer,"[b] but it can be either a Mahāyāna or Hīnayāna Superior's consciousness.

As was mentioned earlier (page 286), the Perfections are presented in monastic textbooks according to the tenets of the Yogāchāra-Svātantrika-Madhyamaka school, which posits different objects for Hearers, Solitary Realizers, and Bodhisattvas—the selflessness of persons for Hearers, the non-difference of entity between subject and object for Solitary Realizers, and non-true existence for Bodhisattvas. Since a knower of paths is a consciousness of a Mahāyāna Superior, it directly knows all three paths, whatever their objects, in the manner of a Mahāyānist—that is, "as not truly existent."[c] Although a knower of bases can be a consciousness of either a Hīnayāna or Mahāyāna Superior, it "is included in a Hīnayāna type of realizer that is posited by way of realizing all bases as without a self of persons."[d] Unlike the definition of "knower of paths," the definition of "knower of bases" is not straightforward but is carefully qualified by "is included in a Hīnayāna type" and "is posited by way of." Denma Lochö Rinpoche comments:

> The fact that [a knower of bases] is posited by way of such a realization means that it either *is* such a realization or is a factor that is conjoined with such a realization.[e]

If it "*is* such a realization," it is simply that of a Hearer Superior. If it "is a factor that is conjoined with such a realization," it can be in the mental continuum of a Bodhisattva Superior or a Buddha.

What would a knower of bases be like in the continuum of a

---

[a] Perfections Transcript, p. 97.

[b] Jam-yang-shay-pa, *Seventy Topics,* quoted in Perfections Transcript, p. 131. Italics mine.

[c] Ibid., p. 90.

[d] Ibid., p. 131.

[e] Perfections Transcript, p. 131. Italics in Transcript.

Mahāyāna Superior? The topics of the category present a range of descriptions of Hīnayāna and Mahāyāna consciousnesses. The first two topics indicate the basic contrast. They are: (1) a knower of bases that, through knowledge, does not abide in [the extreme of] cyclic existence (*shes pas srid la mi gnas pa'i gzhi shes*) and (2) a knower of paths that, through compassion, does not abide in the extreme of peace (*snying rjes zhi la mi gnas pa'i lam shes*).[a] The first type of consciousness can be that of either a Hīnayānist or a Mahāyānist; the knowledge by which it does not abide in the extreme of cyclic existence is explained by Denma Lochö Rinpoche as "realization of the selflessness of the person or of the sixteen attributes of the four noble truths."[b] These are the objects of observation of Hearers. The second type of consciousness can be only that of a Mahāyānist; an illustration of it is "the compassion in the continuum of one on the Mahāyāna path of meditation."[c] Although it is included among the topics of knower of bases, it is not, itself, a knower of bases but a knower of paths. As Denma Lochö Rinpoche explains,

> This is because it would not be feasible for a knower of bases not to abide in peace through compassion....The reason...is that the great compassion of a Bodhisattva, which is the wish himself to relieve all sentient beings from suffering, is a main object of cultivation in the Mahāyāna. This is not so in the Hīnayāna. Therefore, it could not be included within a Hīnayāna type of realizer, as knowers of bases are.[d]

Although neither type of consciousness abides in the extreme of cyclic existence, the first type may abide in the extreme of peace.

The remaining topics suggest further possibilities of meaning within the basic contrast. The third topic—knower of bases that is distant from the effect mother [that is, Buddhahood] (*'bras yum la ring ba'i gzhi shes, phalabhūtamātur dūribhūtavastujñāna*)—and the fifth—knower of bases, classed as discordant, that is bound by the conception of signs [of true existence] (*mtshan 'dzin gyis bcings pa'i mi mthun phyogs kyi gzhi shes*)—are mutually inclusive with the first topic and with "Hīnayāna knower of bases,"[e] whereas the fourth topic—knower of bases that is close to the effect mother (*'bras yum la nyes pa'i gzhi shes,*

---

[a] Jam-yang-shay-pa, *Seventy Topics,* quoted in Perfections Transcript, pp. 132, 134, 137.

[b] Perfections Transcript, p. 132.

[c] Jam-yang-shay-pa, *Seventy Topics,* quoted in Perfections Transcript, p. 137.

[d] Perfections Transcript, p. 137.

[e] Jeffrey Hopkins, trans. and comp., "Topics of Enlightenment," pp. 53, 55.

phalabhūtamātur āsannibhūtavastujñāna)—and the sixth—knower of bases classed as an antidote, conjoined with antidotes to the conception of signs (*mtshan 'dzin gyi gnyen pos zin pa'i gnyen po phyogs kyi gzhi shes*)—are mutually inclusive with each other and with "Mahāyāna knower of bases."[a] Thus, although none of the topics is mutually inclusive with the second, which is a knower of paths, the pattern of contrast continues through the first six topics; different aspects of meaning are suggested by the various mutually inclusive terms. The seventh topic, training in a knower of bases (*gzhi shes sbyor ba, vastujñānaprayoga*), is specifically "a Bodhisattva's yoga included in a Hīnayāna type of realizer."[b] The eighth topic—equality in [the mode of] apprehension of training [in a knower of bases] (*sbyor ba'i 'dzin stangs mnyam pa nyid*)—is, as the topic itself indicates, "an aspect of cultivating" the seventh. The ninth topic, path of seeing, includes both Hīnayāna and Mahāyāna types of consciousness, since, as Jam-yang-shay-pa indicates, it refers to the paths of seeing of all three vehicles.[c]

Thus, the Ge-luk presentations of the three exalted knowers provide a theoretical framework that allows Mahāyānists, as Mahāyānists, to engage in Hīnayāna practices. It is this framework that allows Bodhisattvas to cultivate the concentrations and formless absorptions within the context of the Perfections.

Study and Meditation as Aspects of Ge-luk Religious Practice

Any examination of Ge-luk texts on the concentrations and formless absorptions has to confront the fact that they are scholastic works about classic Buddhist meditations that are not practiced in Tibet now and, as far as we know, were never practiced in Tibet. Two questions arise, both related to a tension between study and meditation as aspects of Ge-luk religious practice:

1 Why do Ge-luk-pas not practice the concentrations and formless absorptions?
2 Why, even though they do not practice the concentrations and formless absorptions, do Ge-luk-pa scholar-monastics continue to study them?

---

[a] Ibid., pp. 54, 55.
[b] Jam-yang-shay-pa, *Seventy Topics,* quoted in Perfections Transcript, p. 147.
[c] Ibid., p. 162.

WHY GE-LUK-PAS DO NOT PRACTICE THE CONCENTRATIONS AND FORMLESS ABSORPTIONS

One answer to the first question appears to be that the concentrations and formless absorptions are associated with the so-called Hīnayāna; a frequently quoted Indian source in these Ge-luk texts is Asaṅga's *Grounds of Hearers* (*śrāvakabhūmi, nyan sa*), intended by Asaṅga and understood by Ge-luk-pa commentators as a description of Hīnayāna practice. This tension between what is perceived as Hīnayānist and what is perceived as Mahāyānist exists even in the Perfection of Wisdom sūtras—the scriptural basis of the Ge-luk presentation of the concentrations and formless absorptions—and in Indian and Tibetan commentaries on the Perfection of Wisdom sūtras.

The Perfection of Wisdom sūtras raise the question of how a Bodhisattva is to practice the concentrations and formless absorptions and, thereby, implies that a Bodhisattva's approach to them is different from a Hearer's. Ge-luk textbooks on the topic of the Perfection of Wisdom attempt to resolve this tension not by changing the character of the original meditations but by distinguishing between the ways in which Hīnayānists and Mahāyānists engage in Hīnayāna practices; they attempt to salvage the concentrations and formless absorptions for the Mahāyāna by demonstrating that Mahāyānists can engage in Hīnayāna practices *as Mahāyānists*. In brief, a Bodhisattva engages in Hīnayāna practices with a Mahāyāna motivation, for the sake of others. Thus, a Bodhisattva who has attained the concentrations and formless absorptions, according to the Perfection of Wisdom sūtras, practices the perfection of giving by dedicating the merit of having attained the concentrations and formless absorptions to the achievement of complete, perfect enlightenment for the sake of all sentient beings; such a Bodhisattva may also teach the concentrations and formless absorptions to sentient beings who need to learn them.

Nevertheless, although they have found a place for the concentrations and formless absorptions in the paradigm of sūtra-system Mahāyāna practice, Tibetan Buddhists do not practice the concentrations and formless absorptions. Rather, they practice Vajrayāna meditations, preceded by the Vajrayāna preliminary practices (*sngon 'gro*). In the Nying-ma, Ka-gyu, and Sa-kya traditions, these include (with slight variations among the three traditions) four ordinary and four extraordinary preliminaries. The four ordinary preliminaries are meditations on leisure and fortune (*dal 'byor, kṣaṇasampad*), the imminence of death (*'chi ba mi rtag pa, maraṇānitya*), actions and their effects, and the sufferings of cyclic existence; the four extraordinary preliminaries are prostrations, done in association with refuge prayers and the generation of the altruistic mind of enlightenment; the Vajrasattva meditation—a practice for confession and purification of misdeeds; maṇḍala offerings, and guru yoga.

Although the Ge-luk-pas also engage in all the practices included in the four extraordinary preliminaries of the other traditions, it may be said that, since the stages-of-the-path meditations prepare students for the Vajrayāna, they serve as the Ge-luk preliminary practices. The stages-of-the-path meditations involve the generation in meditation of the three principal aspects of the path—the thought definitely to leave cyclic existence, the altruistic mind of enlightenment, and the view of emptiness. The four ordinary preliminaries of the other three traditions correspond to the generation of the thought definitely to leave cyclic existence in the Ge-luk stages-of-the-path meditations. What is most important in this context is that the preliminary practices of all four traditions explicitly include the generation of great compassion and the altruistic mind of enlightenment.

It may be that explicit association with great compassion and the altruistic mind of enlightenment is precisely what the concentrations and formless absorptions are felt to lack; for, according to the Perfection of Wisdom sūtras, it is only the Bodhisattva's dedication of merit at the end of the meditation session that marks his or her cultivation of the concentrations and formless absorptions as Mahāyānist. (If Tibetans practiced the concentrations and formless absorptions, they would probably also begin the session, as they begin most meditation sessions of whatever sort, by taking refuge and generating the altruistic mind of enlightenment. Nevertheless, although a meditative absorption of a concentration or formless absorption cultivated during the middle of the session might be subtly affected by the force of prior attitudes, the altruistic practices at the beginning and end of the session would not change the main features of the meditative absorption, such as the branches of a concentration—that is, the mental factors associated with it that characterize it as a concentration of a given level—or the object of observation of a given formless absorption.)

A clue to the difference between the two types of practice can be found in an apparently minor point made by Gedün Lodrö in his discussion of the cultivation of calm abiding, which must be attained before cultivation of the actual meditative absorption of the first concentration:

> [T]he mind need not be overly withdrawn inside for laxity to

> arise. For example, if, while you are in meditative stabilization on the body of a Buddha, love and compassion arise, these are not actual instances of love and compassion but are cases of laxity. One would think that love and compassion would be included among virtuous phenomena, but here they are deceivers and a type of subtle laxity.[a]

In the cultivation of calm abiding, then, even apparent virtues such as love and compassion are considered to be inappropriate, for what is sought is the ability to focus on an object of observation, not a sense of closeness to sentient beings. In the seven cause-and-effect quintessential instructions for the generation of the altruistic mind of enlightenment, however, love and compassion are cultivated as the fourth and fifth steps, respectively, and the arising of love and compassion in a meditator cultivating an altruistic mind of enlightenment would indicate that the practitioner was succeeding. It is at least possible that what came to be preferred are types of meditation that include and develop the meditator's altruistic motivation, not merely his or her skill.

When Ge-luk-pas give practical instructions in the cultivation of calm abiding according to sūtra-system methods, they teach it in the context of stages-of-the-path meditations, outside the system of the concentrations and formless absorptions. There are two ways of teaching stages-of-the-path meditations. In one, that of Tsong-kha-pa's *Great Exposition of the Stages of the Path* (*lam rim chen mo*), calm abiding, followed by special insight realizing emptiness, are attained by sūtra-system methods before entry into the Vajrayāna; although special insight—mutually inclusive with a union of calm abiding and special insight—is achieved through a method similar to the first of Asaṅga's seven mental contemplations for the first concentration—called the mental contemplation of individual knowledge of the character—meditators do not go on to achieve an actual meditative absorption of the first concentration; because they do not cultivate the concentrations and formless absorptions, their practice does not mainly emphasize dexterity in meditation. Thus, although calm abiding and special insight are attained, skill in meditation is not achieved at the expense of altruistic motivation or wisdom. In the approach to stages-of-the-path meditations usually taught to beginners nowadays—that of Tsong-kha-pa's *Three Principal Aspects of the Path*—calm abiding and special insight are not even mentioned; only the initial, conceptual, finding of

[a] Gedün Lodrö, p. 175. For a discussion of the fault of laxity in the cultivation of calm abiding, see pages 144ff. above.

the view of emptiness is achieved before entry into the Vajrayāna, and calm abiding and special insight are achieved later, by Vajrayāna methods.

In an ultimate mind of enlightenment—that is, a Bodhisattva's direct cognition of emptiness—a conventional altruistic mind of enlightenment is not manifest. However, a Bodhisattva directly cognizing emptiness has already achieved an altruistic mind of enlightenment; according to Ge-luk-pa scholars associated with Go-mang College of Dre-pung Monastic University, that altruistic mind of enlightenment exists subliminally at the time of the Bodhisattva's direct cognition of emptiness; it is not merely added at the end, like a dedication of merit after a session of meditation in an actual absorption of a concentration. Thus, a Bodhisattva's direct cognition of emptiness is colored by subliminal compassion. Gedün Lodrö, a Go-mang scholar, remarks of an ultimate mind generation that

> [i]f one does not directly realize emptiness within a conventional altruistic mind generation, one does not have an ultimate mind generation; the meditator has to realize emptiness directly while abiding in a conventional mind generation in order to have an ultimate one. Thus, Hearers and Solitary Realizers, even though they realize emptiness directly, do not have an ultimate mind generation.[a]

He also remarks that "in the continuum of a person on the uninterrupted path of a Mahāyāna path of seeing, there is a conventional altruistic mind generation, but this is a subtle consciousness."[b]

As a possible answer to the question, "Why do Ge-luk-pas not practice the concentrations and formless absorptions?"—especially in relation to the Vajrayāna preliminary practices and deity yoga—Roger J. Corless suggests a "movement from enstatic withdrawal to compassionate outreach" that may be found in other religions as well as Buddhism; he remarks, "There is certainly a similar tension in Christianity, even within a single figure such as St John of the Cross." Corless cites Paul Griffiths' article "Concentration or Insight: The Problematic of Theravāda Buddhist Meditation-Theory" to call attention to the two apparently contradictory systems of meditation in Theravāda—calm (Pāli, *samatha*) and insight (Pāli, *vipassanā*). Griffiths argues "that not only are there to be found in the Pāli sources two distinct and to some

---

[a] Gedün Lodrö, p. 336.
[b] Ibid., p. 244.

degree opposed theories of what salvation is, but that there are also two separate and uneasily combined sets of meditative practices leading to these different goals," which the Theravāda tradition has tried to reconcile in various ways; he argues, further, "that from the point of view of the uncommitted observer of the tradition [namely, himself] such attempts remain, finally, unsatisfactory."[a] Although Corless does not explicitly posit a direct correspondence between calm and insight, on the one hand, and enstatic withdrawal and compassionate outreach, on the other, he implies some such relationship, with the resultant problematical implied consequence that insight is somehow more compassionate than calming meditation, which he seems to equate with enstatic withdrawal:

> My guess is that both forms of mind-training were current in early Buddhism, but that enstatic withdrawal was seen as more and more selfish in favour of the "waking up" into compassionate activity of true Buddha-activity. The great stress on karuṇā in all Mahāyāna practices as against the supposed elitism of the Hīnayāna may be a remnant of a controversy over this issue.[b]

Thus, Corless also suggests, probably correctly, that one reason Mahāyānists did not practice the concentrations and formless absorptions was the association of those meditations with the so-called Hīnayāna. However, the apparent contradiction between calm and insight which he and Griffiths discuss may be less relevant to Ge-luk presentations of calm abiding and special insight and of the concentrations and formless absorptions than to Theravāda presentations because, unlike modern Theravādins, Ge-luk-pas do not have a practice tradition divided into two distinct vehicles, calm (Pāli, *samathayāna*) and bare insight (Pāli, *suddhavipassanāyāna*). The latter type of practice is a mindfulness (Pāli, *sati*; *dran pa, smṛti*) meditation consisting of

---

[a] Paul J. Griffiths, "Concentration or Insight: The Problematic of Theravāda Buddhist Meditation-Theory," *JAAR*, 49:4 (1981), 605.

Strictly speaking, calm (Pāli, *samatha*) and insight (Pāli, *vipassanā*) in Theravāda are not equivalents of calm abiding (*zhi gnas, śamatha*) and special insight (*lhag mthong, vipaśyanā*) in the Tibetan Ge-luk tradition developed from Vasubandhu's *Treasury of Manifest Knowledge* and its *Autocommentary* and the works of Asaṅga, especially his *Grounds of Hearers*. According to Harvey Aronson (in conversation), the equivalent in Theravāda of *zhi gnas* is *upacāra*, or "access [concentration/stabilization]." Moreover, *vipassanā* is not *lhag mthong* (*vipaśyanā*) because the latter is achieved by means of analysis done on the basis of a fully qualified *zhi gnas* (*śamatha*) and is considered to be necessarily a union of *zhi gnas* (*śamatha*) and *lhag mthong* (*vipaśyanā*).

[b] Roger J. Corless, letter of December 9, 1984.

analysis based on observation.

Although Buddhaghosa's *Path of Purification* cannot be read literally as a description of practice—least of all, of modern practice—Buddhaghosa describes mindfulness of breathing, as well as cultivation of the four mindful establishments (Pāli, *satipaṭṭhāna*; *dran pa nye bar bzhag pa, smṛtyupasthāna*) in great detail. It appears, however, that a meditation tradition consisting of analysis based on observation—inductive reasoning within meditation—was not transmitted to Tibet; what Ge-luk-pa writers call analytical meditation is syllogistic reasoning within meditation. Thus, Jam-yang-shay-pa fails to recognize the possibility of an "analytical meditation" based on observation even when he cites passages on breath meditation from Vasubandhu's *Treasury of Manifest Knowledge* and, especially, Asaṅga's *Grounds of Hearers*, that appear to describe it.[a]

Moreover, R. M. L. Gethin suggests the apparent contradiction between calm and insight may be exaggerated even in Theravāda by an excessive reliance on the threefold structural division of Buddhaghosa's *Path of Purification* into "'conduct', 'consciousness', and 'understanding.'" According to Gethin,

> This separating out of the three categories is certainly a useful device for a presentation of the Buddhist path, but the structure of the *Visuddhimagga* can make it appear that much of the account of the development of *samatha* given under the heading "purification of consciousness" (*citta-visuddhi*) has rather little bearing on the remaining five "purifications," which are therefore to be understood more or less exclusively in terms of wisdom and insight. The result of following Buddhaghosa too closeley [*sic*] can be a rather distorted and misleading account of Theravādin meditation theory. My point here is not that Buddhaghosa gets it wrong, but that in failing to have an adequate grasp of the theory of meditation presented in the Nikāyas and Abhidhamma, modern scholars misunderstand Buddhaghosa.[b]

Gethin points out that the Nikāyas and Abhidhamma seem "to make clear and emphasize the ancient conception of the path as the yoking

---

[a] See page 115.

[b] R. M. L. Gethin, *The Buddhist Path to Awakening: A Study of the Bodhi-Pakkhiyā Dhammā* (Leiden, New York, Köln: E. J. Brill, 1992), p. 350. Thanks to Karen Lang for calling my attention to Gethin's work.

together of calm and insight."[a]

Another reason that the apparent contradiction between calm and insight may be less relevant to Ge-luk presentations of calm abiding and special insight and of the concentrations and formless absorptions than to Theravāda presentations is that the Ge-luk-pas follow Vasubandhu's *Treasury of Manifest Knowledge* in positing a union of calm abiding and special insight and in regarding the concentrations as states in which calm abiding and special insight are balanced; they also follow Asaṅga in maintaining that the achievement of special insight is one of the preparations for the first concentration. Thus, in Corless' terms, both calm abiding and special insight, in the Ge-luk sūtra-system tradition, are to be weighed on the side of enstatic withdrawal rather than compassionate outreach. The Ge-luk tradition, however, appears to offer a *balance* between enstatic withdrawal and compassionate outreach—rather than a movement from the first to the second, as Corless suggests—since one version of the stages-of-the-path meditations includes both the cultivation of a union of calm abiding and special insight realizing emptiness, outside the system of the concentrations and formless absorptions, on the one hand, and the explicit cultivation of great compassion and the altruistic mind of enlightenment, on the other.

Collett Cox mentions Griffiths' description of a "tension or dichotomy...between insight meditation and concentrative meditation" as only one of several attempts by Western academics to account for the relationship between them. In "Attainment through Abandonment: The Sarvāstivādin Path of Removing Defilements," a study of the path-structure in Sarvāstivādin Abhidharma, she suggests

> an alternative explanation, neglected in previous studies, to this tension between the cognitive and meditative—namely, a final goal that subsumes knowledge and concentration as equally cooperative means rather than mutually exclusive ends. This inclusive goal is the abandonment of specific defilements (*kleśaprahāṇa*) and the ultimate destruction of all fluxes (*āsravakṣaya*); extensive textual evidence both from early canonical texts and from Abhidharma materials argues that this—not concentration or knowledge alone—represents the final goal in many segments of the Buddhist tradition.[b]

---

[a] Ibid., p. 350.

[b] Collett Cox, "Attainment through Abandonment: The Sarvāstivādin Path of Removing Defilements," *Paths to Liberation: the Mārga and Its Transformations in Buddhist Thought,*

Although the final goal for Mahāyānists is not the abandonment of defilements but the attainment Buddhahood for the sake of all sentient beings, this concern with the abandonment of defilements—designated by many names, as Cox points out, in many numerical lists[a]—is reflected in Ge-luk-pa presentations of the concentrations and formless absorptions, especially in discussions of the preparations, which are explained as techniques for abandoning, or at least suppressing, the afflictive emotions pertaining to the level below the one the meditator is trying to attain. Moreover, since the Ge-luk-pas, unlike the Sarvāstivādins discussed by Cox, posit a distinction between temporary abandonment, or mere suppression, of afflictive emotions and final abandonment from the root, they are usually careful to distinguish between the two modes of abandonment.[b]

Gimello sees calming as preparatory to insight, or discernment (*vipaśyanā*), "[i]n all versions of the story of the Buddha's life and in all systematic curricula of [Buddhist] meditation":

> While it is true that discernment is not to be attained without some degree of calming as precondition, it is no less true that calming itself, without discernment, is of no soteric avail whatsoever. The differences among the various regimens of Buddhist meditation do not put this in question. Such differences have only to do with the relative proportions of the two ingredients....[c]

He further relates "the subordination of calming to discernment in Buddhist meditation" to the development, in "the later scholastic (*abhidharma*) traditions of Buddhism," of "a distinction between the mundane (*laukika*) and the supramundane (*lokottara*) cultivations (*bhāvanā*)," the former involving "nurturing at any one point on the path an aversion for the lower stage, once it has been reached, and by conceiving an aspiration for the next higher stage," and the latter, "the review of the 'truths' of Buddhism."[d] This distinction is also reflected in the Ge-luk presentation—from Manifest Knowledge sources—of the mundane and supramundane paths, of preparations having the aspect of

ed. Robert E. Buswell, Jr. and Robert M. Gimello, Kuroda Institute Studies in East Asian Buddhism 7 (Honolulu: University of Hawaii Press, 1992) p. 66.

[a] Ibid., pp. 68–69.

[b] Ibid., p. 79. For Ge-luk positions, see above, page 194, and Gedün Lodrö, pp. 241–44, 297.

[c] Gimello, "Mysticism and Meditation," p. 185.

[d] Ibid., pp. 185–86.

grossness/peacefulness and of those having the aspect of the truths.

Discussing the understanding of emptiness in Ge-luk-pa Prāsaṅgika, in which, at higher levels of the path, "analysis *itself* induces a state of calm abiding on emptiness," Anne Klein suggests that "[i]n order to make the case that conceptual analysis leads to nonconceptual experience, it becomes necessary to soften the boundaries around the functions of calming and insight." Instead of an apparent contradiction between calm and insight or a movement from one to the other, or even a balance, she describes a "profound compatibility between calming and insight" that "culminates in the apparent unification of these two into a single consciousness." In the Ge-luk-pa "account of the progressive stages leading to Buddhahood," she recognizes "two mental gestures," which she identifies, in terms superficially resembling those used by Corless, as "opening consciousness to encompass the spacelike, unconditioned emptiness, and withdrawing the mind from sense objects through cultivating various stages of concentration and absorption"—or, in brief, as "expansion and withdrawal." Unlike Corless, however, she relates the expansive gesture to the realization of emptiness, not to compassion.[a] Unlike Corless, she has no reason to suggest that either of these mental gestures is more compassionate than the other, since, as stages leading to Buddhahood in a Mahāyāna system—that is, as

---

[a] Anne C. Klein, "Mental Concentration and the Unconditioned: A Buddhist Case for Unmediated Experience," *Paths to Liberation,* pp. 271, 278; also *Path to the Middle: Oral Mādhyamika Philosophy in Tibet; The Oral Scholarship of Kensur Yeshey Tupden* (Albany, NY: State University of New York Press, 1994), pp.15–16; see also 12–15.

As Hopkins points out in a comment on Klein's terminology, calm abiding cannot be described as "just withdrawal," since, when calm abiding is attained, "the mind is as if mixed with space." Indeed, according to Jam-yang-shay-pa, one of the signs of calm abiding is the vanishing of all coarse appearances, "whereupon there is the dawning of a sense that the mind is mixed with space" (*sems nam mkhar 'dres nyams 'char,* Jam-yang-shay-pa, *Concentrations,* 161.2). However, the process of cultivating calm abiding involves a withdrawal from sense objects; calm abiding cannot be achieved with a sense consciousness, and the achievement of calm abiding is marked by the stoppage of the sense consciousnesses; coarse appearances to the sense consciousnesses are the most obvious of those that vanish with the achievement of calm abiding (see Gedün Lodrö, pp. 236–37). Moreover, the "sense that the mind is mixed with space" is to be distinguished from the spacelike meditative equipoise (*mnyam bzhag nam mkha' lta bu*) realizing emptiness, since, even though the achievement of calm abiding is marked by "a sense that the mind is mixed with space," the object of observation of calm abiding can be either emptiness or—more often—a conventional phenomenon such as the body of a Buddha. Therefore, although calm abiding is not "just withdrawal" but includes certain elements of expansion, it is probably correct to say that it consists *mainly* of withdrawal.

practices of a Bodhisattva—both must not only be motivated by compassion but be preceded by the attainment of an altruistic mind of enlightenment that marks the beginning of the Mahāyāna path of accumulation. Thus, although it would be reasonable to say (1) that Ge-luk-pas did not practice the concentrations and formless absorptions because cultivation of those meditative absorptions continued to be associated with the Hīnayāna despite their presentation in the Mahāyāna topic of the Perfection of Wisdom and (2) that they, like members of the other orders of Tibetan Buddhism, engaged in explicitly Mahāyāna practices instead, it would probably not be correct to attribute the non-practice of the concentrations and formless absorptions to the supposed tension between calming and insight and to describe that supposed tension in terms of the absence or presence of compassion.

Why Ge-luk-pas Continue to Study the Concentrations and Formless Absorptions

In brief, Ge-luk-pas study presentations of the concentrations and formless absorptions for three reasons. The first reason, discussed in Chapter 10, is that, since the concentrations and formless absorptions are mentioned in accounts of the life of Shākyamuni Buddha, Buddhists cannot easily ignore them. Although no Buddhist in any tradition is expected to imitate in his or her own life every episode in the life of the founder, accounts of Shākyamuni Buddha's life present a model of progress from an apparently ordinary, unenlightened state to a state of complete enlightenment and, thereby, give the practitioner hope of making similar progress. That model includes, before Shākyamuni Buddha's attainment of enlightenment and subsequent career of teaching, episodes of apparent trial and error, among them his practice of the two highest formless absorptions—the meditative absorption of nothingness and that without discrimination and without non-discrimination—under non-Buddhist teachers. After he concluded that these meditative absorptions, although not absolutely to be avoided, are not, in themselves, means to liberation, he returned to an earlier experience of the meditative absorption of the first concentration, attained the remaining concentrations, and achieved enlightenment on the basis of the fourth concentration. Among Ge-luk-pas, who do not practice the concentrations and formless absorptions, close study of the characteristics of these meditative absorptions and the methods of attaining them maintains and strengthens the scholar-monk's connection to Shākyamuni Buddha's life and attainment of enlightenment.

The second reason for the study of the concentrations and formless absorptions, discussed in Chapter 11 and to some extent also in Chapter 2, is the relationship of these meditations to traditional Buddhist cosmology, since rebirth in any of the levels of the Form or Formless Realm is held to be caused by the attainment of the corresponding meditative absorption. The third is that they are mentioned in a major Mahāyāna scriptural source, the Perfection of Wisdom sūtras, and in Indian and Tibetan commentaries on the Perfection of Wisdom sūtras; therefore, they are studied in Ge-luk monastic universities as part of the topic of the Perfections.

This list of reasons, however, bypasses the deeper implications of the question, which have to do with the nature of devotional scholarship, of study as religious practice. Cox's comment about Abhidharma—"Perhaps attempts at interpretation must recognize that, within the perspective of Abhidharma, the theoretical enterprise is itself an integral part of practice"[a]—is also true of Ge-luk-pa scholasticism. One function of study as a religious practice is to sustain a group's connection with a model even when the model, for whatever reason, is no longer practiced in its original form, and even if—as Cox suggests may be the case for descriptions of path-structure in Abhidharma texts[b]—the original practice, which is no longer known, may not correspond to its later representation. Traditional Jews, for example, study in detail institutions that ceased to exist when the Second Temple was destroyed. Similarly, by immersing themselves in the details of the concentrations and formless absorptions as they are described in Buddhist scriptures and commentaries, Buddhist scholars, whether Theravādin or Ge-luk-pa, vividly reconstruct for themselves, in imagination, what they take to be the practice of predecessors, beginning with Shākyamuni Buddha, whose meditative attainments they regard as superior to their own. In addition, Ge-luk-pa scholar-monastics connect with the paradigm of ideal Bodhisattva practice set forth in the Perfection of Wisdom sūtras and their commentaries, and they explain the correspondence between the actual absorptions of the concentrations and formless absorptions and the levels of the Form and Formless Realms of Buddhist cosmology to ordinary beings, even non-meditators, to establish ethical and soteriological guidelines.

Ge-luk-pa scholar-monastics often spend more than twenty years completing a complex and competitive educational program

---

[a] Cox, "Attainment through Abandonment," *Paths to Liberation*, p. 65.

[b] Ibid., p. 64.

culminating in the degree of ge-shay; they study and debate—and, in the process, compare and evaluate—Indian and earlier Tibetan Buddhist commentaries, as well as the monastic textbooks of their own and other colleges within the monastic universities. As is shown in Chapter 1 (page 23), they regard themselves as the heirs of the textual lineage of Ka-dam-pas, who, in turn, traced their lineage, through Atisha, to the Indian monastic universities. Chapter 1 (page 14) also demonstrates, through an analysis of Jam-yang-shay-pa's *Analytical Delineation of the Presentation of the Three—Hearing, Thinking, and Meditating*—a discussion of Vasubandhu's presentation of the classic triad of hearing, thinking, and meditating in the *Treasury of Manifest Knowledge* (6.5) and its *Autocommentary*—that the Ge-luk-pas explicitly recognize study as an aspect of religious practice and, as such, classify study as an aspect of hearing, or learning.[a] Gimello suggests that the function of the wisdom arisen from hearing, or "insight born of learning," is "not descriptive or cognitive but connative, corrective, performative."[b] He observes that this type of wisdom, "the degree of insight achievable by the logical or rational analysis of teaching,"

---

[a] The importance of hearing as a religious activity is indicated even in basic Tibetan Buddhist classifications of sense objects based on those in Vasubandhu's *Treasury of Manifest Knowledge* and Asaṅga's *Summary of Manifest Knowledge*. The divisions of visible forms, odors, tastes, and tangible objects merely describe how these objects are perceived. Visible forms are divided into colors and shapes, with the former being subdivided into primary and secondary colors, and so on. Odors are divided into fragrant and unfragrant. Tastes are divided into sweet, sour, and so on. Tangible objects are divided into elements (earth, water, fire, and wind) and tangible objects arisen from elements, with the latter being divided into smoothness, roughness, and so on. In the division of sounds, however, consciousness becomes a factor; sounds are divided into sounds caused by elements conjoined with consciousness and sounds caused by elements not conjoined with consciousness, with each of these being subdivided into articulate and inarticulate sounds. Only then are pleasant and unpleasant—categories descriptive of perception—introduced as further subdivisions, and even some of the sub-subdivisions have illustrations that refer to the hearing of teaching. For example, words of doctrine serve as an illustration of pleasant articulate sounds caused by elements conjoined with consciousness. Illustrations of pleasant and unpleasant articulate sounds caused by elements not conjoined with consciousness are, respectively, words of doctrine taught by trees rustled by a Buddha's extraordinary powers and words of scolding from a tree rustled by a Buddha's extraordinary powers. Despite the later development of meditation techniques based on visualization, there is no corresponding division of visible forms into those conjoined with consciousness—such as written letters or religious images—or not conjoined with consciousness, such as trees (see Hopkins, *Meditation on Emptiness*, pp. 220–32).

[b] Robert Gimello, "Mysticism in Its Contexts," *Mysticism and Religious Traditions*, ed. Steven T. Katz (New York: Oxford University Press, 1983), p. 71.

> is the kind and measure of insight attainable in the study of scripture or in attendance upon the instruction of a teacher. It is held, admittedly, to be by itself quite insufficient for liberation. But as often and as strongly as its sufficiency is denied, its necessity is affirmed.[a]

Since Ge-luk-pa scholar-monastics are *religious* scholars whose prolific writings are intended to direct students, even in the debating courtyard, toward the wisdom arisen from hearing, Donald S. Lopez has raised questions concerning the status of their work in a Western academic context. In *A Study of Svātantrika,* he demonstrates that, despite the factors of time and distance that separate them from their Indian sources, Ge-luk-pa scholars approach Indian Buddhist texts from within what they assume to be a shared a Buddhist culture. He also shows that the Ge-luk system is synthetic, since Ge-luk-pa scholars "were forced to construct a Svātantrika system from the sources before them."[b] Although Svātantrika presents its own special problems, Lopez's argument can be extended to other areas of Ge-luk scholarship.

It is precisely the system-building aspect of Ge-luk scholarship, however, that makes it potentially interesting in its own right to Western Buddhologists. Because both Ge-luk-pas and traditional Jews consider study to be an important part of a religious life, and because both Ge-luk and Talmudic scholarship are similar in their concern for constructing religious systems that rely on earlier texts of their respective religions as sources, it is possible that Western Buddhologists studying Ge-luk scholarship can profitably incorporate some of the concepts and methods Jacob Neusner has developed for the Western academic study of the Talmud within the history of religions, despite the very different concerns of Buddhist and Jewish scholarly system-builders.

Of particular interest are Neusner's distinctions between the literary and theological senses of "tradition" and between "tradition" in the literary sense and "system." He regards the literary formation of a traditional body of religious writing as

> an incremental and linear process,...a chain of transmission of received materials, refined and corrected but handed on not

---

[a] Ibid., p. 72.

[b] Donald S. Lopez, *A Study of Svātantrika* (Ithaca, NY: Snow Lion Publications, 1987), pp. 27–30. Citing Kenneth L. Pike's *Language in Relation to a Unified Theory of the Structure of Human Behavior* (2nd rev. ed. [The Hague: Mouton and Co., 1967]), Lopez uses the categories *emic* and *etic,* introduced by Pike to identify two ways of viewing a given culture—from within it and from outside it.

> only unimpaired, but essentially intact.[a]

As Neusner uses the term in this context, "tradition" in the theological sense refers to "content and structure"—something "deriving from an indeterminate past" and "having authority for future generations." Indeed, both types have such authority—theological tradition because of the "content and structure" of what is transmitted and literary tradition because of the nature of the process of transmission.[b]

In distinguishing between "tradition" in the literary sense and "system," Neusner's main criterion is the role of reasoning in the body of work he is examining; it is his emphasis on the role of reasoning that makes his analysis especially applicable to the study of Ge-luk religious scholarship. His axiom is that "a traditional religion cannot constitute a systemic statement, and a systemic statement is not compatible with a process of tradition," since the incremental process of tradition overrides the processes of reasoning, whereas system-building relies on them.[c] Thus, he sees the Babylonian Talmud as not traditional in the literary sense but, rather, as systemic. He admits that, in the theological sense, it is

> a profoundly traditional document, laying forth in its authorship's terms and language the nature of the Judaic tradition, that is, Judaism, as that authorship wishes to read the tradition and have it read.[d]

But it is not traditional in the literary sense: it

> knows not traditions to be recited and reviewed but merely sources, to be honored always but to be used only when pertinent to a quite independent program of thought.[e]

The same, with a change of religious references, can probably be said of the work of Tsong-kha-pa and his Ge-luk-pa followers.

Application of some of Neusner's methods would allow Buddhologists to ask of Tsong-kha-pa and the Ge-luk-pa system-builders who followed him the same questions Neusner asks of the authorship of the

---

[a] Jacob Neusner, "At Stake in Systemic Analysis: Is Judaism a Traditional Religion?" in *First Principles of Systemic Analysis: The Case of Judaism Within the History of Religions* (Lanham, MD: University Press of America, 1987), p. 132.

[b] Ibid., p. 133.

[c] Ibid., p. 133.

[d] Ibid., p. 134.

[e] Ibid., p. 135.

Babylonian Talmud: What is their program; what criteria have they used with respect to their sources; why have they made the choices of selection and omission they have made? Such an approach would allow a shift in perspective from a distinction between original and synthetic—that is, between source texts presumed to be early, and therefore pure, and later syntheses, graded on the basis of how accurately they reflect the early texts but considered suspect merely because they are late and synthetic—to a distinction between mere transmission and a reasoned system built by evaluation of sources and deliberate selection of specific points in them. The system could then be approached as an object of academic research in its own right. A study of how a single Ge-luk presentation of the concentrations and formless absorptions uses one of its sources or a few related sources is beyond the scope of the present work; such a study would illuminate the process of Ge-luk system-building and the program of the builders by considering not only points cited with approval or explicitly refuted, as has been done here, but also those that are ignored.

Other Academic Approaches to the Concentrations and Formless Absorptions

In *Buddhist Thought in India*, Edward Conze remarks that "unfortunately the Buddhist theory of transic experiences is one of the least explored parts of Buddhism, and much of it we simply do not understand."[a] Unfortunately too, the availability of translated texts has not prevented misunderstanding even of Theravāda presentations. Winston L. King, in *Theravāda Meditation: The Buddhist Transformation of Yoga,* demonstrates misunderstanding of basic Buddhist doctrines common to all the Buddhist traditions that include presentations of the concentrations and formless absorptions. Among his misunderstandings is the relationship between the mundane and supramundane paths. He assumes, on the basis of scholastic descriptions of the meditator's subjective experience, that "being outside the time-space series during jhānic moments, the meditator does not perform any actions in thought, word, or deed that have kammic potential," although he acknowledges, inconsistently, the "meticulously worked out correlation of meditational attainment stages with rebirth levels" in the Pāli canon and

---

[a] Edward Conze, *Buddhist Thought in India*, first pub. 1962 (Ann Arbor: University of Michigan Press: Ann Arbor Paperbacks, 1973), p. 253.

Buddhaghosa's *Path of Purification.*[a] However, Theravādins and Ge-luk-pas agree that whatever causes rebirth in cyclic existence must be an action—and, therefore, have what King calls "kammic potential"—and that a mundane concentration or formless absorption attained by a human being is a mental action causing such rebirth. Thus, King misunderstands the relationship between the meditative absorptions of the concentrations and formless absorptions and Buddhist cosmology—a shared premise of Theravāda, Indian, and Tibetan presentations of the concentrations and formless absorptions—and, thereby, attributes to the mundane meditative absorptions greater transformative and liberative power than they are traditionally considered to have.

Mircea Eliade's classic work on the history of religions, *Yoga: Immortality and Freedom,* discusses several systems, primarily Indian but also including Chinese alchemy, from the point of view of apparent similarities of goal, technique, psychological and physical experience, and underlying structure and imagery. According to Eliade's interpretation, all the systems he discusses have an "initiatory structure" involving death to profane life "followed by a rebirth to another mode of being—that represented by liberation."[b] Eliade implies that this structure is universal and overrides cultural differences, although he also claims—somewhat inconsistently—not that yoga, in its various forms, *is* an initiation but, rather, that yoga and initiation are analogous:

> The analogy between Yoga and initiation becomes even more marked if we think of the initiatory rites—primitive or other—that pursue the creation of a "new body," a "mystical body" (symbolically assimilated, among the primitives, to the body of a newborn infant. Now, the "mystical body," which will allow the yogin to enter the transcendent mode of being, plays a considerable part in all forms of Yoga, and especially in tantrism and alchemy. From this point of view Yoga takes over and, on another plane, continues the archaic and universal symbolism of initiation....[c]

Although this is not the place to discuss Eliade's work in detail, it should be noted that his positing of a universal initiatory structure

---

[a] Winston L. King, *Theravāda Meditation: The Buddhist Transformation of Yoga* (University Park and London: The Pennsylvania State University Press, 1980), pp. 49, 86.

[b] Mircea Eliade, *Yoga: Immortality and Freedom,* trans. Willard R. Trask; Bollingen Series, vol. 5 (New York: Pantheon, 1958); first pub. as *Le Yoga. Immortalité et Liberté* (Paris: Librairie Payot, 1954), p. 5.

[c] Ibid., p. 6.

imposes an artificial homogeneity both on dissimilar traditions from diverse cultures and, in his chapter "Yoga Techniques in Buddhism," on dissimilar practices, meditative and non-meditative, within a single religious tradition. He plausibly identifies as initiatory the ceremony of Buddhist monastic ordination, a non-meditative ritual that includes the giving up of one's family name and previous social status and the taking of a new name as a child of the Buddha's Shākya (*śākya*) clan. He then imposes the same basic initiatory structure, with its associated scriptural imagery of the sword drawn from the scabbard and the snake emerging from its newly shed skin, on Pāli scriptural descriptions of the meditative, and therefore very different, activities of realizing *nirvāṇa*, mindfulness of breathing, and successively attaining the concentrations and formless absorptions.[a]

Because they do not readily fit his scheme, Eliade misunderstands both the nature of insight and the role of analysis within meditation. Therefore, he overstates what he calls "the tension between the 'philosophers' and the 'disciples of Yoga.'" He describes Vasubandhu's *Treasury of Manifest Knowledge* as an attempt

> to rationalize mystical experiences, to interpret them in terms of the school; not that he denies the value of "yogic ecstasy," but, writing on the *abhidharma*, the "supreme *dharma*," he is determined to remain on the plane of "philosophy." For this kind of "supreme knowledge" is supposed to achieve the same result as yogic practice.[b]

He describes Buddhaghosa's *Path of Purification* similarly. According to him,

> "Buddhaghoṣa's [*sic*] *Visuddhimagga*...shows the same orientation. The stages of meditation are classified, justified by canonical texts, interpreted "rationally."...The last chapter of his long work is entitled "On the Advantages of Developing Understanding," and one section of it is devoted to showing that ecstasy (*nirodha*, "arrest of states of consciousness") can be attained through the intellect alone.[c]

Eliade seems to assume that meditation leads to a non-intellectual "experience" and that intellectual understanding and meditation are

---

[a] Ibid., pp. 165, 168, 169–73.

[b] Ibid., p. 192.

[c] Ibid., pp. 192–93.

mutually exclusive. According to him, any system emphasizing yogic practice, whether Patañjali's or that of the Buddhist Yogāchāra school, results in "an 'experience' that is enstatic, suprasensory, and extrarational"[a]—and incompatible with analysis. Thus, unlike his Buddhist sources, he does not even consider the relationship between calm and insight as meditative practices.

The relationship between calm and insight is of concern to Paul Griffiths, whose approach to the question will be discussed below (page 304). In *On Being Mindless*, he focuses on the status of consciousness (or rather, the lack of it) in the meditative absorption of cessation according to Theravāda interpretations of it.[b] He also considers the interpretations of Vasubandhu's *Treasury* and its *Autocommentary*, as well as the Yogāchāra tradition. The present study does not concern itself with the meditative absorption of cessation but confines itself for the most part to the four concentrations and the four formless absorptions. However, Griffiths' major innovation, in both *On Being Mindless* and his dissertation, "Indian Buddhist Meditation-Theory: History, Development and Systematization"—his use of the psychological terms "psychotropic technique" and "altered state of consciousness," among others—is worth consideration here.

Griffiths uses "psychotropic technique" to refer to methods of altering consciousness and "altered state of consciousness" to refer to the effects of those methods.[c] In "Indian Buddhist Meditation-Theory," although not in *On Being Mindless,* these terms are generally replaced by their initials—"altered states of consciousness" by "ASC" and "psychotropic technique" by "PT," in the manner of psychologists; Griffiths also introduces two new psychological terms—"observationally analytic technique" (OAT), as a subdivision of "psychotropic technique," and "concentrative enstatic technique" (CET).[d] Considerably later in "Indian Buddhist Meditation-Theory," he concedes that "[t]he Sanskrit terms *śamatha* and *vipaśyanā* are in fact the Buddhist equivalents of our more clumsy neologisms concentrative enstasy and observational analysis."[e]

---

[a] Ibid., p. 37.

[b] Paul J. Griffiths, *On Being Mindless: Buddhist Meditation and the Mind-Body Problem* (La Salle, IL: Open Court, 1986),

[c] Paul J. Griffiths, "Indian Buddhist Meditation-Theory: History, Development and Systematization" (Unpublished dissertation: University of Wisconsin—Madison, 1983), pp. 48–49.

[d] Ibid., pages 90, 122, 231 ff.; the initials OAT first appear, without reference to previous mention of the term, on p. 122.

[e] Ibid., p. 581.

Griffiths plausibly uses the term "altered state of consciousness" to designate meditative states such as the concentrations and formless absorptions, the meditative absorption of non-discrimination (*asaṃjñāsamāpatti*, which he calls the "attainment of unconsciousness"), and the "attainment of cessation" (*nirodhasamāpatti*). However, he is not consistent, since he discusses and charts the entire system of the concentrations and formless absorptions in the *Treasury* and its *Autocommentary*, as well as in Asaṅga's *Summary of Manifest Knowledge*, under the category "concentrative enstatic techniques." Although he refers to the meditative states of the concentrations and formless absorptions, in the context of the *Treasury* also, as altered states of consciousness, he does not assign the preparations (*sāmantaka;* "liminal *dhyānas*" in Griffiths' terminology), which are the means of attaining them, to a separate category. It could be argued, however, that in Griffiths' psychological terminology the *sāmantaka* might be called "psychotropic techniques," since, as Griffiths correctly points out, "the liminal dhyānas...do most of the actual soteriological work of the path of cultivation in the *AKBh* [the *Treasury of Manifest Knowledge* and its *Autocommentary*]," whereas "the root attainments become little more than effects of the practice of the liminal *dhyānas*, ASC's...in which the practitioner can rest as a reward for his work in the liminal stages."[a]

Griffiths' discussion of whether to call the initial stage of mindfulness of breathing, as presented in the *Ānāpānasatisutta,* a psychotropic technique, suggests that the precision of his method is limited:

> ...bearing in mind that our working definition of a PT was anything designed to alter consciousness, it is perhaps not proper to call this initial stage of mindfulness of breathing a PT at all since it is not supposed to change anything but merely to observe. We may note, though, that even the practise of this simple observational technique is likely to alter breath rhythms...[b]

Griffiths seems to be arguing that, although breath rhythms are not consciousness, *something* will change, even if what changes is not the meditator's consciousness; therefore, since the initial stage of mindfulness of breathing is *tropic*, even if not precisely *psycho*tropic, it may be proper to call the initial stage of mindfulness of breathing a psychotropic technique. This is shaky reasoning, at best. Moreover, Griffiths overlooks a key aspect of the meditator's psychological development—

---

[a] Ibid., p. 249.

[b] Ibid., p. 112.

namely, that in the frame of reference of the *Ānāpānasatisutta,* the initial stage of mindfulness of breathing requires development of the habit of mere observation by someone who has not previously engaged in it. That is to say, through a subtle redirection of consciousness, the meditator begins to develop mindfulness. If it is appropriate to call the initial stage of mindfulness of breathing a psychotropic technique, it is appropriate not because this initial stage changes the meditator's breath rhythm (although it does) but because the initial development of mindfulness is a technique capable of producing further alterations of the meditator's consciousness. Thus, the application of a modern psychological term to a classic description of a Buddhist meditative practice can only be as good as the analysis of the psychological factors involved.

Griffiths seems to prefer the psychological terms to the Buddhist ones mainly because "the study of altered states of consciousness (ASC's) has, in the last twenty years or so, become a respectable field of psychological investigation"; therefore, he introduces

> the technical language spawned by this burgeoning field...in an attempt to lend an air of detached phenomenological precision to our analysis of complex and often esoteric Buddhist ideas.[a]

Although a clear comparison of Buddhist and contemporary clinical psychologies of meditation can indeed shed light on both, the substitution of psychological technical terms, or their initials, for Buddhist technical terms implicitly posits as given a correspondence that needs to be demonstrated and, thereby, obscures the elements being compared. It is difficult, moreover, to see how such substitution, especially of initials, meets the standard of "clear, precise, and elegant English" Griffiths demanded in his article "Buddhist Hybrid English."[b] Even the clearest comparison of two technical presentations is likely to use the technical terms of both and, therefore, to be technical, whereas Griffiths' original demand can be met only if Buddhist technical terms are translated into, or explained in, ordinary non-technical English.

An important function of the study of commentarial traditions, such as those of both the Ge-luk-pas and Theravādins, is that such study can uncover previous discussions of major questions that also concern modern academic scholars, so that the latter do not have to think in a vacuum. The relationship between calm and insight is an

---

[a] Ibid., p. 599.

[b] Paul J. Griffiths, "Buddhist Hybrid English," *JIABS*, 4:2 (1981), 24.

example of such a major area of concern, as is the related question of the role of hearing and thinking in the seven mental contemplations ("seven acts of attention" in Griffiths' translation). Griffiths notes that

> phenomenologically they fit very well into the category that we have labelled observationally analytic technique....Thus, according to Asaṅga and Sthiramati, the *dhyānas*—states which we have seen to be defined in these texts as paradigmatically consisting in enstasy—are apparently to be obtained by observationally analytic processes in which the practitioner brings intellectual/verbal faculties to bear on his psychological condition....
>
> There are problems with such a view of the means by which the *dhyānas* are obtained, even if we restrict it to the *dhyānas* of form, since it is not clear to what extent the faculties of intellectual and verbal analysis can operate in these enstatic states. The problem becomes insuperable, however, when we consider the formless states....[a]

Griffiths raises here a question that Ge-luk-pa commentators, especially Jam-yang-shay-pa, considered at great length, especially with regard to the mental contemplation of individual knowledge of the character. They consider it from two related points of view: the level of that mental contemplation and, from a cosmological perspective, how beings of the Form and Formless Realms cultivate it. Their treatment of these questions is discussed detail above (pages 206ff.). If Griffiths were less committed to leaving aside "the frequently distorting perspectives of the Tibetan and Chinese traditional understandings of Indian Buddhism,"[b] he would find that Ge-luk-pa thinkers have anticipated some of his theoretical concerns.

Another function of commentary is the close reading of key passages in the source texts, as well as discussion and debate of various interpretations. Thus, the study of such commentaries can prevent some obvious misreadings out of context. Stephan V. Beyer, for example, in "The Doctrine of Meditation in the Hīnayāna," identifies the first two branches of the first concentration as "discursive thought" (*rtog pa, vitarka;* translated here as "investigation") and "reasoning" (*dpyod pa, vicāra;* translated here as "analysis"). This type of translation is valid for Vasubandhu's *Treasury of Manifest Knowledge,* on which he has based his

---

a Paul J. Griffiths, "Indian Buddhist Meditation-Theory," pp. 561–62.

b Ibid., p. 4.

description, and for traditions based on it, but it is not valid for all Hīnayāna schools because the Theravādins, whom he would presumably include among Hīnayānists, consider the four concentrations (Pāli, *jhāna*) to be pure calm (Pāli, *samatha*) without analysis, and, therefore, interpret *vitarka* (Pāli, *vitakka*) in the first concentration as "initial application of mind," or "applied thought" and *vicāra* as "sustained application of mind," or "sustained thought."[a]

In his article "Mysticism and Meditation," Robert M. Gimello discusses Buddhist explanations of meditation practice, from a variety of Buddhist traditions, in relation to Western theories of mysticism. His summary of the system of the concentrations and formless absorptions is clear and generally accurate. Nevertheless, when he cites Asaṅga's description of calm and insight from the *Summary of Manifest Knowledge* (in Hsüan-tsang's translation), he describes it as "one of the typical scholastic definitions of this pair...late (*c.* fourth century AD) but reflective of the mainstream of the tradition."[b] This passage includes a list of nine items that Gimello understands as characteristics of calming. The sixteenth-century Tibetan scholar Paṇ-chen Sö-nam-drak-pa, however, points out that the nine items in the list are actually the nine mental abidings that are preliminary to calm abiding. It is amusing, though no worse, to find a modern Western scholar in the position of Paṇ-chen Sö-nam-drak-pa's sixteenth-century Tibetan opponent, who cites this passage to support the absurd position that "The nine mental abidings...are calm abidings." It is to be hoped that increased familiarity with the type of close reading done in the Ge-luk scholastic tradition will prevent such misreadings.

Conclusion

According to the editors of *Paths to Liberation*, one of the volume's purposes is to introduce into the comparative study of religion the Buddhist concept of mārga, or path, as a possible cross-cultural category parallel to the Western concept "soteriology," but without the implication of divine, rather than human, "salvific activity." They describe "mārga theory, or...'soteriology' in the Buddhist sense," as

> generally speaking, the theory according to which certain

---

[a] Buddhaghosa, *Path of Purification*, trans., Ñyāṇamoli, IV.88–92, vol. 1, pp. 147–49. For additional discussion of this point, see page 255, note c above.

[b] Robert M. Gimello, "Mysticism and Meditation," *Mysticism and Philosophical Analysis*, ed. Steven T. Katz (New York: Oxford University Press, 1983), p. 180.

> methods of practice, certain prescribed patterns of religious behavior, have transformative power and will lead, somehow necessarily, to specific religious goals.[a]

The virtual non-mention of the concentrations and formless absorptions in *Paths to Liberation*—except, most notably, in Klein's article—serves as a reminder that the concentrations and formless absorptions in themselves are not presented as *the* Buddhist path.[b] Nevertheless, it is in the category of "mārga theory, or...'soteriology' in the Buddhist sense" that Ge-luk presentations of the concentrations and formless absorptions belong. Indeed, these presentations may be described, in part, as an attempt to construct a general mārga theory from within a Mahāyānist scholastic perspective, since they delineate various ways in which the concentrations and formless absorptions intersect with other presentations of Buddhist path-structure, and with Buddhist interpretations of non-Buddhist paths as well. The Ge-luk-pas pay particular attention to these points of intersection in their discussions of the relationship of the meditative absorptions of the concentrations and formless absorptions to Buddhist cosmology, the mundane and supramundane paths, and the five paths—of accumulation, preparation, seeing, meditation, and no more learning—that culminate in the goals of Hīnayānists and Mahāyānists—Foe Destroyerhood and Buddhahood, respectively. Thus, their presentations of the concentrations and formless absorptions function as maps of a territory on which various religious paths can be traced, and can be consulted to orient students of any of those paths. Moreover, although many of the building-blocks of Ge-luk systematic presentations of the concentrations and formless absorptions are known from Indian sources, the system itself, developed and still studied in monastic universities in which study is a major component of the religious life, has a unique cultural flavor.

---

[a] Robert E. Buswell, Jr., and Robert M. Gimello, "Introduction," *Paths to Liberation*, pp. 1–3.

[b] Paul Griffiths, in *On Being Mindless*, presents the concentrations and formless absorptions, together with their corresponding cosmological realms, in a chart of what he calls "the path of cultivation (*bhāvanāmārga*)." Although he points out that the *bhāvanāmārga*, as he charts it, "is actually only (part of) one of the many soteriological paths described in the *AKBh* [the *Treasury of Manifest Knowledge* and its *Autocommentary*]," he does not mention here the more common use of the term *bhāvanāmārga* to refer to the fourth of the five paths of the *Treasury* and its *Autocommentary* (Griffiths, *On Being Mindless*, pp. 120–21; however, he mentions *bhāvanāmārga* as one of the five paths in "Indian Buddhist Meditation-Theory," p. 230).

PART THREE: *TRANSLATIONS*

Tsong-kha-pa's *Notes on the Concentrations and Formless Absorptions*

and

Kön-chok-jik-may-wang-po's *Condensed Statement of (Jam-yang-shay-pa's) "Great Exposition of the Concentrations and Formless Absorptions," An Excellent Vase of Eloquence Presenting the Concentrations and Formless Absorptions*

Translator's Introduction: The Form of the Text and Translation

The text of Tsong-kha-pa's *Notes on the Concentrations and Formless Absorptions* suggests that it is, indeed, a set of notes; it lacks several of the parts of a complete Tibetan book, such as the expression of worship, the promise to compose the book, and the concluding verses and dedication. It is probably a student's lecture notes rather than Tsong-kha-pa's own writing. As such, it is somewhat unsatisfactory—rather like borrowing someone else's notes for a missed class. Although later Geluk-pas, such as Gedün Lodrö, assume that the note taker has represented Tsong-kha-pa's own system accurately, Tsong-kha-pa's voice does not always come through as it does in his own writing.

Like the lecture notes of modern students, the *Notes* is often written in phrases rather than sentences; it alternates between outline and exposition. It is also careless about parallelisms, both between the contents-outlines (*sa bcad*) and topic headings and in repeated passages.

The contents-outlines are sketchy at best—often mere lists of phrases, with items omitted. At one point (*Notes,* 9.6), a topic is called "fourth" when nothing has been identified as "first," "second," or "third"; it turns out that the actual third topic was omitted in the contents-outline. To clarify the contents-outlines and supply the note-taker's omissions, I have followed outline form and, from I.A onward, have filled in the contents-outline in brackets according to the usual expository form of contents-outlines in Tibetan books.

Tsong-kha-pa's
Notes on the Concentrations and Formless Absorptions

[The Main Topics]

[I.] The causes through which the concentrations and formless absorptions are attained[a]
[II.] The entities that are attained[b]
[III.] The attainers—the persons who are the basis
[IV.] The signs of the attainment of such

I. [The Causes through Which the Concentrations and Formless Absorptions Are Attained]

[A.] The explanation of the means of attaining the first concentration
[B.] Indication that [the means of attaining] the remaining [concentrations and formless absorptions] are similar to that

[A. The Explanation of the Means of Attaining the First Concentration]

This section has three topics:

[1.] Ascertainment of the number of mental contemplations
[2.] Identification of the individual [seven mental contemplations]
[3.] Opinions on where the ninth path [of release] is included

[1. Ascertainment of the number of mental contemplations]

There are the mental contemplations of thorough knowledge of the character, arisen from belief, thorough isolation, joy-withdrawal, analysis, final training, and the fruit of final training.

---

[a] Tsong-kha-pa, *Notes,* 2.1, reading *'thob byed kyi rgyu* instead of *thob byed kyi rgyu.* Jeffrey Hopkins' emendation. P6148, vol. 154, 170.2.2; Ngawang Gelek Demo, vol. 27, 544.1, and Guru Deva, vol. *tsha,* 800.1, agree with this text.

[b] Tsong-kha-pa, *Notes,* 2.1, reading *gang thob* instead of *gang gis thob.* Jeffrey Hopkins' emendation. P6148, vol. 154, 170.2.2; Ngawang Gelek Demo, vol. 27, 544.1, and Guru Deva, vol. *tsha,* agree with this text.

Question: What are the reasons for positing seven mental contemplations?

Answer: Since there are three in terms of causal preparations, three in terms of entity, and one in terms of effect, seven are posited.

Question: What are posited as the three in terms of cause?

Answer: Two [are posited] as causes of generating what has not been generated; one [is posited] as the cause of enhancing what has already been generated. The two—thorough knowledge of the character and arisen from belief—are posited as the first [the causes generating what has not been generated]. [3] [The mental contemplation of] analysis is posited as the second [the cause of enhancing what has already been generated].

Question: What are the reasons for positing three in terms of entity?

Answer: [The mental contemplation of] thorough isolation is posited as the antidote for the three great objects of abandonment of the lower level; [the mental contemplation of] joy-withdrawal, as the antidote for the three middling [objects of abandonment of the lower level]; the mental contemplation of final training, as the antidote for the three small [objects of abandonment of the lower level].

Moreover, this way of presenting the six preparations is in terms of separating from attachment to the lower level by way of the mundane path having the aspects of grossness/peacefulness, but the preparations for the first concentration are not limited to these six, since, in the preparations for the first concentration, there occur the uncontaminated paths of seeing, meditation, and no more learning which are generated as entities of the not-unable. [Hence, the mental contemplation called the not-unable is a seventh preparation.]

[2.] Individual identification [of the seven mental contemplations]

[The mental contemplation of] thorough knowledge of the character. That which familiarizes with grossness/peacefulness by way of either a mixture of hearing and thinking or either of those, [reflecting] that the Desire Realm, relative to the First Concentration, is gross by reason of involving many afflictive emotions, very great suffering, and a short life-span, whereas the First Concentration, being the opposite of those, is peaceful, is the mental contemplation of thorough knowledge of the character.

Etymology: [4] By reason of familiarizing with the individual characters of the two, the Desire Realm and the First Concentration, as gross and peaceful [respectively], it is called [the mental contemplation of thorough knowledge of the character]. It is included within the level of the Desire Realm.

The mental contemplation arisen from belief. That which serves as a cause of thorough isolation which reaches [a union of] calm abiding and special insight, having passed beyond hearing and thinking in dependence upon having become well acquainted with grossness/peacefulness by way of [the mental contemplation of] thorough knowledge of the character, is [the mental contemplation arisen from belief].

Etymology: By reason of being the mental contemplation which arises in dependence upon having believed in the grossness and peacefulness [of the Desire Realm and the First Concentration, respectively] through hearing and thinking in the context of [the mental contemplation of] thorough knowledge of the character, it is called [the mental contemplation arisen from belief]. It is included within the level of the first concentration.

The mental contemplation of thorough isolation. That mental contemplation which is the state that acts as an antidote to the three great objects of abandonment of the Desire Realm in dependence upon having meditated on grossness/peacefulness by way of the mental contemplation arisen from belief is the mental contemplation of thorough isolation.

Etymology: By reason of being the mental contemplation that initially isolates the mental continuum from the afflictive emotions pertaining to the Desire Realm by way of [having meditated on grossness/peacefulness by way of the mental contemplation arisen from belief], it is called [the mental contemplation of thorough isolation].

The mental contemplation of joy-withdrawal. The state that is the mental contemplation that acts as the antidote to the three middling [cycles of] afflictive emotions pertaining to the Desire Realm in dependence upon having familiarized with grossness/peacefulness by way of[a] thorough isolation.

Etymology: By reason of there being enhancement in body and mind

---

[a] Tsong-kha-pa, *Notes,* 4.4, reading *rab dben gyis* instead of *rab dben gyi.* Jeffrey Hopkins' emendation. P6148, vol. 154, 170.4.1; Ngawang Gelek Demo, vol. 27, 546.6, and Guru Deva, vol. *tsha,* 802.2, agree with this text.

by way of a small [degree of] joy and bliss, included within the level of the first concentration, which are produced from isolation when one is released from the three middling [cycles of] afflictive emotions pertaining to the Desire Realm through [having familiarized with grossness/peacefulness by way of thorough isolation], it [is called the mental contemplation of joy-withdrawal].

The mental contemplation of analysis. When one has abandoned most of the afflictive emotions pertaining to the Desire Realm, one generates an awareness thinking, "I have abandoned them entirely." At that point, in order to investigate whether or not one has entirely abandoned the afflictive emotions pertaining to the Desire Realm, one takes to mind a sign of something attractive included within the level of the Desire Realm and, when one sees that desire is generated for that [object], meditates again on grossness/peacefulness in order to abandon the remaining objects of abandonment. [This] is [the mental contemplation of analysis].

Etymology: [By reason of] one's investigating whether or not one has abandoned the afflictive emotions pertaining to the Desire Realm, it [is called the mental contemplation of analysis]. [5]

The mental contemplation of final training. The mental contemplation which is the state that acts as an antidote abandoning the three small Desire Realm [objects] to be abandoned by meditation, in dependence upon one's having become well acquainted with such grossness/peacefulness by way of the mental contemplation of analysis, is [the mental contemplation of final training].

Etymology: By reason of being the last mental contemplation in which there are three antidotes that abandon afflictive emotions pertaining to the Desire Realm, it [is called the mental contemplation of final training].

The mental contemplation that is the fruit of final training. By reason of being the mental contemplation that experiences a path of meditation that is released from the small of the small [cycles of] afflictive emotions pertaining to the Desire Realm by way of the mental contemplation of final training, it is [called] the mental contemplation that is the fruit of final training.

[3.] Opinions on where the ninth path [of release] is included

Question: Is the ninth path of release, which is released from the ninth [cycle of] afflictive emotions pertaining to the lower level, generated as an entity of an actual absorption or a preparation?

Answer: In the system of Asaṅga's *Summary of Manifest Knowledge* the ninth path of release, which is released from the ninth [cycle] of afflictive emotions pertaining to the lower level, is necessarily generated as the entity of an actual absorption of the upper level.

In the system of Vasubandhu's *Treasury of Manifest Knowledge*, there are cases of generating the path of release that is released from the ninth [cycle of] afflictive emotions pertaining to the Desire Realm and the ninth paths of release that are released from the ninth [cycles of] afflictive emotions pertaining to the First, Second, and Third Concentrations as entities of either an actual absorption or a preparation. From the Fourth Concentration through the Peak of Cyclic Existence, the ninth paths of release that are released from the ninth [cycles of] afflictive-emotions-to-be-abandoned-by-meditation of their own lower level are necessarily generated as the entities of actual absorptions of [their respective upper levels].

The *Treasury* also gives a reason for asserting such—[namely,] that in general the feeling of the preparations is necessarily equanimity. The feelings of the actual absorptions of the two—the first and second concentrations—have mental bliss (*yid bde*) and the feeling of the actual absorption of the third concentration has the feeling of mental bliss (*tshor ba sems bde*), and therefore, because there are faculties of feeling of dissimilar type, it is difficult to shift faculties [of feeling from equanimity to bliss]; therefore, [6] such [namely, that in the system of Vasubandhu's *Treasury of Manifest Knowledge,* the ninth paths of release that are released from afflictive emotions pertaining to the Desire Realm and to the First, Second, and Third Concentrations may be generated as entities of either an actual absorption or a preparation] is presented.

Since the feeling of the actual absorptions of the fourth concentration and above is necessarily equanimity, therefore, because the faculties of feeling do not differ in type, it is easy to shift faculties; therefore, such [namely that in the system of Vasubandhu's *Treasury of Manifest Knowledge,* from the Fourth Concentration through the Peak of Cyclic Existence, the ninth paths of release are necessarily generated as actual absorptions] is presented. Accordingly, [in both systems] the nine uninterrupted paths that abandon the nine [cycles of] afflictive-emotions-to-be-abandoned-by-meditation of the lower level and the first eight paths of release of those [uninterrupted paths] are necessarily preparations.

[B.] Indication that [the Means of Attaining] the Remaining [Concentrations and Formless Absorptions] Are Similar to That

According to the explanation for the preparations for the first concentration, so, similarly, is it also for the preparations ranging from [those for] the second concentration to [those for] the peak of cyclic existence.

The features of dissimilarity. If [someone having] a Desire Realm basis cultivates the eight [sets of] preparations, there is cultivation with respect to the first mental contemplation [that is, the mental contemplation of individual knowledge of the character] as a mixture of hearing and thinking, but if it is cultivated [by someone having] a Form Realm basis, there are no states arisen from thinking. [If it is cultivated by someone having] a Formless Realm basis, there are also no states arisen from hearing, and it is attained by birth.

The mental contemplations of joy-withdrawal of the first two concentrations have the feelings of joy and bliss, but the mental contemplation of joy-withdrawal of the third concentration has the feeling of bliss, and the mental contemplations of joy-withdrawal of the fourth concentration and [the absorptions] above it are explained as merely seeing abandonment of the objects of abandonment as a good quality, for there are no feelings of joy and bliss included in their levels; and the first mental contemplation that is a preparation for any [of the eight] should be known as included within the lower level.

With respect to the way the preparations having the aspects of grossness/peacefulness abandon the afflictive emotions of the lower level, the Vaibhāṣhika system [asserts] that the preparations must simultaneously abandon the two, the lower level's objects of abandonment to be abandoned by seeing and by meditation, and the Sautrāntika system asserts that they abandon only the lower level's objects of abandonment to be abandoned by meditation. Also, the preparations need not entirely abandon even the lower level's coarse objects of abandonment to be abandoned by meditation; it is like the afflicted intellect of a common being having a Desire Realm basis who attains an actual absorption of the first concentration. Through this, one should also know the remaining levels. [7]

From among the eight [sets of] preparations, the preparations for the first concentration have two [types]—pure and uncontaminated; some assert them as having three [types—the three being pure, uncontaminated,] and having relishing [that is, afflicted]. The five remaining preparations [that is, the seven preparations excluding the mental contemplations of a beginner and of analysis] of the second concentration and above must be pure.

II. The Entities That Are Attained[a]

[This section has four topics:]

[A.] Afflicted [absorptions]
[B.] Pure actual [absorptions]
[C. Uncontaminated absorptions][b]
[D.] Analysis of the presentation of those [absorptions]

[A. Afflicted absorptions]

This section has three topics:

[1.] What bases are afflicted
[2.] By what phenomena they are made afflicted
[3.] How they are made afflicted

[1.] What bases are afflicted

There are eight bases that are afflicted: the four pure actual absorptions of the four concentrations and the four pure actual absorptions of the four formless absorptions. Uncontaminated [absorptions] are not bases that are afflicted because they are not capable of being made afflicted.

[2.] By what phenomena they are made afflicted

There are four phenomena by which [the pure actual absorptions of the four concentrations and the four formless absorptions] are made

---

[a] Tsong-kha-pa, *Notes,* 7.2, reading *gang thob par bya ba'i ngo bo la* instead of *gang gis*...Jeffrey Hopkins' emendation. P6148, vol. 154, 171.1.7; Ngawang Gelek Demo, vol. 27, 550.3, and Guru Deva, vol. *tsha,* 805.2, agree with this text. (This head corresponds to 2.1, which was emended to *gang thob pa'i ngo bo* instead of *gang gis thob pa'i ngo bo;* see page 329, note b.)

[b] Adding *snyoms 'jug zag med* from 9.4, which has *snyoms 'jug zag med gang zhe na* without a topic head. The question looks like part of the preceding topic, but that is impossible, since pure and uncontaminated absorptions are mutually exclusive. Moreover, the outline for the next topic is given at 9.6 under the heading, "With respect to the fourth" (*bzhi pa la*). All four texts agree at this point in listing the topics as three rather than four and in omitting the third topic, uncontaminated absorptions.

afflicted: attachment to an upper realm, pride, doubt, and [bad] view. Anger is not a phenomenon by which they are made afflicted because someone having a basis of an upper realm does not have anger.

Question: If ignorance is a phenomenon by which [the pure actual absorptions of the four concentrations and the four formless absorptions] are made thoroughly afflicted, in what way does [ignorance] make them afflicted?

[*Answer:*] The faculty of ignorance makes [absorptions] have the affliction of doubt. Hence, there is also an explanation that the two, doubt and ignorance, operate together.

[3.] How they are made afflicted

How they are made afflicted by desire. When set in equipoise in any of the eight pure actual absorptions of the four concentrations and [four] formless absorptions, one generates attachment toward the object of observation in those absorptions. When the continuum of the absorption has come into similar association with attachment, [the absorption] is made afflicted by attachment, which has become dominant.

How they are made [afflicted] by pride. [8] When set in equipoise in any of those eight [pure actual absorptions of the four concentrations and four formless absorptions], one generates a mind having the aspect of being puffed up [with the thought, "Only] I have attained such an absorption; it has not been [attained] by anyone else." When the continuum of those absorptions has come into similar association with pride, [the absorption] is made afflicted by pride.

How they are made [afflicted] by doubt. When set in equipoise in any of those eight [pure actual absorptions of the four concentrations and four formless absorptions], by the force of obscuration concerning what is and is not a path, one generates doubt wondering whether these [absorptions] are paths of liberation or not. When the continuum of those absorptions has come into similar association with doubt, [the absorption] is made afflicted by doubt.

How they are made [afflicted] by [bad] view. While[a] possessing in one's continuum the first three [bad] views, one attains in one's continuum

---

[a] Tsong-kha-pa, *Notes*, 8.3, reading *ngang nas* instead of *dang nas*, following Guru Deva, vol. *tsha*, 806.4. P6148, vol. 154, 171.3.2, and Ngawang Gelek Demo, vol. 27, 551.6 agree with this text.

any of the eight—the pure actual absorptions of the four concentrations and the four formless absorptions.[a] When set in that equipoise, one generates the view which is the conception [of a bad view] as supreme, which observes the first three [bad] views thinking, "The attainment of such an absorption is by the force of those supreme views."[b] When the continuum of those absorptions has come into similar association with [bad] view, [the absorption] is made afflicted by [bad] view.

The two, the western Vaibhāṣhikas and Asaṅga's *Summary of Manifest Knowledge*, agree in considering the afflicted absorptions to be fourfold in terms of predominant attachment, and so forth. The Kashmīri Vaibhāṣhikas assert [afflicted absorptions] only in terms of predominant attachment.

[B. PURE ACTUAL ABSORPTIONS]

Question: What are the pure actual absorptions?

Answer: They are said to be cases of actual absorptions of the concentrations[c] and formless absorptions serving as factors of mundane virtue.

The reason they are said to be pure. Because of the mental factor of non-attachment—that is, similar association with the virtuous root that reverses [attachment]—or [because of] reversing attachment—that is, separating from the manifest entanglements of one's own level—they are called pure or thoroughly purified.

[Divisions.] When [pure actual absorptions] are divided, there are pure [actual absorptions] concordant with degeneration, concordant with abiding, [9] concordant with enhancement, and concordant with definite differentiation. The seven actual absorptions except for the actual absorption of the peak of cyclic existence have all four of these, but the actual absorption of the peak of cyclic existence has three, excluding that concordant with enhancement.

---

[a] Tsong-kha-pa, *Notes,* 8.3, reading *gzugs med* instead of *gzugs me.* P6148, vol. 154, 171.3.2; Ngawang Gelek Demo, vol. 27, 551.6, and Guru Deva, vol. *tsha,* 806.4, have the correct reading.

[b] Tsong-kha-pa, *Notes,* 8.4 (also P6148, vol. 154, 171.3.3; Ngawang Gelek Demo, vol. 27, 552.1, and Guru Deva, vol. *tsha,* 806.4), omitting punctuation after *lta ba mchog tu gyur pa.*

[c] Tsong-kha-pa, *Notes,* 8.6, reading *bsam gtan dang* instead of *bsam gtan dang po.* Jeffrey Hopkins' emendation. P6148, vol. 154, 171.3.5; Ngawang Gelek Demo, vol. 27, 552.3, and Guru Deva, vol. *tsha,* 806.6, agree with this text.

What are the four?

A pure actual absorption concordant with degeneration is a pure actual absorption concordant with the generation of an affliction immediately after itself.

The second, [**a pure actual absorption concordant with abiding**, is a pure actual absorption] concordant with the generation of a pure [actual absorption] of its own level without generation of an afflicted absorption immediately after itself.

The third, [**a pure actual absorption concordant with enhancement**, is a pure actual absorption] concordant with the generation of a pure [actual absorption] of a higher level without generation of [a pure actual absorption of its own level] immediately after itself.

The fourth, [**a pure actual absorption concordant with definite differentiation**, is a pure actual absorption] concordant with the generation of an uncontaminated absorption without generation of [a pure actual absorption of a higher level] immediately after itself.

[C. Uncontaminated Meditative Absorptions]

Question: What are uncontaminated meditative absorptions?

Answer: Meditative absorptions of the concentrations and formless absorptions that are generated as the entity of a supramundane path are called [uncontaminated absorptions]. Moreover, there are uncontaminated paths that are generated as entities of the six levels of concentration and the first three formless absorptions, but there is no uncontaminated path which is generated as an entity of the peak of cyclic existence or of the Desire Realm because the peak of cyclic existence [has] a very unclear movement of discrimination and because a Desire Realm [mind] is an entity of distraction.

[D.] Analysis of the Presentation of Those Absorptions

[This sections has three topics,] the explanations of:

[1.] The branches of the concentrations
[2.] The objects of observation and subjective aspects of the formless absorptions
[3.] The effects of having cultivated those

The branches of the concentrations

[This section] has three [topics]:

[a.] The differences between what substantially exists and what imputedly exists[a]
[b.] Identification of the individual branches
[c.] The reason for the definiteness of the number

[The differences between what substantially exists and what imputedly exists]

When these are divided in terms of name, there are eighteen; these refer to the five branches each in the first and third concentrations and the four branches each in the second and fourth.

Question: What are these? [10]

Answer: The branches of the first concentration [are] the five: the two, investigation and analysis; the two, joy and bliss, and meditative stabilization. The branches of the second concentration are the four: internal clarity,[b] joy and bliss, and meditative stabilization. The branches of the third concentration are the five[c] mindfulness, introspection, the compositional factor of equanimity, the feeling of bliss, and meditative stabilization. The branches of the fourth concentration are the four: completely pure mindfulness, completely pure equanimity, neutral feeling, and meditative stabilization.

[The system of Vasubandhu's *Treasury of Manifest Knowledge*.] When these branches are condensed into substantial entities, according to the system of Vasubandhu's *Treasury of Manifest Knowledge*, they are included in eleven substantial entities: the two, investigation and

---

[a] Tsong-kha-pa, *Notes*, 9.6, reading *btags* instead of *rtags*. Jeffrey Hopkins' emendation. *rdzas btags* is an abbreviation of *rdzas yod dang btags yod kyi*. P6148, vol. 154, 171.4.6, reads *brtags*. Ngawang Gelek Demo, vol. 27, 553.5, and Guru Deva, vol. *tsha*, 808.1, agree with this text.

[b] Tsong-kha-pa, *Notes*, 10.1 (P6148, vol. 154, 171.4.8; Ngawang Gelek Demo, vol. 27, 554.1, and Guru Deva, vol. *tsha*, 808.3): *rab dang* is translated throughout as "internal clarity" in accordance with Tsong-kha-pa's own usage in his discussion of that branch at 12.3 (P6148, vol. 154, 172.2.3; Ngawang Gelek Demo, vol. 27, 556.6, and Guru Deva, vol. *tsha*, 810.6), where he has *nang rab dang*.

[c] Tsong-kha-pa, *Notes*, 10.1, following Guru Deva, vol. *tsha*, 808.3, in reading *gsum pa'i yan lag lnga* instead of *gsum pa'i yan lag bzhi*. P6148, vol. 154, 171.4.8, and Ngawang Gelek Demo, vol. 27, 554.1, agree with this text.

analysis; joy; very purified bliss; meditative stabilization; internal clarity; mindfulness; introspection; the compositional factor of equanimity; the feeling of mental bliss; the feeling of equanimity, making eleven.

How they are included [in those substantial entities]: The two joys of the first two concentrations are included in the substantial entity of joy; the two blisses of the first two concentrations are included in the substantial entity of the bliss of pliancy; meditative stabilization is included in the substantial entity of meditative stabilization; the mindfulness of the last two concentrations are included in the substantial entity of mindfulness; the two compositional factors of equanimity of the last two concentrations are included in the substantial entity of the compositional factor of equanimity.

[The system of Asaṅga's *Summary of Manifest Knowledge*.] According to the system of Asaṅga's *Summary of Manifest Knowledge*, they are asserted as nine substantial entities. They are included in the nine: the two, investigation and analysis; the feeling of mental bliss (*tshor ba yid bde*); meditative stabilization; the compositional factor of equanimity; mindfulness; introspection; the feeling of mental bliss (*tshor ba sems bde*), and the feeling of equanimity.

How they are included in those [substantial entities]. The joy and bliss of the first two concentrations are included in the substantial entity of the feeling of mental bliss (*tshor ba yid bde*); meditative stabilization, mindfulness, and the compositional factor of equanimity are [treated] similar[ly to the treatment in Vasubandhu's *Treasury of Manifest Knowledge*]; since internal clarity includes the three—mindfulness, introspection and equanimity—it has no separate substantial entity.

The four identifications of the individual branches

THE BRANCHES OF THE FIRST CONCENTRATION

[Investigation and analysis.] Investigation is imputed to either intention or wisdom that is internal expression which thoroughly examines the mere entity of the meaning. Analysis is imputed to the factor of either intention[a] or wisdom that is internal expression which analyzes in detail the reason for [the meaning]. The Sautrāntikas and above assert that these two arise alternately but do not arise simultaneously. The Vaibhāṣhika system asserts the two, investigation and analysis, as substantially existent minds having the aspects [respectively] of

[a] Tsong-kha-pa, *Notes*, 11.1, reading *sems pa* instead of *sems dpa'*. P6148, vol. 154, 172.1.1; Ngawang Gelek Demo, vol. 27, 555.3, and Guru Deva, vol. *tsha*, 809.4 agree with this text.

coarseness and fineness, and they assert that those two, on the occasion of a mere actual absorption of the first concentration, arise simultaneously and do not arise in stages.

[Joy and bliss.] With respect to bliss, the system of Vasubandhu's *Treasury of Manifest Knowledge* asserts that, since it is the bliss that is the mental factor of pliancy, it is not a feeling, but that joy is the feeling of mental bliss (*tshor ba yid bde*). According to the system of Asaṅga's *Summary of Manifest Knowledge*, the single mental factor that is generated in the sphere of one main mental consciousness and experiences refreshment [is posited as] bliss from the point of view of its helping the body—that is, the sense powers together with their bases—[and it is posited as] joy from the point of view of its refreshing mental bliss (*yid bde*), together with its sphere. It is posited as those two from the point of view of [its having] different functions, but they do not have different substantial entities; this is explained in [Yashomitra's] *Commentary on (Asaṅga's) "Summary of Manifest Knowledge."*

[Meditative stabilization.] Meditative stabilization is the mental factor of one-pointedness that causes the mind and mental factors that are in similar association with it to be collected on one object of observation.

When treated in this way, the three—the two, investigation and analysis, and meditative stabilization—of the system of Asaṅga's *Summary of Manifest Knowledge* are included in the aggregate of compositional factors, and the two—joy and bliss—are included in the aggregate of feeling. [The four]—the two, investigation and analysis, bliss, and meditative stabilization—of the system of Vasubandhu's *Treasury of Manifest Knowledge* are included in the aggregate of compositional factors, and joy is included in the aggregate of feeling.

[The special actual absorption of the first concentration.]
Question: What is this which is called a special actual absorption of the first concentration?

Answer: With reference to an absorption of the first concentration, [12] it is called a special actual absorption of the first concentration with respect to a mere separation from attachment to investigation, and since, moreover, from among the five branches of the first concentration, investigation is the coarsest, separation from attachment to investigation occurs without separation from attachment to the other branches. Therefore, with respect to the first [concentration], a special actual absorption of the first concentration is posited, but since, with respect to the branches of the remaining concentrations, there is no such feature [of one branch being coarser than the others], a special actual absorption is not posited.

THE ACTUAL ABSORPTION[a] OF THE SECOND CONCENTRATION

Internal clarity. It is explained in Vasubandhu's *Treasury of Manifest Knowledge* that [internal clarity] is the faith of conviction in having definitely emerged from the first concentration of the system of Vasubandhu's *Treasury*. [Internal clarity] is explained in Asaṅga's *Compendium of Ascertainments* as the three—mindfulness, introspection, and the compositional factor of equanimity—that are included within the level of the second concentration.[b] The meaning of internal clarity is that it has thoroughly pacified the distraction of the investigation and analysis of the first concentration,[c] which disturbed one's continuum.

[The remaining branches. The explanation of] the three—the two, **joy** and **bliss**, and **meditative stabilization**—is like the explanation of the branches of the first concentration in the individual systems of Vasubandhu's *Treasury of Manifest Knowledge* and Asaṅga's *Grounds of Hearers*.

THE BRANCHES OF THE THIRD CONCENTRATION

From among the five [branches], **mindfulness** is the mental factor, included within the level of the third concentration, which holds on without forgetfulness to the object of observation that is the preceptual instruction of the third concentration; **introspection** is the mental factor, included within the level of the third concentration, which inspects for laxity and excitement; the **compositional factor of equanimity** is the mental factor, included within the level of the third concentration, which is without the inequality of the faults of laxity and excitement; the **feeling of bliss** is a mental factor—[namely,] the experience of refreshment—generated as a concomitant of a single main mental

---

[a] Tsong-kha-pa, *Notes*, 12.2-3, following Guru Deva's reading, *gnyis pa'i dngos gzhi la*, instead of *gnyis pa'i gzhi la* ("the bases [that is, branches] of the second [concentration]") here and at P6148, vol. 154, 172.2.3 and Ngawang Gelek Demo, vol. 27, 556.6. *dngos* is written below the line. Whatever the reading, the heading is an example of the note-taker's faulty parallelism, since the corresponding headings for the other three concentrations are in terms of the branches of those concentrations, not in terms of the actual absorption.

[b] Asaṅga, *Compendium of Ascertainments*, P5539, vol. 111, 14.2.1.

[c] Tsong-kha-pa, *Notes*, following Guru Deva, vol. *tsha*, 811.1, and P6148, vol. 154, 172.2.5, in reading *bsam gtan dang po* instead of *bsam gtan po*. Ngawang Gelek Demo, vol. 27, 557.1, agrees with this text.

consciousness; **meditative stabilization** is as [explained] above.

Question: What is the difference between the joy of the first two concentrations and the bliss of the third? [13]

Answer: Although they are similar in being mental factors generated as concomitants of a single main mental consciousness that experiences refreshment,[a] [this experience] is called joy at the time of pacification of the faults of very great fluctuation with respect to the object [and is called] bliss at the time of the third concentration, which pacifies that [joy], but it is not called joy.

The Vaibhāṣhikas assert that the mental factor of bliss of the first two concentrations is the bliss of pliancy.

The Sautrāntikas ask: While there is[b] a pliancy more marvelous than [that of] the first two concentrations in the third and fourth, why have you not also mentioned the bliss of pliancy [as a branch of the third and fourth concentrations—this being absurd]? Having refuted [the position that the bliss of the first two concentrations is the bliss of pliancy, the Sautrāntikas] assert their own system's bliss of the first [two] concentrations as being the mental factor generated as a concomitant of a single main physical consciousness that experiences refreshment—[that is to say, a bliss concomitant with] a sense consciousness.

The Branches of the Fourth Concentration

From among the four [branches], **completely pure mindfulness** is the mental factor, released from the eight faults of concentration, which holds on without forgetfulness to the object of observation that is the preceptual instruction of the fourth concentration; the **completely pure compositional factor of equanimity** is the mental factor, released from the eight faults of concentration, which is without the inequality of the faults of laxity and excitement; **neutral feeling** is a mental factor generated as a concomitant of a single main mental consciousness, is a feeling of neither refreshment nor anguish, and is a release from the eight faults of concentration which is an experience of neutral

---

[a] Tsong-kha-pa, *Notes,* 13.1, following Guru Deva, vol. *tsha,* 811.5 in reading *sim* instead of *sims.* Ngawang Gelek Demo, vol. 27, 557.5 agrees with this text. P6148, vol. 154, 172.3.2, reads *sem.*

[b] Tsong-kha-pa, *Notes,* 13.2, following P6148, vol. 154, 172.3.4; Ngawang Gelek Demo, vol. 27, 558.1, and Guru Deva, vol. *tsha,* 812.1, in reading *yod bzhin du* instead of *yad bzhin du.*

[feeling]; **meditative stabilization** is as [explained] above.

Question: Why is introspection mentioned as a branch of the third concentration [but] not mentioned as [a branch of] the fourth concentration?

Answer: Since, in the fourth concentration, one is released from the eight faults of concentration, there is no need to inspect for laxity and excitement; therefore, [introspection] is not posited as a branch.

The eight faults of concentration are the two, investigation and analysis; the two, joy and bliss; the two, suffering and mental discomfort; and the two, exhalation and inhalation, [making] eight. Moreover, with respect to the explanation of investigation, analysis, joy, and bliss as faults of concentration, they are faults in terms of levels other [than their own], [14] but they are not faults relative to their own level.

The reason for the definiteness of the number

Question: What is the reason for the branches of the four concentrations being definite as fives and fours?[a]

Answer: The branches of the actual [meditative absorptions] of the concentrations are not definite as these [that is, limited to these] because there are many [branches of] actual meditative absorptions of concentrations which are not any of these branches.

Question: In terms of what meaning are the branches posited as fives and fours?

Answer: In terms of including the main [branches].

Question: In terms of what are the main [branches] included?

Answer: The main are included in terms of antidotal, benefit, and basis branches.

[The first concentration.] The two, the investigation and analysis of the first concentration, are the antidotal branches because they bring about separation from attachment to the afflictions of the lower level.

---

[a] Tsong-kha-pa, *Notes,* 14.1, reading *lnga dang bzhir,* as in 14.2, instead of *bzhi dang lngar.* The latter is inaccurate, since the first and third concentrations each have five branches and the second and fourth each have four, and is another example of the notetaker's faulty parallelism. P6148, vol. 154, 172.4.2; Ngawang Gelek Demo, vol. 27, 559.1, and Guru Deva, vol. *tsha,* 812.6, agree with this text.

Moreover, the way in which the two, investigation and analysis, act as antidotes is in consideration of their being continuations of the investigation and analysis of the preparations; however, the investigation and analysis of the actual absorption merely act to increase[a] the distance from the lower level but are not actual antidotes that abandon [the afflictions of the lower level]. The two, joy and bliss, are the benefit branches because they are generated from having abandoned the afflictions of the lower level. Meditative stabilization is the basis branch because the antidotal branches—investigation and analysis—and the benefit branches—joy and bliss—are generated in dependence upon it.

[The second concentration.] The internal clarity of the second concentration is the antidotal branch because it abandons the investigation and analysis of the first. The way it serves [as this] is similar to that explained above [with regard to the antidotal branches of the first concentration]. The way in which joy and bliss serve as the benefit branches is also similar to [that explained] earlier. Meditative stabilization is also similar to [that explained] earlier.

[The third concentration.] The three—the mindfulness, introspection, and the compositional factor of equanimity of the third concentration—are the antidotal branches [because] they abandon the joy of the second concentration. The other [branches] are similar to [those explained] earlier.

[The fourth concentration.] The completely pure mindfulness and the completely pure compositional factor of equanimity of the fourth concentration [15] are the antidotal branches, since they abandon the bliss of the third. The feeling of equanimity is the benefit branch. Meditative stabilization is the basis branch.

Question: What are the differences among the concentrations in terms of their branches?

[*Answer:*] With respect to the branches of the first two concentrations, there is a difference with respect to the completion or non-completion of meditative stabilization. With respect to the branches of the last two concentrations, there is a difference with respect to the completion or non-completion of help.

Question: What is the reason for positing four concentrations?

---

[a] Tsong-kha-pa, *Notes,* 14.4, reading *sring* instead of *srid.* P6148, vol. 154, 172.4.6, reads *srid.* Ngawang Gelek Demo, vol. 27, 559.5, and Guru Deva, vol. *tsha*, 813.3, also appear to have *srid* but are not clear.

[*Answer:*] Four are posited in terms of definite emergence from faculties of feeling: It is explained in Asaṅga's *Compendium of Ascertainments* that the first is posited in terms of definite emergence from the faculty of the feeling of mental discomfort (*tshor ba yid mi bde'i dbang po*); the second is posited in terms of definite emergence from the faculty of the feeling of suffering (*tshor ba sdug bsngal gyi dbang po*); the third is posited in terms of definite emergence from the faculty of the feeling of mental bliss (*tshor ba yid bde'i dbang po*); the fourth is posited in terms of definite emergence from the faculty of the feeling of bliss (*tshor ba bde ba'i dbang po*).[a]

Having treated them that way, the same work calls the joy and bliss of the first concentration the joy and bliss generated from isolation; it calls the joy and bliss of the second concentration the joy and bliss generated from meditative stabilization; and it calls the bliss of the third concentration the bliss that is without joy. Accordingly, the second concentration is posited by way of discarding the investigation and analysis of the first concentration; the third concentration is posited by way of discarding the joy of the second; and the fourth is posited by way of discarding the bliss of the third. Therefore, the concentrations are explained as passing beyond the lower level by way of their branches.[b]

Analysis of the objects of observation and subjective aspects of the formless absorptions

[Limitless space.] From among the four [limitless space, limitless consciousness, nothingness, and the peak of cyclic existence], the object of observation and subjective aspect of limitless space [are as follows]: A person who has attained the fourth concentration, [16] having seen the fourth concentration as gross, [thinks] for the sake of overcoming it, "The fourth concentration is gross, and limitless space is peaceful, and these are just space." The discrimination of form, which is such appearances as blue and yellow; the discrimination of obstructiveness, which is such appearances as buildings and walls; and the discrimination of various appearances such as groves and rivers vanish in dependence upon one's having become well acquainted for a long time with grossness and peacefulness. When one enters an absorption observing the

[a] Asaṅga, *Compendium of Ascertainments,* P5539, vol. 111, 14.1.1–7 (paraphrase).

[b] Tsong-kha-pa, *Notes,* 15.7, reading *yan lag gi* instead of *yan lag ga.* P6148, vol. 154, 173.1.2; Ngawang Gelek Demo, vol. 27, 561.3, and Guru Deva, vol. *tsha,* 814.6, have the correct reading.

coarse aggregates that are the basis[a] of the name and just space, that is the absorption that is the sphere of limitless space.

[Limitless consciousness.] The object of observation and subjective aspect of the sphere of limitless consciousness[b] [is as follows]: A person who has attained an absorption of the sphere of limitless space, having seen the discrimination of the sphere of limitless space as gross, [thinks] for the sake of overcoming it, "Gross," with respect to limitless space and, "Peaceful" with respect to the sphere of limitless consciousness. In dependence upon having become well acquainted for a long time with grossness and peacefulness, one overcomes the discrimination of limitless space; the discrimination that observes the aggregates of one's own level that are the basis[c] of the name, [thinking,] "Consciousness is limitless," is the absorption of the sphere of limitless consciousness.

[Nothingness.] The object of observation and subjective aspect of the sphere of nothingness [is as follows]: A person who has attained an absorption of the sphere of limitless consciousness, having seen the discrimination of the sphere of limitless consciousness as gross, for the sake of overcoming it [thinks], "Gross," with respect to the sphere of limitless consciousness and, "Peaceful," with respect to the sphere of nothingness. In dependence upon having become well acquainted for a long time with grossness and peacefulness, one overcomes the discrimination of limitless consciousness. [Thinking,] "There is not even any object of observation that has form or is formless," one enters an absorption observing the coarse aggregates that are the basis[d] of the name; [17] that is the absorption of the sphere of nothingness.

---

[a] Tsong-kha-pa, *Notes,* 16.2, reading *ming gzhi'i phung po* instead of *ming bzhi'i phung po.* Jeffrey Hopkins' emendation. P6148, vol. 154, 173.1.5; Ngawang Gelek Demo, vol. 27, 561.6, and Guru Deva, vol. *tsha,* 815.3, agree with this text. However, in "name and form," the fourth of the twelve links of dependent-arising, the four mental aggregates are the basis of the name.

[b] Tsong-kha-pa, *Notes,* 16.3, reading *rnam shes mtha' yas skye mched kyi dmigs rnam* instead of *nam mkha' mtha' yas skye mched kyi dmigs rnam.* P6148, vol. 154, 173.1.6; Ngawang Gelek Demo, vol. 27, 561.6, and Guru Deva, vol. *tsha,* 815.3, agree with this text.

[c] Tsong-kha-pa, *Notes,* 16.5, reading *ming gzhi'i phung po* instead of *ming bzhi'i phung po.* Jeffrey Hopkins' emendation. P6148, vol. 154, 173.1.8; Ngawang Gelek Demo, vol. 27, 562.3, and Guru Deva, vol. *tsha,* 815.5, agree with this text.

[d] Tsong-kha-pa, *Notes,* 16.7, reading *ming gzhi'i phung po* instead of *ming bzhi'i phung po.* Jeffrey Hopkins' emendation. P6148, vol. 154, 173.2.3; Ngawang Gelek Demo, vol. 27, 562.5, and Guru Deva, vol. *tsha,* 816.1-2, agree with this text.

[The peak of cyclic existence.] The object of observation and subjective aspect of the sphere of no discrimination and no non-discrimination [is as follows]: A person who has attained an absorption of the sphere of nothingness, having seen the discrimination of the sphere of nothingness as gross, [thinks] for the sake of overcoming it, "The utter non-existence of discrimination is thorough obscuration. Coarse discrimination is an ache that is an effect of illness. That state in which coarse discrimination does not exist and subtle [discrimination] is not non-existent is peaceful; it is auspicious; it is definite emergence." In dependence upon having become well acquainted for a long time with grossness and peacefulness, [thinking,] "Coarse discrimination does not exist and subtle [discrimination] is not non-existent," one enters an absorption observing the coarse aggregates of one's own level that are the basis[a] of the name; that is the absorption of [the sphere of] no discrimination and no non-discrimination.

Accordingly, the sphere of limitless consciousness is posited by way of discarding the sphere of limitless space; the sphere of nothingness [is posited] in dependence upon discarding [limitless consciousness, and] the sphere of without discrimination and without non-discrimination [is posited] in dependence upon discarding [nothingness]. Therefore, the formless absorptions are said to pass beyond the lower level by way of the object of observation.

Explanation of the effects of having cultivated those [absorptions]

These [effects] are the birth concentrations and the birth formless absorptions. By having cultivated the three [types]—small, middling, and great—with respect to each of the absorptions of the concentrations, one achieves the three [types of] birth in each of the Four Concentrations. Moreover, since most of the factors of the mundane beings of the Concentrations, which are attained through birth there, are fruitional effects of the concentrations that are [actual] absorptions, and the mundane environments of [the Concentrations] are owned effects of [the concentrations that are actual absorptions, these fruitional and owned effects] are birth concentrations. Similarly, with respect to the absorptions of the formless absorptions, by having cultivated the three

[a] Tsong-kha-pa, *Notes*, 17.3, reading *ming gzhi'i phung po* instead of *ming bzhi'i phung po*. Jeffrey Hopkins' emendation. P6148, vol. 154, 173.2.7; Ngawang Gelek Demo, vol. 27, 563.3, and Guru Deva, vol. *tsha*, 816.5, agree with this text.

[types]—small, middling, and great, [18] one achieves the birth of a being of the Formless Absorptions. Since most of the factors attained from birth by sentient beings who are born in [the Formless Absorptions] are fruitional effects of the absorptions of the formless absorptions, [these fruitional effects] are birth formless absorptions.

Concerning the meaning of small, middling, and great: If one has neither intense nor continual application, that is the small [type]; if one has either [intense or continual application, but not both, that is] the middling [type]; if one has both, [that is] the great [type].

[III.] The Attainers—The Persons Who Are the Basis

Except for the sphere of nothingness, the other seven [absorptions are attained by] someone having the basis of either their own level or the level below them, but the sphere of nothingness [is attained by] those having the basis of the three—its own level, the level below it, and the level above it.

[IV.] Explanation of the Signs of Attainment

It is explained in Asaṅga's *Grounds of Hearers* that signs arise—namely, that the sign of the attainment of the absorptions of the concentrations is, for instance, the appearance that one's body is sinking and that the sign of the attainment of the absorptions of the formless absorptions is, for instance, the appearance that one's body is flying in space.

[This was] put together by the glorious Lo-sang-drak-pa [that is, Tsong-kha-pa]. Best of fortune!

Kön-chok-jik-may-wang-po's *Condensed Statement of (Jam-yang-shay-pa's) "Great Exposition of the Concentrations and Formless Absorptions," An Excellent Vase of Eloquence Presenting the Concentrations and Formless Absorptions*

[538]

Namo gurumunīndrāya!

I prostrate myself in homage in the presence of the inseparable ones:
Mañjughoṣha, treasury of the doctrine of ten million Ones Gone Thus (*de bzhin gshegs pa, tathāgata*);
Tsong-kha-pa, sovereign of the complete teaching;
The one with the name Jam-yang, scholar who increased good explanation without precedent.[a]

I bow to the assembly of spiritual guides, skilled proponents
Who satisfy those of small awareness with the essence
Of the nectar of good explanation, [drawn by] the bees
Of individual investigation from the open saffron-flower of great mercy.

Listen in this way, you who desire knowledge of the principles
Of the yoga of the union of calm abiding and special insight,
That which brings vast joy to the minds of the Subduers
And is the basis of achieving immeasurable qualities worthy of praise!

The explanation[b] here of the presentation of the highway of all yogis of the three times, [539] the basis of all the great meditative stabilizations—the meditative absorptions of the concentrations and formless absorptions—has three [topics]: the explanations of (1) the basis of cultivation; (2) the meditative stabilizations of the concentrations and formless absorptions that are to be cultivated; and (3) enumeration of the meditative stabilizations of Buddhas and Bodhisattvas in dependence upon that.

---

[a] Jam-yang is Mañjughoṣha; "the one with the name Jam-yang" is Jam-yang-shay-pa.

[b] *De la,* "with respect to that," has not been translated when it merely serves as a paragraph marker and has no specific referent.

1 THE BASIS OF CULTIVATION

This section has two topics: the explanations of the physical and mental bases.

THE PHYSICAL BASIS

REFUTATION [OF MISTAKEN OPINIONS]

First debate

Incorrect position: In [someone having] a physical basis of the three bad transmigrations or [the northern continent] Unpleasant Sound, there is [retention of] possession of actual meditative absorptions already attained.

Correct position: It follows that that is incorrect because whoever is a person of an upper realm who is about to die and who is definite to be reborn in [a bad transmigration or Unpleasant Sound] in the next birth necessarily degenerates from the actual meditative absorption of that [upper realm]. This is because (1) whoever is [a person of an upper realm who is about to die and who is definite to be reborn in a bad transmigration or Unpleasant Sound] necessarily manifests gross craving, and so forth, which is included within the level of the Desire Realm and (2) a person who simultaneously possesses in his or her continuum manifest afflictions of the Desire Realm and an actual meditative absorption does not occur.

Second debate

Incorrect position: It follows that there exists a new generation of an actual meditative absorption of a concentration in [someone having] the physical basis of [any of] the three bad transmigrations [hell beings, hungry ghosts, and animals] [540] because there exists a new generation of the four immeasurables in [someone having] a physical basis of [any of the three bad transmigrations]. This is because a new generation of the two, [great] love and great compassion, exists in [someone having] the physical basis of [any of the bad transmigrations].

Correct position: It is not entailed [that if a new generation of the two, great love and great compassion, exists in someone having the physical basis of any of the bad transmigrations, a new generation of the four immeasurables in someone having such a physical basis necessarily exists].

The reason [namely, that a new generation of the two, great love and great compassion, exists in someone having the physical basis of any of the bad transmigrations] is established because new generation of the seven cause-and-effect quintessential instructions [for generating the altruistic mind of enlightenment] exists in [someone having such a basis].

Incorrect position with respect to that: New generation of a Mahāyāna altruistic intention to become enlightened does not exist in [someone having] a physical basis of the bad transmigrations because there is no new generation of the four immeasurables in [someone having] a physical basis of [the bad transmigrations].[a]

Correct position: It is not entailed [that if there is no new generation of the four immeasurables in someone having a physical basis of the bad transmigrations, there is necessarily no new generation of a Mahāyāna altruistic intention to become enlightened in someone having a physical basis of the bad transmigrations]. The reason [namely, that there is no new generation of the four immeasurables in someone having a physical basis of the bad transmigrations] is established because (1) according to Asaṅga's *Summary of Manifest Knowledge*, the four immeasurables are necessarily actual meditative absorptions and (2) according to Vasubandhu's *Treasury of Manifest Knowledge*, immeasurable joy is explained as existing in the first two concentrations and the other three [immeasurables—love, compassion, and equanimity] are explained as existing in the six—the not-unable preparation, the special first concentration, and the four concentrations.[b] It is entailed [that since, according to Asaṅga's *Summary of Manifest Knowledge,* the four immeasurables are necessarily actual meditative absorptions and, according to Vasubandhu's *Treasury of Manifest Knowledge,* immeasurable joy is explained as existing in the first two concentrations and the other three immeasurables as existing in the six—the not-unable, the special first concentration, and the four concentrations—there is necessarily no new generation of the four immeasurables in someone having a

[a] Great love and great compassion are, respectively, the fourth and fifth of the seven.

[b] Vasubandhu, *Treasury of Manifest Knowledge* and *Autocommentary on the "Treasury of Manifest Knowledge,"* 8.31a–b (P5591, vol. 115, 276.1.6–7; Shastri, part 4, pp. 1172–73; La Vallée Poussin, 16:5, p. 199; Pruden, vol. 4, p. 1267).

physical basis of the bad transmigrations] because, no matter which of those systems one follows, there is no generation of those [immeasurables] in the three bad transmigrations.

Third debate

Incorrect position: Gods who are about to take rebirth[a] in the three bad transmigrations exist.

Correct position: This is incorrect because whoever is about to take rebirth in [a bad transmigration] must be an intermediate-state being.

Fourth debate

Incorrect position: When an aeon is destroyed, those in the bad transmigrations are persons who must newly achieve a meditative absorption upon being born in the happy transmigrations.

Correct position: It follows that this is also incorrect because (1) with respect to those in the bad transmigrations, there are also cases of those who are definite to attain liberation before [the destruction of the aeon]; (2) also, before that, there are those whose karmic obstructions are used up, and (3) there are also those who are definite to be reborn in the bad transmigrations of another world-system without their karmic obstructions being used up.

Fifth debate

Incorrect position: Whoever is a being of the bad transmigrations [541] is necessarily someone who possesses strong karmic obstructions in his or her continuum.

Correct position: It [absurdly] follows that the subject, someone in a bad transmigration who, having used up his or her strong karmic obstructions, is about to die and is definite to attain a basis of leisure and fortune in the next life, [possesses strong karmic obstructions in his or her continuum] because of being [someone in the bad transmigrations].

Sixth debate

Incorrect position: In a basis of one's own level, there is no cultivation of an actual meditative absorption of one's own level, but in a basis of a

---

[a] Literally "assume the birth state."

lower level, there is cultivation of an actual meditative absorption of an upper level, and in a basis of an upper level, there is no cultivation of an actual meditative absorption of a lower level because Vasubandhu's *Treasury of Manifest Knowledge* [8.19c–d] says [according to the opponent's incorrect translation]:

> In a basis of one's own or a lower level in the concentrations and formless absorptions,
> There is no need [to cultivate a meditative absorption of] a lower [level].[a]

Correct position: It is not entailed [that this passage from Vasubandhu's *Treasury of Manifest Knowledge* means that in a basis of one's own level, there is no cultivation of an actual meditative absorption of one's own level, but in a basis of a lower level, there is cultivation of an actual meditative absorption of an upper level, and in a basis of an upper level, there is no cultivation of an actual meditative absorption of a lower level].

It [absurdly] follows that this passage indicates that in a basis of one's own level, there is no cultivation of an actual meditative absorption of one's own level because you have accepted [that in a basis of one's own level, there is no cultivation of an actual meditative absorption of one's own level]. You cannot accept [that that passage from Vasubandhu's *Treasury of Manifest Knowledge* indicates that in a basis of one's own level, there is no cultivation of an actual meditative absorption of one's own level] because this passage indicates that there are cases of actualizing the eight concentrations and formless absorptions in a basis of either one's own or a lower level.

Incorrect position with respect to that: It follows that there is no cultivation of an actual meditative absorption of a lower level in a basis of an upper level because Vasubandhu's *Autocommentary on the "Treasury of Manifest Knowledge"* says:

> *Question:* Why does someone who is born in an upper [level] not actualize a lower level of meditative absorption?
>
> *Answer:* It is thus that that [person] "has no need [to cultivate] the lower [meditative absorption]." That person has not the least need of the substantial entity of the lower meditative

---

[a] Vasubandhu, *Treasury of Manifest Knowledge,* 8.19c–d (P5591, vol. 115, 274.3.6–7; Shastri, part 4, p. 1158; La Vallée Poussin, 16:5, p. 175; Pruden, vol. 4, p. 1250).

absorption because it is inferior.[a]

Correct position: It is not entailed [that this passage means that there is necessarily no cultivation of an actual meditative absorption of a lower level in a basis of an upper level]. This is because such is the case in general, but as an exception, it is explained that there is a cultivation of a meditative absorption of [the level of] Nothingness in [that is, by persons having] a basis of the Peak of Cyclic Existence. This is because Vasubandhu's *Treasury of Manifest Knowledge* [8.20a–b] says:

> A Superior in the Peak of Cyclic Existence exhausts contamination [542]
> Having actualized [a meditative absorption of the level of] Nothingness.[b]

It is entailed [that this passage means that there is a cultivation of a meditative absorption of the level of Nothingness in a basis of the Peak of Cyclic Existence] because, although in general there is no need to cultivate a meditative absorption of a lower level in a basis of an upper level, since the mind of the Peak of Cyclic Existence has unclear discrimination, it is not suitable as a [mental] basis of a supramundane path that eliminates cyclic existence for the Hīnayāna, and therefore, it must depend on some lower level,[c] and moreover, since the realms and objects of observation are close, there is the exception that there is one that depends on Nothingness.

Seventh debate

Incorrect position in dependence upon the mere literal reading of Asaṅga's "Summary of Manifest Knowledge": Whatever is a meditative absorption of the peak of cyclic existence is necessarily not a supramundane path.

Correct position: It [absurdly] follows that the subject, a newly attained meditative absorption of the peak of cyclic existence in the continuum of a Superior, [is not a supramundane path] because of being [a meditative absorption of the peak of cyclic existence].

You cannot accept [that a newly attained meditative absorption of

---

[a] Vasubandhu, *Autocommentary on the "Treasury of Manifest Knowledge,"* 8.19c–d (P5591, vol. 115, 274.3.7–8; Shastri, part 4, p. 1158; La Vallée Poussin, 16:5, p. 175; Pruden, vol. 4, p. 1250).

[b] Vasubandhu, *Treasury of Manifest Knowledge,* 8.20a–b (P5591, vol. 115, 274.3.8; Shastri, part 4, p. 1159; La Vallée Poussin, 16:5, p. 175; Pruden, vol. 4, p. 1251).

[c] 542.2, omitting *phyir* before *'og sa gcig.*

the peak of cyclic existence in the continuum of a Superior is not a supramundane path] because it is a supramundane path. It follows [that it is a supramundane path] because of being a Superior path.[a] This is because it is among the eight newly attained meditative absorptions in the continuum of a Superior.

Eighth debate

Incorrect position: Whatever is a meditative absorption of the peak of cyclic existence necessarily does not have the aspect of non-true existence.

Correct position: It [absurdly] follows that the subject, a meditative absorption of the peak of cyclic existence which serves as the mental basis of an uninterrupted path of the Mahāyāna path of meditation, [does not have the aspect of non-true existence] because of being [a meditative absorption of the peak of cyclic existence].

Ninth debate

Incorrect position: Whatever is a meditative absorption of the peak of cyclic existence necessarily has an unclear object of observation and subjective aspect.

Correct position: There is no definiteness [in the entailment that whatever is a meditative absorption of the peak of cyclic existence necessarily has an unclear object of observation and subjective aspect] because of [the meditative absorption of the peak of cyclic existence] in the continuum of a Buddha Superior.

OUR OWN SYSTEM

Those who have [committed] the powerful actions of abandoning the doctrine or the [five] heinous crimes, which have been accumulated but not yet purified, can neither newly generate meditative absorptions nor keep what has already been generated because they have very strong karmic obstructions. [543] Neuter persons, eunuchs, androgynes, and so forth, do not have new generation of these [meditative absorptions] because they have very great afflictive obstructions. Those in the three bad transmigrations [hell beings, hungry ghosts, and animals], sentient beings without discrimination, and those having a basis

---

[a] That is to say, a path in the continuum of a Superior.

in [the continent] Unpleasant Sound have no new generation of these [meditative absorptions] because they have very strong fruitional obstructions and because those in the bad transmigrations are strongly tormented by suffering and also by reason of [the fact that] those in Unpleasant Sound and without discrimination cannot do much investigation and analysis.

Those having a basis in Unpleasant Sound, neuter persons, eunuchs, androgynes, or [those having a basis in] the bad transmigrations do not have either new generation or continued possession of the preparations for the concentrations on up because (1) in order to attain [new generation of the preparations for the concentrations], one must have concentrative discipline and (2) there is no generation of either concentrative discipline or a vow of individual liberation or a bad vow [for those having such bases]. Demigods also cannot [generate the preparations for the concentrations on up] because they have very strong obstructions of jealousy and of [being that kind of] transmigrator.

Therefore, those with a physical basis of humans of the [other] three continents have new generation [of the concentrations and formless absorptions] because (1) they have new generation of the three—concentrative discipline, [vows of] individual liberation, and uncontaminated discipline and (2) the meditative absorptions of the concentrations and their discipline are equivalent in terms of basis [that is, who can have them]. Those with a basis of [any of the] six [types of] gods of the Desire Realm and with a basis of the Form Realm also have new generation because they have new generation of concentrative discipline.

There is cultivation of a meditative absorption of a lower level by those with a basis of an upper level because there is a final meditative stabilization in the continuum of a Hearer Superior who has a basis of the Fourth Concentration [544] and because there are leapover meditative absorptions (*thod rgyal gyi snyoms 'jug, vyutkrāntakasamāpatti*) in the continuum of a Bodhisattva Superior who has a basis of [the Fourth Concentration], as well as others.

There is cultivation of the eight concentrations and formless absorptions by those who have bases of their own and lower levels because (1) with respect to the meditative absorption of the peak of cyclic existence, for instance, there is actualization of the eight ranging from its own level, the Peak of Cyclic Existence, to a lower level, the Desire Realm, and similarly, with respect to [the actual meditative absorption of] nothingness, there is actualization of the seven ranging from its own level down to the Desire Realm and (2) it is permissible to extend the reasoning in this way for the remaining [meditative absorptions].

There is new attainment of the actual meditative absorptions in the basis of a Hearer because, although whoever is either a Stream Enterer or a Once Returner has necessarily not attained [the actual meditative absorptions], whoever is either a Non-Returner or a Foe Destroyer has necessarily attained them.

Dispelling objections

First debate

Incorrect position: It follows that there are humans who are about to be born as gods of the Form Realm because there are humans who are about to be born in the Form Realm.

Correct position: It is not entailed [that since there are humans who are about to be born in the Form Realm, there are necessarily humans who are about to be born as gods of the Form Realm].

Another incorrect position: It follows that there are no humans who are about to be born as gods because there are no humans who are about to be born as gods of the Desire or Form Realms.

Correct position: It is not entailed [that since there are no humans who are about to be born as gods of the Desire or Form Realms, there are necessarily no humans who are about to be born as gods].

You cannot accept [that there are no humans who are about to be born as gods] because there are humans who are about to be born as gods of the Formless Realm. It follows [that there are humans who are about to be born as gods of the Formless Realm] because, to be born as a god of the Formless Realm, one does not have to pass through an intermediate state.

Another incorrect position: It follows that there are humans who are about to be born in the bad transmigrations because there are humans who are about to achieve an intermediate state of the bad transmigrations.

Correct position: It is not entailed [that since there are humans who are about to achieve an intermediate state of the bad transmigrations, there are necessarily humans who are about to be born in the bad transmigrations].

Second debate

Incorrect position: There are those in Unpleasant Sound who, having died, are definite to be born in an upper realm without being interrupted by another birth-state.

Correct position: It follows that this is incorrect because whoever is a being in Unpleasant Sound is necessarily born as any of the six types of gods of the Desire Realm in the next birth. [545]

Third debate

Incorrect position: It follows that there is a common locus of being a Desire Realm mind and being an uninterrupted path of the path of meditation because [a meditative absorption of] the peak of cyclic existence is [a common locus of being a mind of the Formless Realm and being an uninterrupted path of the path of meditation]. If you accept [that there is a common locus of being a Desire Realm mind and being an uninterrupted path of the path of meditation], it follows that the subject, [the common locus of being a Desire Realm mind and being an uninterrupted path of the path of meditation], is a mind of non-equipoise because of being a mind that is included within the level of non-equipoise.

Correct position: It is not entailed [that a mind included within the level of non-equipoise is necessarily a mind of non-equipoise].

The reason [namely, that the common locus of being a Desire Realm mind and being an uninterrupted path of the path of meditation is a mind that is included within the level of non-equipoise] is established because it is a Desire Realm mind.

Another incorrect position: It follows that there is a common locus of being a Desire Realm mind and being the uninterrupted path of the path of seeing because you have accepted [that there is a common locus of being a Desire Realm mind and being an uninterrupted path of the path of meditation].

Correct position: It is not entailed [that since there is a common locus of being a Desire Realm mind and being an uninterrupted path of the path of meditation, there is necessarily a common locus of being a Desire Realm mind and being the uninterrupted path of the path of seeing] because Gyel-tsap's *Explanation of (Maitreya's) "Ornament for Clear Realization," Ornament for the Essence* says:

[Haribhadra] explains in [his] *Great Commentary* [*on Maitreya's "Ornament for Clear Realization"*] that the path of meditation [can] depend upon a Desire Realm mind and the peak of cyclic existence, but I think that this cannot characterize the path of seeing.[a]

Mental Bases

Refutation [of mistaken opinions]

First debate

Incorrect position: Whatever is a mental basis of a given consciousness is necessarily of a similar type to that consciousness and acts as its substantial cause.
Correct position: It [absurdly] follows that whatever is a mental basis of a Mahāyāna altruistic mind generation is necessarily a substantial cause of [that altruistic mind generation][b] because [according to you] your thesis [that whatever is a mental basis of a given consciousness is necessarily of a similar type to that consciousness and acts as its substantial cause] is correct.

If you accept [that whatever is a mental basis of a Mahāyāna altruistic mind generation is necessarily its substantial cause], it [absurdly] follows that the subject, the faith that serves as the mental basis of Mahāyāna altruistic mind generation, is necessarily its substantial cause because you have accepted [that whatever is a mental basis of a Mahāyāna altruistic mind generation is necessarily its substantial cause]. You cannot accept [that the faith that serves as the mental basis of a Mahāyāna altruistic mind generation is necessarily its substantial cause] because whatever is a substantial cause of a main consciousness or a [main] mind must be either a [main] mind or the mental constituent.

Moreover, it follows that [the position that the faith which serves as the mental basis of a Mahāyāna altruistic mind generation is necessarily its substantial cause] is incorrect because, on the one hand, accompanying mental factors act as mental bases of main minds, and on the other, faith and aspiration, individually, [546] act as mental bases of

---

[a] Gyel-tsap, *Explanation of (Maitreya's) "Ornament for Clear Realization," Ornament for the Essence* (Buxaduor: n.p. 1967?), 164b.3.

[b] What is substituted for "a given consciousness" is "a Mahāyāna altruistic mind generation."

effort, concentration, and so forth.

The first reason [namely, that accompanying mental factors act as mental bases of main minds] is established because, when one sets [the mind] one-pointedly in meditative equipoise on one's object, the element of qualities [that is, emptiness—that meditative equipoise being] induced by the faith of conviction which is a gaining of ascertaining knowledge with respect to that [object]—that mind has been generated in the entity of that faith, and at that time such faith is the mental basis of that [mind which is in one-pointed meditative equipoise on emptiness]. This is because, although [something] may be simultaneous [with it], if that something has not become of the entity of it and is a different entity, it cannot be posited as the mental basis of that something.

The second reason [namely, that faith and aspiration, individually, act as a mental basis of effort, concentration, and so forth] is established because, when one makes effort for the sake of an object of observation with strong force of faith and aspiration, [the mental factor of effort] becomes of the entity of that [faith and aspiration] without the dissipation of the force of that faith and aspiration, at which time those two such [faith and aspiration] are the mental basis of that effort, and it is the same sort of thing for other [mental factors and consciousnesses].

Our Own System

Although we use the mere verbal convention "based on" for a [given] consciousness' acting as a substantial cause of a [given] mind, and so forth, this is not posited as the meaning of mental basis in this context because, if it were posited this way, there would be the fault that one would have to assert many [things] that are explained as unsuitable to be mental bases, such as that there are non-virtuous consciousnesses for which virtuous consciousnesses act as the mental basis. Therefore, the meaning of [mental basis] does not at all occur in earlier and later cause and effect.

With respect to the subject, the ninth mental abiding and the meditative absorptions ranging from [those of] the first concentration to the peak of cyclic existence, there is a mode of their acting as the mental bases of paths that depend[a] on them because, just as when iron is burned, the iron becomes of the entity of the fire, those [meditative absorptions] act as the mental bases of [paths] by way of paths' becoming of their entities.

---

[a] 546.5, reading *brten pa* instead of *rten pa,* following Jam-yang-shay-pa, *Concentrations,* 39.7 and *Collected Works,* vol. 12, 37.5.

DISPELLING OBJECTIONS

First debate

Incorrect position: It follows that whatever is a mental basis of [a given] path is necessarily that path [547] because the mode of [the path's] becoming [the mental basis of that path] exists.

Correct position: It is not entailed [that if the mode of a path's becoming the mental basis of that path exists, then whatever is a mental basis of a given path is necessarily that path]. This is because, although a [main] mind associated with hatred becomes of the entity of hatred, it is not hatred [which is a mental factor].

Second debate

Incorrect position: It follows that [a given] earlier mind is the mental basis of a later mind because (1) [the earlier mind] is a mind and (2) that earlier mind is the basis of that later mind.

Correct position: It is not entailed [that if a given earlier mind is a mind and that earlier mind is the basis of that later mind, the earlier mind is necessarily the mental basis of the later mind].

Incorrect position with respect to that: It follows that it *is* entailed [that if a given earlier mind is a mind and that earlier mind is the basis of that later mind, the earlier mind is necessarily the mental basis of the later mind] because there is a name for an earlier mind's acting as the basis of a later mind.

Correct position: It is also not entailed [that if there is a name for an earlier mind's acting as the basis of a later mind, then, if the earlier mind is a mind and that earlier mind is the basis of that later mind, the earlier mind is necessarily the mental basis of the later mind] because this is called "the basis which is the similar immediately preceding condition." It follows [that this is called "the basis which is the similar immediately preceding condition"] because the inability of an earlier virtuous mind of the Desire Realm to serve as the basis of a later mind of the Formless Realm is described as its not being able to serve as a basis which is a similar immediately preceding condition of that [mind].

Third debate

Incorrect position: It follows that the subject, the faith that serves as the mental basis of a Mahāyāna altruistic mind generation, possesses the aspect of faith because of being faith.

Correct position: It is not entailed [that whatever is faith necessarily possesses the aspect of faith]. You cannot accept [that the faith that serves as the mental basis of a Mahāyāna altruistic mind generation possesses the aspect of faith] because it possesses the aspect of a wish. It follows [that it possesses the aspect of a wish] because of being faith that is a wish [to attain].

2 THE MEDITATIVE STABILIZATIONS OF THE CONCENTRATIONS AND FORMLESS ABSORPTIONS THAT ARE TO BE CULTIVATED

[547.5]

The presentation of the concentrations and formless absorptions that are to be cultivated has two [parts]: explanation of the presentation of the preparations, the means of attainment, and explanation of the actual meditative absorptions that are to be attained.

EXPLANATION OF THE PRESENTATION OF THE PREPARATIONS, THE MEANS OF ATTAINMENT

This has two [parts]: explanation of the two, calm abiding and special insight, which include all meditative stabilizations, and explanation of the mode of entering into meditative absorption in the eight concentrations and formless absorptions by way of the seven mental contemplations.

EXPLANATION OF THE TWO, CALM ABIDING AND SPECIAL INSIGHT, WHICH INCLUDE ALL MEDITATIVE STABILIZATIONS

This has two [parts]: explanation of actual calm abiding and special insight and explanation of the mode of training individually in calm abiding and special insight.

Explanation of actual calm abiding and special insight

[Refutation of mistaken opinions]

FIRST DEBATE

Incorrect position: [548] Asaṅga's *Summary of Manifest Knowledge* says: "What is calm abiding? It is as follows:...,"[a] and the *Sūtra Unraveling the Thought* says:

> Also, Maitreya, all the mundane and supramundane virtuous

---

[a] Asaṅga, *Summary of Manifest Knowledge,* P5550, vol. 112, 263.2.8–263.3.1; Rahula, trans., *Le Compendium de la super-doctrine*, p. 126. Paṇ-chen Sö-nam-drak-pa, "Concentrations," 155b.1–2 cites the complete passage.

> phenomena of Hearers, Bodhisattvas, and Ones Gone Thus are to be known[a] as fruits of calm abiding and special insight.[b]

Whatever is the calm abiding explicitly indicated in those two texts is necessarily calm abiding. Whatever is the special insight explicitly indicated in [those two texts] is necessarily special insight.

Correct position: With respect to the first [wrong opinion, that whatever is the calm abiding explicitly indicated in those two texts is necessarily calm abiding], it [absurdly] follows that the subject, the meditative stabilizations from the meditative stabilization of the first mental abiding through the meditative stabilization of the ninth mental abiding, [is calm abiding] because of [being calm abidings explicitly indicated in those two texts].[c]

With respect to the second [wrong opinion, that whatever is the special insight explicitly indicated in those two texts is necessarily special insight], it [absurdly] follows that the subject, wisdom consciousnesses that distinguish phenomena, that thoroughly distinguish [phenomena], and so forth, are special insights because of being special insights explicitly indicated in those two [texts]. It follows [that wisdom consciousnesses that distinguish phenomena, that thoroughly distinguish phenomena, and so forth, are special insights explicitly indicated in those two texts] because, since those wisdom consciousnesses are in the class of special insight, they, having been designated by the name of special insight, are indicated with reference to their effect. [It is stated] thus in Tsong-kha-pa's [great and medium-length] *Exposition of the Stages of the Path.*

SECOND DEBATE

Incorrect position: The non-existence of intensity in the factor of clarity in a non-scattering[d] mind is calm abiding, and the existence of that [intensity in the factor of clarity in a non-scattering mind] is special insight.

Correct position: It [absurdly] follows that the meaning of the passage in

---

[a] 548.2, reading *rig par bya'o* instead of *rigs par bya'o.*

[b] Lamotte, *Saṃdhinirmocanasūtra*, pp. 111, 227.

[c] The subject comes from the Asaṅga citation, which goes on to list the nine mental abidings. Paṇ-chen Sö-nam-drak-pa also has a debate on this citation. (*Meditative States,* pp. 170, 236 n.25; Walpola Rahula, trans., *Le Compendium de la super-doctrine (philosophie) (Abhidharmasamuccaya) d'Asaṅga* [Paris: École française d'extrême-orient, 1971], p. 126).

[d] 548.5, reading *mi 'phro bar* instead of *mi 'gro bar.*

the *Cloud of Jewels Sūtra* (*ratnameghasūtra, dkon mchog sprin gyi mdo*)—"Calm abiding is a one-pointed mind. Special insight is correct individual analysis"—is not established because [according to you] calm abiding is not posited as a one-pointed meditative stabilization and special insight is not posited [549] as a wisdom consciousness that analyzes—that individually investigates phenomena correctly. This is because [according to you] both calm abiding and special insight are posited as solely the clear meditative stabilization of a one-pointed mind. This is because [according to you] the factor of stability in that clear meditative stabilization is calm abiding and the factor of clarity, special insight. You have asserted the reason [namely, that the factor of stability in that clear meditative stabilization is calm abiding and the factor of clarity, special insight].

It is entailed [that if the factor of abiding in that clear meditative stabilization is calm abiding and the factor of clarity, special insight, then both calm abiding and special insight are necessarily to be posited as solely the clear meditative stabilization of a one-pointed mind] because all meditative stabilizations that are free of laxity and excitement necessarily have both abiding in a one-pointed mind and intensity of clarity. This is because all meditative stabilizations that are free of laxity have intensity of clarity and all meditative stabilizations that are free of excitement have the factor of stability.

THIRD DEBATE

Incorrect position: The definition of a calm abiding is:

> a steady meditative stabilization in which the prominence[a] of laxity and excitement has been broken and the mind is one-pointed.

Correct position: It [absurdly] follows that the subject, the meditative stabilization of the ninth mental abiding, which is a Desire Realm mind, is calm abiding because of being a steady meditative stabilization in which the prominence of laxity and excitement has been broken.

The reason [namely, that the meditative stabilization of the ninth mental abiding, which is a Desire Realm mind, is a steady meditative stabilization in which the prominence of laxity and excitement has been broken and the mind is one-pointed] is established because, at the time of [the ninth mental abiding], the fault of laxity and excitement does not exist and one has already gained a steady meditative

[a] 549.3, reading *dbal chag* instead of *dbal chog.*

stabilization in which the prominence or intensity of those [namely, laxity and excitement] has been broken. This is because Tsong-kha-pa's *Great Exposition of the Stages of the Path* says:

> Although, having attained the ninth mind [of the Desire Realm], one has not purposely made the exertion of entering into equipoise, one's mind goes entirely into meditative stabilization.[a]

You cannot accept the root statement [that the meditative stabilization of the ninth mental abiding, which is a Desire Realm mind, is calm abiding] because it is a meditative stabilization before one has attained pliancy. It is entailed [that whatever is a meditative stabilization before one has attained pliancy is necessarily not calm abiding] because, until one has attained pliancy, that meditative stabilization is a similitude of calm abiding, but when one has attained pliancy, it is posited as calm abiding.

Moreover, it [absurdly] follows that the subject, the meditative stabilization of the ninth mind of the Desire Realm, [550] is of a level of equipoise[b] because [according to you] it is calm abiding. You have asserted the reason [namely, that the ninth mind of the Desire Realm is calm abiding].

It is entailed [that whatever is calm abiding is necessarily of a level of equipoise] because, in terms of arising from training, the attainment of calm abiding, the attainment[c] of a mind included within the level of equipoise, the attainment of a mind included within the levels of an upper realm, the attainment of a preparation for the first concentration, the attainment of the preparation [called] the not-unable, the attainment of a lesser meditative stabilization or one-pointed mind included within the levels of an upper realm, and the attainment of physical and mental pliancy are simultaneous. This is because Asaṅga's *Grounds of Hearers* says:

> The signs of having a mental contemplation of a beginner are these: the attainment of a lesser [kind of the] mind involved in the Form Realm in this way, and the attainment of lesser [kinds of] the four—physical pliancy, mental pliancy, and a

---

[a] Tsong-kha-pa, *Great Exposition of the Stages of the Path* (Dharamsala: shes rig par khang, no date), 724.4–5.

[b] 550.1, reading *mnyam par bzhag pa'i sa'i* instead of *mnyam par bzhag sa'i sa.*

[c] 550.1, reading *thob pa* instead of *thab pa.*

lesser one-pointed mind....[a]

It is entailed [that this passage from Asaṅga's *Grounds of Hearers* means that, in terms of arising from training, the attainment of calm abiding, the attainment of a mind included within the level of equipoise, the attainment of a mind included within the levels of an upper realm, the attainment of a preparation for the first concentration, the attainment of the preparation called the not-unable, the attainment of a lesser meditative stabilization or one-pointed mind included within the levels of an upper realm, and the attainment of physical and mental pliancy are simultaneous] because "beginner" means one who is new or unfamiliar; "mental contemplation" is posited as calm abiding; "having" (*bcas pa*) is posited as possessing or having (*yod pa*) that; and "the signs of [having the mental contemplation of a beginner]" is to be taken as the signs of having just attained calm abiding.

If you accept the root statement [that the meditative stabilization of the ninth mind of the Desire Realm is of a level of equipoise], it [absurdly] follows that the subject, [the meditative stabilization of the ninth mind of the Desire Realm], is without contrition, is generated by supreme joy and bliss, and is conjoined with pliancy because [according to you] (1) it is a meditative stabilization included within the levels of an upper realm; (2) the meditative stabilizations [included within the levels of the upper realms] must have those features, and (3) there is the correct distinction that, although a Desire Realm mind does not possess those [features], it has a thorough contemplation.

Fourth debate

Incorrect positions: (1) The nine mental abidings are minds. (2) The nine [mental abidings] are mental contemplations.

Correct position: [551] It follows that both are incorrect because the nine [mental abidings] are meditative stabilizations. This is because the nine [mental abidings] are similitudes of calm abiding.

Fifth debate

Incorrect position: A wisdom consciousness that is associated with the first mental abiding is the first mental abiding from the point of view of

---

[a] Asaṅga, *Grounds of Hearers*, Tibetan Sanskrit Works Series, vol. 14, p. 433; P5537, vol. 110, 115.1.1–2.

its entity.[a]

Correct position: It [absurdly] follows that the subject, [a wisdom consciousness that is associated with the first mental abiding], is in the class of calm abiding because you have asserted [that a wisdom consciousness that is associated with the first mental abiding is the first mental abiding from the point of view of its entity].

You cannot accept [that a wisdom consciousness that is associated with the first mental abiding is in the class of calm abiding] because it is in the class of special insight. This is because it is a wisdom consciousness that thoroughly analyzes phenomena.

SIXTH DEBATE

Incorrect position: The four mental engagements[b] in the context of newly achieving calm abiding are mental contemplations.[c]

Correct position: This is incorrect because those four [mental engagements] are similitudes of calm abiding.

Incorrect position: It [absurdly] follows that [the four mental engagements] in the context of newly achieving special insight are also [mental contemplations] because you have asserted [that the four mental engagements in the context of newly achieving calm abiding are mental contemplations].

Another incorrect position: You cannot accept [that the four mental engagements in the context of newly achieving calm abiding are mental contemplations] because they are in the class of special insight. This is because they are in the class of special insight from the point of view of their concomitants.

Correct position: It is not entailed that whatever is in the class of special insight from the point of view of its concomitants is necessarily in the class of special insight.

---

[a] It is the first mental abiding from the point of view of its concomitants, not from the point of view of its entity.

[b] *yid byed, manaskāra.*

[c] *yid byed, manaskāra.*

SEVENTH DEBATE[a]

Incorrect position: When one is meditating on emptiness, ascertainment of emptiness is induced [by reasoning]. Then, within non-degeneration of the mode of apprehension of emptiness, setting [the mind] non-analytically is the mode of sustaining the full form of the view of emptiness or special insight into it.

Correct position: It [absurdly] follows that the subject, such meditation, is the mode of cultivating the wisdom and special insight realizing emptiness because [according to you] it is the mode of cultivating the view and special insight realizing emptiness. You have accepted the reason [namely, that such meditation is the mode of cultivating the view and special insight realizing emptiness].

You cannot accept [that such meditation is the mode of cultivating the wisdom and special insight realizing emptiness] because it is the mode of cultivating the calm abiding and meditative stabilization realizing emptiness. This is because it is stabilizing meditation realizing emptiness.

It is entailed [that whatever is stabilizing meditation realizing emptiness is necessarily the mode of cultivating the calm abiding and meditative stabilization realizing emptiness] because stabilizing meditation realizing emptiness [552] is the cultivation of meditative stabilization on [emptiness] and the cultivation of calm abiding [having emptiness as its object of observation], and analytical meditation realizing emptiness is the cultivation of wisdom [realizing emptiness] and the cultivation of special insight [realizing emptiness].

EIGHTH DEBATE

Incorrect position: There is a wisdom arisen from meditating on emptiness as object of observation in the path of accumulation of one who is definite in the Mahāyāna lineage.

Correct position: It follows that this is incorrect because the attainment of the wisdom arisen from meditating on such, of the special insight on such, and of the heat [stage of the] Mahāyāna path of preparation are simultaneous.

Incorrect position with respect to that: It follows that [someone on the path

[a] This debate is given in somewhat different form in Hopkins, *Meditation on Emptiness*, pp. 557–58, from Jam-yang-shay-pa's *Great Exposition of the Concentrations and Formless Absorptions*, pp. 69–70.

of accumulation who is definite in the Mahāyāna lineage] attains [a wisdom arising from meditating on emptiness as object of observation] because a wisdom consciousness associated with calm abiding [observing emptiness] is such. It follows [that a wisdom consciousness associated with calm abiding observing emptiness is such] because (1) it is a state arisen from meditation [on emptiness as object of observation] and (2) it is a wisdom consciousness.

Correct position: In one aspect, it is not entailed [that whatever arises from meditating on emptiness as object of observation and is a wisdom consciousness is necessarily a wisdom consciousness associated with calm abiding observing emptiness].

Ninth debate

Incorrect position: There is no [mental contemplation of] individual knowledge of the character viewing grossness/peacefulness in which a calm abiding which is a mental contemplation of the level of equipoise acts as the mental basis.[a]

Correct position: It follows that that is incorrect because there is the correct distinction that, although there is individual knowledge of the character for which [calm abiding] acts as the mental basis, those two are not fit to be associated. The reason [namely, that there is the correct distinction that, although there is individual knowledge of the character for which calm abiding acts as the mental basis, those two are not fit to be associated] is established because at that time calm abiding, as well as [those consciousnesses] that are associated with it, has become somewhat hidden, and individual knowledge of the character, as well as [those consciousnesses] that are associated with it, has become manifest. This is because, with respect to those two, until the attainment of a union [of calm abiding and special insight], when one is manifest the other becomes hidden, as in the example of scales.

Tenth debate

Incorrect position: It follows that the explanation of the practice of calm abiding and special insight[b] individually is incorrect because there is a simultaneous attainment of calm abiding and special insight observing emptiness. It follows [that there is a simultaneous attainment of calm

---

[a] 552.2–3, reading *yid byed kyi zhi gnas kyis* instead of *yid byed kyis zhi gnas kyi.*

[b] 552.6. Literally, "of both calm abiding and special insight" (*zhi lhag gnyis ka'i*).

abiding and special insight observing emptiness] because [553] it is permissible to cultivate special insight [observing emptiness] without achieving calm abiding by way of the nine mental abidings observing emptiness.

Correct position: It is not entailed [that if it is permissible to cultivate special insight observing emptiness without achieving calm abiding by way of the nine mental abidings observing emptiness, there is necessarily a simultaneous attainment of calm abiding and special insight observing emptiness] because there is the correct distinction that, although a calm abiding observing emptiness must precede attainment of special insight observing emptiness, it is not necessary definitely to achieve calm abiding by way of the nine mental abidings observing emptiness. It follows [that there is the correct distinction that, although a calm abiding observing emptiness must precede attainment of special insight observing emptiness, it is not necessary definitely to achieve calm abiding by way of the nine mental abidings observing emptiness] because if one has achieved, by way of the nine mental abidings, a calm abiding observing either the mode or [any of] the varieties before [attaining special insight observing emptiness], it is sufficient [to attain special insight observing emptiness] by way of that [calm abiding]. This is because, after achieving calm abiding [observing any of] the varieties, one comes to achieve calm abiding observing emptiness at the time of individual knowledge of the character realizing emptiness. This is because, when pliancy is induced in doing stabilizing meditation on emptiness at the end of analyzing emptiness at the time of individual knowledge [of the character], one attains calm abiding observing emptiness.

ELEVENTH DEBATE

Incorrect position: There is no definiteness about the order of meditation for newly achieving calm abiding and special insight because Asaṅga's *Summary of Manifest Knowledge* says, "Some achieve special insight but have not achieved calm abiding...."[a]

Correct position: It is not entailed [that this passage means that there is no definiteness about the order of meditation for newly achieving calm abiding and special insight] because, since there are the two,

[a] Asaṅga, *Summary of Manifest Knowledge,* P5550, vol. 112, 263.3.3–4; Rahula, trans., *Le Compendium de la super-doctrine,* p. 126. Paṇ-chen Sö-nam-drak-pa, "Concentrations," 155a.3 cites the rest of the sentence.

concordant and fully qualified, with respect to the special insight explicitly indicated in this [passage], (1) in terms of the concordant, the meaning is that, having attained analytical meditation observing the mode or [any of] the varieties, one also again achieves the stabilizing meditation of the nine mental abidings and (2) in terms of the fully qualified, the meaning is that there is effort to attain the calm abiding included within an actual concentration in dependence upon special insight observing selflessness.

The first reason [namely, that in terms of the concordant, the meaning is that, having attained analytical meditation observing the mode or any of the varieties, one also easily achieves the stabilizing meditation of the nine mental abidings] is established because [554] the meaning is that, having attained the four—thorough differentiation, and so forth—observing the mode or any of the varieties, one makes effort in the nine mental abidings. The reason [namely, that the meaning is that, having attained the four—thorough differentiation and so forth—observing the mode or any of the varieties, one makes effort in the nine mental abidings] is established because Asaṅga's *Actuality of the Grounds* says, "Moreover, from suffering [through] the path,...right after that, one sets the mind and does not do analysis."[a]

It is entailed [that this passage means that the meaning of the previously cited passage is that, having attained the four—thorough differentiation, and so forth—observing the mode or any of the varieties, one makes effort in the nine mental abidings] because "right after that" indicates that at the time of the uninterrupted paths one does analytical meditation and at the time of the paths of release one does stabilizing meditation.

TWELFTH DEBATE

Incorrect position: There is no simultaneous attainment of the two, calm abiding and special insight, because there is none in terms of arising from training.

---

[a] Asaṅga, *Actuality of the Grounds,* P5536, vol. 109, 283.4.2–3. Paṇ-chen Sö-nam-drak-pa cites the passage in full (Paṇ-chen Sö-nam-drak-pa, "Concentrations," 155a.5–6). Kön-chok-jik-may-wang-po abridges and paraphrases the end of the sentence (*rnam par 'byed par mi byed do,* "does not do analysis," whereas Paṇ-chen Sö-nam-drak-pa, "Concentrations," 155a.6 and P5536, vol. 109, 283.4.3 read "*chos rnam par 'byed par mi byed do,* "does not engage in differentiating phenomena." Paṇ-chen Sö-nam-drak-pa also gives the next sentence, *de lhag pa'i shes rab de nyid la brten nas lhag ba'i sems la sbyor bar byed do,* "In dependence upon just this special wisdom, that [person] trains in the special mind [namely, an actual first concentration]."

Correct position: It is not entailed [that if there is no simultaneous attainment of the two, calm abiding and special insight, in terms of arising from training, there is necessarily no simultaneous attainment of them].

You cannot accept [that there is no simultaneous attainment of the two, calm abiding and special insight] because (1) there is attainment of the four actual meditative absorptions of the concentrations by the force of nature and (2) at the time of [that attainment] one must simultaneously attain the two, calm abiding and special insight.

The first reason [namely, that there is attainment of the four actual meditative absorptions of the concentrations by the force of nature] is easy.

The second reason [namely that at the time of that attainment, one, must simultaneously attain the two, calm abiding and special insight] is established because whatever person has attained an actual meditative absorption of a concentration is necessarily a person who has attained both calm abiding and special insight. It follows [that whatever person has attained an actual meditative absorption of a concentration is necessarily a person who has attained both calm abiding and special insight] because there are each of the entailments that (1) whatever is a wisdom consciousness that is an actual meditative absorption of a concentration is necessarily a special insight and (2) whatever meditative stabilization is [an actual meditative absorption of a concentration] is necessarily a calm abiding.

THIRTEENTH DEBATE

Incorrect position: After achieving calm abiding, one does only analytical meditation.

Correct position: It follows that that [position] is incorrect because, if one did such, on this occasion of newly achieving special insight, the former calm abiding would become non-existent and because it is the system of both sūtra and mantra that, if one analyzes too much, one comes under the influence of excitement, and if one stabilizes without analysis, laxity and lethargy are generated. [555]

Our own system

There are five parts: (1) the benefits of the cultivation of the two, calm abiding and special insight; (2) how those two include all meditative stabilizations; (3) the reasons for the necessity of cultivating both; (4)

the stages; (5) individual explanations [of each].

(1) The benefits of the cultivation of the two, calm abiding and special insight. Although all the good qualities of the Mahāyāna and Hīnayāna are not included in the fruit of mere actual calm abiding and special insight, they are definitely included in the fruit of the practice of those two because, with respect to the good qualities of the Mahāyāna and Hīnayāna, without depending on the practice of either meditative stabilization or wisdom—[that is,] on [the practice] of either stabilizing meditation or analytical meditation—no attainment whatever appears. The reason [namely that, with respect to the good qualities of the Mahāyāna and Hīnayāna, without depending on the practice of either meditative stabilization or wisdom—that is, on the practice of either stabilizing meditation or analytical meditation—no attainment whatever appears] is established because those [good qualities] that depend on meditation are attained in dependence upon either analytical or stabilizing meditation, but those that do not depend on [meditation, such] as the good qualities arisen from hearing, arise from the practice of either a one-pointed mind or wisdom—that is, hearing or thinking.

(2) How those two [calm abiding and special insight] include all meditative stabilizations. All meditative stabilizations are included in those two because all non-Buddhist and Buddhist meditative stabilizations are included in those two in terms of their manner of practice.

(3) The reasons for the necessity of cultivating both. One who wishes to abandon the obstructions must cultivate both calm abiding and special insight because one cannot see reality clearly by means of either by itself,[a] without cultivating both. The reason [namely, that one cannot see reality clearly by means of either by itself, without cultivating both] is established because, although one has a steady meditative stabilization in which there is no investigation, if there is no wisdom consciousness realizing reality, realization of the mode of being does not occur, and although one realized reality, if one did not have a steady meditative stabilization, clear seeing of the meaning-generality of the mode of being would not occur.

(4) The order [of achieving calm abiding and special insight]. [556] In this context of new achievement, one must initially generate calm abiding and, after that, special insight because, without the generation of

---

[a] 555.5, reading *gang rung re res* instead of *gang rung res,* following Jam-yang-shay-pa, *Concentrations,* 102.7.

such, no achieving of special insight would occur.

In the context of Highest Yoga Tantra, there is a generation of special insight realizing selflessness without the previous achievement of calm abiding because, by reason of having overcome all coarse conceptuality through having greatly trained in analysis—that is, the spreading out and collecting back in [of vajras, for instance] at the time of just the eighth or ninth mental abiding, one's meditative stabilization and pliancy are much greater, by way of the empowering blessing of the object of observation and the essence of the object-of-observation condition, than they would have been if one had attained [meditative stabilization and pliancy before doing the spreading out and collecting back in].

The reason [namely that, by reason of having overcome all coarse conceptuality through having greatly trained in analysis that is, the spreading out and collecting back in of vajras, for instance at the time of just the eighth or ninth mental abiding, one's meditative stabilization and pliancy are much greater, by way of the empowering blessing of the object and the essence of the object-of-observation condition, than they would have been if one had attained meditative stabilization and pliancy before doing the spreading out and collecting back in] is established because, in this context of Highest Yoga Tantra in which there is a generation of special insight observing emptiness without one's having first passed through analytical meditation observing emptiness, there is generation simultaneously of the two, calm abiding and special insight.

Also, for understanding the view and realizing selflessness, it is not necessary for calm abiding to precede [understanding the view and realizing selflessness] because, although one has not attained calm abiding, there are many cases of developing experience with respect to [the view] upon analyzing one-pointedly, as in [realizing] impermanence and [generating] the altruistic mind of enlightenment, for example.

On high [Bodhisattva] grounds, even without dependence upon calm abiding, there are cases of developing experience arisen from analytical meditation with respect to selflessness because, on high [Bodhisattva] grounds, there are cases of developing experience arisen from meditation without depending upon pliancy. It is entailed [that if, on high Bodhisattva grounds, there are cases of developing experience arisen from meditation without depending upon pliancy, then on high Bodhisattva grounds, even without dependence upon calm abiding, there are cases of developing experience arisen from analytical meditation with respect to selflessness] because, for common beings, states arisen from meditation do not develop until the attainment of special pliancy, but on high [Bodhisattva] grounds, there are uninterrupted paths even with Desire Realm minds. This is because, even in the systems of all four schools of tenets, [557] there are no states not arisen from meditation among either uninterrupted paths or paths of release.

Question: Are states arisen from meditation not differentiated according to whether one has attained pliancy?

[Answer:] Although, with respect to beginners, whether [a path consciousness is a state arisen from meditation] is differentiated according to whether one has attained pliancy and a preparation for the first concentration, and so forth, such is not definite with respect to high [Bodhisattva] grounds. Therefore, there is a meaning of "arisen from meditation" because the development of experience through the power of meditation in which [one's mind] has become singly of the nature only of meditation, having passed beyond states arisen from thinking, is such.

Explanation of the mode of training individually in calm abiding and special insight

This [has three parts]: the explanations of (a) calm abiding, (b) special insight, and (c) the mode of union [of calm abiding and special insight].

Explanation of calm abiding

The definition of a calm abiding is:

> a meditative stabilization arisen from meditation which is conjoined with special pliancy.

There is an etymology because, since the mind, having pacified distractions to external objects, abides internally on an object of observation, it is called [calm abiding].

With respect to prerequisites, there are many [presentations] because there are the six explained in Kamalashīla's *Stages of Meditation* and the thirty-four explained in Asaṅga's *Grounds of Hearers*.

There are objects of observation because there are the four—pervasive objects of observation, and so forth.[a] When the first,

[a] The four are: pervasive objects of observation (*khyab pa'i dmigs pa, vyāpyālaṃbana*), objects of observation for purifying behavior (*spyad pa rnam sbyong gi dmigs pa,*

pervasive objects of observation, is divided, there are the four: the two images from the point of view of the observing [consciousness, observing the] the limits of phenomena (*dngos po'i mtha' la dmigs pa, vastvantālaṃbana*) from the point of view of the object observed, and thorough achievement of the purpose (*dgos pa yongs su grub pa, kṛtyānuṣṭāana*) from the point of view of the fruit. There is a meaning of the first two [analytical image (*rnam par rtog pa dang bcas pa'i gzugs brnyan, savikalpakapratibimba*) and non-analytical image (*rnam par mi rtog pa'i gzugs brnyan, nirvikalpakapratibimba*)] because "conceptual" (*rnam par rtog pa, savikalpaka*) and "non-conceptual" (*rnam par mi rtog pa, nirvikalpaka*) refer to analytical and non-analytical, and "image" (*gzugs brnyan, pratibimba*) [or "reflection"] refers to the dawning of the object of observation.

When the second, objects of observation for purifying behavior,[a] is divided, [558] there are the five: ugliness as an antidote to desire, love as an antidote to hatred, dependent-arising as an antidote to obscuration, the divisions of the constituents as an antidote to pride, and meditation on exhalation and inhalation as an antidote to excessive discursiveness.

When the third, objects of observation for [developing] skill, is divided, there are the five: skill with respect to the aggregates, the constituents, the sources, dependent-arising, and the appropriate and the inappropriate.

The fourth, objects of observation for purifying afflictions, has two [types] because there are the two, (1) the factor of grossness/peacefulness according to the mundane path and (2) impermanence, and so forth[—that is,] the sixteen [attributes of the four truths] and so forth—according to the supramundane path.[b]

---

caritaviśodanālaṃbana), objects of observation for [developing] skill (*mkhas pa'i dmigs pa, kauśalyālaṃbana*), and objects of observation for purifying afflictive emotions (*nyon mongs rnam sbyong gi dmigs pa, kleśaviśodanālaṃbana*).

[a] 557.6, reading *spyad pa* instead of *dpyad pa.*

[b] "Impermanence, and so forth—the sixteen," as the text literally reads, refers in a condensed form to the sixteen aspects of the four truths (See *Meditation on Emptiness,* pp. 292–96, and *Meditative States,* pp. 134–43). The second "and so forth" refers to the three selflessnesses that are the objects of observation of Hearers, Solitary Realizers, and Bodhisattvas according to the Yogāchāra-Svātantrika-Madhyamaka school of tenets, traditionally used in Ge-luk monastic universities for teaching the topic of the Perfection of Wisdom and its subtopics, including the concentrations and formless absorptions. The three selflessnesses are, respectively, non-existence of a self-sufficient person, non-existence of subjects and objects as different entities, and non-existence of truly existent phenomena (See ibid., p. 298, chart 36).

There is meditation on certain objects of observation by certain persons, for although, in general, there is no need to delimit the objects of observation of calm abiding, those with excessive desire, and so forth, should definitely use ugliness, and so forth, because one does not succeed in the generation of a steady meditative stabilization without controlling the prominence of [a predominant] affliction by way of that object of observation. Persons who have behaviors of equal afflictions or who have slight afflictions do not definitely have to observe a specific object of observation [from among these] because, even though they depend on any among the specific objects of observation previously explained, they will easily achieve [calm abiding].

It is better to observe the body of a Buddha than [to observe] all those objects of observation [previously explained] because, in addition to having all the functions which the other objects of observation have, it acts as the two, the generator of meditative stabilization and that which quickly completes the collections even in each session of mindfulness [on a Buddha's body].

How to Achieve Calm Abiding

[559]

This has two parts: the actual [mode of achievement] and the measure of having achieved [calm abiding].

[Actual Mode of Achievement of Calm Abiding]

This has two parts: explanation of the mode of achieving [calm abiding] by way of the eight applications [that is, antidotes] that abandon the five faults and explanation of the way in which the nine mental abidings, the four mental engagements, and the six powers arise at that time.

Explanation of the Mode of Achieving [Calm Abiding] by Way of the Eight Applications [That Is, Antidotes] That Abandon the Five Faults

When a beginner newly works at achieving meditative stabilization, it is necessary to achieve[a] [meditative stabilization] by way of eight applications which abandon five faults because it is necessary to achieve by way of the eight: the four—faith, aspiration, exertion, and pliancy—as antidotes to laziness; mindfulness as an antidote to forgetting the

[a] 559.4, reading *bsgrub* instead of *bsgrab.*

object of observation; introspection as an antidote to non-identification of laxity and excitement; with respect to the antidote when laxity and excitement arise, application as an antidote to non-application; and when the prominence of laxity and excitement has been broken, non-application as an antidote to the exertion of application.

At the time of training (*sbyor*), there is the fault of laziness because one will not connect (*sbyor*) to meditative stabilization. When laziness is divided, there are three [types of] laziness—of neutral activities, attachment to bad activities, and inferiority.

When one exerts oneself for the sake of meditative stabilization, forgetting the instruction, and so forth, is a fault[a] because, if one forgets the object of observation at that time, one will not enter into equipoise. When [forgetting the instruction] is divided, there are two in terms of laxity and excitement.

At the time of entering into equipoise, the two, laxity and excitement, are faults because they cause non-serviceability of mind.

When laxity and excitement arise, non-exertion is a fault because, as a result of [non-exertion], those two [laxity and excitement] will not be pacified. When [non-exertion] is divided, there are three [types of] non-exertion in terms of the three [types of] laziness.

When one is free from laxity and excitement, application [of the antidotes] is a fault [560] because, since the mind has been distracted by such application, meditative stabilization cannot increase. When [over-application] is divided, there are two [types of mistaken] exertion in the antidotes—[one] when even subtle laxity does not exist and [the other] when even subtle excitement does not exist. The boundaries are the ninth mental abiding and above.

The definition of laxity is:

> an internal distraction which is a mental factor that slackens the intensity of the mind's clarity when one cultivates virtue.

When [laxity] is divided, there are the two, virtuous and neutral. The entities of the two, laxity and lethargy, are dissimilar because lethargy is a factor of obscuration and accompanies all afflictions, [whereas] laxity does not accompany desire, hatred, and so forth, at all. Those two [laxity and lethargy] have dissimilar functions because lethargy makes the mind and body dull, [whereas] laxity does not do so.

The definition of excitement is:

---

[a] 559.5, reading *nyes pa* instead of *tes pa.*

> a secondary[a] affliction, belonging to the class of desire, which is a non-pacification with respect to a pleasant object and a scattering to the outside, its function being to interrupt [the cultivation of] calm abiding.

When [excitement] is divided, there are the two, afflicted aspiration and [afflicted] wishing, and the five desires with respect to the five sense-objects. With respect to scattering, since there is scattering to various [objects], virtuous and non-virtuous, it is not the same as excitement.

There is a definition of effort, which is an antidote to laziness, because "that intention which observes and is enthusiastic about a virtuous object of observation" is [the definition]. There is that which is exertion but is not effort because exertion toward a neutral object is such. There is that which is effort but is not exertion because that which is enthusiastic about virtue but does not apply itself is such. There is a possibility which is both because exertion which is enthusiastic about virtue is such.

There is aspiration in this [context] because the aspiration that seeks the good qualities of meditative stabilization [561] is such.

There is faith because the faith of conviction in the good qualities of meditative stabilization is such.

There is a fifth antidote because mindfulness which does not forget the object of observation is such.

There is a sixth antidote because introspection which investigates,[b] in dependence upon mindfulness, whether or not the mind is cut off from the object of observation by laxity, excitement, and so forth, is such.

There is a seventh antidote because the intention that consists of exertion in applying antidotes when laxity and excitement arise is such.

There is an eighth antidote because, when the prominence of laxity and excitement has been subdued, the compositional factor of equanimity [or, desisting from application] causes the mind to enter into its natural state at the time of the mental engagement of spontaneous engagement and above is such. This does not exist below the eighth mental abiding.

---

a 560.4, reading *nye nyon* instead of *nya nyon.*

b 561.2, reading *rtog* instead of *rtogs.* Jam-yang-shay-pa's *Great Exposition of the Concentrations and Formless Absorptions* (148.4) also reads *rtog.*

Explanation of the Way in Which the Nine Mental Abidings, the Four Mental Engagements, and the Six Powers Arise at That Time

This has three parts: explanation of how the four mental engagements arise with the nine mental [abidings]; explanation of the nine mental abidings, and explanation of how [the nine mental abidings] are achieved by way of the six powers.

[Explanation of how the four mental engagements arise with the nine mental abidings]

[The explanation of how the four mental engagements arise with the nine mental abidings] exists because (1) in the first and second mental abidings, the mental engagement of forcible engagement arises; (2) in the third through the seventh [mental abidings], the mental engagement of interrupted engagement arises; (3) in the eighth [mental abiding], the mental engagement of uninterrupted engagement arises; (4) in the ninth [mental abiding], the mental engagement of engagement without exertion arises.[a]

[Explanation of the nine mental abidings]

(1) The first of the nine mental abidings that precede calm abiding, setting the mind only inside, exists because the first meditative stabilization, or imputed[b] mental contemplation, which, having withdrawn from all external objects of observation [562] and pursuant to the hearing of the instruction, focuses on an object of observation internally, is such.

(2) The entity of the second [mental abiding], continuous setting, exists because the second meditative stabilization, which is able to prolong to some extent the continuum of the mind's [remaining] without distraction on the object of observation, is such.[c]

(3) The entity of the third [mental abiding], resetting, exists because the third meditative stabilization, which quickly recognizes distraction and again binds the mind to the object of observation with the mindfulness [of a practitioner] whose mind has become somewhat

---

[a] Engagement without exertion is also known as spontaneous engagement (*lhun grub tu 'jug pa, anābhogavāhana*).

[b] 562.1, reading *btags pa ba* instead of *dag pa ba*, following Jam-yang-shay-pa, *Collected Works*, vol. 12, 138.7.

[c] "Entity" means definition.

familiar with the object of observation, is such.

(4) The entity of the fourth [mental abiding], close setting, exists because the fourth meditative stabilization, which sets [the mind] better [on the object of observation], having withdrawn the mind from the vast [array of] objects of observation by the influence of mindfulness, is such.[a]

(5) The entity of the fifth [mental abiding], disciplining, exists because the fifth meditative stabilization, which takes joy in the good qualities of meditative stabilization in dependence upon powerful introspection, is such.

(6) The entity of the sixth mental abiding, pacifying, exists because the sixth meditative stabilization, which blocks distraction in dependence upon [powerful] introspection, is such.

(7) The entity of the seventh mental abiding, thorough pacifying, exists because the seventh meditative stabilization, which pacifies mental attachment [to attributes of the Desire Realm], mental discomfort, lethargy and sleep, and so forth, is such.

(8) The entity of the eighth mental abiding, making one-pointed, exists because the eighth meditative stabilization, which has the capacity to set continuously in meditative stabilization without the interruption of even subtle laxity or excitement, is such.

(9) The entity of the ninth mental abiding, setting in equipoise, exists because the ninth meditative stabilization, which is the self-flowing dawning of meditative stabilization without reliance on striving and exertion, is such.

[Explanation of how the nine mental abidings are achieved by way of the six powers]

[563] The first mental abiding is achieved by the power of hearing; the second mental abiding, by the power of thinking; the third and fourth [mental abidings], by the power of mindfulness; the fifth and sixth, by the power of introspection; the seventh and eighth, by the power of effort; and the ninth mental abiding, by the power of familiarity.

[Measure of Having Achieved Calm Abiding]

There is a measure of having achieved calm abiding because [calm abiding] is achieved when the ninth mental abiding is conjoined with

[a] This is the point at which the practitioner's mind stops scattering to other objects of observation.

special pliancy. There is an order of generating pliancies and achieving calm abiding because a slight pliancy is generated at the beginning of the ninth mental abiding; after that, mental pliancy is generated; after that, physical pliancy is generated; in dependence upon that, a great sense of physical bliss is generated; by the force of that, the bliss of mental pliancy is generated; and calm abiding is achieved simultaneously with the attainment of an unfluctuating pliancy in which the mind abides vividly on the object of observation, the feverish joy immediately after the generation of physical pliancy having diminished a little.

Pliancy is a factor of serviceability that is included within either the form aggregate or the aggregate of compositional factors. The two, the assumption of bad physical states and physical pliancy, are form aggregates and tangible objects; the two, the assumption of bad mental states and mental pliancy, are mental-factor compositional factors.

Explanation of special insight

The definition of a special insight is:

> a wisdom consciousness that thoroughly differentiates phenomena and is conjoined with special pliancy that is induced by the power of analysis. [564]

There are prerequisites of special insight because there are the three, reliance on an excellent being, and so forth.[a]

When special insight is divided into four, there are the four: (a) the two, thorough differentiation observing the varieties and very thorough differentiation observing the mode; and also (b) with respect to each of those two, investigation, which is differentiation of coarse meaning, and analysis, which is differentiation of subtle meaning.

When [special insight] is divided into three, there are the three special insights of the three approaches; there are the three—special insight that arises from signs, special insight that arises from thorough examination, and special insight that arises from individual analysis.

When it is divided into six, when one has thoroughly examined and investigated meaning, things, character, class, time, and reasoning,

---

[a] These three are: reliance on an excellent being, to have thoroughly sought much hearing of the doctrine, and proper contemplation of the meaning heard. (Jam-yang-shay-pa, *Concentrations,* 162.2–3. See Hopkins, *Meditation on Emptiness,* p. 92. Hopkins notes in conversation that Jam-yang-shay-pa's source, which he does not cite, is Tsong-kha-pa's *Middling Exposition of the Stages of the Path.*)

there are the six [types of] special insight of individual analysis. Therefore, the approaches of the four special insights—thorough differentiation, and so forth—are the three [approaches—special insight that arises from signs, and so forth], and with respect to the examinations, they are posited as six.

There is an etymology because, since it sees beyond or more specially than calm abiding, it is explained as special insight.

There is a mode of cultivating special insight in this context of a beginner's newly achieving special insight because it is cultivated through [a beginner's] having alternated analytical and stabilizing meditations.

There is a measure of having achieved special insight because, by the power of analysis which analyzes in this way, one attains special pliancy and, simultaneously, one attains special insight, a union of calm abiding and special insight, the mental contemplation of belief, and a mental contemplation that is a purifier of afflictions. [565]

Mode of union of calm abiding and special insight

There is a mode of union of calm abiding and special insight because an operation having in association the two—special insight, which thoroughly differentiates phenomena, and one-pointed calm abiding—at one time in equal power, is such.

Dispelling objections

FIRST DEBATE

Incorrect position: It follows that all the good qualities of the three vehicles are included in the fruits of cultivating in meditation the two, calm abiding and special insight, because they are included in the fruits of practicing those two.

Correct position: It is not entailed [that if all the good qualities of the three vehicles are included in the fruits of practicing the two, calm abiding and special insight, they are necessarily included in the fruits of cultivating those two in meditation].

The reason [namely, that all the good qualities of the three vehicles are included in the fruits of practicing the two, calm abiding and special insight] is established because there are the three—hearing, thinking, and meditating—in the practice of both of those.

Second Debate

Incorrect position: It follows that the two, calm abiding and special insight, do not arise simultaneously because Tsong-kha-pa's *Great Exposition of the Stages of the Path* says, "Moreover, they are not simultaneous, but...they are experienced in a continuum."[a]

Correct position: It is not entailed [that this citation from Tsong-kha-pa's *Great Exposition of the Stages of the Path* means that the two, calm abiding and special insight, do not arise simultaneously] because the meaning of that [passage] is that the two, special insight which analyzes and the stabilizing meditation that abides at the end of analysis, do not come simultaneously [when one is cultivating special insight].

Third Debate

Incorrect position: It follows that it is incorrect to say that at that time [of the union of calm abiding and special insight] the powers of the two [calm abiding and special insight] are equal in strength because, when one analyzes, there is a greater power of special insight and, when one stabilizes, there is a greater power of calm abiding. It follows [that when one analyzes, there is a greater power of special insight and, when one stabilizes, a greater power of calm abiding] because, at that time, [the power of analysis] induces a powerful calm abiding.

Correct position: It is not entailed [that if, at that time, the power of analysis induces a powerful calm abiding, then, when one analyzes, there is necessarily a greater power of special insight and, when one stabilizes, a greater power of calm abiding].

The reason [namely, that at that time, the power of analysis induces a powerful calm abiding] is established because, at that time, as great as the power of analysis is, so great is the power of calm abiding, and as great as the power of calm abiding is, so great is the power of analysis.

Incorrect position with respect to that: It follows that, at that time, there is no analysis with respect to [the object of observation] because, at that time, [the practitioner] abides one-pointedly on [the object of observation].

Correct position: It is not entailed [that if the practitioner abides one-pointedly on the object of observation at that time, there is necessarily

---

[a] Tsong-kha-pa, *Great Exposition of the Stages of the Path* (Dharamsala: shes rig par khang, no date), 1061.5.

no analysis with respect to the object of observation at that time].

FOURTH DEBATE

Incorrect position: It follows that, at that time [of the union of calm abiding and special insight], one observes a single object of observation[a] [566] because observing only a single object of observation is the meaning of one-pointedness. This is because observing only one's own object of observation is the meaning of [one-pointedness].

Correct position: It is not entailed [that if observing only one's own object of observation is the meaning of one-pointedness, observing only a single object of observation is necessarily the meaning of one-pointedness] because the term "observing only one's own object of observation" eliminates that which is not [one's own object of observation] but does not eliminate that one's own object of observation may be manifold.

FIFTH DEBATE

Incorrect position: It follows that whatever is special insight in this context must be analytical meditation because stabilizing meditation is the cultivation of calm abiding.

Correct position: It is not entailed [that if stabilizing meditation is the cultivation of calm abiding, then whatever is special insight in this context must be analytical meditation].

The reason [namely, that stabilizing meditation is the cultivation of calm abiding] is established because the three—the cultivation of calm abiding, stabilizing meditation, and the cultivation of meditative stabilization—are mutually inclusive, and the three—the cultivation of wisdom, analytical meditation, and the cultivation of special insight—are mutually inclusive.

You cannot accept [that whatever is special insight in this context must be analytical meditation] because there is also a stabilizing meditation with respect to [special insight in this context]. This is because special insight that arises from signs is stabilizing meditation.

---

[a] 565.6, reading *gcig la dmigs par thal* instead of *gcig la ma dmigs par thal.*

Mode of Entering into Meditative Absorption in the Eight Concentrations and Formless Absorptions by Way of the Seven Mental Contemplations

[566.4]

Refutation [of mistaken opinions]

First debate

Incorrect position: The calm abiding in the continuum of a person who has just attained calm abiding is both a beginner at mental contemplation and the mental contemplation of a beginner.

Correct position: It [absurdly] follows that the subject, [the calm abiding in the continuum of a person who has just attained calm abiding], is the ninth mental abiding because [according to you] it is a beginner at mental contemplation. It is entailed [that whatever is a beginner at mental contemplation is necessarily the ninth mental abiding] because the mental contemplation [of a beginner] is calm abiding and a beginner at [mental contemplation—that is, calm abiding] must be posited as a person who possesses in his mental continuum a meditative stabilization that is a precursor to [mental contemplation—that is, calm abiding] and because the boundaries also are posited as ranging from someone who has the ninth mental abiding to someone who has not yet attained calm abiding. [567]

If you accept the root statement [that the calm abiding in the continuum of a person who has just attained calm abiding is the ninth mental abiding] it absurdly follows that the subject, [the calm abiding in the continuum of a person who has just attained calm abiding], is both a person who has not yet achieved calm abiding and a mental contemplation because you have accepted [that the calm abiding in the continuum of a person who has just attained calm abiding is the ninth mental abiding].

Second debate

Incorrect position: The mental contemplation of individual knowledge of the character is[a] a mental contemplation that purifies afflictive emotions.

---

[a] 567.1, reading *yid byed yin zer ba* instead of *yid byed min zer ba.*

Correct position: It follows that this statement is incorrect because [the mental contemplation of individual knowledge of the character] is the mental contemplation of a beginner at purifying afflictive emotions. The reason [namely, that the mental contemplation of individual knowledge of the character is the mental contemplation of a beginner at purifying afflictive emotions] is established because, with respect to "mental contemplation of a beginner" in this context, there are those two types [namely, calm abiding and the mental contemplation of individual knowledge of the character]. It follows [that with respect to "mental contemplation of a beginner" in this context, there are those two types—namely, calm abiding and the mental contemplation of individual knowledge of the character] because, with respect to [the term] "beginner" in this context, there are two types: a beginner at mental contemplation and a beginner at purifying afflictive emotions.

Moreover, it follows that [the statement that the mental contemplation of individual knowledge of the character is a mental contemplation that purifies afflictive emotions] is incorrect because "purifying afflictive emotions" must refer to the mental contemplation of belief and above. It follows [that "purifying afflictive emotions" must refer to the mental contemplation of belief and above] because a yogi is posited as a beginner from the point of having just attained the ninth mental abiding up to, but not including, the mental contemplation of belief; a yogi is posited as one who purifies afflictive emotions from the mental contemplation of belief through the mental contemplation of final training, and the mental contemplation that is the fruit of final training is posited as having passed beyond the mental contemplations that purify afflictive emotions.

THIRD DEBATE

Incorrect position: That which is among the six—the mental contemplation of individual knowledge of the character, and so forth—necessarily has the aspect of grossness/peacefulness.

Correct position: It follows that this statement is incorrect because, except for the mental contemplation of analysis, the five preparations each have the two, the aspect of the truths and the aspect of grossness/peacefulness.

FOURTH DEBATE

Incorrect position: For each of the nine cycles, the mundane uninterrupted paths that are preparations have the aspect of grossness and peacefulness [that is, both the aspect of grossness and the aspect of peacefulness].

Correct position: It [absurdly] follows that the subject, [for each of the nine cycles, the mundane uninterrupted paths that are preparations], have the aspect of peacefulness [568] because you have accepted [that for each of the nine cycles, the mundane uninterrupted paths that are preparations have the aspect of grossness and peacefulness]. You cannot accept [that for each of the nine cycles, the mundane uninterrupted paths that are preparations have the aspect of peacefulness] because, of those two [grossness and peacefulness], they have the aspect of grossness. It follows [that of the two, grossness and peacefulness, they have the aspect of grossness] because they are mundane uninterrupted paths. It is entailed [that whatever is a mundane uninterrupted path necessarily has the aspect of grossness] because the mundane uninterrupted paths have the scope of only the lower level and of the two [grossness and peacefulness] have only the aspect of grossness, whereas the mundane paths of release have the scope of only the upper level and of the two [grossness and peacefulness] have only the aspect of peacefulness.

Fifth Debate

Incorrect position: The mental contemplation of individual knowledge of the character having the aspect of grossness/peacefulness that is a preparation for the first concentration is included within the level of meditative equipoise.

Correct position: It follows that this statement is incorrect because [the mental contemplation of individual knowledge of the character having the aspect of grossness/peacefulness that is a preparation for the first concentration] is included within the level of the Desire Realm. It follows [that it is included within the level of the Desire Realm] because it is an awareness of either hearing or thinking included in the continuum of a being having a Desire Realm basis.

Another [incorrect position]: It follows that the subject, [the mental contemplation of individual knowledge of the character having the aspect of grossness/peacefulness that is a preparation for the first concentration], is not conjoined with the pliancy of an upper realm because it is an awareness included within the level of the Desire Realm.

Correct position: It is not entailed [that whatever is an awareness included within the level of the Desire Realm is necessarily not conjoined with the pliancy of an upper realm].

Another [incorrect position]: Whatever is a mental contemplation of individual knowledge of the character is necessarily included within [the level of] non-equipoise.

Correct position: It follows that this is incorrect because (1) the mental contemplations of individual knowledge of the character for the second concentration and above are each included within the level of meditative equipoise and (2) according to Tsong-kha-pa's *Golden Rosary*, they are also each included within the level of non-equipoise.

The first reason [namely, that the mental contemplations of individual knowledge of the character for the second concentration and above are each included within the level of meditative equipoise] is established because, in the upper realms, there are those who achieve a causal meditative absorption for birth in the next higher level. It is entailed [that if, in the upper realms, there are those who achieve a causal meditative absorption for birth in the next higher level, then the mental contemplations of individual knowledge of the character for the second concentration and above are each necessarily included within the level of meditative equipoise] because, at that time, even from the point of view of their basis, object of observation, and so forth, they do not belong to the Desire Realm.[a]

The second reason [namely, that according to Tsong-kha-pa's *Golden Rosary*, they are also each included within the level of non-equipoise] is established because Tsong-kha-pa's *Golden Rosary* says: [569]

> Because of this reasoning, if one cultivates the remaining [concentrations and formless absorptions] within a basis of a lower level, it is to be asserted that the first mental contemplation [that is, the mental contemplation of individual knowledge of the character] is also of a lower level.[b]

---

[a] "And so forth" refers to the rest of the five associations (*mtshungs par ldan pa, saṃprayukta*). According to the system of Asaṅga's *Summary of Manifest Knowledge*, followed by Jam-yang-shay-pa and Kön-chok-jik-may-wang-po, the five are basis, object of observation and subjective aspect, time, substantial entity, and realm and level. (See Hopkins, *Meditation on Emptiness*, p. 236, which also sets forth the slightly different system of Vasubandhu's *Treasury of Manifest Knowledge*.)

[b] Tsong-kha-pa, *Golden Rosary*, *Collected Works*, vol. 17 (New Delhi: Guru Deva, 1979), 480.4.

Sixth debate

Incorrect position: If one cultivates the mental contemplation of individual knowledge of the character within a Form Realm basis, there are no states arisen from hearing, and if one cultivates it in a Formless Realm basis, there are no [states arisen from] either hearing or thinking.

Correct position: It follows that this is incorrect because (1) these two exist in the Form Realm and (2) both of these also exist in the Formless Realm.

The first reason [namely, that the two, states arisen from hearing and states arisen from thinking, exist in the Form Realm] is established because, since one has clairvoyance in [the Form and Formless Realms], one can easily achieve [states arisen from] hearing and thinking.

The second reason [namely, that both states arisen from hearing and states arisen from thinking exist in the Formless Realm] is established because, in the [Formless Realm], there are both states arisen from hearing that think about the meaning of that concerning which, although one had heard it in a former lifetime, one did not gain ascertainment and also states arisen from thinking about that concerning which one gained ascertainment.

Seventh debate

Incorrect position: Each of the eight [sets of] preparations—the preparations for the first concentration, and so forth—has two [types]: pure and uncontaminated.

Correct position: It follows that that is incorrect because, although the preparations for the first concentration have [both types, pure and uncontaminated], the preparations for the second concentration and above are necessarily pure.

Eighth debate

Incorrect position: Whatever is among the eight meditative absorptions is necessarily a mental contemplation that is the fruit of final training.

Correct position: It [absurdly] follows that the subject, each of the seven meditative absorptions of the second concentration and above in the continuum of a simultaneous Foe Destroyer,[a] is [a mental

[a] See Hopkins, *Meditation on Emptiness*, pp. 104–108, for the eight levels of approaching and abiding in the fruits of a Stream Enterer, Once Returner, Non-Returner, and Foe

contemplation that is the fruit of final training] because of being [among the eight meditative absorptions]. If you accept [that each of the seven meditative absorptions of the second concentration and above in the continuum of a simultaneous Foe Destroyer is a mental contemplation that is the fruit of final training], it [absurdly] follows with respect to the subject, [each of the seven meditative absorptions of the second concentration and above in the continuum of a simultaneous Foe Destroyer], that there exists for each its mental contemplation of final training which is its cause because you have accepted [that each of the seven meditative absorptions of the second concentration and above in the continuum of a simultaneous Foe Destroyer is a mental contemplation that is the fruit of final training].

If you accept [that, with respect to each of the seven meditative absorptions of the second concentration and above in the continuum of a simultaneous Foe Destroyer, there exists for each its mental contemplation of final training which is its cause], it [absurdly] follows that they are actual meditative absorptions attained by the power of cultivating the preparations for their level!

You cannot accept [that they are actual meditative absorptions attained by the power of cultivating the preparations for their level] because [570] they are attained by the power of having separated from the coarse afflictive emotions pertaining to the lower level without having cultivated [the preparations] for one's own level. It follows [that they are attained by the power of having separated from the coarse afflictive emotions pertaining to the lower level without having cultivated the preparations for one's own level] because they are actual meditative absorptions of the second concentration and above in the continuum of a simultaneous [Foe Destroyer].

Our own system

This has two parts: mode of entering into meditative absorption in the first concentration by way of the seven mental contemplations and indication similarly [of the mode of entering into meditative absorption] in the remaining levels by way of [the seven mental contemplations].

Destroyer, and the distinction between the gradual and simultaneous abandonment of afflictions.

Mode of entering into meditative absorption in the first concentration by way of the seven mental contemplations

[This section has] two parts: the mode of entering into meditative absorption in the first concentration by way of mundane mental contemplations having the aspect of grossness/peacefulness and the explanation of the mode of entering [into meditative absorption in the first concentration] by way of supramundane mental contemplations having the aspect of the truths.

MODE OF ENTERING INTO MEDITATIVE ABSORPTION IN THE FIRST CONCENTRATION BY WAY OF MUNDANE MENTAL CONTEMPLATIONS HAVING THE ASPECT OF GROSSNESS/PEACEFULNESS

This has three parts: definition, divisions, and explanation of the ascertainment of the number.

DEFINITION

The definition of a preparation for a concentration is:

> a mental contemplation that is a training for entering into an actual meditative absorption of a concentration.

DIVISIONS

When [preparations for the concentrations] are divided, there are the four [sets of] preparations for the four concentrations.

When preparations for the first concentration are divided, there are two types: preparations for the first concentration having the aspect of grossness/peacefulness and [preparations] for the first concentration having the aspect of the truths.

[PREPARATIONS FOR THE FIRST CONCENTRATION HAVING THE ASPECT OF GROSSNESS/PEACEFULNESS]

The definition of a mental contemplation of a beginner is:

> a mental contemplation included within either the precursors for the attainment of calm abiding or the precursors for the attainment of special insight.

When [mental contemplations of a beginner] are divided, there are three types: the mental contemplation of a beginner at mental contemplation, the mental contemplation of a mere beginner, and the mental contemplation of a beginner at purifying afflictive emotions. The ninth mental abiding, the calm abiding of one who has just attained [calm abiding], and the mental contemplation of individual knowledge of the character are posited, respectively, as illustrations of the three. [571]

The definition of a preparation for the first concentration in terms of the mundane is:

> a mental contemplation included in the class of preparations for the first concentrations having the aspect of grossness/peacefulness.

When these are divided, there are seven: the mental contemplation of a mere beginner, and so forth.

The definition of a mental contemplation of individual knowledge of the character which is a mundane preparation for the first concentration is:

> a taking to mind by a beginner at purifying afflictive emotions which is mainly analysis having individually distinguished the Desire Realm as faulty and the First Concentration as having good qualities, and so forth, in dependence upon calm abiding.[a]

The two, [mental contemplation of individual knowledge of the character which is a mundane preparation for the first concentration] and mental contemplation of a beginner at purifying afflictive emotions which is a mundane [preparation] for the first concentration, are mutually inclusive.

The definition of a mental contemplation of belief which is a mundane preparation for the first concentration is:

> the first taking to mind purifying afflictive emotions, which,

---

[a] The term translated as "mental contemplation" (*yid la byed pa, manaskāra*) literally means a doing or making in the mind, or a taking to mind, and "taking to mind," in this definition and the others in this series, is literally "mental contemplation" (*yid la sems pa*). The English term "mental contemplation" reflects the meaning given in this series of definitions. Since "mental contemplation" and "taking to mind" are synonyms and since the general term, in English, needs to be a noun, the two terms have been transposed; the general term *yid la byed pa* has been translated throughout as "mental contemplation," as though it were *yid la sems pa,* and *yid la sems pa,* in this series of definitions, has been translated as "taking to mind," as though it were *yid la byed pa.* The term "taking to mind" makes it clear that the "contemplation" of "mental contemplation" does not mean mere gazing at the object, as "contemplation" often does in English.

> having passed beyond hearing and thinking with respect to the grossness/peacefulness of [the Desire Realm and the First Concentration, respectively], is mainly special insight—ranging from the attainment of special pliancy by way of analytical meditation up to, but not including, the generation of an actual antidote to the great coarse afflictive emotions pertaining to the Desire Realm.

The definition of a mental contemplation of thorough isolation which is a mundane preparation for the first concentration is:

> the second taking to mind purifying afflictive emotions, which abides in the type of causing the mere suppression of any of the three cycles of the corresponding great coarse afflictive emotions pertaining to the Desire Realm in terms of viewing the lower or upper level as either faulty or having good qualities, [respectively].[a]

When [mental contemplations of thorough isolation which are mundane preparations for the first concentration] are divided, there are three mundane uninterrupted paths, three [mundane] paths of release, and [572] three mundane [mental contemplations] of thorough isolation that are neither [uninterrupted paths nor paths of release].

The boundaries range from the mundane uninterrupted path that causes the suppression of the great of the great coarse afflictive emotions pertaining to the Desire Realm up to, but not including, generation of the mental contemplation of joy-withdrawal.

The definition of a mental contemplation of either withdrawal or joy that is a mundane preparation for the first concentration is:

> the third taking to mind purifying afflictive emotions, which abides in the type of causing the mere suppression of any of the three cycles of the corresponding middling coarse afflictive emotions pertaining to the Desire Realm in dependence upon a union of calm abiding and special insight, having such aspects of grossness/peacefulness.

When [mental contemplations of either withdrawal or joy that are mundane preparations for the first concentration] are divided, there

---

[a] "Which abides in the type" means that there are exceptions. The type that is neither an uninterrupted path nor a path of release is an obvious exception, since it does not suppress afflictive emotions. There is also some question whether the path of release fulfills the definition, since it is a state of having suppressed afflictive emotions.

are a) the two: mental contemplations of joy and of withdrawal; and b) mundane uninterrupted paths, [mundane] paths of release, and mental contemplations of joy-withdrawal that are neither of the two [mundane uninterrupted paths or paths of release], and so forth.

The boundaries range from the uninterrupted path that is the antidote to the great of the middling [coarse afflictive emotions pertaining to the Desire Realm] up to, but not including, generation of the mental contemplation of final training.

The definition of a mental contemplation of analysis that is a mundane preparation for the first concentration is:

> the fourth taking to mind purifying mundane afflictive emotions which analyzes, after separation from attachment to the three cycles of middling coarse afflictive emotions pertaining to the Desire Realm, whether one has separated from the small [coarse afflictive emotions pertaining to the Desire Realm].

When [mental contemplations of analysis that are mundane preparations for the first concentration] are divided, there are the three mental contemplations that analyze whether one has separated from attachment to the three cycles of small coarse afflictive emotions pertaining to the Desire Realm.

The boundaries range from the subsequent attainment of the third path of release of the mental contemplation of joy-withdrawal until before connection to the third mundane uninterrupted path of the mental contemplation of final training [573] because, when one has separated from attachment to the three [cycles of] middling [coarse afflictive emotions pertaining to the Desire Realm], there is one [period of] analysis wondering whether one has separated from attachment to all the afflictive emotions pertaining to the Desire Realm; there is a similar [period of] analysis when one has separated from attachment to the great of the small [coarse afflictive emotions pertaining to the Desire Realm]; and when one has separated from attachment to the middling of the small [coarse afflictive emotions pertaining to the Desire Realm], there is [a period of] analysis in detail, since it seems that one has completely abandoned [the coarse afflictive emotions pertaining to the Desire Realm].

The definition of a mental contemplation of final training that is a mundane preparation for the first concentration is:

> the fifth taking to mind purifying afflictive emotions, which abides in the type of causing the mere suppression of any of the three cycles of the corresponding small coarse afflictive

> emotions pertaining to the Desire Realm in dependence upon a union of calm abiding and special insight having such aspects of grossness/peacefulness.

When [mental contemplations of final training that are mundane preparations for the first concentration] are divided, there are three mundane uninterrupted paths, two paths of release, and [a type] that is neither. The path of release induced by the third uninterrupted path is an actual meditative absorption of the first concentration.

The definition of a mundane mental contemplation that is the fruit of final training for the first concentration is:

> an actual meditative absorption of the first concentration which abides in the type of the path of release induced by the ninth mundane uninterrupted path.

When [mundane mental contemplations that are the fruit of final training for the first concentration] are divided, there are the five—investigation, analysis, joy, bliss, and meditative stabilization.[a]

[Preparations for the First Concentration Having the Aspect of the Truths]

In terms of the supramundane path: The definition of a supramundane preparation for the first concentration is:

> a preparation for the first concentration included within that which has the aspect of any of the selflessnesses or the attributes of the four truths.

When [supramundane preparations for the first concentration] are divided, there are the six—the mental contemplation of a beginner, and so forth—having the aspect of [any of] the three selflessnesses, and so forth, [574] because the first three preparations, up to the mental contemplation of belief, have only a conceptual [type] having the aspect of selflessness [or the sixteen attributes of the four truths], and the three—thorough isolation, and so forth—each have two [types]: conceptual and non-conceptual.

---

[a] Since these five—investigation, analysis, joy, bliss, and meditative stabilization—are the branches of the first concentration, this division supports the definition: the mental contemplation that is the fruit of final training for the first concentration is an actual absorption of the first concentration because it has all the branches of the first concentration.

The definition of a supramundane [mental contemplation] of a mere beginner that is a preparation for the first concentration is:

> a mere beginner's preparation having the aspect of any of the three selflessnesses.

One can extend the reasoning similarly for the remaining ones.

Although someone who has just attained simultaneous Foe Destroyerhood has attained an actual first concentration, he has not attained the actual meditative absorptions of the seven remaining [concentrations and formless absorptions] because (1) when the eight actual meditative absorptions are newly attained, they must be manifestly generated,[a] and (2) since the first exists manifestly in his continuum, the remaining ones cannot become manifest. Nevertheless, a [simultaneous] Foe Destroyer need not achieve [the remaining concentrations and formless absorptions] by way of the preparations possessing [the usual] objects of observation and aspects because the preparations conquer the afflictive emotions of the lower [level], but [a simultaneous Foe Destroyer] has already conquered those [afflictive emotions]. This is because, although he does not achieve [the remaining concentrations and formless absorptions] in that way, he can enter into any meditative absorption he wishes.

Ascertainment of the Number

For the achievement of the actual meditative absorptions by way of the preparations, the number is definite as seven mental contemplations because those seven are sufficient.[b] (1) Someone who has not generated the preparations that abandon the afflictive emotions pertaining to the Desire Realm [needs] the two, the mental contemplations of individual knowledge of the character and belief, in order to generate them; (2) the mental contemplation of analysis is needed for enhancing what has already been done; (3) with respect to the entities of the paths that abandon the afflictive emotions pertaining to the Desire Realm, there are the three—thorough isolation, which abandons the three cycles of great [afflictive emotions]; joy-withdrawal, which abandons the three cycles of middling [afflictive emotions, and] final training, which abandons the three cycles of small afflictive emotions; (4) in terms of effect,

---

[a] Someone who has just attained simultaneous Foe Destroyerhood has the capacity to attain the seven remaining concentrations and formless absorptions but has not yet done so.

[b] "By way of the preparations" eliminates the simultaneous Foe Destroyer.

there is [575] the mental contemplation that is the fruit of final training. This is because, with respect to even the order of those mental contemplations, although, according to the mundane path, [the mental contemplation of] analysis is generated only after [that of] joy-withdrawal, at the time of the supramundane path, the generation of [the mental contemplation of] analysis occurs before joy-withdrawal.

There are many ways of setting forth conventions of paths concerning these preparations because the conventions of the four paths, of the mundane and supramundane paths, and so forth, are used.[a]

The first reason [namely, that the convention of the four paths is used for the preparations] is established because the convention "path of training"[b] is used for the two, [the mental contemplations of] individual knowledge of the character and belief; the convention "uninterrupted path" is used for the two, thorough isolation and final training; the convention "path of enhancement" is used for [the mental contemplation of] analysis; and the convention of the four paths is used for joy-withdrawal.[c]

The second reason [namely, that the conventions of the mundane and supramundane paths, and so forth, are used] is established because the convention of the mundane path is used for the preparations having the aspects of grossness/peacefulness, and the convention of the supramundane path is used for those having the aspect of the truths.

Although the proponents of Vasubandhu's *Treasury of Manifest Knowledge* assert that the feeling of the preparations is necessarily equanimity, such is not asserted on this occasion because [on this occasion] they have the feeling of bliss.[d]

---

[a] According to Jam-yang-shay-pa, the four paths referred to here are the path of training (*sbyor ba'i lam*), the uninterrupted path (*bar chad med pa'i lam*), the path of release (*rnam par grol ba'i lam*), and the path of enhancement (*khyad par gyi lam*) (Jam-yang-shay-pa, *Concentrations*, 240.6–241.1). "And so forth" refers to the nine cycles of a path of meditation, which Jam-yang-shay-pa explains in relation to mundane and supramundane paths of meditation.

[b] *sbyor lam* is translated as "path of training" here because Jam-yang-shay-pa explains that this is not "the path of preparation" in the context of the five paths (Jam-yang-shay-pa, *Concentrations*, 241.2–3) and because the translation "preparation," in that context, is based on an oral explanation specific to that context.

[c] Jam-yang-shay-pa does not explicitly assign "path of release" to specific preparations. He explains in detail the convention of the four paths in relation to joy-withdrawal (Jam-yang-shay-pa, *Concentrations*, 242.6–243.1).

[d] Vasubandhu, *Treasury of Manifest Knowledge*, 8.22a–b (P5591, vol. 115, 274.5.2; Shastri, part 4, p. 1161; La Vallée Poussin, 16:5, p. 178; Pruden, vol. 4, p. 1253). "This occasion" refers to the Mahāyāna presentations. Jam-yang-shay-pa cites Asaṅga's *Grounds of*

MODE OF ENTERING INTO MEDITATIVE ABSORPTION IN THE FIRST CONCENTRATION BY WAY OF SUPRAMUNDANE MENTAL CONTEMPLATIONS HAVING THE ASPECT OF THE TRUTHS

There is a way of entering into meditative absorption in the first concentration by way of the seven supramundane mental contemplations having the aspect of the truths because, for Hearers who proceed simultaneously, (1) there is cultivation of the two having the aspect of the truths—calm abiding and the mental contemplation of individual knowledge of the character—at the time of the path of accumulation; (2) a state arisen from meditation which analyzes the object, selflessness; the mental contemplation of belief; the heat stage of the Hearer path of preparation; and the small forbearance of non-fear with respect to selflessness are attained simultaneously; (3) the middling forbearance of non-fear with respect to selflessness and the peak [stage of the Hearer path of preparation] are attained simultaneously; [576] (4) the great forbearance of non-fear with respect to [selflessness] and the forbearance stage [of the Hearer path of preparation] are attained simultaneously; (5) the path that is a facsimile of direct realization—the appearance of duality with respect to selflessness having vanished—and the supreme [mundane] quality [of the Hearer path of preparation] are attained simultaneously; (6) all four of those are the occasion of [the mental contemplation of] belief having the aspect of the truths; (7) the path of seeing and [the mental contemplation of] thorough isolation are simultaneous; (8) after that, when one has abandoned the nine cycles of afflictive emotions to be abandoned by meditation by way of the remaining preparations—[the mental contemplation of] analysis, and so forth—the attainment of the ninth path of release, the attainment of an actual first concentration, and the attainment of Foe Destroyerhood are simultaneous.

Indication similarly [of the mode of entering into meditative absorption] in the remaining [concentrations and formless absorptions] by way of [the seven mental contemplations]

According to the mundane path, [everything] ranging from entering into actual meditative absorption, when one has achieved the first concentration by way of the seven mental contemplations, up to the peak

---

Hearers and Tsong-kha-pa's *Golden Rosary* (Jam-yang-shay-pa, *Concentrations,* 244.5–245.1).

of cyclic existence, is similar. This is because, when an actual first concentration is newly achieved in terms of being arisen from training, no matter whether it is mundane or supramundane, the preparations are definitely needed. However, with respect to the remaining [levels], there is attainment of the actual meditative absorptions in terms of being arisen from training without their being preceded by [their respective] preparations.[a]

Dispelling objections

FIRST DEBATE

Incorrect position: It follows that it is not correct to posit the ninth path of release as an actual meditative absorption of the first concentration because [the ninth path of release] has two [types]: an actual meditative absorption and a preparation. It follows [that it has two types: an actual meditative absorption and a preparation] because it has such in the Vaibhāṣhika system.

Correct position: It is not entailed [that if the ninth path of release has two types—an actual meditative absorption and a preparation—in the Vaibhāṣhika system, it necessarily has two types]. The reason [namely, that the ninth path of release has two types—an actual meditative absorption and a preparation—in the Vaibhāṣhika system] is established because, in [the Vaibhāṣhika] system, the ninth mundane path of release for the first three concentrations has two [types]—a preparation and an actual meditative absorption—and the ninth mundane path of release for the fourth concentration and above necessarily has only an actual meditative absorption. [577] This is because Vasubandhu's *Treasury of Manifest Knowledge* [6.48a–c] says:

> That concentration which has conquered over the three levels
> Or [is] the path of release at the end among the preparations
> Is not among the preparations for the higher [concentrations and formless absorptions.[b]

---

[a] There *is* such attainment because a simultaneous Foe Destroyer who has attained an actual first concentration does not have to do the preparations for the remaining seven levels to attain the actual absorptions.

[b] Vasubandhu, *Treasury of Manifest Knowledge,* 6.48a–c (P5591, vol. 115, 253.2.4, 6; Shastri, part 3, p. 976; La Vallée Poussin 16:3, pp. 237–38; Pruden, vol. 3, pp. 988–89). This debate refutes Paṇ-chen Sö-nam-drak-pa's interpretation of this verse (*Meditative States,* pp. 153–54).

The ninth path of release is a mental contemplation that is the fruit of final training. According to Jam-yang-shay-pa's and Kön-chok-jik-may-wang-po's interpretation of

SECOND DEBATE

Incorrect position: It follows that the third concentration and those above it have the feeling of joy because [the third concentration and those above it] have mental contemplations of joy.

Correct position: It is not entailed [that if the third concentration and those above it have mental contemplations of joy they necessarily have the feeling of joy] because, although [the third concentration and those above it] do not have the joy of [the branches] joy and bliss, the convention "joy" is used for the clarifying of the mind [in the paths of release of the mental contemplation of joy-withdrawal].

THIRD DEBATE

Incorrect position: It follows that the subject, the mental contemplation of analysis that is a preparation for the first concentration, is included in an upper realm because it is included in the six levels of concentration.[a]

Correct position: It is not entailed [that whatever is included in the six levels of concentration is necessarily included in an upper realm]. You cannot accept [that the mental contemplation of analysis that is a preparation for the first concentration is included in an upper realm].

Moreover, it [absurdly] follows that the subject, [the mental contemplation of analysis that is a preparation for the first concentration],

---

the Vaibhāṣhika position, it can be a preparation for the first, second, and third concentrations because, according to the Vaibhāṣhikas, the preparations have the feeling of equanimity, whereas the first three concentrations have the feeling of bliss. A meditator of dull faculties would find it difficult to change from equanimity to bliss, whereas a meditator of sharp faculties would find it easy. Therefore, for a meditator of dull faculties, the ninth path of release would be a preparation, whereas, for a meditator of sharp faculties, it would be an actual absorption. However, the ninth path of release would not be among the preparations for the fourth concentration or for the formless absorptions—the "higher [concentrations and formless absorptions]" mentioned in the verse—because the fourth concentration and the formless absorptions have the feeling of equanimity, not the feeling of bliss. Therefore, according to Jam-yang-shay-pa's and Kön-chok-jik-may-wang-po's interpretation of the Vaibhāṣhika system, no change of feeling would be necessary at that point.

Jam-yang-shay-pa holds that "the positing of the feeling of equanimity as a branch [of the preparations] is concordant with Vasubandhu's *Treasury of Manifest Knowledge.* It is not concordant with Asaṅga's *Grounds of Hearers*" (Jam-yang-shay-pa, *Concentrations,* 257.5–6).

[a] The six levels of concentration are the preparations, the mere first concentration, the special first concentration, and the second, third, and fourth concentrations.

is a causal meditative absorption of the first concentration because of being a preparation for the first concentration.[a]

It is not entailed [that whatever is a preparation for the first concentration is necessarily a causal meditative absorption of the first concentration].

If you accept [that the mental contemplation of analysis that is a preparation for the first concentration is a causal meditative absorption of the first concentration], it [absurdly] follows that [the mental contemplation of analysis that is a preparation for the first concentration] is a meditative absorption because you have accepted [that the mental contemplation of analysis that is a preparation for the first concentration is a causal meditative absorption of the first concentration].

You cannot accept [that the mental concentration of analysis that is a preparation for the first concentration is a meditative absorption] because it is an awareness that analyzes in that way in a subsequent attainment.

FOURTH DEBATE

Incorrect position: It follows that a newly attained mundane path of meditation in the continuum of a Superior is necessarily a path of meditation because [a newly attained mundane path of meditation in the continuum of a Superior] is necessarily a path of a Superior.[b]

Correct position: It is not entailed [that if a newly attained mundane path of meditation in the continuum of a Superior is necessarily a path of a Superior, it is necessarily also a path of meditation].

You cannot accept [that a newly attained mundane path of meditation in the continuum of a Superior is necessarily a path of meditation] because [a newly attained mundane path of meditation in the continuum of a Superior can also be] the two, a path of seeing and a Hearer path of no more learning.[c]

FIFTH DEBATE

Incorrect position: It follows that the subject, a mundane mental

[a] The preparations for the first concentration are absorptions included within the level of the first concentration, but they are not actual absorptions.

[b] The reason establishes that *'phags lam,* literally "Superior path," means "path of a Superior" (*'phags pa'i lam*).

[c] This is really a question of entailment. It is not *necessarily* a path of meditation because there are two other possibilities.

contemplation of analysis, has the aspect of either grossness or peacefulness because it is mundane preparation.

Correct position: It is not entailed [that whatever is a mundane preparation necessarily has the aspect of either grossness or peacefulness].

You cannot accept [that a mundane mental contemplation of analysis has the aspect of either grossness or peacefulness] because [a mundane mental contemplation of analysis] necessarily analyzes only whether one has separated from the three cycles of small coarse afflictive emotions pertaining to the Desire Realm. [578]

SIXTH DEBATE

Incorrect position: It follows that the subject, a simultaneous Foe Destroyer, is a Foe Destroyer who is released from the factors of both [the afflictive obstructions and obstructions to meditative absorption] because, among [simultaneous Foe Destroyers], there are cases of those who are [released from the factors of both the afflictive obstructions and obstructions to meditative absorption].[a]

Correct position: It is not entailed [that if, among simultaneous Foe Destroyers, there are cases of those who are released from the factors of both the afflictive obstructions and obstructions to meditative absorption, a simultaneous Foe Destroyer is necessarily a Foe Destroyer who is released from the factors of both the afflictive obstructions and obstructions to meditative absorption].

SEVENTH DEBATE

Incorrect position: It follows that the subject, the obstructions to meditative absorption, are obstructions to omniscience because (1) they are obstructions and (2) they [can] exist in the continuum of a Foe Destroyer.

Correct position: It is not entailed [that whatever is an obstruction and

---

[a] In other words, if a simultaneous Foe Destroyer generates all eight concentrations and formless absorptions, he or she is released from obstructions to absorption. Moreover, such a person does not need to generate the second concentration and the levels above it by means of the preparations for them; it seems that all he or she has to do is to think of the branches or object of observation of the concentration or formless absorption in question. There are many Foe Destroyer who do this and who, therefore, do not have obstructions to absorption. However, the statement would not apply to all simultaneous Foe Destroyers because it would not apply to someone who has just attained simultaneous Foe Destroyerhood.

can exist in the continuum of a Foe Destroyer is necessarily an obstruction to omniscience] because there are [also] the two—Non-Returners and Hearer Foe Destroyers—who abandon them.[a]

EXPLANATION OF THE ACTUAL MEDITATIVE ABSORPTIONS THAT ARE TO BE ATTAINED

This has three parts: the explanations of (1) the entities of the concentrations and formless absorptions; (2) the features of the branches, objects of observation, and subjective aspects; and (3) the effects attained.

ENTITIES OF THE MEDITATIVE ABSORPTIONS OF THE CONCENTRATIONS AND FORMLESS ABSORPTIONS

This has three parts: refutation [of mistaken opinions], presentation [of our own system], and dispelling objections.

Refutation [of mistaken opinions]

FIRST DEBATE

Incorrect position: The definition of a meditative absorption is:

> a consciousness that is either a main [mind—that is,] meditative stabilization—or a mental factor in its "retinue."

Correct position: It [absurdly] follows that there are mental factors in the "retinue" of meditative stabilization because [according to you] the definition [of "meditative absorption" as a consciousness that is either a main mind—that is, meditative stabilization—or a mental factor in its "retinue"] is correct. You cannot accept [that there are mental factors in the "retinue" of meditative stabilization] because meditative stabilization is a mental factor. This is because, with respect to the positing of minds and mental factors as main and in the "retinue" [respectively], that which exists independently with respect to the basis, and so forth,

---

[a] A Non-Returner has the first concentration because Non-Returners overcome all nine cycles of afflictive emotions pertaining to the Desire Realm; that is what makes them Non-Returners. However, the correct position implies that a Non-Returner could have all eight absorptions, including that of the peak of cyclic existence. It is this type of person—someone who has generated all eight absorptions—who does not have obstructions to absorption.

Hearer Foe Destroyer are probably specified because Solitary Realizer Foe Destroyers are necessarily simultaneous.

is presented as the main [mind], and that which does not exist [independently with respect to the basis, and so forth] is presented as in the "retinue."

Second debate

Incorrect position: It follows that the subject, a meditative absorption of the first concentration having the aspects of grossness/peacefulness, views the upper realm as peaceful because, between having the aspect of grossness or [that of] peacefulness, it is a viewing as peaceful.

Correct position: It is not entailed [that whatever, between having the aspect of grossness or that of peacefulness, is a viewing as peaceful necessarily views the upper realm as peaceful].

If you accept [that a meditative absorption of the first concentration having the aspects of grossness/peacefulness views the upper realm as peaceful], it [absurdly] follows that it is a viewing [of the upper realm] as a true cessation!

You cannot accept [that a meditative absorption of the first concentration having the aspects of grossness/peacefulness views the upper realm as a true cessation] [579] because it must be posited relatively in terms of positing that is relative to a place of relation.

Third debate

Incorrect position: Whatever is an actual meditative absorption of the first concentration has necessarily separated from attachment to the level below.

Correct position: It [absurdly] follows that the subject, a mere actual meditative absorption of the first concentration in the continuum of a [non-Buddhist] Outsider who has attained the eight concentrations and formless absorptions, [has separated from attachment from the level below] because of being [an actual meditative absorption of the first concentration].[a]

You cannot accept [that a mere actual meditative absorption of the first concentration in the continuum of a [non-Buddhist] Outsider who has attained the eight concentrations and formless absorptions has separated from attachment to the level below] because he is a person

[a] A mere actual meditative absorption of the first concentration has both investigation and analysis and has the feeling of bliss, whereas a special actual meditative absorption of the first concentration has only analysis and has the feeling of equanimity.

who has in his continuum attachment included within the level of the Desire Realm.

Moreover, it [absurdly] follows that whatever is an actual meditative absorption of the second concentration has necessarily separated from the investigation and analysis of the first concentration because [according to you] your thesis [that whatever is an actual meditative absorption of the first concentration has necessarily separated from attachment to the level below] is correct.

You cannot accept [that whatever is an actual meditative absorption of the second concentration has necessarily separated from the investigation and analysis of the first concentration] because there are investigation and analysis in the continuum of a being of the Second Concentration who possesses in his continuum an actual second concentration. It follows [that there are investigation and analysis in the continuum of a being of the Second Concentration who possesses in his continuum an actual second concentration] because the eye and ear consciousnesses exist in the continuum [of a being of the Second Concentration].

It is entailed [that if the eye and ear consciousnesses exist in a being of the Second Concentration, there are necessarily investigation and analysis in the continuum of a being of the Second Concentration who possesses in his continuum an actual second concentration] because any [main] consciousness which is a sense consciousness necessarily has investigation and analysis in its "retinue."

At the time of challenge to the entailment [that if the eye and ear consciousnesses exist in a being of the Second Concentration, there are necessarily investigation and analysis in the continuum of a being of the Second Concentration], the reason [namely, that the eye and ear consciousnesses exist in the continuum of a being of the Second Concentration] is established because the distinction is correct that [in the Second Concentration] the three—eye, ear, and body [main] consciousnesses—and, for each, the investigation and analysis that are in the "retinue" of these three, exist but that they are included in the level of the First Concentration.

FOURTH DEBATE

Incorrect position: Whatever is an actual meditative absorption of the first concentration necessarily possesses five branches—investigation, analysis, and so forth.[a]

---

[a] The five branches are investigation, analysis, joy, bliss, and meditative stabilization.

Correct position: It [absurdly] follows that the subject, a special actual meditative absorption of the first concentration, [possesses five branches—investigation, analysis, and so forth] because [of being an actual meditative absorption of the first concentration].

You cannot accept [that a special actual meditative absorption of the first concentration possesses five branches—investigation, analysis, and so forth] because a special actual meditative absorption of the first concentration necessarily does not have the investigation that is a changeable mental factor [580] and [necessarily] has as its feeling the feeling of equanimity.

FIFTH DEBATE

Incorrect position: If something is the investigation, analysis, and so forth, that is a branch of a lower concentration, it is necessarily an obstruction with respect to a higher concentration or in [the higher concentration's] dissimilar class.

Correct position: It [absurdly] follows that the subject, the investigation and analysis that are branches of the first concentration in the continuum of a Bodhisattva on the path of preparation who is of definite lineage from the beginning and who has attained the five powers, [are obstructions with respect to the second concentration or in its dissimilar class] because they are the investigation and analysis that are branches of a lower concentration].[a]

You cannot accept [that the investigation and analysis that are branches of the first concentration in the continuum of a Bodhisattva on the path of preparation who is of definite lineage from the beginning and who has attained the five powers are obstructions with respect to the second concentration or in its dissimilar class] because they do not obstruct [the second concentration]. This is because, although the contextual etymology is propounded in many [texts], they do not obstruct the first concentration. This is because, similarly, the second concentration is not obstructed by investigation and analysis; the third, by joy; or the fourth, by endeavor in the apprehension of phenomena. It follows [that the second concentration is not obstructed

---

[a] The subject rules out someone who had attained concentrations as a Hearer before entering the Bodhisattva path.

The five powers are included in the thirty-seven harmonies with enlightenment. They are: faith, effort, mindfulness, meditative stabilization, and wisdom, and they are attained on the heat and peak levels of the path of preparation (Hopkins, *Meditation on Emptiness*, p. 206).

by investigation and analysis; the third, by joy; or the fourth, by endeavor in the apprehension of phenomena] because this person has attained a power of meditative stabilization such that these are not obstructed.

Moreover, fling [such consequences] with regard to [these] in the continuum of a Buddha Superior or a Bodhisattva Superior.

Sixth Debate

Incorrect position: When pure meditative absorptions are divided, there are the four: concordant with degeneration, concordant with abiding, concordant with enhancement, and concordant with definite differentiation. The respective definitions of the four—concordant with degeneration, and so forth—are posited as:

(1) a meditative absorption concordant with the generation of its dissimilar class immediately after itself;

(2) [a meditative absorption concordant with] the generation of a meditative absorption of its own level immediately after itself;

(3) [a meditative absorption concordant with] the generation of a meditative absorption of a higher level immediately after itself;

(4) a meditative absorption concordant with the generation of the uncontaminated immediately after itself.

Correct position: It [absurdly] follows that the subject, an actual meditative absorption of the first concentration that alternates with a Desire Realm mind in the descending [order] in the continuum of a Bodhisattva Superior, [581] is concordant with degeneration because of fulfilling the first definition [namely, a meditative absorption concordant with the generation of its dissimilar class immediately after itself].[a]

The reason [namely, that an actual meditative absorption of the first concentration that alternates with a Desire Realm mind in the descending order in the continuum of a Bodhisattva Superior is a meditative absorption concordant with the generation of its dissimilar class immediately after itself] is established because it is a meditative

[a] The subject refers to a Bodhisattva Superior's generation of the actual meditative absorptions of the concentrations and formless absorptions in ascending order, from the first concentration to the peak of cyclic existence; then in descending order, from the peak of cyclic existence to the first concentration; and then back to the fourth concentration. Each of these actual meditative absorptions is alternated with a Desire Realm mind.

absorption that generates a consciousness of the Desire Realm immediately after itself.

It is entailed [that whatever is a meditative absorption that generates a consciousness of the Desire Realm immediately after itself is necessarily a meditative absorption concordant with the generation of its dissimilar class immediately after itself] because the two—a Desire Realm mind in the continuum of a learner and the discursiveness of the Desire Realm—are its dissimilar class. This is because it is an actual meditative absorption of the first concentration in the continuum of a learner.

It is entailed [that if it is an actual meditative absorption of the first concentration in the continuum of a learner, the two—a Desire Realm mind in the continuum of a learner and the discursiveness of the Desire Realm—are necessarily its dissimilar class] because an actual meditative absorption of the first concentration has five types in its dissimilar class. It follows [that an actual meditative absorption of the first concentration has five types in its dissimilar class] because there are the five:

1 the two, attachment to the Desire Realm and a harmful mind;
2 the two, harmfulness and discursiveness;
3 the two, suffering and mental discomfort;
4 deviant ethics; and
5 distraction.

This is because, similarly, there are five in the dissimilar class of the second concentration, four in the dissimilar class of the third concentration, and eight in the dissimilar class of the fourth concentration.

The first reason [namely, that there are five in the dissimilar class of the second concentration] is established because there are the five:

1 attachment to the First Concentration;
2 investigation and analysis;
3 suffering;
4 excitement; and
5 incomplete meditative stabilization.[a]

The second reason [namely, that there are four in the dissimilar class of the third concentration] is established because there are the

[a] Excitement in this context seems to go with investigation and analysis, which prevent the completion of meditative stabilization. It is not the excitement that is a fault in the cultivation of calm abiding.

four:

1 attachment to the Second Concentration;
2 joy;
3 bliss; and
4 incomplete meditative stabilization.

The third reason [namely, that there are eight in the dissimilar class of the fourth concentration] is established because Vasubandhu's *Treasury of Manifest Knowledge* [8.11] says:

> Because of being released from the eight faults,
> The fourth concentration is unfluctuating.
> They are: investigation, analysis, the two breaths,
> And the four—[feeling of] pleasure, and so forth.[a]

You cannot accept the root statement [namely, that an actual meditative absorption of the first concentration that alternates with a Desire Realm mind in the descending order in the continuum of a Bodhisattva Superior is concordant with degeneration] because there is no concordance with degeneration in the continuum of a Bodhisattva Superior. [582]

Moreover, it follows that those definitions are not correct because there is also generation of that concordant with degeneration and that concordant with abiding immediately after that concordant with degeneration; except for that concordant with definite differentiation, there is generation of the [other] three immediately after that concordant with abiding; except for that concordant with degeneration, there is generation of the [other] three immediately after the third concordance [that concordant with enhancement]; and there is generation of itself immediately after the fourth concordance [that concordant with definite differentiation]. This is because Vasubandhu's *Treasury of Manifest Knowledge* [8.18a–b] says:

> Immediately after that concordant with degeneration, and so forth,
> There are two, three, three, and one.[b]

---

[a] Vasubandhu, *Treasury of Manifest Knowledge,* 8.11 (P5591, vol. 115, 273.1.5–6; Shastri, part 4, p. 1150; La Vallée Poussin, 16:5, p. 161; Pruden, vol. 4, p. 1239).
[b] Ibid., 8.18a–b (P5591, vol. 115, 274.1.8; Shastri, part 4, p. 1157; La Vallée Poussin, 16:5, p. 172; Pruden, vol. 4, p. 1248).

Our own system

This section has two parts: explanation of the concentrations and formless absorptions and explanation of the distinctions of entering into and rising from [the meditative absorptions of the concentrations and formless absorptions], and so forth.

Explanation of the concentrations and formless absorptions

This section has two parts: the explanation of the four concentrations by way of[a] the branches and the explanation of the four formless absorptions by way of the objects of observation and subjective aspects.

EXPLANATION OF THE FOUR CONCENTRATIONS BY WAY OF THE BRANCHES

This section has four parts: definition, etymologies, divisions, and the individual meanings of the divisions.

DEFINITION

The definition of an actual meditative absorption of a concentration is:

> a consciousness that is either a meditative stabilization posited from the point of view of possessing antidotal, benefit, and basis branches or that possessing association with it.

ETYMOLOGIES

Because of doing contemplation (*sems par byed pa*), it is called a concentration (*bsam gtan*), and because it engages the mind and mental factors equally (*cha mnyam du 'jug pa*) on the object of observation, it is called a meditative absorption (*snyoms 'jug*).

DIVISIONS

When [concentrations] are divided by way of[b] what branches are attained and what branches are set aside, there are four [types of division—namely, the four concentrations]. [583] When they are divided in terms of the basis, there are two types: those in the continua of

---

[a] 582.4, reading *yan lag gi sgo nas* instead of *yan lag gi sgos.*

[b] 582.6, reading *thob gtong gis* instead of *thob gtong gi.*

common beings and of Superiors. In terms of cause and effect, there are the two, causal concentrative meditative absorptions and concentrations that are resultant births. In terms of substantial entity, there are the three: afflicted, pure, and uncontaminated. In terms of objects of observation and subjective aspects, there are the two: pure mundane virtues and uncontaminated [concentrations] having the aspect of the truths.

THE INDIVIDUAL MEANINGS OF THE DIVISIONS

There are four [concentrations] in terms of the branches because (1) the [meditative absorption] of the first concentration is posited in terms of possessing branches antidotal to the level below—namely, investigation and analysis; (2) the [meditative absorption] of the second concentration is posited in terms of possessing, as its antidotal branch, internal clarity, which separates from attachment to the two, investigation and analysis; (3) the [meditative absorption] of the third concentration is posited in terms of having as its antidotal branches mindfulness, introspection, and equanimity, which separate from attachment to the joy of the second concentration; (4) the meditative absorption of the fourth concentration is posited in terms of possessing as its antidotal branches mindfulness and equanimity, which separate from the bliss of the third concentration. This is because Vasubandhu's *Treasury of Manifest Knowledge* [8.2a–b] says:

> ...which has abandoned the former branches
> Possessing analysis, joy, and bliss...[a]

There is a way of passing [from one level to the next higher one] by way of the branches because, although the higher [meditative absorptions] have not abandoned the branches of the lower, they, having separated from those as their branches, abide by way of other branches.[b]

The definition of an actual meditative absorption of the first concentration is:

> a meditative absorption of an upper level which is posited in terms of possessing analysis as an antidotal branch, joy and

[a] Vasubandhu, *Treasury of Manifest Knowledge,* 8.2a–b (P5591, vol. 115, 270.4.6–7; Shastri, part 4, p. 1129; La Vallée Poussin, 16:5, p. 132; Pruden, vol. 4, pp. 1218–19).

[b] In other words, the higher absorptions do not abandon the branches of the lower, but they get rid of them, or separate from them. Kön-chok-jik-may-wang-po does not want to use the word *spangs* ("abandon") here.

> bliss as benefit branches, and meditative stabilization as the basis branch. [584]

When [actual meditative absorptions of the first concentration] are divided, there are the two, mere and special. The definition of a mere actual meditative absorption of the first concentration is:

> a meditative absorption of an upper level that possesses investigation as the antidotal branch.

This is because Vasubandhu's *Treasury of Manifest Knowledge* [8.7a–b] says:

> The first [concentration] has five [branches]:
> Investigation, analysis, joy, bliss, and meditative stabilization.[a]

The definition of a special actual meditative absorption of the first concentration is:

> a meditative absorption of an upper level which, having separated from [possessing] investigation as its branch by way of its antidotal [branch] analysis, possesses meditative stabilization as its basis branch and the feeling of equanimity as its benefit branch.

This is because Vasubandhu's *Treasury of Manifest Knowledge* [8.22d–8.23b].says: "The special concentration, [having separated] also from investigation," and, "Three aspects, without pleasure and without suffering."[b]

There is a reason why the first concentration has the two types, mere and special, and the remaining three concentrations do not have [such a division] because, in the first concentration, it is possible to separate from attachment to some [that is, a certain one] of its branches even though one does not separate from attachment to that level, whereas in the second concentration, and so forth, that is not possible.

The definition of an actual meditative absorption of the second concentration is:

> an actual meditative absorption of an upper level possessing internal clarity as the antidotal branch, joy and bliss as the

---

[a] Vasubandhu, *Treasury of Manifest Knowledge,* 8.7a–b (P5591, vol. 115, 271.5.6–272.1.5; Shastri, part 4, p. 1140; La Vallée Poussin, 16:5, p. 147; Pruden, vol. 4, p. 1229).

[b] Ibid., 8.22d–8.23b (P5591, vol. 115, 274.5.8, 275.1.1–2, 275.1.4; Shastri, part 5, p. 1162; La Vallée Poussin, 16:5, p. 180–82; Pruden, vol. 4, pp. 1254–55).

> benefit branches, and meditative stabilization as the basis branch.

This is because Vasubandhu's *Treasury of Manifest Knowledge* [8.7c] says:

> The second has four branches:
> Internal clarity, joy, and so forth.[a]

The definition of an actual meditative absorption of the third concentrations is:

> an actual meditative absorption of an upper level possessing the three—mindfulness, introspection, and the compositional factor of equanimity—as the antidotal branches, bliss that is free of joy as the benefit branch, and meditative stabilization as the basis branch. [585]

This is because Vasubandhu's *Treasury of Manifest Knowledge* [8.8a–b] says:

> The third has five [branches]: equanimity,
> Mindfulness, introspection, bliss, and the basis.[b]

The definition of an actual meditative absorption of the fourth concentration is:

> an actual meditative absorption possessing [entirely pure] mindfulness and the entirely pure compositional factor of equanimity as the antidotal branches, neutral feeling as the benefit branch, and meditative stabilization as the basis branch.

This is because Vasubandhu's *Treasury of Manifest Knowledge* [8.8c–d] says:

> The final [concentration] has four [branches]: mindfulness, equanimity,
> That [feeling] without bliss and without pain, and meditative stabilization.[c]

The definition of a causal meditative absorption of a concentration

---

[a] Ibid., 8.7c (P5591, vol. 115, 271.5.6–272.1.5; Shastri, part 4, p. 1140; La Vallée Poussin, 16:5, p. 147; Pruden, vol. 4, p. 1229).

[b] Ibid., 8.8a–b (P5591, vol. 115, 271.5.6–272.1.5; Shastri, part 4, p. 1140; La Vallée Poussin, 16:5, p. 147; Pruden, vol. 4, p. 1229).

[c] Ibid., 8.8c–d (P5591, vol. 115, 271.5.6–272.1.5; Shastri, part 4, p. 1140; La Vallée Poussin, 16:5, p. 147; Pruden, vol. 4, p. 1229).

is:

> a consciousness that either is a one-pointed mind that possesses antidotal, benefit, and basis branches and passes beyond the level below it by way of generation [of the branches] or possesses association with that.

When these meditative absorptions possess following, in this context they possess the four non-physical aggregates because there is no form following the mind. This is because even the concentrative disciplines and the uncontaminated disciplines are posited in relation to either contemplation or seed.[a]

The definition of a resultant-birth concentration is:

> a contaminated [phenomenon] included within either a fruitional effect, a causally concordant effect, or a possessional effect of cultivating, in another birth, a concentration that is a causal meditative absorption.

When [resultant-birth concentrations] are divided, there are fruitional effects—that is, the appropriative aggregates in the continuum of a Form Realm being; possessional effects—that is, an inestimable mansion, and so forth; and causally concordant effects—that is, the actual meditative absorptions, and so forth, [586] of the four concentrations attained by birth, in the continuum of [a Form Realm being].

When actual meditative absorptions of the concentrations are divided from the point of view of substantial entity, there are the three: afflicted, pure, and uncontaminated.

The *afflicted* has three parts: definition, divisions, and that basis which is afflicted.

Definition. The definition of an afflicted actual meditative absorption of a concentration is:

> (1) that which is the continuation of the substantial entity of a pure actual meditative absorption of a concentration that is its substantial cause and (2) that which has come to be associated with any of [the four]—attachment, [bad] view, pride, or ignorance—which are neutral.

Divisions. When [afflicted actual meditative absorptions of the concentrations] are divided, fundamentally there are the four afflicted

[a] These disciplines are not posited in relation to form—even non-revelatory form. (The meaning of "following" is not clear.)

[meditative absorptions] of the four concentrations, and secondarily each of the four [concentrations] has the four [meditative absorptions] possessing any of the four afflictive emotions—attachment, and so forth.

The definition of an afflicted meditative absorption of the first concentration is:

> the substantial entity of a meditative absorption of the first concentration which is a continuation of the type of a former pure actual meditative absorption of a concentration and has come to be associated with any of the four [afflictive emotions]—attachment, and so forth—of its own level.

The definition of a meditative absorption of the first concentration possessing attachment is:

> the type of the substantial entity of a meditative absorption of the first concentration associated with attachment of its own level.

Extend this to the others in that way.

That basis which is afflicted. There is a meditative absorption that is the basis which is afflicted because a pure actual meditative absorption of any of the four concentrations is posited as such. Uncontaminated meditative absorptions are not posited as such because there is no way in which the later continuation of the substantial entity of uncontaminated [meditative absorptions] can arise [587] even associated with any of those afflictive emotions.

The western Vaibhāṣhikas assert afflicted meditative absorptions as [having] four [types] because Vasubandhu's *Treasury of Manifest Knowledge* [5.21] says:

> The western Vaibhāṣhikas say these are four:
> Attachment, view, pride, and obscuration.[a]

The Kashmīri Vaibhāṣhikas assert that afflicted meditative absorptions necessarily are in association only with attachment as their concomitant because Vasubandhu's *Treasury of Manifest Knowledge* says, "Possessing attachment, which is associated with relishing (*ro myang tshungs ldan, āsvādanasaṃprayukta*)."[b]

---

[a] Vasubandhu, *Treasury of Manifest Knowledge,* 5.21 (P5591, vol. 115, 227.1.1–2; Shastri, part 3, pp. 795–96; La Vallée Poussin, 16:4, p. 43; Pruden, vol. 3, p. 799).

[b] Vasubandhu, *Treasury of Manifest Knowledge* and *Autocommentary on the "Treasury of Manifest Knowledge,"* 8.6b–c (P5591, vol. 115, 271.5.1–4; Shastri, part 4, p. 1169; La Vallée

[Afflicted meditative absorptions] are also similar in the formless absorptions.

When *pure* actual meditative absorptions of concentrations are divided, there are four types: concordant with degeneration, concordant with abiding, concordant with enhancement, and concordant with definite differentiation.

The definition of an actual meditative absorption of a concentration concordant with degeneration is:

> a pure actual meditative absorption of a concentration concordant with the generation of an afflictive emotion of its own or a lower level immediately after itself.

The definition of an actual meditative absorption of a concentration concordant with abiding is:

> a pure actual meditative absorption of a concentration that induces another pure [actual meditative absorption] of the same level as itself immediately after itself.

The definition of an actual meditative absorption of a concentration concordant with enhancement is:

> an actual meditative absorption of a concentration that induces a pure actual meditative absorption of a higher level than itself immediately after itself.

The peak of cyclic existence does not have a type concordant with enhancement.

The definition of an actual meditative absorption of a concentration concordant with definite differentiation is:

> a pure actual meditative absorption of a concentration immediately after which an uncontaminated path is manifestly generated. [588]

When uncontaminated meditative absorptions are divided, there are two types: a contaminated, conceptual type and an uncontaminated type free from conceptuality.

Explanation of the Four Formless Absorptions by Way of the Objects of Observation and Subjective Aspects

This section has four parts: definition, etymology, explanations of the

---

Poussin, 16:5, pp. 144–46; Pruden, vol. 4, p. 1228).

meanings of the divisions, and the explanation of the distinction of the existence or non-existence of branches.

Definition. The definition of an actual meditative absorption of a formless absorption is:

> an actual meditative absorption of an upper [level], having the type of being posited from the point of view of its object of observation and subjective aspect without having branches, which arises from having familiarized oneself again and again, mainly by way of calm abiding, with any of the discriminations of space, and so forth, upon having viewed as coarse any of the discriminations of form, space, consciousness, and nothingness for one's awareness at the time of training.

Etymology. With respect to the subject, [a formless absorption,] there is a reason for its being called a meditative absorption of a formless absorption because it is called formless since the discrimination of form has been destroyed or because there is not the least form, and it is called [a meditative absorption] since it causes the mind and mental factors to engage equally in the object of observation.

Explanations of the meanings of the divisions. When [formless absorptions] are divided, there are the four, limitless space, and so forth. The definition of an actual meditative absorption of limitless space is:

> an actual meditative absorption of an upper level which enters into equipoise by way of calm abiding with respect to space as limitless, upon the destruction of the discrimination of form, and which is posited in terms of its object of observation and subjective aspect without possessing branches. [589]

The definition of an actual meditative absorption of limitless consciousness is:

> [an actual meditative absorption of an upper level] which enters into equipoise by way of calm abiding with respect to consciousness as limitless, upon the destruction of the discrimination of space [and which is posited in terms of its object of observation and subjective aspect without possessing branches].

The definition of an actual meditative absorption of nothingness is:

> [an actual meditative absorption of an upper level] which enters into equipoise by way of calm abiding with respect to the factor of there being nothing to be apprehended, upon the

> destruction, moreover, of the discrimination of consciousness [and which is posited in terms of its object of observation and subjective aspect without possessing branches].

The definition of an actual meditative absorption without discrimination and without non-discrimination is:

> [an actual meditative absorption of an upper level] which enters into equipoise by way of calm abiding with respect to the factor of coarse discrimination's being non-existent but subtle discrimination's not being non-existent, and upon the destruction, moreover, of the discrimination of nothingness [and which is posited in terms of its object of observation and subjective aspect without possessing branches.

By the statement of qualification [that is, "which is posited in terms of"], the [formless absorptions] having the aspect of the truths are included.

Each [of the formless absorptions] has the two types—contaminated and uncontaminated—and the two types—causal meditative absorptions and resultant-birth absorptions—and so forth.

The distinction of the existence or non-existence of branches. None of the upper and lower [schools of tenets] asserts branches of the actual meditative absorptions of the formless absorptions because the convention of branches of [the formless absorptions] is not stated in any sūtra or [commentarial] treatise (*bstan bcos, śāstra*). Another reason is that, when the meditative absorptions of the formless absorptions are newly achieved, one enters [into meditative absorption] by way of the later object of observation and subjective aspect upon leaving the discrimination of the previous object of observation, and, therefore, the formless absorptions are posited as passing [to the next higher level] by way of their objects of observation and subjective aspects. [590]

The distinctions of entering into and rising from [the meditative absorptions of the concentrations and formless absorptions], and so forth

This section has three parts: (1) the distinctions of entering into and rising; (2) the distinctions of the mode of abandoning the dissimilar class; (3) the distinctions between complete and incomplete meditative stabilization.

The distinctions of entering into and rising. According to the tenets held in common with the lower [schools], when one enters into or rises from a meditative absorption of a given level, although there are sentient beings who can enter into and rise from pure and uncontaminated meditative absorptions computed, for instance, from the first concentration through the third concentration, there is none who can do so having crossed four levels because of being distant by way of the four distances—that is, basis, object of observation, subjective aspect, and level of meditative absorption. This is because Vasubandhu's *Treasury of Manifest Knowledge* says:

> Immediately after an uncontaminated [meditative absorption],
> Pure [meditative absorptions] are generated ranging over three [levels], upward or downward.
> After the pure [meditative absorptions], it is the same.[a]

According to the higher schools of tenets, there is generation of each of seventeen meditative absorptions immediately after each of the eight concentrations and formless absorptions because there is generation, for each, of each of the pure and uncontaminated eight concentrations and formless absorptions—that is, sixteen—and the meditative absorption of cessation—that is, seventeen.

The distinctions of the mode of abandoning the dissimilar class. Although Bodhisattvas deliberately abandon utterly the afflictive emotions included within ignorance and view, together with their dormancies, it is not the case that they do not engage in manifestly generating desire and attachment for the Desire Realm and the upper realms on certain occasions because there is engagement in generating them for the sake of others.

The distinctions between complete and incomplete meditative stabilization. [There are distinctions of completeness and incompleteness in the concentrations] because, although the two, the first and second concentrations, are similar in terms of being mere firm meditative stabilization, and so forth, they differ in the completeness of the strength of meditative stabilization; although the two, the second and third concentrations, are similar in just the completeness of meditative stabilization, [591] they differ in the completeness of the strength of help; although the two, the third and fourth concentrations, are similar in just the completeness of meditative stabilization and help, they differ in the completeness of purification of the faults of fluctuation.

[a] Vasubandhu, *Treasury of Manifest Knowledge*, 8.15 (P5591, vol. 115, 273.4.8–273.5.4; Shastri, part 4, pp. 1154–55; La Vallée Poussin, 16:5, pp. 168–69; Pruden, vol. 4, p. 1245).

The first reason [namely, that although the two, the first and second concentrations, are similar in being mere firm of meditative stabilization, and so forth, they differ in the completeness of the strength of meditative stabilization] is established because, at the time of the first concentration, since investigation and analysis cause the mind to fluctuate and not be peaceful and fluctuation again and again interrupts the continuum of peacefulness in one-pointedness of mind, the strength of meditative stabilization is incomplete, [whereas], at the time of the second concentration, the strength of [meditative stabilization], which has separated from [investigation and analysis], is complete.

The second reason [namely, that although the two, the second and third concentrations, are similar in just the completeness of meditative stabilization, they differ in the completeness of the strength of help] is established because at the time of the second concentration, since it is polluted by the fault of joy, the strength of help is incomplete, [whereas], at the time of the third concentration, since one has separated from the three entanglements of investigation, analysis, and joy, the strength of the three—the compositional factor of equanimity, mindfulness, and introspection—is complete.

The third reason [namely, that although the two, the third and fourth concentrations, are similar in just the completeness of meditative stabilization and help, they differ in the completeness of purification of the faults of fluctuation] is established because there is the correct distinction that in the fourth concentration, since one has become purified of the eight faults, there is completion of entirely pure equanimity and mindfulness, [whereas], in the three lower concentrations, there is no [completion of entirely pure equanimity and mindfulness].

Dispelling objections

First debate

Incorrect position: It follows that whatever is an actual meditative absorption of a concentration necessarily possesses its branches because [according to you] your definition [of an actual meditative absorption of a concentration as "a consciousness that is either a meditative stabilization posited from the point of view of possessing antidotal, benefit, and basis branches or that possessing association with it"] is correct.

If you accept [that whatever is an actual meditative absorption of a concentration necessarily possess its branches], it [absurdly] follows that the subject, an actual meditative absorption of the second concentration in the continuum of a Foe Destroyer of simultaneous abandonment, [592] [possesses the branches of the second concentration] because of being [an actual meditative absorption of the second concentration]. You have accepted the entailment [that whatever is an actual meditative absorption of the second concentration necessarily possesses the branches of the second concentration.

If you accept [that an actual meditative absorption of the second concentration in the continuum of a Foe Destroyer of simultaneous abandonment possesses the branches of the second concentration], it [absurdly] follows that the subject, [an actual meditative absorption of the second concentration in the continuum of a Foe Destroyer of simultaneous abandonment], possesses the antidotal branches [of the second concentration] because you have accepted [that an actual meditative absorption of the second concentration in the continuum of a Foe Destroyer of simultaneous abandonment possesses the branches of the second concentration].

If you accept [that an actual meditative absorption of the second concentration in the continuum of a Foe Destroyer of simultaneous abandonment possesses the antidotal branches of the second concentration], it [absurdly] follows that it is a direct continuation of the antidotes that conquered over the level below at the time of the preparations for [the second concentration] because you have accepted [that an actual meditative absorption of the second concentration in the continuum of a Foe Destroyer of simultaneous abandonment possesses the antidotal branches of the second concentration].

Correct position: It is not entailed [that if an actual meditative absorption of the second concentration in the continuum of a Foe Destroyer of simultaneous abandonment possesses the antidotal branches of the second concentration, it is necessarily a direct continuation of the antidotes that conquered over the level below at the time of the preparations for the second concentration].

You cannot accept [that an actual meditative absorption of the second concentration in the continuum of a Foe Destroyer of simultaneous abandonment is a direct continuation of the antidotes that conquered over the level below at the time of the preparations] because [an actual meditative absorption of the second concentration in the continuum of a Foe Destroyer of simultaneous abandonment] is not preceded by its preparations.

Incorrect position: With respect to the challenge to the entailment [that if an actual meditative absorption of the second concentration in the continuum of a Foe Destroyer of simultaneous abandonment possesses the antidotal branches of the second concentration, it is necessarily a direct continuation of the antidotes that conquered over the level below at the time of the preparations for the second concentration], such is entailed because whatever is an antidotal branch of [a concentration] must be a continuation of that which conquered over the level below at the time of its preparations. It follows [that whatever is an antidotal branch of a concentration must be a continuation of that which conquered over the level below at the time of its preparations] because Tsong-kha-pa's *Golden Rosary of Eloquence* says:

> Moreover, [the antidotal branches] are a continuation of the antidotes of the time of the preparations; at the time of the actual meditative absorption, they merely lengthen the distance from the level below but are not actual antidotes that abandon it.[a]

Correct position: It is not entailed [that this citation from Tsong-kha-pa's *Golden Rosary of Eloquence* means that whatever is an antidotal branch of a concentration must be a continuation of that which conquered over the level below at the time of the preparations] because, in terms of that which is preceded by its preparations, it is a continuation of them; however, whether it is preceded by [its preparations] or not, in the actual meditative absorption the so-called antidotal branches are not [antidotes] that abandon that which has not been abandoned; rather, the meaning is that they merely lengthen the distance from the afflictive emotions, and so forth, of the level below.

SECOND DEBATE

Incorrect position: It follows that whatever is a pure actual meditative absorption is necessarily among the four—that which is concordant with degeneration, abiding, enhancement, or definite differentiation—because those four [types] are explained with respect to [pure actual meditative absorptions].

Correct position: It is not entailed [that since those four types—concordant with degeneration, abiding, enhancement, and definite differentiation—are explained with respect to pure actual meditative absorptions, whatever is a pure actual meditative absorption is

[a] Tsong-kha-pa, *Golden Rosary*, *Collected Works*, vol. 17 (New Delhi: Guru Deva, 1979), 492.3.

necessarily among those four].

If you accept [that whatever is a pure actual meditative absorption is necessarily among the four—concordant with degeneration, abiding, enhancement, and definite differentiation], it [absurdly] follows that the subject, each of the eight pure meditative absorptions at the time of becoming absorbed in the eight pure meditative absorptions in the descending order, [is among the four—concordant with degeneration, abiding, enhancement, and definite differentiation] because of being [a pure meditative absorption.]

[The Features of] the Branches and of the Objects of Observation and Subjective Aspects

Refutation [of mistaken opinions] [593]

First debate

Incorrect position: Whatever is either investigation or analysis is necessarily not a wrong consciousness.

Correct position: It [absurdly] follows that the subject, analysis which is a changeable [mental factor] that accompanies a sense consciousness perceiving a snow mountain as blue, is not a wrong consciousness because of being either investigation or analysis.

Second debate

Incorrect position: The definition of investigation which is a changeable [mental factor] is:

> a mental factor that examines merely gross aspects of names together with their meanings.

The definition of analysis which is a changeable [mental factor] is:

> a mental factor that analyzes finely.

Correct position: With respect to the first [definition], it [absurdly] follows that the subject, the investigation that is a branch of a first concentration [and] that has become an uninterrupted path of the path of seeing, is [a mental factor that examines merely gross aspects of names together with their meanings] because of being [investigation which is a changeable mental factor].

If you accept [that the investigation that is a branch of a first concentration which has become an uninterrupted path of the path of seeing is a mental factor that examines merely gross aspects of names together with their meanings], it [absurdly] follows that it apprehends term and meaning as suitable to be mixed!

With respect to the second [definition], it [absurdly] follows that the subject, the special insight which finely analyzes its object and which is an actual fourth concentration, is [analysis which is a changeable mental factor] because of being [a mental factor that analyzes finely]. The reason [namely, that the special insight which finely analyzes its object and which is an actual fourth concentration is a mental factor which analyzes finely] is established because it is a special insight which finely analyzes its object. This is because it is that subject [namely, the special insight which finely analyzes its object and which is an actual fourth concentration]. It follows [that it is the special insight which finely analyzes its object and which is an actual fourth concentration] because there is [a special insight which finely analyzes its object and which is an actual fourth concentration].

[You cannot accept that the special insight which finely analyzes its object and which is an actual fourth concentration is analysis which is a changeable mental factor] because, since there is steady meditative stabilization in the second concentration and above, although one analyzes finely, it is explained that both investigation and analysis do not exist from the point of view that [such analysis] does not generate stress in the mind.

THIRD DEBATE

Incorrect position: It follows that the subject, the analysis which is a branch of the first concentration in the continuum of a common being, is a fault of concentration in the continuum of that [being] because of being a fault of the fourth concentration in the continuum of that [being].

Correct position: It is not entailed [that whatever is a fault of the fourth concentration in the continuum of a certain being is necessarily a fault of concentration in the continuum of that being].

You cannot accept [that the analysis which is a branch of the first concentration in the continuum of a common being is a fault of concentration in the continuum of that being] [594] because it is a branch of a concentration in the continuum of that [being]. This is because it is among the eighteen branches of the concentrations in the continuum of [a common being].

Fourth Debate

Incorrect position: There are no differences in how investigation and analysis are asserted in the four schools of tenets.

Correct position: It follows that that is incorrect because (1) The Vaibhāṣhikas treat the entities of those two [investigation and analysis] as [investigation's] being a mental factor that acts coarsely and [analysis,] a mental factor that acts finely, whereupon they assert that [investigation and analysis] occur as concomitants of a single mind; (2) the Sautrāntikas treat those two [investigation and analysis] as coarse and fine awarenesses that motivate speech expressing[, respectively,] the entity and features of an object, whereupon they assert that these do not arise as concomitants of a single mind; (3) the Cittamātrins and those above posit those two [investigation and analysis] from the point of view of coarse and fine engagement in their objects and coarse and fine functioning.

The first reason [namely, that the Vaibhāṣhikas treat the entities of those two, investigation and analysis, as investigation's being a mental factor that acts coarsely and analysis, a mental factor that acts finely, whereupon they assert that investigation and analysis occur as concomitants of a single mind] is established because they assert that, although the two [investigation and analysis] arise as concomitants of a single mind, investigation does not act very coarsely and analysis does not act very finely. This is because Vasubandhu's *Treasury of Manifest Knowledge* [2.33] says: "Investigation and analysis are coarse and fine."[a]

The second reason [namely, that the Sautrāntikas treat those two [investigation and analysis] as coarse and fine awarenesses that motivate speech expressing, respectively, the entity and features of an object whereupon they assert that these do not arise as concomitants of a single mind] is established because they assert that the explanation that there are five branches of an actual first concentration means that [the five branches] are included in [that] level, but those two [investigation and analysis] are not possessed as concomitants of a single mind. This is because Vasubandhu's *Autocommentary on the "Treasury of Manifest Knowledge"* [2.33] says, "They are explained as the five branches from [the point of view of] level, but they are not from [the same] moment."[b]

---

[a] Vasubandhu, *Treasury of Manifest Knowledge*, 2.33 (P5591, vol. 115, 147.3.3; Shastri, part 1, pp. 204–207; La Vallée Poussin, 16:1, p. 173; Pruden, vol. 1, pp. 202–204).

[b] Vasubandhu, *Autocommentary on the "Treasury of Manifest Knowledge,"* 2.33 (P5591, vol. 115, 147.3.5; Shastri, part 1, pp. 204–207; La Vallée Poussin, 16:1, pp. 175–76; Pruden, vol. 1, pp. 202–204).

The third reason [namely, that the Cittamātrins and those above posit those two, investigation and analysis, from the point of view of coarse and fine engagement in their objects and coarse and fine functioning] is established because investigation is posited as engaging coarsely in its object in dependence upon either intention or wisdom, and analysis is posited as engaging finely in its object in dependence upon [either intention or wisdom]. [595]

FIFTH DEBATE

Vaibhāṣhika position with respect to the distinction between joy and bliss: The two blisses of the first and second concentrations and of the third concentration have the same name but different meanings because, in the first two concentrations, pliancy is posited as bliss, but in the third concentration, a mental feeling—intention—is posited as bliss.

The first reason [namely, that in the first two concentrations, pliancy is posited as bliss] is established because (1) joy is mental bliss and (2) if two blissful feelings arose as the concomitants of a single mental consciousness, the similarity of substantial entity would be lost. The first reason [namely, that joy is mental bliss] is established because Vasubandhu's *Treasury of Manifest Knowledge* [8.9c–d] says: "Because of two scriptural passages, joy is mental bliss."[a] The second reason [namely, that if two blissful feelings arose as the concomitants of a single mental consciousness, the similarity of substantial entity would be lost] is easy.

The second root reason [namely, that in the third concentration, a mental feeling—intention—is posited as bliss] is established because Vasubandhu's *Treasury of Manifest Knowledge* says: "With respect to the third concentration, the mental [feeling] is the faculty of bliss."[b]

Sautrāntika position with respect to the distinction between joy and bliss: It follows that that is incorrect because "bliss" in "the joy and bliss that are branches of concentrations" must refer only to physical feeling. This is because Vasubandhu's *Autocommentary on the "Treasury of Manifest Knowledge"* says: "Others say, '...Also, in the [first] three concentrations, only physical bliss is presented as a branch.'"[c]

---

[a] Vasubandhu, *Treasury of Manifest Knowledge,* 8.9c–d (P5591, vol. 115, 272.2.2, 272.5.6; Shastri, part 4, pp. 1151–58; La Vallée Poussin, 16:5, pp. 150, 158–60; Pruden, vol. 4, p. 1237).

[b] Ibid., 2.7c–d (P5591, vol. 115, 140.4.5; Shastri, part 1, p. 146; La Vallée Poussin, 16:1, p. 114; Pruden, vol. 1, p. 160).

[c] Vasubandhu, *Autocommentary on the "Treasury of Manifest Knowledge,"* 8.9b (P5591, vol.

SIXTH DEBATE

Incorrect position: It follows that the internal clarity that is a branch of the second concentration is faith because the Vaibhāṣhikas assert such.

Correct position: It is not entailed [that if the Vaibhāṣhikas assert such, the internal clarity that is a branch of the second concentration is necessarily faith].

The reason [namely, that the Vaibhāṣhikas assert such] is established because Vasubandhu's *Treasury of Manifest Knowledge* [8.9c] says: "Internal clarity is faith."[a]

You cannot accept [that the internal clarity that is a branch of the second concentration is faith] because [the internal clarity that is a branch of the second concentration] is threefold: mindfulness, introspection, and equanimity.

Our own system

[596] This section has three parts: the entities, enumeration, and mode of possession of the branches.

The entities of the branches

The definition of the investigation that is a changeable [mental factor] is:

> a changeable mental factor that is posited in terms of motivating internal expression [or] speech and which engages its object coarsely and engages it with an aspect of examination in dependence upon either intention or wisdom.

Stating "intention or wisdom" indicates the substantial entity. Stating "coarsely and [...] examination" indicates the features of the mode of engagement. Stating "motivating internal expression [or] speech" indicates the features of the entity. Stating "posited in terms of" includes some which do not have all of those features. There is a purpose for stating variously, "either intention or wisdom" because the distinction is known that, when the object has not been settled, one relies mainly on intention, and when it has been settled, one relies mainly on wis-

115, 272.2.5–6; Shastri, part 4, p. 1143; La Vallée Poussin, 16:5, p. 150; Pruden, vol. 4, p. 1232).

[a] Vasubandhu, *Treasury of Manifest Knowledge,* 8.9c (P5591, vol. 115, 272.2.2, 272.5.6; Shastri, part 4, pp. 1151–58; La Vallée Poussin, 16:5, pp. 150, 158–60; Pruden, vol. 4, p. 1236).

dom. This is because Yashomitra's *Commentary on (Asaṅga's) "Summary of Manifest Knowledge"* says, "The reference of 'dependence upon intention or wisdom' is to the states of non-realization and realization, respectively."[a]

The definition of the investigation that is a branch of the first concentration is:

> (1) [a changeable mental factor that is posited in terms of motivating internal expression or speech and which engages its object coarsely and engages it with an aspect of examination in dependence upon either intention or wisdom]; (2) that which possesses association with its concomitant, the meditative stabilization of an actual first concentration.

When [the investigation that is a branch of the first concentration] is divided, there are two types: conceptual and non-conceptual. Whatever is [the investigation that is a branch of the first concentration] is necessarily only a mental consciousness and virtuous. If one eliminates the general substantial entity, a prime cognizer that is [the investigation that is a branch of the first concentration] is necessarily either a mental direct perceiver or a yogic perceiver.

The definition of the analysis that is a changeable [mental factor] is:

> a changeable mental factor that is posited in terms of individual analysis [597] from the point of view of finely engaging in the features, and so forth, of its object in dependence upon either intention or wisdom.

The fineness of the [engagement] is posited as fine analysis of the features, parts, and so forth, whether the object is coarse or subtle. Whatever analyzes in that way is not necessarily the analysis that is this [type of branch of a concentration] because it must be a changeable [mental factor] analyzing in that way.

The definition of the analysis that is a branch of the first concentration is:

> (1) [a changeable mental factor that is posited in terms of motivating internal expression or speech and which engages its ob-

---

[a] Yashomitra, *Commentary on (Asaṅga's) "Summary of Manifest Knowledge,"* P5554, vol. 113, 88.1.6. Kön-chok-jik-may-wang-po's citation reads...*mngon par mi rtogs pa dang mngon par rtogs pa'i gnas skabs*...whereas P5554 (and Jam-yang-shay-pa, *Concentrations*, 390.7) read...*mngon par mi rtog pa dang mngon par rtog pa'i gnas skabs*...—apparently a textual error.

> ject coarsely and engages it with an aspect of examination in dependence upon either intention or wisdom]; (2) that which possesses association with its concomitant, the meditative stabilization of an actual first concentration.

The divisions of [the analysis that is a branch of the first concentration] are similar to those of [the investigation that is a branch of the first concentration].

In general, with respect to joy, there are four possibilities between joy (*dga' ba, prīti*) and faith (*dad pa, śraddhā*) because afflicted joy must be taken as craving and non-afflicted [joy] as faith. The joy that is a branch in this context is posited as the joy that is a feeling possessing joy that makes the mind joyful because positing a mental feeling as such is the thought of Asaṅga's *Grounds of Hearers,* and so forth.

The bliss [that is a branch in this context] is also posited as a mental feeling—that is, a contemplation—because it is posited as something that, in dependence upon mental pliancy, satisfies the mind and is concordant with generating a bliss of physical serviceability. For that reason, with respect to "body" in the phrase in a sūtra, "Bliss is experienced by the body," the two, a physical body and a mental body, are asserted, and there is the distinction that the Vaibhāṣhikas assert that it is only a mental body and the Sautrāntikas assert that it is only a physical body. This is because Tsong-kha-pa's *Golden Rosary of Eloquence* says:

> The explanation [of bliss] as the experience of pliancy by a physical body and the experience of bliss by a mental feeling [598] does not accord with the assertion [of the experiencer of bliss as referring] to only the physical body just explained and the mental body as asserted by the Vaibhāṣhikas.[a]

There is a reason why the bliss of pliancy is generated in the first three concentrations and is not generated in the fourth because of the fact that, in the first three [concentrations], bliss is not viewed as a fault and one attains its cause, serviceability of body and mind that is concordant with the generation of bliss, whereas the fourth concentration has separated from attachment to bliss.

There is a reason why joy is generated in the first two concentrations [but] is not generated in the third because the first two concentrations do not stop joy upon viewing it as a fault, whereas the third

[a] Tsong-kha-pa, *Golden Rosary, Collected Works,* vol. 17 (New Delhi: Guru Deva, 1979), 488.5–6.

concentration, viewing joy as a fault of fluctuation, and so forth, does not allow it to be generated.

The definition of the joy that is a branch of the first concentration is:

> (1) that which possesses association with its concomitant, the meditative stabilization of an actual first concentration; (2) a refreshing mental feeling that generates great joy in the mind.

The definition of the bliss that is a branch of the first concentration is:

> (1) [that which possesses association with its concomitant, the meditative stabilization of an actual first concentration]; (2) a refreshing mental feeling that generates bliss in the mind by way of serviceability of body.

This is because joy and bliss are posited individually in terms of isolating the way in which a single mental feeling helps the body and mind. This is because Tsong-kha-pa's *Golden Rosary of Eloquence* says:

> Therefore, the explanation in Yashomitra's *Commentary on (Asaṅga's) "Summary of Manifest Knowledge"* agrees with that in Asaṅga's *Grounds of Hearers*; [Yashomitra explains that] the two—(1) the feeling experiencing refreshment that accompanies the mental consciousness and that helps the body by making the body, which is the basis of the sense powers, serviceable and (2) the aspect of joy, which refreshes the mental consciousness associated with it, together with its concomitants, and thereby helps the mind [599] —are posited, respectively, as bliss and joy.[a]

The definition of the meditative stabilization that is a branch of the first concentration is:

> a mental factor that is an actual first concentration that causes the mind and mental factors associated with it to gather in a single object of observation and that ascertains its object.

The definition of the internal clarity that is a branch of the second concentration is:

> that which (1) is associated with its concomitant, the meditative stabilization of an actual second concentration and (2)

[a] Ibid., 488.6–489.2.

> is any of [the three]—mindfulness, introspection, and the compositional factor of equanimity that have separated from the entanglements of investigation and analysis.

The definition of the joy that is a branch of the second concentration is:

> that which (1) is associated [with its concomitant, the meditative stabilization of an actual second concentration] and (2) is the mental feeling that possesses the joy generated from a meditative stabilization isolated from investigation and analysis.

The definition of the bliss that is a branch of the second concentration is:

> that which (1) is associated [with its concomitant, the meditative stabilization of an actual second concentration] and (2) is the refreshing mental feeling induced by the physical serviceability generated from a meditative stabilization isolated from investigation and analysis.

The definition of the meditative stabilization that is a branch of the second concentration is:

> that which (1) is associated with its concomitants, the branches—joy, and so forth—of the second concentration and (2) is a one-pointedness of mind that has separated from the entanglements of investigation and analysis.

The definition of the equanimity that is a branch of the third concentration is:

> that which (1) is associated with its concomitant, the meditative stabilization of an actual third concentration and (2) is a compositional factor that acts as the mental factor of equanimity which has separated from attachment to investigation, analysis, and joy [and thus is] undisturbed by them. [600]

The definition of the mindfulness that is a branch of the third concentration is:

> that which (1) is associated [with its concomitant, the meditative stabilization of an actual third concentration] and (2) is that mindfulness which apprehends either the object of observation or subjective aspect of stopping the entanglement of joy.

The definition of the introspection that is a branch of the third concentration is:

> that which (1) is associated [with its concomitant, the meditative stabilization of an actual third concentration] and (2) is a wisdom consciousness that inspects whether one abides in that mindfulness which apprehends either the object of observation or the subjective aspect of stopping the entanglement of joy.

The definition of the bliss that is a branch of the third concentration is:

> that which (1) is associated [with its concomitant, the meditative stabilization of an actual third concentration], and (2) is that bliss which causes the two—the physical and mental bodies—to be refreshed [and is] a mental feeling that has separated from the entanglement of joy.

The definition of the meditative stabilization that is a branch of the third concentration is:

> a one-pointedness of mind which does not have joy and which is associated with its concomitants, the branches [equanimity, mindfulness, introspection and bliss].

The definition of the completely pure equanimity that is a branch of the fourth concentration is:

> that which (1) is associated with its concomitant, the meditative stabilization of an actual fourth concentration and (2) is the compositional factor of equanimity which has separated from the fluctuation of the eight faults.

The definition of the completely pure mindfulness that is a branch of the fourth concentrations is:

> that which (1) is associated [with its concomitant, the meditative stabilization of an actual fourth concentration] and (2) is that mindfulness which is without the fluctuation of the eight faults.

The definition of the neutral feeling that is a branch of the fourth concentration is:

> that which (1) is associated [with its concomitant, the meditative stabilization of an actual fourth concentration and (2) is that mental feeling which experiences satisfaction and pain as equal.

The definition of the meditative stabilization that is a branch of the fourth concentration is:

that which (1) is associated with its concomitants, the branches—mindfulness, and so forth—of an actual fourth concentration and (2) is a one-pointedness of mind which does not fluctuate by way of the eight faults.

In general, these [branches], investigation and analysis [and so forth] are not necessarily faults of concentration [601] because they also exist in a Buddha. Although investigation, analysis, and so forth, that are branches of the respective lower concentrations in the continuum of a sentient being are faults in relation to the higher concentrations, they are not faults of concentration because they are the branches of [the lower concentrations].

There is a reason why, although the three—mindfulness, introspection, and the compositional factor of equanimity—are present at the time of the first concentration, they are not mentioned as branches because it is by reason of [the fact that], at that time, there is strong fluctuation due to investigation and analysis and [those three] are not predominant like other branches. This is because Tsong-kha-pa's *Golden Rosary of Eloquence* says:

> Although these three—mindfulness, introspection, and the compositional factor of equanimity—are present in the first concentration, they are polluted by investigation and analysis.[a]

There is a reason why, although those three [mindfulness, introspection, and the compositional factor of equanimity] are posited as mere branches at the time of the second concentration, they are not mentioned individually by name, for (1) although, at that time, one has done the task of stopping the faults of investigation and analysis of those three [mindfulness, introspection, and the compositional factor of equanimity], one comes under the influence of fluctuation due to joy, and (2) they are posited as an antidotal branch for the sake of knowing that "the 'investigation' of 'investigation and analysis' is merely pacified" and are indicated by the name of internal clarity. This is because Tsong-kha-pa's *Golden Rosary of Eloquence* says:

> Also, in the second concentration, since they are obstructed by the fault of joy, [mindfulness, introspection, and the compositional factor of equanimity] are not mentioned by their own names but are designated by the name of internal clarity.[b]

---

[a] Ibid., 490.4.

[b] Ibid., 490.4–5.

There is a reason why [mindfulness, introspection, and the compositional factor of equanimity] are mentioned individually by name at the time of the third concentration and are posited as branches, for, since they do their respective work individually at that time without the faults of investigation, analysis, and joy, they are mentioned individually as branches by their own names. This is because Tsong-kha-pa's *Golden Rosary of Eloquence* says: "Here, since they have separated from those faults, [602] they are mentioned by their own names."[a]

There is a reason why, in the fourth concentration, the two, mindfulness and equanimity, are not only mentioned as branches by their own names but also mentioned in terms of complete purity, whereas introspection is not posited, for, since one has separated from all faults of fluctuation at that time, the two [mindfulness and equanimity] are not only mentioned by their own names but are indicated by the term "completely pure," and since, here, there is no need for watchfulness out of qualms of distraction due to those faults, introspection is not posited as a branch. This is because Vasubandhu's *Treasury of Manifest Knowledge* [8.11b] says: "The fourth is unfluctuating."[b]

The enumeration [of the branches]

With respect to the branches of those concentrations, there is a reason for their enumeration as five and four because, although there are many consciousnesses that are also concomitants and helpers for each of the actual concentrations, they are posited as such in terms of three causes. This is because they are posited as five and four in terms of the three—the antidotal branches which are the causes of abandoning harm, the benefit branches which are the causes of achieving help. and the branch that is the basis of those two.

The mode of possession [of the branches]

There is a way in which one possesses or does not possess investigation and analysis and a way in which one possesses or does not possess joy and bliss, for it is not just whether these exist in a person's continuum but whether they are possessed in association with that meditative absorption without being stopped, upon viewing whether or not they are faults in that [person's continuum].

---

[a] Ibid., 490.5.

[b] Vasubandhu, *Treasury of Manifest Knowledge,* 8.11b (P5591, vol. 115, 273.1.5–6; Shastri, part 4, p. 1150; La Vallée Poussin, 16:5, p. 161; Pruden, vol. 4, p. 1239).

Dispelling objections

First debate

Incorrect position: It follows that whatever is an actual concentration is necessarily equally calm abiding and special insight because, owing to the equality of such, a path is necessarily easier. This is because Vasubandhu's *Treasury of Manifest Knowledge* says: [603] "...of the concentrations,..."[a]

Correct position: [That Vasubandhu's *Treasury of Manifest Knowledge* says this] does not entail [that, owing to the equality of calm abiding and special insight, a path is necessarily easier].

You cannot accept [that, owing to the equality of calm abiding and special insight, a path is necessarily easier] because special insight predominates in a special actual first concentration, but it is not an easy path to generate.

Second debate

Incorrect position: Whatever is a preparation is necessarily predominantly a consciousness of special insight because, since such is necessarily so, those are necessarily paths which are difficult to generate. This is because Vasubandhu's *Treasury of Manifest Knowledge* says: "...other grounds..."[b]

Correct position: [That Vasubandhu's *Treasury of Manifest Knowledge* says this] does not entail [that since whatever is a preparation is necessarily predominantly a consciousness of special insight, those are necessarily paths which are difficult to generate].

It [absurdly] follows that the subject, the preparation of one who has just attained calm abiding [that is, calm abiding itself] is predominantly a consciousness of special insight because of being a preparation].

You cannot accept [that the preparation of one who has just attained calm abiding is predominantly a consciousness of special insight] because, aside from mere calm abiding, special insight has not been achieved and because [one's] meditation is still mainly stabilizing meditation.

---

[a] This citation is too fragmentary to permit identification.

[b] This citation is too fragmentary to permit identification.

THIRD DEBATE

Incorrect position: It follows that among the branches of the third concentration there is subtle mental bliss because Asaṅga's *Grounds of Hearers* says: "When one enters into a meditative absorption of the third concentration, mental bliss vanishes."[a]

Correct position: [That Asaṅga's *Grounds of Hearers* says this] does not entail [that among the branches of the third concentration there is subtle mental bliss]. This is because in that [statement] he is thinking of coarse mental bliss.

You cannot accept [that among the branches of the third concentration there is subtle mental bliss] because the first concentration is posited in terms of separation from attachment to the coarse feeling of pain; the second, in terms of separation from attachment to the assumption of bad states of [feeling], which are subtle; the third, in terms of separation from attachment to the mental bliss of the second concentration and below, which is the coarse feeling of bliss; and the fourth, in terms of separation from attachment to the faculty of bliss of the third concentration, which is subtle.

FOURTH DEBATE

Incorrect position: It [absurdly] follows that each of the two, investigation and analysis, has different substantial entities at one time because [according to you] each of these also has the two substantial entities of intention and wisdom. [604]

Correct position: In one aspect, it is not entailed [that if each of the two, investigation and analysis, has the two substantial entities of both intention and wisdom, each necessarily has different substantial entities at one time] because, although each of these does not occur for those two [investigation and analysis] at one time, in general each has intention and wisdom.

FIFTH DEBATE

Incorrect position: It follows that whatever is investigation that is a changeable mental factor is necessarily either intention or wisdom because whatever is [investigation that is a changeable mental factor] is necessarily the substantial entity of either intention or wisdom.

[a] Asaṅga, *Grounds of Hearers,* Tibetan Sanskrit Works Series, vol. 14, p. 453; P5537, vol. 110, 118.5.8.

Correct position: It is not entailed [that if whatever is investigation that is a changeable mental factor is necessarily the substantial entity of either intention or wisdom, then whatever is investigation that is a changeable mental factor is necessarily either intention or wisdom].

The Effects Attained

Asaṅga's *Summary of Manifest Knowledge* says:

> Because of cultivation of the first concentration to a small, middling, and great [degree], there are the three rebirths of the First Concentration. As in the First Concentration, so also, in the remaining ones, there are similarly three rebirths of concentration.[a]

[a] Asaṅga, *Summary of Manifest Knowledge,* P5550, vol. 112, 261.2.5–6; Rahula, trans., *Le Compendium de la super-doctrine,* p. 112. In Kön-chok-jik-may-wang-po, *Condensed Statement,* 604.3, the final *pa'i phyir* is grammatically unnecessary; the corresponding section of Jam-yang-shay-pa's text (Jam-yang-shay-pa, *Concentrations,* 415.6) also has an unnecessary *phyir.*

3 ENUMERATION OF THE MEDITATIVE STABILIZATIONS [OF BUDDHAS AND BODHISATTVAS] IN DEPENDENCE UPON THAT

[604.3]

With respect to the subject, that which is to be known here, there are limitless meditative stabilizations of Buddhas and Bodhisattvas which depend even on each of the meditative absorptions of the concentrations and formless absorptions because, like the limitless enumeration of meditative stabilizations that depend on the first concentration, those of the remaining [concentrations and formless absorptions] are similar[ly limitless].

* * * * *

[I] say:

It is suitable to praise those scholarly rulers of the nāgas
Who play in the ocean of the Omniscient One's speech
Having depths of scripture and reasoning which are not manifest
And thousands of series of waves of pure refutation and proof.
Having condensed the essence of the vast great texts
For the sake of beings who take intense fright at them,
I give this excellent vase of the ambrosia of good explanation.
May unbiased aspirants have a feast! [605]
May whatever actuality of virtue is attained from striving here
Put an end to the darkness of the mistaken conception of true existence
In the sky of the minds of the nine [levels] of limitless beings
Through the union of the sun and moon of calm abiding and special insight!

With respect to this *Condensed Presentation of the Concentrations and Formless Absorptions, An Excellent Vase of the Ambrosia of Eloquence,* I thought that, although the *Great Analysis of the Scope of the Concentrations and Formless Absorptions* by the sovereign of the complete teachings, the great, omniscient lord of scholars and adepts Jam-yang-shay-pay-dorjay is a jewel-like, unprecedented good explanation providing limitless analytical approaches for scholars, since, because of the times, it is difficult for those of weak intelligence and exertion to assimilate it, it would help me and those of similar lot if there were a condensation of it. The monk of much hearing, a proponent of reasoning, Kön-chok-jik-may-wang-po, abridging words of [Jam-yang-shay-pa's] *Great Exposition of the Concentrations and Formless Absorptions,* has stated [the topics] in condensation without contradicting the meaning of the thought [of Jam-yang-shay-pa]. Since, when debating, there are also distinctions to be drawn throughout [the text], if[a] those of unrestricted intelligence analyze [these topics] finely without bifurcation of understanding and reasoning, in not much [time], the lotus of discrimination will open.

[a] 605.5, reading *mdzad na* instead of *mdzad ni.*

DETAILED OUTLINE

GLOSSARIES

1 English-Tibetan-Sanskrit

English	*Tibetan*	*Sanskrit*
abandonment	spangs pa	prahāṇa
abandoning the doctrine	chos spong	
Abider in the Fruit of Foe Destroyer	dgra bcom 'bras gnas	arhattvaphalasthita
absorption	snyoms 'jug	samāpatti
absorption of cessation	'gog pa'i snyoms 'jug	nirodhasamāpatti
achieving	sgrub pa	pratipatti
achieving armor	go sgrub	saṃnāhapratipatti
achieving through engagement	'jug sgrub	prasthānapratipatti
achieving definite emergence	nges 'byung sgrub pa	niryāṇapratipatti
achieving the collections	tshogs sgrub	saṃbhārapratipatti
action	las	karma
actual meditative absorption	dngos gzhi'i snyoms 'jug	maulasamāpatti
adamantine posture, vajra	rdo rje skyil krung	vajrāsana
posture		
afflicted	nyon mong can	kliṣṭa
afflictive emotion	nyon mongs	kleśa
afflictive obstruction	nyon mongs kyi sgrib pa	kleśāvaraṇa
aggregate	phung po	skandha
aging and/or death	rga shi	jarāmaraṇa
altruistic mind of enlightenment	byang chub kyi sems	bodhicitta
analytical image	rnam par rtog pa dang bcas pa'i gzugs brnyan	savikalpikapratibimba
analysis	dpyod pa	vicāra
analytical meditation	dpyad sgom	
androgyne	mtshan gnyis pa	ubhayavyañjana
anger	khong khro	pratigha
animal	dud 'gro	tiryañc
antidotal mental contemplation	gnyen po yid la byed pa	
antidote	'du byed pa	abhisaṃskāra
application	'du byed pa	abhisaṃskāra
Approacher to Foe Destroyer	dgra bcom zhugs pa	arhattvapratipannaka
appropriate and the inappropriate	gnas dang gnas ma yin pa	sthānāsthāna
arisen from hearing	thos byung	śrutamayī
arisen from meditation	sgom byung	bhāvanāmayī
arisen from thinking	bsam byung	cintāmayī

English	*Tibetan*	*Sanskrit*
aspect, subjective aspect	rnam pa	ākāra
aspiration	'dun pa	chanda
aspiration to attributes of the Desire Realm	'dod pa la 'dun pa	kāmacchanda
aspirational prayer	smon lam	praṇidhāna
attachment	sred pa	tṛṣṇā
attainment subsequent [to meditative equipoise]	rjes thob	pṛṣṭhalabdha
Avalokiteshvara	spyan ras gzigs	avalokiteśvara
awareness	blo	buddhi, dhī
Awareness and Knowledge	blo rig	
bad discipline	sdom min	asaṃvara
bad transmigration	ngan 'gro	durgati
basis	rten	āśraya
basis	gzhi	vastu
basis of designation	gdags gzhi	
beginner	las dang po pa	ādikarmika
beginner at mental contemplation	yid la byed pa las dang po pa	manaskārādikarmika
beginner at purifying the afflictive emotions	nyon mongs rnam par sbyong ba'i las dang po pa	kleśaviśuddhyādikarmika
being of great capacity	skyes bu chen po	
being of middling capacity	skyes bu 'bring	
belligerence	khro ba	krodha
benefit	phan yon	anuśaṃsa
birth	skye ba	jāti
blame	smad pa	nindā
bliss	bde ba	sukha
Bodhisattva	byang chub sems dpa'	bodhisattva
Bodhisattva who is one lifetime away from achieving Buddhahood	skye ba gcig gis thogs pa'i byang chub sems dpa'	
body consciousness	lus kyi rnam par shes pa	kāyavijñāna
Born from Merit	bsod nams skyes	puṇyaprasava
Brahmā Type	tshangs ris	brahmakāyika
branch	yan lag	aṅga
Bright Light	'od gsal	ābhāsvara
Buddha	sangs rgyas	buddha
Buddha field	sangs rgyas kyi zhing	buddhakṣetra
Buddhist [Insider]	nang pa	
Buddhist of dull faculties	dbang rdul gyi nang pa	
Buddhist of sharp faculties whose virtuous roots are not thoroughly ripened	dbang rnon gyi dge rtsa yongs su ma smin pa	
calm abiding	zhi gnas	śamatha

English	*Tibetan*	*Sanskrit*
calm abiding with signs	mtshan ma dang bcas pa'i zhi gnas	
calm abiding without signs	mtshan ma med pa'i zhi gnas	
category, thing	dngos po	vastu
causal meditative absorption	rgyu snyoms 'jug	*kāraṇasamāpatti
causal collection, prerequisite	tshogs bsten pa	
causally concordant application	rgyu mthun pa'i sbyor ba	
causally concordant effect	rgyu mthun gyi 'bras bu	niṣyandaphala
central channel	rtsa dbu ma	
cessation	'gog pa	nirodha
change	yongs su sgyur ba	vivartanā
channel	rtsa	nāḍi
character, definition	mtshan nyid	lakṣaṇa
Chittamātra	sems tsam pa	cittamātra
clairvoyance	mngon shes	abhijñā
class	phyogs	pakṣa
clear light	'od gsal	prabhāsvara
close setting	nye bar 'jog pa	upasthāpana
Cloudless	sprin med	anabhraka
coarse conceptuality, discursiveness	rnam rtog	vikalpa
coarse pliancy	rags pa'i shin sbyangs	
collection of merit	bsod nams gyi tshogs	puṇyasaṃbhāra
collection of wisdom	shes rab gyi tshogs	prajñāsaṃbhāra
common being	so so'i skye bo	pṛthagjana
complete training in the aspects	rnam rdzogs sbyor ba	sarvākārābhisaṃbhodha
compositional action	'du byed kyi las	saṃskārakarma
compositional factor	'du byed	saṃskāra
concentration	bsam gtan	dhyāna
concentrative discipline	bsam gtan gyi sdom pa	dhyānasaṃvara
conception of a [bad] view as supreme	lta ba mchog 'dzin	dṛṣṭiparāmarśa
conception of ethics and systems of behavior as supreme	tshul khrims dang brdul zhugs mchog 'dzin	śīlavrataparāmarśa
concomitant	grogs	sahāya
concordant mental contemplation	rjes su mthun pa las byung ba'i yid byed	
concordant with abiding	gnas pa cha mthun	sthitibhāgīya
concordant with definite differentiation	nges 'byed cha mthun	nirvedhabhāgīya
concordant with degeneration	nyams pa cha mthun	hānabhāgīya
concordant with enhancement	khyad par cha mthun	viśeṣabhāgīya
confession	bshags pa	deśanā
consciousness	rnam shes	vijñāna

English	*Tibetan*	*Sanskrit*
consequence	thal 'gyur	prasaṅga
constituents	khams	dhātu
contact	reg pa	sparśa
contents-outline	sa bcad	
continuous application	rtag sbyor	
continuous setting	rgyun du 'jog pa	saṃsthāpana
continuum	rgyud	saṃtāna
correctly assuming consciousness	yid dpyod	*manaḥ parīkṣā
counting	grangs pa	gaṇanā
covetousness	brnab sems	abhidhyā
cyclic existence	'khor ba	saṃsāra
definition, character	mtshan nyid	lakṣaṇa
demigod	lha ma yin	asura
dependent-arising	rten cing 'brel bar 'byung ba	pratītyasamutpāda
Desire Realm	'dod khams	kāmadhatu
Desire Realm mind	'dod sems	
desire	'dod chags	rāga
desisting from application	'du byed btang snyoms	
discipline	sdom pa	saṃvara
discipline of individual emancipation	so mthar gyi sdom pa	pratimokṣasaṃvara
disciplining	dul bar byed pa	damana
discrimination	'du shes	saṃjñā
discursiveness, coarse conceptuality	rnam rtog	vikalpa
disgrace	ma snyan grags	ayaśas
distraction	rnam par g.yeng ba	vikṣepa
Doctrine, phenomenon, quality, topic	chos	dharma
doubt	the tshom	vicikitsā
drop	thig le	bindu
earth	sa	pṛthivī
effect	'bras bu	phala
effort	brtson 'grus	vīrya
effort arising from application	sbyor ba las byung ba'i	
effort which is insatiable	chog ma shes pa'i brtson grus	
eight worldly concerns	'jig rten chos brgyad	aṣtalokadharma
element	'byung ba	bhūta
emptiness	stong pa nyid	śūnyatā
equanimity	btang snyoms	upekṣā
eunuch	ma ning	paṇḍaka
exalted knower	mkhyen pa	jñāta
exalted knower of all aspects	rnam pa thams cad mkhyen pa nyid, rnam mkhyen	sarvākārajñatā
exalted knower of bases	gzhi shes	vastujñatā

English	*Tibetan*	*Sanskrit*
exalted wisdom of meditative equipoise	mnyam bzhag ye shes	samāhitajñāna
Excellent Appearance	gya nom snang ba	sudṛśa
excitement	rgod pa	auddhatya
excitement and contrition	rgod pa dang 'gyod pa	auddhatyakaukṛtya
exertion	rtsol ba	vyāyāma
exhalation	dbugs 'byung pa	praśvāsa
exhalation and inhalation of the breath	dbugs 'byung rngub	ānāpana
existence	srid pa	bhava
extreme	mtha'	anta
eye consciousness	mig gi rnam par shes pa	cakṣurvijñāna
eye sense power	mig gi dbang po	cakṣurindriya
factor of clarity	gsal cha	
factor of stability	gnas cha	
factor of subjective clarity	dvang cha	
faith	dad pa	śraddhā
faith of clarity	dvang ba'i dad pa	*prasādaśraddhā
faith of conviction	yid ches pa'i dad pa	*abhisaṃpratyaya-
faith that is a wish to attain	'thob 'dod pa'i dad pa	*abhilāṣaśraddhā śraddhā
fame	snyan grags	yaśas
familiarity	yongs su 'dris pa	paricaya
fault	nyes dmigs	ādīnava
fault	skyon	apakṣāla
feeling	tshor ba	vedanā
feeling of mental bliss	tshor ba yid bde, tshor ba sems bde	
final analysis	mtha' dpyod	
fire	me	tejas
first concentration	bsam gtan dang po	prathamadhyāna
Five Pure Places	gnas gtsang lnga	pañcaśuddhāvāsakāyika
Foe Destroyer	dgra bcom pa	arhan
following	rjes su 'gro ba	anugama
forcible engagement	sgrim ste 'jug pa	balavāhana
forgetting the instruction	gdam ngag brjed pa	avavādasammoṣa
form	gzugs	rūpa
form aggregate	gzugs kyi phung po	rūpaskandha
Form Body	gzugs sku	rūpakāya
Form Realm	gzugs khams	rūpadhātu
formless absorption	gzugs med kyi snyoms 'jug	ārūpyasamāpatti
Formless Realm	gzugs med khams	ārūpyadhātu
fortune	'byor ba	kṣaṇa
four immeasurables	tshad med bzhi	catvary apramāṇāni
fourth concentration	bsam gtan bzhi pa	caturthadhyāna
fruit	'bras bu	phala

English	*Tibetan*	*Sanskrit*
fruitional effect	rnam smin gyi 'bras bu	vipākaphala
fruitional obstruction	rnam smin gyi sgrib pa	*vipākāvaraṇa
gain	rnyed pa	lābha
Ge-luk-pa	dge lugs pa	
ge-shay	dge bshes	
general character, generally characterized phenomenon	spyi'i mtshan nyid	sāmānyalakṣaṇa
general meaning commentary	spyi don	
generic image, meaning-generality	don spyi	arthasāmānya
god	lha	deva
grasping	len pa	upādāna
great	chen po	adhimātra
Great Brahmā	tshangs chen	mahābrahmaṇa
great compassion	snying rje chen po	mahākaruṇā
Great Completeness	rdzogs chen	
great element	'byung ba chen po	mahābhūta
Great Fruit	'bras bu che	bṛhatphala
great love	byams pa chen po	mahāmaitri
great of the great	chen po'i chen po	adhimātrādhimātra
great of the middling	'bring gi chen po	madhyādhimātra
great of the small	chung ngu'i chen po	mṛdvadhimātra
Great Perception	shin tu mthong ba	sudarśana
grossness/peacefulness	zhi rags	*śāntaudārika
ground	sa	bhūmi
Grounds and Paths	sa lam	bhūmimārga
hand symbol	phyag mtshan	mudrā
happiness	bde ba	sukha
happy transmigration	bde 'gro	sugati
harmfulness	gnod sems	vyāpāda
hatred	zhe dang	dveṣa
haughtiness	rgyags pa	mada
having the aspect of grossness/peacefulness	zhi rags rnam can	
having the aspect of the truths	bden pa rnam can	
Hearers	nyan thos	śrāvaka
hearing	thos pa	śruta
heinous crime	mtshams med pa	ānantarya
hell	dmyal ba	naraka
hell being	dmyal ba	nāraka
help	phan 'dogs pa	
hidden, subliminal	lkog gyur	parokṣa
Highest Yoga Tantra	bla med kyi rgyud	anuttarayogatantra
Hīnayāna	theg dman	hīnayāna
human	mi	manuṣya

English	*Tibetan*	*Sanskrit*
hungry ghost	yi dvags	preta
ignorance	ma rig pa	avidyā
immediately preceding condition	de ma thag rkyen	samanantarapratyaya
immeasurable equanimity	btang snyoms tshad med	
imminence of death	'chi ba mi rtag pa	maraṇānitya
impermanence	mi rtag pa	anitya
In Front of Brahmā	tshangs mdun	brahmapurohita
individual emancipation	so sor mthar pa	pratimokṣa
inestimable mansion	gzhal med khang	*amātragṛha
inferential cognition	rjes dpag	anumāna
inhalation	dbugs rngub pa	śvāsa
instruction, preceptual instruction	gdams ngag	avavāda
intellect	yid	manas
intense application	gus sbyor	
intensity	ngar	
intermediate state	bar do	antarābhāva
internal clarity	nang rab tu dvang ba	adhyātmasamprasāda
interrupted engagement	bar du chad cing 'jug pa	sacchidravāhana
introspection	shes bzhin	samprajanya
investigation	rtog pa	vitarka
investigation	nye bar rtog pa	upalakṣaṇā
jealousy	phrag dog	irṣyā
joy	dga' ba	prīti
Ka-dam-pa	dka' gdams pa	
Ka-gyu	bka' brgyud	
karmic obstruction	las sgrib	karmāvaraṇa
knower	rig pa	saṃvedana
knower of bases	gzhi shes	vastujñatā
knower of paths	lam shes	mārgajñatā
lama	bla ma	guru
laxity	bying ba	laya
laziness	le lo	kausīdya
laziness of inadequacy	sgyid lugs pa'i le lo	
laziness of neutral activities	snyoms las kyi le lo	
laziness which is an attachment to bad activities	bya ba ngan zhen gyi le lo	
leapover absorptions	thod rgyal gyi snyoms 'jug	vyutkrāntakasamāpatti
leisure	dal ba	saṃpad
leisure and fortune	dal 'byor	kṣaṇasampad
lethargy	rmugs pa	styāna
lethargy and sleep	rmugs pa dang gnyid	styānamiddha
liberation	thar pa	vimokṣa

English	*Tibetan*	*Sanskrit*
life faculty	srog gi dbang po	jivitendriya
Limitless Bliss	tshad med bde	apramāṇaśuba
limitless consciousness	rnam shes mtha' yas	vijñānāntya
Limitless Light	tshad med 'od	apramāṇābhā
limitless space	nam mkha' mtha' yas	ākāśānantya
Little Bliss	bde chung	parīttaśuba
Little Light	'od chung	parīttābhā
logical reasoning	'thad sgrub kyi rigs pa	upapattisādhanayukti
loss	ma rnyed pa	alābha
love	byams pa	maitri
love observing mere sentient beings	sems can tsam la dmigs pa'i byams pa	*sattvālaṃbanā maitri
love observing phenomena	chos la dmigs pa'i byams pa	*dharmālaṃbanā maitri
love observing the unapprehendable	dmigs med la dmigs pa'i byams pa	*anālaṃbanā maitri
Mādhyamika	dbu ma pa	mādhyamika
main mind	gtso sems	
Mahāyāna	theg chen	mahāyāna
Mahāyāna [altruistic] mind generation	theg chen sems bskyed	mahāyānacittotpāda
making one-pointed	rtse gcig tu byed pa	ekotīkaraṇa
Manifest Knowledge	chos mngon pa	abhidharma
meaning	don	artha
meaning-generality, generic image	don spyi	arthasāmānya
meditating	sgom pa	bhāvanā
meditative absorption	snyoms 'jug	samāpatti
meditative absorption of cessation	'gog pa'i snyoms 'jug	nirodhasamāpatti
meditative equipoise	mnyam bzhag	samāhita
meditative stabilization	ting nge 'dzin	samādhi
meditative stabilization of the ninth mind of the Desire Realm	'dod sems dgu pa'i ting nge 'dzin	
mental abiding	sems gnas	cittasthiti
mental basis	sems rten	
mental bliss	yid bde	saumanasya
mental body	yid lus	
mental consciousness	yid kyi rnam shes	manovijñāna
mental contemplation	yid la byed pa	manaskāra
mental contemplation arisen from belief	mos pa las byung ba'i yid byed	adhimokṣikamanaskāra
mental contemplation of a mere beginner	las dang po pa tsam gyi yid byed	
mental contemplation of analysis	dpyod pa yid byed	mīmāṃsāmanaskāra

English	*Tibetan*	*Sanskrit*
mental contemplation of final training	sbyor mtha'i yid byed	prayoganiṣṭhamanaskāra
mental contemplation of individual investigation	so sor rtog pa yid la byed pa	
mental contemplation of individual knowledge of the character	mtshan nyid so sor rig pa'i yid byed	lakṣaṇapratisaṃvedī-manaskāra
mental contemplation of joy-withdrawal	dga' ba sdud pa'i yid byed	ratisaṃgrāhaka-manaskāra
mental contemplation of thorough isolation	rab tu dben pa'i yid byed	prāvivekyamanaskāra
mental contemplation of thorough knowledge of the character	mtshan nyid rab tu rig pa'i yid byed	
mental contemplation that is the fruit of final training	sbyor ba mtha'i 'bras bu yid byed	prayoganiṣṭaphala-manaskāra
mental discomfort	yid mi bde	daurmanasya
mental engagement	yid la byed pa	manaskāra
mental factor	sems byung	caitta
mere absorption of an actual first concentration	bsam gtan dang po'i dngos gzhi'i snyoms 'jug tsam po ba	
merit, meritorious	bsod nams	puṇya
middling	'bring	madhya
middling of the great	chen po'i 'bring	adhimātramadhya
middling of the middling	'bring gi 'bring	madhyamadhya
middling of the small	chung ngu'i 'bring	mṛdumadhya
mind	sems	citta
mind of enlightenment	byang chub kyi sems	bodhicitta
mindful establishment	dran pa nye bar bzhag pa	smṛtyupasthāna
mindfulness	dran pa	smṛti
misapprehension of the supreme	lta ba mchog 'dzin	dṛṣṭiparāmarśa
miserliness	ser sna	mātsarya
mode	ji lta ba	
mode of subsistence	gnas lugs	
momentary training	skad cig ma'i sbyor ba	kṣaṇikaprayoga
monastic discipline	'dul ba	vinaya
monastic textbook	yig cha	
mount	bzhon pa	
mundane path	'jig rten pa'i lam	laukikamārga
mutually exclusive	'gal ba	viruddha
nāga, dragon, snake	klu	nāga
name	ming	nāman
name and form	ming gzugs	nāmarūpa
neuter person	za ma	ṣaṇḍha
neutral	lung du ma bstan pa	avyākṛta

English	*Tibetan*	*Sanskrit*
neutral feeling	btang snyoms	upekṣā
neutral feeling	tshor ba btang snyoms	*upekṣāvedanā
neutral feeling	sdug bsngal ma yin bde ba yang ma yin	aduḥkhāsukhavedanā
nine mental abidings	sems gnas dgu, sems gnas pa rnam pa dgu	navākārā cittasthiti
ninth mind of the Desire Realm	'dod sems dgu pa	
nirvāṇa	mya ngan las 'das pa	nirvāṇa
non-analytical image	rnam par mi rtog pa'i gzugs brnyan	nirvikalpakapratibimba
non-application	'du mi byed pa	anabhisaṃskāra
non-associated compositional factor	ldan min 'du byed	viprayuktasaṃskāra
Non-Buddhist, Outsider	phyi rol pa	
non-discrimination	'du shes me pa	asaṃjnā
non-revelatory form	rnam par rig byed ma yin pa'i gzugs	avijñaptirūpa
non-shame	ngo tsha med pa	āhrikya
non-virtue, non-virtuous	mi dge ba	akuśala
Not Great	mi che ba	avṛha
Not Low	'og min	akaniṣṭha
Non-Returner	phyir mi 'ong	anāgāmin
not-unable	mi lcog med	anāgamya
nothingness	ci yang med	akiṃcanya
Nying-ma	rnying ma	
object	yul	viṣaya
object of knowledge	shes bya	jñeya
object of observation	dmigs pa	ālambana
object of observation for [developing] skill	mkhas pa'i dmigs pa, mkhas par byed pa'i dmigs pa	kauśalyālambana
object of observation for purifying afflictive emotions	nyon mongs rnam sbyong gi dmigs pa	kleśaviśodanālambana
object of observation for purifying behavior	spyad pa rnam sbyong gi dmigs pa	caritaviśodanālambana
obscuration	gti mug	moha
observed-object condition	dmigs rkyen	ālambanapratyaya
observing the limits of phenomena	dngos po'i mtha' la dmigs pa	vastvantālambana
obstruction	sgrib pa	āvaraṇa
offer one's realization	rtogs ba phul ba	
omen of pliancy	shin sbyangs skye ba'i snga bltas	
Once Returner	phyir 'ong	sakṛdāgāmin
One Gone Thus	de bzhin gshegs pa	tathāgata
operative consciousness	'jug shes	

English	*Tibetan*	*Sanskrit*
Outsider, Non-Buddhist	phyi rol pa	
pacifying	zhi bar byed pa	śamana
path	lam	mārga
path of accumulation	tshogs lam	saṃbhāramārga
path of meditation	sgom lam	bhāvanāmārga
path of no more learning	mi slob lam	aśaikṣamārga
path of preparation	sbyor lam	prayogamārga
path of release	rnam grol lam	vimuktimārga
path of seeing	mthong lam	darśanamārga
peak of cyclic existence	srid rtse	bhavāgra
peak training	rtse sbyor	mūrdhaprayoga
perfection of wisdom	shes rab kyi pha rol tu phyin pa, sher phyin	prajñāpāramitā
Perfections	phar phyin	pāramitā
person	gang zag	pudgala
pervasive object of observation	khyab pa'i dmigs pa	vyāpyālambana
phenomenon, quality, topic, Doctrine	chos	dharma
physical basis	lus rten	
placement	'jog ba	sthāna
pliancy	shin sbyangs	praśrabdhi
pliancy difficult to analyze	brtags par dka' ba'i shin sbyangs	
pliancy easy to analyze	brtags par sla ba'i shin sbyangs	
possessional effect	bdag 'bras	adhipatiphala
power	stobs	bala
praise	bstod pa	praśaṃsa
Prāsaṅgika	thal 'gyur pa	prāsaṅgika
preceptual instruction, instruction	gdams ngag	avavāda
predisposition	bags chags	vāsanā
preliminary practices	sngon 'gro	
preparation	nyer bsdogs	sāmantaka
preparatory training	ngon 'gro'i sbyor ba	
prerequisite, causal collection	tshogs bsten pa	
pride	nga rgyal	māna
pure	dag pa	śuddha
purifying	yongs su dag pa	pariśuddhi
purifying	rnam sbyong	viśodana
quality, Doctrine, phenomenon, topic	chos	dharma
quintessential instruction	man ngag	upadeśa
reality	de kho na nyid	tathatā
reasoning	rigs pa	yukti

English	*Tibetan*	*Sanskrit*
reasoning of dependence	ltos pa'i rigs pa	apekṣāyukti
reasoning of nature	chos nyid kyi rigs pa	dharmatāyukti
reasoning of the performance of function	bya ba byed pa'i rigs pa	kāryakāraṇayukti
reasoning that establishes correctness	'thad sgrub kyi rigs pa	upapattisādhanayukti
refuge	skyabs	saraṇa
resentment	'khon 'dzin	upanāha
resetting	slan te 'jog pa	avasthāpana
resultant-birth meditative absorption	'bras bu skye ba'i snyoms 'jug	*kāryasamāpatti
resultant-birth state	'bras bu skye ba	
rhinoceroslike Solitary Realizer	bse ru lta bu rang sangs rgyas	khaḍgaviṣāṇakalpa pratyekabuddha
root afflictive emotion	rtsa ba'i nyon mongs	mūlakleśa
Sa-kya	sa skya	
Sautrāntika	mdo sde pa	sautrāntika
scattering	'phro ba	
seal	phyag rgya	mudrā
second concentration	bsam gtan gnyis pa	dvitīyadhyāna
secondary afflictive emotion	nye ba'i nyon mongs	upakleśa
selflessness	bdag med	nairātmya
selflessness of persons	gang zag gi bdag med	pudgalanairātmya
sense consciousness	dbang shes	indriyajñāna
sense power	dbang po	indriya
sentient being	sems can	sattva
separation from attachment	chags bral	kāmād virakta
serial training	mthar gyis sbyor ba	anupūrvaprayoga
setting in equipoise	mnyam par 'jog pa	samādhāna
setting the mind	sems 'jog pa	cittasthāpana
seven cause-and-effect quintessential instructions	rgyu 'bras man ngag bdun	
signless	mtshan med	animitta
simultaneous	gcig car	sakṛt
slackness	zhum pa	
sleep	gnyid	middha
small	chung ngu	mṛdu
small of the great	chen po'i chung ngu	adhimātramṛdu
small of the middling	'bring gi chung ngu	madhyamṛdu
small of the small	chung ngu'i chung ngu	mṛdumṛdu
Solitary Realizer	rang sangs rgyas	pratyekabuddha
space	nam mkha'	ākāśa
special being of small capacity	skyes bu chung ngu khyad par can	

English	*Tibetan*	*Sanskrit*
special absorption of an actual first concentration	bsam gtan dang po'i dngos gzhi'i snyoms 'jug khyad par can	
special insight	lhag mthong	vipaśyanā
special insight without signs	mtshan ma med pa'i lhag mthong	
specific character, specifically characterized phenomenon	rang gi mtshan nyid	svalakṣaṇa
sphere	skye mched	āyatana
spiritual community	dge 'dun	saṃgha
spiritual friend, spiritual guide	dge ba'i bshes gnyen	kalyāṇamitra
spontaneous engagement	lhun grub tu 'jug pa	anābhogavāhana
stabilization, meditative stabilization	ting nge 'dzin	samādhi
stabilizing meditation	'jog sgom	
stage of completion	rdzogs rim	niṣpannakrama
stages of the path	lam rim	
Stream Enterer	rgyun zhugs	śrotāpanna
subjective aspect, aspect	rnam pa	ākāra
subliminal, hidden	lkog gyur	parokṣa
substantial cause	nyer len	upādāna
substantially existent	rdzas su yod pa	dravyasat
subtle pliancy	phra ba'i shin sbyangs	
suffering	sdug bsngal	duḥkha
suffering of conditioning	'du byed kyi sdug bsngal	saṃskāraduhkhatā
Superior	'phags pa	ārya
suppression	nyams smad	
supramundane path	'jig rten las 'das pa'i lam	lokottaramārga
supreme mundane qualities	'jig rten pa'i chos kyi mchog	laukikāgryadharma
Svātantrika	rang rgyud pa	svātantrika
syllogism	sbyor ba	prayoga
tangible object	reg bya	spraṣṭavya
tangible-object sphere	reg bya'i skye mched	spraṣṭavyāyatana
tenets	grub mtha'	siddhānta
terminological division	sgras brjod rigs kyi sgo nas dbye ba	
textual [lineage]	gzhung pa pa	
thing, category	dngos po	vastu
thinking	bsam pa	cintā
third concentration	bsam gtan gsum pa	tritīyadhyāna
thorough achievement of the purpose	dgos pa yongs su grub pa	kṛtyānuṣṭāna
thorough enwrapment	kun sbyor	saṃyojana
thorough pacifying	nye bar zhi bar byed pa	vyupaśamana
thorough purity	yongs su dag pa	pariśuddhi

English	*Tibetan*	*Sanskrit*
thoroughly clear mental contemplation	rab tu dvang ba yid la byed pa	
Three Jewels	dkon mchog gsum	triratna
time	dus	kāla
topic, Doctrine, phenomenon, quality	chos	dharma
training	bslab pa	śikṣā
treatise	bstan bcos	śāstra
true cessations	'gog pa'i bden pa	nirodhasatya
true origins	kun 'byung bden pa	samudayasatya
true paths	lam gyi bden pa	mārgasatya
true sufferings	sdug bsngal bden pa	duḥkhasatya
Truth Body	chos sku	dharmakāya
Truth Body, the fruit	'bras bu chos sku	*phaladharmakāya
Tsong-kha-pa	tsong kha pa	
Unadorned Foe Destroyer	dgra bcom rgyan med	
uncommon empowering condition	thun mong ma yin pa'i bdag rkyen	asādhāranadhipati-pratyaya
uncontaminated	zag med	anāsrava
undisturbed effort	mi 'thugs pa'i brtson grus	
unfluctuating	mi g.yo ba	āniñjya
uninterrupted engagement	chad pa med par 'jug pa	niśchidravāhana
uninterrupted path	bar chad med lam	ānantaryamārga
union of calm abiding and special insight	zhi lhag zung 'brel	śamathavipaśyanā-yuganaddha
unpleasant	mi sdug pa	aśubha
Unpleasant Sound	sgra mi nyan	kuru
Vaibhāṣhika	bye brag smra ba	vaibhāṣika
Vairochana	rnam par snang mdzad	vairocana
vajra posture, adamantine posture	rdo rje skyil krung	vajrāsana
Vajrasattva	rdo rje sems dpa'	vajrasattva
vajra nodes	rdo rje gzegs ma	
varieties	ji snyed pa	
Vast Bliss	bde rgyas	śubakṛtsna
view, [bad] view	lta ba'	dṛṣṭi
view holding to an extreme	mthar 'dzing pa'i lta ba	antagrāhadṛṣṭi
view of the transitory collection [as real I and mine]	'jig tshogs la lta ba	satkāyadṛṣṭi
virtue, virtuous	dge ba	kuśala
virtuous root	dge ba'i rtsa ba	kuśalamūla
virtuous spiritual friend	dge ba'i bshes gnyen	kalyāṇamitra
water	chu	āp
wind	rlung	vāyu

English	*Tibetan*	*Sanskrit*
wind	rlung	prāṇa
wisdom	shes raba	prajñā
wisdom of individual analysis	so sor rtog pa'i shes rab	
Wisdom Truth Body	ye shes chos sku	jñānadharmakāya
without discrimination and without non-discrimination	'du shes med 'du shes med min	naivasaṃjñānāsaṃjñā
Without Pain	mi gdung ba	atapas
wrong view	log lta	mithyādṛṣṭi
yoga of a beginner at mental contemplation	yid la byed pa las dang po pa'i rnal 'byor	manaskārādikarmika-[yoga]
yoga of one whose mental contemplation is perfected	yid la byed pa yongs su rdzogs pa'i rnal 'byor	atikrāntamanaskāra-[yoga]
yoga of someone who is practiced	yongs su sbyangs pa byas pa'i rnal 'byor	kṛtaparicaya[yoga]
Yogāchāra	rnal 'byor spyod pa	yogācāra

2 Tibetan-Sanskrit-English

Tibetan	*Sanskrit*	*English*
kun 'byung bden pa	samudayasatya	true origins
kun sbyor	saṃyojana	thorough enwrapment
klu	nāga	nāga
dka' gdams pa		Ka-dam-pa
bka' brgyud		Ka-gyu
lkog gyur	parokṣa	hidden, subliminal
skad cig ma'i sbyor ba	kṣaṇikaprayoga	momentary training
skyabs	saraṇa	refuge
skye mched	āyatana	sphere
skye ba	jāti	birth
skye ba gcig gis thogs pa'i byang chub sems dpa'		Bodhisattva who is one life-time away from achieving Buddhahood
skyes bu chung ngu khyad par can		special being of small capacity
skyes bu chen po		being of great capacity
skyes bu 'bring		being of middling capacity
skyon	apakṣāla	fault
dkon mchog gsum	triratna	Three Jewels
khams	dhātu	constituents
khong khro	pratigha	anger
khyad par cha mthun	viśeṣabhāgīya	concordant with enhancement
khyab pa'i dmigs pa	vyāpyālambana	pervasive object of observation
khro ba	krodha	belligerence
mkhas pa'i dmigs pa, mkhas par byed pa'i dmigs pa	kauśalyālambana	object of observation for [developing] skill
mkhyen pa	jñāta	exalted knower
'khon 'dzin	upanāha	resentment
'khor ba	saṃsāra	cyclic existence
gang zag	pudgala	person
gang zag gi bdag med	pudgalanairātmya	selflessness of persons
gus sbyor		intense application
go sgrub	saṃnāhapratipatti	achieving armor
gya nom snang ba	sudṛśa	Excellent Appearance
grangs pa	gaṇanā	counting
grub mtha'	siddhānta	tenets
grogs	sahāya	concomitant
dga' ba	prīti	joy
dga' ba sdud pa'i yid byed	ratisaṃgrāhakamanaskāra	mental contemplation of joy-withdrawal

Tibetan	*Sanskrit*	*English*
dge ba	kuśala	virtue, virtuous
dge ba'i rtsa ba	kuśalamūla	virtuous root
dge ba'i bshes gnyen	kalyāṇamitra	virtuous spiritual friend
dge lugs pa		Ge-luk-pa
dge bshes		ge-shay
dge 'dun	saṃgha	spiritual community
dgos pa yongs su grub pa	kṛtyānuṣṭāna	thorough achievement of the purpose
dgra bcom rgyan med		Unadorned Foe Destroyer
dgra bcom pa	arhan	Foe Destroyer
dgra bcom 'bras gnas	arhattvaphalasthita	Abider in the Fruit of Foe Destroyer
dgra bcom zhugs pa	arhattvapratipannaka	Approacher to Foe Destroyer
'gal ba	viruddha	mutually exclusive
'gog pa	nirodha	cessation
'gog pa'i snyoms 'jug	nirodhasamāpatti	meditative absorption of cessation
'gog pa'i bden pa	nirodhasatya	true cessations
rga shi	jarāmaraṇa	aging and/or death
rgod pa	auddhatya	excitement
rgod pa dang 'gyod pa	auddhatyakaukṛtya	excitement and contrition
rgyags pa	mada	haughtiness
rgyu snyoms 'jug	*kāraṇasamāpatti	causal meditative absorption
rgyu mthun gyi 'bras bu	niṣyandaphala	causally concordant effect
rgyu mthun pa'i sbyor ba		causally concordant application
rgyu 'bras man ngag bdun		seven cause-and-effect quintessential instructions
rgyud	saṃtāna	continuum
rgyun du 'jog pa	saṃsthāpana	continuous setting
rgyun zhugs	śrotāpanna	Stream Enterer
sgom pa	bhāvanā	meditating
sgom byung	bhāvanāmayī	arisen from meditation
sgom lam	bhāvanāmārga	path of meditation
sgyid lugs pa'i le lo		laziness of inadequacy
sgra mi nyan	kuru	Unpleasant Sound
sgras brjod rigs kyi sgo nas dbye ba		terminological division
sgrib pa	āvaraṇa	obstruction
sgrim ste 'jug pa	balavāhana	forcible engagement
sgrub pa	pratipatti	achieving
nga rgyal	māna	pride
ngan 'gro	durgati	bad transmigration
ngar		intensity
nges 'byung sgrub pa	niryāṇapratipatti	achieving definite emergence

Tibetan	*Sanskrit*	*English*
nges 'byed cha mthun	nirvedhabhāgīya	concordant with definite differentiation
ngo tsha med pa	āhrikya	non-shame
ngon 'gro'i sbyor ba		preparatory training
dngos po	vastu	thing, category, phenomenon
dngos po'i mtha' la dmigs pa	vastvantālambana	observing the limits of phenomena
dngos gzhi'i snyoms 'jug	maulasamāpatti	actual meditative absorption
mngon shes	abhijñā	clairvoyance
sngon 'gro		preliminary practices
ci yang med	akiṃcanya	nothingness
gcig car	sakṛt	simultaneous
chags bral	kāmād virakta	separation from attachment
chad pa med par 'jug pa	niśchidravāhana	uninterrupted engagement
chu	āp	water
chung ngu	mṛdu	small
chung ngu'i chen po	mṛdvadhimātra	great of the small
chung ngu'i 'bring	mṛdumadhya	middling of the small
chen po	adhimātra	great
chen po'i chung ngu	adhimātramṛdu	small of the great
chen po'i chen po	adhimātrādhimātra	great of the great
chen po'i 'bring	adhimātramadhya	middling of the great
chog ma shes pa'i brtson grus		effort which is insatiable
chos	dharma	phenomenon, quality, topic, Doctrine
chos sku	dharmakāya	Truth Body
chos mngon pa	abhidharma	Manifest Knowledge
chos nyid kyi rigs pa	dharmatāyukti	reasoning of nature
chos la dmigs pa'i byams pa	*dharmālaṃbanā maitri	love observing phenomena
chos spong		abandoning the doctrine
'chi ba mi rtag pa	maraṇānitya	imminence of death
ji lta ba		mode
ji snyed pa		varieties
'jig rten chos brgyad	aṣṭalokadharma	eight worldly concerns
'jig rten pa'i lam	laukikamārga	mundane path
'jig rten las 'das pa'i lam	lokottaramārga	supramundane path
'jig rten pa'i chos kyi mchog	laukikāgryadharma	supreme mundane qualities
'jig tshogs la lta ba	satkāyadṛṣṭi	view of the transitory collection [as real I and mine]
'jug sgrub	prasthānapratipatti	achieving engagement
'jug shes	operative consciousness	
'jog sgom		stabilizing meditation
'jog ba	sthāna	placement
rjes thob	pṛṣṭhalabdha	attainment subsequent [to meditative equipoise]

Tibetan	*Sanskrit*	*English*
rjes dpag	anumāna	inferential cognition
rjes su 'gro ba	anugama	following
rjes su mthun pa las byung ba'i yid byed		concordant mental contemplation
nyan thos	śrāvaka	Hearers
nyams pa cha mthun	hānabhāgīya	concordant with degeneration
nyams smad		suppression
nye bar rtog pa	upalakṣaṇā	investigation
nye bar 'jog pa	upasthāpana	close setting
nye bar zhi bar byed pa	vyupaśamana	thorough pacifying
nye ba'i nyon mongs	upakleśa	secondary afflictive emotion
nyer bsdogs	sāmantaka	preparation
nyer len	upādāna	substantial cause
nyes dmigs	ādīnava	fault
nyon mongs	kleśa	afflictive emotion
nyon mongs kyi sgrib pa	kleśāvaraṇa	afflictive obstruction
nyon mong can	kliṣṭa	afflicted
nyon mongs rnam par sbyong ba'i las dang po pa	kleśaviśuddhyādikarmika	beginner at purifying the afflictive emotions
nyon mongs rnam sbyong gi dmigs pa	kleśaviśodanālambana	object of observation for purifying afflictive emotions
gnyid	middha	sleep
gnyen po yid la byed pa		antidotal mental contemplation
mnyam par 'jog pa	samādhāna	setting in equipoise
mnyam bzhag	samāhita	meditative equipoise
mnyam bzhag ye shes	samāhitajñāna	exalted wisdom of meditative equipoise
rnying ma		Nying-ma
rnyed pa	lābha	gain
snyoms 'jug	samāpatti	meditative absorption, absorption
snyoms las kyi le lo		laziness of neutral activities
snyan grags	yaśas	fame
snying rje chen po	mahākaruṇā	great compassion
ting nge 'dzin	samādhi	meditative stabilization, stabilization
gti mug	moha	obscuration
btang snyoms	upekṣā	equanimity, neutral feeling
btang snyoms tshad med		immeasurable equanimity
rtag sbyor		continuous application
rtog pa	vitarka	investigation
rtogs ba phul ba		offer one's realization
rten	āśraya	basis
rten cing 'brel bar 'byung ba	pratītyasamutpāda	dependent-arising

Tibetan	*Sanskrit*	*English*
brtags par dka' ba'i		pliancy difficult to
shin sbyangs		analyze
brtags par sla ba'i shin sbyangs		pliancy easy to analyze
bstan bcos	śāstra	treatise
lta ba	dṛṣṭi	view, [bad] view
lta ba mchog 'dzin	dṛṣṭiparāmarśa	conception of a [bad] view as supreme; misapprehension of the supreme
ltos pa'i rigs pa	apekṣāyukti	reasoning of dependence
stong pa nyid	śūnyatā	emptiness
stobs	bala	power
bstod pa	praśaṃsa	praise
thal 'gyur	prasaṅga	consequence
thal 'gyur pa	prāsaṅgika	Prāsaṅgika
thar pa	vimokṣa	liberation
the tshom	vicikitsā	doubt
thig le	bindu	drop
thun mong ma yin pa'i	asādhāranadhipatipratyaya	uncommon empowering
bdag rkyen		condition
theg chen	mahāyāna	Mahāyāna
theg chen sems bskyed	mahāyānacittotpāda	Mahāyāna [altruistic] mind generation
theg dman	hīnayāna	Hīnayāna
thod rgyal gyi snyoms 'jug	vyutkrāntakasamāpatti	leapover absorptions
thos pa	śruta	hearing
thos byung	śrutamayī	arisen from hearing
mtha'	anta	extreme
mtha' dpyod		final analysis
mthar gyis sbyor ba	anupūrvaprayoga	serial training
mthar 'dzing pa'i lta ba	antagrāhadṛṣṭi	view holding to an extreme
mthong lam	darśanamārga	path of seeing
'thad sgrub kyi rigs pa	upapattisādhanayukti	logical reasoning; reasoning that establishes correctness
'thob 'dod pa'i dad pa	*abhilāṣaśraddhā	faith that is a wish to attain
dag pa	śuddha	pure
dad pa	śraddhā	faith
dal ba	kṣaṇa	leisure
dal 'byor	kṣaṇasampad	leisure and fortune
dud 'gro	tiryañc	animal
dul bar byed pa	damana	disciplining
dus	kāla	time
de kho na nyid	tathatā	reality
de ma thag rkyen	samanantarapratyaya	immediately preceding condition

Tibetan	*Sanskrit*	*English*
de bzhin gshegs pa	tathāgata	One Gone Thus
don	artha	meaning
don spyi	arthasāmānya	generic image, meaning-generality
dvang cha		factor of subjective clarity
dvang ba'i dad pa	*prasādaśraddhā	faith of clarity
dran pa nye bar bzhag pa	smṛtyupasthāna	mindful establishment
dran pa	smṛti	mindfulness
gdags gzhi		basis of designation
gdams ngag	avavāda	instruction, preceptual instruction
gdam ngag brjed pa	avavādasammoṣa	forgetting the instruction
bdag 'bras	adhipatiphala	possessional effect
bdag med	nairātmya	selflessness
bde 'gro	sugati	happy transmigration
bde rgyas	śubakṛtsna	Vast Bliss
bde chung	parīttaśuba	Little Bliss
bde ba	sukha	bliss, happiness
bden pa rnam can		having the aspect of the truths
mdo sde pa	sautrāntika	Sautrāntika
'du byed kyi sdug bsngal	saṃskāraduhkhatā	suffering of conditioning
'du byed kyi las	saṃskārakarma	compositional factor
'du byed btang snyoms		desisting from application
'du byed pa	abhisaṃskāra	application, antidote
'du mi byed pa	anabhisaṃskāra	non-application
'du shes	saṃjñā	discrimination
'du shes med 'du shes med min	naivasaṃjñānāsaṃjñā	without discrimination and without non-discrimination
'du shes med pa	asaṃjnā	non-discrimination
'dun pa	chanda	aspiration
'dul ba	vinaya	monastic discipline
'dod khams	kāmadhatu	Desire Realm
'dod chags	rāga	desire
'dod pa la 'dun pa	kāmacchanda	aspiration to attributes of the Desire Realm
'dod sems		Desire Realm mind
'dod sems dgu pa		ninth mind of the Desire Realm
'dod sems dgu pa'i ting nge 'dzin		meditative stabilization of the ninth mind of the Desire Realm
rdo rje skyil krung	vajrāsana	adamantine posture, vajra posture
rdo rje gzegs ma		vajra nodes
rdo rje sems dpa'	vajrasattva	Vajrasattva

Tibetan	*Sanskrit*	*English*
ldan min 'du byed	viprayuktasaṃskāra	non-associated compositional factor
sdug bsngal	duḥkha	suffering
sdug bsngal bden pa	duḥkhasatya	true sufferings
sdug bsngal ma yin bde ba	aduḥkhāsukhavedanā	neutral feeling
	yang ma yin	
sdom pa	saṃvara	discipline
sdom min	asaṃvara	bad discipline
nang pa		Buddhist [Insider]
nang rab tu dvang ba	adhyātmasamprasāda	internal clarity
nam mkha'	ākāśa	space
nam mkha' mtha' yas	ākāśānantya	limitless space
gnas cha		factor of stability
gnas dang gnas ma yin pa	sthānāsthāna	appropriate and the inappro-priate
gnas pa cha mthun	sthitibhāgīya	concordant with abiding
gnas gtsang lnga	pañcaśuddhāvāsakāyika	Five Pure Places
gnas lugs		mode of subsistence
gnod sems	vyāpāda	harmfulness
rnam pa	ākāra	aspect, subjective aspect
rnam grol lam	vimuktimārga	path of release
rnam rtog	vikalpa	discursiveness, coarse concep-tuality
rnam pa thams cad mkhyen	sarvākārajñatā	exalted knower of all
pa nyid, rnam mkhyen		aspects
rnam par rtog pa dang	savikalpikapratibimba	analytical image
	bcas pa'i gzugs brnyan	
rnam par snang mdzad	vairocana	Vairochana
rnam par mi rtog pa'i gzugs	nirvikalpakapratibimba	non-analytical image
	brnyan	
rnam par g.yeng ba	vikṣepa	distraction
rnam par rig byed ma yin	avijñaptirūpa	non-revelatory form
	pa'i gzugs	
rnam sbyong	viśodana	purifying
rnam smin gyi sgrib pa	*vipākāvaraṇa	fruitional obstruction
rnam smin gyi 'bras bu	vipākaphala	fruitional effect
rnam rdzogs sbyor ba	sarvākārābhisaṃbhodha	complete training in the as-pects
rnam shes	vijñāna	consciousness
rnam shes mtha' yas	vijñānānantya	limitless consciousness
rnal 'byor spyod pa	yogācāra	Yogāchāra
brnab sems	abhidhyā	covetousness
dpyad sgom		analytical meditation
dpyod pa	vicāra	analysis

Tibetan	*Sanskrit*	*English*
dpyod pa yid byed	mīmāṃsāmanaskāra	mental contemplation of analysis
spangs pa	prahāṇa	abandonment
spyad pa rnam sbyong gi dmigs pa	caritaviśodanālambana	object of observation for purifying behavior
spyan ras gzigs	avalokiteśvara	Avalokiteshvara
spyi don		general meaning commentary
spyi'i mtshan nyid	sāmānyalakṣaṇa	general character, generally characterized phenomenon
sprin med	anabhraka	Cloudless
phan 'dogs pa		help
phan yon	anuśaṃsa	benefit
phar phyin	pāramitā	Perfections
phung po	skandha	aggregate
'phags pa	ārya	Superior
phyag rgya	mudrā	seal
phyag mtshan	mudrā	hand symbol
phyi rol pa		Non-Buddhist, Outsider
phyir mi 'ong	anāgāmin	Non-Returner
phyir 'ong	sakṛdāgāmin	Once Returner
phyogs	pakṣa	class
phra ba'i shin sbyangs		subtle pliancy
phrag dog	irṣyā	jealousy
'phro ba		scattering
bags chags	vāsanā	predisposition
bar chad med lam	ānantaryamārga	uninterrupted path
bar do	antarābhāva	intermediate state
bar du chad cing 'jug pa	sacchidravāhana	interrupted engagement
bya ba ngan zhen gyi le lo		laziness which is an attachment to bad activities
bya ba byed pa'i rigs pa	kāryakāraṇayukti	reasoning of the performance of function
byang chub sems dpa'	bodhisattva	Bodhisattva
byang chub kyi sems	bodhicitta	mind of enlightenment, altruistic mind of enlightenment
byams pa	maitri	love
byams pa chen po	mahāmaitri	great love
bying ba	laya	laxity
bye brag smra ba	vaibhāṣika	Vaibhāṣhika
bla med kyi rgyud	anuttarayogatantra	Highest Yoga Tantra
'byor ba	saṃpad	fortune
bla ma	guru	lama
blo	buddhi, dhī	awareness
blo rig		Awareness and Knowledge

Tibetan	*Sanskrit*	*English*
dbang rdul gyi nang pa		Buddhist of dull faculties
dbang rnon gyi dge rtsa yongs su ma smin pa		Buddhist of sharp faculties whose virtuous roots are not thoroughly ripened
dbang po	indriya	sense power
dbang shes	indriyajñāna	sense consciousness
dbu ma pa	mādhyamika	Mādhyamika
dbugs rngub pa	śvāsa	inhalation
dbugs 'byung pa	praśvāsa	exhalation
dbugs 'byung rngub	ānāpana	exhalation and inhalation of the breath
'byung ba	bhūta	element
'byung ba chen po	mahābhūta	great element
'bras bu	phala	effect, fruit
'bras bu skye ba		resultant-birth state
'bras bu skye ba'i snyoms 'jug	*kāryasamāpatti	resultant-birth meditative absorption
'bras bu che	bṛhatphala	Great Fruit
'bras bu chos sku	*phaladharmakāya	Truth Body, the fruit
'bring	madhya	middling
'bring gi chung ngu	madhyamṛdu	small of the middling
'bring gi chen po	madhyādhimātra	great of the middling
'bring gi 'bring	madhyamadhya	middling of the middling
sbyor mtha'i yid byed	prayoganiṣṭhamanaskāra	mental contemplation of final training
sbyor ba	prayoga	syllogism
sbyor ba mtha'i 'bras bu yid byed	prayoganiṣṭaphala-manaskāra	mental contemplation that is the fruit of final training
sbyor ba las byung ba'i brtson grus		effort arising from application
sbyor lam	prayogamārga	path of preparation
ma ning	paṇḍaka	eunuch
ma rnyed pa	alābha	loss
ma snyan grags	ayaśas	disgrace
ma rig pa	avidyā	ignorance
man ngag	upadeśa	quintessential instruction
mi	manuṣya	human
mi rtag pa	anitya	impermanence
mi dge ba	akuśala	non-virtue, non-virtuous
mi sdug pa	aśubha	unpleasant, the
mi gdung ba	atapas	Without Pain
mi lcog med	anāgamya	not-unable
mi che ba	avṛha	Not Great
mi slob lam	aśaikṣamārga	path of no more learning
mi 'thugs pa'i brtson grus		undisturbed effort

Tibetan	*Sanskrit*	*English*
mi g.yo ba	āniñjya	unfluctuating
mig gi rnam par shes pa	cakṣurvijñāna	eye consciousness
mig gi dbang po	cakṣurindriya	eye sense power
ming	nāman	name
ming gzugs	nāmarūpa	name and form
me	tejas	fire
mos pa las byung ba'i yid byed	adhimokṣikamanaskāra	mental contemplation arisen from belief
mya ngan las 'das pa	nirvāṇa	nirvāṇa
dmigs pa	ālambana	object of observation
dmigs rkyen	ālambanapratyaya	observed-object condition
dmigs med la dmigs pa'i byams pa	*anālaṃbanā maitri	love observing the unapprehendable
dmyal ba	naraka	hell
dmyal ba	nāraka	hell being
rmugs pa	styāna	lethargy
rmugs pa dang gnyid	styānamiddha	lethargy and sleep
smad pa	nindā	blame
smon lam	praṇidhāna	aspirational prayer
tsong kha pa		Tsong-kha-pa
gtso sems		main mind
rtsa	nāḍi	channel
rtsa ba'i nyon mongs	mūlakleśa	root afflictive emotion
rtsa dbu ma		central channel
rtse gcig tu byed pa	ekotīkaraṇa	making one-pointed
rtse sbyor	mūrdhaprayoga	peak training
rtsol ba	vyāyāma	exertion
brtson 'grus	vīrya	effort
tshangs chen	mahābrahmaṇa	Great Brahmā
tshangs mdun	brahmapurohita	In Front of Brahmā
tshangs ris	brahmakāyika	Brahmā Type
tshad med bde	apramāṇaśuba	Limitless Bliss
tshad med bzhi	catvary apramāṇāni	four immeasurables
tshad med 'od	apramāṇābhā	Limitless Light
tshul khrims dang brdul zhugs	śīlavrataparāmarśa	conception of ethics and systems of behavior as supreme
tshogs sgrub	saṃbhārapratipatti	achieving the collections
tshogs bsten pa		prerequisite, causal collection
tshogs lam	saṃbhāramārga	path of accumulation
tshor ba	vedanā	feeling
tshor ba btang snyoms	*upekṣāvedanā	neutral feeling
tshor ba yid bde		feeling of mental bliss
tshor ba sems bde		feeling of mental bliss
mtshan nyid	lakṣaṇa	character, definition

Tibetan	*Sanskrit*	*English*
mtshan nyid rab tu rig pa'i yid byed		mental contemplation of thorough knowledge of the character
mtshan nyid so sor rig pa'i yid byed	lakṣaṇapratisaṃvedī-manaskāra	mental contemplation of individual knowledge of the character
mtshan gnyis pa	ubhayavyañjana	androgyne
mtshan ma dang bcas pa'i zhi gnas		calm abiding with signs
mtshan ma med pa'i zhi gnas		calm abiding without signs
mtshan ma med pa'i		special insight without
lhag mthong		signs
mtshan med	animitta	signless
mtshams med pa	ānantarya	heinous crime
rdzas su yod pa	dravyasat	substantially existent
rdzogs chen		Great Completeness
rdzogs rim	niṣpannakrama	stage of completion
zhi gnas	śamatha	calm abiding
zhi bar byed pa	śamana	pacifying
zhi rags	*śāntaudārika	grossness/peacefulness
zhi rags rnam can		having the aspect of grossness/peacefulness
zhi lhag zung 'brel	śamathavipaśyanā-yuganaddha	union of calm abiding and special insight
zhum pa		slackness
zhe dang	dveṣa	hatred
gzhal med khang	*amātragṛha	inestimable mansion
gzhi	vastu	basis
gzhi shes	vastujñatā	knower of bases, exalted knower of bases
bzhon pa		mount
gzhung pa pa		textual [lineage]
za ma	ṣaṇḍha	neuter person
zag med	anāsrava	uncontaminated
gzugs	rūpa	form
gzugs kyi phung po	rūpaskandha	form aggregate
gzugs sku	rūpakāya	Form Body
gzugs khams	rūpadhātu	Form Realm
gzugs med kyi snyoms 'jug	ārūpyasamāpatti	formless absorption
gzugs med khams	ārūpyadhātu	Formless Realm
'og min	akaniṣṭha	Not Low
'od chung	parīttābhā	Little Light
'od gsal	ābhāsvara	Bright Light
'od gsal	prabhāsvara	clear light

Tibetan	*Sanskrit*	*English*
yan lag	aṅga	branch
yi dvags	preta	hungry ghost
yig cha		monastic textbook
yid	manas	intellect
yid kyi rnam shes	manovijñāna	mental consciousness
yid ches pa'i dad pa	*abhisaṃpratyayaśraddhā	faith of conviction
yid bde	saumanasya	mental bliss
yid dpyod	*manaḥ parīkṣā	correctly assuming consciousness
yid mi bde	daurmanasya	mental discomfort
yid la byed pa	manaskāra	mental contemplation, mental engagement
yid la byed pa las dang po pa	manaskārādikarmika	beginner at mental contemplation
yid la byed pa las dang po pa'i rnal 'byor	manaskārādikarmika[yoga]	yoga of a beginner at mental contemplation
yid la byed pa yongs su rdzogs pa'i rnal 'byor	atikrāntamanaskāra[yoga]	yoga of one whose mental contemplation is perfected
yid lus		mental body
ye shes chos sku	jñānadharmakā	Wisdom Truth Body
yongs su sgyur ba	vivartanā	change
yongs su dag pa	pariśuddhi	purifying, thorough purity
yongs su 'dris pa	paricaya	familiarity
yongs su sbyangs pa byas pa'i rnal 'byor	kṛtaparicaya[yoga]	yoga of someone who is practiced
yul	viṣaya	object
rags pa'i shin sbyangs		coarse pliancy
rang gi mtshan nyid	svalakṣaṇa	specific character, specifically characterized phenomenon
rang rgyud pa	svātantrika	Svātantrika
rang sangs rgyas	pratyekabuddha	Solitary Realizer
rab tu dvang ba yid la byed pa		thoroughly clear mental contemplation
rab tu dben pa'i yid byed	prāvivekyamanaskāra	mental contemplation of thorough isolation
rig pa	saṃvedana	knower
rigs pa	yukti	reasoning
reg pa	sparśa	contact
reg bya	spraṣṭavya	tangible object
reg bya'i skye mched	spraṣṭavyāyatana	tangible-object sphere
lam	mārga	path
lam gyi bden pa	mārgasatya	true paths
lam rim		stages of the path
lam shes	mārgajñatā	knower of paths
las	karma	action
las sgrib	karmāvaraṇa	karmic obstruction

Tibetan	*Sanskrit*	*English*
las dang po pa	ādikarmika	beginner
las dang po pa tsam gyi yid byed		mental contemplation of a mere beginner
lung du ma bstan pa	avyākṛta	neutral
lus kyi rnam par shes pa	kāyavijñāna	body consciousness
lus rten		physical basis
le lo	kausīdya	laziness
len pa	upādāna	grasping
log lta	mithyādṛṣṭi	wrong view
rlung	vāyu, prāṇa	wind
shin tu mthong ba	sudarśana	Great Perception
shin sbyangs	praśrabdhi	pliancy
shin sbyangs skye ba'i snga bltas		omen of pliancy
shes bya	jñeya	object of knowledge
shes bzhin	samprajanya	introspection
shes rab	prajñā	wisdom
shes rab kyi pha rol tu phyin pa, sher phyin	prajñāpāramitā	perfection of wisdom
shes rab gyi tshogs	prajñāsaṃbhāra	collection of wisdom
bshags pa	deśanā	confession
sa	pṛthivī	earth
sa	bhūmi	ground
sa skya		Sa-kya
sa bcad		contents-outline
sa lam	bhūmimārga	Grounds and Paths
sangs rgyas	buddha	Buddha
sangs rgyas kyi zhing	buddhakṣetra	Buddha field
sems	citta	mind
sems can	sattva	sentient being
sems can tsam la dmigs pa'i byams pa	*sattvālaṃbanā maitri	love observing mere sentient beings
sems rten		mental basis
sems gnas	cittasthiti	mental abiding
sems gnas dgu	navākārā cittasthiti	nine mental abidings
sems gnas pa rnam pa dgu	navākārā cittasthiti	nine mental abidings
sems byung	caitta	mental factor
sems tsam pa	cittamātra	Chittamātra
sems 'jog pa	cittasthāpana	setting the mind
ser sna	mātsarya	miserliness
so mthar gyi sdom pa	pratimokṣasaṃvara	discipline of individual emancipation
so so'i skye bo	pṛthagjana	common being
so sor rtog pa yid la byed pa		mental contemplation of individual investigation

Tibetan	*Sanskrit*	*English*
so sor rtog pa'i shes rab		wisdom of individual analysis
so sor mthar pa	pratimokṣa	individual emancipation
gsal cha		factor of clarity
bsam pa	cintā	thinking
bsam gtan	dhyāna	concentration
bsam gtan gyi sdom pa	dhyānasaṃvara	concentrative discipline
bsam gtan dang po	prathamadhyāna	first concentration
bsam gtan dang po'i dngos gzhi'i snyoms 'jug khyad par can		special absorption of an actual first concentration
bsam gtan dang po'i dngos gzhi'i snyoms 'jug tsam po ba		actual absorption of a mere first concentration
bsam gtan gnyis pa	dvitīyadhyāna	second concentration
bsam gtan bzhi pa	caturthadhyāna	fourth concentration
bsam gtan gsum pa	tritīyadhyāna	third concentration
bsam byung	cintāmayī	arisen from thinking
bse ru lta bu rang sangs rgyas	khaḍgaviṣāṇakalpapratyekabud-dha	rhinoceroslike Solitary Realiz-er
bsod nams	puṇya	merit, meritorious
bsod nams kyi tshogs	puṇyasaṃbhāra	collection of merit
bsod nams skyes	puṇyaprasava	Born from Merit
bslab pa	śikṣā	training
srid pa	bhava	existence
srid rtse	bhavāgra	peak of cyclic existence
sred pa	tṛṣṇā	attachment
srog gi dbang po	jivitendriya	life faculty
slan te 'jog pa	avasthāpana	resetting
lha	deva	god
lha ma yin	asura	demigod
lhag mthong	vipaśyanā	special insight
lhun grub tu 'jug pa	anābhogavāhana	spontaneous engagement

3 Sanskrit-Tibetan-English

Sanskrit	*Tibetan*	*English*
akaniṣṭha	'og min	Not Low
akiṃcanya	ci yang med	nothingness
akuśala	mi dge ba	non-virtue, non-virtuous
aṅga	yan lag	branch
atapas	mi gdung ba	Without Pain
atikrāntamanaskāra[yoga]	yid la byed pa yongs su rdzogs pa'i rnal 'byor	yoga of one whose mental contemplation is perfected
aduḥkhāsukhavedanā	sdug bsngal ma yin bde ba yang ma yin	neutral feeling
adhipatiphala	bdag 'bras	possessional effect
adhimātra	chen po	great
adhimātramadhya	chen po'i 'bring	middling of the great
adhimātramṛdu	chen po'i chung ngu	small of the great
adhimātrādhimātra	chen po'i chen po	great of the great
adhimokṣikamanaskāra	mos pa las byung ba'i yid byed	mental contemplation arisen from belief
adhyātmasamprasāda	nang rab tu dvang ba	internal clarity
anabhisaṃskāra	'du mi byed pa	non-application
anabhraka	sprin med	Cloudless
anāgamya	mi lcog med	not-unable
anāgāmin	phyir mi 'ong	Non-Returner
anābhogavāhana	lhun grub tu 'jug pa	spontaneous engagement
*anālaṃbanā maitri	dmigs med la dmigs pa'i byams pa	love observing the unapprehendable
anāsrava	zag med	uncontaminated
anitya	mi rtag pa	impermanence
animitta	mtshan med	signless
anugama	rjes su 'gro ba	following
anuttarayogatantra	bla med kyi rgyud	Highest Yoga Tantra
anupūrvaprayoga	mthar gyis sbyor ba	serial training
anumāna	rjes dpag	inferential cognition
anuśaṃsa	phan yon	benefit
anta	mtha'	extreme
antagrāhadṛṣṭi	mthar 'dzing pa'i lta ba	view holding to an extreme
antarābhāva	bar do	intermediate state
apakṣāla	skyon	fault
apekṣāyukti	ltos pa'i rigs pa	reasoning of dependence
apramāṇaśuba	tshad med bde	Limitless Bliss
apramāṇābhā	tshad med 'od	Limitless Light
abhijñā	mngon shes	clairvoyance
abhidharma	chos mngon pa	Manifest Knowledge
abhidhyā	brnab sems	covetousness
*abhilāṣaśraddhā	'thob 'dod pa'i dad pa	faith that is a wish to attain

Sanskrit	*Tibetan*	*English*
*abhisaṃpratyayaśraddhā	yid ches pa'i dad pa	faith of conviction
abhisaṃskāra	'du byed pa	application, antidote
*amātragṛha	gzhal med khang	inestimable mansion
ayaśas	ma snyan grags	disgrace
artha	don	meaning
arthasāmānya	don spyi	generic image, meaning-generality
arhattvapratipannaka	dgra bcom zhugs pa	Approacher to Foe Destroyer
arhattvaphalasthita	dgra bcom 'bras gnas	Abider in the Fruit of Foe Destroyer
arhan	dgra bcom pa	Foe Destroyer
alābha	ma rnyed pa	loss
avalokiteśvara	spyan ras gzigs	Avalokiteshvara
avavāda	gdams ngag	instruction, preceptual instruction
avavādasammoṣa	gdam ngag brjed pa	forgetting the instruction
avasthāpana	slan te 'jog pa	resetting
avijñaptirūpa	rnam par rig byed ma yin pa'i gzugs	non-revelatory form
avidyā	ma rig pa	ignorance
avṛha	mi che ba	Not Great
avyākṛta	lung du ma bstan pa	neutral
aśubha	mi sdug pa	unpleasant
aśaikṣamārga	mi slob lam	path of no more learning
aṣṭalokadharma	'jig rten chos brgyad	eight worldly concerns
asaṃjñā	'du shes me pa	non-discrimination
asaṃvara	sdom min	bad discipline
asādhāranadhipatipratyaya	thun mong ma yin pa'i bdag rkyen	uncommon empowering condition
asura	lha ma yin	demigod
ākāra	rnam pa	aspect, subjective aspect
ākāśa	nam mkha'	space
ākāśānantya	nam mkha' mtha' yas	limitless space
ādikarmika	las dang po pa	beginner
ādīnava	nyes dmigs	fault
ānantarya	mtshams med pa	heinous crime, crime of immediate retribution
ānantaryamārga	bar chad med lam	uninterrupted path
ānāpana	dbugs 'byung rngub	exhalation and inhalation of the breath
āniñjya	mi g.yo ba	unfluctuating
āp	chu	water
ābhāsvara	'od gsal	Bright Light
āyatana	skye mched	sphere
ārūpyadhātu	gzugs med khams	Formless Realm
ārūpyasamāpatti	gzugs med kyi snyoms 'jug	formless absorption

Sanskrit	*Tibetan*	*English*
ārya	'phags pa	Superior
ālambana	dmigs pa	object of observation
ālambanapratyaya	dmigs rkyen	observed-object condition
āvaraṇa	sgrib pa	obstruction
āśraya	rten	basis
āhrikya	ngo tsha med pa	non-shame
indriya	dbang po	sense power
indriyajñāna	dbang shes	sense consciousness
irṣyā	phrag dog	jealousy
upakleśa	nye ba'i nyon mongs	secondary afflictive emotion
upadeśa	man ngag	quintessential instruction
upanāha	'khon 'dzin	resentment
upapattisādhanayukti	'thad sgrub kyi rigs pa	logical reasoning, reasoning that establishes correctness
upalakṣaṇā	nye bar rtog pa	investigation
upasthāpana	nye bar 'jog pa	close setting
upādāna	nyer len	substantial cause
upādāna	len pa	grasping
upekṣā	btang snyoms	equanimity, neutral feeling
*upekṣāvedanā	tshor ba btang snyoms	neutral feeling
ubhayavyañjana	mtshan gnyis pa	androgyne
ekotīkaraṇa	rtse gcig tu byed pa	making one-pointed
auddhatya	rgod pa	excitement
auddhatyakaukṛtya	rgod pa dang 'gyod pa	excitement and contrition
kalyāṇamitra	dge ba'i bshes gnyen	spiritual friend, spiritual guide
karma	las	action
karmāvaraṇa	las sgrib	karmic obstruction
kāmacchanda	'dod pa la 'dun pa	aspiration to attributes of the Desire Realm
kāmadhatu	'dod khams	Desire Realm
kāmād virakta	chags bral	separation from attachment
kāyavijñāna	lus kyi rnam par shes pa	body consciousness
*kāraṇasamāpatti	rgyu snyoms 'jug	causal meditative absorption
kāryakāraṇayukti	bya ba byed pa'i rigs pa	reasoning of the performance of function
*kāryasamāpatti	'bras bu skye ba'i snyoms 'jug	resultant-birth meditative absorption
kāla	dus	time
kuru	sgra mi nyan	Unpleasant Sound
kuśala	dge ba	virtue, virtuous
kuśalamūla	dge ba'i rtsa ba	virtuous root
kṛtaparicaya[yoga]	yongs su sbyangs pa byas pa'i rnal 'byor	yoga of someone who is practiced

Sanskrit	*Tibetan*	*English*
kṛtyānuṣṭāna	dgos pa yongs su grub pa	thorough achievement of the purpose
kauśalyālambana	mkhas pa'i dmigs pa, mkhas par byed pa'i dmigs pa	object of observation for [developing] skill
kausīdya	le lo	laziness
krodha	khro ba	belligerence
kliṣṭa	nyon mong can	afflicted
kleśa	nyon mongs	afflictive emotion
kleśaviśuddhyādikarmika	nyon mongs rnam par sbyong ba'i las dang po pa	beginner at purifying the afflictive emotions
kleśaviśodanālambana	nyon mongs rnam sbyong gi dmigs pa	object of observation for purifying afflictive emotions
kleśāvaraṇa	nyon mongs kyi sgrib pa	afflictive obstruction
kṣaṇa	dal ba	leisure
kṣaṇasampad	dal 'byor	leisure and fortune
kṣaṇikaprayoga	skad cig ma'i sbyor ba	momentary training
khaḍgaviṣāṇakalpapratyekabuddha	bse ru lta bu rang sangs rgyas	rhinoceroslike Solitary Realizer
gaṇanā	grangs pa	counting
guru	bla ma	lama
cakṣurindriya	mig gi dbang po	eye sense power
cakṣurvijñāna	mig gi rnam par shes pa	eye consciousness
caturthadhyāna	bsam gtan bzhi pa	fourth concentration
catvāry apramāṇāni	tshad med bzhi	four immeasurables
caritaviśodanālambana	spyad pa rnam sbyong gi dmigs pa	object of observation for purifying behavior
citta	sems	mind
cittamātra	sems tsam pa	Chittamātra
cittasthāpana	sems 'jog pa	setting the mind
cittasthiti	sems gnas	mental abiding
cintā	bsam pa	thinking
cintāmayī	bsam byung	arisen from thinking
caitta	sems byung	mental factor
chanda	'dun pa	aspiration
jarāmaraṇa	rga shi	aging and/or death
jivitendriya	srog gi dbang po	life faculty
jāti	skye ba	birth
jñāta	mkhyen pa	exalted knower
jñānadharmakāya	ye shes chos sku	Wisdom Truth Body
jñeya	shes bya	object of knowledge
tathatā	de kho na nyid	reality
tathāgata	de bzhin gshegs pa	One Gone Thus
tiryañc	dud 'gro	animal
tṛṣṇā	sred pa	attachment

Sanskrit	*Tibetan*	*English*
tejas	me	fire
tritīyadhyāna	bsam gtan gsum pa	third concentration
triratna	dkon mchog gsum	Three Jewels
damana	dul bar byed pa	disciplining
darśanamārga	mthong lam	path of seeing
durgati	ngan 'gro	bad transmigration
duḥkha	sdug bsngal	suffering
duḥkhasatya	sdug bsngal bden pa	true sufferings
dṛṣṭi	lta ba'	view, [bad] view
dṛṣṭiparāmarśa	lta ba mchog 'dzin	conception of a [bad] view as supreme, misapprehension of the supreme
deva	lha	god
deśanā	bshags pa	confession
daurmanasya	yid mi bde	mental discomfort
dravyasat	rdzas su yod pa	substantially existent
dvitīyadhyāna	bsam gtan gnyis pa	second concentration
dveṣa	zhe dang	hatred
dharma	chos	phenomenon, quality, topic, Doctrine
dharmakāya	chos sku	Truth Body
dharmatāyukti	chos nyid kyi rigs pa	reasoning of nature
*dharmālaṃbanā maitri	chos la dmigs pa'i byams pa	love observing phenomena
dhātu	khams	constituent
dhī	blo	awareness
dhyāna	bsam gtan	concentration
dhyānasaṃvara	bsam gtan gyi sdom pa	concentrative discipline
naraka	dmyal ba	hell
navākārā cittasthiti	sems gnas dgu, sems gnas pa rnam pa dgu	nine mental abidings
nāga	klu	nāga
nāḍi	rtsa	channel
nāman	ming	name
nāmarūpa	ming gzugs	name and form
nāraka	dmyal ba	hell being
nindā	smad pa	blame
nirodha	'gog pa	cessation
nirodhasatya	'gog pa'i bden pa	true cessations
nirodhasamāpatti	'gog pa'i snyoms 'jug	meditative absorption of cessation
niryāṇapratipatti	nges 'byung sgrub pa	achieving definite emergence
nirvāṇa	mya ngan las 'das pa	nirvāṇa
nirvikalpakapratibimba	rnam par mi rtog pa'i gzugs brnyan	non-analytical image

Sanskrit	*Tibetan*	*English*
nirvedhabhāgīya	nges 'byed cha mthun	concordant with definite differentiation
niśchidravāhana	chad pa med par 'jug pa	uninterrupted engagement
niṣpannakrama	rdzogs rim	stage of completion
niṣyandaphala	rgyu mthun gyi 'bras bu	causally concordant effect
nairātmya	bdag med	selflessness
naivasaṃjñānāsaṃjñā	'du shes med 'du shes med min	without discrimination and without non-discrimination
pakṣa	phyogs	class
pañcaśuddhāvāsakāyika	gnas gtsang lnga	Five Pure Places
paṇḍaka	ma ning	eunuch
paricaya	yongs su 'dris pa	familiarity
pariśuddhi	yongs su dag pa	purifying, thorough purity
parīttaśuba	bde chung	Little Bliss
parīttābhā	'od chung	Little Light
parokṣa	lkog gyur	hidden, subliminal
pāramitā	phar phyin	Perfections
puṇya	bsod nams	merit, meritorious
puṇyaprasava	bsod nams skyes	Born from Merit
puṇyasaṃbhāra	bsod nams gyi tshogs	collection of merit
pudgala	gang zag	person
pudgalanairātmya	gang zag gi bdag med	selflessness of persons
pṛthagjana	so so'i skye bo	common being
pṛthivī	sa	earth
pṛṣṭhalabdha	rjes thob	attainment subsequent [to meditative equipoise]
prajñā	shes rab	wisdom
prajñāpāramitā	shes rab kyi pha rol tu phyin pa, sher phyin	perfection of wisdom
prajñāsaṃbhāra	shes rab gyi tshogs	collection of wisdom
praṇidhāna	smon lam	aspirational prayer
pratigha	khong khro	anger
pratipatti	sgrub pa	achieving
pratimokṣa	so sor mthar pa	individual emancipation
pratimokṣasaṃvara	so mthar gyi sdom pa	discipline of individual emancipation
pratyekabuddha	rang sangs rgyas	Solitary Realizer
pratītyasamutpāda	rten cing 'brel bar 'byung ba	dependent-arising
prathamadhyāna	bsam gtan dang po	first concentration
prabhāsvara	'od gsal	clear light
prayoga	sbyor ba	syllogism
prayoganiṣṭaphalamanaskāra	sbyor ba mtha'i 'bras bu yid byed	mental contemplation that is the fruit of final training
prayoganiṣṭhamanaskāra	sbyor mtha'i yid byed	mental contemplation of final training
prayogamārga	sbyor lam	path of preparation

Sanskrit	*Tibetan*	*English*
praśaṃsa	bstod pa	praise
praśrabdhi	shin sbyangs	pliancy
praśvāsa	dbugs 'byung pa	exhalation
prasaṅga	thal 'gyur	consequence
*prasādaśraddhā	dvang ba'i dad pa	faith of clarity
prasthānapratipatti	'jug sgrub	achieving engagement
prahāṇa	spangs pa	abandonment
prāṇa	lung	wind
prāvivekyamanaskāra	rab tu dben pa'i yid byed	mental contemplation of thorough isolation
prāsaṅgika	thal 'gyur pa	Prāsaṅgika
prīti	dga' ba	joy
preta	yi dvags	hungry ghost
phala	'bras bu	effect, fruit
*phaladharmakāya	'bras bu chos sku	Truth Body, the fruit
bala	stobs	power
balavāhana	sgrim ste 'jug pa	forcible engagement
bindu	thig le	drop
buddha	sangs rgyas	Buddha
buddhakṣetra	sangs rgyas kyi zhing	Buddha field
buddhi	blo	awareness
bṛhatphala	'bras bu che	Great Fruit
bodhicitta	byang chub kyi sems	mind of enlightenment, altruistic mind of enlightenment
bodhisattva	byang chub sems dpa'	Bodhisattva
brahmakāyika	tshangs ris	Brahmā Type
brahmapurohita	tshangs mdun	In Front of Brahmā
bhava	srid pa	existence
bhavāgra	srid rtse	peak of cyclic existence
bhāvanā	sgom pa	meditating
bhāvanāmārga	sgom lam	path of meditation
bhāvanāmayī	sgom byung	arisen from meditation
bhūta	'byung ba	element
bhūmi	sa	ground
bhūmimārga	sa lam	Grounds and Paths
mada	rgyags pa	haughtiness
madhya	'bring	middling
madhyamadhya	'bring gi 'bring	middling of the middling
madhyamṛdu	'bring gi chung ngu	small of the middling
madhyādhimātra	'bring gi chen po	great of the middling
manas	yid	intellect
manaskāra	yid la byed pa	mental contemplation, mental engagement

Sanskrit	*Tibetan*	*English*
manaskārādikarmika	yid la byed pa las dang po pa	beginner at mental contemplation
manaskārādikarmika[yoga]	yid la byed pa las dang po pa'i rnal 'byor	yoga of a beginner at mental contemplation
*manaḥ parīkṣā	yid dpyod	correctly assuming consciousness
manuṣya	mi	human
manovijñāna	yid kyi rnam shes	mental consciousness
maraṇānitya	'chi ba mi rtag pa	imminence of death
mahākaruṇā	snying rje chen po	great compassion
mahābrahmaṇa	tshangs chen	Great Brahmā
mahābhūta	'byung ba chen po	great element
mahāmaitri	byams pa chen po	great love
mahāyāna	theg chen	Mahāyāna
mahāyānacittotpāda	theg chen sems bskyed	Mahāyāna [altruistic] mind generation
mātsarya	ser sna	miserliness
mādhyamika	dbu ma pa	Mādhyamika
māna	nga rgyal	pride
mārga	lam	path
mārgajñatā	lam shes	knower of paths
mārgasatya	lam gyi bden pa	true paths
mithyādṛṣṭi	log lta	wrong view
middha	gnyid	sleep
mīmāṃsāmanaskāra	dpyod pa yid byed	mental contemplation of analysis
mudrā	phyag rgya	seal
mudrā	phyag mtshan	hand symbol
mūrdhaprayoga	rtse sbyor	peak training
mūlakleśa	rtsa ba'i nyon mongs	root afflictive emotion
mṛdu	chung ngu	small
mṛdumadhya	chung ngu'i 'bring	middling of the small
mṛdumṛdu	chung ngu'i chung ngu	small of the small
mṛdvadhimātra	chung ngu'i chen po	great of the small
maitri	byams pa	love
moha	gti mug	obscuration
maulasamāpatti	dngos gzhi'i snyoms 'jug	actual meditative absorption
yaśas	snyan grags	fame
yukti	rigs pa	reasoning
yogācāra	rnal 'byor spyod pa	Yogāchāra
ratisaṃgrāhakamanaskāra	dga' ba sdud pa'i yid byed	mental contemplation of joy-withdrawal
rāga	'dod chags	desire
rūpa	gzugs	form
rūpakāya	gzugs sku	Form Body

Sanskrit	*Tibetan*	*English*
rūpadhātu	gzugs khams	Form Realm
rūpaskandha	gzugs kyi phung po	form aggregate
lakṣaṇa	mtshan nyid	character, definition
lakṣaṇapratisaṃvedī-manaskāra	mtshan nyid so sor rig pa'i yid byed	mental contemplation of individual knowledge of the character
laya	bying ba	laxity
lābha	rnyed pa	gain
lokottaramārga	'jig rten las 'das pa'i lam	supramundane path
laukikamārga	'jig rten pa'i lam	mundane path
laukikāgryadharma	'jig rten pa'i chos kyi mchog	supreme mundane qualities
vajrasattva	rdo rje sems dpa'	Vajrasattva
vajrāsana	rdo rje skyil krung	adamantine posture, vajra posture
vastu	gzhi	basis
vastu	dngos po	category
vastujñatā	gzhi shes	knower of bases, exalted knower of bases
vastvantālambana	dngos po'i mtha' la dmigs pa	observing the limits of phenomena
vāsanā	bags chags	predisposition
vāyu	rlung	wind
vikalpa	rnam rtog	discursiveness, coarse conceptuality
vikṣepa	rnam par g.yeng ba	distraction
vicāra	dpyod pa	analysis
vicikitsā	the tshom	doubt
vijñāna	rnam shes	consciousness
vijñānānantya	rnam shes mtha' yas	limitless consciousness
vitarka	rtog pa	investigation
vinaya	'dul ba	monastic discipline
vipaśyanā	lhag mthong	special insight
vipākaphala	rnam smin gyi 'bras bu	fruitional effect
*vipākāvaraṇa	rnam smin gyi sgrib pa	fruitional obstruction
viprayuktasaṃskāra	ldan min 'du byed	non-associated compositional factor
vimuktimārga	rnam grol lam	path of release
vimokṣa	thar pa	liberation
viruddha	'gal ba	mutually exclusive
vivartanā	yongs su sgyur ba	change
viśeṣabhāgīya	khyad par cha mthun	concordant with enhancement
viśodana	rnam sbyong	purifying
viṣaya	yul	object
vīrya	brtson 'grus	effort
vedanā	tshor ba	feeling
vaibhāṣika	bye brag smra ba	Vaibhāṣhika

Sanskrit	*Tibetan*	*English*
vairocana	rnam par snang mdzad	Vairochana
vyāpāda	gnod sems	harmfulness
vyāpyālambana	khyab pa'i dmigs pa	pervasive object of observation
vyāyāma	rtsol ba	exertion
vyutkrāntakasamāpatti	thod rgyal gyi snyoms 'jug	leapover absorptions
vyupaśamana	nye bar zhi bar byed pa	thorough pacifying
śamatha	zhi gnas	calm abiding
śamathavipaśyanā-yuganaddha	zhi lhag zung 'brel	union of calm abiding and special insight
śamana	zhi bar byed pa	pacifying
*śāntaudārika	zhi rags	grossness/peacefulness
śāstra	bstan bcos	treatise
śikṣā	bslab pa	training
śīlavrataparāmarśa	tshul khrims dang brdul zhugs mchog 'dzin	conception of ethics and systems of behavior as supreme
śuddha	dag pa	pure
śubakṛtsna	bde rgyas	Vast Bliss
śūnyatā	stong pa nyid	emptiness
śraddhā	dad pa	faith
śrāvaka	nyan thos	Hearers
śruta	thos pa	hearing
śrutamayī	thos byung	arisen from hearing
śrotāpanna	rgyun zhugs	Stream Enterer
śvāsa	dbugs rngub pa	inhalation
ṣaṇḍha	za ma	neuter person
saṃgha	dge 'dun	spiritual community
saṃjñā	'du shes	discrimination
saṃtāna	rgyud	continuum
saṃnāhapratipatti	go sgrub	achieving armor
saṃpad	'byor ba	fortune
samprajanya	shes bzhin	introspection
saṃbhārapratipatti	tshogs sgrub	achieving the collections
saṃbhāramārga	tshogs lam	path of accumulation
saṃyojana	kun sbyor	thorough enwrapment
saṃvara	sdom pa	discipline
saṃsāra	'khor ba	cyclic existence
saṃskārakarma	'du byed kyi las	compositional factor
saṃskāraduhkhatā	'du byed kyi sdug bsngal	suffering of conditioning
saṃsthāpana	rgyun du 'jog pa	continuous setting
sakṛt	gcig car	simultaneous
sakṛdāgāmin	phyir 'ong	Once Returner
sacchidravāhana	bar du chad cing 'jug pa	interrupted engagement
samanantarapratyaya	de ma thag rkyen	immediately preceding condition

Sanskrit	*Tibetan*	*English*
samādhi	ting nge 'dzin	meditative stabilization, stabilization
samāpatti	snyoms 'jug	meditative absorption, absorption
samāhita	mnyam bzhag	meditative equipoise
samāhitajñāna	mnyam bzhag ye shes	exalted wisdom of meditative equipoise
samudayasatya	kun 'byung bden pa	true origins
saṃvedana	rig pa	knower
satkāyadṛṣṭi	'jig tshogs la lta ba	view of the transitory collection [as real "I" and mine]
sattva	sems can	sentient being
*sattvālaṃbanā maitri	sems can tsam la dmigs pa'i byams pa	love observing mere sentient beings
samādhāna	mnyam par 'jog pa	setting in equipoise
saraṇa	skyabs	refuge
sarvākārajñatā	rnam pa thams cad mkhyen pa nyid, rnam mkhyen	exalted knower of all aspects
sarvākārābhisaṃbhodha	rnam rdzogs sbyor ba	complete training in the aspects
savikalpikapratibimba	rnam par rtog pa dang bcas pa'i gzugs brnyan	analytical image
sahāya	grogs	concomitant
sāmantaka	nyer bsdogs	preparation
sāmānyalakṣaṇa	spyi'i mtshan nyid	general character, generally characterized phenomenon
siddhānta	grub mtha'	tenets
sukha	bde ba	bliss, happiness
sugati	bde 'gro	happy transmigration
sudarśana	shin tu mthong ba	Great Perception
sudṛśa	gya nom snang ba	Excellent Appearance
sautrāntika	mdo sde pa	Sautrāntika
saumanasya	yid bde	mental bliss
skandha	phung po	aggregate
styāna	rmugs pa	lethargy
styānamiddha	rmugs pa dang gnyid	lethargy and sleep
sthāna	'jog ba	placement
sthānāsthāna	gnas dang gnas ma yin pa	appropriate and the inappropriate
sthitibhāgīya	gnas pa cha mthun	concordant with abiding
sparśa	reg pa	contact
spraṣṭavya	reg bya	tangible object
spraṣṭavyāyatana	reg bya'i skye mched	tangible-object sphere
smṛti	dran pa	mindfulness
smṛtyupasthāna	dran pa nye bar bzhag pa	mindful establishment
svalakṣaṇa	rang gi mtshan nyid	specific character, specifically characterized phenomenon

Sanskrit	*Tibetan*	*English*
svātantrika	rang rgyud pa	Svātantrika
hānabhāgīya	nyams pa cha mthun	concordant with degeneration
hīnayāna	theg dman	Hīnayāna

LIST OF ABBREVIATIONS

P = *Tibetan Tripiṭaka,* Peking edition (Tokyo-Kyoto: Tibetan Tripiṭaka Research Foundation, 1955-1962).

Gedün Lodrö = Gedün Lodrö, *Walking Through Walls: A Presentation of Tibetan Meditation,* trans. and ed. by Jeffrey Hopkins (Ithaca, NY: Snow Lion Publications, 1992; restructured as *Calm Abiding and Special Insight: Spiritual Transformation through Meditation.* Ithaca, New York: Snow Lion Publications, 1998). References are to the 1992 edition.

La Vallée Poussin = Louis de La Vallée Poussin, trans. and ed., *L'abhidharmakośa de Vasubandhu, Mélanges Chinois et Bouddhiques* 16 (reprinted 1971).

Manual of Abhidhamma = Nārada Mahā Thera, ed. and trans., *A Manual of Abhidhamma, Being "Abhidhammattha Sangaha" of Bhadanta Anuruddhācariya* (Kandy, Sri Lanka: Buddhist Publication Society, 1975).

Meditative States = Lati Rinpoche, Denma Lochö Rinpoche, Leah Zahler, and Jeffrey Hopkins, *Meditative States in Tibetan Buddhism* (London: Wisdom Publications, 1983; revised edition, 1996). References are to the 1983 edition.

Perfections Transcript = Denma Lochö Rinpoche and Jeffrey Hopkins, "The Seventy Topics" (unpublished transcript).

Pruden = Leo M. Pruden, trans., *Abhidharmakośabhāṣyam by Louis de La Vallée Poussin,* 4 vols. (Berkeley: Asian Humanities Press, 1988–90).

Shastri = Dwarikadas Shastri, ed., *Abhidharmakośa & Bhāṣya of Ācārya Vasubandhu* (Varanasi: Bauddha Bharati, 1971).

BIBLIOGRAPHY

1 WORKS IN TIBETAN AND SANSKRIT

SŪTRAS

Cloud of Jewels Sūtra
ratnamegha
dkon cog sprin gyi mdo
P879, vol. 35

Extensive Sport Sūtra
lalitavistarasūtra
rgya cher rol pa'i mdo
P763, vol. 27

Heap of Jewels Sūtra
mahāratnakūṭadharmaparyāyaśatasāhasrikagranthasūtra
dkon mchog brtsegs pa chen po'i chos kyi rnam grangs le'u stong phrag brgya pa'i mdo
P760, vol. 22–24

Sūtra Unraveling the Thought
saṃdhinirmocanasūtra
dgongs pa nges par 'grel pa'i mdo
P774, vol. 29
Edited Tibetan text (transliterated) and French translation: Étienne Lamotte, trans. and ed. *Saṃdhinirmocanasūtra: L'Explication des mystères*. Louvain: Bibliothèque de l'université, 1935.
English translation: John Powers. *Wisdom of Buddha: The Saṃdhinirmocana Mahāyāna Sūtra.* Berkeley: Dharma Publishing, 1995. Also: Thomas Cleary. *Buddhist Yoga: A Comprehensive Course.* Boston: Shambhala, 1995.

Twenty-five Thousand Stanza Perfection of Wisdom Sūtra
pañcaviṃśatisāhasrikāprajñāpāramitāsūtra
shes rab kyi pha rol tu phyin pa stong phrag nyi shu lnga pa
P731, vol. 18–19
English translation: Edward Conze. *The Large Sūtra on Perfect Wisdom.* Berkeley: University of California Press, 1975.

TREATISES

Āryadeva (*'phags pa lha*, second–third century C.E.)
Four Hundred
catuḥśataka
bstan bcos bzhi brgya
P5246, vol. 95
Edited Tibetan and Sanskrit fragments along with English translation: Karen Christina Lang. *Āryadeva's Catuḥśataka: On the Bodhisattva's Cultivation of Merit and Knowledge.* Indiske Studier 7. Copenhagen: Akademisk Forlag, 1986.

Asaṅga (*thogs med*, fourth century)
Compendium of Ascertainments
nirṇayasamgrahaṇī/viniścayasamgraha
gtan la dbab pa bsdu ba
P5539, vol. 110–111

Summary of Manifest Knowledge
abhidharmasamuccaya
mngon pa kun btus
P5550, vol. 112
Sanskrit text: *Abhidharma Samuccaya of Asaṅga*. Pralhad Pradhan, ed. Visva-Bharati Series, vol. 12. Santiniketan: Visva-Bharati, 1950.
French translation: Walpola Rahula, trans. *Le Compendium de la super-doctrine (philosophie) (Abhidharmasamuccaya) d'Asaṅga*. Paris: École française d'extrême-orient, 1971.
English translation: Walpola Rahula. *Abhidharmasamuccaya: The Compendium of the Higher Teaching (Philosophy) by Asaṅga*. Trans. Sara Boin-Webb. Fremont, Calif.: Asian Humanities Press, 2001.
Grounds of Hearers
śrāvakabhūmi
nyan sa
P5537, vol. 110
Sanskrit text: *Śrāvakabhūmi*. Karunesha Shukla, ed. Tibetan Sanskrit Works Series, vol. 14. Patna: K. P. Jayaswal Research Institute, 1973.
Also: Alex Wayman. *Analysis of the Śrāvakabhūmi Manuscript*. University of California Publications in Classical Philology, vol. 17. Berkeley and Los Angeles: University of California Press, 1961.
Grounds of Yogic Practice/Actuality of the Grounds
yogācāryābhūmi/bhūmivastu
rnal 'byor spyod pa'i sa/sa'i dngos gzhi
P5536, vol. 109–11

Ashvaghoṣha (*rta dbyangs*)
Buddha's Deeds
buddhacaritanāmamahākavya
sangs rgyas kyi spyod pa shes bya ba'i snyan ngag chen po
P5356, vol. 129
English translation: E. H. Johnston. *The Buddhacarita; or, Acts of the Buddha*. First pub. 1936. Delhi: Oriental Books Reprint Corp., 1972.

Atisha (982–1054)
Lamp for the Path to Enlightenment
bodhipathapradīpa
byang chub lam gyi sgron ma
P 5343, vol. 103
English translation: Richard Sherburne, S.J. *A Lamp for the Path and Commentary of Atīśa*. London: George Allen & Unwin, 1983.
Commentary on the Difficult Points of "Lamp for the Path to Enlightenment"
bodhimārgapradīpapañjikā
byang chub lam gyi sgron ma'i dka' 'grel
P5344, vol. 103

Fourth Paṇ-chen Lama, Lo-sang-pel-den-ten-pay-nyi-ma (*blo bzang dpal ldan bstan pa'i nyi ma*, 1781-1852/4)
Instructions on (Tsong-kha-pa's) "Three Principal Aspects of the Path"
lam gyi gtso bo rnam pa gsum gyi khrid yig
folio publication in India, n.d.
English translation: Geshe Wangyal. In *The Door of Liberation*. Third edition, revised. Boston: Wisdom Publications, 1994. Second edition, New York: Lotsawa, 1978; first edition, New York: Girodias, 1973. Also: Geshe Lhundup Sopa and Jeffrey Hopkins. In *Cutting Through Appearances: The Practice and Theory of Tibetan Buddhism*. Ithaca, NY: Snow Lion Publications, 1989. First edition pub. 1976 as *Practice and Theory of Tibetan Buddhism*.

Gyel-tsap (*rgyal tshab dar ma rin chen*, 1364–1432)

Ornament for the Essence/Explanation Illuminating the Meaning of (Maitreya's) "Treatise of Quintessential Instructions on the Perfection of Wisdom, Ornament for Clear Realization" Together with Its Commentaries, Ornament for the Essence

rnam bshad snying po'i rgyan/shes rab kyi pha rol tu phyin pa'i man ngag gi bstan bcos mngon par rtogs pa'i rgyan gyi 'grel pa don gsal ba'i rnam bshad snying po'i rgyan

Buxaduor: n.p. 1967?

Jam-yang-shay-pa (*'jam dbyangs bzhad pa*, 1648–1721)

Analytical Delineation of the Presentation of the Three—Hearing, Thinking, and Meditating: Clearing Away the Darkness of Bad Views

thos bsam sgom gsum gyi rnam bzhag mtha' dpyod kyi sgo nas gtan la 'bebs pa lta ngan mun sel

Varanasi: Pleasure of Elegant Sayings Printing Press, 1964.

Also: *The Collected Works of 'Jam-dbyaṅs-bzad-pa'i-rdo-rje:* Reproduced from Prints from the Bkra-sis-'khyil Blocks, vol. 12. New Delhi: Ngawang Gelek Demo, 1974.

Eloquent Presentation of the Eight Categories and Seventy Topics, The Sacred Word of the Guru Ajita

dngos po brgyad don bdun cu'i rnam bzhag legs par bshad pa mi pham bla ma'i zhal lung

The Collected Works of 'Jam-dbyaṅs-bzad-pa'i-rdo-rje: Reproduced from Prints from the Bkra-sis-'khyil Blocks, vol. 15. New Delhi: Ngawang Gelek Demo, 1974.

Great Exposition of the Concentrations and Formless Absorptions/Treatise on the Presentations of the Concentrative and Formless Absorptions, Adornment Beautifying the Subduer's Teaching, Ocean of Scripture and Reasoning, Delighting the Fortunate

bsam gzugs chen mo/bsam gzugs kyi snyoms 'jug rnams gyi rnam par bzhag pa'i bstan bcos thub bstan mdzes rgyan lung dang rigs pa'i rgya mtsho skal bzang dga' byed).

Folio printing in India; no publication data.

Also: *The Collected Works of 'Jam-dbyaṅs-bzad-pa'i-rdo-rje:* Reproduced from Prints from the Bkra-sis-'khyil Blocks, vol. 12. New Delhi: Ngawang Gelek Demo, 1974.

Jinaputra. *See* Yaśomitra

Kamalashīla (*pad ma'i ngang tshul*; c.740-795)

Stages of Meditation

bhāvanākrama

sgom pa'i rim pa

P5310, 5311, 5312, vol. 102

Sanskrit texts: *First Bhāvanākrama*. G. Tucci, ed. *Minor Buddhist Texts*, II. Serie Orientale Roma IX, 2. Rome: ISMEO, 1958; *Third Bhāvanākrama*. G. Tucci, ed. *Minor Buddhist Texts*, III. Serie Orientale Roma XLIII. Rome: ISMEO, 1971.

Kön-chok-jik-may-wang-po (*dkon mchog 'jigs med dbang pa*, 1728–91)

Condensed Statement of (Jam-yang-shay-pa's) "Great Exposition of the Concentrations and Formless Absorptions"/An Excellent Vase of Eloquence Presenting the Concentrations and Formless Absorptions

bsam gzugs chen mo las mdor bsdus te bkod pa bsam gzugs kyi rnam bzhag legs bshad bum bzang

The Collected Works of Dkon-mchog-'jigs-med-dbaṅ-po, the Second 'Jam-dbyaṅs-bzad-pa of La-braṅ Bkra-śis-'khyil; Reproduced from Prints from the Bkra-sis-'khyil Blocks, vol. 6. New Delhi: Ngawang Gelek Demo, 1972.

Precious Garland of Tenets/Presentation of Tenets, A Precious Garland

grub pa'i mtha'i rnam par bzhag pa rin po che'i phreng ba

Dharamsala: Shes rig par khang, 1969.

English translation: Geshe Lhundup Sopa and Jeffrey Hopkins. In *Cutting Through Appearances: The Practice and Theory of Tibetan Buddhism*. Ithaca, NY: Snow Lion Publications, 1989. First edition pub. 1976 as *Practice and Theory of Tibetan Buddhism*.

Presentation of the Grounds and Paths, Beautiful Ornament of the Three Vehicles

sa lam gyi rnam bzhag theg gsum mdzes rgyan

The Collected Works of Dkon-mchog-jigs-med-dbaṅ-po, the Second 'Jam-dbyaṅs-bzad-pa of La-braṅ

Bkra-śis-'khyil; Reproduced from Prints from the Bkra-sis-'khyil Blocks, vol. 7. New Delhi: Ngawang Gelek Demo, 1972.
Also: Buxaduor: Gomang, 1965.

Maitreya (*byams pa*)
Ornament for Clear Realization
abhisamayālaṃkāra
mngon par rtogs pa'i rgyan
P5184, vol. 88
Sanskrit: *Abhisamayālaṃkāra-Prajñāpāramitā-Upadeśa-Śāstra.* Th. Stcherbatsky and E. Obermiller, ed. Bibliotheca Buddhica 23. rpt: Osnabrück: Biblio Verlag, 1970.
English translation: Edward Conze. *Abhisamayālaṅkāra.* Serie Orientale Roma 6. Rome: ISMEO, 1954.
Ornament for the Mahāyāna Sūtras
mahāyānasūtrālaṃkārakārikā
theg pa chen po'i mdo sde'i rgyan gyi tshig le'ur byas pa
P5521, vol. 108
Sanskrit text: Sitansusekhar Bagchi. *Mahāyāna-Sūtrālaṃkāraḥ of Asaṅga* [with Vasubandhu's commentary]. Buddhist Sanskrit Texts, 13. Darbhanga, India: Mithila Institute, 1970.

Nāgārjuna (*glu sgrub,* first–second century C.E.)
Friendly Letter
suhṛllekha
bshes pa'i spring yig
P5409, vol. 103
Edited Tibetan text and English translation: Lozang Jamspal, Ven. Ngawang Samten Chophel, and Peter Della Santina. *Nāgārjuna's Letter to King Gautamiputra.* Delhi: Motilal Banarsidass, 1978.

Nga-wang-lo-sang-gya-tso (*ngag dbang blo bzang rgya mtsho,* Fifth Dalai Lama, 1617–1682)
Sacred Word of Mañjushrī
byang chub lam gyi rim pa'i 'khrid yig 'jam pa'i dbyangs kyi zhal lung
Thim-phu: Kun-bzang stobs-rgyal, 1976.
English translation (Perfection of Wisdom chapter): Jeffrey Hopkins. *Practice of Emptiness: The Perfection of Wisdom Chapter of the Fifth Dalai Lama's "Sacred Word of Manjuśrī."* Dharamsala: Library of Tibetan Works and Archives, 1974.

Nga-wang-pel-den (*ngag dbang dpal ldan,* b. 1797)
Annotations for (Jam-yang-shay-pa's) "Great Exposition of Tenets," Freeing the Knots of the Difficult Points, Precious Jewel of Clear Thought
grub mtha' chen mo'i mchan 'grel dka' gnad mdud grol blo gsal gces nor
Sarnath: Pleasure of Elegant Sayings Press, 1964.

Paṇ-chen Sö-nam-drak-pa (*paṇ chen bsod nams grags pa,* 1478–1554)
General Meaning of (Maitreya's) "Ornament for Clear Realization"/Eloquent Explanation of the Meaning of (Gyel-tsap's) "Explanation Illuminating the Meaning of (Maitreya's) 'Treatise of Quintessential Instructions on the Perfection of Wisdom, Ornament for Clear Realization,' Together with Its Commentaries, Ornament for the Essence," A Lamp Illuminating the Meaning of the Mother [Perfection of Wisdom Sūtras]
phar phyin spyi don/shes rab kyi pha rol tu phyin pa'i man ngag gi bstan bcos mngon par rtogs pa'i rgyan 'grel pa dang bcas pa'i rnam bshad snying po rgyan gyi don legs par bshad pa yum don gsal ba'i sgron me
Buxaduor: Nang bstan shes rig 'dzin skyong slob gnyer khang, 1963.

Rājaputra Yaśomitra (*rgyal po'i sras grags pa'i bshes gnyen*)
Explanation of (Vasubandhu's) "Treasury of Manifest Knowledge"
abhidharmakośaṭīkā
chos mngon pa'i mdzod 'grel bshad
P5593, vol. 116

Sanskrit text: In *Abhidharmakośa & Bhāṣya of Ācārya Vasubandhu with Sphuṭārtha Commentary of Ācārya Yaśomitra.* Dwarikadas Shastri, ed. Bauddha Bharati Series, no. 5. Varanasi: Bauddha Bharati, 1971.

Shāntideva (*zhi ba lha*, eighth century)

Engaging in the Bodhisattva Deeds

bodhi[sattva]caryāvatāra

byang chub sems dpa'i spyod pa la 'jug pa

P5272, vol. 99

Sanskrit and Tibetan edition: *Bodhicaryāvatāra.* Vidhushekara Bhattacharya, ed. Bibliotheca Indica, vol. 280. Calcutta: The Asiatic Society, 1960.

English translation: Stephen Batchelor. *A Guide to the Bodhisattva's Way of Life.* Dharamsala: LTWA, 1979. Also: Marion Matics. *Entering the Path of Enlightenment.* New York: Macmillan, 1970. Also: Kate Crosby and Andrew Skilton. *The Bodhicaryāvatāra.* Oxford: Oxford University Press, 1996. Also: Padmakara Translation Group. *The Way of the Bodhisattva.* Boston: Shambhala, 1997. Also: Vesna A. Wallace and B. Alan Wallace. *A Guide to the Bodhisattva Way of Life.* Ithaca, N.Y.: Snow Lion Publications, 1997.

Contemporary commentary: Geshe Kelsang Gyatso. *Meaningful to Behold.* London: Wisdom Publications, 1980.

Sthiramati (*blo gros brtan pa,* fl. late fourth century)

Explanation of (Vasubandhu's) "Commentary on (Maitreya's) 'Ornament for the Mahāyāna Sūtras'"

sūtrālaṃkārāvṛttibhāṣya

mdo sde'i rgyan gyi 'grel bshad

P5531, vol. 108

Tsong-kha-pa Lo-sang-drak-pa (*tsong kha pa blo bzang grags pa,* 1357–1419)

Concise Meaning of the Stages of the Path

lam rim bsdus don/byang chub lam gyi rim pa'i nyams len gyi rnam gzhag mdor bsdus

The Collected Works of Rje Tsoṅ-kha-pa Blo-bzaṅ-grags-pa, vol. kha

New Delhi: Ngawang Gelek Demo, 1975ff.

Golden Rosary of Eloquence/Extensive Explanation of (Maitreya's) "Ornament for Clear Realization, Treatise of Quintessential Instructions on the Perfection of Wisdom," As Well As Its Commentaries

legs bshad gser gyi phreng ba/shes rab kyi pha rol tu phyin pa'i man ngag gi bstan bcos mngon par rtogs pa'i rgyan 'grel pa dang bcas pa'i rgya cher bshad pa

P6150, vol. 154

Also: *The Collected Works of Rje Tsoṅ-kha-pa Blo-bzaṅ-grags-pa,* vol. 25. New Delhi: Ngawang Gelek Demo, 1975ff.

Also: *Collected Works,* vol. 17. New Delhi: Guru Deva, 1979.

Great Exposition of the Stages of the Path/Stages of the Path to Enlightenment Thoroughly Teaching All the Stages of Practice of the Three Types of Beings

P6001, vol. 152

Also: Dharamsala: Shes rig par khang, n.d.

Also: New Delhi: Ngawang Gelek Demo, 1975ff.

Edited Tibetan: Tsultrim Kelsang Khangkar. *The Great Treatise on the Stages of the Path to Enlightenment (Lam Rim Chen Mo).* Japanese and Tibetan Buddhist Culture Series, 6. Kyoto: Tibetan Buddhist Culture Association, 2001.

English translation: Lamrim Chenmo Translation Committee. *The Great Treatise on the Stages of the Path to Enlightenment.* 3 vols. Joshua W.C. Cutler, editor-in-chief, Guy Newland, editor. Ithaca, N.Y.: Snow Lion Publications, 2000-2004.

English translation of the part on the excessively broad object of negation: Elizabeth Napper. *Dependent-Arising and Emptiness,* 153-215. London: Wisdom Publications, 1989.

English translation of the part on the excessively narrow object of negation: William Magee. *The Nature of Things: Emptiness and Essence in the Geluk World,* 179-192. Ithaca, N.Y.: Snow Lion Publications, 1999.

English translation of the parts on calm abiding and special insight: Alex Wayman. *Calming the Mind and Discerning the Real*, 81-431. New York: Columbia University Press, 1978; reprint, New Delhi, Motilal Banarsidass, 1979.

Illumination of the Thought: Extensive Explanation of (Chandrakīrti's) "Supplement to (Nāgārjuna's) 'Treatise on the Middle'"

dbu ma la 'jug pa'i rgya cher bshad pa dgongs pa rab gsal

P6143, vol. 154

English translation (first five chapters): Jeffrey Hopkins. In *Compassion in Tibetan Buddhism*. Valois, N.Y.: Snow Lion Publications, 1980.

English translation (chap. 6, stanzas 1-7): Jeffrey Hopkins and Anne C. Klein. In Anne C. Klein, *Path to the Middle: Madhyamaka Philosophy in Tibet: The Oral Scholarship of Kensur Yeshay Tupden*, 147-183, 252-271. Albany, N.Y.: State University of New York Press, 1994.

Notes on the Concentrations and Formless Absorptions

bsam gzugs zin bris

P6148, vol. 154

Also: modern block print, n.p., n.d.

Also: *The Collected Works of Rje Tsoṅ-kha-pa Blo-bzaṅ-grags-pa*, vol. 27. New Delhi: Ngawang Gelek Demo, 1975ff.

Also: *Collected Works*, vol. *tsha*. New Delhi: Guru Deva, 1979.

The Three Principal Aspects of the Path

lam gtso rnam gsum/tsha kho dpon po ngag dbang grags pa la gdams pa

P6087, vol. 153

English translation: Geshe Wangyal. In *The Door of Liberation*. Third edition, revised. Boston: Wisdom Publications, 1994. Second edition, New York: Lotsawa, 1978; first edition, New York: Girodias, 1973. Also: Geshe Lhundup Sopa and Jeffrey Hopkins. In *Cutting Through Appearances: The Practice and Theory of Tibetan Buddhism*. Ithaca, NY: Snow Lion Publications, 1989. First edition pub. 1976 as *Practice and Theory of Tibetan Buddhism*.

Vasubandhu (*dbyig gnyen*, fl. 360)

Treasury of Manifest Knowledge

abhidharmakośakārikā

chos mngon pa'i mdzod kyi tshig le'ur byas pa

P5590, vol. 115

Explanation of the "Treasury of Manifest Knowledge"

abhidharmakośabhāṣya

chos mngon pa'i mdzod kyi bshad pa

P5591, vol. 115

Sanskrit text: *Abhidharmakośa & Bhaṣya of Ācārya Vasubandhu with Sphuṭārtha Commentary of Ācārya Yaśomitra*. Dwarikadas Shastri, ed. Bauddha Bharati Series, no. 5. Varanasi: Bauddha Bharati, 1971.

French translation: Louis de La Vallée Poussin. *L'abhidharmakośa de Vasubandhu*. First pub. Paris: Geuthner, 1923–31. Mélanges Chinois et Bouddhiques 16 (reprinted 1971).

English translation: Leo M. Pruden. *Abhidharmakośabhāṣyam by Louis de La Vallée Poussin*. 4 vols. Berkeley: Asian Humanities Press, 1988–90.

Yaśomitra (*grags pa'i bshes gnyen*; indexed in P as Jinaputra [*rgyal ba'i sras*])

Commentary on (Asaṅga's) "Summary of Manifest Knowledge"

abhidharmakośaṭīkā

chos mngon pa'i 'grel bshad

P5554, vol. 113

2 Other Works

Aronson, Harvey B., trans. and ed. "The Buddhist Path: A Translation of the Sixth Chapter of the First Dalai Lama's *Path of Liberation*: The Path of Preparation and The Path Directly Seeing the

Truths." Parts 1 and 2: *Tibet Journal* 5:3 and 4 (1980); part 3, unpublished ms.

Buddhaghosa. *The Visuddhi-Magga of Buddhaghosa*. C.A.F. Rhys Davids, ed. First pub. 1920. London: Pali Text Society: Routledge & Kegan Paul, 1975. English translation: Buddhaghosa, *The Path of Purification (visuddhimagga)*. Ñyāṇamoli, trans. 2 vols. Berkeley and London: Shambhala, 1976.

Bu-tön (*bu ston*, 1290–1364). *History of Buddhism*, Part 2: *The History of Buddhism in India and Tibet*. E. Obermiller, trans. Heidelberg: n.p., 1932.

Buswell, Robert E., Jr., and Robert M. Gimello. "Introduction." *Paths to Liberation: The Mārga and Its Transformations in Buddhist Thought*. Robert E. Buswell, Jr. and Robert M. Gimello, eds. Kuroda Institute Studies in East Asian Buddhism 7. Honolulu: University of Hawaii Press, 1992.

Conze, Edward. *Buddhist Thought in India*. First pub. 1962 Ann Arbor: University of Michigan Press: Ann Arbor Paperbacks, 1973.

Cox, Collett. "Attainment through Abandonment: The Sarvāstivādin Path of Removing Defilements." In *Paths to Liberation: the Mārga and Its Transformations in Buddhist Thought*. Robert E. Buswell, Jr. and Robert M. Gimello, eds. Kuroda Institute Studies in East Asian Buddhism 7. Honolulu: University of Hawaii Press, 1992.

Deikman, Arthur J. "Experimental Meditation." In *Altered States of Consciousness*. Charles T. Tart, ed. New York: Wiley, 1969.

Eliade, Mircea. *Yoga: Immortality and Freedom*. Trans. Willard R. Trask. Bollingen Series, vol. 5. New York: Pantheon, 1958.

Gethin, R. M. L. *The Buddhist Path to Awakening: A Study of the Bodhi-Pakkhiyā Dhammā*. Leiden, New York, Köln: E. J. Brill, 1992.

Gimello, Robert M. "Mysticism and Meditation." In *Mysticism and Philosophical Analysis*. Steven T. Katz, ed. New York: Oxford University Press, 1978.

———. "Mysticism in Its Contexts." In *Mysticism and Religious Traditions*. Steven T. Katz, ed. New York: Oxford University Press, 1983.

Gö-lo-tsa-wa (*'gos lo tsa ba gzhon nu dpal*, 1392–1481). *The Blue Annals* (*deb ther sngon po*). George N. Roerich, trans. First pub. 1949. Delhi: Motilal Banarsidass, 1976.

Griffiths, Paul J. "Buddhist Hybrid English: Some Notes on Philology and Hermeneutics for Buddhologists." *JIABS*, 4:2 (1981), 17–32.

———. "Concentration or Insight: The Problematic of Theravāda Buddhist Meditation-Theory." *JAAR*, 49:4 (1981), 605–24.

———. "Indian Buddhist Meditation-Theory: History, Development and Systematization." Ph.D. dissertation, University of Wisconsin—Madison, 1983.

———. *On Being Mindless: Buddhist Meditation and the Mind-Body Problem*. La Salle, IL: Open Court, 1986.

Gunaratana, Henepola. *The Path of Serenity and Insight: An Explanation of the Buddhist Jhānas*. Delhi: Motilal Banarsidass, 1985.

Gyatso, Tenzin, Fourteenth Dalai Lama. *Kindness, Clarity, and Insight*. Ithaca, NY: Snow Lion Publications, 1984.

Hopkins, Jeffrey. *Emptiness Yoga: The Middle Way Consequence School*. Ithaca, NY: Snow Lion Publications: 1987.

———. *Meditation on Emptiness*. London: Wisdom Publications, 1983; rev. ed., Boston, Ma.: Wisdom Publications, 1996.

Hopkins, Jeffrey, trans. and comp. "Topics of Enlightenment." Unpublished compilation from monastic textbooks on the Perfections, University of Virginia.

Khetsun Sangpo Rinpoche. *Tantric Practice in Nying-ma*. Trans. and ed. by Jeffrey Hopkins. London: Rider, 1982; reprint, Ithaca, N.Y.: Snow Lion Publications, 1983.

King, Winston L. *Theravāda Meditation: The Buddhist Transformation of Yoga*. University Park and London: The Pennsylvania State University Press, 1980.

Klein, Anne C. "Mental Concentration and the Unconditioned: A Buddhist Case for Unmediated Experience." In *Paths to Liberation: the Mārga and Its Transformations in Buddhist Thought*. Robert E. Buswell, Jr. and Robert M. Gimello, eds. Kuroda Institute Studies in East Asian Buddhism 7. Honolulu: University of Hawaii Press, 1992.

———. *Path to the Middle: Madhyamaka Philosophy in Tibet: The Oral Scholarship of Kensur Yeshay Tupden.* Albany, NY: State University of New York Press, 1994.

Lang, Karen Christina. "Lord Death's Snare: Gender-Related Imagery in the Theragāthā and the Therīgāthā." *Journal of Feminist Studies in Religion,* 2:2 (1986).

Lati Rinpoche. *Mind in Tibetan Buddhism: Oral Commentary on Ge-shay Jam-bel-sam-pel's* Presentation of Awareness and Knowledge. Elizabeth Napper, ed. and trans. Ithaca, NY: Snow Lion Publications, 1980.

Lati Rinpoche, Denma Lochö Rinpoche, Leah Zahler, and Jeffrey Hopkins. *Meditative States in Tibetan Buddhism.* London: Wisdom Publications, 1983; rev. ed., Boston: Wisdom Publications, 1997.

Levinson, Jules Brooks. "The Process of Liberation and Enlightenment in the Buddhism of Tibet." M.A. thesis, University of Virginia, 1983.

Lochö Rinpoche, Denma, and Jeffrey Hopkins. "Grounds and Paths: Lectures by Denma Lochö Rinpoche on Kön-chok-jik-may-wang-po's *A Presentation of the Grounds and Paths: An Ornament Beautifying the Three Vehicles.*" University of Virginia: unpublished transcript.

———. "The Seventy Topics." University of Virginia: unpublished transcript.

Lodrö, Geshe Gedün. *Walking through Walls: A Presentation of Tibetan Meditation,* Jeffrey Hopkins, trans. and ed. Anne C. Klein and Leah Zahler, co-editors. Ithaca, New York: Snow Lion Publications, 1992; restructured as *Calm Abiding and Special Insight: Spiritual Transformation through Meditation.* Ithaca, New York: Snow Lion Publications, 1998.

Lopez, Donald S. *The Heart Sūtra Explained: Indian and Tibetan Commentaries.* Albany, NY: State University of New York Press, 1988.

———. *A Study of Svātantrika.* Ithaca, NY: Snow Lion Publications, 1987.

The Majjhima-Nikāya. Vol. 1. V. Trenckner, ed. First pub. 1888. London: Pali Text Society: Luzac, 1964. English translation: *The Collection of the Middle Length Sayings.* I. B. Horner, trans. Pali Text Society Translation Series, no. 29. First pub. 1954. London: Luzac, 1967.

Napper, Elizabeth. *Dependent-Arising and Emptiness.* Boston and London: Wisdom Publications, 1989.

Nārada Mahā Thera, ed. and trans. *A Manual of Abhidhamma, Being "Abhidhammattha Sangaha" of Bhadanta Anuruddhācariya.* Kandy, Sri Lanka: Buddhist Publication Society, 1975.

Newland, Guy. *Compassion: A Tibetan Analysis; A Buddhist Monastic Textbook.* London: Wisdom Publications, 1984.

Neusner, Jacob. "At Stake in Systemic Analysis: Is Judaism a Traditional Religion?" In *First Principles of Systemic Analysis: The Case of Judaism Within the History of Religions.* Lanham, MD: University Press of America, 1987.

Obermiller, E. "The Doctrine of Prajñā-pāramitā as exposed in the Abhisamayālaṃkāra of Maitreya." *Acta Orientalia* 9 (1932).

Wylie, Turrell. "A Standard System of Tibetan Transcription." *HJAS* 22 (1959), 261–76.

Zwilling, Leonard. "Homosexuality as Seen in Indian Buddhist Texts." *Buddhism, Sexuality, and Gender.* José Ignacio Cabezón, ed. Albany, NY: State University of New York Press, 1992.